THE PATH TO THE BERLIN WALL

Critical Stages in the History of Divided Germany

Manfred Wilke

Translated from the German by Sophie Perl

berghahn
NEW YORK · OXFORD
www.berghahnbooks.com

Published in 2014 by
Berghahn Books
www.berghahnbooks.com

English-language edition
©2014 Berghahn Books

German-language edition
©2011 Ch. Links Verlag, Berlin
Der Weg zur Mauer: Stationen der Teilungsgeschichte

The translation of this work was funded by Geisteswissenschaften International—
Translation Funding for Humanities and Social Sciences from Germany, a joint initiative of the
Fritz Thyssen Foundation, the German Federal Foreign Office, the collecting society VG WORT
and the Börsenverein des Deutschen Buchhandels (German Publishers & Booksellers Association)

Library of Congress Cataloging-in-Publication Data

Wilke, Manfred.
  [Weg zur Mauer. English]
  The path to the Berlin Wall : critical stages in the history of divided Germany / Manfred Wilke ;
translated from the German by Sophie Perl.
     p. cm.
  "Der Weg zur Mauer."
  Includes bibliographical references and index.
  ISBN 978-1-78238-288-1 (hardback : alk. paper) — ISBN 978-1-78238-289-8 (ebook)
  1. German reunification question (1949–1990) 2. Berlin Wall, Berlin, Germany, 1961–1989.
3. Germany (East)—Boundaries—Germany (West) 4. Germany (West)—Boundaries—
Germany (East) 5. Germany (East)—History. 6. Germany (East)—Politics and government.
7. Germany (East)—Social conditions. I. Title.
  DD257.25.W47913 2014
  943.087—dc23   2013029913

British Library Cataloguing in Publication Data
A catalogue record for this book is available from the British Library.

Printed on acid-free paper

ISBN: 978-1-78238-288-1 hardback   ISBN: 978-1-78238-289-8 ebook

This volume was originally published as part of the series *Publications on the Berlin Wall and Flight to the West* by the Berlin Wall Foundation and the Institute of Contemporary History, Munich–Berlin

This book is dedicated to:

- — my friend Jürgen Fuchs, who intervened in the realities of dictatorship and division in his and our "own affairs,"
- — Bärbel Bohley, the voice and face of the Peaceful Revolution in the GDR, which caused the Wall to fall,
- — Helmut Kohl, who as federal chancellor of the Federal Republic of Germany made German unification a political reality,

and my academic mentors Siegfried Braun, Karlheinz Messelken, and Theo Pirker.

The Wall is actually an obsession, it takes over people's thoughts in the East and West. That is why there is no real debate; it actually stands in the way and destroys any truly constructive opportunities.

—Bärbel Bohley, 1989

CONTENTS

FOREWORD

In early 2011, the Berlin Wall Foundation (Stiftung Berliner Mauer) initiated a book series that, in accordance with the Foundation's purpose, aims to make various aspects of the history of divided Germany and inter-German migration accessible to a broader public. All of the volumes in this series examine facets of the Berlin Wall and the emigration movement out of the German Democratic Republic (GDR) as contributions to and results of German division and the East–West conflict of the twentieth century.

The series comprises five volumes in total, a culmination of the interdisciplinary research project "The Berlin Wall as a Symbol of the Cold War: From an Instrument of SED Domestic Policy to a Monument of International Significance," funded by the German Research Foundation (Deutsche Forschungsgemeinschaft). This project was carried out from 2007 to 2010 under the leadership of Prof. Leo Schmidt, chair of historic preservation at the Brandenburg University of Technology, Cottbus; Prof. Manfred Wilke of the Institute of Contemporary History, Munich–Berlin; and Dr. Winfried Heinemann of the Military History Research Institute of the Bundeswehr, Potsdam. It aimed to investigate the Berlin Wall through the interconnected dimensions of political demands, material execution, and military implementation with a goal of studying as comprehensively as possible the Wall's multilayered meaning and expression as an extraordinary historical monument of the twentieth century.

In addition to filling in missing pieces in the fields of contemporary history, military history, and monument preservation, this project also looked at the implications of the Wall beyond academic frameworks. Even during the early stages of the research process, questions were developed across disciplines to ensure that results within each field could also enrich the other fields. As a consequence, the project's conclusions provide a solid foundation for discussions of the Wall in civil society by expanding the scientific base of knowledge and using an interdisciplinary approach (as well as many research perspectives) to position "competing" narratives in relation to each other.

As the inaugural volume of the German book series, Manfred Wilke's study provides deep insights into the decisions and events leading up to the Wall's construction. By setting German–German postwar history against the international backdrop of the Cold War, the author illuminates the complex relations that paved the way for the Berlin Wall. And, thanks to this English translation, his findings will now be accessible to a broader international public.

This volume not only represents an important contribution to the daily work of the Berlin Wall Foundation, but it is also an eye-opener—especially for international readers—to the history of German division and its global roots and consequences. The book examines an era that did not end until the Peaceful Revolution of 1989, a movement that capitalized on a favorable international political constellation but ultimately came from the people themselves. In the fall of 1989, peaceful East German protesters demonstrated that freedom and democracy were stronger than the conviction of East German Communists that they could permanently keep this freedom out of the population's reach. Over the course of the previous decades, those who had simply wanted to leave their country were ostracized, imprisoned, injured, or killed. This violation of human rights contributed to a political system that could not exist without an "Antifascist Protection Rampart"—and the system collapsed as soon as the Wall fell.

The Berlin Wall Foundation would first like to thank the author of this nuanced study, which sheds light on important new primary source material. Many thanks also to Dr. Susanne Muhle and Dr. Gerhard Sälter of the Berlin Wall Foundation for their thorough reading of the first draft, and to Margret Kowalke-Paz from the Ch. Links Verlag for editing and supervising the German publication. Sophie Perl translated the German manuscript with the greatest thoroughness, diligence, and patience. Finally, I would like to thank the German publisher, Christoph Links, and the American publisher, Marion Berghahn, who have both supported this publication project with energy and enthusiasm.

Axel Klausmeier
Director, Berlin Wall Foundation
April 2013

Abbreviations

AdBIK	Archive of the Ludwig Boltzmann Institute for Research on War Consequences, Graz
BArch	Bundesarchiv (Federal Archives of Germany)
BStU	Bundesbeauftragte(r) für die Unterlagen des Staatssichheitsdienstes der ehemaligen DDR (Federal Commissioner for the Records of the State Security Service of the Former German Democratic Republic)
BVerG	Bundesverfassungsgericht (Federal Constitutional Court of Germany)
CD	Diplomatic Corps (from the French: *corps diplomatique*)
CDU	Christian Democratic Union
CIA	Central Intelligence Agency
Comecon	Council for Mutual Economic Assistance
CPSU	Communist Party of the Soviet Union
CSU	Christian Social Union in Bavaria
DKP	Deutsche Kommunistische Partei (German Communist Party)
DM	Deutsche Mark (also D-mark)
DPRK	Democratic People's Republic of Korea
DWK	Deutsche Wirtschaftskommission (German Economic Commission)
EAC	European Advisory Commission
ECSC	European Coal and Steel Community
EDC	European Defense Community
EEC	European Economic Community
EFTA	European Free Trade Association
ERP	European Recovery Program (Marshall Plan)
Euratom	European Atomic Energy Community

FDGB	Freier Deutscher Gewerkschaftsbund (Free German Trade Union Federation)
FDJ	Freie Deutsche Jugend (Free German Youth)
FDP	Free Democratic Party
FRG	Federal Republic of Germany (in German: Bundesrepublik Deutschland, or BRD)
FRUS	Foreign Relations of the United States
FU	Freie Universität
GDR	German Democratic Republic (in German: Deutsche Demokratische Republik, or DDR)
GRU	Glavnoye Razvedyvatelnoye Upravleniye (Main Intelligence Directorate), USSR
GSFG	Group of Soviet Forces in Germany
gulag	Glavnoye Upravleniye Lagerei (Main Camp Administration), USSR
HA	*Hauptabteilung* (main department)
HVA	Hauptverwaltung Aufklärung (Main Reconnaissance Administration in the Ministry for State Security), GDR
IfZ	Institut für Zeitgeschichte (Institute of Contemporary History)
KGB	Komitet Gosudarstvennoi Bezopasnosti (Committee for State Security), USSR
KP	Kommunistische Partei (Communist Party)
KPD	Kommunistische Partei Deutschlands (Communist Party of Germany)
KPSS	Communist Party of the Soviet Union
LDPD	Liberal Democratic Party of Germany
LEW	Lokomotivbau-Elektrotechnische Werke (Locomotive and Electrotechnical Works)
MfAA	Ministerium für Auswärtige Angelegenheiten (Ministry of Foreign Affairs)
MfS	Ministerium für Staatssicherheit (Ministry for State Security)
MVD	Ministerstvo Vnutrennikh Del (Ministry of Internal Affairs), USSR
NATO	North Atlantic Treaty Organization
NKGB	Narodny Komissariat Gosudarstvennoi Bezopasnosti (People's Commissariat for State Security), USSR
NKVD	Narodny Komissariat Vnutrennikh Del (People's Commissariat for Internal Affairs), USSR

NSDAP   Nationalsozialistische Deutsche Arbeiterpartei (National Socialist German Workers' Party)

NVA   Nationale Volksarmee (National People's Army), GDR

OEEC   Organization of European Economic Cooperation

PB   Politburo of the SED

PKWN   Polski Komitet Wyzwolenia Narodowego (Polish Committee of National Liberation)

RGANI   Rossiiskii gosudarstvennyi arkhiv noveishei istorii (Russian State Archive of Contemporary History)

RIAS   Rundfunk im amerikanischen Sektor (Radio in the American Sector)

SAG   *sowjetische Aktiengesellschaft* (Soviet joint-share company)

SAPMO   Stiftung Archiv der Parteien und Massenorganisationen der DDR im Bundesarchiv (Foundation Archives of Parties and Mass Organisations of the GDR in the Federal Archives)

SBZ   Sowjetische Besatzungszone (Soviet occupation zone)

SED   Sozialistische Einheitspartei Deutschlands (Socialist Unity Party of Germany)

SKK   Sowjetische Kontrollkommission (Soviet Control Commission)

SMAD   Sowjetische Militäradministration in Deutschland (Soviet Military Administration in Germany)

SPD   Social Democratic Party

SU   Soviet Union

UN   United Nations

USSR   Union of Soviet Socialist Republics

ZAIG   Zentrale Auswertungs- und Informationsgruppe (Central Analysis and Information Group of the MfS), GDR

ZK   Zentralkomitee (Central Committee)

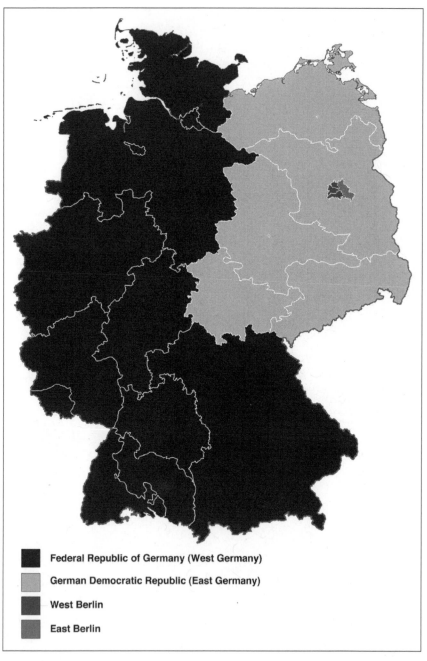

Federal Republic of Germany (West Germany)

German Democratic Republic (East Germany)

West Berlin

East Berlin

Map of Germany, 1949–89, showing West Germany, East Germany, and Berlin

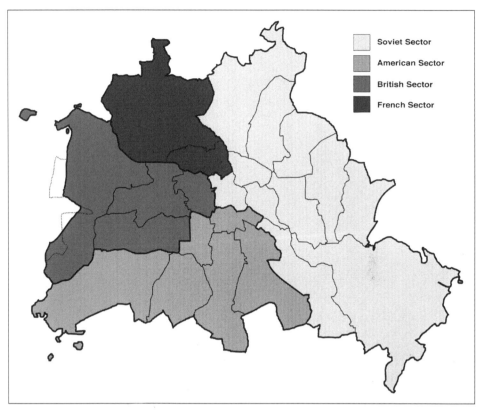

Map of Berlin, 1949–89, showing the American, British, French, and Soviet sectors

INTRODUCTION

The Berlin Wall was a multifaceted, concrete border. It split the city in two, forming part of both the inner-German division and the cleft between the Soviet Empire and the Western European democracies. After its construction in 1961, the Wall came to symbolize the division of Germany and the oppositional forces of dictatorship and freedom; internationally, it remained the most indelible image of the Cold War. In May 1989, before anyone in Germany sensed the Wall's fall just a few months later, Gerald R. Kleinfeld, founder and executive director of the German Studies Association, spoke at a congress in West Berlin. "For the Americans," he said, "the Wall is a symbol of injustice, of inhumanity, of a disrespect for human rights; perhaps it is more important than for some West Germans and West Berliners. . . . The United States is here because of national interests, but also because of political ideals. This is precisely the point. Every American Administration advocates the right of the German people to self-determination. Public support is broad and deep. When the Wall turned twenty-five, even provincial newspapers in the United States contained comprehensive coverage of the history and significance of this monument."[1] After Berliners toppled the Wall on 9 November 1989, its fall embodied German reunification and, in the broader European context, the end of Communist dictatorship in Central and Eastern Europe and the Soviet Union. Indeed, the Berlin Wall represented Europe's transition into a new era.

This book traces the path that led to the Wall's construction. It begins in 1945, when the conditions and motivations to follow that path emerged in the aftermath of the Second World War. Led by Adolf Hitler, the Third Reich had provoked the war by attacking Poland in 1939; it ended on 8 May 1945 with the unconditional capitulation of the German Wehrmacht. Over the course of World War II, through the National Socialists' systematic annihilation of the European Jews and racist war of obliteration and repression against the Slavic populations, the German people took on a heavy burden of moral debt—one whose effects still play out today. The Allied armies of Great Britain, France, the United States, and especially the Soviet Union were the forces that defeated Hitler and freed the Germans from the National Socialist dictatorship. For the war and for this form of freedom, the Germans paid a high price: millions of people perished, millions more were displaced, and Germany lost its eastern provinces. The country surrendered unconditionally to the occupying powers and relinquished its sovereignty.

This book focuses on the following topics and developments:

1. The significance of borders in postwar Germany, which delimited the spheres of influence in Europe and were shaped by the Cold War between the Soviet Empire and the democracies of the West, led by the United States.
2. The political decisions that shaped the oppositional approaches to rebuilding political systems in the Soviet and Western occupation zones and led to the founding of two German states.
3. The role and significance of Berlin, especially West Berlin, in the Germany policy of the Soviet Union and the Socialist Unity Party of Germany (Sozialistische Einheitspartei Deutschlands, or SED).
4. The question of responsibility for building the Berlin Wall.
5. The role of the nuclear stalemate between the United States and the Soviet Union in resolving the second Berlin Crisis, which lasted for four years.
6. The significance of the Berlin Wall for West German politics, especially concerning the goal of achieving German unity.

This analysis takes as its starting point the new, postwar borders drawn through Germany by the occupying powers. Borders denote the spatial limits not only of territories but also of political and social structures, as well as international spheres of influence. The zonal borders in occupied Germany provided the basis of each occupation power's political developments within its respective zone; these, in turn, led to the emergence of different political and economic systems, culminating in the creation of two German states. By the time this occurred in 1949, the conflict between West and East had already become the Cold War, and the frontline ran straight through Germany and Berlin.

Political decisions are at the core of this book's focus. They represent commitments to certain paths of conflict resolution and, after they have been made, rule out potential alternatives in domestic and foreign policy. Before the founding of the two German states, decisions were made in London, Moscow, Paris, and Washington. Disagreement over the borders of Germany and Berlin constituted one of many points of contention in the imminent conflict among the powers, which continued to have sway over German fortune; both West and East Germany joined the antagonistic system of alliances in 1955 through membership in NATO and the Warsaw Pact. The analysis here concentrates on major turning points in the political decision-making processes on both sides of the Iron Curtain that eventually led to the division of the country.

The book explores these processes in three parts. Part I examines the relationship between the division of Germany and the polarized postwar European order, which manifested itself concretely in the new German borders. Indeed, the zonal borders determined the shape of both German states. One important difference between the emergence of the German Democratic Republic (GDR) and the Federal Republic of Germany (FRG) is that the future Communist leaders of the GDR had already begun preparations for the state-to-be while in exile in Moscow during the war. In 1944, this cadre of the KPD was already contemplating the fundamental question facing German politics after Hitler: Which way would Germany sway, to the East or to the West? Wilhelm Pieck and Walter Ulbricht already saw themselves as the "state-building party" and were certain that their political rise in the Soviet zone would be guaranteed by the occupying power. One of Joseph V. Stalin's early accomplishments thus came as no surprise: in June 1945, he charged the German Communists in his occupation zone with taking over state leadership—a move that was not annulled until 1990, by the last general secretary of the Communist Party of the Soviet Union (CPSU), Mikhail S. Gorbachev.

The second part of this book focuses on the two Berlin Crises and the construction of the Berlin Wall. The analysis follows the Soviet Union's political goals throughout the crises that it started, as well as the interaction between the Soviet Union and its East German partners, the leaders of the SED. Reactions from the West also play an important role, in particular the political decision-making processes in America, within the Western alliance, in the West German government, and in the West Berlin Senate. Out of this complex landscape, a transformation took place in the relationship between the West Germans, defeated in the Second World War, and the Allied victors: over the course of Western integration, the occupied became partners and the occupiers protectors. The dream of unifying Germany through a national consensus that included the Communists—a proposal that seemed self-evident right after the war—dissipated with the confrontation between Social Democrats and Communists over their forced fusion into the SED within the Soviet zone. The Social Democrats called for a vote on the fusion by all party members, but this only materialized in West Berlin. It was the first step toward the city's political division, which followed in 1948.

Meanwhile, under Konrad Adenauer, West Germany's first federal government aspired relentlessly to integrate itself into the West. To Adenauer, the three Western powers were advocates for and guarantors of German self-determination in the four-power negotiations over a peace treaty with Germany and the reestablishment of a single German nation-state, as the 1945 Potsdam Agreement had promised. A reliable partner in the Western alliance, Adenauer hoped to use his stronger position over the Soviet Union to negotiate unification based on free elections throughout the entire country.

The Berlin Crises of 1948–49 and 1958–62 were very much related to each other. In order to understand them in the context of Communist policy, it is crucial to examine the people's uprising against the SED dictatorship in the GDR on

17 June 1953. Unrest began on 16 June with a strike by construction workers on Berlin's Stalinallee, and only the intervention of Soviet troops restored and secured SED power. The GDR confronted a crisis situation for the first time. With the SED directly facing dissatisfaction and rejection, the state party's relationship to its people fundamentally changed. The events of 17 June 1953 were a shock not only to the SED in the GDR, but also to the new Soviet leadership after Stalin's death. The next three years brought the Polish October and the tragedy of the Hungarian Revolution. These uprisings destroyed the illusion that Communist parties could instate their political systems in Eastern Europe without resistance of any kind; simultaneously, the ideological myth of a common political identity shared among state party and state citizens dissolved. Still, when the Soviet Union and the GDR tried in 1958 to change the status quo in Berlin, they succeeded in eliciting international recognition of the GDR, thus cementing the existence of the East German state.

17 June should also be seen as emblematic of a crisis phenomenon in the young GDR state. The crisis was not *solved* by repressing the revolt but rather shelved and stored away. It endured, however, perhaps its most visible sign the persistent emigration of the East German population. The currents of crisis intensified at the end of the 1950s, reacting to economic expansion measures that aimed to compete with West Germany but were impeded by a dependence on West German supplies and still called for the collectivization of East German agriculture. This book discusses the ways in which emigration and economic crisis influenced decision-making processes and sketches the resulting shift in political priorities in both East Berlin and Moscow.

The analysis of the second Berlin Crisis concentrates primarily on the process of political coordination between the SED and the CPSU. These discussions took place only at the highest level. Fundamental agreements on political tactics emerged from personal conversations between Walter Ulbricht and Nikita S. Khrushchev in Moscow, which, in this book, are analyzed for the first time based on protocols from the meetings. Especially clear throughout the conversations is the asymmetrical relationship between two unequal partners. The analysis of these documents was made possible through cooperation with Gerhard Wettig, who has published a thorough account of Khrushchev's policy toward the West from 1955 to 1964.[2] In portraying the communication between the two party leaders, this book attempts to identify and examine the differences between Khrushchev's and Ulbricht's interests.

Part III, entitled "The End of the Second Berlin Crisis," examines the factors that led Khrushchev to authorize building a wall through Berlin on 13 August 1961. By broadening the analytical perspective to include the interests of the Soviet Union, one of two world powers, the discussion sketches the real danger of nuclear war in Europe and its connection to the Soviet Berlin Ultimatums of 1959 and 1961. The analysis focuses on the ways in which the military plans of the United States and the Soviet Union, as well as the two powers' relationship to each other, determined the course of the crisis and ruled out certain solutions. In contrast to the first Berlin Crisis, the nuclear standoff between the superpowers dominated the security politics of the second crisis. Part III looks at how this constellation and the challenge of avoiding nuclear war influenced the decision-making processes in Moscow and Washington.

Through the author's involvement in the project, "The Vienna Summit between Kennedy and Khrushchev in June 1961"[3] at the Ludwig Boltzmann Institute for Research on War Consequences in Graz, this book was able to draw on a further body of documents related to the Soviet decision-making process during the second Berlin Crisis. In particular, these materials conveyed the deep significance of the Berlin conflict for international politics, painting a nuanced picture of the course of events over several different phases, each shaped by specific political interests and priorities. Furthermore, this material provided answers to a central question: What situation and which political conditions motivated the decision to build the Berlin Wall? With these new resources, it was possible to capture the decision-making process itself, as well as the key events that determined its path.

The research for this book benefitted further from an enlightening interview with the former deputy head of operations for the Group of Soviet Forces in Germany (GSFG), Colonel General Anatoli Grigoryevich Mereshko.[4] Mereshko was able to clarify significant pieces of information regarding the course of military planning for the construction of the Berlin Wall, going far beyond the general scope of knowledge on this topic.

Finally, on an orthographic note, there were two ways of denoting the Western and Eastern sectors of Berlin in Germany before 1990. The West German government and the Berlin Senate used "West-Berlin" and its analogous "Ost-Berlin." These remain the standard German spellings today, equivalent to the English "West Berlin" and "East Berlin." The GDR and the Soviet Union preferred to write "Westberlin" as one word. The term for East Berlin in the GDR changed over time: it began after the war as "democratic Berlin," later evolving into "Berlin, Capital of the GDR" (Berlin—Hauptstadt der DDR). Each name expresses a different legal interpretation of Berlin's status: the West made reference to a shared four-sector city; the East integrated the eastern part into the rest of the GDR and emphasized the special political unit of "Westberlin." Because of this difference, both versions (West Berlin and Westberlin) appear in the translations of primary source documents, depending on the original text. In general, all quotations from German sources have been translated into English by the translator of this volume.

To conclude, I would like to thank the people and institutions whose cooperation was indispensible to writing and publishing this book. Among them are Leo Schmidt and Winfried Heinemann, my partners in the interdisciplinary research project, "The Berlin Wall as a Symbol of the Cold War: From an Instrument of SED Domestic Policy to a Monument of International Significance," which received generous support from the German Research Foundation. Our cooperation revealed the extent to which the architecture of the border as a permanent component of East German state iconography was directly tied to domestic and foreign policy—an insight that has only grown stronger through outstanding interdisciplinary work. Horst Möller, director of the Institute of Contemporary History (IfZ) in Munich and Berlin, allowed me to conduct research for this book as a visiting scholar at the IfZ. Stefan Karner, director of the Ludwig Boltzmann Institute for Research on War Consequences in Graz, integrated me into his institute's international research project on the Vienna Summit. Many thanks also to Gerhard Wettig and Peter Ruggenthaler for providing access to the Soviet files. The Foundation Archives of Parties and Mass Organisations of the GDR in the Federal Archives (SAPMO) lent active support to my research on the policies of the SED; thank you especially to Ute Räuber. My good friend Wilhelm Mensing read through and corrected the first manuscript of the book with a keen critical eye, a task that Susanne Muhle and Gerhard Sälter of the Berlin Wall Foundation saw through to the end. Thank you also to my daughters, Cornelia and Julia, for their assistance with many technical aspects of the process, and a special thanks to my wife, Karin, for her encouragement and help during my work on this book. The English translation was made possible through a grant from the International Humanities program of the Fritz Thyssen Foundation, for which I am deeply grateful. Finally, I would like to thank the translator, Sophie Perl, for a fruitful and trusting collaboration.

Notes

1. Quoted in Manfred Wilke, "Sternstunde der deutsch-amerikanischen Allianz: 9. November 1989," in *Germany and America: Essays in Honor of Gerald R. Kleinfeld*, ed. Wolfgang-Uwe Friedrich (New York, 2001), 215.
2. Gerhard Wettig, ed., *Chruschtschows Westpolitik 1955–1964: Gespräche, Aufzeichnungen und Stellungnahmen*, vol. 3: *Die Kulmination der Berlin-Krise (Herbst 1960 bis Herbst 1962)* (Munich, 2011).
3. Stefan Karner et al., eds., *Der Wiener Gipfel 1961: Kennedy—Chruschtschow* (Innsbruck, 2011). A revised English edition of this volume has been published as part of the Harvard Cold War Studies Book Series: Günter Bischof, Stefan Karner, and Barbara Stelzl-Marx, eds., *The Vienna Summit and Its Importance in International History* (Lanham, MD, 2013).
4. Manfred Wilke and Alexander Vatlin, "'Arbeiten Sie einen Plan zur Grenzordnung zwischen beiden Teilen Berlins aus!': Interview mit Generaloberst Anatolij Grigorjewitsch Mereschko," trans. Tatiana Timofeeva, *Deutschland Archiv* 44, no. 2 (2011): 89–96.

Part I

THE POLARIZATION OF POSTWAR EUROPE

Chapter 1

THE ALLIED WAR CONFERENCES AND EUROPE'S POSTWAR ORDER

The unconditional capitulation of the German Wehrmacht on 8 May 1945 meant the self-inflicted collapse of the German Reich as a major European power. However, the Allied victory did not create a political vacuum in Central Europe. Compared to the period before the Second World War, the international political constellation in Europe had undergone a fundamental change: the Soviet Union and the United States had risen to the status of dominant world powers, shaping politics on the continent and in Germany for decades to come.

The United States of America and the Anti-Hitler Coalition's Goals for Peace: The Atlantic Charter of 1941

The Anti-Hitler Coalition among Great Britain, the Soviet Union, and the United States developed as an alliance of necessity early on, following the German attack on the Soviet Union and the United States' entry into World War II in 1941. An odd combination of the Atlantic democracies and the dictatorial Soviet Union, the coalition based its rhetoric on the fight against the National Socialist Third Reich. Even before the United States entered the war, American President Franklin D. Roosevelt had already summed up the coalition's key message: "In his annual speech before Congress on 6 January 1941, he enumerated for the American people four basic human liberties at stake in the war against the Axis powers: freedom of expression and religion, freedom from want, and freedom from fear."[1] Together with British Prime Minister Winston Churchill, Roosevelt formulated the ideational basis for a fight against the Axis powers at their first summit meeting in Newfoundland on 12 August 1941.

The Atlantic Charter gave the Anti-Hitler Coalition's war a democratic, progressive goal: "After the final destruction of Nazi tyranny," it read, "[Churchill and Roosevelt] hope to see established a peace which will afford to all nations the means of dwelling in safety within their own boundaries, and which will afford assurance that all the men in all the lands may live out their lives in freedom from fear and want." Peace should be achieved through "the establishment of a wider and permanent system of general security." Despite maintaining neutrality at this time, the American government was already aligning itself with the Third Reich's most powerful enemy by setting common goals. At the center of the charter were the universal rights of all peoples "to choose the form of Government under which they will live; and [Churchill and Roosevelt] wish to see sovereign rights and self-government restored to those who have been forcibly deprived of them." Among its goals in war, the charter denounced "territorial changes that do not accord with the freely expressed wishes of the peoples concerned."[2] With this democratic rhetoric, any divergent interests of the signatories could be overlooked; the Soviet Union joined the United States and Great Britain in recognizing the principles of the Atlantic Charter on 1 January 1942. Actual discrepancies among the countries' views only became apparent to the United States and Great Britain in 1944, with the question of Poland's right to self-determination.

Moreover, the power-political interests of the Allied powers were purposefully veiled through rhetoric. Simplified concepts of friend and enemy in this, the most immense war in the history of humankind, were crafted to help bring about the Anti-Hitler Coalition's victory. This eloquence also permeated the Declaration on Liberated Europe of February 1945, signed in Yalta by Roosevelt, Churchill, and Stalin. The three powers agreed to coordinate their policies in order to solve "the political and economic problems of liberated Europe in accordance with democratic principles."[3] The declaration of intent also encompassed Germany—even though it would remain under Allied control—in order to "destroy German militarism and Nazism and to ensure that Germany will never again be able to disturb the peace of the world."[4] But the rhetoric soon faded as the opposing interests of the Communist Soviet Union and the Western democracies formed the new, polarized power constellation of the Cold War.

The Soviet Precedent in 1944 Poland and Churchill's Warning about the Iron Curtain in 1945

The terms "spheres of influence" and "spheres of interest" never appeared in the rhetoric above, but they had a significant impact on the actions of each superpower. This became especially clear toward the end of the war, with an agreement signed by Winston Churchill and Joseph V. Stalin in October 1944 delimiting Great Britain's and the Soviet Union's zones of influence in the Balkan region.[5] In fact, the Soviet Union would later cut off Great Britain's secured influence in Romania, Bulgaria, and Hungary. Likewise, the accord did not hold up in Yugoslavia, where the Communists, led by Josip Broz Tito, took undivided power. In Greece, the Soviet Union found itself at a disadvantage: with British and American forces against them, the Communists suffered defeat in a bloody civil war, after which the monarchy was reinstated. Disappointment over the violation of this "Percentages Agreement" likely nudged Churchill toward his early confrontational course with the Soviet Union after victory in 1945.

With the Soviet Army's victory over the German Wehrmacht, the Soviet Union could be confident, at least militarily, in the implementation of its imperial perspectives in Eastern and Southern Europe. By 1945, the army's success had also engendered the political drive. After the war and the defeat of the German empire, the Soviet Union rose to become the strongest power in continental Europe.'

The Soviet Commissariat for Foreign Affairs deliberated on the spheres of influence in Europe with the clear objective of securing the conquered areas within its own sphere of interest. In consequence, all of the plans put forth came down to dividing Europe. A brief note by Maxim M. Litvinov, director of the Commission for Postwar Order—and also the Soviet ambassador to the United States[6]—exemplifies the imperial perspectives of Soviet foreign policy. Before the conference in Yalta, Litvinov sketched out what he perceived to be the American president's vision of postwar Europe: "As a realist, perhaps Roosevelt personally understands that the development of spheres, zones, or blocks in Europe is unavoidable. Still, out of respect for public opinion, he refuses in any way to condone it." On the contrary, he believed, Roosevelt would try to pressure England and the Soviet Union "to refrain from building blocs." Litvinov then described the Soviet Union's maximum sphere of interest, "or better yet, security zone," as comprising "Finland, Norway, Sweden, Poland, Hungary, Czechoslovakia, Romania, Yugoslavia, Bulgaria, and Turkey." He imagined that the British security zone would include "Holland, Belgium, France, Spain, Portugal, and Greece." A neutral zone, in which both sides would "work together through permanent consultation on the basis of common principles," would consist of Denmark, Germany, Austria, Switzerland, and Italy. Great Britain would probably "protest [the inclusion of] Norway, Sweden, Turkey, and Yugoslavia in the Soviet zone and demand the expansion of its own zone to encompass Sweden, Norway, Denmark, and Italy. These countries will likely be the subject of haggling and compromise no matter what."[7] The premise of Litvinov's (false) prognosis was that the Americans would retreat from Europe as they did after the First World War, allowing the European powers to reinstate their classic zones of influence over the continent. After the "haggling" subsided, the only remaining country would be Germany, where both sides would exercise joint supremacy on the basis of "common principles"—Litvinov's only prediction that turned out to be true.

For the Soviet Union, preparations to delimit the competing powers' spheres of interest entailed the immediate establishment of Soviet-friendly regimes throughout the area of Soviet influence. Poland became the first country in which the Soviet Army succeeded in extending Soviet hegemony by instating Polish Communist rule even before the war ended. Vis-à-vis its Western allies, the Soviet Union implemented a policy of faits accomplis in Poland. After 22 June 1944, two different governments lay claim to Polish rule: "the government-in-exile in London, which tried in vain to intervene in Poland's domestic developments, and the Lublin government, which came into being after the Red Army crossed the Bug and advanced to the Vistula."[8] The Lublin Committee, officially the Polish Committee of National Liberation (PKWN), comprised members of the Moscow-based Union of Polish Patriots and cadres of the Polish Communist Party. The latter had changed its name to the Polish Workers' Party in 1938 after being disbanded by the Communist International. The PKWN did not include members of the National Council of Poland, which formed the basis of the government-in-exile in London.

The secret of the "Polish model" rested in the establishment of the "National Committee" as a provisional government after the Soviet Army's military victory. Led more or less openly by the newly founded Communist Party, the Committee aimed to initiate the transformation of Poland's political and social order. Coordination with Soviet interests in Poland occurred through the "Moscow cadre" at the head of the new Communist Party: Communists in Soviet exile who had survived Stalin's terror toward his own guard in the 1930s.[9]

In this "model," which then expanded to include the Eastern and Southeastern European countries, historian Leonid Gibianski sees "the solution to a dilemma that many authors have so heavily debated: whether Stalin's policy toward Eastern Europe was based on his revolutionary postulates or rather on the security interests of the USSR."[10] For Gibianski, this is a petty disagreement. Stalin himself viewed the power of the Communist Party in the Soviet Union along the continuum of the Russian Empire. At the Kremlin's private ceremony in 1937 to honor the twentieth anniversary of the Bolshevik Revolution, Stalin explicitly praised the imperial heritage of the Czars. Georgi Dimitrov noted Stalin's words: "But [the Czars] did accomplish one important thing: they scraped together a giant empire—all the way to Kamchatka. We inherited this state. And we, the Bolsheviks, have consolidated this state for the first time."[11]

With his reference to the "giant empire," Stalin integrated Russian nationalism into the party ideology. The long-emphasized "proletarian internationalism" of the Communist International, founded in 1919, receded to the background of Soviet propaganda, serving primarily to secure the loyalty of outside Communist parties to the Soviet Union.

The strengthening of Communist Party power beyond the borders of the USSR thus contributed to "guaranteeing the security of the Soviet borders while at the same time expanding the 'sphere of socialism,' taking a further step toward the so-called 'world revolution.'"[12] The imperial goals of the state and the ideological-political projections of the Communist Party were thus indistinguishable in Soviet policy, having "melted into a single, uniform whole."[13] Here, Gibianski draws on Isaac Deutscher, who calls these two components a "paradox" and explains it through the history of Bolshevism and the Soviet victory in the Second World War: "For more than two decades [Stalin] had preached the gospel of socialism in one country and violently asserted the self-sufficiency of Russian socialism. In practice, if not in precept, he had made Russia turn her back upon world revolution—or was it Russia that had made him turn his back upon it? Now, in his supreme triumph, he disavowed, again in practice if not in precept, his own gospel; he discarded his own canon of Russia's self-sufficiency and revived her interest in international revolution."[14] Whereas early Bolshevism had counted on organizing the world revolution from Moscow but carrying it out through the national parties of the Communist International, Stalin's version of the world revolution, both during and after the war, depended entirely on the tanks of the Soviet Army. As the war ended in victory and Stalin entered talks with the Western powers over the new European order, he replaced his "socialism in one country" doctrine with something new: "socialism in one zone."[15]

The "Polish model" synthesized both components of this revolutionary imperialism. Communist parties in the Soviet zone were bolstered into power in their respective countries after the Soviet Army's victory. But they received this power on loan from Moscow and could not exercise autonomy over the fundamental decisions affecting their states. It was precisely this course of action by the Soviet Union in Poland that alarmed Winston Churchill: he sensed that the Western powers would face a new conflict after the end of World War II—this time with the Soviet Union. In Germany, too, the Polish model was used to ensure the Communist rise to power in the Soviet occupation zone.

In Yalta, at the February 1945 summit conference of the "Big Three" (Stalin, Roosevelt, and Churchill), the Soviet Union's actions in Poland represented the central point of contention. In view of the ongoing war against the German Reich and the presence of the Soviet Army in Poland, the Western powers accepted the Lublin Committee's transformation into a provisional Polish government. Most importantly, they agreed to forgo control of the upcoming Polish elections.[16] Beginning in Poland, the Soviet Union built up its Eastern and Central European empire, for which the occupation zone in Germany formed the keystone in Central Europe.

Frightened, British and French politicians wondered whether the United States would remain a counterweight to the Soviet Union in Western Europe. Four days after the unconditional capitulation of the German Wehrmacht, Churchill set down on paper his fears regarding the politics of the continent's new dominant power. Writing to the new American president, Harry S. Truman, successor of the deceased Franklin D. Roosevelt, Churchill described his concerns: "An iron curtain is drawn down upon [the Soviet] front. We do not know what is going on behind. There seems little doubt that the whole of the regions east of the line Lübeck–Trieste–Corfu will soon be completely in their hands."[17] Churchill added that this also applied to regions of Germany east of the Elbe that had been conquered by the U.S. Army; the Americans were set to withdraw from these areas because they were part of the Soviet zone. Thus the key concept was coined for the dividing line between spheres of influence and political systems in the European postwar landscape: the Iron Curtain. In the summer of 1945, the future development of Europe depended heavily on the United States' policy and presence on the continent.

In contrast to Churchill, Truman did not perceive an acute Soviet threat in mid 1945. Truman also wanted to end the ongoing war in Asia with the help of the Soviet Union. Indeed, he convinced the USSR to enter into the war against Japan and founded the United Nations with its partnership. Truman celebrated the signing of the UN Charter in 1945 with "Roosevelt-like rhetoric, as a 'one-time chance' to establish the 'rule of reason' worldwide."[18] The UN Charter cemented the "fundamental right of nations to self-determination"[19] that the Big Three had tabled; earlier that year, the right to self-determination in the UN Charter had still met with resistance among the Western colonial powers. Truman began to pull American troops out of Europe in the summer of 1945. At the Potsdam Conference of the three victorious powers, the American president hoped to implement the negotiated Allied control systems in Germany and Austria with Stalin's help. In general, he envisioned cooperating with the Soviet Union to create a common policy for European peace.

The decline of the European powers in world politics coincided with a radical change in the international standing of the United States: "[It] had become the strongest military power in the world. The country's self-evident distance from the rest of the world in the years before World War II decreased at a rapid pace. As an occupation force in Germany and Japan, and with the goal of transforming both countries into democratic nations, the United States committed de facto to a long-term presence in Europe and the Far East. The Soviet Union's military and political encroachment on these regions provoked concerns of imminent Soviet domination."[20] In contrast to the period after the First World War, American troops remained in Western Europe to defend democracy and the free market economy.

Raymond Aron, a French sociologist who worked in London alongside Charles de Gaulle for a liberated France during World War II, already drew consequences from the new constellation of world power in the summer of 1945. In particular, he saw implications for the relationship between France and Germany. He spoke out decisively against the popular French demand that Germany should be punished, arguing that "Hitler himself had assumed the task."[21] He no longer saw Germany as a special danger now that the international political constellation had fundamentally shifted. The significance of Europe in the context of world politics was diminishing. The Germans themselves were forced to confront "the definitive inferiority of the Central European countries in relation both to the Soviet Union and to Western democracies."[22] To Aron, the new constellations of power made the division of Germany inevitable. He advised France to join Great Britain and the United States in helping to rebuild a destroyed West Germany.

Yalta: Controlling Germany without Dismembering It

Concerning Germany, the conference in Yalta was a turning point: the Allied powers abandoned plans to divide the continent as they had discussed during the war. One example from December 1941 suffices to clarify. Just a few days after the

Japanese attack on Pearl Harbor and the United States' entry into the war, Stalin and the British foreign minister, Anthony Eden, negotiated the lines demarcating spheres of influence in a future postwar Europe. The Soviet dictator demanded that the British government "immediately" recognize the western border of the USSR as it had been drawn in the Treaty of Non-aggression between the German Reich and the Soviet Union in 1939.[23] In a secret supplementary protocol, Berlin and Moscow had agreed to split Poland between the two powers, while the Soviet Union would absorb into its sphere of interest the Baltic states, the Bukovina, and regions surrendered by Finland in the subsequent Winter War of 1939–40. At the meeting between Stalin and Eden, the Soviet Commissariat for Foreign Affairs once again compiled secret supplementary protocols, this time addressing the borders of Germany. An undated draft suggested separating Germany "into several independent states" and dividing East Prussia between the Soviet Union and Poland.[24] The starting point of these discussions was the western border of the Soviet Union as of 22 June 1941, which, to Stalin, was nonnegotiable.

During these negotiations to secure the Allied spheres of influence, German troops stood just before Moscow. Stalin's demand that Britain recognize the Soviet Union's western border gained force after the Soviet victory in Stalingrad, when the Big Three met for the first war conference in Teheran in 1943.[25] Discussions of Germany's future tended to favor dividing up the territory. In Yalta in February 1945, however, the general mood toward these plans changed. Still, the conditions of capitulation discussed at the conference included the option of "dismembering" the country, and a special committee was created to explore this possibility.[26]

Soviet Foreign Minister Vyacheslav M. Molotov advised the Soviet representative to this committee to frame the division of Germany as just one "potential perspective." He justified this by arguing that the Western powers, "who brought up the question of dividing Germany in the first place, are now hoping to shift responsibility for the division onto the USSR in order to tarnish our country in the eyes of the international public."[27] Eden, the British foreign minister, reminded all parties debating the division that the Anti-Hitler Coalition had one primary goal toward Germany: to prevent renewed German aggression. This would be achieved through disarmament and demilitarization, as well as the dismantling of and control over German industry; but "a further instrument would be the division of Germany—'if necessary.'"[28] On March 26, 1945, the Soviet side agreed that dividing the country was "one way to exert pressure over Germany, in case other means prove to be ineffective in rendering the country harmless."[29] Meanwhile, the U.S. State Department positioned itself against the proponents of dismembering Germany. President Roosevelt accepted that the joint Control Council created in Yalta would exercise centralized control over developments in Germany. After its establishment, he believed, there would be no way for Germany to be divided.

Thus, even before the unconditional capitulation of the German Wehrmacht, the Allied victors had already decided to treat Germany as a single nation. The Big Three promised that it was not their intention "to destroy the people of Germany, but only when Nazism and Militarism have been extirpated will there be hope for a decent life for Germans, and a place for them in the comity of nations."[30] To the liberated peoples of Europe the three powers guaranteed "the right . . . to choose the form of government under which they will live."[31] This fundamental right specifically did not apply to Germany, which was viewed as an occupied enemy state not entitled to select its own government.

The foundation of joint supremacy in Germany was laid in London by Great Britain, the United States, and the Soviet Union at the European Advisory Commission (EAC), which had been established in 1943. For the historian Rolf Steininger, the EAC's significance is clear: "It was a decision specifically by this commission that had a fateful impact on Germany. On 15 January 1944, the British representative, Sir William Strang, presented a proposal to the commission to divide Germany into three zones: one each for the Soviet Union, the United States, and Great Britain. He also envisioned that troops of the other two powers would be stationed in each occupation zone."[32] The Soviet Union accepted the principle of occupation zones but insisted upon a system in which only the occupation power could station troops in its respective zone, and the high commander of those troops would exercise full supremacy. On that January day in the fifth year of the war, Gladwyn Jebb, chairman of the British planning committee, prophetically recognized the implications of this proposal: "That particular map produced at that particular moment, may prove to be of considerable significance in the history of Europe."[33] His prediction was correct. What began as simply a line to demarcate the transitional Soviet zone later became the border that divided Germany into two states and Europe into two blocs.

In Yalta, the Big Three confirmed the agreements made at the EAC and expanded them into the conference resolution. The plan called for the establishment of a central Control Commission to ensure coordinated administration and checks, "consisting of the Supreme Commanders of the Three Powers with headquarters in Berlin."[34] France was also offered an occupation zone and a seat in the Control Council. With a resolution encompassing the unconditional capitulation of the German Wehrmacht, the allocation of occupation zones, and the founding of the Control Council, all necessary structures were in place for the Allies to assume control of Germany.

After its surrender, Germany became an object of conflict among the victors even before German politicians could get involved on either side. Stalin was the first Allied leader to present himself to the Germans as a friend. On 9 May, he announced to the German people on the occasion of victory: "Germany has suffered a blow to its head. The German troops have capitulated. The Soviet Union celebrates its victory, even though it has no intention of dividing up or annihilating Germany."[35]

In his examination of the Allied Control Council, Gunther Mai concludes that by early summer 1945, the German population was already treated as little more than an object in Allied debates about Germany. Calls for a unified Germany were instruments used by the Allies in their conflicts with one another. The elevated positions and demands usually targeted the other occupation powers, serving as "tools of pressure and objects of negotiation rooted in zonal or national interests, but not representative of any obligation toward the German people."[36] Mai substantiates this theory by analyzing the behavior of the Allied powers toward pan-German political organizations, especially considering that the "democratization" of Germany had been a common goal of war: "Neither in Yalta nor at the EAC was the approval of [German] parties and unions tied to particular conditions that the Allied powers defined. But after the Soviet Union refused to engage in any debate over the substantive aspects of common occupation policy at the EAC, its pushiness to move forward no doubt aroused bafflement and mistrust—especially since the four supreme commanders had just met for direct negotiations on 5 June."[37] Stalin was certainly aware of the systemic political differences between the visions of his capitalist Allies and his own ideas of "democratization," in following with the Polish example. After Hitler's defeat, these differences would define postwar politics among the powers.

Germany's Forced Reorientation

Liberation and Occupation Rule

In Yalta, the Big Three demanded Germany's unconditional capitulation. Churchill described what this would entail for the Germans in plain terms: "submitting to the will of the victors."[38] The defeat represented, and still represents today, liberation from the National Socialist dictatorship that many Germans enthusiastically followed into war. The price of this liberation was high. Soldiers from numerous nations paid for it with their lives; Poles, Russians, Ukrainians, Americans, British, French, Norwegians, Serbians, and many others died while liberating their countries and Europe from German occupation and opening the gates of the concentration and extermination camps.

At the moment of German capitulation, only concentration camp survivors and German opponents of National Socialism could see the liberation as such and embrace it with full gratitude. German soldiers marching as prisoners of war (eleven million in total, of whom hundreds of thousands died in Soviet captivity), as well as the approximately fourteen million refugees and displaced persons from the lost German territories in the East, searching for a new home, suffered the reality of defeat in this war that Germany began. Their fates most clearly embody the Germans' change in status after the capitulation of the Wehrmacht. National Socialist ideology had elevated them to the "master race"; now they were hungry masses, homeless and without a homeland, at the mercy of decisions by foreign occupation powers, the enemies of yesterday. Along with those who had evacuated the bombed German cities, these parts of the German population could only be thankful that death on the fronts and in the bombing raids had finally reached an end. In this collapsed society, people's political agendas were limited to survival, maintaining a living space, and looking for work, on which the distribution of ration cards for food depended. Hunger and the search for lost relatives dominated the daily routine. The black market functioned as a place to exchange goods and helped people survive in the scarce economy.

Indeed, "the German people have begun to atone for the terrible crimes committed under the leadership of those whom, in the hour of their success, they openly approved and blindly obeyed."[39] With this observation about German atonement, the communiqué from the Potsdam Conference made an important differentiation: it distinguished between the National Socialists and the population that had "blindly obeyed" them. This difference was a crucial step for the Allies, paving the way to carry out the "denazification" of the German people and to discuss questions—both for and with the Germans—of responsibility and guilt for the dictatorship, war, and genocide.

The call to prosecute Nazi criminals also rose from the liberated prisoners of Buchenwald, who came from many European nations. On 19 April 1945, following their liberation, the survivors took an oath on Buchenwald's *Appellplatz* in memory of the fifty-one thousand people who had died in the concentration camp:

> One thought animated us: Our cause is just—
> > Victory must be ours!
> In many languages we led the same hard and pitiless fight full of sacrifice, and this
> > fight is not yet over. There are still Nazi flags flying!
> The murderers of our comrades are still living!
> Our sadistic tormentors are still free!
> That is why we swear here before the whole world, on this place of Fascist horrors:
> > We will only give up the fight when the last of the guilty
> > has been judged by the tribunal of all nations![40]

The vision of the future should be a "new world of peace and freedom. . . . We owe this to our murdered comrades and their families."[41]

Heinz Brandt was among those who pledged to this authentically anti-fascist oath. Looking back, he remarked:

> We have the present again. Our oath—looking toward the future—also swears to the past. We believe that what lies behind us will always bind us together. Elated, we linger in the moment. We do not ask ourselves what exactly should never happen again. Auschwitz?
> Unconsciously we understand this NEVER AGAIN to be all encompassing, as absolute as everything we have experienced and encountered in the past twelve years.
> Everything seems simple today. Tomorrow everything will already be in doubt.
> . . . Today we are united in common horror at the crimes of the past. Tomorrow we will be split in our interpretations of the crimes of the present.[42]

It is not without sorrow that Brandt describes the impending split among the anti-fascists who gathered on Buchenwald's *Appellplatz* as comrades in suffering. The survivors of National Socialist crimes were not capable of formulating a general ethics of human rights that would extend to their own future behavior and definitively rule out torture, arbitrary imprisonment, terror as political means, and camps comparable to the ones they had just survived. Of the sense of commonality, little remained beyond the will to bring the National Socialist perpetrators to justice; the shared traumatic memories could do little more than nudge a survivor in trouble to ask a favor of a comrade from a different political camp, "for the sake of the past." In addition to divergent views of other crimes against humanity, such as the atomic bomb dropped on Hiroshima or the vast landscape of Soviet gulag camps, political goals quickly divided the surviving prisoners of Buchenwald. The Communists, for example, wanted not only a democracy but an "anti-fascist democracy" in order to establish their political monopoly on power.

The Question of Guilt

The Allied declaration of German guilt applied to and affected the entire population: one of the stated goals was "to convince the German people that they have suffered a total military defeat and that they cannot escape responsibility for what they have brought upon themselves, since their own ruthless warfare and the fanatical Nazi resistance have destroyed [the] German economy and made chaos and suffering inevitable."[43] Through their military presence, the occupation powers prevented silence and repression concerning the question of guilt among the German people. The punishment of war criminals and the denazification of Germany represented Allied goals whose implementation also helped to legitimate the occupation rule.

The philosopher Karl Jaspers was one of the first to frame the (externally posed) question of guilt as a problem that could hinder a new, democratic beginning and the creation of a new national identity. In this respect, the anti-fascism instrumentalized in the East of Germany was already showing itself to be problematic. The war and its conclusion had traumatized German self-conception. Collective pride in the nation, as it exists elsewhere in the world, had been shattered by the nationalist excess of the National Socialists. Germans found themselves with an identity problem that, at times, even led to the phenomenon of German self-hatred. This problem intensified with the claim by both German states, both founded in 1949, to embody the "true" Germany.

Jaspers posed a central question: What does guilt mean in relation to the National Socialist dictatorship, the war, and the crimes committed during the war, if the Germans themselves live on—despite this assignment of guilt—and wish to rebuild their country? His answer was fundamental: "It is a vital question for the German soul. No other way can lead to a regeneration that would renew us from the source of our being. That the victors condemn us is a political fact which has the greatest consequences for our life, but it does not help us in the decisive point, in our inner regeneration."[44] To make the question of guilt more straightforward, easier to grasp, Jaspers distinguished among criminal, political, moral, and metaphysical guilt. In their implications, however, all of these categories amounted to the same thing. For example, the conditions under which political guilt and crimes could thrive were rooted in moral "lapses." The German change of course toward democracy and the rule of law must begin by addressing the question of guilt in Germany itself, Jaspers believed, through introspection by each individual person. This challenge was not meant to evoke backward-looking contrition over past events that could no longer be changed; instead, self-reflection would give Germans the drive to shape their future: "Clarification of guilt is at the same time clarification of our new life and its possibilities. From it spring seriousness and resolution."[45] Jaspers was convinced: "We have to get our spiritual bearings in Germany, with one another. We have no common ground yet. We are seeking to get together."[46]

Jaspers's piece was of programmatic character for the political culture of post-war Germany. It drew a clear moral line between National Socialist barbarian-ism (which, through German actions, had led to war and genocide) and a future German democracy. With this political-moral boundary in place, Germans began the agonizing dialogue, extending over several subsequent generations, about the darkest chapter of their twentieth-century history. Members of the "experience generation" (*Erlebnisgeneration*), who had witnessed Nazi Germany and the Second World War firsthand, reacted in large part by remaining quiet or trying to justify their acceptance of the dictatorship.

The dissolution of the National Socialist Party and the Allied denazification process sentenced the perpetrators to silence. War criminals were successively con-victed and executed in Allied courts. The German language produced new words and concepts, for example, *Vergangenheitsbewältigung* (coming to terms with the past), *Geschichtspolitik* (history politics), and *Gedenkstätten* (memorial sites) for victims of the dictatorship and the German resistance against the Nazi regime. The word *Wiedergutmachung* (reconciliation, or, literally, "making things better again") took on a new political meaning; now it denotes compensation for the victims of National Socialist rule, especially survivors of the genocide of the European Jews. To com-pensate for the destruction of their countries during the war, the Allies (particu-larly the Soviet Union) demanded reparations through the dismantling of German industrial complexes. Jaspers considered *Wiedergutmachung* to be an indispensible component of taking political responsibility toward those who were "deported, robbed, pillaged, tortured, and exiled by the Hitler régime"; at the same time, *Wiedergutmachung* represented a necessary process of moral "purification" for the German people.[47]

The political-cultural line dividing National Socialism from the postwar period symbolized a fundamental differentiation that would heavily influence the fate of divided Germany. Jaspers describes a process of turnaround that can only succeed through individual introspection, an outlook that draws on Christian ideals of man and the concept of a responsible citizen in a democratic republic. The path to Jaspers's goal is inextricably linked to a right to free expression and open, heated debate.

The Communists, meanwhile, followed an opposite strategy in their "anti-fascist fight" after the Allied victory. They focused on pushing the cultural substance and values of their anti-fascism, over which they maintained a political monopoly. Anti-fascism and the legacy of Communist victims who fought against the National Socialist dictatorship legitimized their strategy of capturing the party's undivided power. In the Communists' ideological self-image, the new order was inseparable from its nemesis, fascism, and they defined this conflict as a question of class. In fascism, the Communists saw a terrorist dictatorship in a capitalist society in crisis. The fascist regime stepped in to reinforce financial capital as the ruling class after the tools of bourgeois democracy (i.e., rule of law and parliamentarianism) had failed to do so and the Socialist revolution began to pose a threat. Out of this depiction came the Communist image of German fascism (i.e., National Socialism): domestically terrorist, outwardly aggressive and imperialist. Since class was the determinant factor, fascism's greatest enemy was the Soviet Union.

Emerging from Catastrophe: Konrad Adenauer, Kurt Schumacher, and Walter Ulbricht

Germany's place in the new, peaceful European order, as well as the future of the German people, was largely in the hands of the Allied victors; they had secured the right to determine the fate of their former enemy.

But what were the expectations of German politicians selected by the occupation powers to build a new, democratic Germany? Their actions, too, depended on decisions by the military leadership in each zone and by the Allied Control Council. The Big Three had vowed not to dismember the country, but they had yet to agree on Germany's internal organization and its position in Europe's postwar order.

On 5 June 1945, the Allied Control Council, consisting of the four supreme commanders of the occupation troops, assumed the highest governmental authority, "including all the powers possessed by the German Government, the High Command and any state, municipal, or local government or authority." After the unconditional surrender of the German Wehrmacht, there was "no central Government or authority in Germany capable of accepting responsibility for the maintenance of order, the administration of the country and compliance with the requirements of the victorious Powers"—at least, this was how the Allies reasoned. France, Great Britain, the United States, and the Soviet Union promised that their assumption of governmental authority would "not affect [*sic*] the annexation of Germany." Furthermore, "The Governments of the United States of America, the Union of Soviet Socialist Republics and the United Kingdom, and the Provisional Government of the French Republic, will hereafter determine the boundaries of Germany or any part thereof and the status of Germany or of any area at present being part of German territory."[48] With this declaration, the four powers made it clear that they would be the ones to draw Germany's new internal and external borders. Germany had lost its sovereignty. Stalin considered it necessary at this point to introduce a German version of the "Polish model" to his Western allies. Simultaneous to the assumption of supreme governmental authority by all four Allies, he moved to make the KPD the "state-building party" in the Soviet zone.

As in Poland, the advancing Soviet Army was followed by three groups from the Moscow cadre of the KPD in April 1945. In Berlin, Sachsen, and Mecklenburg-Vorpommern (Sobottka Group), these three groups helped the central political administration of the Soviet Army set up German administrations directly after the war. The "Ulbricht Group" in Berlin and the "Ackermann Group" in Dresden (for Sachsen) proved to be especially important.[49]

Kurt Schumacher was one of the first German politicians in the British zone to think fundamentally about the consequences of the German defeat, which for him had meant liberation. After a ten-year imprisonment in the Dachau Concentration Camp, he began after the war to rebuild the Social Democratic Party of Germany (SPD) in Hannover. To Schumacher, the end of World War II was the "hour of great transformation"[50] for his compatriots. In the SPD's first programmatic document from 1945, he emphasized German responsibility for the national catastrophe that yielded the present situation:

> The time has come to tell the German people that they will now experience the inevitable consequences of events that were, in large part, their own fault. Because broad swaths of the population wanted and tolerated a government that evaded any form of outside control, now the Germans will be controlled by foreign powers. Because the Third Reich tried to obliterate and bleed other populations dry, now Germany lies shattered on the ground. Because the Hitler Regime pillaged and looted Europe, today we will lose our most important means of production. Every disgrace, every torturous moment and difficulty is the result of the Third Reich.[51]

Nevertheless, without wavering, Schumacher demanded respect for Germany's self-determination: "The German Reich must be preserved as a unity of state and nation!"[52] In his conception of German politics, Schumacher built continuity with the Weimar Republic, longing for the Germans to have a democratic nation-state. The document was an appeal to the Allied powers after they had already decided to reduce the territory in the East, divide the country into four occupation zones, and subject Berlin to the joint control of the four powers.

Meanwhile, Konrad Adenauer, formerly a politician for the Catholic Centre Party in the Rhineland, contemplated the same concerns as Churchill. In the summer of 1945, he wrote: "Russia shies away more and more from cooperating with the other major powers and acts in its occupied areas entirely according to its own whim. In the *Länder* [states] that it controls, economic and political foundations have been laid that are completely different from the rest of Europe. The separation between Eastern Europe, the Russian area, and Western Europe is already a fact. . . . The part of Germany not occupied by Russia is an integrated part of Western Europe."[53]

Without reservations, Adenauer recognized the security interests of France and Belgium vis-à-vis Germany. He saw only one possible solution to the problem at hand: namely, through the "economic interdependency of West Germany, France, Belgium, Luxembourg, Holland" and perhaps England, with the goal of building a "union of Western European countries."[54] To the former lord mayor of Cologne, the German nation-state as it existed under Bismarck was history. The international political constellation made the achievement of German sovereignty, particularly in West Germany, contingent upon the formation of a Western European union. Addressing two American officers, he called on the United States in June 1945 to recognize its responsibilities. If the Americans didn't change their policy, he argued, "Germany would be lost to Bolshevism."[55] He urged them to consider the consequences of dividing Europe and Germany: "In the Russian-dominated territories of Eastern and Central Europe, a hegemonic system has emerged, structured according to Soviet principles; the Western European states need to build their own counter bloc—ideally in the form of an economic and political union. The parts of Germany not occupied by Russia should comprise a federal republic and act in close connection to the Western European democracies. Economic interdependency would best fulfill both the security interests and the economic demands of Germany's neighbors."[56] Hans-Peter Schwarz emphasizes the foresight of Adenauer's analysis in 1945, against the tangled backdrop of Germany's shattered society. Despite the complexity of the situation, Adenauer shaped his politics around the founding of a West German federal republic.

Adenauer shared this early acceptance of lost German unity with a politician who owed his top position in the KPD to the Soviet Union, and who would later become Adenauer's East German adversary: Walter Ulbricht. In January 1946, the KPD held a "national convention" (*Reichsberatung*) to lay the foundations for the SED, a unified party made up of Communists and Social Democrats. In his closing speech, Ulbricht linked the Communist rise to power within the German workers' movement to the question of national unity. Addressing the West German Social Democrats, who rejected the founding of the SED, he argued that it was "an illusion to believe that the unification of Germany and the nation can take place without the working class at the helm. Cementing the unity of our action by combining the two workers' parties is thus the fundamental decision for the future of the whole nation. This decision must be made now."[57]

Whereas Schumacher acted upon the wishes of democrats liberated from National Socialism, who longed for a single, German republic, Adenauer and Ulbricht based their politics on the reality of the emerging spheres of interest in Europe. For Ulbricht, close ties to Soviet policy and subordination to Soviet decisions were the foundation of his personal position of power, as well as his party's standing within the Soviet zone. Adenauer had to and wanted to depend on the Western powers, especially the Americans, to realize the reconstruction of German democracy in the Western zones. Adenauer and Ulbricht embodied the fundamental question in German politics after Hitler: In which direction should the country go—to the East or to the West? Both politicians were aware of their limited room to maneuver, but they were willing to use that space as efficiently as possible.

Most Germans were not ready to give up their nation-state after 1945, and the goal of German unity dominated all party programs. Germans expected their politicians to do everything possible to overcome the zonal borders. Anything else would have been unthinkable; after all, the internal German demarcation lines divided families. Looking back, the German Bundestag's Enquete Commission on the History and Consequences of the SED Dictatorship concluded: "The national feeling of belonging together, which endured over several decades, was ultimately rooted in interpersonal relationships. In the GDR, 65–70 percent of citizens maintained contact to relatives and/or friends in the Federal Republic, while 32–35 percent of West Germans maintained contacts in the GDR."[58]

Only the reality of the Cold War in and around Germany, added to a generational shift, began to diminish the goal of German unification. Still, the Germans' feeling of belonging together remained strong enough to bring about the Peaceful Revolution in the GDR in 1989 and the reunification of Germany in 1990.

Potsdam 1945

The European War ended in May, but in Asia, Japan ploughed on. Right after the Potsdam Conference concluded, President Truman gave the command—while still in Potsdam—to drop the atomic bomb on Hiroshima, forcing Japan to capitulate. The world entered the nuclear era, a critical juncture in the history of humankind. The timing of the Big Three summit in Potsdam was at first a point of contention: Should the meeting take place before or after victory over Japan? That was the question. Churchill took the initiative on 6 May by requesting a conference to discuss and reach agreement on the subsequent Allied cooperation in Germany and the rest of Europe. If it proved impossible to reconcile with the Soviet Union, the alternative was already clear: the world's division "into an Anglo-American bloc and a Soviet camp."[59]

Soviet Deputy Foreign Minister Litvinov warned Molotov on 3 June to hurry up. The conference absolutely needed to begin before the end of the Pacific War. "Our main [negotiation] partners—the United States and England—are completely absorbed in worrying about a successful end to the war in Japan; we, in contrast, are free of commitment. This situation places us in an extraordinarily advantageous position compared to our partners." Litvinov continued that since the Western powers expected the Soviet Union to participate in the Pacific War, "they will be more inclined toward concessions now than they will be after a victorious conclusion to the war in the East."[60] Both Churchill and Litvinov already saw the world as two polarized camps beginning to define their spheres of interest.

The Potsdam summit of the Big Three (17 June to 2 August 1945) marked the beginning of the path to a divided postwar Europe. Stalin, Churchill, Churchill's successor Clement R. Attlee, and Roosevelt's successor Harry S. Truman sketched out Europe's postwar organization and set into motion the inter-Allied control mechanism for Germany that they had agreed to in Yalta. At the beginning of the Potsdam Conference, mistrust already prevailed among the members of the "Anti-Hitler Coalition," and the negotiations only served to reinforce the separate spheres of influence. The clearest sign of the war coalition's deterioration was the decision to postpone formulating a peace treaty with Germany. This problem would be addressed by a council formed at the conference, comprising the foreign ministers of the four occupation powers.

In Potsdam, Churchill posed the question of which German borders the negotiation partners should use; in other words, "What do we mean by Germany?" Stalin answered that "Germany is what it has become after the war. No other Germany exists." Truman agreed: "Everything collapsed in 1945; Germany does not actually exist." Stalin added that it was now "a geographical term" and proposed that the powers "determine the Western border of Poland, and then the German question will be clearer." To emphasize Germany's fall from its position of power, he declared: "This is a country that has no government and no fixed borders, because the borders have not yet been decided by our troops. Germany has no troops whatsoever, not even border troops; it is divided into occupied zones. So go ahead, define what Germany is! It is an utterly defeated country."[61]

The "German question" thus asserted itself as a new problem in international politics. The Council of Foreign Ministers from the four Allied powers was unable to solve this problem definitively; instead it cemented the division, which then evolved into an enduring European problem.

The Potsdam Conference shifted its focus away from Germany's peace treaty. "Essentially up until the beginning of the occupation of Germany, the American government had no clear political concept for its future policy."[62] Above all, the Americans wanted to continue cooperating with the Soviet Union with respect to occupation policy, involving France as well but also working against the "establishment of a hegemonic European power." With the Germans incapacitated, this type of hegemony was only imaginable in the form of either France or Russia, assuming that one of them was able to take control of Germany.[63] Great Britain took a pragmatic approach to Germany, concentrating on overcoming the economic emergency and supporting "Germany's internal renewal and transformation into a democratic country."[64] France, meanwhile, held fast to "a classic alliance model" and pursued "a policy of balance among the old European powers, especially regarding the French–Soviet relationship. . . . Its goal was chiefly security vis-à-vis Germany, as well as Germany's domination and control."[65] Alone among the Western powers, France maintained an annexation policy in Saarland; however, in contrast to areas beyond the Oder-Neisse line, the German population there was not expelled.

Unknown in Potsdam were the Soviet goals and motives: If they were defensive, then the Soviet Union simply aimed to secure its own territory. Or did the

USSR also have "dreams of expanding"[66] to Western Europe? For the historian Hanns Jürgen Küsters, these two sets of goals are not contradictory but rather strategically reconcilable. Convincingly, he argues that especially concerning the German question, it was essential for the Soviets to "keep all options open and accept certain delays with the expectation that this would improve their own position."[67]

At the conference, the Soviet Union pursued priorities other than the preservation of the German nation-state. The Soviets considered the collection of reparations from Germany to be of utmost urgency. Indeed, the fulfillment of reparation duties and the dismantling of German industry were goals that convinced all three Allied powers to continue viewing Germany as an economic unity. Furthermore, the three powers could agree on the political foundations of their respective occupation policies in Germany, according to plans made in Yalta:

1. Demilitarization of the country, including industrial disarmament, in order to prevent Germany from ever again exercising imperial politics in Europe.
2. A ban on the NSDAP and its subgroups; the denazification of the country and the trials of war criminals in Allied military courts or at the international court in Nuremberg.
3. The Allied powers had already assumed supreme governmental authority and did not allow for the establishment of a pan-German government. The Allies' determination on this point was already clear from their "assumption of supreme authority with respect to Germany" on 5 June 1945. They did not intend to annex Germany; rather, the four powers wanted to ensure that the Germans would not be able to shirk their obligations regarding conditions for peace, future borders, and reparations owed, as they had done in part after the First World War.

The Allies' intent to exercise absolute control over German capacities appeared without ambiguity in the Berlin Declaration of 5 June 1945:

> The Allied Representatives will impose on Germany additional political, administrative, economic, financial, military and other requirements arising from the complete defeat of Germany. The Allied Representatives, or persons or agencies duly designated to act on their authority, will issue proclamations, orders, ordinances and instructions for the purpose of laying down such additional requirements, and of giving effect to the other provisions of this Declaration. All German authorities and the German people shall carry out unconditionally the requirements of the Allied Representatives, and shall fully comply with all such proclamations, orders, ordinances and instructions.[68]

4. Military governments were established in the individual occupation zones, headed by the supreme commanders of their respective armed forces. These military governors had a double function: within their occupation zones they were the sole leaders, but as members of the Control Council they were

responsible for Germany as a whole. However, "in practice, the function as a zone commander proved to be much more real and effective than that as a member of the Control Council."[69]

5. Of critical importance for the future border through Germany was the division of the country into four occupation zones and the governance of Greater Berlin through an Allied command, referred to by all sides as the "Allied Kommandatura." The control mechanism put in place evidenced the diminishing trust among the Allies that their occupation policy goals truly overlapped. In each occupation zone, the military government was the highest authority over all German administrative structures. The short-lived Allied Control Council had no German administration of its own and functioned only in consensus; each of the powers had the right to veto the council's decisions.

   As a result, the Potsdam decision to establish national secretariats in order to reinforce Germany's economic unity was vetoed by the French occupation power in the fall of 1945. The Control Council thus lacked a German administrative structure to institutionally protect the economic unity of the country; the French occupation power would not allow it.

6. In order to realize Germany's democratization, democratic parties and associations were permitted in all occupation zones.

7. Regarding the Oder-Neisse line, the Soviet and Polish governments had already acted: German territory beyond this line was already under Polish and Soviet administration.

George F. Kennan, American diplomat and expert on the Soviet Union, sharply criticized the direction of America's Germany policy in Potsdam:

> The idea of a Germany run jointly with the Russians is a chimera. The idea of both the Russians and ourselves withdrawing politely at a given date and a healthy, peaceful, stable, and friendly Germany arising out of the resulting vacuum is also a chimera. We have no choice but to lead our section of Germany—the section of which we and the British have accepted responsibility—to a form of independence so prosperous, so secure, so superior, that the East cannot threaten it. This is a tremendous task for Americans. But it is an unavoidable one; and along these lines, not along the lines of fumbling unworkable schemes of joint military government, must lie our thinking.[70]

Kennan's critique turned out to be valid. The "Polish model" of Soviet democratization policy in Germany began with the reconstruction of state administrations and a Magistrat (the city's executive governing body) in Berlin and throughout the rest of the Soviet zone, and proved incompatible with American and British visions of rebuilding democracy. Aside from the Communists, all other political parties in the Western zones strove for a democratic republic based on the rule of law. By enabling German self-determination within their occupation zones, the Western powers lay the groundwork for the FRG's later integration into the West.

But one question remains: What consequences did Potsdam have for the Germans? The coalition of necessity to fight a common war against the German Reich soon dissolved in the face of the Allied powers' competing interests. These opposing goals—rooted in different worldviews, economic systems, and political orders—were fought out in the occupation zones of Germany, always with reference to the victors' original rights of 1945. The occupation powers would continue to insist upon these rights until 1990.

Germany found itself in a strange position. The country was divided but at the same time unified under the supreme authority of the occupation powers' Control Council. With the Soviet zone, part of Germany would soon belong to the Soviet sphere of influence in Europe, while the Western zones would begin in 1948 to join the Western economic and security alliances. Notwithstanding the antagonism between the different political and social orders, Germany remained unified in one respect: the four Allied victors of World War II were unwavering—throughout their various conflicts—in their responsibility toward Germany as a whole. This became especially clear in the crises over Berlin with its special four-power status.

The borders between the Soviet zone and the three Western occupation zones increasingly divided not only Germany but also the rest of the continent. The reconstruction of German statehood in the individual occupation zones played out parallel to the development of clashing interests between the Soviet Union and the Western powers, which soon took on a name of its own: the Cold War.

Notes

1. Klaus Schwabe, *Weltmacht und Weltordnung: Amerikanische Außenpolitik von 1898 bis zur Gegenwart—Eine Jahrhundertgeschichte* (Paderborn, 2006), 117.
2. "Declaration of Principles issued by the President of the United States and the Prime Minister of the United Kingdom (Atlantic Charter)," 14 August 1941, *NATO e-Library*, http://www.nato.int/cps/en/natolive/official_texts_16912.htm.
3. "Report of the Crimea Conference (Communiqué Issued at the End of the Conference)," in U.S. Dept. of State, *Foreign Relations of the United States (FRUS), Diplomatic Papers: The Conferences at Malta and Yalta, 1945* (Washington, 1955), 972.
4. Ibid., 970.
5. See Rolf Steininger, *Deutsche Geschichte: Darstellung und Dokumente in vier Bänden*, vol. I, *1945–1947* (Frankfurt, 2002), 29.
6. Litvinov served as deputy foreign minister from 1941 to 1946; from 1941 to 1943 he was also the Soviet ambassador to Washington.
7. "Aufzeichnung von Litvinov," 11 January 1945, in *Die UdSSR und die deutsche Frage 1941–1948: Dokumente aus dem Archiv für Außenpolitik der Russischen Föderation*, ed. Jochen P. Laufer and Georgij P. Kynin (Berlin, 2004), vol. I, 521–22.
8. Jens Hacker, *Der Ostblock: Entstehung, Entwicklung und Struktur 1939–1980* (Baden-Baden, 1983), 9.

9. In 1938, the executive committee of the Communist International dissolved the Polish party, claiming that it was a party of agents. Not until the CPSU's 20th Party Congress in 1956 was this decision declared unjustified. See Reinhard Crusius and Manfred Wilke, "Polen und Ungarn 1956: Eine Dokumentation," in *Entstalinisierung: Der XX. Parteitag der KPdSU und seine Folgen*, ed. Reinhard Crusius and Manfred Wilke (Frankfurt am Main, 1977), 98.

10. Leonid Gibianskij, "Osteuropa: Sicherheitszone der UdSSR, sowjetisiertes Protektorat des Kreml oder Sozialismus 'ohne Diktatur des Proletariats'? Zu den Diskussionen über Stalins Osteuropa-Politik am Ende des Zweiten Weltkrieges und am Anfang des Kalten Krieges," *Forum für Osteuropäische Ideen- und Zeitgeschichte* 8, no. 2 (2004): 131.

11. Georgi Dimitroff, *Tagebücher 1933–1943*, ed. Bernhard H. Bayerlein (Berlin, 2000), vol. 1, 162.

12. Gibianskij, "Osteuropa," 131.

13. Ibid.

14. Isaac Deutscher, *Stalin: A Political Biography* (London, 1949), 552.

15. Ibid.

16. See Zbigniew K. Brzezinski, *Der Sowjetblock: Einheit und Konflikt*, trans. Karl Römer (Cologne, 1962), 31.

17. "Prime Minister Churchill to President Truman," London, 12 May 1945, in U.S. Dept. of State, *FRUS, Diplomatic Papers: The Conference of Berlin (The Potsdam Conference), 1945* (Washington, 1960), vol. 1, 9.

18. Schwabe, *Weltmacht*, 152.

19. Peter J. Opitz, *Die Vereinten Nationen: Geschichte, Struktur, Perspektiven* (Munich, 2002), 77.

20. Schwabe, *Weltmacht*, 161–62.

21. Raymond Aron, *Memoirs: Fifty Years of Political Reflection*, trans. George Holoch (New York, 1990), 145.

22. Ibid., 153.

23. "Unterredung zwischen Stalin und Eden," 16 December 1941, in Laufer and Kynin, *UdSSR*, vol. 1, 24.

24. "Entwurf eines Zusatzprotokolls," December 1941, in Laufer and Kynin, *UdSSR*, vol. 1, 32.

25. See Alexander Fischer, ed., *Teheran, Jalta, Potsdam: Die sowjetischen Protokolle von den Kriegskonferenzen der "Großen Drei"* (Cologne, 1968), 86–87.

26. Ibid., 191–92.

27. "Molotov an Gusev," 24 March 1945, in Laufer and Kynin, *UdSSR*, vol. 1, 555.

28. Quoted in Theodor Eschenburg, ed., *Jahre der Besatzung 1945–1949*, vol. 1 of *Geschichte der Bundesrepublik Deutschland*, ed. Karl Dietrich Bracher et al. (Stuttgart/Wiesbaden, 1983), 301.

29. Ibid., 301.

30. "Report of the Crimea Conference," in U.S. Dept. of State, *FRUS: Malta and Yalta*, 971.

31. Ibid., 972.

32. Steininger, *Deutsche Geschichte*, vol. 1, 19.

33. Tony Sharp, *The Wartime Alliance and the Zonal Division of Germany* (Oxford, 1975), 57.

34. "Report of the Crimea Conference," in U.S. Dept. of State, *FRUS: Malta and Yalta*, 970.

35. Josef W. Stalin, "Ansprache des Genossen J. W. Stalin an das Volk, 9. Mai 1945," in Josef W. Stalin, *Reden, Interviews, Telegramme, Befehle, Briefe und Botschaften, Mai 1945–Oktober 1952*, ed. Parteihochschule "Karl Marx" beim ZK der SED (n.c., n.d.), 5.

36. Gunther Mai, "Alliierter Kontrollrat," in *Deutschland unter alliierter Besatzung 1945–1949/55*, ed. Wolfgang Benz (Berlin, 1999), 40.

37. Gunther Mai, *Der Alliierte Kontrollrat in Deutschland 1945–1948: Alliierte Einheit—deutsche Teilung?* (Munich, 1995), 118.

38. Fischer, *Teheran*, 112.

39. "Report on the Tripartite Conference of Berlin (Communiqué No. 1384)," Babelsberg, 2 August 1945, in U.S. Dept. of State, *FRUS: Conference of Berlin*, vol. 2, 1501.

40. "Der Schwur von Buchenwald," 19 April 1945, Stiftung Gedenkstätte Buchenwald, http://www.buchenwald.de/files/downloads/Schwur-D.pdf. English and German versions of this

text were read aloud by the former prisoners of Buchenwald on 19 April 1945; however, there are strong indications that the German version was the original. The text quoted here is a translation of the German, based closely on the English version of 19 April 1945.

41. Ibid.

42. Heinz Brandt, *Ein Traum, der nicht entführbar ist* (Munich, 1967), 166–67.

43. "Report on the Tripartite Conference of Berlin," in U.S. Dept. of State, *FRUS: Conference of Berlin*, vol. 2, 1502.

44. Karl Jaspers, *The Question of German Guilt*, trans. E. B. Ashton (New York, 2000), 22.

45. Ibid., 113.

46. Ibid., 5.

47. Ibid., 113.

48. "Declaration Regarding the Defeat of Germany and the Assumption of Supreme Authority by the Allied Powers," Berlin, 5 June 1945, in U.S. Dept. of State, *Documents on Germany, 1944–1985* (Washington, 1985), 33.

49. See Rainer Behring and Mike Schmeitzner, *Diktaturdurchsetzung in Sachsen: Studien zur Genese der kommunistischen Herrschaft 1945–1952* (Cologne, 2003).

50. Kurt Schumacher, "Für ein neues, besseres Deutschland! (Ein Aufruf zur Besinnung und geistigen Umkehr)," in Kurt Schumacher, *Nach dem Zusammenbruch: Gedanken über Demokratie und Sozialismus* (Hamburg, 1948), 10.

51. Kurt Schumacher, "Konsequenzen deutscher Politik (Forderungen und Ziele der SPD)," in Schumacher, *Zusammenbruch*, 17.

52. Schumacher, "Für ein neues, besseres Deutschland!," 12.

53. Quoted in Hans-Peter Schwarz, *Vom Reich zur Bundesrepublik: Deutschland im Widerstreit der außenpolitischen Konzeptionen in den Jahren der Besatzungsherrschaft 1945–1949*, 2nd ed. (Stuttgart, 1980), 425.

54. Ibid.

55. Quoted in Henning Köhler, *Adenauer: Eine politische Biografie* (Berlin, 1997), vol. 1, 332.

56. Schwarz, *Reich*, 425–26.

57. Walter Ulbricht, "Die Aufgaben der KPD im Kampf um die Herstellung der Einheit der Arbeiterklasse: Schlusswort auf der Reichsberatung der KPD in Berlin am 8. und 9. Januar 1946," 9 January 1946, in Walter Ulbricht, *Zur Geschichte der deutschen Arbeiterbewegung*, vol. 2, *1933–1946*, supplementary volume (Berlin (East), 1966), 340.

58. "Bericht der Enquete-Kommission," in *Materialien der Enquete-Kommission: Aufarbeitung von Geschichte und Folgen der SED-Diktatur in Deutschland*, ed. Deutscher Bundestag (Baden-Baden, 1995), vol. 1, 478.

59. Manfred Görtemaker, "Potsdamer Konferenz (17.7.–2.8.1945)," in Benz, *Deutschland unter alliierter Besatzung*, 214.

60. "Litvinov an Molotov," 3 July 1945, in Laufer and Kynin, *UdSSR*, vol. 2, 40–41.

61. Quoted in Fischer, *Teheran*, 214–15.

62. Hanns Jürgen Küsters, *Der Integrationsfriede: Viermächte-Verhandlungen über die Friedensregelung mit Deutschland 1945–1990* (Munich, 2000), 71.

63. Ibid., 72.

64. Ibid., 82.

65. Ibid., 86.

66. Ibid., 93.

67. Ibid.

68. "Declaration Regarding the Defeat of Germany and the Assumption of Supreme Authority by the Allied Powers," Berlin, 5 June 1945, in U.S. Dept. of State, *Documents on Germany*, 37–38.

69. Richard Thilenius, *Die Teilung Deutschlands: Eine zeitgeschichtliche Analyse* (Hamburg, 1957), 133.

70. George F. Kennan, *Memoirs: 1925–1950* (Boston, 1967), 258.

Chapter 2

NEW BORDERS FOR GERMANY

Poland's Borders and the Separation of Austria and the Eastern Provinces

In their war plans, the members of the Anti-Hitler Coalition took the German borders of 1937 as their starting point: all revisions by the National Socialists after 1938 were automatically dismissed. This included the Anschluss of Austria and the integration of the Sudetenland into the German Reich in 1938. Austria was thus restored to an independent state, and the Sudetenland was returned to Czechoslovakia.

There were qualitative differences in the implications of these new borders. The separation of the eastern territories by drawing Poland's borders permanently changed Germany's territorial composition. Germany ceased to be a major European power—and this allowed for the emergence of a new constellation of players whose spheres of interest ran right through the country. At the Potsdam Conference of 1945, a compromise on the structure of reparations represented the first steps toward separating the Soviet and Western zones. It was a preliminary decision on the borders of the two German states, but the frontiers lasted until 1990, taking on fundamental significance for the history of divided Germany.

Decisions over the eastern border of Germany took place at the Allied war conferences in Tehran in 1943 and Yalta in February 1945; de facto, they were also decisions about the new Polish borders. The crystallization of Poland's eastern border with the Soviet Union represented Britain and America's willingness in Tehran to recognize the western Soviet border as it stood in 1941. The "Big Three" (Stalin, Churchill, and Roosevelt) agreed at the same meeting to set Poland's western border at the Oder. Stalin then laid Soviet claim to the ice-free ports in Königsberg and Memel, as well as their surrounding areas.[1] Poland's new western border was finalized in Yalta in February 1945. Poland was to receive compensation for its loss of land in the East, which was not specified further, in the form of "substantial accessions of territory."[2] Regarding the exact shape of the borders, the Soviet foreign minister hoped to discuss the details with the provisional Polish government.

Here, too, the Soviet leadership instated a policy of faits accomplis. The Soviets and the provisional Polish government signed a resolution on 21 April 1945 stating that all territories east of the Oder captured by the Soviet Army were now under Polish authority.[3] Without consultation with the Western powers, the Polish administration took over these former German territories while the Soviet government took Königsberg and northern East Prussia. Stalin's concession to the British and Americans at the summit in Potsdam was his willingness to postpone finalizing these borders until a peace treaty could be drawn.[4] At the same time, the victorious powers all agreed on the "removal of Germans from Poland, Czechoslovakia and Hungary."[5] With the Western powers in support of this population transfer, the separation of Germany's eastern territories was essentially complete. But the border's status under international law still seemed open; for refugees and expellees from East Prussia, Pomerania, eastern parts of Brandenburg, and Silesia, it remained the one hope they had of returning to their former homeland. This question was only clarified officially through the process of German reunification in 1990, when reunified Germany recognized the Oder-Neisse line as its eastern border.

The Demarcation Lines of the Occupation Zones

The Allies drew demarcation lines within Germany in September 1944, in reaction to the Soviet Army's unstoppable march forward while the Western powers still fought in France. It seemed possible at the time that the Soviet Army could penetrate deep into central Germany before the Americans and British could even cross the Rhine. Looking to protect themselves if this turned out to be the case, the Western powers wanted the Soviet Union to enter into a binding agreement. In Yalta the following year, the Allies agreed to establish occupation zones in which only the respective occupation power could exercise authority. The Soviet Union would occupy the East of Germany, Great Britain the Northwest, the United States the Southwest and Bremen, as well as the port of Bremerhaven, and France the West. As the headquarters of the Allied Control Council, Greater Berlin would be omitted from the distribution of zones, divided into four sectors, and governed by an Allied Kommandatura.[6]

The four zones differed from each other sharply in size, economic potential, and population: "With 22.3 million inhabitants, the British zone was the most populous, followed by the Soviet zone with 17.3 million (not counting Berlin with 3.18 million). . . . In terms of area, the Soviet and the American zones were nearly the same size, each occupying approximately 30 percent of the entire territory. The British zone was slightly smaller, at 27 percent, while the French zone was the smallest in terms of both population (5.9 million) and size (approximately

43,000 square kilometers including the Saar region, totaling 12 percent of the entire territory)."[7]

From an economic perspective, the British zone was most important industrially for rebuilding the country; after the separation of the industrial regions in Upper Silesia, the Ruhr Valley provided the highest concentration of raw material industry in Germany. "According to the production statistics of 1936, 87 percent of German coal production, 72 percent of iron making, and 72 percent of raw steel extraction fell within the British zone."[8] The processing industries in both the American and the Soviet zones relied on coal and steel shipments from the Ruhr.

Within the individual zones, the military governments retained preexisting *Länder* (states) such as Bavaria, Schleswig-Holstein, Saxony, Thuringia, and the Hanseatic cities of Bremen and Hamburg. In addition, they created new territorial units. Prussia, Germany's largest *Land*, proved especially problematic: after its eastern provinces were severed from Germany, the remaining Prussian territory was divided once more by the zonal borders. The occupation powers dissolved Prussia de facto in 1945. Provisional German administrations were established immediately in the intact Prussian provinces in all occupation zones; otherwise the regions were absorbed into new territorial entities. In this way, the Soviet zone of 1945 encompassed the province of Saxony, which was later split into Saxony-Anhalt and Mecklenburg-Vorpommern; likewise, the American zone included Hessen and Württemberg-Baden, and the French zone Rhineland-Palatinate and Württemberg-Hohenzollern—Württemberg had been divided to French advantage. After the founding of the FRG, Württemberg-Baden became the nucleus of Baden-Württemberg, a *Land* created in 1952 that included Württemberg-Hohenzollern. Baden, occupied by the French, voted to join this temporary "southwestern state" in 1951. These events represented not only a reunification of Württemberg but also the only German-initiated revision to the *Länder* borders set by the Allies.

The new organization of *Länder* in the British zone took on particular significance for the development of West Germany. In 1946, the British created two large *Länder* with low population densities: Lower Saxony and North Rhine-Westphalia, the latter a combination of the Prussian provinces Rhineland and Westphalia. This step by Great Britain also secured the Ruhr Valley from French annexation plans and the Soviet Union's claim to control. The founding of North Rhine-Westphalia on 23 August 1946 coincided with the creation of a unified economic area in the American and British zones.[9]

In the same year, France erected a customs border between the Saar region and the rest of the French occupation zone. The Saar was then directly linked to France through an economic union, but it retained political autonomy and was treated as a third German state. Later, however, the French government failed in its attempt to permanently detach the Saar region from Germany by signing a treaty to this end with the FRG in the context of a European statute. In a popular referendum on 23 October 1955, Saarland's inhabitants decided against the statute, with a 67.7 percent majority of eligible voters supporting reintegration into Germany. Following the German–French Saar Treaty of October 1956, "Saarland returned to

West Germany as a federal *Land* on 1 January 1957."[10] After a transitional period, the Federal Republic reincorporated Saarland's economy in 1959. The region's reintegration followed Article 23 of Germany's Basic Law (Grundgesetz), which allowed for the accession of "other parts of Germany" into its scope of authority.

The creation of new *Länder* from Prussian provinces ended in the four zones in 1946. Since Prussia no longer existed as an entity, a formal decision by the Allied Control Council was unnecessary. Still, in February 1947, the council officially declared Prussia's dissolution, arguing that "Prussia was a hotbed of militarism and reaction in Germany."[11] This statement was especially beneficial to the territorial interests of the Soviet Union, which, together with Poland, had taken control of the Prussian provinces in eastern Central Europe. In their view, the declaration served as further recognition of their acquired territories by the Western powers.

Reparations Borders

In Yalta in 1945, the three powers essentially gave up their plans to dismember Germany; it was to be treated as a unified economic region under Allied occupation. Abandoning these plans also tied in to another decision: the Big Three obliged Germany to "compensate" (*wiedergutmachen*; literally, to make things better again) for damages to the Allied countries during the war. After the Yalta Conference, a new joint Allied commission set to work in Moscow to determine an appropriate "compensation of damage."[12]

The war caused particularly grave destruction in the Soviet Union, especially resulting from Germany's "scorched earth" strategy unleashed upon the troops' withdrawal. In 1942, the USSR established the first state commission to assess war damages. In 1943 came the Government Commission for Compensation for Damages Caused to the USSR by Hitler Germany and its Followers.[13] The work of this commission, based in the Soviet Ministry of Foreign Affairs, led to the Soviet demand in Yalta that Germany pay a total of $20 million, of which the USSR should receive $10 million. This sum did not represent financial obligations but rather the dismantling and transfer of factories, as well as the requirement that Germany hand over goods in production. The amount also included labor by German prisoners of war. The question of reparations produced a sharp split between the Soviet Union and the Western powers, proving to be an explosive factor in plans for German economic unity in Potsdam later that year.

The Allied victors knew it would be impossible for Germany to compensate fully for the damages it had caused during the war. Thus, Yalta's general resolution contained a limitation, stating that Germany was to pay reparations "to the greatest extent possible."[14] This limitation came mostly from Churchill, who questioned "whether Germany was in a position at all to deliver on high reparations payments. He mentioned the 'phantom of a starving Germany' with its eighty million people, whose provisions could become a major problem."[15] Roosevelt, in contrast, accepted Stalin's demands vis-à-vis Germany as the starting point for negotiations.

The Yalta resolution disguised fundamental differences in opinion among the powers regarding reparations, which, in turn, reflected diverging interests. The Soviet Union not only was aware of this but also aspired to use it politically. Toward the end of 1945, Maxim Litvinov suggested that the Soviet Union support France's push to weaken Germany, in contrast to the Anglo-American "inclination" to "preserve Germany as a more or less unified, large state."[16] In return for supporting France's power politics, the Soviet Union hoped to gain a share of control in the Ruhr Valley.

Reparations demands also reflected the Allied powers' own economic systems. Scheduled reparations payments from Germany were a top priority for the Soviet Union, whereas the reconstruction of a unified German nation-state through compromise with the Anglo-Americans was not. To boost its centrally managed economy, the Soviet Union focused on dismantling and transferring entire German industrial plants and absorbing the goods that were currently in production. "Moreover, Moscow assumed that German labor would benefit not only postwar reconstruction but also further industrialization [in the Soviet Union]."[17] German reparations functioned as free supplies to the central economic administration of the Soviet Union.

In January 1946, speaking to Molotov and Lavrentiy P. Beria, Stalin reportedly took the position that "Germany, with its workforce, equipment, experience, and capabilities, must be used to its limits."[18] In substance, this view reflected perfectly the tactics of Soviet policy toward Germany. Communists were established as the dictatorial state party in the Soviet zone, and the societal structures were Sovietized. At the same time, the Soviet Union adhered to the system of joint control over Germany, hoping to increase its influence in the Western occupation zones— not least for the sake of increased reparations. This tactic did not rule out conflict with the Western powers but aimed to avoid military confrontation. "The Soviets cemented their power position in Germany as much as possible, pushing it as far as the Western allies would tolerate politically and the shared system of responsibility would withstand legally."[19]

The Americans and the British, meanwhile, had other economic interests. Moreover, they were wary of Germany's political and economic failure to pay reparations after the First World War. The United States was fundamentally against reparations, arguing that they would disrupt the exchange relationships of the market. Instead, the Americans wanted to build a multilateral "world economic system,"[20] a position that Britain supported. The British were also critical that the extensive dismantling of German industry would greatly decrease capacities to rebuild the country. Furthermore, the Western powers worried about the provision of goods to the German people, as well as the question of who would pay for those goods. Both the British and the Americans wanted to avoid a situation in which their own taxpayers would have to pay for the costs of occupying Germany. However, this goal required allowing the German economy to recover after just a short period of reparations and limiting the dismantling of German industry to disarmament. In this way, industrial production would be able to create a surplus in German exports, thus financing the occupation and the import of basic goods.

The Americans countered the Soviet proposals in Potsdam with a suggestion that would have far-reaching implications: each power should only extract reparations from its own occupation zone. The Soviet Union accepted this compromise on the condition that the Western zones transfer additional dismantled industrial plants and machines to the Soviet zone. In exchange for some of these costs, the Soviets would provide food and raw materials to the Western zones. This was the division of Germany based on reparations politics, following the American initiative to prevent the Soviet Union from tapping into German economic potential beyond the borders of the Soviet zone.

At the same time, the Americans still believed in sharing the administration of the German economic area with the Soviet Union through the Control Council. France was not present at the Potsdam Conference, and the French government was determined to "use German resources indiscriminately for the economic reconstruction of France."[21] Access to reparations was one reason why the French government used its veto in the Control Council to prevent the establishment of a German central administration. France did not consider a pan-German economic policy—even one directed by the Control Council—to be in its best interests. The autonomy of the individual occupation zones and the specific interests of their military governments parceled out the German economic region with sweeping consequences. The old web of supply relationships among the German regions, a system built on the regional division of labor, was completely disrupted: "Domestic commerce was superseded by complicated, essentially foreign trade relationships between the German occupation zones."[22]

It was not until the spring of 1946 that the first interzonal commerce agreements were signed between individual German states. The American military governor, General Lucius D. Clay, reported to Washington in May 1946 "that each of the occupation zones represented a hermetically isolated economic region after one year of allied rule. This seemed catastrophic for both the economies of the individual zones and the economic development of Germany as a whole."[23] The situation contradicted an American vision of the German economic area as a pool that "would necessitate a comprehensive exchange of resources among the individual zones."[24] To motivate France and the Soviet Union toward a more constructive policy in the Control Council, Clay halted the dismantling of industry in the American zone in May 1946, as well as the shipments of reparations to France and the Soviet Union. This step signaled the end of reparations in the Western occupation zones but fell short of the goal of rebuilding Germany's economic unity. Clay drew important conclusions from this failure. In May 1946, "as a way out of the economically and politically unbearable situation," he suggested that Washington "begin rebuilding German economic unity through a fusion of zones, at first between the American and British zones."[25]

By the end of 1945 and beginning of 1946, the Soviet occupation power was no longer primarily concerned with the "disarmament of Germany." More important was the army's access to nuclear weapons, and for this, the Soviet occupation zone played a significant role. Since the summer of 1942, Russian physicists had worked to develop an atomic bomb; these efforts intensified greatly in the summer of 1945, when the Americans used the weapon for the first time—just days after the end of the Potsdam Conference. Stalin gave the orders. The Soviet atomic project had brilliant physicists at its disposal, who, like Pjotr Kapitsa, were among the pioneers of nuclear physics.[26] In the spring of 1945, the advancing Soviet troops were accompanied by Soviet physicists, with the goal of securing uranium and laying the groundwork for "the total material and personal 'exploitation' of German atomic research."[27] On 20 August 1945, a special task force formed from members of the State Defense Committee, with Lavrentiy P. Beria at its head. Only the NKVD was in a position to provide adequate resources to support the bomb project as a top priority on all levels.[28] In 1945, the Soviet Union possessed mostly underdeveloped sources of uranium deposits in Central Asia. After Allied victory, further deposits became available in Saxony, which was part of the Soviet occupation zone. The Soviet Special Committee on the Atomic Bomb decided in August 1945 "to undertake an expedition for the NKVD to explore Saxon ore."[29] Sure enough, the geologists found what they were looking for; however, it took until 1947 to start the SDAG Wismut company and begin mining uranium. The presence of uranium may have provided another reason for the Soviets to reject the American proposal of German demilitarization at the Paris conference of foreign ministers in 1946.

The Moscow conference of foreign ministers in March 1947 did not lead to an agreement over the German question either. Instead, like the London conference nine months later, the meeting was "pure diplomatic show business in which the rhetoric of a unified Germany, polished and recited by both sides, served to impress the Germans in each side's region of power and saddle responsibility onto the other side for the relentlessly persistent development of two German states."[30] In Moscow, reparations became an object of diplomatic sparring once again. "Foreign Minister Molotov accused the Americans of taking more than $10 million in reparations from Germany in the form of patents and other technical 'know-how'; American Secretary of State [George] Marshall rejected this indignantly as simply 'fantastic.'"[31] The actual extent of "intellectual reparations" paid to the Americans by Germany has since become known. Right after the end of the war, approximately one thousand German scientists were brought to the United States along with their teams, of which Wernher von Braun and his rocket builders from Peenemünde are the most prominent examples. Denazification did not apply to these groups, nor to the scientists recruited for Soviet nuclear and rocket programs; demilitarization and industrial disarmament were only meant for Germany. The Americans also began a microfilm project to copy scientific results from corporate archives and patents from the German patent office in order to secure them for their own purposes. "More than 30 km of film were required to record the most important patents"[32]—material that the German Ministry of Commerce made available to American firms.

For the economy and society of the Soviet zone, reparations took on a greater weight and much deeper significance. André Steiner distinguishes five waves of industrial dismantling in the Soviet zone up until the spring of 1948. Some sectors lost 75 to 80 percent of their 1945 capacities through this process; the airplane industry was dismantled completely and transferred east. The disassembly of train tracks reduced the train network by half compared to 1938, a change reflected in the reduction of locomotives and railway cars. The portion of the Soviet zone/ GDR's GNP devoted to reparations payments reached 48.8 percent in 1946, sinking to 14.6 percent by 1952.[33] In the summer of 1946, the Soviet Union changed its reparations politics, shifting its focus to removing goods from current production rather than dismantling German industry. Large industrial plants set for destruction were transformed into Soviet joint-share companies (SAGs), whose production primarily satisfied reparations schedules.

In connection with its new reparations policy, the Soviet Military Administration in Germany (SMAD) took on a "forceful role in interzonal commerce."[34] At the Central Administration for Trade and Supply (Zentralverwaltung für Handel und Versorgung), a new department formed to take charge of interzonal and foreign commerce. The Leipzig Trade Fair was reopened, and for the first time the SMAD allowed cash transactions in interzonal trade. The military administration's interest in interzonal commerce was related to the fulfillment of reparations obligations: it was the only way to balance out the lack of raw materials and industrial goods in the Soviet zone. After negotiating with the Soviets, representatives from the Western zones' chambers of commerce reported "that the Russians' interest lay not in the state of Thuringia but in the deliveries of reparations payments from Thuringia. . . . It became apparent that they urgently needed materials in order to prevent the industry from coming to a halt within the next two to three months. Out of this desperation, the Russians were willing to make certain sacrifices."[35] The Soviet Union was the only occupation power to maintain control over all imports to and exports from its zone.

The importance of reparations for the Soviet Union becomes clear in the statute of the Soviet Control Commission (SKK) from 1949. The third entry in a list of the SKK's tasks reads: "Ensuring the fulfillment of obligations by the German government concerning deliveries of reparations and the settlement of occupation costs."[36] Only after 17 June 1953 did the USSR allow the government of the GDR to retain goods from its current production, handing over the SAGs in Soviet possession to the GDR. Wismut became a German–Soviet joint-share company. The Soviet minister of foreign commerce, Anastas J. Mikojan, explained that uranium mining held great importance "for the security and defense not only of the Soviet Union, but also of the GDR."[37]

Berlin: The Four-Sector City

As the headquarters of the Allied Control Council, Berlin was a separate area of occupation. The Allied Kommandatura held governing authority, comprised of the city commandants of all four powers. The city was split into four sectors that reflected the division of Germany: Soviet forces occupied the east and the center, British troops held six districts in the northwest, of which they gave two northern districts to France, and American troops occupied the southwest.[38]

With the Soviet Union's pullout from the Berlin Kommandatura in the days leading up to the Berlin Blockade, the joint, four-power administration ended. Leaving the Kommandatura on 1 June 1948, the Soviet representative articulated for the first time "that Berlin lay in the Soviet occupation zone. The Soviet Union repeated the statement in a note to the Western powers on 14 June 1948."[39] The USSR and, after its founding, the GDR maintained this position adamantly. Later, during the Berlin Crises, it became the basis for their demand that Berlin's status change. However, the end of the four-power Kommandatura did not terminate the city's four-power status; it was simply the end of joint administration. Until December 1948, each of the four military governments maintained supreme authority in its respective sector, dividing Berlin both politically and administratively. But on 21 December 1948, the three Western city commandants declared that the Allied Kommandatura had resumed its work despite the Soviet Union's unilateral withdrawal. They considered it their duty to "resume joint authority over the German institutions," as described in the preliminary constitution of Berlin from 1946.[40]

Geographically, Berlin did lie in the Soviet occupation zone, and the Western powers needed transit routes through the Soviet zone in order to provide their troops with adequate supplies. In all of the negotiations over Germany and Berlin, the question of free access to the Berlin sectors occupied by the United States, Great Britain, and France had never been addressed. The Western powers had assumed that the agreement to create sectors in Berlin would "automatically entail a right to free access, as well as the provision of food, energy, water, and other necessities."[41]

Only the Western powers' air travel to Berlin had been regulated by the Control Council on 30 November 1945. The Council had established three air corridors to and from Hamburg, Frankfurt, and Bückeburg (in the district of Schaumburg, in western Lower Saxony), as well as a control space over Berlin (ten nautical miles around Tempelhof). In Berlin, the Control Council had created an air safety control center to oversee air traffic within Berlin's air space.[42] This system remained in place until 1990, and during the Berlin Airlift in 1948, the Soviet air safety control officers continued to perform their duties. The rules were simple: "Flights to and from Berlin had to register [with air safety control] and, as a matter of routine, received permission to fly."[43] In this way, air traffic remained regulated through an inter-Allied agreement, and the Soviet Union had no interest in breaking the arrangement. But until the Four Power Agreement on Berlin of 1971, the central conflict between the Western powers and the Soviet Union revolved around the transit routes between West Germany and West Berlin.

All confrontations in Berlin had one thing in common: all four parties respected the city's four-power status and insisted on their right to maintain the situation, as well as their veto right with regard to Germany as a whole. The Western powers reiterated these rights with the founding of NATO in 1949, in a guarantee of security and assistance for West Berlin: "In Article 5 of the North Atlantic Treaty, the parties agreed 'that an armed attack against one or more of them in Europe or North America shall be considered an attack against them all and consequently they agree that, if such an armed attack occurs, each of them . . . will assist the Party or Parties so attacked.' Article 6 of the North Atlantic Treaty held special meaning for Berlin, stating that such an attack included 'an armed attack . . . on the territory of any of the Parties in Europe or North America' or on the occupation forces of any party in Europe."[44] Through Article 6, the demilitarized Federal Republic of Germany and West Berlin came under NATO's protection.

In political reality, the four-power status remained the common foundation for compromise among the powers. This became especially clear during the two Berlin Crises, the division of the city in 1948, the erection of the Berlin Wall in 1961, and the signing of the Four Power Agreement in 1971, which guaranteed the Western powers safe passage through the GDR to West Berlin and opened mostly unrestricted transit routes through the GDR for West Berliners.

Under the supremacy of the four powers, the creation of two German states with opposing political and economic systems paralleled Berlin's split into two parts. The city's division had already begun in 1945–46, and a fundamental conflict arose with the founding of the SED in 1946. Opposing interests among the powers in Berlin manifested themselves in the political goals of German politicians, particularly the Social Democrats and the Communists, and contributed to the collapse of joint Allied control over the Germans.

These processes affected not only the city itself but also the region surrounding Berlin. In 1945, the occupation powers seemed not to think through the consequences of the inter-Allied conflict situation; after all, Berlin's special status was only intended to be a transitional phase until the four powers could agree on a solution to the German question. The isolation of Berlin from the other occupation zones—a solution desired by all of the occupation powers—had a significant impact on the historical region of Berlin-Brandenburg, which had expanded through industrialization and oriented itself entirely toward Berlin. The region included Berlin proper, divided in two after 1948, and the East German cities of Potsdam and Frankfurt (Oder) after 1952. Until the erection of the Berlin Wall, the border in this area remained relatively porous; it took years for this complex urban and suburban space to sever itself completely from West Berlin. Until 1961, *Grenzgänger* (border crossers) from the GDR worked in and commuted to factories in West Berlin.[45]

But very quickly, a divided region emerged that was entirely unique in postwar Europe. It developed out of interactions among Germans who were busy reorganizing their political system in West Berlin or working to build a new state in the GDR; out of the individual occupation powers on the one hand and their interests and conflicts on the other. Berlin constituted an intersection

of international, national, and regional history. Nowhere in Europe, perhaps nowhere in the world, were regional and international history as intertwined as in the area of Berlin. Equally unique, the politics and society of this intermeshed and divided region embodied the larger Cold War—both in its dangerous crises and its periods of de-escalation. In the divided city of millions, the East–West conflicts (Berlin Crises) were more volatile than they were elsewhere; at the same time, attempts at conflict resolution and alternatives to confrontation (travel permit regulation, the Berlin Agreement [of 1971]) took shape more quickly than in other theaters of the Cold War.[46]

The year 1952 signaled a dramatic turning point with the fortification of the "western border" between the GDR and the Federal Republic, along with the severe restriction of movement by people from West Berlin into the GDR. After 1 June 1952, West Berliners could no longer travel easily to the GDR; now they had to apply for a permit to enter the country, and these applications only rarely gained approval. The purchase of food and other products in East Berlin was prohibited to residents of West Berlin beginning in November. The SMAD and SED leaders successively destroyed city-wide transit and supply networks: 1948 brought the administrative separation of sewage and electricity systems; 1949 ushered in the division of gas and water supplies; and in 1952, the telephone network and public transportation system were split in two.[47] The East German Reichsbahn cut off West Berlin from long-distance trains into the GDR. The interzonal trains now ended at Zoologischer Garten, and the exquisite stations in the western part of the city fell into disrepair.[48]

Upon the founding of the two German states in 1949 and the development of their respective policies toward Berlin, the two new governments had to recognize the rights of the Allied powers in Berlin. The Parliamentary Council (Parlamentarischer Rat), which included five nonvoting representatives from West Berlin, opted to include Greater Berlin as a federal state of West Germany through Article 23 of the Basic Law. However, the three Western Allied military governors suspended Berlin's designation as a *Land* of the Federal Republic, making it clear in their approval of the Basic Law that the city would not fall under the Federal Government's control. Instead they insisted on maintaining Berlin's four-power status, the basis of their presence there. Jens Hacker elaborates on this point: "On the other hand, they [the Western powers] did not raise any objections to the way in which Berlin (West) was, in many respects, treated by the Federal Republic as if it were one of the *Länder*. Out of their responsibility to the whole of Germany, the Western Allies recognized and supported the close political and economic ties between Berlin and the Federal Republic."[49]

The City Council (Stadtverordnetenversammlung), which had formed in West Berlin, accepted the Basic Law on 19 May 1949. At the same time, the body announced its intention "to coordinate its work with the development of the Federal Republic within the framework set by the Western Allies."[50] Legally, West Berlin was not a state of the Federal Republic; however, the Allies declined to suspend Article 87 of the 1950 Berlin Constitution, which allowed the Abgeordnetenhaus (Berlin's parliament, a successor to the City Council) to vote on and pass federal laws. The city's ties to West Germany were politically reinforced by the presence of federal institutions in Berlin and the election of Berlin's representatives to the Bundestag by the Abgeordnetenhaus.

West Berlin's de facto integration occurred in 1952 through the Law on the Position of Berlin in the Financial System of the Federal Republic. "Through this law, the city was integrated into the financial and legal system of the Federal Republic. Berlin's financial, customs, and postal administrations came under the authority of their respective federal ministries."[51] The Bundestag justified sending federal aid to Berlin because it saw West Germany as the protector of German democracy. Berlin should be capable "of providing economic and social protection to its population as required by its special situation, and of fulfilling its duties as the capital of a unified Germany."[52] Berlin had become the stage upon which the competition of systems played out.

In rebuilding the destroyed East Berlin, the SED took a firm position with its "Reconstruction Law," passed by the provisional People's Chamber (Volkskammer) in 1950: "The reconstruction of Berlin as the capital of Germany is one of the GDR's tasks. It requires the participation of the entire country's population, especially all construction workers. Together with the Magistrat of Greater Berlin, the Ministry of Construction will assume the task of planning and directing the reconstruction process."[53] Frankfurter Allee underwent a major transformation, making way to showcase Socialist housing under the banner of a new name: Stalinallee. The politicians in charge were certain that their ideological system would prevail. Rudolf Herrnstadt, editor-in-chief of the SED's central publication *Neues Deutschland*, evoked the future to promote the construction project and impress upon the architects the weight of their responsibility: "At the beginning of this era we are rebuilding the destroyed capital of Germany. The houses we build will have a perspective that spans centuries. They will stand in a unified, new, strong, democratic Germany."[54] He emphasized the symbolism of rebuilding Berlin, writing that the Germans needed "a national capital once again as a political necessity in the fight against American imperialism."[55] On 16 June 1953, it was the "construction workers" of Stalinallee who initiated the uprising against the SED dictatorship.

In the competition between the two halves of Berlin, West Berlin had a stronger pull than its eastern counterpart. In addition to being a destination for refugees from the East, West Berlin fulfilled many roles for people in its surrounding region. It was a shopping paradise, providing everyday goods in scarce supply in the GDR. It was an information exchange for Western culture, art, and entertainment. It was a workplace for tens of thousands of border crossers, a place of education for schoolchildren and university students, and a meeting point for all Germans in the divided country. "This 'magnetism' of West Berlin also had such a massive effect because the areas of Brandenburg closest to Berlin had a particularly high population density. In the 1950s, over 50 percent of residents in the district of Potsdam lived in towns that directly bordered West Berlin."[56]

In the 1952 General Treaty with the Western Allies, which went into effect in 1954, the Federal Republic recognized the rights of the Western powers to continue exercising their responsibilities vis-à-vis Berlin and Germany as a whole. The Western powers promised that they would "[consult] 'the Federal Republic on the exercise of their rights concerning Berlin,' in order to enable German assistance to the city and ensure that Berlin's population would have a voice in the Federal Republic. Regarding the FRG, the Western Allies reserved all rights agreed to by the four powers concerning movement between West Germany and Berlin."[57]

When the Allied war coalition placed Berlin under a four-power administration, it assumed that the city would remain Germany's capital. But after the founding of the two German states, this function ceased to exist. The Bundestag chose Bonn in November 1949 as its provisional seat of government—a move that reflected the Basic Law, which saw the Federal Republic as a temporary entity, the democratic core of Germany. The decision to make Bonn the temporary political center did not question Berlin as the future capital of a reunified Germany, which is also evident in the Berlin Law of 1952. The Soviet zone agreed, establishing the SMAD office and the SED party headquarters in East Berlin. Article 2, paragraph 2 of the 1949 East German Constitution declared that "the capital of the Republic is Berlin," reflecting the constitution's pan-German character. "After the constitution of 1949 was only put into effect within the Soviet zone, this sentence could either claim symbolic significance with reference to all of Germany, or it could mean that Berlin was the capital of the GDR. In the GDR, the sentence was interpreted in the latter sense."[58] Both German states held fast to Berlin as the capital of Germany at the moment of their founding. But the longer the country's division persisted, the more Berlin's status as capital faded in West Germany. In contrast, the GDR tried hard to mold Berlin into its capital, but the integration of East Berlin into the GDR was a lengthy administrative process. With the January 1957 Law on the Local Organs of State Power, East Berlin assumed its place in the centralist establishment of the state administration, with the People's Chamber and the Council of Ministers as its two main political bodies.[59]

After the founding of the GDR, the Soviet Union transitioned its military administration into a Control Commission following the example of the Western powers, which dissolved their military governments after the founding of the FRG and transferred control to high commissions. The Soviet Union's official documents avoided a clear description of its occupation rights in Berlin, instead subsuming the topic in references to agreements made at the Potsdam Conference in 1945. But the USSR continued to insist upon its rights to Berlin as a whole. Army general Vasily Chuikov, first chairman of the Soviet Control Commission (the successor to the Soviet Military Administration), described the commission's task as "supervising the implementation of the Potsdam agreements and the other joint decisions by the four powers with regard to Germany."[60] Five years later, in 1954, the Soviet government granted the GDR sovereignty. But the accompanying declaration included caveats: "The Soviet Union will maintain functions in the

GDR that are essential to guaranteeing security and that reflect the Soviet Union's responsibilities resulting from the various four-power agreements."[61]

Berlin's status had very different implications for East and West Germany. Together with its Western partners, the FRG wanted to maintain the city's unusual position to the greatest extent possible. With West Berlin's geographical separation from the rest of the Federal Republic, the presence of the Western powers guaranteed the city's protection. For the SED leadership, the Western powers' presence—along with their military members' unrestricted access to the "capital of the GDR"—was a daily reminder of the GDR's limited sovereignty and the failure of two Soviet attempts to nullify Berlin's special status. In the history of divided Germany, Berlin was the dynamic factor that always prevented the two German states from sealing themselves off completely. It was the factor that kept the German question unanswered and the decisions by competing ideologies open long enough for Berliners to break through the Wall on 9 November 1989 and transform the situation forever. The following day, Soviet leadership informed the SED that the border to the Federal Republic was the GDR's problem, but the opening of the Wall in Berlin affected "the interests of the Allies." In response to this accusation by Viacheslav Kochemasov, Soviet ambassador to East Berlin, Egon Krenz, general secretary of the SED, replied: "But at this point, that is nothing more than a theoretical question. Life gave its answer last night. The opening of the border could have only been prevented through military means. It would have resulted in a terrible bloodbath."[62]

Interzonal Trade: An Economic Safety Pin
Holding the Divided Country Together

The Potsdam Conference created a dualism between zonal autonomy and claimed economic unity, which ultimately destroyed the established trade relationships within the German economy. The zones became "closed 'customs areas,' since each occupation power was motivated to maintain control over the capacities within its own zone. But none of the zones was self-sustaining—perhaps the British and Soviet zones were the closest to it. Interzonal commerce came to replace the lacking economic unity. With its help, unsolved problems could be overlooked: [the system] enabled an exchange of resources between the zones but in principle did not infringe upon the zonal autonomy of the occupation powers."[63] This solution accommodated the requirements of Germany's economic geography without demanding a uniform economic order among the zones.

The Soviet side understood that the fusion of the British and American zones to create the Bizone not only aided the economic reconstruction of the two zones; the Bizonal administration also represented a functioning German apparatus in the West. The Germans and the two Western powers then succeeded in boosting the economies of both zones. From the perspective of the SMAD, this step laid the economic foundation "for West Germany's isolation. From this point onward, we can observe the de facto creation of a West German state."[64]

Speaking to Vladimir S. Semyonov, political advisor to Marshal Vasily D. Sokolovsky (head of the SMAD), SED leaders Wilhelm Pieck and Otto Grotewohl openly stated that they had "no interest at present in eliminating the zonal borders." The position of the Soviet sphere of influence and the power interests of SED leadership were thus identical with regard to the border: it had to be sealed in order to give "the new democratic order of the Soviet zone" time to consolidate.[65]

The volume of interzonal commerce increased steadily until April 1948, and its course was influenced by three developments: "the founding of the Bizone, the gradual transition to central economic planning in the Soviet zone, and the Marshall Plan."[66] But with the Berlin Blockade by the Soviet Union beginning in June 1948, interzonal trade came to a tentative halt. The Western powers answered the barred transit routes to Berlin with a suspension of interzonal commerce and used it as a way to apply pressure to the Soviet Union. This comes through in a conversation between the military governors Lucius Clay and Vasily D. Sokolovsky on 3 July 1948. Sokolovsky complains about the disruption to interzonal commerce, which "was the 'most important' source of trade for the Soviet zone. Now the Soviets would have to undergo a cumbersome reorientation toward the East. Clay answered smugly that he was prepared to end the block as soon as the 'technical difficulties' impeding interzonal transit were rectified."[67] Meanwhile, the German economic administrations on both sides of the border demanded the deliveries that had been laid out in the relevant agreements. The economic administration of the Bizone, for example, made sure "that the Western Allies' (implicit) goal to declare the Soviet zone a separate country for the political purpose of trade was snuffed out at the very beginning."[68]

The blockade turned into a political failure on the part of Soviet leadership. Cutting off interzonal trade had dire implications for both the economy of the Soviet zone and the delivery of reparations to the USSR, and this became increasingly evident. In 1949, American and Soviet diplomats met at the UN to discuss the situation, and the USSR accepted the American demand to end the blockade two weeks before the next conference of foreign ministers. But the meeting in Paris could not halt preparations for the founding of the two German states; on the first day of the conference, the West German Parliamentary Council announced its new Basic Law. Still, the foreign ministers reached an agreement on interzonal trade that would have fundamental significance for inter-German economic relations until 1990. The agreement created an economic safety pin that held together the two future German states.

The 1949 conference of foreign ministers in Paris recommended that the economic administrations of the Eastern and Western zones "facilitate commerce between the zones through a trade and economic agreement."[69] Since the founding of two German states was imminent, this agreement on interzonal trade stood as a remnant of the Potsdam Agreement, in which the Soviet Union, Great Britain, and the United States had agreed to treat Germany as an economic unity.

> But in the meantime, the two separate currency reforms stood in the way of a regulated exchange of goods; the Ostmark's lack of convertibility demanded a special mode of conversion between the two currencies. Following instructions from the Western powers, West German representatives were to negotiate a new interzonal trade agreement. This agreement was signed in Frankfurt am Main on 8 October [1949] between the Economic Administration Department [of the Western zones] and the German Economic Commission of the Soviet zone. The Frankfurt Agreement already contained the fundamental principles of the . . . Berlin Agreement of 20 September 1951, which would remain valid until reunification. In terms of policy on Germany, the political core of the Berlin Agreement was its scope of application. It referred not to political units but rather to the currency areas of the D-mark (West) and the D-mark (East). With this currency clause, Berlin (West) and Berlin (East) were automatically included in the agreement. In contrast to all inter-German agreements reached after that point, this document elegantly avoided questions about Berlin's status.[70]

The forty-year span of interzonal trade is historically significant because it represents the oldest and most stable component of the entire inter-German relationship. "Over many long years, this was the only area of the relationship regulated by contract. Because of its origin and legal foundations, inter-German trade was an anomaly without parallels."[71] For the Federal Republic, the economic significance of interzonal trade was minimal in comparison to foreign trade; still, it remained politically important. This became clear in 1960: after the GDR began requiring special permits from citizens of the FRG to visit East Berlin, the Federal Republic announced that it would cancel the trade agreement at the end of the year. The Soviet party leaders pressured the SED to offer concessions in order to put the agreement back into effect.[72] The economy of the GDR could never afford to forgo inter-German trade completely.[73] Apart from the political significance of inter-German commerce, there were also companies in the Federal Republic interested in maintaining economic relations with the GDR. Inter-German trade (*innerdeutscher Handel*), as it was called after the FRG officially recognized the GDR, constituted a web of political, technological, and economic interests in both German states.[74] In 1989, Egon Krenz, the new general secretary of the SED, demonstrated the lasting importance of inter-German trade for the SED state. He attempted to negotiate a credit for the GDR worth billions of marks with West Germany's Federal Government in Bonn. Helmut Kohl refused to grant the credit and changed the conditions of exchange for the SED state. In 1989, he was less concerned with relief efforts or improvements to inter-German travel than with the systemic political transformation of the GDR. The chancellor laid out the conditions of capitulation as a prerequisite to West German financial aid: an end to the SED's monopoly on power, the approval of new political parties, and free elections to the People's Chamber. With German reunification in 1990, the economic safety pin of inter-German trade became obsolete—but, from the Federal Government's point of view, it had fulfilled its purpose.

The Interzonal Pass: Initial Efforts to Control Travel to and from the East

Interzonal trade during the occupation period after the war was tied to a strict regulation of movement among the individual zones. The Allied Control Council's Second Proclamation in 1945 prevented German nationals "from leaving German territory except as authorized or directed by the Allied Representatives."[75] Germans' freedom of movement among the zones rested completely in Allied hands.

After the decision to combine the British and American zones but before the formal fusion took place, the Control Council supported an expansion of interzonal trade in 1946 and created the Interzonal Pass with Directive 43. The pass served the express purpose of facilitating commercial exchange between the zones. It was granted by the military command or a representative of the military government in the applicant's place of residence. Travel through multiple zones was recorded in the pass. "Upon arrival at the destination, the pass must be registered within 24 hours by either a Military Government or by the Burgermeister, according to the discretion of the Zone Commander."[76] By possessing this pass, the traveler also had a right to rations of food and fuel. The interzonal pass became synonymous with control over the Germans' freedom of movement, and all of the rules dictated in its bureaucracy appeared in the GDR's subsequent travel laws. The pass's period of validity varied among the zones, and after the three Western zones fused together, they no longer required the pass at all. For travel between the Soviet zone and "Trizonesia," as people called the unified economic area before the founding of the FRG, the pass continued to be required until its repeal in 1953.

Even before the founding of the two German states, their paths already diverged in terms of freedom of movement. In the Federal Republic, this freedom was a constitutional right of every citizen. Over the course of Western integration, the FRG removed customs borders to many of its neighboring countries, as well as the cumbersome procedure of acquiring an entry visa. A passport sufficed to cross its borders. For the citizens of the GDR, however, things developed differently. After the currency reform in 1948 and the Berlin Blockade by the Soviet occupation power, the Soviet authorities instated a visiting permit for travelers from the West, which, along with the interzonal pass, was required to enter the Soviet zone and later the GDR. From 1952 onward, the GDR militarily fortified its border to the FRG, closing it off to travel. Inter-German travel was permitted at just a handful of border crossings; in divided Berlin, the sector border and the municipal transportation systems were controlled at several checkpoints. In 1952, the Soviet Union rejected a request by the SED to completely seal off the sector border to the West.

But despite the SED's efforts, none of its measures sufficed to prevent or even hamper people's flight from the GDR. Thus, soon after declaring sovereignty from the Soviet Union, the GDR passed the Passport Law of 1954 requiring that all persons crossing the border of the GDR carry a passport. Paragraph 8 addressed "German nationals" (i.e., citizens of the GDR), and stated that "Whoever leaves the territory of the German Democratic Republic for another country without permission . . . will be punished with a prison sentence of up to three years."[77] With this document, emigrating from the GDR became a punishable crime, even though the GDR had not yet declared the FRG and West Berlin to be a separate country. Negotiations by the four powers over a German peace settlement were still in process.

The GDR's new passport law of 1957 criminalized leaving the country without permission; preparing to leave, as well as assisting others to flee, likewise became a "crime against the state order" of the GDR. The tightening of the passport law followed from a speech by Walter Ulbricht, in which he characterized "fleeing the republic" as "betraying the peaceful interests of the people." Emigration would only benefit "West Germany, the base of NATO."[78] Thus, the GDR used its penal code to secure its exterior border from the inside as well.[79]

In the penal code of 1968, "unlawful border crossing" became punishable according to §213, and that paragraph remained valid until 1989. The special part of the penal code that regulated military crimes, among other things, described "desertion" in §254 as being "motivated by the goal of leaving the territory of the GDR or purposefully remaining abroad." Desertion constituted a "serious crime"; perpetrators from the National People's Army and the border troops would receive a sentence of "two to ten years." Further paragraphs added to §213 by criminalizing the "unlawful establishment of connections" (§219), meaning connections to people from Western countries abroad, including the Federal Republic, who "make it their goal to disrupt the state order of the German Democratic Republic." Aid from the West to people fleeing the East was a crime as well and qualified as "human trafficking" (§132) under the GDR's penal code.[80]

Still, political penal code was not enough to cut down on mass emigration; the SED's goal required the government to implement a stronger system of secret police surveillance over the society of the GDR. Controlling exit from and entry to the GDR became a central task of the Ministry for State Security (Ministerium für Staatsicherheit, or MfS). Expanding the network of "unofficial employees" (*inoffizielle Mitarbeiter*) in the years after the Wall was built also served to obstruct flight from the GDR, contributing to the MfS's "total and ubiquitous surveillance"[81] of the population, which the last SED government finally acknowledged on 15 January 1990.

The Inter-German Emigration Movement, 1945–1989/90

After World War II, "truncated Germany" (Rumpfdeutschland)[82] became a destination of immigration. The Federal Republic's claim to be the "legal successor" of the German Reich and the sole representative of all Germans laid the constitutional basis for taking in refugees, which also applied to people fleeing the GDR and ethnic German repatriates from Poland, Romania, and later the Soviet Union.

Over the course of the war, the panicked flight of German populations from the eastern territories of the German Reich, which had become military fronts, as well as the Allied decisions to reshape Germany's external borders,[83] caused millions of Germans to lose their homes and homelands. In 1945, the expulsion of ethnic Germans began in West Prussia, Silesia, Pomerania, and the Sudetenland. 1946–47 brought the organized removal of ethnic German minorities from Poland and Czechoslovakia. These people, who suddenly found themselves homeless, were settled in the Soviet and Western occupation zones. Of the approximately 12.45 million expellees, about 4.5 million arrived in the Soviet zone and 7.95 million in the three Western zones.[84]

The Allied distribution of expellees among the four occupation zones took place in a rather arbitrary way. Border crossings, mostly from the Soviet zone to the Western zones, occurred primarily to reunite families in the years right after the war—a trend evident in the government statistics as well. Of the 2,103,100 people who crossed the zonal borders into the West between 1945 and 1949, 1,307,400 were expellees who originally arrived in the Soviet zone. After the founding of the GDR, the proportion of emigrants to the FRG born in the territory of the Soviet zone increased steadily. By the time the Berlin Wall was built, official statistics in West Germany recorded 4,722,500 immigrants from the Soviet zone/GDR to the FRG or West Berlin. Of them, 2.2 million were expellees from the East, while 2.5 million were born within the territory of the Soviet zone/GDR.[85]

Three large waves of emigration occurred in the history of the GDR. These either caused state crises or resulted from them, and were rooted in the politics of the SED and the constant comparison of systems—on an individual and collective level—by the East German population. The first emigration wave began in 1952, after the SED announced its plan to "build the foundations of socialism" at its Second Party Congress; it culminated in the uprising of 17 June 1953. In 1952 and 1953 combined, 513,783 people left the GDR. The second wave was precipitated by the collectivization of agriculture during the Berlin Crisis of 1960, as well as by the subsequent decline in the food supply. The increase in refugees during the first eight months of 1961 also reflected a general fear among the population that Berlin's sector borders would soon close. In 1960 and 1961 combined, 406,214 people fled the territory of the SED—and it was this massive flight that triggered the erection of the Berlin Wall.[86]

The summer of 1989 brought the third and last wave of emigration from the GDR. It provoked the Peaceful Revolution, which led to the end of the SED state and to German reunification. In this third wave before the fall of the Wall on 9

November 1989, refugees mostly fled via Hungary, Czechoslovakia, or Poland; in total, 343,854 people left that year. In 1990 the trend of emigration let up slightly, but 238,384 people still made their way to the West.[87]

On 1 July 1989, the West German Federal Ministry of the Interior compiled a summary of the immigration movements from the Soviet zone/GDR to the Western zones/FRG. For the current year, the immigration processing centers had already registered 55,970 applicants from the GDR. The Ministry identified three different phases of movement. The first spanned from the end of the war to 31 December 1948, during which 732,100 immigrants were registered. The second phase lasted from 1 January 1949 to 12 August 1961 and encompassed 2,686,942 people. Finally, between 13 August 1961 and 31 December 1988, 616,051 people relocated from East to West Germany. Altogether, official statistics counted 4,025,093 immigrants. The third phase was largely comprised of people who had received permission from the GDR administration to leave (382,481 in total). By contrast, just 40,101 refugees fled during that time.[88]

Following the Eastern Treaties in the early 1970s and the Basic Treaty (Grundlagenvertrag) between the Federal Republic and the GDR in 1972, the amount of approved emigration steadily increased. This reflected "relief efforts" (*menschliche Erleichterungen*) by the West German government on the one hand and the GDR's need for Western currency on the other. After the Basic Treaty, inter-German relations were based on an exchange of relief measures, specifically concerning travel, in return for Western currency. One of the most striking episodes in this arena of inter-German relations was the West German government's successful effort from 1961 to 1989 to buy the freedom of 33,755 political prisoners from prisons throughout the GDR. This humanitarian instrument of West German policy was developed in 1962 and "conducted through the charitable Diakonisches Werk, the social welfare organization of the protestant church. The Diakonisches Werk acted as an intermediary, providing 'administrative assistance' to the West German government. In total, approximately 3.4 billion [D-marks] of federal funds were transferred by the end of the GDR." The sum was transferred in the form of goods. "The purchase of people's freedom did not only include prisoners. Under certain conditions, the Federal Republic would also make financial transfers to the GDR in order to reunite families. In this way, [the FRG] facilitated the emigration of 2,000 children, for example, who had been split from their parents after the Berlin Wall was built. The number of family reunions overseen by the West German government in the context of these 'special efforts,' that is, enabled through financial payments to the GDR, is estimated to be around 250,000 cases for the period until 1989."[89]

Notes

1. Fischer, *Teheran*, 86–87.
2. "Report of the Crimea Conference," in U.S. Dept. of State, *FRUS: Malta and Yalta*, 974.
3. See Thilenius, *Teilung*, 73–79.
4. See ibid.
5. "Report on the Tripartite Conference of Berlin," in U.S. Dept. of State, *FRUS: Conference of Berlin*, vol. 2, 1511.
6. See Dietrich Rauschning, ed., *Rechtsstellung Deutschlands: Völkerrechtliche Verträge und andere rechtsgestaltende Akte* (Munich, 1985), 6–10.
7. Christoph Kleßmann, *Die doppelte Staatsgründung: Deutsche Geschichte 1945–1955* (Bonn, 1991), 67.
8. Ibid., 70.
9. See Oliver Harvey, "Die zukünftige Deutschlandpolitik," memorandum to the Foreign Office, 24 May 1946, in Steininger, *Deutsche Geschichte*, vol. 1, 229–44.
10. Thilenius, *Teilung*, 98.
11. Gerd Heinrich, *Geschichte Preußens: Staat und Dynastie* (Frankfurt am Main, 1981), 530.
12. "Report of the Crimea Conference," in U.S. Dept. of State, *FRUS: Malta and Yalta*, 971.
13. See Jochen Laufer, "Die Reparationsplanungen im sowjetischen Außenministerium während des Zweiten Weltkrieges," in *Wirtschaftliche Folgelasten des Krieges in der SBZ/DDR*, ed. Christoph Buchheim (Baden-Baden, 1995), 21–44. "Reparations are forced economic payments made after a war by the defeated to the victor, without claiming to even out the difference between the defeated and the victorious." Jörg Fisch, *Reparationen nach dem Zweiten Weltkrieg* (Munich, 1992), 17.
14. "Report of the Crimea Conference," in U.S. Dept. of State, *FRUS: Malta and Yalta*, 971.
15. Steininger, *Deutsche Geschichte*, vol. 1, 32.
16. Laufer and Kynin, *UdSSR*, vol. 2, 191.
17. André Steiner, *Von Plan zu Plan: Eine Wirtschaftsgeschichte der DDR* (Bonn, 2007), 24.
18. Küsters, *Integrationsfriede*, 205.
19. Ibid.
20. Christoph Buchheim, "Kriegsschäden, Demontagen und Reparationen: Deutschland nach dem zweiten Weltkrieg," in Deutscher Bundestag, *Materialien der Enquete-Kommission: Aufarbeitung*, vol. 2, 1038.
21. Hermann Graml, "Die deutsche Frage," in Eschenburg, *Besatzung*, 328.
22. Werner Abelshauser, *Deutsche Wirtschaftsgeschichte seit 1945* (Munich, 2004), 85.
23. Graml, "Deutsche Frage," 335.
24. Buchheim, "Kriegsschäden," 1050.
25. Graml, "Deutsche Frage," 341.
26. For more information on the Soviet physicists participating in the atomic project, see Michael Morozow, *Die Falken des Kreml: Die sowjetische Militärmacht von 1917 bis heute* (Munich, 1982), 318–27.
27. Rainer Karlsch, *Uran für Moskau: Die Wismut—Eine populäre Geschichte* (Bonn, 2007), 39.
28. Ibid., 44–45. From 1934 to 1946, the People's Commissariat for Internal Affairs (NKVD) was concerned primarily with security policy in addition to intelligence. In 1945, actual "espionage" in the sense of foreign intelligence and counterintelligence fell under the authority of the People's Commissariat for State Security (NKGB), which had operated as a separate branch of the NKVD since 1943. The NKVD became the Ministry of Internal Affairs (MVD) in 1946, out of which the most well-known Soviet intelligence agency emerged in 1954, the Committee for State Security (KGB).
29. Ibid., 47.
30. Graml, "Deutsche Frage," 372.
31. Steininger, *Deutsche Geschichte*, vol. 1, 283.
32. Ibid., 284; see also Abelshauser, *Wirtschaftsgeschichte*, 82–84.
33. Steiner, *Plan*, 24–35.

34. Mai, *Kontrollrat*, 193.
35. Ibid., 194.
36. "Statut der Sowjetischen Kontrollkommission in Deutschland," in Elke Scherstjanoi, *Das SKK Statut: Zur Geschichte der Sowjetischen Kontrollkommission in Deutschland 1949 bis 1953* (Munich, 1998), 119.
37. "Protokoll der Eröffnungssitzung der Regierungsdelegationen der Sowjetunion und der DDR," Moscow, 20 August 1953, Stiftung Archiv der Parteien und Massenorganisationen der DDR im Bundesarchiv (SAPMO-BArch), NY 4890/471, 3.
38. See "Protokoll über die Besatzungszonen in Deutschland und die Verwaltung von Groß-Berlin," in Rauschning, *Rechtsstellung*, 3.
39. Siegfried Mampel, *Die sozialistische Verfassung der Deutschen Demokratischen Republik: Kommentar* (Frankfurt am Main, 1982), 152.
40. Udo Wetzlaugk, *Berlin und die deutsche Frage* (Cologne, 1985), 66.
41. Volker Koop, *Kein Kampf um Berlin? Deutsche Politik zur Zeit der Berlin-Blockade 1948/1949* (Bonn, 1998), 18.
42. See ibid., 26–29.
43. Jörg Friedrich, *Yalu: An den Ufern des dritten Weltkrieges* (Berlin, 2007), 85.
44. Wetzlaugk, *Berlin*, 80; for the full text of this treaty, see NATO, "The North Atlantic Treaty," 4 April 1949, Washington, *NATO e-Library*, http://www.nato.int/cps/en/natolive/official_texts_17120.htm.
45. For more on this topic, see Frank Roggenbuch, *Das Berliner Grenzgängerproblem: Verflechtung und Systemkonkurrenz vor dem Mauerbau* (Berlin, 2008).
46. Michael Lemke, introduction to *Schaufenster der Systemkonkurrenz: Die Region Berlin-Brandenburg im Kalten Krieg*, ed. Michael Lemke (Cologne, 2006), 7.
47. See Gerhard Kunze, *Grenzerfahrungen: Kontakte und Verhandlungen zwischen dem Land Berlin und der DDR 1945–1989* (Berlin, 1999), 16–18; Steffen Alisch, *"Die Insel sollte sich das Meer nicht zum Feind machen!" Die Berlin-Politik der SED zwischen dem Bau und dem Fall der Mauer* (Munich, 2004), 51–54; Gerhard Sälter, *Grenzpolizisten: Konformität, Verweigerung und Repression in der Grenzpolizei und den Grenztruppen der DDR (1952–1965)* (Berlin, 2009), 38–46.
48. Winfried Roth, *Die Insel: Eine Geschichte West-Berlins 1948 bis 1990* (Munich, 2009), 87.
49. Jens Hacker, *Die Rechtslage Berlins: Die Wandlungen in der sowjetischen Rechtsauffassung* (Bonn, 1965), 38; see also Wetzlaugk, *Berlin*, 99–105.
50. Ernst R. Zivier, *Der Rechtsstatus des Landes Berlin: Eine Untersuchung nach dem Viermächte-Abkommen vom 3. September 1971* (Berlin (West), 1977), 26.
51. Wetzlaugk, *Berlin*, 120.
52. Ibid.
53. Wolfgang Ribbe, *Berlin 1945–2000: Grundzüge der Stadtgeschichte* (Berlin, 2002), 93.
54. Rudolf Herrnstadt, "Über den Baustil, den politischen Stil und den Genossen Henselmann," *Neues Deutschland*, 29 July 1951, quoted in Irina Liebmann, *Wäre es schön? Es wäre schön! Mein Vater Rudolf Herrnstadt* (Berlin, 2008), 312.
55. Ibid., 312.
56. Lemke, *Schaufenster*, 19.
57. Hacker, *Rechtslage*, 38–39.
58. Mampel, *Verfassung*, 131.
59. Ibid., 136–37.
60. "Erklärung des Vorsitzenden der SKK zur Übergabe von Verwaltungsfunktionen an Deutsche," 11 November 1949, in *Dokumente des geteilten Deutschland: Quellentexte zur Rechtslage des Deutschen Reiches, der Bundesrepublik Deutschland und der Deutschen Demokratischen Republik*, ed. Ingo von Münch (Stuttgart, 1968), 326.
61. Ibid., 330.
62. Hans-Hermann Hertle, *Chronik des Mauerfalls: Die dramatischen Ereignisse um den 9. November 1989* (Augsburg, 2006), 231.

63. Mai, *Kontrollrat*, 187.
64. "Bericht von Gribanov: Die Positionen der Alliierten in Deutschland nach der Moskauer SMID-Tagung," 12 September 1947, in Laufer and Kynin, *UdSSR*, vol. 3, 403.
65. "Unterredung Semenovs mit Pieck und Grotewohl," 27 October 1947, in Laufer and Kynin, *UdSSR*, vol. 3, 429–30.
66. Mai, *Kontrollrat*, 197.
67. Ibid., 201.
68. Ibid., 202.
69. Maria Haendcke-Hoppe-Arndt, "Interzonenhandel/innerdeutscher Handel," in Deutscher Bundestag, *Materialien der Enquete-Kommission: Aufarbeitung*, vol. 5/2, 1545.
70. Ibid., 1545–46.
71. Ibid., 1544.
72. See chapter 12 of this volume.
73. See Jörg Roesler, "Handelsgeschäfte im Kalten Krieg: Die wirtschaftlichen Motivationen für den deutsch-deutschen Handel zwischen 1949 und 1961," in Buchheim, *Wirtschaftliche Folgelasten*, 193–220.
74. See Siegfried Kupper, "Innerdeutscher Handel," in *DDR-Handbuch*, ed. Bundesministerium für innerdeutsche Beziehungen, 3rd ed. (Bonn, 1985), vol. I, 643–53.
75. "Proclamation No. 2: Agreement on Certain Additional Requirements to be Imposed on Germany," in Allied Control Authority Germany, *Enactments and Approved Papers of the Control Council and Coordinating Committee*, vol. I, *1945* (Berlin, 1946), 83.
76. "Directive 43: Procedure for the Issue to German Civilians of Single Round-Trip Interzonal Passes for a Journey Outside the Zone for Purposes of Interzonal Trade," in Allied Control Authority Germany, *Enactments and Approved Papers of the Control Council and Coordinating Committee*, vol. 5, *1 October 1946–31 December 1946* (Berlin, n.d.), 86.
77. "Paßgesetz der Deutschen Demokratischen Republik vom 13.9.1954," in Münch, *Dokumente*, 361–82; see also Sälter, *Grenzpolizisten*, 15–24. The term *deutsche Staatsangehörige* (German nationals) was used until 1961, when it was replaced with the phrase, *Bürger der DDR einschließlich ihrer Hauptstadt (demokratisches Berlin)* (citizens of the GDR including its capital, democratic Berlin). East German citizenship was not defined or regulated by law until 1967; according to the text of this law, residents of the GDR had been granted citizenship upon the state's founding. See Mampel, *Verfassung*, 583.
78. Walter Ulbricht, "Über die Vereinfachung des Staatsapparates und die Änderung der Arbeitsweise der Mitarbeiter des Staatsapparates. Referat vor dem Zentralkomitee der SED, 10.–12.7.1957," in Walter Ulbricht, *Die Entwicklung des deutschen volksdemokratischen Staates 1945–1958* (Berlin [East], 1958), 535.
79. See Walther Rosenthal, *Das neue politische Strafrecht der "DDR"* (Frankfurt am Main, 1968).
80. Ministerium für Justiz/Akademie für Staats- und Rechtswissenschaften der DDR, ed., *Strafrecht der Deutschen Demokratischen Republik: Kommentar zum Strafgesetzbuch* (Berlin [East], 1984), 327–28.
81. "Zwischenbericht der Regierung Modrow: 'Die Staatssicherheit in Liquidation,'" in Karl Wilhelm Fricke, *MfS intern: Macht, Strukturen, Auflösung der DDR-Staatssicherheit* (Cologne, 1991), 189. See also Gerhard Sälter, "Fluchtverhinderung als gesamtgesellschaftliche Aufgabe," in *Die Mauer: Errichtung, Überwindung, Erinnerung*, ed. Klaus-Dietmar Henke (Munich, 2011), 152–62.
82. Michael Kubina and Manfred Wilke, "Aufnahme von Flüchtlingen aus der SBZ/DDR in der Bundesrepublik" (manuscript, Berlin, 2005), 28.
83. See "Report on the Tripartite Conference of Berlin," in U.S. Dept. of State, *FRUS: Conference of Berlin*, vol. 2, 1511.
84. See Heike Amos, *Die Vertriebenenpolitik der SED 1949 bis 1990* (Munich, 2009), 15. It is not possible here to elaborate on the controversy regarding these statistics; the numbers are simply meant to convey the massive scope of the transfer of German populations from the former eastern territories.

85. Karl F. Schumann, "Flucht und Ausreise aus der DDR insbesondere im Jahrzehnt ihres Unterganges," table 1, "Flucht aus der SBZ/DDR bis zum 13.8.1961," in Deutscher Bundestag, *Materialien der Enquete-Kommission: Aufarbeitung*, vol. 5/3, 2397.

86. Table 5, "Fluchtbewegungen aus der DDR und dem Ostsektor von Berlin (1949–1961)," in *Mauerbau und Mauerfall: Ursachen—Verlauf—Auswirkungen*, ed. Hans-Hermann Hertle, Konrad H. Jarausch, and Christoph Kleßmann (Berlin, 2002), 312.

87. Hertle et al., *Mauerbau*, 312–14.

88. Hanns Jürgen Küsters and Daniel Hofmann, eds., *Dokumente zur Deutschlandpolitik: Deutsche Einheit. Sonderedition aus den Akten des Bundeskanzleramtes 1989/90* (Munich, 1998), 347–48. A third group, "Other," included 13,872 people in this third phase, but the statistics provide no explanation for the difference between the given total number of immigrants during this period (616,051) and the sum of these three groups (436,454).

89. Kubina and Wilke, "Aufnahme," 42–43.

Chapter 3

TWO GERMAN STATES

After May 1945, each Allied command exercised sovereign authority within its occupation zone. The Allied Control Council was comprised of the four supreme commanders, who could only act on unanimous decisions—each of the four powers could block the others through a veto. The Control Council did not have its own German administrative structure to span the zonal borders; thus, the reorganization of German statehood and the process of reconstruction began separately in each of the four zones, following the organizational and political directives of the respective occupation power. Disagreements among the four powers concerning the approval of political parties foreshadowed later conflicts over Germany's political order, which played out both between the Soviet Union and the Western powers and among the German politicians themselves. The fractured landscape of German political parties laid the groundwork for the founding of two German states.

Conflicts over the German Party System and the Democratic Elections of 1946

At the end of 1945, Soviet leadership (i.e., Joseph V. Stalin as general secretary of the Communist Party of the Soviet Union (CPSU), commander-in-chief of the Soviet Forces, and head of state) began to undertake major changes to the party system in the Soviet occupation zone. With massive pressure, Stalin pushed to implement the KPD's monopoly on power. At the Control Council, the Soviet Military Administration (SMAD) had already agreed with the Western powers to hold democratic elections in order to establish legitimate local administrations and state governments in all four zones and Berlin. But the election results in Hungary and Austria in the fall of 1945 were a shock to Soviet leadership: the Communist parties had clearly lost.

First among the occupation powers, the Americans held local elections in their zone in late January 1946. Here, too, the KPD was the unambiguous loser. In Berlin and the Soviet zone, elections were to take place later that year. The election results in the American zone sent a clear signal to the Soviets, which emerges in a report to the Soviet Foreign Ministry by Vladimir S. Semyonov,[1] political advisor to the head of the Soviet Military Administration. In it, he refrains from sugar-coating the KPD's defeat, turning his attention instead to the political goals of the American approach. The Americans and British understood "democratization" as the supervised development of German self-government and a parliamentary republic based on free elections. In their view, only a democratic Germany could recover its sovereignty. Thus, not only were elections important for the acceptance of Communists in Germany, but they also served as an instrument in the struggle for "the German soul." For Soviet leaders, "democratization" had an entirely different meaning. In the Soviet zone and the Soviet sector of Berlin, "democratization" meant establishing the Communist monopoly on power. The results of the local elections in the American zone had demonstrated something important to the SMAD: with free elections, the Soviets' goal would remain unattainable. Semyonov therefore demanded that the elections scheduled in the Soviet zone for the fall of 1946 be planned as quickly as possible.[2]

By June 1945, the Soviet occupation power had approved four "anti-fascist democratic" parties in the Soviet zone without discussing the move with the other occupation powers: the KPD, the SPD, the Christian Democratic Union (CDU), and the Liberal Democratic Party (LDPD). These constituted the four-party, anti-fascist democratic "block." The SMAD's main task during these months was to prepare for the fusion of the SPD and the KPD[3] and to suppress the two bourgeois parties, especially the CDU, that had been approved in June 1945. Compared to the Communists, the bourgeois parties faced clear boundaries regarding what they could and could not do. Sergei I. Tiulpanov, director of the Propaganda Administration within the SMAD, described this in a portrait of the CDU from December 1945:

> The Christian Democratic Union is a party that stands up for the interests of the middle and upper class, as well as the nobility. Hermes and Schreiber, the leaders of the Christian Democratic Union, tried to transform the Union into a harbor for reactionary figures who made it their mission to obstruct all democratic measures by the four-party block (land reform, school reform, aid to new farmers, etc.). They refused to support the resolutions of the Berlin Conference[4] and openly expressed their resentment over Germany's eastern border; they accused the allies of wanting to eliminate "militarism with militaristic means" and denied that the German people were responsible for the war. . . . Now Hermes and Schreiber have been kicked out of their leadership positions. More progressive elements from the provinces have joined the executive board of the CDU, ready to work toward strengthening the antifascist block and closely cooperating with the Soviet Military Administration.[5]

Although the CDU did not have many members, Tiulpanov wrote, the party might still be able to attract a significant number of votes.

The Social Democrats (SPD) were the greatest problem facing the occupation power and the KPD in the Soviet zone in December 1945. The Soviet Union had counted on their consent throughout Germany to a fusion with the KPD to form the Socialist Unity Party of Germany (SED), along with their willing submission to the Communist claim on power. But led by Kurt Schumacher, the Social Democrats in the West rejected this plan; therefore, fusion could only occur within the Soviet zone.

In March 1946, Semyonov called Schumacher a "minion of the British and the right-wing SPD leaders in the British, American, and French occupation zones," who had been able to "pass resolutions at the Social Democratic conferences in the Western zones that rejected the creation of a unified workers' party." Schumacher justified his actions with a critique of the KPD, which Semyonov cites: "Communist politics are not politics of the German people and not politics of international socialism . . . Communist politics in Germany have failed theoretically and practically in the same way that every dictator's politics have failed. This is clearest in the Russian occupation zone. The Social Democrats refuse to act as blood donors, to make their blood available to the weaker organism of the Communist Party."[6] According to Semyonov, Schumacher saw German Communists as "usurpers" and "agents of Moscow." The assertion that Schumacher was a "minion" of the British also seemed plausible. No leading German politician could wage such an overt confrontation with the interests of the Soviet occupation power in 1945 without the backing of another major power. Inevitably, this led Moscow to ask what the British were really up to in Germany and Berlin.

The decision to eliminate the SPD came from Moscow. On 23 January 1946, General Lieutenant Fedor E. Bokov, the political member of the SMAD's military council, informed Wilhelm Pieck, chairman of the KPD, that Stalin wanted to "expedite" the campaign to join the two parties—unification should take place as soon as possible, ideally by 1 May. With respect to the "party program, decisions would all be made in Moscow."[7] Pieck's notes on Walter Ulbricht's trip to Moscow from 28 January to 6 February 1946 suggest that Stalin approved of Ulbricht's proposed plan for unification within the Soviet zone, confirmed the KPD's political line, and saw the party unification as a pan-German process. But "as part of a political 'minimalist program,' the possibility existed to simply change the name of the KPD to 'Unity Party' in the Western zones in order to reiterate German unity."[8] With this, Stalin chose a name for the new party: the Socialist Unity Party of Germany (Sozialistische Einheitspartei Deutschlands, or SED).[9] The dependence of KPD leadership on Stalin and his directives regarding German politics "can hardly be overestimated. Without the approval of CPSU leadership, any decision on the party's sociopolitical strategy would have been unthinkable."[10] Stalin did concede that in contrast to Russia, the path to power in Germany must account for the parliamentary traditions of the West; the party could not immediately begin establishing a dictatorship of the proletariat. In her examination of the

KPD's alliance policy, Friederike Sattler notes that directly after Ulbricht's return to Germany, the party's programmatic approach to this "transition" was "laid out thoroughly in Anton Ackermann's oft-cited article, 'Is There a Special German Path to Socialism?'"[11]

Only in Berlin was the KPD forced to address openly the conflict over its fusion with the SPD. Against the will of the SPD's central committee, Berlin's Social Democrats held a plebiscite within the party to vote on the fusion. In the Eastern sector, the Soviet Command forbade the vote, citing a formal error on the part of the applicant (the SPD). Thus, it could only take place among SPD members in the Western sectors of Berlin on 31 March 1946. "Of the 32,547 eligible voters, 23,755 participated in the vote. The first question read: 'Do you support an immediate fusion of the two workers' parties?' 19,529 members (82.2 percent) voted 'No,' and only 2,937 (12.3 percent) voted 'Yes.'"[12] Unimpressed by the Social Democrats' vote in West Berlin and the firm stance of the SPD in the West against the politics of the KPD, the Communists took action to found the SED in the Soviet zone and East Berlin.

Immediately following the SED's inaugural party convention, the head of the SMAD approved the party on 23 April and informed the Control Council. But the intrazonal fusion of parties (with its aim to reach the rest of Germany) was a strain on Allied occupation policy in Germany. Semyonov recognized this at once: "The significance of uniting the KPD and the SPD extends far beyond the borders of the zone and has awakened the interest of the international public."[13] In May, he informed the Foreign Ministry[14] of the consequences the Western Allies drew from the founding of the SED: "The Allies have taken a position of delay and postponement and have not yet approved the SED in either Berlin or the Western zones of Germany."[15] In fact, the Allied Kommandatura in Berlin had instated a downright blockade. The Western Allies moved to recognize the SPD, which reorganized itself in the Western sectors following the founding of the SED. For the SPD, the Allies only needed to recognize the new district boards; the SED, in contrast, was an entirely new party, and it was up to the Control Council to decide on its fate. "The recognition of the SEP [meaning the SED] throughout all of Germany and in the Western sectors of Berlin is one of the most important questions at this time."[16] At the end of May, Semyonov asked the head of the SMAD, Marshal Vasily D. Sokolovsky, to tell the Propaganda Administration

> to get together with SED leadership and think about the best way to achieve the approval of the SEP [i.e., SED] organization in the Western zones. It is imperative today that we solve the question of how the fusion between the Communist Party and the Social Democrats in the Western zones should move forward: through a referendum, as the Allies wish, or through a split by way of a vote as it happened in Berlin, which will certainly meet with long-term resistance among the Allied occupation authorities. Perhaps we should try to set a precedent in the American zone by registering the SEP in order to unite the parties while following all of the rules of "democracy," as the Americans would prefer.[17]

In the same context, Semyonov warned against the detrimental effects of mutual "non-recognition" for the situation in Berlin, meaning a refusal to recognize the SED in the Western sectors and the SPD in the Eastern sector. His warning led to action: on 31 May, the reciprocal blockade within the Allied Kommandatura ended. The SED was permitted in the Western sectors of Berlin, and the SPD in the Soviet sector.[18] In the Western occupation zones, however, the Soviets had to give up on their goal of SED recognition by the Control Council; the Western powers rejected it plainly.[19]

The Establishment of Communist Party Rule in the Soviet Zone

Moscow Plans, 1944

Even during the war, the Soviet Union had already begun to plan out Germany's new beginning. Parallel to committees at the People's Commissariat for Foreign Affairs responsible for planning a new European order, a working group of KPD cadres formed in Moscow in early 1944. It was their task, according to the CPSU, to develop a political concept for Germany's transformation after Hitler, based on the assumption of Allied occupation. Not wanting to disturb the harmony of the war alliance, Soviet leadership advised the KPD working group in 1944 that they should avoid using the words "socialism" and "revolution" in their plans. With this in mind, the group chose programmatic phrases such as "anti-fascist democratic regime" and "parliamentary republic"[20] in the KPD's founding proclamation of June 1945. These types of formulations aimed to disguise the KPD's intention to take over leadership of the new republic.

The Moscow working group consisted of only the most experienced cadres of the KPD, who had worked in the apparatus of the Communist International and, in large part, had passed through its International Lenin School. Some of them had even worked for the Soviet secret service. In any case, the character of the future KPD was incontrovertible: it would remain a "Marxist-Leninist revolutionary party" following the example of the Soviet Bolsheviks.

The fundamental question in German politics after Hitler had already crystallized by 1944: Which direction would the country sway—to the East, toward the Soviet Union, or to the West, toward Great Britain and the United States? Wilhelm Florin, who led the working group together with Wilhelm Pieck, answered this question on 6 March 1944 with a clear set of rules dictating the party's language. He instructed the group to avoid asking the question openly, in order to obscure its consequences:

> We must say: Peace and friendship with all of our neighbors, and especially close friendship with the Soviet Union.
> We must prepare ourselves today for a tomorrow in which the issue of close friendship with the Soviet Union will become an issue affecting Germany and the

livelihood of the German people, and, much more so than today, it will be the dividing line between reaction and progress.[21]

Conversely, the Soviet Union also needed a strong Communist Party in post-Hitler Germany; as Florin wrote, "Germany without a strong Communist Party is a danger to the Soviet Union."[22] In order to orient Germany toward the East and split the German bourgeoisie through an adroit policy of alliances, the new KPD had to avoid its revolutionary, Weimar-era demand for a "Soviet Germany." Thus, the KPD's appeal of June 1945 specifically stated: "We believe it would be the wrong approach to impose the Soviet system upon Germany; this approach would not reflect the current conditions of German development."[23] It was a tactical formulation that used the word "current" to conceal the KPD's basic strategy.

Florin saw the conflict over Germany's orientation toward the East or the West as inevitable: "The national problem today and tomorrow consists of fighting against the one-sided Western orientation that Fascism is trying to push through, and preventing Germany from falling into foreign hands to be used as a new instrument against peace with the Soviet Union."[24] As early as one year before the end of the war, Florin projected the emerging spheres of influence in Europe onto future fronts of hostile domestic confrontation in Germany. He drew a line between the political powers in Germany and predicted that their positions toward the Soviet Union would mark the major rift in postwar German politics. As for the KPD, Florin reinforced the self-image of his cadre, drawing on a dogma already formed in the 1920s: protection of the Soviet Union remained the highest maxim of KPD policy. Only the Soviet Union could and would guarantee the establishment of the KPD's political power within its occupation zone.

The Moscow cadres of this KPD working group were already aware in 1944 that the defeat of the National Socialist dictatorship would produce a new international political constellation in which Germany would no longer be a major player. The world powers of the future would be the Soviet Union, Great Britain, and the United States. Influenced by their experience after the First World War, the group overestimated the importance of Great Britain; otherwise, their predictions proved correct and became their guiding principles in postwar Germany.

This version of Communist postwar policy took as its starting point the new international political constellation after the war. The party's primary goal would be to steer Germany toward the East. The future leaders of the KPD already viewed themselves as the "state-building party" in the Soviet occupation zone. While still in exile in Moscow, Wilhelm Pieck emphasized that the goals of the Soviet occupation power and the KPD were identical. In contrast, the Communists predicted enmity from the occupation powers of the Western zones.

In the immediate aftermath of the war, the Moscow cadres of the KPD in Soviet exile formed a bridge between the Soviet political officers and the German population, swiftly helping to establish administrative structures in the *Länder*, cities, and municipalities. At first, this occurred on a pluralist basis. The Communists held back when it came to filling government administrations; in the large cities, they mostly took charge of three key areas: personnel management (which was centralized from the very beginning), national education, and the police. Parallel to the creation of the Allied Control Council in June 1945, Stalin summoned Walter Ulbricht, Gustav Sobottka, and Anton Ackermann to Moscow. He ordered Pieck, Ulbricht, and Ackermann to rebuild the KPD, designated the members of the Central Committee as the provisional party leadership, and approved the founding proclamation of the KPD. Pieck and Ulbricht would be responsible for maintaining contact with the head of the SMAD.[25] At the same time, the SMAD published its founding document and its Order No. 2, which permitted the establishment of unions and the four anti-fascist democratic parties.

The Soviet Military Administration and the Establishment of a Communist Party Dictatorship

Marshal Georgy Zhukov is said to have called out to the soldiers of his Berlin garrison in May 1945: "We have stormed Berlin, but the fight for the Germans' souls still lies ahead. It will be a difficult battle, and our front line is right here. I would like to think that a brilliant victory awaits us on this front, too."[26] In order to achieve the victory Zhukov spoke of, the KPD's leadership position was a strategic precondition (in a Marxist-Leninist sense) for Soviet policy toward Germany. Because the Soviet Union exercised occupation authority together with the three Western democracies, it would have to achieve KPD leadership through the establishment of a German party system. To this end, the SMAD immediately approved four anti-fascist democratic parties in its zone, which it then controlled rigorously.

But in its fight for the "German soul," the Soviet Union had already lost an important battle, right in the midst of its military triumph. The Soviet path to victory was marred by atrocities, looting, and the widespread rape of women. Especially these rapes "became the Germans' primary aversion to building closer connections with the Soviet Union."[27] The transgressions of Soviet soldiers were preceded by the war of annihilation that National Socialist Germany had waged against the Soviet Union. It was, after all, the Soviet Army that liberated Auschwitz and other death camps in Poland.

In accordance with the Allied agreements of 5 June 1945, the Soviet Military Administration exercised supreme governmental authority within its occupation zone. Jan Foitzik characterizes the administration's structure and legal position as "extraordinarily complex" and "original."[28] This special complexity refers to the many Soviet institutions that had immediate access to the occupation administration. Fundamental to the constellation was the "omnipotence of Stalin," who intervened directly and constantly in the work of the SMAD. The Central Committee of the CPSU also had access to the SMAD,[29] as did the People's Commissariat/Ministry of the Interior, led by Lavrentiy P. Beria. Beria's ministry included Colonel General Ivan Serov, Marshal Zhukov's deputy, and was responsible for the civil administration of the Soviet zone from 1945 to 1947.[30] Serov was also in charge of approving the personal composition of the new German administration and heading the Soviet secret police in the occupation zone. His department took up this latter task immediately by building a "network of secret German employees."[31]

The relationship between the SMAD and the KPD/SED was of utmost importance for the transition from the Soviet zone to the GDR. Led by the Moscow cadre, the party served a double function: it was a "dependent component of the occupation structure, subject to the occupation power's control and intervention. At the same time, the KPD/SED formed the most important connection between the SMAD and the general population."[32] However, the party leadership also enjoyed "direct connections" to the decision-making center in Moscow, which were independent of the SMAD and could undermine its authority. The Moscow cadre also bridged the SMAD and the KPD/SED in Berlin. These party functionaries had returned from Soviet exile to occupy a key role in the establishment of Communist dictatorship. Among this group were Walter Ulbricht, Wilhelm Pieck, Anton Ackermann, Otto Winzer, Rudolf Herrnstadt, and Wilhelm Zaisser; Ulbricht stood out early as the central figure, assuming responsibility for managing relations with the occupation power.[33] But all of these men held integral positions in their party and in the new state. "The corps of German Communist functionaries consisted of about five hundred people that the Soviet Military Administration (SMAD) could rely on in 1945. They were sworn to the infallible authority of the CPSU and its leader, Stalin. The subordinate relationship worked in two ways: it was Communist, 'party-based,' and 'internationalist,' and it was founded upon the dominance of the victor over the defeated."[34]

The Moscow cadres' understanding of their role within these various structures strongly influenced the perspectives of many SMAD officers. As Sergei I. Tiulpanov, director of the Propaganda and Information Administration, writes in his memoirs, it was clear "that the officers of the Propaganda Administration of the SMAD, especially the members of the CPSU, paid special regard to their contacts and cooperation with the founding organization of the KPD, as well as with the heads of the party in the various states and provinces."[35] These contacts were necessary in order to make the correct "personnel selection" among the Germans in each locality. The consequences of this personnel policy within the state administration of the Soviet zone—which corresponded to an "increase in function of the KPD/SED"[36]—led to the establishment of the SED dictatorship by the Soviet occupation power.[37] This was the Soviet path to a divided Germany.

The German Economic Commission: Preparations to Found the New State

Through Order No. 32 on 12 February 1948, the SMAD commanded the German Economic Commission (Deutsche Wirtschaftskommission, or DWK) to function from then on "as the central body responsible for economic planning and administration with full government authority throughout the entire Soviet zone." In contrast to other SMAD orders, this one was published openly. The DWK was to "take over the reconstruction of the peace industry in the Soviet occupation zone of Germany, as well as the coordination of the German central adminis- tration for the individual economic branches."[38] The commission was given the right to "determine and issue binding decrees and instructions consistent with the orders set forth by the Soviet Military Administration to all German institu- tions within the territory of the Soviet occupation zone, as well as to enforce their implementation." Monitoring reparations deliveries to the Soviet Union also fell among the duties of the DWK, "which, of course, carried out its tasks under the supervision of the SMAD"; the DWK continued to function as an instrument of Soviet power.[39] Before publishing or publicizing any fundamental decision, the commission had to present it to the military administration first. Heinrich Rau, minister of economic affairs for the state of Brandenburg, was made director of the DWK, and in 1949 he became a member of the SED's politburo. Rau's two deputies were Bruno Leuschner, head of the economics division in the executive committee of the SED, and Fritz Selbmann, minister of economic affairs for the state of Saxony, both longtime cadres of the KPD. With the establishment of the DWK, central economic planning could begin in the Soviet zone; the commission organized an exchange of currency following the Western currency reform in 1948 before centralizing the "finance and credit economy."[40]

The state order implemented by the Soviet Union in its occupation zone relied on the Communist Party's monopoly on power. Pro forma elections, always accom- panied by propaganda, had no real influence on the political decision-making pro- cesses of the SED leadership. Through the DWK, the occupation power managed to establish a centralist state administration including the German Administration of the Interior (Deutsche Verwaltung des Inneren) even before the founding of the GDR. In keeping with this goal, the SMAD told SED leaders in May 1948 to already think of the SED as "the party in power."[41] On an official level, this meant eliminating the residual independence of the regional (*Länder*) administrations. The SED carried out this task through the interior ministers of each state—they became "party ministers"[42] who coordinated the de facto subordination of the *Län- der* administrations to the directives of the German Administration of the Interior.

But contrary to the hopes of its leaders, the SED was not yet entrusted with rebuilding the state. When they met with the head of the SMAD to ask

"whether [a] government [in the] Eastern zone" should be built, they were swiftly turned down: "[Only] the Econo[mic] Commiss[ion] for now." At a high-level meet- ing with Sokolovsky, the establishment of an Eastern state was only considered as the (probable or possible) result of international developments. Pieck's notes read: "Perspective—development of the int[ernational] situation—Western powers— Western state—Sov[iet] zone—autonomy/government—parliament." Pushing for- ward with the "Socialist development" that Ulbricht had proclaimed in the party's executive committee appealed even less to the SMAD. The subject of "socialism in

the Soviet zone" only came up at the meeting once, and then only on a low level. . . .
On the highest level, the "intensification of the class struggle" took priority; the
development of a social order in the Soviet zone was not discussed between the
SMAD and the SED leadership.[43]

It was also not within the SMAD's authority to make such fundamental decisions;
Moscow was responsible for these types of questions. The "international situation" that Marshal Sokolovsky evoked in order to postpone the SED's plans to
build an Eastern state referred primarily to negotiations among the four powers to
solve the Berlin Crisis of 1948–49.

The "Party of Power": Party Cleansing and the Stalinization of the SED

Following the course set directly after the war, and in preparation to found the
new state, the leaders of the SED transformed their party into an instrument of
dictatorship. As early as 1948, the SED openly made itself known to the German
people and to its own members as the party of the proletarian dictatorship. This
was part of the German and Soviet Communists' self-image, influenced by their
party's Leninist-Stalinist ideology. With the DWK's first semi-annual plan for
1948, Ulbricht instructed his fellow party leaders "to take direct charge of execut-
ing the plan: 'One can say that with the adoption of this plan, our party's leaders
find themselves for the first time in a position to systematically lead the political,
economic, and organizational work not only of the Party but also of the entire
economic and state apparatus.'"[44] Thus, there was a clear connection between the
establishment of a centrally planned economy and the transformation of the SED
into a "Stalinist state party": "The SED was to transition from a Socialist mass
party into a Stalinist state party, in which the party leadership alone—in direct
accordance with Soviet instructions—decided on the goals and content of [state]
policy, and a strictly hierarchical apparatus of full-time party functionaries—with
the support of a disciplined membership—ensured the unconditional implementation of this policy. In this system, the enforcement of long-term economic plans
took on extraordinary importance, with the goal of integrating East German economic potential into the emerging 'Eastern camp.'"[45]

In 1948–49, the SED became a "new type of party" based on a Stalinist structure. Leadership apparatuses were centralized with the creation of a "small secretariat of the politburo" under the direction of Ulbricht—who, like Stalin, now
called himself the general secretary. The first task at hand was to organize the
SED's First Party Congress in January 1949, which would conclude the transition
from a Socialist mass party into this "new type of party." This conference constituted one of the high points in the "Stalinization campaign," as Hermann Weber
notes, with delegates passing a resolution that held up this transformation as the
party's primary duty: "Today, the SED stands before the immense and historic

task of ensuring the democratic reconstruction of the Eastern zone; upon this foundation, [the party] will wage its fight for Germany's democratic unification, for peace, and for progressive development. The party can only fulfill these duties by working tirelessly to develop the SED into a new kind of party, a Marxist-Leninist revolutionary party. Forward under the invincible banner of Marx, Lenin, and Stalin." Within the party, the regime modeled itself after the Soviet example: "Democratic centralism" became the overriding principle of party building, while factions and groups within the SED were forbidden. Above all, "it was mandatory for all SED members to swear loyalty to Stalin's CPSU and to the 'leading role of the Soviet Union.'"[46]

Another factor in this transformation was the inner-party struggle against "Social Democracy," or, as it was also described, against the "Schumacher agents." Two years after the forced fusion of the SPD and the KPD in the Soviet zone, this meant that SED members were to weed out all traditions of German Social Democracy within the party—on the orders of the CPSU. In order to fulfill this demand, the SED underwent an internal "cleansing" process, for which it established institutions of surveillance within the party itself.[47]

Several more waves of "party cleansing" in the SED followed this initial procedure, ensuring its transition to a Stalinist state party. Between 1948 and 1952, the Communists began by purging the Unity Party of Social Democrats, followed by alleged "Trotskyists" and "Titoists." Members whom the Party Control Commission (Partei-Kontrollkommission, or PKK) "exposed as party enemies" were expelled from the party and often lost their jobs; some even faced imprisonment. The year 1951 marked a high point in "party cleansing"; of the SED's 1,603,754 members in December 1949, only 1,256,002 remained by December 1951. Thus, the campaign affected hundreds of thousands of people.[48] This "exchange" of cadres and members turned the SED into a disciplined ideological machine to govern the German "people's democracy." Many Social Democrats and Communists refused to wait idly for their expulsion or imprisonment; instead they crossed the so-called "green border" into the Federal Republic and published their experiences in memoirs. The most prominent example was Wolfgang Leonhard, the youngest member of the Ulbricht Group in 1945, whose biography permanently shaped the image of the GDR within West Germany.[49]

The Founding of the GDR

The founding of the German Democratic Republic took place on 7 October 1949, apparently in reaction to the founding of the FRG on 7 September 1949, when the West German Bundestag convened and elected Konrad Adenauer as chancellor. In fact, Stalin and the SED leaders had decided on their method for founding the East German state in a conversation in Moscow in December 1948.[50]

Since the state apparatus of the GDR already functioned in the form of the DWK, it was possible, from a propagandistic point of view, to wait out the founding of the FRG in order to blame the West for Germany's division. In September 1949 the Western state came into being, signaling the need to make a decision in the East. Stalin summoned the SED leadership to Moscow once more. Before the meeting, the heads of the SED had sent a letter to Stalin describing their vision of building a provisional "German government in the Soviet occupation zone." They requested that he hand over the administration of the Soviet zone to the new government-to-be and transition the SMAD into a "Soviet Control Commission." One section of this letter described the KPD's quest for German unity and its fight against "the West German government," in order to "expose [it] as an instrument of the Western powers."[51] The politburo of the CPSU's Central Committee approved the SED's plan to found the new state, but with one modification: "The new government, approved at last, was not permitted to call itself the 'German government,' which would imply that it claimed exclusive representation of all Germans. Stalin insisted on using the formulation 'provisional government of the German Democratic Republic,' which left the territory of the GDR open to interpretation. On 5 October, after introducing the program agreed to in Moscow, Pieck stated that the 'provisional government' was not meant to indicate a government of all of Germany but rather a government of the German Democratic Republic."[52]

"Despite its own separatist development," the GDR still claimed to be "the protector of German unity."[53] The "People's Congress Movement," initiated and steered by the SED, provided a glow of plebiscitary legitimacy to the founding of the Communist state. The third People's Congress in 1949 elected a "German People's Council" that only consisted of representatives from the Soviet zone, although the previous People's Congresses had also included delegates from the Western zones. After the passage of West Germany's Basic Law, the People's Congress voted on a text that would become the Constitution of the GDR on 7 October 1949. The German People's Council thus served as the provisional People's Chamber of the GDR.

Up until the end of SED rule, the party legitimized the East German state by quoting from a congratulatory telegram sent by Stalin to the president and the prime minister of the GDR, Wilhelm Pieck and Otto Grotewohl (in the final years, of course, without naming the sender): "The creation of the peace-loving German Democratic Republic is a turning point in the history of Europe. There is no doubt that the presence of a peace-loving, democratic Germany in addition to the existence of the peace-loving Soviet Union rules out the possibility of new wars in Europe, bringing an end to the bloodbath in Europe and rendering the enslavement of European countries by the world imperialists impossible. . . . If you lay the cornerstone of a united, democratic, and peace-loving Germany, you will also accomplish a great achievement for all of Europe by guaranteeing stable peace."[54] Stalin's order to the leaders of the GDR was clear: the new state was the "cornerstone" of a "united Germany." This "united Germany" in his understanding could only be achieved through a fight against the Western powers and the West German state that they had erected. With two states and Berlin divided, Germany now belonged to both international political camps and took on a central role in the competition and struggle between the two systems.

The Federal Republic of Germany: The West German State

Preliminary Decisions at the Conference of Foreign Ministers, Paris, 1946

Discussions to sign a peace treaty with Germany were tabled in Potsdam in 1945 and deferred to the foreign ministers of the four Allied powers. By the end of 1947, the foreign ministers had met four times without reaching a positive conclusion. To the contrary: their meetings served as stepping-stones toward the division of Germany. The border between the Western zones and the Soviet zone cemented itself as the line delimiting the systems of the East and West, and two German states emerged. Parallel to these developments, public opinion in the United States and Great Britain changed with regard to the Soviet Union and its politics— a transformation that had direct consequences for the joint Allied control of Germany.

Winston Churchill initiated this change in public opinion with a speech in Fulton, Missouri, on 5 March 1946. In it he asked the Western democracies to face the Soviet threat head on, which also meant reconciling with the Germans. "The long-term solution," as Henry Kissinger quoted Churchill later, "was European unity, 'from which no nation should be permanently outcast.' Churchill, the first and leading opponent of the Germany of the 1930s, thus became the first and leading advocate of reconciliation with the Germany of the 1940s. Churchill's central theme, however, was that time was not on the side of the democracies, and that an overall settlement should urgently be sought."[55] Churchill had two central theses regarding the postwar situation in Europe: first, that Europe was split power-politically, with the Soviet Empire and the Western democracies on either side of the conflict. Second, that the Western European democracies could only protect themselves from renewed German aggression by including Germany in an integrated Europe.

Concerning the development of the Federal Republic, the conference of foreign ministers in Paris in April 1946 was of central importance. It was at this meeting that the conflict over Germany's reconstruction came to a head. Whereas Soviet policy concentrated on the establishment of Communist Party leadership within its zone, the Western powers focused their Germany policy on economic reconstruction and the establishment of a functioning democracy. American Secretary of State James F. Byrnes presented a plan for a peace agreement with Germany "that contained a twenty-five-year period of German neutralization in the form of full disarmament and demilitarization."[56] According to this plan, the four powers would pull their occupation troops out of Germany; at the same time, Byrnes announced that the United States would maintain a longer-term presence in Europe. Proposals for this type of agreement had first been floated in the spring of 1945. In an earlier conversation with Stalin, Byrnes had gained the impression that it would be possible to agree with the Soviets on a peace treaty of this kind.[57] However, Stalin had already taken a "dismissive position" internally as early as September of 1945. "For him it was clear that the treaty went against the USSR's objectives."[58] The plan was also "unacceptable" to the SMAD, which emphasized the intertwined relationship between Germany's "disarmament" and its "democratization." Once again, two levels of Soviet policy emerged. The presence of Soviet troops in Germany served both goals and was indispensable to their implementation. To Marshal Sokolovsky and his political advisor Semyonov, this aspect was "central to our decision to position ourselves against the American proposal."[59]

The Byrnes Plan, along with the simultaneous consolidation of the British and American zones, was a way for the Americans to "test" Soviet intentions: "If Stalin had accepted the proposal, this would have meant giving up the policy of spheres of influence and could have supported the basis for a cooperative occupation policy in Germany. But his rejection of the plan led directly to consolidating the defensive Western positions. The division of Europe was inevitable if the Western Allies wanted to win West Germany for their own zone of influence and put a cap on reparations. Thus, Germany's division was pre-programmed from that point onward."[60]

In Paris, discussions revolved once more around Germany's status as a unified economic territory. The extent of reparations that each power should extract from Germany led to major conflict between the Western powers and the Soviet Union. The Soviet government demanded the sum of $20 million, insisted upon additional reparations deliveries from the Western zones, and called for a limit to German industrial production. This policy of non-decision regarding the reconstruction of Germany—already a year after the war ended—seemed particularly problematic to the Western powers. Within their occupation zones, the Western powers felt obliged to use their own taxpayer money to cope with German hunger and misery. Weakened by the war and struggling to keep up with the responsibilities of its empire, Great Britain was at the end of its economic capacities. The British government was most concerned in Paris with clarifying the German question: Was is possible to reach an understanding with the Soviet Union, or should the British and Americans—already confronted with France's claim to the Ruhr Valley—focus on the economic consolidation of their occupation zones? Throttling German industrial capabilities would seriously compromise the reconstruction of Western Europe, which demanded increasing quantities of coal and steel from the Ruhr. With these considerations in mind, British Foreign Minister Ernest Bevin submitted an "official declaration" after Molotov, the Soviet foreign minister, had turned down the American proposal of German demilitarization. It read as an ultimatum:

If the four powers were unable to come to an agreement, [Bevin's] government found it necessary to organize its zone independently of the other zones and to export goods on a dollar basis. The British government was no longer willing to borrow dollars in order to buy food for the Germans within its own zone. . . . Considering the situation, only Byrnes could feel confident in this ultimatum. Immediately afterward, he submitted his own declaration stating that the United States was ready to band together with any other occupation power—or multiple other occupation powers—in order to unify the zones economically."[61]

With these exchanges, the Anti-Hitler Coalition's 1944–45 vision of jointly governing Germany failed; the contrasting interests of the parties involved were irreconcilable.

The Bizone: A Decision to Rebuild Germany

The situation in Germany in 1946 hardly inspired rebuilding the destroyed country. American military governor Clay reported to Washington "that each of the four occupation zones represented an almost hermetically sealed economic space just one year into Allied rule, and that this was catastrophic for both the economies of each individual zone and the economic development of Germany as a whole."[62] In his opinion, the British and American zones had the most in common—an analysis that led to the first steps of founding the West German state after the 1946 conference of foreign ministers in Paris failed.

After Paris, the British and Americans decided to combine the three Western occupation zones into one unified economic territory. "The British cabinet advocated the fusion on 25 June: economic and political necessities demanded it. Bevin argued that [the British] could not abandon the Americans; two days earlier, an internal briefing with representatives from the military government had dispelled any remaining doubt he might have had."[63] Byrnes announced the change in American Germany policy in a September 1946 speech in Stuttgart, the headquarters of the Regional Council (Länderrat) in the American zone. He stressed that the United States emphatically supported the "economic unification of Germany"[64] in order to overcome the zonal borders. The primary goal of military occupation was to "demilitarize and de-Nazify Germany but not raise artificial barriers to the efforts of the German people to resume their peacetime economic life."[65] He linked the push for German economic unity with the reclamation of German self-determination:

It is the view of the American Government that the German people throughout Germany, under proper safeguards, should now be given the primary responsibility for the running of their own affairs. . . . The United States favors the early establishment of a provisional German government for Germany. . . . While we shall insist that Germany observe the principles of peace, good-neighborliness, and humanity, we do not want Germany to become the satellite of any power or powers or to live under a dictatorship, foreign or domestic. The American people hope to see peaceful, democratic Germans become and remain free and independent.[66]

With this speech, the first of its kind after the war, the secretary of state presented the Germans "with a perspective for the first time, with a way out of the misery. And he made it clear that unlike after World War I, the American troops would stay in Germany and Europe as long as necessary and would not, as President Roosevelt had casually remarked in Yalta, pull out after two years." The Bavarian economic minister at the time, Ludwig Erhard, wrote: "Since the collapse [of Nazi Germany], nothing has felt as liberating as this speech by the secretary of state, proclaiming his will to give the Germans a chance to shape their own destiny."[67]

The integration of the British and American zones to create the Bizone in January 1947 led to the economic results that both governments had hoped for; the Germans and the Anglo-Americans succeeded in stimulating the economies in both zones. Meanwhile, the Soviets understood well that more than economic rebuilding was at stake. With the reorganization of the Bizonal structures in June and July 1947, a system of functioning German administrations emerged in the West. At the same time, from the perspective of the Soviets, this step laid the economic foundation "for West Germany's isolation. From this point onward, we can observe the de facto creation of a West German state."[68] In retrospect, Walter Ulbricht interpreted this decision by the two Western powers as the beginning of division and the "restoration of power to the militarists and revanchists in West Germany."[69] He used this historical argument in Moscow in 1961 to justify closing the sector borders in Berlin for the citizens of the GDR.

Fundamental Decisions for the West German State

The London conference of foreign ministers on Germany took place from 25 November to 15 December 1947 and ended without the participants reaching any conclusion or setting a date for the next round of negotiations. After the meeting, Washington and London agreed that the path of the "Western solution, which had already been weighed and thought out, must now be implemented without further hesitation." Great Britain and the United States would have to negotiate the founding of the new state with France, which had based its Germany policy on a single imperative up until that point: "to establish final and definitive security vis-à-vis Germany—that was the focus."[70] In view of developments in the East–West conflict over the first half of 1948, the French political elite slowly began to understand the necessity of this step. Robert Schuman, a Lorrainer and the French prime minister beginning in November 1947, was convinced "that a new kind of European solution to the German problem would also serve France's interests better than a second Versailles."[71]

The Soviet Union saw this step by the Western powers as a breach of the Potsdam agreements and left the Allied Control Council on 20 March 1948. This demonstrative termination of four-power control over Germany was among several countermeasures taken by the Kremlin that March. Deputy Foreign Minister Andrei A. Smirnov, who was also director of the European Department, wrote Molotov a memorandum that summarized the situation in view of Soviet interests in Germany: "Under these circumstances, we cannot content ourselves any longer with protesting against the separate actions of the Western powers that fundamentally threaten our interests in Germany and Europe. Therefore, we should also take concrete measures that will not only limit the independent actions of the USA, England, and France in Germany, but will also enable us to actively obstruct their plans to build a Western bloc that includes Germany."[72] If the Western powers rejected the Soviet offer, it would be a clear sign that they had "definitively dispensed with a solution to the German question on the basis of the Potsdam decisions."[73] Thus, the control mechanisms in Germany that the Allies had agreed upon would lose their validity. (The Soviet Union continued to use this line of argumentation later, during the second Berlin Crisis.) Moreover, through the presence of the Western powers in Berlin, Smirnov argued, the Soviet zone was essentially open in contrast to the three Western zones. Because of this, the Soviet government found itself forced "to close its zone."[74] Thus, the fundamental idea to close the inner German border—"measures to seal off the zone (protect the borders)"[75]—took form.

The Soviet foreign ministry had little involvement in the implementation of these countermeasures. "Stalin summoned the director of the Soviet Military Administration in Germany (SMAD) to Moscow in order to discuss the details with him and with members of the Politburo. With their participation, he formulated a plan of action on 15 March, followed by secret orders for its execution."[76] The Soviet leadership was ready to use the geopolitical position of Berlin, as well as the transit routes to and from the city, for the USSR's measures against the Western powers:

> The transportation routes between the Western sectors of Berlin and the Western zones of Germany were to be limited by increasingly strict controls before being closed entirely, making it impossible for the Western powers to maintain a continued presence in the city. . . . If the three Western states agreed to the Soviet Union's terms of negotiation, they would be giving up the basis of their shared plans for West Germany. If they rejected them, it would signal their intention to abandon the Potsdam decisions. This would render all agreements invalid with regard to the joint Allied control mechanism and the division of the occupied territory—the basis of the Western powers' rights to remain in Berlin.[77]

For the Western powers, however, the die had already been cast. After the London meeting, there was no turning back.

Currency Reform and the Social Market Economy

Simultaneous to negotiations among the Western powers, a currency reform was being prepared in the three Western zones. Both the Soviet side and the American side had been planning this step since 1947. When the Soviet Union left the Control Council, Washington decided not to pursue Germany-wide reform any longer, but to carry it out in the three Western zones instead. Berlin would remain the exception, with its currency under four-power control. The Soviets rejected this proposal, leading to the introduction of the Deutsche Mark (DM or D-Mark) in the Western sectors of Berlin. The currency reform favored people who owned capital and property; market shares were exchanged at a face value of one to one, while savings accounts drastically decreased in value. By eliminating the Reichsmark, the currency reform addressed the severe effects of inflation from the war. The scarce economy of the postwar period made way for an extensive array of goods in retail stores, and the psychological implications of the currency reform's "showcase effect" had great significance for the West German self-image. "For most people at that time, it was neither the passage of the Basic Law on 23 May 1949 nor the establishment of parliament in Bonn on 7 September 1949 that symbolized a decisive new beginning for the state and the economy; it was rather 20 June 1948"[78]—the day of the currency reform. That day also marked the end of people's hopes for renewed economic unity in Germany.

One the same day the currency reform was announced, the Bizonal Economic Council approved a bill by Ludwig Erhard, director of the economic administration, calling for changes to the government's economic control. This "Law of Basic Principles" (Leitsätzegesetz) marked the birth of a free market economy, ending government regulation of prices and supplies. Parallel to the introduction of the Deutsche Mark, Erhard "eliminated controlled prices in the most important economic areas. 'The only valid ration card today is the Deutsche Mark,' he announced in his radio speech."[79] Erhard's decision was an economic success, proving to be the most important administrative measure for the transformation of West Germany's economic system into a social market economy.

A Constituent Assembly for West Germany

In early June 1948, the three Western powers agreed in London on the path to founding a West German state. The Germany communiqué of 7 June 1948, "more than any other document, was the birth certificate of the Federal Republic. The sober message announcing the new West German state read as follows: 'The delegates have agreed to recommend to their governments that the military governors should hold a joint meeting with the Ministers-President of the western zone in Germany. At that meeting the Ministers-President will be authorized to convene a Constituent Assembly in order to prepare a constitution for the approval of the participating states.'"[80]

The London decision sent a clear message that the Western powers were no longer willing to negotiate indefinitely with the Soviet Union over a peace agreement for Germany. Moscow answered by blocking the transit routes to West Berlin beginning on 24 June, ostensibly to carry out "repair work."

On 1 July, the three Western military governors handed over the "Frankfurt Documents" to the ministers-president of the eleven states in the Western zones. They requested that the ministers call a constituent assembly for the West German state-to-be, "convening at the latest by 1 September 1948."[81] The answer from the ministers-president led to a crisis in their relations with the Western powers; they refused to call the constituent assembly, not wanting German politics to be responsible for the country's division. For the same reason, they also rejected the idea of a referendum on the constitution for a provisional West German state. Their argument was fundamental: this process should only take place with a constitution designated for all of Germany. At the same time, they underlined their readiness "to participate in the founding of the West German state and welcomed the Allies' plan to create an Occupation Statute that would legally regulate the relation between the Allies and the Germans."[82] Since the German politicians did not question the core issue (the founding of the West German state), the Allies made a terminological concession to the ministers-president: "Instead of 'Constitution,' they could call it 'Basic Law'; instead of a 'constituent assembly,' they could call it the 'Parliamentary Council.'"[83] In the end, the Allies did away with the constitutional referendum that they had ordered as well.

Carlo Schmid, minister of justice from Württemberg-Hohenzollern and head of the Parliamentary Council's executive committee, attributed the Allied concessions—as well as the Germans' willingness to compromise—to the influence of Ernst Reuter. As governing mayor of Berlin, Reuter framed the Berlin Blockade and the situation in the Eastern zone as factors that made it impossible to turn down the offer of the Western powers. The West German state would represent the foundation of democracy for all Germans, and Reuter emphasized the "provisional character of any political organization established in divided Germany." He asserted categorically

that we, in the free West, had to meet as a parliamentary body and create a constitution for the free part of Germany that represented a positive answer to the London recommendations. This was especially important for the sake of Berlin . . . whose blockade had to be broken and whose battle against the violent measures of the Soviet Union had to be waged—not in order to reestablish the status quo ante, but rather to integrate [the city] into the part of Germany "to which we belong according to our political conviction and to which we are bound for economic reasons, for better or for worse." . . . We could not travel the path from non-sovereignty to full sovereignty all at once; we had to peel back the occupation powers' claims to authority one by one, until they could no longer refuse the Germans sovereignty. Furthermore, we would have a fully valid mandate: not only Berlin but also the people of the Soviet occupation zone saw the "consolidation of the West as an elementary prerequisite for the improvement of their situation, as well as for the return of the

East to a common motherland." These arguments, especially concerning the East and Berlin, convinced the ministers-president, who Ernst Reuter believed could only benefit from the measures put forth in the London recommendations.[84]

The decision by the ministers-president to found West Germany did not free them from the dilemma they faced: the necessity to rebuild the country and reestablish German self-administration on the one hand, and the inevitable division of Germany on the other. Many still hoped that the concept of a democratic core state would work. General Clay reassured the ministers-president in his zone:

> Consoling [them], the departing general commented that this would finally bring the possibility of incorporating the Eastern zone into the Federal Republic. With this, he evoked a central argument of American Germany policy that first evolved at the Paris conference and went on to be the most frequently posed solution to the German question: annexation of the Eastern zone. It seemed to be an ideal way out of the dilemma in which West Germans found themselves. The goal encompassed both Western integration and reunification, both Marshall Plan and national unity. In 1949, it did not seem foolish to aim for this type of maximal program.[85]

Even Semyonov, political advisor to the head of the Soviet Military Administration, mentioned this approach to Pieck. Building two German states could only advance the goal of German unity if one of the two achieved victory over the other: "In a conversation with Semyonov on 10 June, Pieck allegedly noted that 'unity through annexation East' [he must have meant: annexation to the East] must occur."[86]

The Marshall Plan

In 1948, the American administration passed a comprehensive economic aid program in order to rebuild and stabilize Western Europe. Secretary of State George B. Marshall introduced the plan in July. Negotiations with the European countries over the European Recovery Program (ERP) were emblematic of the divided continent: "The Soviet Union rejected the American concept as dollar diplomacy and forced its Eastern European satellite states to distance themselves from the program as well."[87] Passed by Congress on 3 April and also referred to as the Marshall Plan, the aid program to rebuild Western Europe specifically included the three Western occupation zones of Germany. But the Americans tied the ERP to one condition: the European governments had to agree on a common economic program in order to use the economic aid in an efficient and targeted way. This condition initiated the European unification process and led to the formation of the Organization of European Economic Cooperation (OEEC) in Paris, which took over the task of distributing and monitoring ERP funds. With the inclusion of the Western zones in the program, West Germany "was already integrated into the Western camp one and a half years before the Federal Republic even came into existence. The inclusion of West Germany in Western Europe and the Atlantic community, along with the democratic development of West Germany, are certainly among the outstanding achievements of the Marshall Plan. The plan had deep consequences for Germany—economically, politically, and also psychologically."[88]

The European Coal and Steel Community

Three years after the Second World War, the security of Western European states against German aggression still played an important role in their foreign policies. With the Marshall Plan, U.S. policy aligned itself with Churchill's position. The danger of German aggression, they believed, would be contained by Germany's European neighbors through its tight integration into the European community. Taking France's security concerns into consideration, an international organization would be formed to control the coal and steel production in the Ruhr Valley. This demand by the French marked the beginning of Western Europe's economic integration. In 1950, Robert Schuman, the former French foreign minister, suggested "placing the entire French and German coal and steel production under a joint, supranational 'High Authority.'" Schuman underlined that European unity could only succeed if the "centuries-old antagonism between France and Germany is extinguished." The joint administration of coal and steel production by the former "weaponsmiths" of both countries, he went on, "would signal that any future war between France and Germany is not only unthinkable but also materially impossible."[89]

In 1950, France, Belgium, West Germany, Italy, Luxemburg, and the Netherlands agreed to establish this "High Authority" in order to form a union of raw materials production. The treaty on the European Coal and Steel Community (ECSC) went into effect in July 1952 with a validity period of fifty years. The politicians involved hoped that the ECSC would also provide an economic basis for the federal union of Western Europe that they desired. Even though this goal never materialized, the ECSC represented the beginning of Europe's supranational integration, born out of France's need for security against renewed German strength.

The Founding of the Federal Republic and the German Basic Law

On 23 May 1949, the Parliamentary Council completed its work by passing the Basic Law of the Federal Republic of Germany. On 14 August 1949, the citizens of the Western zones elected their representatives to the German Bundestag for the first time. The Christian Democratic Union (CDU), along with its sister party, the Christian Social Union (CSU) of Bavaria, emerged as the strongest faction in the newly elected Bundestag, followed by the Social Democratic Party and a variety of smaller parties. The CDU was led by Konrad Adenauer, who had already made a name for himself as president of the Parliamentary Council. He was elected by the Bundestag as federal chancellor on 15 September. Four years after the end of the war, Germans possessed an elected government once again. The FRG saw itself as the democratic core state for all Germans—a claim reinforced in the preamble to the Basic Law, as well as in the articles that followed. The document's provisional character came through in the period of validity stated in Article 146: "This Basic Law becomes invalid on the day on which a Constitution adopted by the German people by means of a free decision becomes effective."[90]

The Parliamentary Council thus provided the FRG with an organizational statute for a federal, republican state. After the National Socialist dictatorship, and in light of the new Communist dictatorship developing in the Soviet zone, the Council created a Basic Law drawing on a concept of humanity in which each person's dignity had intrinsic value, and freedom and equality were central principles of state unity. The Parliamentary Council wanted to establish a fundamental order bound to basic values. It would be the opposite of a totalitarian state, in which the party's exclusive governing power enabled it to suppress the human dignity, power interests, and freedom of the individual and reject the principle of equality before the law. Heinrich Oberreuter remarks on this new approach in Germany's constitutional history: "The ideologically neutral state—for the sake of humanity and freedom—is not neutral in its values. Because of this, its constitution can encompass 'the basic ethical consensus of the nation.'"[91]

The members of the Parliamentary Council were aware that with regard to the state's population and territory, the Federal Republic's constitutional foundation could only encompass part of the German nation. But they acted as representatives of a core German state, as did their counterparts in East Berlin. "In its 'partial identity' as a continuation of the German Reich, the Federal Republic represented the idea of a larger whole, which did not coincide with the reality of the 'double state founding' [*doppelte Staatsgründung*]. Rather, an extraordinary harmony pervaded the beginning of German division. Both here and there, in the West and in the East, the 'double state founding' took place with a certain pathos of unity." The idea of standing for a greater whole that could not yet be achieved came out of the active initiative "of the Federal Republic's first Federal President, Theodor Heuss, and found its expression in the preamble to the Basic Law."[92] Several of the following articles served to constitutionally cement the character of the Federal Republic as the core state of Germany.

For forty years, the preamble remained nothing more than a postulate. But it is important to emphasize the role of the Federal Constitutional Court (Bundesverfassungsgericht) in reinforcing these "core state articles" of the Basic Law. The Constitutional Court repeatedly used its jurisdiction to strengthen the fundamental consensus of 1949, when the founding of the two half-states took place according to Allied orders, limiting Germany's right to self-determination in the West and suspending it altogether in the East. The significance of this consensus from 1949 diminished in the media and political debates of the later Federal Republic, as West German identity became increasingly trapped in a contemporary outlook that had given up on the nation and the core state as expressed in the Basic Law. But by protecting the core state ideal against these changes in public opinion, the

Constitutional Court safeguarded the legal mechanisms needed to carry out a swift reunification as it finally occurred in 1990, following Article 23 of the Basic Law.

According to the preamble of the Basic Law, the Parliamentary Council "also acted on behalf of those Germans to whom participation was denied. The entire German people is called upon to achieve, by free self-determination, the unity and freedom of Germany."[93] The Constitutional Court stated in 1956 that "all political state institutions of the Federal Republic of Germany must understand from this document that they should strive for the unification of Germany with all of their strength; they should orient their measures toward this goal; and they should use the applicability to this goal as a scale by which to evaluate all of their political actions."[94] Thus, the preamble was interpreted as a legal norm with immediate validity. Finding a path to reunification belonged in the political domain, but the principle of reunification, according to the Constitutional Court, also meant forbidding all actions and agreements that went against established legal positions or obstructed or impaired reunification.

The Constitutional Court defended this interpretation of the law in several verdicts, especially in connection with complaints of unconstitutionality regarding the Eastern Treaties signed under the Brandt-Scheel government. With its verdict, the Court defended the Basic Law's core state concept against members of the federal governing coalition and a media-propagated zeitgeist that advocated "facing reality."[95]

Article 23 of the Basic Law contained an offer to the Eastern states to join the West and, up until its annulment through the Unification Treaty of 23 September 1990, read as follows: "For the time being, this Basic Law applies in the territory of the Länder Baden, Bavaria, Bremen, Greater Berlin, Hamburg, Hesse, Lower-Saxony, North-Rhine-Westphalia, Rhineland-Palatinate, Schleswig-Holstein, Württemberg-Baden and Württemberg-Hohenzollern. It is to be put into force in other parts of Germany on their accession."[96] Here, too, the interpretation reflects a belief in the continued existence of the German Reich as a nation-state under international law, which had also manifested itself in the veto rights of the Allied victors. Article 23 created the practical possibility of successively expanding the territory in which the Basic Law applied, based on the right of Germans to self-determination. With the Eastern Treaties of the early 1970s, the social-liberal government took the position that Article 23 had been realized with Saarland's accession in 1957 and thus rendered obsolete. However, the Constitutional Court declared that there were still other parts of Germany to which accession must remain open. In its verdict, the court cited Article 7 of the General Treaty (in addition to the Basic Law) and concluded that it was unaffected by the Eastern Treaties. The Constitutional Court prioritized the Western Treaties over the Eastern Treaties, emphasizing that the Federal Republic still had an obligation toward the Western powers to cooperate "to achieve, by peaceful means, their common aim of a reunified Germany enjoying a liberal-democratic constitution, like that of the Federal Republic, and integrated within the European community."[97]

According to Article 116 of the Basic Law, a person does not have "Federal Republic" citizenship but rather "German" citizenship. This article draws on the 1913 Nationality Law of the German Empire and States (Reichs- und Staatsangehörigkeitsgesetz) and also reflects a legal insistence on the enduring German Reich as a political body under international law. At first, the GDR followed the same interpretation. But from the early 1950s onward, it distanced itself increasingly from this perspective, passing a law in 1967 to establish "citizenship of the German Democratic Republic." For the FRG and its stance on uniform German citizenship, the move changed nothing. Even the Basic Treaty of 1972 between the FRG and the GDR had negligible influence on West Germany's concept of German citizenship. The Constitutional Court stated in unmistakable terms: "A German citizen under the Basic Law does not only mean a citizen of the Federal Republic of Germany . . . irrespective of any regulation of citizenship law in the German Democratic Republic."[98] Thus, the court prevented a weakening in the FRG's position on the citizenship question, a weakening that the Federal Government accepted and took for granted. Soon after the Basic Treaty was signed, the Federal Foreign Office changed its guidelines for dealing with citizens of the GDR: instead of a right to diplomatic protection, GDR citizens would only have access to "politically" or "ethically" motivated aid. But the Constitutional Court put a stop to these changes, too—a decision that had tremendous importance for citizens of and refugees from the GDR.

In its verdict, the Constitutional Court went well beyond the question of West Germany's obligation to protect all Germans. It obliged every new government not only to remind "the public consciousness . . . of commonalities" between East and West Germany, but also to keep the public alert to "the ideological, political, and social differences between daily life and legal order in the Federal Republic of Germany and daily life and legal order in the German Democratic Republic. Any attempt to constrict the West German government in its freedom and constitutional obligation to represent the interests of free and democratic order by asserting that it is acting against the substance and spirit of the Treaty [i.e., the Basic Treaty with the GDR in 1972] and thereby interfering with the domestic affairs of the German Democratic Republic" was, according to the Constitutional Court, "in itself a breach of the Treaty." In fact, the Court considered the Basic Treaty to be an additional legal basis for the West German government, "in fulfilling its constitutional duties, to do everything possible to change and dismantle these inhuman conditions," specifically "the Wall, barbed wire, death strip, and command to shoot."[99] The legal foundation built on the verdicts of the Constitutional Court set clear legal barriers and goals for West German politics, even if their interpretation found less and less resonance within the political sphere.

While Article 23 and the principle of reunification provided a specific goal and a possible path to achieve that goal, the regulation of citizenship and the assertion of free movement for all Germans in Article 11 (and 117) of the Basic Law had eminent practical significance for each individual refugee from the Soviet zone/GDR, as well as for the politics of receiving immigrants in West Germany.

"Freedom of movement denotes the right to stay and live in any place within the federal territory, unimpeded by the government, or to travel to the federal territory for this purpose."[100]

Notes

1. In his memoirs, Semyonov describes a personal meeting with Stalin at the Kremlin on 11 April 1945, during which he was named director of a special commission of the Soviet government. From Berlin, the commission would make sure that the directives of the supreme commander were being followed. See Wladimir S. Semjonow, *Von Stalin bis Gorbatschow. Ein halbes Jahrhundert in diplomatischer Mission 1939–1991* (Berlin, 1995), 161–75.
2. "Bericht von Semenov," 2 March 1946, in Laufer and Kynin, *UdSSR*, vol. 2, 268.
3. The Social Democrats' fight against this fusion is described thoroughly in Harold Hurwitz, *Demokratie und Antikommunismus in Berlin nach 1945*, vol. 4, *Die Anfänge des Widerstandes* (Cologne, 1990).
4. By this Tiulpanov means the Potsdam Conference of 1945.
5. Laufer and Kynin, *UdSSR*, vol. 2, 229.
6. Vladimir S. Semyonov, "Informationsbrief Nr. 1: Über die politische Lage in Deutschland," February 1946, in ibid., 275.
7. See Rolf Badstübner and Wilfried Loth, eds., *Wilhelm Pieck: Aufzeichnungen zur Deutschlandpolitik 1945–1953* (Berlin, 1994), 63.
8. Friederike Sattler, "Bündnispolitik als Problem des zentralen Parteiapparates der KPD 1945/46," in *Anatomie der Parteizentrale: Die KPD/SED auf dem Weg zur Macht*, ed. Manfred Wilke (Berlin, 1998), 190.
9. Badstübner and Loth, *Wilhelm Pieck*, 68.
10. Andreas Malycha and Peter Jochen Winters, *Die SED: Geschichte einer deutschen Partei* (Munich, 2009), 46.
11. Sattler, "Bündnispolitik," 190.
12. Steininger, *Deutsche Geschichte*, vol. 1, 177.
13. "Politischer Bericht von Semenov," 9 March 1946, in Laufer and Kynin, *UdSSR*, vol. 2, 276.
14. The Council of People's Commissars (Rat der Volkskommissare) changed its name to the Council of Ministers (Ministerrat) in March 1946; accordingly, the Commissariats became Ministries.
15. "Politischer Bericht von Semenov," 9 May 1946, in Laufer and Kynin, *UdSSR*, vol. 2, 391.
16. Ibid., 391.
17. "Semenov an Sokolovskij," late May 1946, in Laufer and Kynin, *UdSSR*, vol. 2, 468.
18. See "Politischer Bericht von Semenov," 22 June 1946, in Laufer and Kynin, *UdSSR*, vol. 2, 520.
19. See Gerhard Wettig, *Bereitschaft zu Einheit in Freiheit? Die sowjetische Deutschland-Politik 1945–1955* (Munich, 1999), 103–9.
20. "Aufruf des ZK der KPD vom 11. Juni 1945," in *"Nach Hitler kommen wir": Dokumente zur Programmatik der Moskauer KPD-Führung 1944/45 für Nachkriegsdeutschland*, ed. Peter Erler, Horst Laude, and Manfred Wilke (Berlin, 1994), 394.
21. Wilhelm Florin, "Die Lage und die Aufgaben in Deutschland bis zum Sturz Hitlers," in Erler et al., *Nach Hitler*, 144.
22. Ibid., 156.

23. "Aufruf des ZK der KPD vom 11. Juni 1945," in Erler et al., *Nach Hitler*, 394.

24. Florin, "Die Lage und die Aufgaben in Deutschland bis zum Sturz Hitlers," in Erler et al., *Nach Hitler*, 145.

25. See Michael Kubina, "Der Aufbau des zentralen Parteiapparates der KPD 1945–1946," in Wilke, *Anatomie*, 49–118.

26. Quoted in Sergej I. Tjulpanow, *Deutschland nach dem Kriege (1945–1949): Erinnerungen eines Offiziers der Sowjetarmee*, ed. Stefan Doernberg, trans. Günter Gossing and Lothar Jäger (Berlin (East), 1986), 15.

27. Norman M. Naimark, *Die Russen in Deutschland: Die sowjetische Besatzungszone 1945 bis 1949* (Berlin, 1997), 170.

28. Jan Foitzik, *Sowjetische Militäradministration in Deutschland (SMAD) 1945–1949: Struktur und Funktion* (Berlin, 1999), 221.

29. Ibid., 227.

30. See ibid., 241.

31. Vladimir V. Sacharov, Dmitrij N. Filippovych, and Michael Kubina, "Tschekisten in Deutschland: Organisation, Aufgaben und Aspekte der Tätigkeit der sowjetischen Sicherheitsapparate in der Sowjetischen Besatzungszone Deutschlands (1945–1949)," in Wilke, *Anatomie*, 293–335. Nikita Petrov has identified nearly one thousand employees of the Soviet secret service who were part of this ubiquitous and anonymous power structure in the Soviet occupation zone. See Nikita Petrov, *Die sowjetischen Geheimdienstmitarbeiter in Deutschland: Der leitende Personalbestand der Staatssicherheitsorgane der UdSSR in der SBZ und der DDR von 1945–1954*, trans. Vera Ammer (Berlin, 2010).

32. Foitzik, *Militäradministration*, 424.

33. See Kubina, "Aufbau," 70.

34. "Schlussbericht der Enquete-Kommission," in *Materialien der Enquete-Kommission: Überwindung der Folgen der SED-Diktatur im Prozess der deutschen Einheit*, ed. Deutscher Bundestag (Baden-Baden, 1999), vol. 1, 682.

35. Tjulpanow, *Deutschland*, 25.

36. Foitzik, *Militäradministration*, 425.

37. Mike Schmeitzner and Stefan Donth, *Die Partei der Diktaturdurchsetzung: KPD/SED in Sachsen 1945–1952* (Cologne, 2002).

38. Winfrid Halder *"Modell für Deutschland": Wirtschaftspolitik in Sachsen 1945–1948* (Paderborn, 2001), 539.

39. Ibid., 540; see also Foitzik, *Militäradministration*, 389.

40. Wolfgang Zank, "Wirtschaftliche Zentralverwaltungen und Deutsche Wirtschaftskommission (DWK)," in *SBZ-Handbuch: Staatliche Verwaltungen, Parteien, gesellschaftliche Organisationen und ihre Führungskräfte in der Sowjetischen Besatzungszone Deutschlands, 1945–1949*, ed. Martin Broszat and Hermann Weber (Munich, 1990), 268.

41. Sattler, "Bündnispolitik," 767.

42. See Hans-Peter Müller, "'Parteiministerien' als Modell politisch zuverlässiger Verwaltungsapparate: Eine Analyse der Protokolle der SED-Innenministerkonferenzen 1946–1948," in Wilke, *Anatomie*, 337–411.

43. Wilfried Loth, *Stalins ungeliebtes Kind: Warum Moskau die DDR nicht wollte* (Berlin, 1994), 143.

44. Andreas Malycha, *Die SED: Geschichte ihrer Stalinisierung 1946–1953* (Paderborn, 2000), 297.

45. Friederike Sattler, *Wirtschaftsordnung im Übergang: Politik, Organisation und Funktion der KPD/SED im Land Brandenburg bei der Etablierung der zentralen Planwirtschaft in der SBZ/DDR 1945–52* (Münster, 2002), vol. 2, 769.

46. Hermann Weber, *Geschichte der DDR*, rev. ed. (1985; repr. Munich, 1999), 119–20.

47. See Malycha, *SED*, 277–435.

48. Malycha, *SED*, 506; see also Karl Wilhelm Fricke, *Opposition und Widerstand in der DDR: Ein politischer Report* (Cologne, 1984).

49. Wolfgang Leonhard, *Die Revolution entlässt ihre Kinder* (Cologne, 1955).

50. Loth, *Stalins ungeliebtes Kind*, 145–48.
51. See "Brief der SED-Führung an Stalin, 19.9.1949," in Steininger, *Deutsche Geschichte*, vol. 2, 103–6.
52. Loth, *Stalins ungeliebtes Kind*, 159.
53. Manfred Koch, "Volkskongreßbewegung und Volksrat," in Broszat and Weber, *SBZ-Handbuch*, 353–54.
54. "Telegramm J. W. Stalins an W. Pieck und O. Grotewohl, 13.10.1949," quoted in Steininger, *Deutsche Geschichte*, vol. 2, 115.
55. Henry Kissinger, *Diplomacy* (New York, 1994), 442.
56. Oliver Jäckel, "Außenministerkonferenz Paris (25.4.–15.5. und 15.6.–12.7.1946)," in Benz, *Deutschland unter alliierter Besatzung*, 219.
57. "Unterredung zwischen Stalin und Byrnes," 24 December 1945, in Laufer and Kynin, *UdSSR*, vol. 2, 226.
58. Laufer and Kynin, *UdSSR*, vol. 2, XCIX.
59. "Entwurf von Sokolovskij und Semenov," 1 March 1946, in Laufer and Kynin, *UdSSR*, vol. 2, 265.
60. Küsters, *Integrationsfriede*, 278.
61. Steininger, *Deutsche Geschichte*, vol. 1, 251–52.
62. Hermann Graml, *Die Alliierten und die Teilung Deutschlands: Konflikte und Entscheidungen 1941–1948* (Frankfurt am Main, 1985), 120.
63. Steininger, *Deutsche Geschichte*, vol. 1, 252.
64. "Address by Secretary of State Byrnes on United States Policy Regarding Germany," Stuttgart, 6 September 1946, in U.S. Dept. of State, *Documents on Germany*, 94.
65. Ibid., 95.
66. Ibid., 96–97.
67. Steininger, *Deutsche Geschichte*, vol. 1, 253.
68. "Bericht von Gribanov: Die Positionen der Alliierten in Deutschland nach der Moskauer SMID-Tagung," 12 September 1947, in Laufer and Kynin, *UdSSR*, vol. 3, 403.
69. Walter Ulbricht, "Rede auf der Tagung der Ersten Sekretäre der kommunistischen und Arbeiterparteien des Warschauer Paktes in Moskau," 3 August 1961, SAPMO-BArch, DY 30/3478.
70. Peter Graf Kielmansegg, *Nach der Katastrophe: Eine Geschichte des geteilten Deutschland* (Berlin, 2000), 38–39.
71. Ibid., 40.
72. "Smirnov an Molotov," 12 March 1948, in Laufer and Kynin, *UdSSR*, vol. 3, 523.
73. Ibid., 524.
74. Ibid., 525.
75. Ibid.
76. Gerhard Wettig, "Die Verhandlungen der Westmächte mit der UdSSR über die Aufhebung der Berliner Blockade 1948: Untersuchungen unter Verwendung sowjetischer Gesprächsprotokolle," *Jahrbuch des Landesarchivs Berlin* (2008): 244.
77. Ibid., 243–44.
78. Abelshauser, *Wirtschaftsgeschichte*, 127.
79. Kleßmann, *Staatsgründung*, 190.
80. Kielmansegg, *Katastrophe*, 40. For the full text of this communiqué, see "Communiqué Issued at the Conclusion of Informal Talks on Germany Among Representatives of France, the United Kingdom, the United States, and the Benelux Countries," London, 7 June 1948, in U.S. Dept. of State, *Documents on Germany*, 143–46.
81. "Die 'Frankfurter Dokumente,' 1.7.1948," in Steininger, *Deutsche Geschichte*, vol. 2, 43.
82. "Antwortnote der westdeutschen Ministerpräsidenten an die Militärgouverneure," in Steininger, *Deutsche Geschichte*, vol. 2, 44–46.
83. Kielmansegg, *Katastrophe*, 66.
84. Carlo Schmid, *Erinnerungen* (Frankfurt am Main, 1980), 332–33.

85. Ibid., 144.

86. Loth, *Stalins ungeliebtes Kind,* 143.

87. Hans-Jürgen Schröder, "European Recovery Program (ERP)," in Benz, *Deutschland unter alliierter Besatzung,* 260.

88. Steininger, *Deutsche Geschichte,* vol. I, 299.

89. Michael Gehler, *Europa: Ideen, Institutionen, Vereinigung* (Munich, 2005), 151.

90. "Basic Law (Constitution) of the Federal Republic of Germany, Approved by the Parliamentary Council in Bonn, May 8, 1949," in U.S. Dept. of State, *Documents on Germany,* 257.

91. Heinrich Oberreuter, *Wendezeiten: Zeitgeschichte als Prägekraft politischer Kultur* (Munich, 2010), 71.

92. Volker Kronenberg, "Die deutsche Perspektive nach der Katastrophe: Nation, Verfassung, Vaterland" (conference paper, German-Russian Conference of Historians, Moscow, 28–30 October 2005), 2–3.

93. "Basic Law (Constitution) of the Federal Republic of Germany," in U.S. Dept. of State, *Documents on Germany,* 221.

94. BVerfG, "Entscheidung im KPD-Prozess," in *KPD-Prozess: Dokumentarwerk zu dem Verfahren über den Antrag der Bundesregierung auf Feststellung der Verfassungswidrigkeit der Kommunistischen Partei Deutschlands vor dem Ersten Senat des Bundesverfassungsgerichts,* ed. Gerd Pfeiffer and Hans-Georg Strickert (Karlsruhe, 1956), vol. 3, 605.

95. See Dieter Blumenwitz, "Die Bedeutung des BVG-Urteils zum Grundlagenvertrag vom 31. Juli 1973 für die deutsche Einigung 1990," lecture, in *Materialien der Enquete-Kommission: Aufarbeitung,* vol. 5/1, 457–67.

96. "Basic Law (Constitution) of the Federal Republic of Germany," in U.S. Dept. of State, *Documents on Germany,* 226.

97. Blumenwitz, "Bedeutung," 461.

98. Ibid., 462.

99. Ibid., 462–63.

100. Dieter Hesselberger, *Das Grundgesetz: Kommentar für die politische Bildung* (Neuwied, 1975), 88.

Chapter 4

WESTERN INTEGRATION AND THE
ESTABLISHMENT OF SOCIALISM
Competing Systems in a Divided Germany

The Federal Republic: Western Integration
and the Reclamation of German Sovereignty

Konrad Adenauer, first chancellor of the Federal Republic of Germany, entered office at the age of seventy-three. After the National Socialists stripped him of his position as lord mayor of Cologne in 1933, he survived the regime's persecution and was among the founders of the Christian Democratic Union (CDU) in the Rhineland in 1945. His realism regarding the situation in postwar Germany comes out in a statement he made as president of the Parliamentary Council during a meeting of the CDU caucus: "We are not mandated by the German people. Our orders come from the Allies."[1] Adenauer's sober "sense of reality" understood the limited "possibilities for the defeated country," and he drew appropriate consequences: "Only patiently, little by little, ready to give without receiving in return, was it possible to move forward. But most importantly: it was essential to lay a foundation of trust; that was the most difficult and most urgent task. 'Step by step, we had to try to rebuild trust in us Germans. The most basic precondition for this in my opinion, was a clear commitment to the West, consistent and unwavering. Our foreign policy needed to be clear, consequential, and open.' These sentences constitute the quintessence of Adenauer's foreign policy for the first few years."[2] Adenauer had a realistic perception of the international situation in Europe, which Peter Graf Kielmansegg summarizes as follows:

> The Soviet Union had made itself ruler of Central and Eastern Europe to the east of the Elbe. "Asia stands at the Elbe," Adenauer wrote in a letter in the spring of 1946. This meant a divided Germany for the foreseeable future. Western Europe had no choice but to come together if it was to survive under these conditions. Thus, Western Germany had to be included in a Western European union. This plan would also address the security concerns of Germany's neighbors, especially

France, in the best way possible. Not that this assessment of the situation already produced a master plan that needed only to be implemented later. The United States, for example, only gradually began to identify itself with Adenauer's political worldview. And tactically [the plan] remained entirely open. But in its main features, Adenauer's vision of the postwar world, as well as his conception of the necessities and possibilities of West German politics within this world, formed early and clearly. Adenauer understood how important it was to take advantage of the historic opportunity that the Western powers offered with the founding of West Germany. It was this ideal match between the pre-existing constellation and the foreign policy vision of the first federal chancellor that enabled the extraordinary rise of the West German state in the years up to 1955. A match that was anything but self-evident: the results of the Bundestag election in 1949 were just as close as the results of the first chancellor's election in parliament.[3]

The first West German government still operated under the status of occupation, which would continue to form the legal basis of relations between the Western powers and the Federal Republic until 1955. "The Allies reserved the right to control the demilitarization of the Ruhr Valley, reparations and restitution, Nazi crimes, and foreign policy, and the Allied high commissioner reserved his right to take over the exercise of force completely if it was necessary 'for security or for maintaining democratic order.'"[4] This ordinance also retained the rights of the Allies to proclaim a state of emergency during serious domestic crises or in the case of war, and to reverse its course through the deployment of Allied troops.

The first revision to this status came with the Petersberg Protocol in November 1949. In it, the Federal Republic gained the right to participate in international organizations, including the Organization for European Economic Cooperation (OEEC), the European Council, and the International Authority for the Ruhr, as well as to "initiate the gradual re-establishment of Consular and Commercial relations."[5] Germans were allowed to begin building ships again, and the Allied policy of industrial disassembly continued only in a limited form. The Western orientation of German foreign policy, which Adenauer saw as irreversible, aimed to rule out any future attempts to implement a "seesaw policy" between West and East—a danger that seemed likely considering Germany's position in between the two camps. Adenauer himself had lived through the consequences of this type of policy, and his strong tie to the West was the result:

> This emerged very consciously from the twofold failure of the Reich, first founded in 1871, which long disturbed the continent with its power-hungry maneuvers before finally shredding it—and itself—to ruins. Every maxim of Adenauer's foreign policy somehow alluded to the failure of German tradition, even in examples that in retrospect seem obvious, such as his commitment to the West. The central statement of foreign policy in the government's declaration of 20 September 1949 read: "There is no doubt in our minds that we belong to the Western European world in terms of both our background and our disposition." In a country that had always understood itself as a country in the middle, this was certainly a new beginning.[6]

The start of the Korean War in June 1950 catalyzed relations between the Western powers and the Federal Republic. With the founding of the North Atlantic Treaty Organization (NATO) in 1949, American and British generals were already aware that they would need West German troops in order to defend Western Europe against the Soviet Union. "But this meant that the Federal Republic had to be released from its status as a quasi-protectorate and assume the role of an ally. This provoked the question of equal standing. The days of the occupation period were numbered."[7] After the beginning of the Korean War, it was not just the West German government that feared an attack by the other side; after all, the East German Volkspolizei had already begun performing military formations at their barracks in 1948.[8] In the summer of 1950, the Federal Republic had no equivalent police force.

Leading up to the New York meeting of the Western powers' foreign ministers in September 1950, the federal chancellor submitted a "security memorandum" on the situation of the FRG that relayed these fears and "demanded the formation of a federal police force." At the same time, he offered the participation of a contingent of German soldiers in the Western defense alliance and requested that the Federal Republic be included in NATO. Adenauer was pursuing two simultaneous goals. Contributing to NATO defense should "guarantee security for the Federal Republic while also obtaining equal standing" among the Western powers. This would "prevent, to the greatest extent possible, a unification of the Western powers and the Soviet Union against the interests of the Germans"—a possibility that he always feared. At the time that Adenauer submitted his memorandum, he had basically already reached an agreement with the United States and Great Britain—without consulting his cabinet—"over the inclusion of the Federal Republic in the military defense of Western Europe. Whether and with what speed this could be realized depended entirely on France."[9]

The foreign ministers of the three Western powers agreed in New York to create a European Defense Community (EDC) that would include West Germany. The realization of this plan required changing the "relationship between the Western Allies and the Federal Republic, which, after all, still stood under the occupation statute: the military occupation would take on a protective function for the Federal Republic, while the FRG would become a kind of 'junior partner' with distinctly broader rights than it had possessed in the past. One-sided obligations would give way to reciprocal obligations."[10] The agreement on the EDC marked a turning point in West Germany's path to sovereignty. With it, the three Western powers recognized the government of the Federal Republic as the single legitimate German government. The state of war with Germany ended, the occupation statute was reevaluated, and economic constraints were loosened. "The Western powers broadened their guarantee of security explicitly to include an attack by the GDR's Volkspolizei."[11] Against the backdrop of the Korean War, decisions emerged from the New York conference of foreign ministers that reflected "expectations of a looming third world war"[12]—at least, this is Hans-Peter Schwarz's interpretation of the Korean War's effects on Western Allied behavior toward West German sovereignty.

The negotiations in New York addressed two treaties: one regarding West Germany's entry into the EDC, and the other, the Germany Treaty (Deutschlandvertrag), with which the Federal Republic would regain its sovereignty. The Germany Treaty could only take effect after the treaty to found the EDC was ratified by all parliaments of the member states. But the French National Assembly refused to endorse it in 1954, forcing the parties to renegotiate West Germany's entry into NATO in the "Paris Treaties" of 1955. Rather than joining a Western European army, the FRG built up its own military forces and entered NATO later that year.

Domestically, ties to the West and the rearmament of the Federal Republic were subject to fierce debate. The SED managed to mobilize not only the West German KPD but also some members of the SPD against the Germany Treaty. Kurt Schumacher, head of the SPD and proponent of the national alternative to the Germany Treaty in 1952, formulated his rejection of the Germany Treaty in the following statement: "Whoever agrees to the Germany Treaty is no longer a German."[13]

Despite opposition, the Germany Treaty finally went into effect on 5 May 1955. "Adenauer's desire to win back full state sovereignty manifested itself in the changes to the Germany Treaty of 23 October 1954. Article I, Paragraph 2 explicitly states: 'The Federal Republic shall have the full power of a sovereign state over its internal and external affairs.' At the same time, a caveat remained in place reserving the rights of the Western powers to retain authority over questions that affected all of Germany or Berlin, as well as to maintain their ongoing military presence."[14] With deep international repercussions that endured until 1989–90, the Germany Treaty's significance for the restoration of German unity cannot be overstated, even if the relevant ordinance had to be rediscovered by many political actors thirty-four years after its ratification. Article 7 obliged the signatory states

> to work together until "a peace settlement of the whole of Germany, freely negotiated between Germany and her former enemies" could materialize, in order "to achieve, by peaceful means, their common aim of a reunified Germany enjoying a liberal-democratic constitution, like that of the Federal Republic, and integrated within the European community." Furthermore, the signatory states were in agreement that "the final determination of the boundaries of Germany must await such settlement." This (controversial) conclusion did not require the Western powers to fight actively for the restoration of Germany's Eastern territories. But even the contractual obligation to keep the question of Germany's borders open was more than the Western powers had wanted to concede.[15]

In 1951–52, Adenauer saw the Federal Republic politically as the core German state, while the GDR represented a territory under foreign rule without the qualities of a state. "This view was shared among all of the democratic parties at that time; it was entirely beyond dispute. If one accepted this idea of the Federal Republic as the core German state, it was certainly logical to project its relations onto a larger Germany . . . that included a liberated Eastern zone. Only in this way could the legitimate security concerns of the Western neighbors be reconciled with Germany's wish to achieve equal standing."[16] By defining reunification through the conditions of the West, Adenauer was able to achieve another goal: "From then on, it would be impossible for the major Allied powers to make agreements based on the Potsdam resolutions at the expense of Germany, their 'bargaining tool.'"[17]

Signing the North Atlantic Treaty in conjunction with the Paris Treaties and the accession of West Germany into the alliance, the member states declared that "They consider the Government of the Federal Republic as the only German Government freely and legitimately constituted and therefore entitled to speak for Germany as the representative of the German people in international affairs."[18] This recognition of the FRG as the sole legitimate German state, acting on behalf of all Germans as the democratic core, blocked all attempts by the Soviet Union until 1971 to achieve equal standing for the GDR as a second legitimate German state in Western Europe.

With the Germany Treaty, the Federal Republic became a partner of the Western powers. At the same time, the failure of the EDC embodied the lasting tension and conflicts in the triangular relationship between Bonn, Washington, and Paris.

The Federal Republic's Alignment with the West and Stalin's Peace Note of 1952

The Western integration of the Federal Republic, the restoration of its sovereignty (limited through the retention of Allied rights for all of Germany), and the creation of a new German army to face the Soviet Union led Stalin to write a note in March 1952 offering to resume negotiations over Germany's peace treaty, its neutralization, the strengthening of his own forces, and free elections. Stalin's goals were clear: he wished to isolate Adenauer politically, prevent the emergence of a sovereign West Germany, and distance the Federal Republic from Western Europe and the United States.

One year earlier, Foreign Minister Andrey J. Vyshinsky had presented Molotov, his predecessor in the politburo in charge of foreign affairs, with an evaluation of the "movement to neutralize Germany."[19] Vyshinsky cited Adenauer's argument against the neutralization of West Germany. The chancellor felt that if neutralized, the Federal Republic "would be pulled into the orbit of Soviet power within just a few years. Moreover, neutralization also presents the danger that the USA could lose interest in Europe. The continent will only be able to exist if the Federal Republic of Germany remains in the Western camp."[20] Adenauer was a decided opponent of West Germany's neutralization.

At the same time, there were neutralists within the Federal Republic who adamantly argued against Adenauer's alignment with the West. According to Vyshinsky, the SED leadership weighed using these voices for their own policy toward the West: "Pieck and Ulbricht do not believe that the SED should take a stand against the proponents [within the FRG] of neutralizing Germany; rather, it should try to join forces with them against remilitarization and against the inclusion of West Germany in the North Atlantic Alliance."[21] Ulbricht, who was responsible for his party's "Western operations," suggested this in part because he had no illusions about the KPD's struggle against the Federal Republic's rearmament. According to his assessment, the Communists only had one more trump with regard to possible four-power negotiations: "Ulbricht thinks it might be possible for the Soviet Union itself, in one form or another, to suggest neutralizing Germany—with the goal of exposing the American warmongers."[22]

One year later, Stalin seized on this thought with the "Peace Note" of 10 March 1952. The moment was well chosen in terms of propaganda, since the Western powers were in the midst of negotiations with the Federal Republic over the Germany Treaty. The SED and KPD's campaign in West Germany against the country's "remilitarization" and its entry into NATO was part of Soviet peace propaganda. In the debate over the Peace Note, Hermann Graml has pointed to the significance of NATO for Soviet security policy and policy toward Germany: "Indeed, Stalin and his aides respected the establishment and existence of this alliance. With reinvigorated energy, they strove to integrate and guard the territories within their own empire whose possession was not challenged by the Western powers with military force."[23] This was especially true of the GDR, despite Soviet propaganda suggesting that German unification was still possible on the basis of a peace treaty that would span the bloc borders.[24]

The Western Allies rejected the Soviet offer to negotiate, just as Adenauer had.[25] In Henry Kissinger's view, Stalin had missed the window of opportunity when this type of offer might have been feasible: "Had Stalin offered the so-called Peace Note four years earlier—before the Berlin Blockade, the Czech coup, and the Korean War—it almost certainly would have stopped German membership in NATO in its tracks. Indeed, it is quite possible that German membership in the Atlantic Alliance would never have been considered."[26] However, a positive response to the note by the West would have contradicted all experiences with Soviet politics since the end of the war. American leaders interpreted Stalin's offer "as merely one more tactic in a Cold War struggle which could only end in victory or defeat. Compromise with Stalin was no longer on the agenda."[27]

As a further reason for the Americans to reject the offer, Kissinger pointed to the danger that would arise from the armed, neutral Germany that the note had suggested: "Even if it had been possible to define German neutrality in such a way as to forestall permanent Soviet intervention and a level of German arms that would not have left Germany at the mercy of the Soviet Union, this would only have restored what had been Europe's dilemma since German unification in 1871. A strong, unified Germany in the center of the Continent pursuing a purely national policy had proved incompatible with the peace of Europe. Such a Germany would be stronger than any of the nations of Western Europe, and probably stronger than all of them combined."[28] Moreover, American leadership feared that a neutral Germany housing fifteen million expellees and refugees (who still viewed the lost eastern territories as their homeland) would pursue a revision-ist policy with regard to the western border of Poland: "It was tempting fate to turn loose a united, neutral Germany so soon after the war."[29] After listing the interests of Germany's European neighbors that discouraged the country's neu-tralization, Kissinger closes his argument with an homage to Adenauer: "Above all, such an outcome would have discredited the greatest German statesman since Bismarck, who bears the historic distinction of having guided Germany away from the legacy of Bismarck."[30]

The GDR in 1952: "Building the Foundations of Socialism"

Even before the SED's Second Party Congress in July 1952 resolved to "build the foundations of socialism" in the GDR, preparations had already been made. Three occurrences closely tied in to this party congress: Stalin's Peace Note on the German question in March 1952; the SED's party cleansing, ongoing since 1948; and the fortification of the demarcation line between East and West Germany, as well as the GDR's increased control of the border between West Berlin and its sur-rounding areas. These measures to ensconce the SED dictatorship were reinforced through a propaganda campaign by the SED and the KPD for a German peace treaty on the one hand and the revolutionary overthrow of the freely elected West German government on the other. The familiar pattern of post-1945 Soviet Ger-many policy repeated itself again: in their own occupation zone, the Soviets cre-ated political faits accomplis but always took care to give the impression (through propaganda and published decisions) that their measures were simply reactions to developments in West Germany. 1952 was no different.

Cementing the Zonal Border and Sealing Off
West Berlin from Its Surrounding Area

After the Western powers uniformly rejected Stalin's Peace Note on 25 March 1952, Stalin met with Pieck in the Kremlin on 1 April. The president of the GDR reported to Stalin that the West German SPD executive would probably turn down the SED's suggestion to build a "unity of action for the peace treaty" out of the two parties and would instead vote for the Federal Republic's Western integration. In their final conversation on 7 April, Pieck noted Stalin's evaluation of the West's reply with the words, "all suggestions rejected so far" and "no com-promises / . . . Atlantic pact—independent state in the West." Stalin approved of the SED's approach, to call more intensely for the "fall" of the government in Bonn. Pieck jotted down: "Unity—peace treaty—agitate further."[31]

The integration of the Federal Republic into the Western alliance allowed West Germany to strengthen its armed forces. Following the logic of the Cold War's bloc confrontation, Stalin anticipated certain consequences for his Germany:

When Pieck tentatively suggested taking "steps toward the establishment of a People's Army rather than a police force," . . . Stalin arranged for comprehensive armament: "Not in steps, but immediately." He already began to develop the details: "9–10 army corps—30 divis[ions]—300,000 [soldiers]/training in S[oviet] U[nion]/youth service," etc. To justify his haste, Stalin pointed out that the "demarcation line" was a "dangerous border": "We have to prepare ourselves for terrorist acts." . . . Even more important to the further development [of the GDR] was Stalin's reaction when Pieck reported "increased enemy activities," specifically mentioning "large-scale farmers" and "churches." Stalin advised Pieck to encircle the large-scale farmers . . . by establishing agricultural cooperatives in the villages as well. In connection with these "collective farms" [*Kolchosen*], he alluded to "the path to Socialism" for the first time.[32]

Even before this conversation with Pieck, Semyon Ignatyev, Soviet minister of state security, had already informed Stalin and the politburo "about the unacceptable condition of the demarcation borders of the German Democratic Republic." The minister reported multiple "border infringements, illegal border crossings, and provocations from the Western occupation powers. The border police was too poorly equipped and could not properly perform its duties. Additionally, the border police personnel included 'unreliable elements'; the force lacked discipline, and alcohol abuse was present."[33]

Stalin decided in May to reinforce the border to the FRG. In addition, the Soviet Control Commission instructed the Central Committee of the SED to formulate a special policy regarding the demarcation line to West Germany and the coastal areas of the GDR. The SED Politburo reacted accordingly. Prime Minister Grotewohl ordered Wilhelm Zaisser, the East German minister of state security, to take immediate measures for the protection of the borders in order to "prevent further infiltration by saboteurs, spies, terrorists, and other pests into the territory of the German Democratic Republic."[34] On 27 May 1952, the minister presented a draft of these regulations. The German Border Police (Deutsche Grenzpolizei) were to implement the following measures:

Directly along the demarcation line, a 10-meter-wide control strip shall be plowed and smoothed.
Fixed streets and railroad embankments are to be torn up and closed with physical barriers. Exceptions to this are the streets and railroad lines of interzonal transit at the set control posts.
The 500-meter-wide protection strip and the 5-kilometer zone shall be marked along the demarcation line with trespassing signs and barriers.[35]

In his chronicle of the "border through Germany," Roman Grafe traces the implementation of these orders using the example of Probstzella, a city in Thuringia. Part of this was "Operation Vermin" (Aktion Ungeziefer), through which approximately eleven thousand people were relocated away from the closed security strip because they were considered unreliable.[36] Klara Gerold, one of the forced evacuees, witnessed the way in which Ulbricht, the master builder of socialism, cultivated one of his most important raw materials: fear. "When the closed zone was established in Probstzella, there was no public protest. People were against it but stayed quiet and became even quieter. . . . Such a dulling [of their wills], and then finally obedience. It was this fear from above and below that allowed it to happen. Fear was the decisive factor. It was always possible that someone could rat you out."[37] The relocation, according to Gerhard Sälter, "left behind an atmosphere of individual fear and general uncertainty in the areas near the border, which significantly increased the political pressure to fit in."[38]

Berlin was included in these measures to close the border. While the border to the Federal Republic could be sealed within a few weeks, the "isolation procedure" in West Berlin proved more complicated: "Because of the many ties between West and East Berlin and the surrounding zonal regions in all areas of civil and economic life, [it could] only be accomplished over the course of a longer process."[39] This began with transportation routes: "Of the 277 streets that led from Westberlin into the Soviet sector and the Soviet zone, 99 were closed by 28 May 1952";[40] by the end of September the number had increased to 200. At various points along the border between West Berlin and Brandenburg, a border strip was drawn similar to the zonal border to the FRG. For the West German government and the broader public, the closing of the inner German border, ordered by the Soviet occupation power and carried out by the GDR government, signaled the prelude to "an intensified Sovietization of Central Germany."[41] The number of refugees increased. As the blocks along the inner German border developed over the following years, Berlin gained more and more importance for people fleeing to the West.

Building Socialism in the GDR and Relations with the Federal Republic

When the SED Party Congress met in July 1952, the politics of the SED and KPD in the Federal Republic had already failed. "The resonance of SED and KPD policy faded more and more. Neither the ban on Communist organizations such as the Free German Youth (Freie Deutsche Jugend, or FDJ) nor the Federal Government's petition to ban the KPD, which stood before the Constitutional Court, elicited mass protests. Plans to mobilize people in West Germany by appealing to a national feeling and a unified country against the 'Adenauer Regime' never achieved success."[42] The Peace Note did nothing to change the situation. Since the SED was busy laying the foundations of socialism in the GDR, its campaign for a neutral Germany that the Western powers rejected served to legitimize the SED state. The West's refusal to accept Stalin's note fueled the push to secure the Socialist core state. This was Stalin's argument at a meeting with the head of the Italian Socialists, Petro Nenni, on 1 July 1952, in which he laid out the consequences of the West's refusal to neutralize all of Germany: Stalin "'assumed that the division of Germany would last for some time.' The Italian Socialist leader gained the impression throughout the conversation that he [Stalin] 'had given up hope for a successful four-power conference at which Germany would be unified through an agreement."[43] One week later, at the Second Party Congress of the SED, Ulbricht announced that the GDR would no longer take into consideration the developments in West Germany and would begin instead to build the foundations of socialism.

Stalin's authorization to lay the "foundations of socialism" in the GDR implied that the Soviet Union would guarantee SED rule in East Germany. The Second Party Congress of the SED, which later became an important step toward building the Berlin Wall, took place from 9 to 12 July 1952 in East Berlin. Coordination between the SED leadership and Moscow had already begun in January. Going through General Vasily Chuikov, head of the Soviet Control Commission, Pieck, Ulbricht, and Grotewohl asked Stalin if he would meet with them at the end of April to discuss preparations for the conference. Andrei Gromyko, deputy foreign minister of the Soviet Union, informed Chuikov that the Central Committee of the CPSU had decided that the SED leaders could "come to Moscow" to discuss the matter.[44] Pieck, Ulbricht, and Grotewohl then traveled there one month earlier than planned.

When the three men arrived in Moscow at the beginning of April, their main concern with regard to the Peace Note was

> to make all future actions seem like counterreactions. In writing, Semyonov and Smirnov conveyed the positions of the GDR leaders to Molotov upon their arrival: "Comrade Pieck plans to report on pan-German issues during the conversation, and one of his questions will address measures in connection with the signing of the 'General Treaty' between the Bonn government and the Western powers. Comrade Pieck believes it will be necessary to undertake appropriate countermeasures in the German Democratic Republic following the signing of the 'General Treaty' and the establishment of West German military units, and especially to reach a decision on the creation of a German National Army." Grotewohl, according to Semyonov and Smirnov, would report on "questions related to state building in the German Democratic Republic" and would go into the issue of "securing democratic legitimacy and taking measures against subversive activities by enemy elements (public trials, publication of verdicts from secret trials, etc.)." Ulbricht intended to pose questions on the economy, as well as the "issue of arming the Volkspolizei with firearms."[45]

These were key questions facing the further development of the GDR as the Socialist core state of Germany. The SED party congress aimed not only to consolidate the GDR but also to endow the developing state with its own societal perspectives through the establishment of Socialist foundations—perspectives that would stand as an alternative to the Federal Republic. SED leaders faced the complex task of protecting their state externally through its integration into the Soviet Empire, while at the same time winning autonomy by distancing it from the Federal Republic, especially with regard to the democratic structures and budding economic prosperity of the West. The SED was pressed for time.[46]

Although the SED had coordinated its moves with Moscow, there was still doubt within the party over whether the Soviets truly supported an announcement at the Second Party Congress about laying the foundations of socialism. To clarify this point, the SED's politburo wrote to Stalin once again on 2 July 1952. The letter addressed three issues: first, the development of the SED into a Marxist-Leninist party; second, the character of the "Adenauer government"; and third, the stage of development in the GDR.[47] The SED only received an answer to its questions (in the affirmative) on the eve of the party congress; Stalin approved of taking an accelerated course toward building the foundations of socialism. Ulbricht then used many of the formulations from the SED politburo's letter in his speech at the party congress.

In view of the still open German question, the SED had needed reassurance that its plans for the socialism project were secure. The most important issue was whether Stalin considered the SED to be a Communist party capable of leading the GDR as a Socialist state; this was contained in the first question. The question concerning the political order of the Federal Republic referenced the provisional character of both German states, aiming to assess the interests of Soviet Germany policy. The SED characterized the "Adenauer government" as a "protectorate of the United States"[48] and claimed that only the GDR's development into a people's democracy, along with the establishment and safeguarding of socialism, could mobilize the West German working class.[49] This step would lay the groundwork for the fall of the "Adenauer government," which the SED encouraged. Furthermore, the SED accused the "American imperialists" of trying to prepare for and set off a new world war; according to this position, "the collapse of the vassal government in Bonn is the prerequisite for the restoration of German unity."[50]

Only with this step, Ulbricht explained, could the results of the Germany Treaty be reversed and the "integration of West Germany into the aggressive North Atlantic bloc"[51] halted. However, he continued with a sober remark that the "patriotic movement and the working class of West Germany are not yet strong enough to prevent Bonn from signing its separate treaty."[52] With this situation in mind, it was crucial to secure the achievements of the "anti-fascist democratic revolution" taking place in the GDR with the help of the Soviet Union by ensuring "that the establishment of socialism in the GDR becomes a fundamental endeavor."[53] Ulbricht would only gain more autonomy for the GDR by aligning his interests with Soviet Germany policy. Thus, his speech also included a prediction of the effect that the SED's Socialist vision would have on West Germany: "The central question is, and will remain, the national question, which has deep social significance. The establishment of Socialism in the GDR and in Berlin can only have a positive effect on the struggle for our own democratic, peace-loving, independent Germany. As we always have, we continue to stand by our proposals to effect a Peace Treaty and the unity of Germany. The question of which societal order will emerge after the unification of Germany shall be decided by the entire German people without any kind of foreign interference."[54]

Ideological formulas aside, Ulbricht proposed three components of future SED policy in the GDR: a "stronger fight against and suppression of the deposed former elite; an even more self-confident 'leading role' for the 'Marxist-Leninist party'; and the massive armament of the GDR."[55] Looking to lay the "foundations of socialism," the SED already possessed state power, and this was the party's "primary instrument" for the collectivization of handicraft and farming enterprises.[56] Thus, the SED expanded its apparatus of repression, established the Ministry for State Security, and concentrated the GDR into a centralist state entity by dissolving the *Länder*. In addition to the fight against independent businesses, handworkers, and farmers, an ideological campaign emerged against the Protestant Church and its work in youth organizations. The well-planned establishment of socialism turned into the first major—fully unplanned—state crisis of the GDR. One of the most important reactions by those who were already or potentially affected was fleeing to the West of Germany.

Notes

1. Köhler, *Adenauer*, vol. I, 472.
2. Kielmansegg, *Katastrophe*, 155.
3. Ibid., 134.
4. Wolfgang Benz, "Besatzungsstatut," in Benz, *Deutschland unter alliierter Besatzung*, 333.
5. "Protocol of Agreements Between the Allied (Western) High Commissioners and the Chancellor of the Federal Republic of Germany, November 22, 1949 (Petersberg Protocol)," in U.S. Dept. of State, *Documents on Germany*, 310.
6. Auswärtiges Amt, ed., *40 Jahre Außenpolitik der Bundesrepublik Deutschland: Eine Dokumentation* (Stuttgart, 1989), 136.
7. Hans-Peter Schwarz, *Die Ära Adenauer: Gründerjahre der Republik, 1949–1957*, vol. 2 of *Geschichte der Bundesrepublik*, ed. Karl Bracher et al. (Stuttgart/Wiesbaden, 1983), 104.
8. See Gerhard Wettig, "Wiederbewaffnung," in *Lexikon des DDR-Sozialismus: Das Staats- und Gesellschaftssystem der Deutschen Demokratischen Republik*, ed. Rainer Eppelmann, Horst Möller, Günter Nooke, and Dorothee Wilms (Paderborn, 1996), 698–700.
9. Andreas Hillgruber, *Deutsche Geschichte 1945–1986: Die "deutsche Frage" in der Weltpolitik* (Stuttgart, 1987), 48–49.
10. Ibid., 49.
11. Steininger, *Deutsche Geschichte*, vol. 2, 150.
12. Schwarz, *Ära Adenauer*, 104.
13. Rudolf Morsey, "Die Deutschlandpolitik der Bundesregierungen Adenauer und die politisch-parlamentarische Diskussion 1949–1963," in Deutscher Bundestag, *Materialien der Enquete-Kommission: Aufarbeitung*, vol. 5/2, 1837.
14. Horst Möller, "Die Deutschlandpolitik von 1949 bis in die sechziger Jahre," in Deutscher Bundestag, *Materialien der Enquete-Kommission: Aufarbeitung*, vol. 5/1, 250. Concerning Berlin, the three Western powers and the Federal Republic agreed to enter into a close cooperation.

15. Morsey, "Deutschlandpolitik," 1836. For the full text of the Germany Treaty, see "Convention on Relations Between the Three Powers and the Federal Republic of Germany, May 26, 1952, As Amended by Schedule I of the Protocol on Termination of the Occupation Regime in Germany, Signed at Paris, October 23, 1954," in U.S. Dept. of State, *Documents on Germany*, 425–30.

16. Schwarz, *Ära Adenauer*, 146.

17. Ibid.

18. NATO, "Resolution of Association by Other Parties to the North Atlantic Treaty, Annex B," 22 October 1954, *NATO e-Library*, http://www.nato.int/cps/en/SID-AC209642-068 C9020/natolive/official_texts_17412.htm.

19. Andrej J. Vyšinskij, "Über die Bewegung für eine Neutralisierung Deutschlands," 18 February 1951, in *Stalins großer Bluff: Die Geschichte der Stalin-Note in Dokumenten der sowjetischen Führung*, ed. Peter Ruggenthaler (Munich, 2007), 56.

20. Ibid.

21. Ibid., 57.

22. Ibid.

23. Hermann Graml, "Eine wichtige Quelle—aber mißverstanden: Anmerkungen zu Wilfried Loth, 'Die Entstehung der "Stalin-Note": Dokumente aus Moskauer Archiven,'" in *Die Stalin-Note vom 10. März 1952: Neue Quellen und Analysen*, ed. Jürgen Zarusky (Munich, 2002), 119.

24. The note and its rejection set off a bitter debate among West German historians over whether a chance had been missed to reunify Germany. See Zarusky, *Stalin-Note*; Wettig, *Bereitschaft*.

25. See Steininger, *Deutsche Geschichte*, vol. 2, 185–87.

26. Kissinger, *Diplomacy*, 498.

27. Ibid., 501.

28. Ibid., 502.

29. Ibid.

30. Ibid.

31. Loth, *Stalins ungeliebtes Kind*, 185.

32. Ibid., 186–87.

33. Ruggenthaler, *Stalins großer Bluff*, 154.

34. Quoted in Roman Grafe, *Die Grenze durch Deutschland: Eine Chronik von 1945 bis 1990* (Berlin, 2002), 39.

35. Ibid. See also Sälter, *Grenzpolizisten*, 24–38.

36. See Inge Bennewitz and Rainer Potratz, *Zwangsaussiedlungen an der innerdeutschen Grenze: Analysen und Dokumente* (Berlin, 1997).

37. Grafe, *Grenze*, 47.

38. Sälter, *Grenzpolizisten*, 31.

39. Bundesministerium für gesamtdeutsche Fragen, ed., *Die Sperrmaßnahmen der Sowjetzonenregierung an der Zonengrenze und um Westberlin* (Bonn, 1953), 25.

40. Ibid.

41. Ibid., 31.

42. Weber, *Geschichte der DDR*, 150.

43. Wettig, *Bereitschaft*, 186.

44. Quoted in Ruggenthaler, *Stalins großer Bluff*, 98–99.

45. Ruggenthaler, *Stalins großer Bluff*, 155–56. The SED used the term "General Treaty" to refer to the Germany Treaty signed on 26 May 1952 by the Federal Republic and the Western powers and tied to the creation of the European Defense Community (EDC).

46. As Hermann Weber writes, "the paths of the two German states and their differently structured societies already began to diverge visibly. Democratic order took shape in the Federal Republic. With the economic upswing, the damages of war began to disappear and living conditions improved dramatically." In contrast, the situation in the GDR was characterized

by economic weakness and political dictatorship. The population's living conditions "led to permanent tensions in the 1950s; they prevented the society's consolidation." Weber, *Geschichte der DDR*, 150.

47. "Brief des Politbüros an J. W. Stalin," 2 July 1952, in Günter Benser, *Als der Aufbau des Sozialismus verkündet wurde: Eine Rückschau auf die II. Parteikonferenz der SED mit Dokumentenanhang* (Berlin, 2002), 57.

48. Walter Ulbricht, "Die gegenwärtige Lage und die neuen Aufgaben der SED," in *Protokoll der Verhandlungen der II. Parteikonferenz der SED, 9. bis 12. Juni 1952 in der Werner-Seelenbinder-Halle zu Berlin* (Berlin (East), 1952), 36.

49. Ibid., 58.

50. "Beschluss der 2. Parteikonferenz der SED: Zur gegenwärtigen Lage und zu den Aufgaben im Kampf für Frieden, Einheit, Demokratie und Sozialismus," in *Dokumente der SED*, vol. 4 (Berlin (East) 1954), 71.

51. Walter Ulbricht, "Die gegenwärtige Lage und die neuen Aufgaben der SED," in *Protokoll der Verhandlungen der II. Parteikonferenz der SED, 9. bis 12. Juni 1952 in der Werner-Seelenbinder-Halle zu Berlin* (Berlin (East), 1952), 36.

52. Ibid., 37.

53. Ibid., 58.

54. Ibid., 61–62.

55. Werner Müller, "Die Zweite Parteikonferenz der SED 1952: Das Regime zeigt sein stalinistisches Gesicht," in *17. Juni 1953: Der Aufstand für die Demokratie*, ed. Jürgen Maruhn (Munich, 2003), 24.

56. See Jens Schöne, *Frühling auf dem Lande? Die Kollektivierung der DDR-Landwirtschaft* (Berlin, 2010).

Chapter 5

THE END OF THE POSTWAR PERIOD

The Geneva Summit and the Transition to "Peaceful Coexistence" in Germany

Before the two German states achieved sovereignty, Joseph V. Stalin died in 1953—a critical turning point in the history of the Soviet Union and the East–West conflict. The years between 1953 and 1958 were marred by crisis in the Soviet Empire: The GDR witnessed a popular uprising against the SED in 1953. Nikita S. Khrushchev, Stalin's successor at the head of the CPSU, exposed Stalin's crimes against his own party at the 20th Party Congress in 1956, causing major unrest in Poland and the Hungarian Revolution, which ended in a bloody defeat at the hands of Soviet troops. The first differences of opinion emerged between the Soviet and the Chinese Communists, both ideologically and with respect to the issue of a Chinese nuclear bomb. Against this backdrop, Khrushchev engaged the Western powers in a new conflict over Berlin, presenting an ultimatum to finalize a peace treaty with Germany and transform West Berlin into a "Free City," which provoked the second Berlin Crisis. In the years leading up to this point, the state of world affairs had changed: the atomic standoff now pushed aside discussions of the German question.

With its entry into the Warsaw Pact in May 1955, the GDR integrated itself further into the Soviet-dominated bloc. Reacting to the sovereignty of both German states, the failure of the Geneva Summit with regard to the German question, and the opening of diplomatic relations with the Federal Republic, the Soviet Union began to pursue a two-state doctrine for Germany, insisting that the German question could only be solved by the Germans themselves within a system of collective European security. To preempt the potential recognition of the GDR by other countries as a second German state, the West German government formulated the "Hallstein Doctrine," reiterating its claim to be the sole legitimate German state on the international stage. After this point, the Federal Republic considered it an unfriendly act for other states to establish diplomatic relations with the GDR, and it condemned this type of action. After Geneva, the Soviet Union proposed forming a confederation between the two German states and integrating the entity into a nuclear-free Central Europe.

Politically, 1956 was dominated by the CPSU's 20th Party Congress. Khrushchev had discovered that one of Stalin's secret speeches called for terror against his own party cadres, and the new party leader condemned his predecessor's "personality cult." Additionally, he revised Lenin's doctrine that called war inevitable as long as the world contained imperialist states. The basic principle of Soviet foreign policy thus became the propagation of "peaceful coexistence" among states with different social orders. Soviet leadership justified this change in ideological dogma by citing the strength of the Socialist position. The group of states under Soviet power represented the heart of this "peaceful camp" in world politics, which—through alliances with workers' movements in the capitalist states of the West and with national liberation movements in the European colonies of Africa and Asia—would be strong enough to suppress the "imperialist warmongers." The Communists understood the concept of peaceful coexistence as a method of class struggle along the world's "lawful path" to socialism, which began with the Russian October Revolution of 1917. Coexistence did not mean accepting the status quo within the various states, especially not in the capitalist societies; instead it referred exclusively to avoiding war among states of different social orders.[1]

The doctrine was formulated as the atomic standoff began to crystallize between the Soviet Union and the United States. With reciprocal nuclear fear tactics and the existent weapon potential on both sides, the two world powers threatened each other in a very direct way. "After this point, the United States and the Soviet Union's main interest was to settle the East–West conflict in Europe through negotiations over controlled disarmament and a European security system."[2] During Khrushchev's tenure in office, the Soviet Union supported nuclear disarmament using the ideological claim to be the peaceful power in world politics. The issue of disarmament was among "the most important priorities of Soviet foreign policy."[3] In light of the mutual threat, the policy of coexistence did have an effect, for example with the cancellation of atomic bomb testing in 1958.[4] This outcome had become possible because the United States also advocated arms control and disarmament. But above all, the military-political side of Soviet nuclear policy aimed to match U.S. capacities in strategic atomic weapons and their launching systems, and that meant armament.

In October 1957, the Soviet Union launched Sputnik, the first satellite sent into orbit, using an intercontinental missile that also had potential for military applications. NATO decided that the Bundeswehr should be equipped with tactical missiles for atomic warheads. The warheads themselves remained under the control of the American forces but were situated in the Federal Republic.

The Geneva Summit of 1955

The constellation that emerged in Europe after 1945 cemented itself in divided Germany as well. On 5 May 1955, the Paris Treaties between the Federal Republic and the three Western occupation powers went into effect, including the Germany Treaty of 1952. The FRG thereby gained sovereignty and became a member of NATO. Just a few days later, the Soviet Union founded the Warsaw Pact, whose membership included East Germany. The Soviet Union then signed a treaty of friendship with the GDR in September 1955, which finally released the latter from its occupation statute.[5]

On the one hand, the new dimensions of war in the nuclear era pushed the German question to the periphery of international politics. On the other hand, a political constellation had emerged whose opposing interests and positions made reconciliation between the Western powers and the Soviet Union seem impossible. This shift in the international political agenda became clear at the July 1955 summit meeting among the four heads of state in Geneva—the first such meeting since Potsdam ten years earlier. In attendance were U.S. President Dwight D. Eisenhower, British Prime Minister Anthony Eden, Soviet Premier Nikolai A. Bulganin, First Secretary of the CPSU Nikita S. Khrushchev, and French Prime Minister Edgar Faure. For the last time until 1990, the four powers discussed the question of Germany's reunification—but did not come to any kind of agreement.

Through the Geneva Summit, the four powers hoped to end the period of confrontation that began directly after the war and enter a new era in East–West relations, one that would determine West German foreign policy as well. The Soviet Union purposefully relegated the topic of German reunification to the background in order to prioritize issues such as arms control and a European security system. The new era drew its contours in "the normalization of East–West relations based on the status quo of a divided Germany. A telegram from Blankenhorn[6] to Adenauer on 20 July remarked that 'the question of reunification is therefore beginning to lose its relevance quite significantly as the no. 1 international source of tension.'"[7] New key concepts became: détente efforts despite existing differences in Germany and Europe; silent acceptance, at least for now, of German division as the status quo; and attempts to find new forms of arms control in order to curb the danger of nuclear war. At the same time (though not specifically at the Geneva Summit), another feature of this era began to take shape: a certain tendency to project the East–West conflict onto countries in Asia and Africa that were either still under colonial rule or right in midst of decolonization. This process especially applied to France and Great Britain, who would lose their colonial empires over the following decade. The Soviet Union supported decolonization politically, through propaganda, and with the delivery of weapons to the national freedom movements.

As a concession to the Federal Republic, however, its Western Allies still insisted on "tying the demand for reunification to the issue of new security agreements" in Europe. A summary of the conference proceedings for the federal chancellor commented that "the Soviets' intransigence vis-à-vis the German question has even exceeded the expectations of Western experts."[8] The Western powers had already committed themselves to German reunification in Article 7 of the Germany Treaty: "Pending the peace settlement, the Signatory States will cooperate to achieve, by peaceful means, their common aim of a reunified Germany enjoying a liberal-democratic constitution, like that of the Federal Republic, and integrated within the European Community."[9] Although the Federal Republic's partners had granted it the right to demand German reunification based on free elections in all of Germany, this could not be implemented at the Geneva Summit "through peaceful means" against the Soviet Union's will—regardless of which Western powers actually wanted German unity. "Adenauer's intuition had proven correct, that the Geneva summit represented a watershed in international politics."[10]

The Beginning of Diplomatic Relations between the Federal Republic and the Soviet Union, and the "Hallstein Doctrine"

After the ratification of the Paris Treaties and the restoration of state sovereignty, the Federal Republic was able to sign treaties and form alliances. The government's first act of foreign policy was to take up diplomatic relations with the Soviet Union. With this step, the FRG entered a second circle of foreign relations: with countries in Central and Eastern Europe. Thus, the new republic forged connections to the power that was protecting the GDR as its own German state and blocking the Western-led path to German unity.

Successful Western integration was already intertwined with economic prosperity, the Federal Republic's critical strength. West Germany had reached the point at which Chancellor Konrad Adenauer believed it could negotiate with the Soviet Union on the basis of its own power. In a letter to the historian Gerhard Ritter in 1952, Adenauer laid out his conviction that this was the correct approach to dealing with the USSR: "With Soviet Russia, it is only possible to negotiate if you are at least equally strong. For that reason I welcome our integration into the Western world. I am convinced that when the Western world is as strong as Soviet Russia, it will be possible to reach an agreement with Soviet Russia—but not earlier. . . . My policy aims to incorporate Germany into the West in order to escape the danger of neutralization, to strengthen the West, and, when the opportunity to negotiate with Russia arises, to have an equal say—it is in the interest of Germany, in the interest of peace."[11]

When Adenauer decided to establish diplomatic relations with the Soviet Union, the outline of his Germany policy was already set: the FRG's claim to be the sole legitimate German state; reservations regarding the border to Poland; and the demand for free, Germany-wide elections, which the Soviet Union would not accept because of the nature of its own political system. Independent negotiations with the Soviet Union on Germany were out of the question for the Federal Republic, especially as the Western powers had agreed by contract to negotiate a path to German reunification based on the demand for free elections. Adenauer was convinced that the Soviet Union would only give in if the West could shape the negotiations from a position of power.

When Adenauer arrived in Moscow with a West German delegation in September 1955, the outlines of both sides' Germany policies were clear. Throughout complex negotiations by the chancellor and his delegation, the FRG's top priority was to build on the establishment of diplomatic relations and effect the release of German prisoners of war and interned civilians. The successful outcome of Adenauer's Moscow trip ingrained itself into German collective memory: "In the Federal Republic, a wave of emotion swept through the country as the men came home from Russian captivity in October 1955. Of the 98,229 prisoners of war known by name, only 9,626 returned—the remaining 1,156,663 German soldiers fighting in the East disappeared without a trace in the Soviet Union. Of the approximately 30,000 interned civilians recorded officially in West Germany, more than 20,000 were repatriated."[12]

With the establishment of diplomatic relations with the Soviet Union, West Germany undermined its claim to be the sole legitimate German state. The government reasoned that as one of the four Allied powers, the Soviet Union held a special status; without its cooperation Germany could never achieve unification. In international politics this step had mixed implications, but the positive aspects outweighed the negative: "The Federal Republic, which still understood itself as the German core state, was now recognized throughout the world—and also by the Soviet power—as a sovereign state. The establishment of diplomatic relations gave Bonn more weight vis-à-vis the Western powers. And in relation to the Soviet Union, the postwar period now ended as well; the first foundations of normalization were in place."[13]

In 1958, Bonn and Moscow came to an agreement on "reciprocal economic relations that included West Berlin."[14] This economic contract represented a dramatic step in the slow "normalization process" between the Federal Republic and the Soviet Union. Economic relations emerged between the two states that forged the greatest alignment of their interests during the period of divided Germany. The Moscow economic agreement stood as a model for similar arrangements between the FRG and the Soviet satellite states. But by the end of Adenauer's time in office, progress in relations between the two states had reached an impasse. Khrushchev had instated a new Soviet policy of intervention and expansion while cementing Germany's division through his Two-State Doctrine, evidenced in the Berlin Ultimatum of 1958, the 1959 "Proposal for a Dictated Peace" in divided Germany, and the erection of the Berlin Wall.[15] Only after the Cuban Missile Crisis in 1962 did the East and the West begin to develop cooperative approaches to détente on the basis of the status quo.

In 1955, however, the West German government found itself confronted with the consequences of resuming diplomatic relations with the Soviet Union. The FRG expected that the Soviet Union would use international negotiations to try to establish the GDR as a second, equally legitimate German state, thereby negating West Germany's claim to be the sole legitimate representative of the German people. Bonn moved to create obstacles. To this end, the Federal Foreign Office of the FRG formulated a maxim, announced in 1958 as the "Hallstein Doctrine," to combat recognition of the GDR by third-party states (aside from the Soviet Union). The West German government persisted in its claim to be the sole legitimate representative of Germany and viewed the establishment of diplomatic relations with the GDR by third-party states as an unfriendly act that it was willing to punish accordingly. For Wilhelm Grewe, who formulated the Hallstein Doctrine, it was "a political maxim that grew out of very sober and practical considerations." The doctrine was

> a reasonable principle, as long as there seemed to be a real chance of effecting fundamental change to the status quo in the foreseeable future. But at the latest with the advent of the nuclear standoff at the end of the 1950s, this . . . became impossible, and the costs of perpetuating the Hallstein Doctrine were not at all proportional to the targeted goal. This made the Hallstein Doctrine into a symbol of the defensive position in which the Federal Republic found itself at the end of the Adenauer era. The centrality of the doctrine gradually decreased as the Federal Republic began to make its way into international waters.[16]

The maxim thus served as part of the prologue to a new Ostpolitik, with which West Germany recognized the realities of the situation and began to participate in shaping them. "Beginning in 1955, the discussion of the GDR's quest for recognition became an increasingly central problem in West Germany's foreign policy and internal debate."[17] Especially for domestic policy, it presented a fundamental conflict around the relationship between West German politics and the goal of German reunification in an international constellation that the Federal Republic could not influence.

Therefore, domestically, the Hallstein Doctrine was more than simply a pragmatic, West German foreign policy maxim; the FRG saw itself as the core state for all Germans and, with its claim to be the sole legitimate German government, demanded the right to participate in Allied negotiations with the Soviet Union on Germany's reunification. The Federal Republic considered it imperative to isolate the GDR, which it saw as a vassal state of the Soviet Union with no democratic legitimacy. Following the abandonment of the Hallstein Doctrine and the recognition of the GDR by others as a second German state, the major point of contention within the Federal Republic—whether implicit or explicit—revolved around the country's self-image: Did the Bonn republic still see itself as the democratic core, as stated in its Basic Law, and did the restoration of German unity remain an enduring state goal?

Peaceful Coexistence in a Divided Germany: The Two-State Doctrine, Plans for a Confederation, and the Rapacki Plan

Following the Geneva Summit, Khrushchev announced a new Soviet policy toward Germany on 26 July 1955 in East Berlin. It was based on the reality of a divided Germany. In it, he declared that there were two German states of equal legal standing and that West Berlin existed under the control of the Western powers. This doctrine would be the starting point for all future negotiations.

Through the Federal Republic's alignment to the West and its subsequent armament, German unification had become more complicated. Without attacking Adenauer explicitly, Khrushchev emphasized that "some statesmen were in a hurry to ratify the Paris Treaties and claimed that by implementing these treaties, West Germany would be able to address the Soviet Union from a stronger position. I think it is obvious to everyone today that these calculations proved wrong." Khrushchev formulated a proposal in East Berlin that would serve as the basis of Soviet Germany policy in the following years: "In the current situation, the only path to German unification is through the creation of a collective European security system, by reinforcing and developing economic and political contacts between the two German states. We cannot solve the German question at the expense of the German Democratic Republic's interests."[18]

This guaranteed that the SED leaders would remain in power: according to the Soviet Union, the "Socialist achievements of the GDR" would no longer be subject to discussion in negotiations on Germany among the four powers. Thus, even before Berlin's sector border was sealed by a wall, the USSR had already vetoed the Western approach to solving the German question. Moreover, as a political consequence, the Soviet doctrine demanded recognition of the GDR, which the Federal Republic had blocked internationally with the Hallstein Doctrine. In order to release itself from obligations arising from the Potsdam Agreement of 1945, the Soviet Union declared German reunification to be a matter between the two German states that could only be solved through their own negotiations with each other.

The SED and the West German political parties continued to maintain the goal of German reunification, which the majority of Germans supported. But the common goal was pursued under the political and economic banners of two antagonistic, competing systems. The political parties in the FRG demanded free elections in all of Germany, confident that the SED's certain loss would dissolve the Communist state. The state party of the GDR hoped to find another path: "The reunification of Germany could only result from the further consolidation of the GDR and a 'powerful people's movement against the NATO policy of West Germany's ruling circles.'"[19] In the public debate between East and West, each state's vision of itself as the core of a future unified Germany managed to reconcile reunification propaganda with goal-oriented consolidation of the state on both sides. But in fact, the two trumpeted paths to reunification were mutually exclusive.

After the CPSU's 20th Party Congress, the SED received orders in the spring of 1956 to apply the new general policy of peaceful coexistence to the German situation. The SED felt that within Germany, the opposing systems of socialism and capitalism were cemented in place. In view of the Two-State Doctrine and the push to establish German unity by consolidating the Socialist core state of the GDR, Ulbricht interpreted the principle of peaceful coexistence to mean that peace—and not the restoration of national unity—was at the heart of the German question. However, he believed that the clash of opposing systems between the two states would have to be resolved through class struggle in West Germany.

The next motivator for the SED to take initiative in its Germany policy came from the Soviet Union, leading up to the 1957 West German Bundestag elections. Following a suggestion from Moscow, the politburo of the SED passed a plan for a German confederation on 29 December 1956. Paul Verner, director of the Western Division, had authored the proposal. It began by citing the troop strength of both states, "GDR: 80–90,000 men; Federal Republic: 110–120,000," and the "renunciation of nuclear weapons." A pan-German council would make the necessary preparations for reunification, including the "creation of a customs and currency union." The published version of the plan did not include the West German measures that the SED politburo considered necessary preconditions of German unification: "for example, neutralizing Germany, overcoming the 'militarist, revanchist, and fascist forces' and 'disempowering the capital monopoly,' . . . converting key industries into property of the people, and reforming the agricultural and school systems according to the model of the Soviet zone/GDR." Thus, the proposed path to German reunification, which seemed plausible at first, actually aimed to transform the social order of the Federal Republic. The plan also included suggestions to mobilize political forces within the FRG in order to "force the separation of West Germany from NATO and the 'creation of a zone of limited armament in Europe.'"[20]

Less than one year after Moscow announced its idea for a confederation, Polish Foreign Minister Adam Rapacki put forth a new suggestion at the UN General Assembly on 2 October 1957. Rapacki proposed creating a nuclear-weapon-free zone in Central Europe that would include Poland, the GDR, and the Federal Republic. Czechoslovakia was added later. Both suggestions shared a—more or less obvious—vision of a neutralized West Germany. The Soviet draft of a German peace treaty in 1959 also demanded the neutralization of a unified Germany, as had Stalin's Peace Note of 1952.

Among the countries included in Rapacki's proposal for a nuclear-free zone, there was only one state in which nuclear arms were even on the table in 1957: the Federal Republic of Germany. The real security-political goal of the Polish plan was to prevent the Bundeswehr from acquiring nuclear weapons through NATO. Militarily, Western agreement to this nuclear-free zone would have meant "that conventional NATO forces, which were already inferior, would have been stripped of their most effective tactical nuclear weapons on German soil. At the same time, Central Europe would not have gained anything in the way of protection from nuclear weapons, considering its geographic proximity to the Soviet Union and the high speed of jet planes and intermediate-range missiles."[21] The Warsaw Pact welcomed the Polish plan, while the NATO states (including the Federal Republic) rejected it. Adenauer saw it as "'a Russian affair.' Implementing it would 'precipitate NATO's collapse.'"[22]

Sputnik and the End of America's "Massive Retaliation" Strategy

Just days after Rapacki introduced his plan to the UN, a Soviet intercontinental missile launched Sputnik, the world's first satellite, into space. Like others, Adenauer was hit by "Sputnik shock" and worried about the stability of the American nuclear shield protecting the Federal Republic. He asked: "Would the USA actually wipe out the Soviet Union with atomic bombs if the situation came down to that? Adenauer increasingly doubted the [United States'] readiness to practice deterrence after it became clear that American cities could be obliterated by Soviet intercontinental missiles in the case of war."[23]

In the intermediate term, Sputnik's launch elicited a change in American military doctrine.[24] President Eisenhower had wanted to confine military spending to justifiable sums. In the Republican tradition, he rejected the idea of expenses financed on credit. Navigating the territory between "welfare state" and "warfare state," Eisenhower tried to limit "warfare" costs and reduce the power of the military and the arms industry accordingly. His farewell speech on 17 January 1961 included an enduring warning about the lurking power of the "military industrial complex."[25]

In order to minimize military spending, Eisenhower had prioritized a nuclearization of American defense and significantly reduced the scope of conventional army units. The corresponding military strategy was referred to as "massive retaliation." It relied on the threat that any attack on the United States or its allies would be answered with a massive strategic nuclear strike, decimating the Soviet Union to Stone Age conditions over a period of two weeks. As long as the Soviet Union posed no real existential threat to the continental United States, which it did not until the mid 1950s, this strategy remained plausible. The "Sputnik shock" of October 1957 derived from the realization by U.S. military planners that the Soviet Union would, in fact, be able to attack the continental territory of the United States with ballistic missiles in the near future. This cast doubt, at least for a time, on the credibility of "massive retaliation." In NATO, various countries had already asked the United States in the fall of 1956 to outfit its European allies with launching systems for tactical nuclear weapons (the warheads themselves would remain under American control). Great Britain tested its own hydrogen bomb in 1957, and France began to develop nuclear weapons as well. The West German government faced the reality that the United States and Britain were arming their troops in the Federal Republic with tactical nuclear weapons, but the Bundeswehr would not have these weapons at its disposal in the case of an emergency. "Had the Federal Republic refused to accept this development, the conventionally armed Bundeswehr would have been the first and largely defenseless victim of attacks from either side if the situation had escalated into conflict," according to Hans-Peter Schwarz. Schwarz adds a further security concern to explain the Bundeswehr's request for launching systems: Adenauer's government strove to gain equal footing as a European power next to France and Great Britain. Because of West Germany's geographic location, it (along with the GDR) would become the battlefield in the case of war. Although the West German government did not aspire to the "nuclear option," this option should, "in principle, remain open."[26]

Through an extensive inquiry by the SPD in the Bundestag, these plans became public and turned into a major issue during the Bundestag elections of 1957. The chancellor fueled the debate by introducing an inappropriate comparison: he asserted that the Federal Republic did not possess strategic nuclear weapons, and "the tactical weapons are nothing more than a further development in artillery. Obviously we cannot afford to refuse our troops access to the newest developments in normal weaponry."[27] In this regard, he erred in both domestic and foreign affairs.

Nuclear Missiles for the Bundeswehr?

Konrad Adenauer won the Bundestag elections of 1957 and gained an absolute majority in parliament for the CDU/CSU. In March 1958, the Bundestag implemented the North Atlantic Council's December 1957 recommendation to arm the Bundeswehr with missiles for nuclear warheads.[28] Indeed, the Bundestag voted to arm the Bundeswehr with delivery weapons for nuclear warheads but tied the decision to a general call for disarmament.

The nuclear weapons themselves remained under the control of and at the disposal of the United States. During the debate in the Bundestag, Federal Defense Minister Franz Josef Strauß reminded the members of parliament that West Germany had declined to possess or produce weapons of mass destruction, and now the country was being threatened by the Soviet Union. "An isolated security policy by the Federal Republic," he stated, "is no longer possible today. Only together with our alliance partners can we take effective measures to prevent the outbreak of war and thereby protect all of Germany."[29] Strauß ended his speech with the following assertion: "Until we succeed in disarmament efforts, the Federal Government cannot, in the interest of West German security, refuse to support the United States' armed forces in our common defense—we cannot prohibit the provision of these weapons, which, in this respect, are of at least the same caliber as those in the Red Army's possession."[30] The opposition SPD contested this policy adamantly. The SPD demanded a popular vote on whether to arm the Bundeswehr with intermediate-range nuclear missiles and, together with the Confederation of German Trade Unions (Deutsche Gewerkschaftsbund), initiated a protest movement with the motto, "Combat nuclear death" (*Kampf dem Atomtod*). In a sense, this marked the beginning of the extra-parliamentary peace movement in the Federal Republic.

With the Bundestag's decision to arm the Bundeswehr with nuclear missiles, Ulbricht considered West Germany to be on a path toward its own "isolation." In his view, this step went against the spirit of the times. All around the world, people advocated ending nuclear tests and prohibiting atomic weapons, but the Bonn government stood "apart and strengthen[ed] its attack position with nuclear weapons."[31] Even before the Bundestag discussed whether to implement the rec-ommendations of the North Atlantic Council, Ulbricht had already reported to Khrushchev on the West German debate over nuclear missiles. The politburo of the SED interpreted the debate as a "change of opinion among the masses in favor of a nuclear-free zone in Europe."[32] During the Bundestag elections, the SED and the prohibited KPD had rallied around the election of the SPD. Now, in support of the KPD's stronger presence in North-Rhine Westphalia, they revised their course as part of the SED's policy toward West Germany. One of the KPD's first decisions in January 1958 was to call for the Social Democrats and the unions to build a "unity of action against armament for nuclear war."[33]

In the Federal Republic, a broad protest movement began to form against Ade-nauer's security policy, and public opinion did, in fact, begin to change. Ulbricht was optimistic that the unions and the frequently evoked "German people" would have the strength to "suppress the atomic warriors in Bonn."[34] The prohibited KPD called on people to "combat nuclear death" and propagated the triad of the Soviet peace cam-paign: "Combat nuclear death! [Stand] against the nuclear armament of the Federal Republic and support a nuclear-free zone in Europe—this is the unifying solution of the powerful people's movement."[35] The protest movement in the Federal Republic was one factor in Ulbricht's calculations that he believed the KPD could influence.

The Founding of the European Economic Community

Wilhelm Grewe, one of the most important figures shaping West German foreign policy at the beginning of the 1950s, summarized the FRG's approach as follows: "Like any other state, it had to provide security and welfare to its population; but in contrast to the others, it was also instructed by its own constitution (Preamble to the Basic Law) to tackle the challenges that emerged from the division of the coun-try and the push by all European nations (including its own) for closer economic, political, and military ties."[36] The first incremental steps toward the economic inte-gration of Western Europe had helped bring prosperity to the six participating states: West Germany, Belgium, the Netherlands, Luxemburg, France, and Italy. In 1956, these states agreed to found a European Economic Community (EEC). Two European treaties were signed in Rome in March 1957: the first concerned the EEC and tasked its member states with establishing a single Western European market; the second created the European Atomic Energy Community (Euratom). This lat-ter organization declared the peaceful use of nuclear energy to be a cooperative project that would benefit the whole community. Great Britain bowed out of the plans by its continental counterparts. France, meanwhile, underwent a dramatic change of course in its European policy after the National Assembly rejected the idea of a European Defense Community (EDC) in 1954. The transformation made the EEC possible: "After its negative decision on the EDC, France suffered several heavy blows. Adding to the French defeat in Indochina and the fiasco of the Suez adventure, uprisings began to occur in Algeria. France faced the still unsolved question of how it would find a reasonable succession to its outdated international and colonial policies. Parallel to the external political uncertainty, inner weakness emerged, surfacing in the form of constant government turnover. Thus, there was a vivid necessity in France to seek support among its European neighbors."[37] Two paths emerged toward Western European integration: some envisaged a supranational Europe, while other pictured an integration that would not interfere with the national sovereignty of each country—in other words, a federal European republic versus a union of sovereign states. Ultimately the latter version triumphed, "headed by a permanent council that would reinforce the common interests of its members and build a framework to coordinate foreign and domestic policy."[38] The politically viable solution of creating a union of states allowed for the future accession of additional states, particularly Great Britain.

Negotiations over the founding of the EEC—which would benefit the GDR through interzonal and later inter-German trade—began after the Geneva Summit. According to Waldemar Besson, by reinforcing the status quo, the EEC eliminated any "international political inhibitions" that Adenauer might have had regarding the strengthening of "Western European regionalism." In early 1956, he gave the green light for German preparations:

> In the guidelines for all federal ministers, he stated that the ongoing negotiations over the EEC should have top priority, stressing that it was also important to emphasize the political character of the new community. Especially telling was Adenauer's reference, once again, to the importance of Western strength against the USSR as a motif of renewed Western reinforcement: "Serious concessions by the Soviet Union cannot be expected as long as Europe's disunity inspires hope that one state or another will cross over to [the USSR], thereby fracturing the cohesion and leading to the gradual incorporation of Europe into the [Soviet] satellite system." Above all, Adenauer saw the EEC as a new manifestation of the European plans from the early 1950s. But now, much more so than before, he had to emphasize that a unified Europe would also contribute to [German] reunification.[39]

The EEC increased the Federal Republic's importance as a state. Whereas domestically, the FRG was nothing more than a supplicant to the United States, in European politics it had already become "an equal among equals, even endowed with a leading role." Besson continues: "Therefore, in addition to Bonn's focus on America, which received special emphasis from 1955 to 1959, it was only natural to develop the impulse toward Western European regionalism. Indeed, it was the high degree of dependence on America that now motivated [West Germany] to turn once more to its European partners. Together it would be easier to confine American pressure to reasonable limits."[40] German–French relations were put to the test—also vis-à-vis London and Washington—during the second Berlin Crisis, after the erection of the Berlin Wall. European integration became and remained a central pillar of West German foreign policy.

The Rome treaties created several new institutions, the most important of which was the EEC Commission in Brussels. This structure represented an economic steering system with independent sovereign powers, superseding national economic policy and embodying Western European supranationality.[41] One precondition for the founding of the EEC was France and Germany's agreement on plans for European integration. Despite this common ground, a discrepancy remained between the interests of the two states.

France was particularly interested in Euratom, deriving from the country's European policy from 1950 onward that German potential should permanently remain under international control. Moreover, plans to create a common market had little resonance within the French protectionist tradition. For the Federal Republic, building a common market was the much more important project: politically because it offered much broader perspectives for the German interest in integration; economically because, as early as the 1950s, it was clear that the West German economy relied heavily on exports.[42]

The customs union applied to all exchanges of goods and to the free movement of goods within the community; this was tied to the freedom of movement for people, services, and capital. Along with other European states that were not part of the EEC (these included Denmark, Norway, Austria, Portugal, Sweden, and Switzerland), Great Britain founded the European Free Trade Association (EFTA), which concentrated on removing obstacles to customs and trade among the member states but refrained from building any supranational structures. With the expansion of the EEC, including the accession of Great Britain (among others), EFTA grew less and less important. The community that evolved from the EEC would go on to become the European Union in 1991. Even then, Adenauer's goal of creating a political union of European states still did not materialize. But the European integration process that began in Western Europe now encompasses the states of Central Europe as well; it continues to move forward and seems irreversible.

Notes

1. Nikita S. Chruschtschow, *Bericht des Zentralkomitees der KPdSU, XX. Parteitag der KPdSU* (n.c., n.d.), 29–37.

2. Morsey, *Deutschlandpolitik*, 1844.

3. Natalja Egorova, "Die Entwicklung sowjetischer Vorschläge zur Abrüstungsfrage und die Einstellung von Atomwaffentests im Vorfeld des Wiener Gipfels und deren Erörterung zwischen Nikita S. Chruščev und John F. Kennedy," in *Der Wiener Gipfel 1961: Kennedy—Chruschtschow*, ed. Stefan Karner et al. (Innsbruck, 2011), 335.

4. "On 31 March 1958, the USSR called upon the U.S. Congress and the parliaments of Europe to cancel their nuclear tests (the USSR cited the danger that the FRG could also arm itself with atomic weapons) and announced its one-sided decision to cancel all of its own atomic and hydrogen bomb testing." On 7 November, American President Eisenhower also announced his decision to cancel future nuclear tests. See Egorova, "Entwicklung," 337.

5. See Rauschning, *Rechtsstellung*, 219–23.

6. Herbert Blankenhorn, a West German diplomat, was director of the Federal Foreign Office's political division from 1951 to 1955.

7. Hans-Peter Schwarz, *Adenauer: Der Staatsmann 1952–1967* (Stuttgart, 1991), 204.

8. Ibid., 204–5.

9. "Convention on Relations Between the Three Powers and the Federal Republic of Germany, May 26, 1952," in U.S. Dept. of State, *Documents on Germany*, 428.

10. Schwarz, *Adenauer: Der Staatsmann*, 207.

11. Quoted in Morsey, *Deutschlandpolitik*, 1839.

12. Schwarz, *Ära Adenauer*, 278.

13. Ibid., 280.

14. Boris Meissner, "Die Bundesrepublik Deutschland und die Sowjetunion: Entwicklung, Stand und Perspektive ihrer Beziehungen," in *Die Sowjetunion und Deutschland von Jalta bis zur Wiedervereinigung* (Cologne, 1995), 134.

15. Ibid.

16. Waldemar Besson, *Die Außenpolitik der Bundesrepublik: Erfahrungen und Maßstäbe* (Munich, 1970), 198–99.

17. Schwarz, *Ära Adenauer*, 280.

18. Quoted in Steininger, *Deutsche Geschichte*, vol. 3, 16–17.

19. Kurt Hager, Secretary of the SED Central Committee, 5–6 May 1958, quoted in Hermann Weber and Fred Oldenburg, *25 Jahre SED: Chronik einer Partei* (Cologne, 1971), 119.

20. "Über die Wiedervereinigung Deutschlands zu einem friedliebenden, demokratischen Staat," quoted in Michael Lemke, *Einheit oder Sozialismus? Die Deutschlandpolitik der SED 1949–1961* (Cologne, 2001), 401–2.

21. Bruno Thoß, *NATO-Strategie und nationale Verteidigungsplanungen: Planung und Aufbau der Bundeswehr unter den Bedingungen einer massiven atomaren Vergeltungsstrategie* (Munich, 2006), 489.

22. Schwarz, *Adenauer: Der Staatsmann*, 382.

23. Ibid., 388.

24. See Winfried Heinemann and Manfred Wilke, "Kein Krieg um Berlin: Sicherheitspolitische Aspekte des Mauerbaus," in *Die Berliner Mauer: Vom Sperrwall zum Denkmal*, ed. Deutsches Nationalkomitee für Denkmalschutz (Bonn, 2009), 35–52.

25. Dwight D. Eisenhower, "Farewell Radio and Television Address to the American People," 17 January 1961, online at http://www.presidency.ucsb.edu/ws/index.php?pid=12086&st=&st1=. On Eisenhower's security policy, see chapters 5 and 6 of John Lewis Gaddis, *Strategies of Containment: A Critical Appraisal of American National Security Policy during the Cold War*, rev. ed. (1982; repr. New York, 2005).

26. Schwarz, *Ära Adenauer*, 359.

27. Quoted in ibid.

28. See Militärgeschichtliches Forschungsamt, ed., *Verteidigung im Bündnis: Planung, Aufbau und Bewährung der Bundeswehr 1950–1972* (Munich, 1975), 85.

29. Franz Josef Strauß, *Die Erinnerungen* (Berlin (West), 1989), 325.

30. Ibid., 326.

31. Walter Ulbricht, "Die Brandstifter im deutschen Haus bändigen: Interview mit dem Direktor des Allgemeinen Deutschen Nachrichtendienstes," 26 March 1958, in Walter Ulbricht, *Zur Geschichte der deutschen Arbeiterbewegung: Aus Reden und Aufsätzen*, vol. 7, *1957–1959* (Berlin (East), 1964), 127.

32. Walter Ulbricht to Nikita S. Khrushchev, Berlin, 9 January 1958, SAPMO-BArch, DY 30/3538.

33. "Beschluss der 8. Tagung des ZK der KPD: Aktionseinheit gegen Atomkriegsrüstung, Januar 1958," in *Die KPD lebt und kämpft: Dokumente der KPD 1956–1962* (Berlin (East), 1963), 166–72.

34. Ibid., 133.

35. "Aufruf des ZK der KPD: Vorwärts zum 1. Mai, dem Kampftag gegen den Atomtod," April 1958, in *Die KPD lebt*, 174.

36. Wilhelm G. Grewe, *Die Deutsche Frage in der Ost-West-Spannung: Zeitgeschichtliche Kontroversen der achtziger Jahre* (Herford, 1986), 115.

37. Besson, *Außenpolitik*, 185–86.

38. Ibid., 186.

39. Ibid., 187–88.

40. Ibid., 185.

41. See Gehler, *Europa*, 169–72.

42. Kielmansegg, *Katastrophe*, 182.

Part II

THE FIGHT FOR BERLIN

Chapter 6

THE FIRST BERLIN CRISIS, 1948–49

Berlin in general, but especially West Berlin, had special importance during the period of divided Germany. The city's enduring four-power status prevented the situation of two Germanys from settling into permanent normality. Its national significance became especially visible on 9 November 1989, when East Berliners broke through the wall that had divided the city and the path to German reunification began.

In 1945, when the four Allied powers took over joint administration of Greater Berlin, comprised of four sectors, no one thought about dividing the city. It had been excluded from the drawing of zones. From Berlin, the headquarters of the Allied Control Council, the Allies planned to coordinate their control over the rest of occupied Germany. None of the four powers gave up its right to this shared status in Berlin until 1990, even though the Soviet Union left the Control Council and the Allied Kommandatura—the mechanisms of joint rule—in 1948. Until 1990, the city's fate remained in the hands of both the Western powers and the Soviet Union. Their common right to retain Berlin's status forced the four powers to negotiate and compromise when conflicts over the city arose. In addition, the two German states had to accept the reserved rights of the Allies in Berlin. The Western powers had refused to allow the West German Basic Law to include Berlin as federal state, and federal laws only applied to West Berlin when the Abgeordnetenhaus (the city's parliament) explicitly adopted them.

Through the Federal Republic's comprehensive economic support to West Berlin, as well as through the introduction of the Deutsche Mark there, special ties emerged between West Berlin and the Federal Republic, enabling residents of West Berlin to see themselves politically and socially as part of the Federal Republic. West Berliners' agreement to let the protective Western powers and their troops remain in Berlin resulted from their experience of two dramatic Berlin Crises, during which the Soviet Union and the SED tried to eliminate the "irritation" of West Berlin from their territory.

Berlin's Historical Significance for the Division of Germany

During the Berlin Crisis of 1948–49, negotiations focused primarily on shaping the United States' and the Soviet Union's spheres of influence in Germany. After leaving the Allied Control Council in 1948, the Soviet Union protested the rights of the Western powers to remain in Berlin. By blockading the routes of access leading to the city's Western sectors, the Soviet Union attempted to force the Western powers to leave Berlin and relinquish the entire city to the Soviet occupation zone. But the Americans and British thwarted these plans with an airlift, and the provision of supplies by air to the Western sectors of Berlin was matched by the powerful determination of West Berliners. Ernst Reuter, the major of West Berlin, personified the will of democracy to survive in the city.

Even if none of the four Allied powers had any intention of building a wall through Berlin in 1945, the foundations of this development already emerged early in the postwar period. The political division of the city in 1948 embodied the conflict not only between the Soviet Union and the Western powers, but also between the Communist leaders of the Soviet zone and the democratic politicians in Berlin. The crisis ended when the Soviet Union conceded to the Western Allies and removed its blockade in 1949. Over the course of this first crisis, the wall through Berlin was already beginning to take shape.

The Berlin Blockade and the American airlift of 1948–49 had a decisive impact on the history of the Federal Republic and West Berlin. The city's governing mayor, Ernst Reuter, was among the fathers of the Basic Law. The Federal Republic subsidized West Berlin, and the protection of the city—both politically and in terms of security—formed a cornerstone in the alliance between the Federal Republic and the United States. Through the existence of West Berlin, the FRG could actively influence public opinion among the population of the GDR, and the divided city with its four-power status demonstrated for more than forty years the abnormality of German division in a Europe consisting of nation-states. In addition to familial ties and the German language, Berlin served as a further link between Germans in the West and Germans in the East. Berlin was the erratic obstacle that prevented the SED and the Soviet Union from hermetically sealing off the GDR from the FRG. Berlin forced the question of German unity to remain open.

A military confrontation between the two world powers never materialized, and the solution to the Berlin Crisis grew out of a mutual recognition that the two blocs' spheres of influence in Germany had become the status quo. The Paris conference of the four powers' foreign ministers in 1949 produced rules regulating interzonal trade between what were now the two currency areas. Even after the end of the Allied Control Council, the four victorious powers still insisted upon their original right to Germany as a whole and with it their right to maintain joint status in Berlin.

The solution to the first Berlin Crisis in 1949 already demonstrated the ways in which joint control without a control council could function on the basis of a shared legal position and respect for the status quo. The Soviet Union's attempt to shift Germany's borders to its own advantage, based on agreements in Yalta, had clearly failed, and this failure laid the foundation for the second Berlin Crisis of 1958–62. Once again, Soviet leadership and the SED would try to precipitate the departure of the Western powers from West Berlin. In both crises, this move led to direct confrontations between the Soviet Union and the United States.

Pivotal Conflicts over Berlin's Political Order after the End of the War

Berlin was conquered by the Red Army. Between May and July 1945, the Soviet occupation power established district administrations and a Magistrat, Berlin's executive cabinet.[1] Conflict among the occupation powers over the German political structures in Berlin began with the Soviet Army's personnel policy directly after its victory. In selecting personnel for the new city administration, the Soviet military commander drew on a task force of German Communists, led by Walter Ulbricht and situated under the main political administration of the occupation forces. Wolfgang Leonhard, the task force's youngest member, gave a detailed description of its role in reorganizing Berlin's district administrations and appointing the first Magistrat. In both the Magistrat and the twenty district offices (Bezirksämter), Communists took over the positions of deputy mayor and head of personnel, as well as responsibilities for education and the police.[2] They also controlled Berlin's broadcasting operations and the *Berliner Zeitung*, Germany's first daily newspaper, under Editor-in-Chief Rudolf Herrnstadt. The rush to build a new city administration certainly reflected the needs of the destroyed metropolis, but it also had a distinctive political background, as highlighted in one of Ulbricht's directives to his task force: "We must concentrate exclusively on the districts in the northwest, southwest, and west of Berlin. In about one month we can count on the arrival of the Western allies. By then, the district administrations in their sectors should already be functioning smoothly." He added: "We can worry about the eastern sectors later, we will have enough time for that."[3] The Ulbricht Group's approach followed the Polish model. It aimed to influence the political leaning of Berlin's new democratic administration even before the work of the Allied Kommandatura began.

The Western powers arrived in Berlin on 4 July 1945. With Commandant Order No. 1 of 11 July 1945, they accepted all of the orders and regulations instated by the Soviet occupation power up until that point. However, this victory of Soviet Germany policy was short-lived. Each of the four occupying powers established a military government within its respective sector, and a tendency soon emerged to seal off each territory like the larger occupation zones. In Berlin, like in the rest of Germany, conflicts among the occupying powers led to a separation into two camps, with the Western Allies on one side and the Soviet Union on the other. The conflicts that arose in the Kommandatura leading up to the Berlin elections (which would shape the city's future political order) seemed to many contemporaries to be "at first pragmatic, temporary, and revocable, but in reality, they were already shaping the structural separation of the sectors that would later prove irreversible"[4] and would lead to the division of the city. Disintegration began with the fracture in Berlin's party system after the KPD and SPD fused together in the Soviet zone to create the SED in April 1946.

Until 1948, the Soviet Union retained the political upper hand in Berlin. But thanks to the presence of the Western powers in the city, the SMAD's move to change the party system within its occupation zone in the winter of 1945–46 led to an open conflict among German politicians over the shape of democracy in Germany. This clash had deep consequences for the unity of Berlin. The Western powers had to determine whether their democratization policy within the Western zones should apply to their sectors of Berlin as well, or whether the harmony of the war alliance should take top priority in their decisions concerning the people of Berlin. Their reaction had a major impact on the future of democracy in Berlin.

The state parliament (Landtag) and municipal elections within the Soviet zone in October 1946 did little to affirm the SED's claim to be the "state party." Even with a massive effort on the part of the occupation power to sway the elections and suppress the bourgeois parties, the SED was unable to gain an absolute majority of votes, despite emerging as the strongest party. Until 1990, these were the last semi-free elections in the Soviet zone/GDR. In Berlin, the city-wide elections of 1946 spelled out a definitive defeat for the SED. With just 19.8 percent, the SED emerged behind the CDU (with 22.2 percent); the overwhelming winner was the SPD with 48.7 percent of the vote.[5] Many SED functionaries acknowledged that the defeat had to do with their party's reputation as the "party of the Russians."[6]

The Social Democrats nominated Ernst Reuter to the new Magistrat after his return from exile in Turkey. He was allowed to assume his position provisionally, but the Soviet military administration demanded a review of his biography by the Allied Kommandatura, which led to his dismissal in early 1947. The Soviet and German Communists still remembered Reuter as the first general secretary of the KPD who had been barred from the party in 1922.[7] Later the same year, the SPD nominated Reuter to the position of Lord Mayor (Oberbürgermeister) of Berlin; the City Council (Stadtverordnetenversammlung) then elected him, but the Soviet occupation power vetoed his entry into office. Only with the city's division in 1948 could Reuter could take up his position as Governing Mayor (Regierender Bürgermeister) of West Berlin. He entered the political stage as a politician who would represent the population of the Western sectors and lead their resistance to the Soviet blockade. Under his leadership, the Western sectors began to see themselves as West Berlin.

Berlin as a Soviet Lever to Shift the Zones of Influence in Germany

The first Berlin Crisis began with plans in the Soviet foreign ministry leading up to the London conference of foreign ministers in December 1947. For Vladimir S. Semyonov, political advisor to the head of the SMAD, and Andrei A. Smirnov, head of the Third European Department in the Soviet foreign ministry, the conference's failure was clear from the outset: "The position of the Anglo-American bloc with regard to reparations, the Ruhr Valley, Bizonal unification, and Germany's economic unity eliminates the possibility of reaching an agreement from the very beginning."[8] Considering the international political developments at the time, this prognosis was a sober statement. Fedor T. Gusev, deputy foreign minister of the USSR, drew logical consequences for Soviet policy on Berlin. He formulated a new interpretation of Greater Berlin's four-power status, which, he argued, was based on the existence of the Control Council and pan-German institutions. If these two prerequisites were gone, the Western powers' claim on their right to remain in Berlin would dissipate.

This interpretation of inter-Allied agreements on Berlin during the war also became the Soviets' central argument during the second Berlin Crisis, in their demand that the Western powers leave the city. In 1947, Gusev claimed that the West was treading a path to German division; therefore, it was

> not necessary to maintain the special zone in cooperation with the English, Americans, and French. The presence of the English and Americans in the zone of Greater Berlin enables them not only to gather information about the situation in the Soviet zone but also to exercise a certain influence over the population of the Soviet zone through their sectors in Berlin. The Soviet Military Administration does not enjoy the same possibilities vis-à-vis the Western zones. . . . If the English and Americans refuse to make concessions to the Soviet Union's entirely legitimate demands for reparations, joint control of the Ruhr Valley, etc. at the upcoming conference of the Council of Foreign Ministers, the Soviet Union may be forced to consider eliminating the zone of Greater Berlin and integrating the entire territory of Berlin into the Soviet zone.[9]

Since the actual outcome of the conference was still unknown, Gusev added a sentence specifying the exact point at which the recommendation would become a necessity if the Soviet Union was to maintain its interests in Germany: "This is, of course, an extreme measure that should only be taken when all hope is lost for reaching an agreement."[10] Only then should the Soviet Union revise the borders of its sphere of influence in Germany and integrate Greater Berlin into its occupation zone. However, Gusev's plan relied on the assumption that the Western Allies would, in fact, depart from Berlin. The London conference of foreign ministers failed as expected and precipitated the end of the Allied Control Council, as well as preparations to found the two German states.

Blockading the transportation routes to Berlin served as leverage for Moscow to integrate Greater Berlin into its own occupation zone. In all of the negotiations over Germany and Berlin, "the question of free access to the sectors of Berlin that the United States and Great Britain—and later France—would occupy had never come up in discussion. Trusting Soviet leadership, the Western powers had assumed that the establishment of sectors in Berlin would automatically entail a right to free access, as well as the provision of food, energy, water, and other necessities."[11]

The head of the SMAD, Marshal Sokolovsky, justified the Soviet Union's departure from the Allied Control Council on 20 March 1948 by arguing that the Western powers had violated the Potsdam agreements (the Soviet Union maintained this assertion during the second Berlin Crisis as well). On 16 June 1948, the Soviet Union left the Allied Kommandatura in Berlin. After that, Sokolovsky began to implement the measures determined at the Kremlin on 15 March:

> On 25 and 27 March, respectively, Sokolovsky issued the top secret Orders No. 002 and 003, which restricted the transportation of persons and goods to a minimum for the Western occupation powers in Berlin, deployed troops at almost division strength to the border of the Western zones, and concentrated four motorized guard battalions all around the city's periphery. 20,000 soldiers and 12,000 men in units from the Ministry of the Interior were transferred from the USSR to the Soviet zone. These measures further reinforced the already significant military advantage over the Western powers. In an armed conflict, [the Western powers] would have had to evacuate their positions not only in Berlin but also throughout the rest of Germany.[12]

First, the Soviets severely limited the Western powers' train connections on the Berlin–Hannover line. Formally this allowed the Soviet Union to avoid breaking any of the Allied agreements, since none of the agreements mentioned ground transportation. Only with regard to air transportation had the Allies agreed to establish a shared air corridor and a jointly run air safety control in Berlin. This functioned all the way through to 1990, and during the Berlin Airlift of 1948, the Soviet air safety control officers continued performing their professional duties.

In the spring of 1948, the SED pushed to found its own state, but Stalin made the final decision. Pieck and Grotewohl flew to Moscow on 26 March. In his report on the situation in Germany, Pieck emphasized the indecision of German developments. The leaders of the SED wanted to know what the Soviet Union suggested. "The pol[itical] mood of the masses [is] influenced by growing opposition among the Allies in the fight for peace, whether democr[atic] or imp[erialistic] peace, and whether unity o[r] the division of Germany, whether democr[atic] development or colonization through the Marshall Plan. To the masses, the opposites [are] not so clear—but their opinions are very strong—whether for or against the Western powers or the Soviet Union. The battle has taken shape especially in Berlin."[13] In his report, Pieck toed the Soviet line when discussing the two camps. He expressed worry over the development in Berlin, which also concerned Stalin: "In October of that year, Pieck noted, elections would take place in Berlin. Pieck did not believe the elections would turn out better for the SED than they had in 1946. [The SED] would be happy to be rid of the Allies in Berlin. Stalin remarked: Okay, let's give it a try through combined efforts, maybe we can drive them away."[14]

The Russian historian Vladimir K. Volkov writes that this topic was not explored in more depth, and indeed, no further elaboration exists. But Stalin had already decided to use Berlin as leverage against the Western powers, forcing them to "correct" their Germany policy. After the disintegration of the Control

Council, the Western powers transferred parts of their personnel to their occupation zones. Semyonov warned Soviet leadership against reading this move the wrong way: "This does not imply that it will be easy to smoke the Western powers out of Berlin. On the contrary: they will cling stubbornly to Berlin and are clearly using the retreat of their extremely bloated local apparatus to give themselves leeway to withstand our pressure."[15]

A corresponding plan to terminate Soviet cooperation in the Berlin Kommandatura, which would end four-power administration in Berlin and force the Western powers to leave the city, has not yet been declassified in Russia. However, Semyonov described this planned action in a telegram of 11 June 1948 as aiming to "'further undermine' the reputation of the Western powers in Germany and Europe."[16] In 1989, former Secretary of State Henry Kissinger asked his former Soviet counterpart, Andrei A. Gromyko, "why Stalin risked the Berlin Blockade directly after such a horrific world war and despite the American nuclear monopoly."[17] Gromyko replied that Stalin had been sure the United States would not deploy nuclear weapons on account of Berlin, and if they had sent military convoys to the city by Autobahn, the Red Army would have stopped them. Stalin explicitly reserved the right to make decisions regarding war and peace for himself. "This meant that at the moment of possible military inferiority, Stalin relied on the means of diplomacy among the great powers and [counted on] the other side's interest in avoiding conflict escalation with all of its consequences."[18] This statement describes the Soviet leader's method of crisis management after the West refused to be intimidated.

Conflict over Berlin's Currency Reform, the Blockade, and the Airlift

As a catalyst for the Berlin Blockade, the Soviet Union chose to use the one-sided currency reform in the Western occupation zones on 20 June 1948:

> Although the Soviets had expected the change in currency for quite some time, they were completely surprised when the Western powers announced on 18 June that it was about to happen. [The Soviet side] had assumed that this step would not occur until August. Thus, measures against West Berlin had not yet attained their full state of constriction; moreover, the planned conference of foreign ministers from the Eastern European states, which was supposed to take place before any currency reform went through, had not yet occurred. The Soviet Military Administration in Germany (SMAD) hastily ordered a halt to all transportation to West Berlin by Autobahn, street, train lines, and shipping routes, and introduced a separate currency in its own zone on 23 June, simultaneous to the West. To this end, the SMAD declared its currency to have exclusive validity in the entire city of Berlin and prohibited the possession of Western money. The following day, the Western powers circulated the Westmark within their sectors. However, they wondered whether this connection to the distant West German currency area was practical and kept open

the possibility of retracting the move by printing a "B" on each of the bills. The Kremlin interpreted this as a refusal to integrate West Berlin into the Western zones. However, this soon proved to be wrong.[19]

By introducing the Ostmark as the only currency for all of Berlin, the Soviet Union tried to substantiate its claim that Berlin belonged economically to the Soviet occupation zone. The SMAD's Order No. 111 stated that "in the area of Greater Berlin, which is located within the Soviet occupation zone and is economically a part of the Soviet occupation zone, the new currency of the Eastern zone is the single legal means of payment."[20] After the departure of the Soviet representative, the Allied Kommandatura no longer functioned as the supreme authority throughout all of Berlin. From that point onward, the SMAD's decrees only carried weight in the Soviet sector, and the three Western city commandants annulled them retroactively for their own sectors.

American Military Governor Clay recognized the seriousness of the situation and of Soviet intentions. Early 1948 had already brought street closures and controls of Western Allied military transports to and from Berlin. The conclusion Clay drew and conveyed to Washington was unambiguous: If we intend to stand up to communism in Europe, then we have to stay in Berlin.[21] At the beginning of the blockade, Robert Murphy, U.S. political advisor on German affairs, took the same position as Clay: "The presence of the Western powers in Berlin had become 'a symbol of resistance to eastern expansionism. It is unquestionably an index of our prestige in central and eastern Europe.' If the Americans and British were to withdraw now, the position of the United States in all of Europe would begin to slip, 'like a cat on a sloping tin roof.'"[22] In other words: If we leave West Berlin, the Soviet Union's next goal will be West Germany. Clay's unflinching position found emphatic support in Ernst Reuter, who had his own fears about the situation. David Barclay writes in Reuter's biography that after early June 1948, Reuter "suspected that the London recommendations by the Allies to create a West German state could mean giving up Berlin."[23] This had to be stopped.

In February 1948, Communists in Czechoslovakia launched a coup that overthrew the country's democratic system and allowed them to assume power. Reuter publicly drew consequences from this at a rally by Berlin's Social Democrats. They demonstrated on 24 June against the Soviet blockade and for the introduction of the Deutsche Mark in the Western sectors. Turning to Prague, Reuter wondered who the next victim of Soviet expansionist policy would be: Finland or Berlin? On behalf of the people of Berlin, he declared that the city had already given a clear answer: "Berlin will not be next! We will use all means at our disposal to fight against the claim to power that will turn us into slaves, that will turn us into Helots of one party. We have already lived under this type of slavery in Adolf Hitler's Reich. We have had enough of it. We refuse to go back!"[24] In this way, he elevated the conflict over Berlin to the context of a larger, more fundamental decision facing the Germans: Which political order would they live in? For the sake of the future, he asked the Western powers to accept the offer of the German Democrats to fight for their own freedom and that of others.

The Western powers were not prepared for a blockade of the transit routes to Berlin, and the Germans possessed neither airplanes nor a sovereign government. Nevertheless, Reuter's voice counted. He told the Western Allies on 25 June that this Berlin Crisis demanded a fundamental decision by the West about the future of Europe: "The Magistrat and the City Council, he said, had done their part to create an anti-Communist atmosphere, and it had worked. But the Allies had to do more. Time was short. Food supplies would last for four more weeks, but the Magistrat and the people of Berlin needed assurance before this point that [the Americans] would and could do something to improve the situation. An early gesture of support—such as flying in provisions for the Berlin population—would be better than nothing, even if it did little to change the supply situation in the long term."[25] To the question of whether the Western sectors could be adequately supplied by air, Reuter's skepticism was understandable. This type of undertaking had never occurred anywhere in the world. In deciding to blockade the city, Soviet leadership had not considered the possibility either. In August 1948, Stalin allegedly expressed his doubt "that the Americans could supply a city as large as Berlin by air for very long."[26]

However, American President Truman had made precisely this decision in July. "In doing so, he had to take aspects of domestic policy, the military, international law, and international politics into consideration. Concerning domestic politics, in the summer of 1948 the United States stood before the beginning of campaign season for the upcoming presidential elections." Truman was running for a second term. An unflinching stance in the East–West conflict and the retention of Berlin garnered the support of "80 percent of the American population, according to polls." Militarily, Berlin signified the first direct confrontation between the two world powers; "any mistake could lead to war, which, considering the overwhelming superiority of the USSR's land forces in Europe (four to one), it would win easily in the beginning stages. The approximately fifty nuclear bombs that stood at the United States' disposal but were not ready for immediate use could not change anything about the situation, even if there was no doubt that the United States would win in the end."[27] After weighing these factors, the American government returned to Clay's suggestion to supply the population of West Berlin with provisions through an airlift. It represented a nonviolent reaction to Soviet tactics.

Clay had calculated that with enough planes, it would be possible to supply the 2.5 million people in the Western sectors of Berlin with the necessary 4,500 tons of goods per day by establishing a shuttle system over flight corridors to the Tempelhof and Gatow airports. This goal was achieved in December 1948, and by early 1949 the daily transportation capacity reached 8,000 tons.[28] This had become possible through the use of larger, four-motor planes.

The West's second nonviolent reaction to the blockade was a trade embargo against the Soviet zone: deliveries from the Western zones were prohibited, causing a drastic cutback in interzonal trade. Ludwig Erhard, director of the Department of Economics in the unified Western economic area, petitioned the Allies to loosen the commercial blockade. Clay rejected Erhard's request and insisted that the embargo on the Soviet zone could only end when the supply of coal and food to the population of West Berlin was secure.[29] During the Berlin Blockade, many examples emerged of Germans from the East and West finding ways around the situation. This also applied to businesses and official institutions in the Soviet zone and East Berlin, since the two separate German currency zones still depended heavily on each other in terms of the division of labor. The Soviet zone in particular relied on deliveries of steel from the Ruhr Valley. Josef Orlopp, head of the (East German) German Economic Commission's Central Department of Interzonal and Foreign Trade, emphasized in April 1949 "that the Soviet zone continued to be dependent upon the West in many respects."[30]

From September 1948 onward, the West extended its counterblockade to include trade with countries in Eastern Europe. The Berlin Blockade ended on 12 May 1949, just a few days before the Paris conference of foreign ministers. The airlift endured a while longer; September brought an end to the most spectacular transportation feat in the history of air travel.

The Division of the City

On 16 June 1948, the Soviet Union terminated its role in the Allied Kommandatura. This move marked the beginning of the city's administrative and political split, which reached completion by the end of that year. Berlin retained its de jure four-power status, but joint administration was shattered. When the Western Allies resumed the work of the Kommandatura on 21 December 1948, they stated that because of the Soviet position, it was "not possible to implement the Kommandatura's decisions in East Berlin."[31] Thus, the second rule of the inter-Allied decision-making mechanism took effect: each occupation power had exclusive authority to exercise control over its respective zone or sector in Berlin.

For the population, the division of Berlin began with the two parallel currency reforms. At first, the Western powers had excluded Berlin from their plans to introduce the new currency. Shortly before going through with the money exchange, they learned that the Soviet Union also intended to carry out a currency reform in its zone and in Berlin. Hoping to quell the tense situation in Berlin, American experts tended toward accepting Soviet currency reform throughout the entire area of the city. But Ernst Reuter petitioned adamantly against it, arguing that the move could only lead to integrating Greater Berlin into the economy of the Soviet zone. Indeed, the SMAD had made this its goal. Reuter demanded the introduction of the Western Deutsche Mark in the Western sectors of Berlin. His reasoning was simple: "Whoever has this currency has power."[32] The Western city commandants allowed Reuter to convince them. They introduced the Deutsche Mark to their sectors, at first with a prominent "B" stamped on each bill, and simultaneously permitted the Ostmark to circulate there as a method of payment as well. West Berlin thus had two currencies until March 1949. After that, Berlin's Western commandants declared the Deutsche Mark to be the only valid currency in West Berlin, strengthening the city's economic ties to West Germany.

With the advent of the blockade on 24 June 1948, "the lights literally went out"[33] for West Berliners as the power plants located in the Eastern part of the city turned off their supplies to the Western sectors. Berlin's City Council and Magistrat both convened in the Soviet sector. On 24 July, the Soviet city commandant ordered supplies to East Berlin to be integrated into the supply system of the Eastern zone, which was under the direction of the German Economic Commission (DWK). This order precipitated a reorganization of capacities in the city's Food Department. A sub-division was created at the Food Office (*Ernährungsamt*) of the Magistrat to provide supplies to the population of West Berlin through food stores in the Eastern sector. The new subdivision was headed by an SED functionary, who then took over all authorities from the SPD council member in the Eastern sector.

This measure took place in the context of an offer by the SMAD to provide the population of the Western sectors with food and fuel during the blockade. Food would come from the state reserves of the USSR, and the DWK was tasked with implementing the supply program.[34] The significance of the Food Office for the undersupplied population was obvious. The Magistrat, which was largely not Communist, agreed on 23 August to transfer the Food Department to the British sector without giving up its authority over the Berlin-wide Food Office. "Under the existential pressure of the early blockade period, 'voting with ration cards' represented a fundamental decision for 920,000 families."[35] At the time of the SMAD's offer, supplies to East Berlin were secure while in West Berlin they literally hung in the air. Had the offer been accepted, the Americans could have spared themselves the entire airlift. "On 4 August, it was calculated that only 21,802 West Berliners had registered in the Eastern sector. The number was even more impressive considering that 100,000 West Berliners still worked in the Eastern sector at that time and risked losing their jobs if they acted contrarily."[36] This represented a clear vote by Berliners for the Western powers to remain in the Western sectors.

The conflict over the Food Office followed the division of the police force, which had resulted from a scandal in November 1947. The Berlin-based journalist Dieter Friede had disappeared without a trace in the Eastern sector. The City Council discussed the case "and, after questioning Mayor Friedensburg [CDU], concluded that (1) the bureau investigating Friede's disappearance had made grave errors, and (2) police leadership was responsible for the silent disappearance of 5,413 people in total (250 per month)."[37] The Soviet Command appointed Paul Markgraf[38] as police chief of Greater Berlin immediately after it occupied the city. In the wake of the Friede case, a majority in the City Council passed a vote of no confidence against Markgraf, and the majority in the Magistrat followed suit soon after. But Markgraf refused to recognize the authority of the Magistrat and referred "to the police force's position directly under the Allied Committee for

Public Security."[39] The Soviet Command prevented Markgraf's dismissal through its veto. For their part, the Western powers suspended Markgraf and provisionally appointed Johannes Stumm as police chief in Berlin. With the transfer of headquarters to West Berlin, "at least for employees loyal to Stumm,"[40] the split of the Berlin police department was practically complete by the end of July—that is, by the beginning of the blockade. Like the police, the fire department was soon divided as well.

Politically, the conflict reached its climax in August and September 1948 with the fight over the freely elected City Council of Berlin, which, like the Magistrat, convened in the Soviet sector. Until August 1948, the SED had hoped for a quick retreat by the Western powers; after that point the party took a different approach. On 30 August, Ulbricht justified the necessity of a single, uniform currency in all of Berlin by insisting upon the city's inclusion in the Soviet zone's economic area. In addition, SED leadership hoped to eliminate the Western powers' "bridgehead" in the Soviet zone through the struggle for "currency unity": "For them, Berlin serves as a bridgehead from which to launch an attack on the economy of the Soviet occupation zone. Therefore, the fight for a unified currency in Berlin is also the fight to ensure the implementation of the two-year plan [for the Soviet occupation zone]."[41] Since the Western powers enjoyed the support of most West Berliners in maintaining this "bridgehead," the SED found itself under pressure, especially in view of the looming second elections to the City Council in December 1948. On 25 August, Hermann Matern, state chair (*Landesvorsitzender*) of the SED in Berlin, presented an "Immediate Program to Save Berlin," demanding "the establishment of unified currency, administration, and provisions for the city."[42] The SMAD criticized Matern's speech internally: the announcement of a "platform" was not enough; he had not addressed the concerns of the people. Pieck noted: "no light—winter distress—coal—heat."[43]

On 26 August, the City Council could not meet because demonstrators mobilized by the SED were blocking City Hall. Matern's "Immediate Program" of 25 August signaled the beginning of the SMAD- and SED-led division of the city. Pieck, chair of the SED, also discussed this topic with Major Smirnov. Under the heading "Bans," he noted, "Agitation in the West, change in the Magistrat's policy = workers to the parliaments. Cleanse the Eastern sector of counterrevolutionary forces, police, administrations, dismissal from posts, arrests." The strategy was clear: "in favor of Magistrat collapse, against new elections."[44]

If 26 August was the dress rehearsal, 6 September was opening night. When the council members tried to enter City Hall, they found it occupied, and protests to the Soviet city commandant elicited no response. City Council member Otto Suhr (SPD) "took the position that 'those who put pressure on a parliament violate the fundamental laws of the democracy and place themselves outside of the law.' He then moved the City Council's meeting place from the Soviet sector to the British sector. The representatives from the SPD, CDU, and LDP followed his call."[45] Without exception, the SED caucus remained in East Berlin and boycotted the West Berlin City Council. With Ottmar Geschke (SED) as its chair, a special parliamentary session took place on 30 November in the Eastern sector with the twenty-three SED representatives, "over 200 delegates from the 'democratic block,' and more than 1,150 delegates from firms and institutions."[46] This assembly removed the elected Magistrat from office; from then on, the SED referred to it as the "splitter Magistrat." Friedrich Ebert (SED) assumed leadership of the new, provisional Magistrat of East Berlin.

The SED led its fight under the banner of national unity. Ulbricht formulated this linguistic rule in October 1948 as follows: "The propaganda of the United States talks about the Soviet Union's inflexible attitude because it wants people to forget that the entire Berlin question would not exist if the Western powers had not introduced this separate currency and if they had not split Germany apart. This is the starting point. Normal conditions can only exist in Germany if the Western Mark is abolished and German unity re-established." Ulbricht never forgot that Germany's future political and economic order was at stake. "It is impossible to disguise the fact that German division occurred precisely because the reactionary forces in the West feared a democratic Germany in which the power of old war criminals and corporate executives would be eliminated."[47]

West Berlin's answer was imparted to the SED by neither a "war criminal" nor a "corporate executive" but by Ernst Reuter, the governing mayor. The democratic parties of Berlin protested on 9 September 1948 with a large rally against the divisive politics of the SED, set before the ruins of the Reichstag. Reuter's address that day became one of the most important speeches in German postwar history. At the time of the demonstration, the Eastern sector had already been "cleansed." Before hundreds of thousands of listeners, Reuter assured the SED that their tactics were useless: "We will return to the Eastern sector of Berlin, and we will return to the Eastern zone of Germany!" Only the moment at which this would happen remained unknown. Reuter was not speaking only for Berliners; he was convinced that the crowd gathered that day represented a majority of Germans in the Eastern zone as well. He emphasized Magdeburg in particular, bridging the present with his own early biography during the first, failed German republic. This traumatic experience, formative for his generation, surely served as a central motivation in his fight for Berlin: "I think of my old city, Magdeburg, where the people elected me as a parliamentary representative, where I served as Lord Mayor before Hitler put us into concentration camps." He advised the SED to choose a new party symbol: "Please, not the handshake but rather the handcuffs that they are placing on Berliners. Handcuffs—the true symbol of these wretched cowards who, for thirty silver pieces, are willing to sell themselves and their people to a foreign power." More eloquent than his counterpart, Ulbricht, Reuter accentuated the national and political opposition between the SED and the democratic parties in the West of Germany and the Western sectors of Berlin. He articulated the desire of Berliners for freedom also from the Western occupation powers, which were gradually transforming into protective forces. With pathos, in words heard around the world and quoted ever since, he called on the Western powers to support Berlin in its fight for freedom and democracy:

"People of the world, people in America, in England, in France, in Italy! Look upon this city and recognize that you cannot, you must not abandon this city and this people! There is only one possibility for all of us: to stand together until this fight has been won, until the fight has been settled through victory over the enemies, through victory over the force of darkness." To Berliners he concluded: "This fight is one that we will win!"[48]

The last two steps toward the political division of Berlin occurred before the end of 1948. On 30 November, a new Magistrat was established in East Berlin. "On the orders of the Soviet city commandant, residents of the Eastern sector were not permitted to participate in the [City Council] elections planned for 5 December 1948."[49] Elections to the City Council could only take place in West Berlin, and with 64.5 percent, the Reuter-led SPD won an overwhelming electoral victory. It was a de facto referendum for West Berlin's self-assertion in the face of the Soviet blockade.

The Ring around Berlin: A New Border

The division of the city made West Berlin a permanent problem for the SED. Ulbricht revived his favorite military analogy of the Western "bridgehead" in October 1948 in order to emphasize its significance for the SED going forward: "The United States and England's policy of using Berlin as a bridgehead not only represents their intention to spread disruptive propaganda but also furthers their goal of disorganizing the economy of the Soviet occupation zone and sneaking spy agents and sabotage troops into the Soviet occupation zone."[50]

This propagandist justification prefaced practical measures from the SMAD and the SED. In October 1948, a new border was established surrounding the entire city: the "ring around Berlin." Its first goal was to sever the mostly unregulated provision of supplies to West Berliners from the nearby areas of Brandenburg: "On 18 October 1948, the Soviet/East zonal side began implementing strict controls not only of the street connections between the Western sectors and their surrounding areas but also of the crossing points between sectors within the city."[51] One day later, the police chief of the *Land* of Brandenburg issued Order No. 53 calling for police action against "hoarders and profiteers." In accordance with this order, East Berlin's police chief commanded all motor vehicles from the Soviet zone or the Eastern sector of Berlin bringing food into the city "to enter through the Eastern sector only."[52] Within the city itself, seventy checkpoints were erected along the sector border. In Berlin's metro system (U- and S-Bahn), the East Berlin police instated forced bag inspections. Surveillance of motor vehicle traffic to West Berlin increased: "Six checkpoints were established in the Eastern sector, at which all vehicles on the way to West Berlin had to register."[53] Mail coming from Western Germany was separated from mail coming from the Eastern zone in order to improve censorship of letter traffic. With the "ring around Berlin," the SMAD and SED established a police regime along Berlin's sector border that already anticipated elements of the border regime to come—but still remained open for residents of Berlin.

Crisis Management as Superpower Diplomacy

The four powers dealt with the Berlin conflict on the basis of their original rights as the Allied victors, and they made sure throughout the confrontation that their communication with each other did not deteriorate with respect to Germany. This common interest meant that each power respected the original rights of the other side. Over the following decades of European and German division, it remained a constant throughout their policies. However, this foundation of Allied Berlin policy irritated the Soviet Union during the two Berlin Crises as it tried to force the Western powers to withdraw from Berlin. Against these attempts, the Western powers always invoked their legal position, which the Soviet Union acknowledged in negotiations.

The Soviet Union started the bargaining game on 14 July 1948 with a note to the Western powers declaring that they had forfeited their rights in Berlin. The Soviets justified this assertion by claiming that the Western powers had violated the Potsdam Agreement. "Even before that point, Major General Kotikov, the Soviet city commandant, had ordered the Magistrat to cut off payments of occupation expenses to the Western powers. Their directives in Berlin were legally void, he argued, just as the Magistrat and the City Council had no legal basis without the approval of the Soviet city commandant."[54] The American government answered with a double strategy. On 17 June, B29 bombers were transferred to England, and simultaneously the three Western powers conveyed an offer to negotiate through their ambassadors in Moscow.

On 2 August, the ambassadors of the three Western powers met with Stalin in Moscow to discuss the problem. He justified the measures taken so far:

> After [the Western powers] had split off the Western part of the country at the London conference, making it a separate state with Frankfurt am Main as its capital and compelling the Eastern side to take analogous steps—to which the Soviet Union had not yet acquiesced—Berlin was no longer the capital of Germany. Now there were two capitals. Since the Western powers had divided the occupied country and Berlin no longer remained the capital of the entire country, they had forfeited their rights to station military forces there. Through their policy of division, they had robbed themselves of their own rights.
>
> This did not mean that the Soviet Union wished to drive the Allied troops out of Berlin. The transportation limitations only served as a defense against the penetration of [Western] currency and the division of Germany into two states as decided in London. The USSR was forced to defend itself. Therefore, it was impossible to talk about these measures without also considering the German question. Stalin concluded his speech with an order to introduce the Ostmark in the Western sectors. There were two currencies in the two basic zones—one in the East and one

in the West—as well as a third one in Berlin, which, needless to say, was "economic nonsense." He found it unacceptable that within the [Soviet] zone, one part of one city existed with its own currency. Berlin would not allow itself to be separated economically and territorially from its surrounding economic region. Did Mr. Smith [the American ambassador to Moscow] think that [the USSR] would tolerate a special currency in a portion of a city surrounded by the Soviet zone? The situation had to end. Thus, it was only logical to eliminate the special currency in Berlin, enabling the creation of a single currency within the Soviet zone until the four powers could finally agree on a uniform currency in all of Germany.[55]

Speaking to the three ambassadors, Stalin listed five issues that the Soviet government wished to see discussed, as well as two conditions required to lift the blockade:

First, [the Soviet government] insisted upon reparations benefitting the countries that suffered under German aggression. If some states declined to ask for these types of payments, that was their own matter. Second, [the USSR] demanded demilitarization; this had not yet taken place. Third, the creation of a single German government based on the resolutions from Yalta and Potsdam. A government was not a government [Stalin argued] without its own currency. When the Western powers created a separate currency, they forced the USSR—against its will—to do the same. Stalin demanded that they reverse the situation that had emerged. [The parties] should arrive at a four-sided agreement over a uniform means of payment for all of Germany. The request affected the currency not only in Berlin but also in the Western zones. As a fourth postulate, the Soviet leader requested that a peace treaty be signed. And finally, he demanded a special four-power regime in the Ruhr Valley, which constituted the industrial center of the Western zones. This list made it clear that Stalin was unwilling to abandon any claim he had articulated toward the Western powers over the previous years. For the time being, the most pressing points were the two conditions he required to lift the blockade: the introduction of the Ostmark in West Berlin and the suspension of the London Agreements.[56]

The Western powers could not accept either condition if they were to realize their project of building a Western state. Negotiations in the summer and fall of 1948 failed. Stalin's demands remained unsatisfied, and he did not succeed in exercising direct influence over the founding of the Western state. Berlin housed two currencies and two political orders. The Wall grew, even as the sector borders remained open.

On 3 October 1948, Molotov suggested convening the Council of Foreign Ministers; the Western powers countered with a demand to lift the blockade of transportation routes. They were supported by the UN General Assembly, which drafted a resolution calling for an immediate end to the blockade of Berlin's transit routes. Küsters emphasizes: "The longer the crisis went on, the more resolute the Americans became in exercising their rights in Berlin and maintaining supplies to the city."[57] Serious talks between Washington and Moscow only opened after the

American presidential election, which Truman won. On 15 February 1949, discussions began between Philip C. Jessup, deputy director of the American mission to the UN, and Jakob A. Malik, permanent representative of the USSR to the UN. At issue was a new conference of foreign ministers at which the German question would be renegotiated. In March, the Soviet side accepted the American demand that it "end the blockade two weeks before the beginning of negotiations by the Council of Foreign Ministers. The West had already achieved its real goal."[58]

In addition, the Soviet side brought interzonal trade into the discussion. With his American counterpart, Malik sounded out "whether lifting the blockade" would signal the resumption of "interzonal trade to its full extent," whether it would be possible to return to the conditions that existed before the blockade. "This would provide significant relief to the Soviets in addressing the supply problems within their occupation zone."[59] The Soviet side also requested assurance from the Western powers that no West German government would be established before or during the conference of foreign ministers. Under these conditions, the Soviets were ready to lift the blockade of West Berlin. The Western powers accepted the conditions as well, and before the Council of Foreign Ministers convened in Paris on 23 May 1949, the Soviet Union lifted the Berlin Blockade on 12 May; simultaneously, the Western powers ended their boycott of interzonal trade.[60]

The combination of ending the blockade and lifting the embargo on interzonal trade managed to bring the crisis to a conclusion. But preparations to found the two states pushed forward inexorably, despite discussions in Paris. The conference resolution confirmed a "modus vivendi among the four powers in their treatment of Germany."[61] Paris also marked the last conference of the Council of Foreign Ministers, even though there was no formal decision to dissolve the body.

Thus, the Soviet Union's attempt to drive the Western powers out of Berlin with the help of the blockade and to integrate Greater Berlin into its own occupation zone had failed by May 1949. The Allied airlift, together with the will of West Berliners to assert their independence, marked a political and psychological milestone in relations between the Germans and the Western occupation powers. At the same time, it deepened the rift between the West and the Soviet Union. Rolf Steininger counts the blockade as "one of the most serious errors in Soviet policy after 1945." By going through with the airlift, the Western powers thwarted the Soviet goal to expel them from the city; they simply refused to leave Berlin. In fact, the opposite occurred. Soviet tactics confirmed the "validity of the Anglo-American course toward the Soviet Union" and created an emotional bond among the Western Allies, the West Germans, and the West Berliners.[62]

In one respect, the Berlin Blockade was a conflict between the United States and the Soviet Union; in another, it was the hour of German decision. In 1944 in Moscow, the Communist Wilhelm Florin had summarized the basic question in German politics after Hitler with the fundamentally accurate phrase: "Eastern or Western orientation."[63] During the blockade, the West Berliners and then the West Germans—the only ones who could still vote—answered this question: they decided on the West. At the same time, the Western powers respected the Soviet Union's rights as a victor within its occupation zone and allowed Berlin's division to proceed, along with the establishment of the SED as the totalitarian state party of the Soviet zone.

Notes

1. The Magistrat of Greater Berlin split in 1948. West Berlin's Magistrat became the Berlin Senate in 1950, while the Magistrat of East Berlin kept its name until reunification.
2. See Leonhard, *Revolution*, 411–500.
3. Ibid., 457.
4. Arthur Schlegelmilch, *Hauptstadt im Zonendeutschland: Die Entstehung der Berliner Nachkriegsdemokratie 1945–1949* (Berlin, 1993), 97.
5. For the individual election results, see Weber, *Geschichte der DDR*, 87–90.
6. Andreas Malycha, *Partei von Stalins Gnaden? Die Entwicklung der SED zur Partei neuen Typs in den Jahren 1946 bis 1950* (Berlin, 1996), 75.
7. Reuter had joined the Bolsheviks as a prisoner of war in Russia in 1917. He then participated in the founding party congress of the KPD in 1918 as a member of the Soviet delegation and was voted first general secretary in 1921. His opponent was Wilhelm Pieck. Reuter's criticism of the KPD culminated in the assertion "that our financial dependence [will lead] to a psychological dependence" on Moscow. Wilhelm Pieck called this statement "disgraceful" at the time. In striving for the "independence of the KPD from the Communist International," Reuter was dismissed from his position and barred from the party in February 1922. He then returned to the SPD, of which he had become a member in 1912. See David E. Barclay, *Schaut auf diese Stadt: Der unbekannte Ernst Reuter* (Berlin, 2000), 96, 196–230.
8. "Aufzeichnung von Smirnov und Semenov: Die bevorstehende Tagung des Rats der Außenminister," 1 November 1947, in Laufer and Kynin, *UdSSR*, vol. 3, 430–31.
9. "Gusev an Molotov: Zur Tagung des Rats der Außenminister in London im November 1947," 17 October 1947, in Laufer and Kynin, *UdSSR*, vol. 3, 424.
10. Ibid.
11. Koop, *Kein Kampf*, 18.
12. Wettig, "Verhandlungen," 244.
13. "Gespräch bei Stalin in Moskau vom 26.3.1948," in Badstübner and Loth, *Wilhelm Pieck*, 191.
14. Harald Neubert, ed., *Stalin wollte ein anderes Europa: Moskaus Außenpolitik 1940 bis 1968 und die Folgen. Eine Dokumentation von Wladimir K. Wolkow* (Berlin, 2003), 175.
15. "Semjonow an das MID," 23 April 1948, in Laufer and Kynin, *UdSSR*, vol. 3, 589.
16. Laufer and Kynin, *UdSSR*, vol. 3, 724.
17. Küsters, *Integrationsfriede*, 383.
18. Ibid.
19. Wettig, "Verhandlungen," 246–47.
20. Gerhard Keiderling, *Berlin 1945–1986: Geschichte der Hauptstadt der DDR* (Berlin (East), 1987), 278.
21. See Friedrich, *Yalu*, 59–67.
22. Quoted in Barclay, *Schaut auf diese Stadt*, 241. For the text of Murphy's original telegram, see "The United States Political Advisor for Germany (Murphy) to the Secretary of State," Berlin,

26 June 1948, in U.S. Dept. of State, *FRUS, 1948*, vol. 2, *Germany and Austria* (Washington, 1973), 919–20.

23. Barclay, *Schaut auf diese Stadt*, 239.

24. Quoted in ibid., 240.

25. Ibid., 242.

26. "Berlin," in *Geschichte der Bundesrepublik Deutschland*, ed. Karl Dietrich Bracher et al., vol. I: *Jahre der Besatzung: 1945–1949*, ed. Theodor Eschenburg (Stuttgart, 1983), 453.

27. Schwabe, *Weltmacht*, 185.

28. See Friedrich, *Yalu*, 83–84.

29. See Koop, *Kein Kampf*, 236.

30. Quoted in ibid., 244.

31. Dieter Mahncke, *Berlin im geteilten Deutschland* (Munich, 1973), 45.

32. "Berlin," in Eschenburg, *Jahre der Besatzung*, 452.

33. Udo Wetzlaugk and Christian Koziol, *Im Überblick: Berlin* (Berlin (West), 1986), 30.

34. See Keiderling, *Berlin*, 288.

35. Udo Wetzlaugk, *Berliner Blockade und Luftbrücke 1948/49* (Berlin, 1998), 52.

36. Ibid., 54.

37. Wetzlaugk and Koziol, *Im Überblick: Berlin*, 129.

38. Paul Markgraf (1910–93) was a captain of the German Wehrmacht when he fell into Soviet captivity at Stalingrad as a prisoner of war. He attended an anti-fascist reeducation program in the USSR before serving as police chief in Berlin from 1945 to 1949, at first responsible for Greater Berlin, after 1948 for East Berlin.

39. Wetzlaugk and Koziol, *Im Überblick: Berlin*, 129.

40. Ibid., 130.

41. Walter Ulbricht, "Demokratische Wirtschaftspolitik und Zweijahrplan: Rede vor Technikern, Ingenieuren, Wirtschaftswissenschaftlern, Aktivisten, Vertretern von Betrieben, Behörden und Organisationen in der Kongreßhalle in Leipzig," 30 August 1948, in Walter Ulbricht, *Zur Geschichte der deutschen Arbeiterbewegung: Aus Reden und Aufsätzen*, vol. 3, *1946–1950*, supplementary volume (Berlin (East) 1971), 544.

42. Keiderling, *Berlin*, 283.

43. "Handschriftliche Notizen von Wilhelm Pieck, o. D., wahrscheinlich zwischen 30.8. und 7.9.1948," in Badstübner and Loth, *Wilhelm Pieck*, 237. In its "Immediate Program" ("Sofort-Programm") of 30 November, the East Berlin Magistrat took these points to heart. The Magistrat promised to take care of coal supplies and improve electricity provisions.

44. Ibid.

45. Ribbe, *Berlin*, 64.

46. Keiderling, *Berlin*, 300.

47. Walter Ulbricht, "Die ideologische Arbeit der Partei in den Betrieben verbessern: Aus dem Referat auf der Transportkonferenz der SED am 28. und 29. Oktober 1948 in Leipzig," 28 October 1948, in Ulbricht, *Arbeiterbewegung*, vol. 3, supplementary volume, 612–13.

48. Ernst Reuter, "Rede auf der Protestkundgebung am 9. September 1948," in Jürgen Weber, *Das Entscheidungsjahr 1948*, vol. 2 of *30 Jahre Bundesrepublik Deutschland*, ed. Bayrische Landeszentrale für politische Bildungsarbeit (Munich, 1982), 228–29.

49. Ribbe, *Berlin*, 66.

50. Walter Ulbricht, "Die ideologische Arbeit der Partei in den Betrieben verbessern," in Ulbricht, *Arbeiterbewegung*, vol. 3, supplementary volume, 612.

51. Koop, *Kein Kampf*, 264.

52. Ibid., 263.

53. Ibid., 265.

54. "Berlin," in Eschenburg, *Jahre der Besatzung*, 454.

55. "Aufzeichnung über das Gespräch Stalins mit den drei westlichen Botschaftern, 2.8.1948," quoted in Wettig, "Verhandlungen," 248.

56. Wettig, "Verhandlungen," 251.
57. Küsters, *Integrationsfriede*, 386.
58. Ibid., 390.
59. Ibid., 391.
60. "Four-Power Communiqué on Arrangements for Lifting the Berlin Blockade Effective May 12," New York, 4 May 1949, in U.S. Dept. of State, *Documents on Germany*, 221.
61. Küsters, *Integrationsfriede*, 428.
62. Steininger, *Deutsche Geschichte*, vol. 2, 29.
63. See Erler, Laude, and Wilke, *Nach Hitler*, 136–58.

Chapter 7

STALIN'S DEATH AND THE FIRST
EXISTENTIAL CRISIS OF THE GDR
17 June 1953

Between the first and second Berlin Crises, the establishment of the "foundations of socialism" in the GDR unleashed the country's first existential crisis with a major wave of emigration and the uprising of 17 June 1953. These events confirmed all of Fedor Gusev's fears in 1947 regarding the significance of West Berlin for the stability of the Soviet zone. The GDR's crisis in the early summer of 1953 occurred after Stalin's death, after a "collective leadership" took power at the head of the CPSU in Moscow. During the uprising, the Soviet Union resolved to defend and stabilize the GDR both internally and externally. As first secretary of the CPSU's Central Committee, Khrushchev was part of the collective leadership in 1953 and participated in this decision; 17 June 1953 was likely a major factor that contributed to his Berlin offensive in 1958.

A "New Course" for the SED

After Stalin's death in March 1953, the new collective leadership in Moscow assessed Socialist progress in the GDR up to that point. In order to stabilize the situation there, the SED was ordered to change its course. The presidium of the Soviet Council of Ministers convened on 27 May to address the issue of Germany. This took place against the backdrop of British Prime Minister Churchill's proposal to hold a summit conference to open a renewed examination of the German question. A meeting of this type did not occur until two years later in Geneva.[1]

According to Andrei A. Gromyko's recollections, Soviet Minister of Internal Affairs Lavrentiy P. Beria questioned the importance of the GDR for Soviet Germany policy: "We need only a peaceful Germany, it does not matter to us whether there will be socialism or not." Regarding the quality of the GDR state, Beria was unambiguous: "What does it amount to, this GDR? It is not even a real state. It is only kept in being by Soviet troops."[2] Molotov allegedly answered, "The Democratic Republic is not inferior to the Federal Republic in any way. I adamantly refuse to accept that kind of attitude toward a friendly country. It has the right to exist as an independent state."[3] The majority of the presidium shared Molotov's position.

The Soviet position paper of early June refers to the high number of refugees as a symptom of the crisis: "From January 1951 to April 1953, 447,000 people fled to West Germany."[4] Among the refugees were also members of the SED and the FDJ. At the root of this critical situation, at least in Moscow's view, were the decisions made at the Second Party Congress of the SED, which Stalin and the CPSU Politburo later approved. By 1953, it was clear that "the domestic and foreign conditions required" to go through with these plans had not been fulfilled.[5] The GDR had to revise its course of action, and the CPSU put forth a list of necessary measures. Among them were: suspension of the forced collectivization of agriculture and private handwork; a review "from the top" of verdicts against victims of the class struggle, followed by their release from prison; and the suspension of the ongoing campaign against the church. The SED was instructed, in its decisions "that aimed to strengthen the GDR, to thoroughly consider the real conditions within the GDR as well as the situation in all of Germany and the situation internationally."[6]

The Soviet Union's biggest nemesis in this "fight for the unification of Germany based on democratic and peaceful foundations" was still Konrad Adenauer. The CPSU demanded that the SED change its approach to the West German Social Democrats in order to achieve "maximum fragmentation of the opponent's strength and to take advantage of any and every oppositional force" against the politics of the Federal Government. "Therefore, since the Social Democratic Party of West Germany (which still includes significant portions of the working class) has opposed the Bonn Agreements—even if it hasn't been sufficiently consistent— the [SED's] completely antagonistic position against that party must, for the present time, come to an end. Wherever and whenever possible, [the SED] should try to organize joint action against Adenauer's politics of division and the imperialist subjugation of Germany."[7] This change in course by the SED remained in place over the following decades, serving years later as a basic reason to accept the Social Democrats' Ostpolitik when renegotiating the status quo of divided Germany.

On 2 June 1953, a delegation from the SED Politburo was summoned to Moscow. The group consisted of General Secretary Walter Ulbricht, Prime Minister Otto Grotewohl, and Fred Oelßner, the member of the politburo responsible for propaganda, and they came to Moscow to receive new political instructions. The "collective leadership" had decided to set a "New Course" that would correct the establishment of socialism in the GDR and revise Stalin's decision of 1952.[8]

The SED delegation stood before a collective leadership that acted as a single entity. The collective's critique of the SED, as well as its cautious critique of

CPSU leadership (in other words, of Stalin) were communicated through carefully selected roles—at least, this is the impression conveyed in Grotewohl's sparse notes. Consistent with hierarchy, Soviet Prime Minister Georgi M. Malenkov opened the discussion with an observation: "Everything must start by changing the conditions in the GDR." Even Beria tried to appease the situation, adding a dose of self-critique: "All of us are responsible for the mistake; no accusations." Molotov continued in this vein, evoking the planned policy's intended effect on West Germany: "Enough errors must be corrected so that all of G.[ermany] sees it."[9] Molotov's demand that the SED visibly correct its erroneous policies corresponds to a communiqué of 9 June 1953 from the SED Politburo, which read: "The politburo of the Central Committee of the SED had reason to believe that the SED and the government of the German Democratic Republic were responsible for a series of mistakes in the past, which manifested themselves in decrees and orders . . . moreover, in implementing these decrees and orders, serious mistakes arose in the districts, counties, and municipalities. One result was that numerous people have left the republic."[10] In fact, this public admission of error by the party-that-never-erred opened a floodgate of dissatisfaction with Communist Party rule and living conditions in the GDR—contrary to the expectations of the SED and leadership in Moscow—and overflowed in the popular uprising on 17 June.

After the SED delegation returned to Berlin, the politburo had less than a week to transform the Soviet instructions into concrete resolutions. The session of 6 June 1953 witnessed an exchange of open, and thus controversial, statements. Rudolf Herrnstadt was the only speaker to argue from the Soviet position with respect to the German question. He highlighted differences in the CPSU's resolutions on this "New Course" and on the decisions from the SED's Second Party Congress in July 1952. In his view, the basic resolution of 1952 was "unrealistic," based on fundamental convictions that were never spoken aloud: "We'll establish socialism, the German question will somehow resolve itself in the meantime, or if it doesn't, it can always be solved with the bayonets of the Soviet Army."[11]

Moscow's new strategy, which tasked the SED with improving living conditions in the GDR, led the SED leaders to take a critical position toward their own policy: "We cannot claim that that we truly took this position, even if we did so in words. Otherwise it would not have been possible for us to find ourselves with 450,000 deserters of the republic, who have now become 450,000 propagandists against us over there."[12]

Herrnstadt reminded himself and the others that the GDR's accelerated armament ordered by Stalin also reflected the Soviet leader's concern that war could break out in Europe just as it did in Korea: "When we announced the 'accelerated establishment of socialism' last summer at the Second Party Congress, I was excited, but I remember being troubled by one thing. If the comrades in Moscow have decided to approve this step—so I thought at the time—then it means that in their view, the goal of 'peaceful unification' has receded to the background to make way for the possibility of armed conflict." He continued with a bitter truth about the defeat of German Communists in the debate to shape Germany after 1945, which was also a debate over Soviet policy toward Germany. Moscow's approval of the slogan "accelerated establishment of socialism" also implied an extremely negative view toward the work of the KPD and SED in terms of the German question, which was so crucial for their political success. Herrnstadt's critique conveyed the succinct assertion that within the historic window of opportunity, which was now essentially closed, the KPD and SED had been unable to "change the power relationship in Germany to our advantage."[13] Presumably Herrnstadt did not rule out the possibility that the Soviet Union could use this "New Course" to sacrifice socialism in the GDR and the separate SED state altogether in international negotiations to solve the German question.

Later, when the SED leadership searched for scapegoats after the 17 June uprising, Ulbricht found them in Wilhelm Zaisser, minister of state security, and Rudolf Herrnstadt. The two men were charged with advocating this particular consequence of the "New Course." In Berlin, Ulbricht repeated one of the accusations that Khrushchev had leveled against Beria, who was imprisoned and executed shortly after 17 June: "A comrade here has posed the very serious question of whether there is a connection between the work of the Herrnstadt/Zaisser group and Beria's case. A comrade minister has explained that Zaisser told him the new strategy entailed compliance to the West and could lead back to the rule of the bourgeoisie. This point of view reflects Beria's political position, which, in turn, is connected to Churchill's whole concept."[14]

Grotewohl's notes from the Moscow visit in early June only show that the "collective leadership," including Beria, presented itself to the SED as a unified body.

The SED State's Crisis of Legitimacy: 17 June 1953

Just a few days after the SED announced its "New Course," the people of the GDR gave their verdict for the first time on the legitimacy of the East German state. On 17 June, strikes and demonstrations took place in more than seven hundred cities in the GDR with the participation of hundreds of thousands of people.[15] They demanded the government's resignation, free elections, and the fall of zonal borders, amounting to the end of the GDR and the beginning of German unification. The Soviet military commandants announced a state of emergency in thirteen districts and fifty-one county seats. No measure by the Soviet chief commissar could have more clearly exposed the German Communists' dependence on the USSR than the "protective" internment of the SED Politburo in Berlin-Karlshorst, which Semyonov ordered on the morning of 17 June.

Soviet diplomat Igor F. Maximychev explains the Soviet occupation power's quick reaction by recalling the experience of the Second World War: "Only eight years had passed since the end of the most bitter war in the history of mankind. It sufficed to paint the unrest on 17 June as an attempt at a 'fascist putsch,' which all USSR media immediately did, in order to eliminate any kind of sympathy with the demonstrators from the outset."[16] Right away, Ulbricht adopted the vilifying term "fascist provocation" to denote the strikes and demonstrations by workers, tainting the incidents with propaganda, as Rudolf Herrnstadt recalled later. Herrnstadt received the order to draft an editorial for *Neues Deutschland*, the party newspaper (*Zentralorgan*) of the SED. This editorial about "Day X" located the causes of the uprising in the West and placed its initiators in the United States and West Germany. By name, the SED denounced Konrad Adenauer; Jakob Kaiser, Adenauer's minster of all-German affairs; Erich Ollenhauer, head of the SPD; and Ernst Reuter, governing mayor of Berlin. The SED accused them of "directly organizing Day X," making them responsible "for the blood that has been lost in the suppression of this fascist adventure."[17]

These assertions intended to absolve the Soviet occupation power and the SED of their responsibility for the death sentences by Soviet court martial and the imprisonment of strikers and demonstrators, at the same time making taboo questions that pointed to "mistakes" by the SED that led to the uprising. Shifting blame to politicians in the Federal Republic also reinforced another taboo, namely questioning why the Soviet occupation power answered the demonstrating workers' demands for better living conditions, free elections, and German reunification by imposing a state of emergency. Prime Minister Grotewohl justified this move to the SED's Central Committee, insisting that it was necessary because the SED itself was too weak to "suppress this provocation with its own strength. We could not have done it. It was easy to determine that the great and profound inner trust [of the East German people in the SED] that must exist in order to go through with this type of action was simply not there."[18] In other words, without the protection of the Soviet occupying power, the SED could not have maintained its rule.

The image of West Germany's threat to socialism in the GDR through its politics and its outpost, West Berlin, became a propaganda stereotype. The Soviet Union and the GDR evoked it again during the second Berlin Crisis to demand "normalization" of the situation in West Berlin and its transformation into a "Free City."

The Soviet Union Guarantees the Existence of the SED State

Only after the Soviet Army had brought "calm and order" to the GDR could the SED resume its governing activities—this time, in a fundamentally different constellation. Under the state of emergency, the Soviet Union had used military means to secure the East German state within its empire, which Ulbricht quickly understood. Now the SED could be confident enough in the security of its plans to establish socialism in the GDR. The Soviet Union had reaffirmed Stalin's approval of an SED-led separate Socialist German state; after this massive show of power, there was no chance that the USSR would simply abandon the GDR. Ulbricht already boasted new self-confidence on 20 June in a conversation in Karlshorst among Chief Commissar Semyonov, Chief of the General Staff

Marshal Sokolovsky, and four top-ranking functionaries of the SED. Herrn-stadt, who was one of the participants, noticed Ulbricht's confidence. Semyonov asked his German counterparts whether it wouldn't be better for them to go to the factories as Lenin and Stalin had always done during times of crisis in the Soviet Union, in order to lead the country from there. Ulbricht retorted gruffly, Herrnstadt wrote later, "but in principle he was correct: 'You yourselves forbade us from going to the factories!' Semyonov responded, taken aback, 'That is no way to argue, Com[rade] Ulbricht, as you are well aware. My instructions only referred to the 17 [June].' Marshal Sokolovsky tried to help our situation, but in fact made it worse. He said quietly: 'The German comrades are probably some-what shocked by the suddenness of the whole thing.' Making reference to that, Ulbricht exclaimed as we were leaving: 'Just let them try one more time to tell me how to behave! Now I am going to do whatever I think is right!' In our bitterness, we all agreed with him."[19]

At this point in time, neither the power struggle in Moscow among the lead-ers of the CPSU nor the leadership crisis of the SED had been solved. Beria's imprisonment on 26 June made way for the rise of the first secretary of the CPSU, Nikita S. Khrushchev, to the apex of power. The decision concerning new SED leadership also occurred in Moscow. At a meeting of the CPSU's Central Com-mittee in early July, the committee members negotiated Beria's case and reached a political conviction of guilt. In connection with this Central Committee con-ference, Ulbricht and Grotewohl traveled once again to the Soviet capital, and the Soviet leaders briefed them on Beria. According to Grotewohl's notes, Soviet Prime Minister Malenkov expressed that "Gr[otewohl] and U.[lbricht] must work together," and "Gr. and U. can found and build up this collective."[20] After this conversation, Ulbricht and Grotewohl had the mandate to solve the SED's crisis according to their own vision—and that is precisely what they did.

Western Initiatives for New Negotiations on Germany

Stalin's death, the collective leadership in Moscow, and the entry into office of a new American president, Dwight D. Eisenhower, brought new movement to the German question internationally. Eisenhower and British Prime Minister Churchill announced preparations for a summit meeting with the new Soviet leaders. In light of this development, which the SPD used to call for a four-power conference on Germany, Adenauer decided to make a statement at the Bundestag on 10 June. He also requested a "four-power conference soon" and presented a five-point program enumerating the following steps to German unification: "Free elections in all of Germany, the creation of a Germany-wide government, the ratification of a freely negotiated peace treaty, the resolution of open territorial questions, and the free-dom to act independently in foreign affairs."[21]

With demands for free elections, the resignation of the GDR government, and German unity, the popular uprising in the GDR on 17 June supported the initiatives of the SPD and the Federal Government. In a 20 June circular by West German State Secretary Walter Hallstein, he asserted that there could be no more doubt in the Western world that "given free elections, the people of the Soviet occupied zone would raise their voices for democratic parties."[22] In a sober tone, he continued: "The Russian relapse into a system based on the naked use of violence should make everyone think again who, cradled in fantasy dreams, recently believed that the necessary conditions already existed for a quick, peaceful agreement with Soviet Russia on the major questions of Europe and Asia hovering over us today." The Federal Republic, Hallstein wrote, should use the popular uprising to force the Western powers to take an active stance for German reunification, "if the weakness shown by the Soviet regime in the past few days is not to go unused. In doing so, the West German government accepts that a permanent solution to the German question would have to accommodate not only the security needs of Germany but also those of all of its neighbors, including the Soviet Union."[23] From the perspective of the West German government, overcoming the East–West antagonism was a necessary condition to solve the German question. Adenauer also took this position in the Bundestag debate on 1 July 1953: "Since Germany's division is a result of the East–West conflict, reunification can only follow from an appeasement of this conflict. Reunification and European cooperation are necessary components of the same policy."[24] The Western powers agreed with the Federal Republic on this point. In mid July, the Western foreign ministers presented an offer to the Soviet Union to hold a conference on the German question. At the top of the agenda were the demand for free elections in all of Germany, the formation of a national assembly, and the election of a pan-German government.

The behavior of the Soviet occupation power in the GDR on 17 June was a shock for Germans on both sides of the zonal border. The population of the GDR was forced to learn that acts of courage and civil disobedience could not solve the German question in the face of military force. Still, their strikes and demonstrations were not in vain. After the uprising, the SED and the Soviet occupation power reacted more sensitively to the needs of the population than they had before, for example by improving the provision of food and supplies and returning the Soviet joint-share companies (*sowjetische Aktiengesellschaften*, or SAGs) to the GDR. The people of the Federal Republic and their politicians had to accept helplessly that a change to the status quo in Germany would not be possible against the ironclad will of the Soviet Union. Soviet tanks on Potsdamer Platz reinforced the view in West Germany that it was the right decision to build ties to the West, contributing significantly to Konrad Adenauer's victory in the Bundestag elections of 1953. The Bundestag commemorated the popular uprising for freedom and unity by passing the "Law for a Day of German Unity" on 4 August 1953, according to which the Bundestag marked every subsequent 17 June with an hour of remembrance. In the preamble to the law, the Federal Republic made a clear declaration that, as the democratic core state, it would not accept the country's permanent division: "On 17 June 1953, the German people in the Soviet occupation zone and East Berlin rose up against the Communist tyranny and manifested their will for freedom, even as they suffered severe casualties. Through this, 17 June has become a symbol of German unity in freedom."[25]

Recognition and Stabilization of the GDR

The Soviet leadership managed to align the stabilization of the GDR with its Germany policy vis-à-vis the Western powers. In their answer to the Western powers' initiative on 15 August 1953, the Soviet leaders abandoned their previous position of treating Germany as a single state. From that point onward, the Soviet Union emphasized the necessity of including the "existing governments" of both German states in negotiations over a peace treaty. This separation of demands for a peace treaty and for state unity evidenced the USSR's recognition of the GDR as an independent state. In 1960, Khrushchev reminded Ulbricht of the fundamental change seven years earlier: "Malenkov and Beria wanted to liquidate the GDR, but we chased one of them away and shot the other, and declared our support for Socialist Germany."[26]

From 20 to 22 August 1953, the Soviet government welcomed Grotewohl and Ulbricht to Moscow as the official government delegation of the GDR with a ceremonious demonstration of protocol. At the Kremlin, Soviet Prime Minister Georgi M. Malenkov outlined the Soviet vision of a pan-German government to the GDR delegation: it would "be built by the parliaments of the GDR and the Federal Republic." Foreign Minister Molotov promised that "the extraction of reparations" would stop by the end of the year. All thirty-three SAGs "in mining, chemistry, and machine construction, among other areas, that had been transferred to the possession of the Soviet government as part of reparations payments" would "be returned . . . without any demand for compensation." Defense Minister Nikolai A. Bulganin announced a decline in occupation costs. Anastas J. Mikoyan, the minister of foreign commerce, handled a particularly sensitive subject: the mining of uranium in the GDR. The mines were indispensable for the Soviet nuclear weapons program and would be converted into a German–Soviet joint-share company (*deutsch-sowjetische Aktiengesellschaft*), since Wismut, the Soviet joint-share company in the nonferrous heavy metal industry, was crucial "to securing the defense not only of the Soviet Union, but also of the GDR," as Mikoyan emphasized. He also disclosed the extent of additional food and raw materials deliveries to the GDR from the Soviet Union. Finally, in a demonstrative gesture, the diplomatic missions in Moscow and East Berlin were converted into embassies.[27]

In his speech thanking the Soviet Union for its help, Grotewohl made reference to the events of June that had obviously sparked the need for this new aid program: "You know that we have been through a period of political and economic conditions in the GDR over these past few months that were, without a doubt, erroneous. We tried to escape from the cycle, but it was clear that this would be completely impossible using our strength alone." Soviet aid, he hoped, "will bring our people to understand that this type of help can only come from true friends."[28] Ulbricht added a propaganda-laden explanation of the events leading up to 17 June and emphasized the significance for Germany of the USSR's response to the Western powers on 15 August 1953. The Soviet Union's recognition of the GDR and its economic aid program would enable the SED "to really push forward, also in West Germany, and emerge from our position of defense. The bandits from West Germany, America, and Bonn have succeeded in planting a fascist organization in the GDR; but now we will be able to unleash a broad movement for German unity."[29] Ulbricht was careful in his speech to align his own positions perfectly with those of his Soviet superiors. This applied not only to strengthening the GDR but also to his request that the Ministry for State Security liquidate any West German "operative centers" remaining on East German territory.[30] Like his Soviet counterpart, he advocated taking initiative on Germany policy in order to sign a peace agreement.

Soviet Prime Minister Malenkov announced the "international state founding" of the GDR by underlining the GDR's pan-German mission: It "is a bastion and a state for the entire German people. A significant responsibility for the future of Germany weighs on the shoulders of the GDR. [The state] is born in order to create a new, great, peace-loving Germany, in order to ensure peace and security throughout Europe and the entire world."[31] This line of reasoning continued in 1955 with the "treaty of friendship" between the GDR and the Soviet Union, "which guaranteed the GDR's total sovereignty. Through the transfer of sovereignty to the GDR, all resolutions by the Control Council from 1945 to 1948 ceased to be valid, but simultaneously the agreement arranged for Soviet troops to remain stationed in the GDR."[32] Furthermore, the treaty reiterated the Soviet Union's veto rights with regard to Germany as a whole.[33]

Notes

1. Kissinger, *Diplomacy*, 510–12.
2. Quoted in Vladislav Zubok and Constantine Pleshakov, *Inside the Kremlin's Cold War: From Stalin to Khrushchev* (Cambridge, MA, 1996), 161.
3. Quoted in Andrej Gromyko, *Erinnerungen*, trans. Hermann Kusterer (Düsseldorf, 1989), 441.
4. "Über die Maßnahmen zur Gesundung der politischen Lage in der Deutschen Demokratischen Republik," in Steininger, *Deutsche Geschichte*, vol. 2, 241.
5. Ibid.
6. Ibid., 246.
7. Ibid.
8. On this, see Manfred Wilke and Tobias Voigt, "'Neuer Kurs' und 17. Juni: Die 2. Staatsgründung der DDR 1953," in *Satelliten nach Stalins Tod: Der "Neue Kurs"; 17. Juni 1953 in der DDR, Ungarische Revolution 1956*, ed. András B. Hegedüs and Manfred Wilke (Berlin, 2000), 24–136.
9. Ibid., 45. This change of course in the GDR also aimed to improve the Soviet Union's position in negotiations on a peace treaty with Germany.

10. "Kommuniqué des Politbüros der SED, 9.6.1953," in Steininger, *Deutsche Geschichte*, vol. 2, 267.

11. Steininger, *Deutsche Geschichte*, vol. 2, 267.

12. Elke Scherstjanoi, "'Wollen wir den Sozialismus?': Dokumente aus der Sitzung des Politbüros der ZK der SED am 6. Juni 1953," *Beiträge zur Geschichte der Arbeiterbewegung* 33, no. 5 (1991): 671.

13. Ibid., 673.

14. "Aus der Geheimrede Walter Ulbrichts vor dem 15. Plenum (Juli 1953)," in Rudolf Herrnstadt, *Das Herrnstadt-Dokument: Das Politbüro der SED und die Geschichte des 17. Juni 1953*, ed. Nadja Stulz-Herrnstadt (Reinbek, 1990), 260.

15. See Ilko-Sascha Kowalczuk, *17. Juni 1953: Volksaufstand in der DDR, Ursachen—Abläufe—Folgen* (Bremen, 2003).

16. Igor F. Maximytschew, "Eine wenig bekannte Seite des 17. Juni 1953," in *Juni 1953 in Deutschland: Der Aufstand im Fadenkreuz von Kaltem Krieg, Katastrophe und Katharsis*, ed. Heiner Timmermann (Münster, 2003), 113.

17. "Über die Lage und die unmittelbaren Aufgaben der Partei," in *Dokumente der Sozialistischen Einheitspartei Deutschlands: Beschlüsse und Erklärungen des Zentralkomitees sowie seines Politbüros und seines Sekretariats*, ed. Zentralkomitee der Sozialistischen Einheitspartei Deutschlands (Berlin (East), 1954), vol. 4, 438.

18. Quoted in Manfred Wilke, *Die Streikbrecherzentrale: Der Freie Deutsche Gewerkschaftsbund (FDGB) und der 17. Juni 1953* (Münster, 2004), 252.

19. Herrnstadt, *Herrnstadt-Dokument*, 87–88.

20. Wilke and Voigt, "Neuer Kurs," 98. For original audio, see Lyndon B. Johnson, "Speech to House of Rep. in Berlin," 19 August 1961, online by George Washington University, National Security Archive, *The Berlin Wall, Fifty Years Ago*, http://www2.gwu.edu/~nsarchive/NSAEBB/NSAEBB354.

21. Ulrich Enders and Konrad Reiser, "Die Bundesregierung im Wahljahr 1953," in *Die Kabinettsprotokolle der Bundesregierung*, vol. 6, *1953*, ed. Hans Booms (Boppard am Rhein, 1989), 55.

22. "Runderlaß des Staatssekretärs Hallstein," in *Akten zur auswärtigen Politik der Bundesrepublik Deutschland: 1953*, ed. Institut für Zeitgeschichte (Munich, 2001), vol. 1, 598.

23. Ibid., 599.

24. *Bulletin des Presse- und Informationsamtes der Bundesregierung* 122 (2 Juli 1953), Bonn, 1034.

25. Quoted in Wilke and Voigt, "Neuer Kurs," 83–84.

26. "Gespräch Chruschtschows mit dem Ersten Sekretär der SED, Walter Ulbricht, am 30. November 1960," Russian protocol, in Wettig, *Chruschtschows Westpolitik*, vol. 3, 43. In the note from the SED files about this conversation, the passage cited is missing. After the events of 17 June 1953, the accusation of wanting to abandon the GDR became an important argument with which Khrushchev and the other members of the presidium of the CPSU's Central Committee justified the imprisonment, conviction, and execution of Beria, their colleague and minister of interior affairs, after 26 July 1953. In 1955, Malenkov, who had been the lead prosecutor at the conference of the Central Committee in early July 1953, was accused of collaborating with Beria and stripped of his position as head of the Council of Ministers.

27. "Protokoll der Eröffnungssitzung der Regierungsdelegationen der Sowjetunion und der DDR," Moscow, 20 August 1953, SAPMO-BArch, NY 4890/471, 3, 4, 9.

28. Ibid., 11.

29. Ibid., 14.

30. See Roger Engelmann and Karl Wilhelm Fricke, *"Konzentrierte Schläge": Staatssicherheitsaktionen und politische Prozesse in der DDR 1953–1956* (Berlin, 1998).

31. "Protokoll der Eröffnungssitzung der Regierungsdelegationen der Sowjetunion und der DDR," Moscow, 20 August 1953, SAPMO-BArch, NY 4890/471, 16.

32. Weber, *Geschichte der DDR*, 177.

33. See "Vertrag über die Beziehungen zwischen der Deutschen Demokratischen Republik und der Union der Sozialistischen Sowjetrepubliken," Moscow, 20 September 1955, in Rauschning, *Rechtsstellung*, 221.

Chapter 8

A Prelude to the Second Berlin Crisis
The SED Party Congress

During each Berlin Crisis, the Soviet Union tried to use an offensive in Berlin to change the status quo in divided Germany to its advantage. The Soviet Union's goal of resolving the problem of West Berlin in a way that would benefit its own interests was evident in both crises. For Nikita S. Khrushchev, leader of the Soviet party and state, Stalin's failure in 1948 and 1949 provided an incentive to remedy the past with his Berlin advance of 1958. In his memoirs, Khrushchev wrote:

> When we began to face up to the problem of West Berlin after Stalin's death, we realized that the agreement which had liquidated the blockade of West Berlin [1948–49] was unfair. The West had managed to exploit the tension generated by the blockade and to impose conditions on East Germany which were even more constraining and one-sided than the ones set by the Potsdam Agreement. The international situation throughout Europe was highly unstable, and therefore internal stabilization was impossible for the German Democratic Republic [East Germany]. Germany was a sort of barometer. The slightest fluctuation in the pressure of the world political atmosphere naturally registered at that point where the forces of the two sides were squared off against each other.
>
> We wanted very much to relieve the tension which was building up dangerously over West Berlin, and we knew that the only way we could do it would be to conclude a peace treaty with the West. This posed a problem: on what basis would it be possible to reach an agreement with the Western powers? It was already too late to talk about a treaty that would reunify Germany because neither East Germany nor West Germany wanted to accept the social-political system of the other side.[1]

The long-term enforcement of SED rule in the GDR was an important motivator behind Khrushchev's Berlin policy, which, in its original goals, extended far beyond Berlin. At the beginning of "his" Berlin Crisis, Khrushchev did not intend to build a wall through the city. He and Ulbricht wanted the Western powers to withdraw from West Berlin so that they could transform it into a "demilitarized

Free City." But the crisis within the GDR, which manifested itself in climbing numbers of refugees and a decline in living standards, gave way to a new constellation in 1960. After the Vienna Summit in June 1961, the Soviet Union felt forced to return to the status quo and close the sector borders with a barbed wire fence, which later became the Wall.

Since the Soviet Union and the GDR were the two states pushing for change in 1958, the analysis of the second Berlin Crisis must focus on the interaction between the two state and party leaders. In addition to coordination and agreement between the supreme power and its vassal state, there were also diverging interests. Central here was the question of Soviet rights to remain in Berlin. Ulbricht wanted the Soviet Union to transfer its authorities to the GDR, including the control of transit routes. But the Soviet Union was primarily interested in an agreement on West Berlin with the United States and its allies, and it refused to give up at any time either its power to control the conflict or its right to remain in Berlin.

In terms of propaganda, the Fifth Party Congress of the SED in June 1958 represented the prologue to the second Berlin Crisis. The SED formulated its Germany policy from a position of perceived strength. Backed by Khrushchev, Ulbricht demanded a German peace treaty based on the Soviet draft of 1952 and put forth an economic strategy to overtake the Federal Republic in terms of workers' living standards. With this "major economic task," the SED wanted to cement socialism's victory in the competition of systems in divided Germany. Especially central to Ulbricht's program on Germany was solving his "Westberlin problem." But in 1958, he was not concerned with closing the border so much as maintaining control over this last remaining gateway to the West for the population of the GDR. He proposed that West Berlin be transformed into a "demilitarized Free City" on the territory of the GDR. The adjective "demilitarized" disguised his demands for the departure of the Western powers from Berlin, accompanied by the GDR's exclusive, unlimited control of West Berlin's transit connections by water, land, and air. The SED had coordinated these stipulations with the Soviet Union's planned offensive in Germany policy. Moreover, the head of the Kremlin believed that his desired "liquidation of the occupation regime in West Berlin" would be welcomed by the German people as liberation from the foreign occupation.[2]

Ulbricht was aware that the SED could not realize these goals relying on its own strength alone; they could only be implemented in conjunction with Soviet negotiations with the Western powers over a German peace treaty. In Ulbricht's view, these negotiations would provide the groundwork to fulfill another, more urgent goal of the SED: international recognition of the GDR as a second German state—a move that the Federal Republic was blocking in the West.

In the end, the SED built a wall through Berlin and closed the one open gateway in the fortified border between its state and the FRG. In light of this outcome, the goals of 1958 seem both insincere and unrealistic. But they cannot be viewed in isolation: setting these goals constituted an important part of the Soviet Union's offensive in Germany policy. Once again, the Soviets were trying to shift the border between spheres of influence in Germany to their territorial advantage and significantly weaken the sway of the United States and NATO in Europe.

At the beginning of their offensive, neither Khrushchev nor Ulbricht could foresee its actual culmination: the wall through Berlin. The SED's interests changed dramatically over the following three years; with the barbed wire fence running through Berlin, the victory of socialism in Germany that the party had hoped for would become its ultimate downfall. Precisely because the symbol of the Berlin Wall tends to overshadow the Wall's actual origins in remembrance culture today, it is important to emphasize the following point: in 1958, no one was concerned with building a wall through Berlin; they were rather concerned with the Western powers' departure from the city and the transformation of West Berlin into a integrated entity to be handed over to the SED state.

The Fifth Party Congress of the SED, 1958

As first secretary of the SED, Walter Ulbricht was the undisputed leader of the party and the state when the SED's Fifth Party Congress convened in July 1958. Ever since Stalin had made him leader of the "state-building" KPD in the Soviet zone in 1945, Ulbricht had mastered the central aspects of his task. He played a major role in using the CPSU as a model to transform the SED into a "new type" of party—one that was capable, in Moscow's view, of leading the GDR as the single state party. Ulbricht's career depended on a strict adherence to the party line of the CPSU, which, after the war, shifted often. The power holders of the GDR were not free to determine their own political line; "the patterns to imitate were dictated externally." The Russian historian Alexander Vatlin argues that it is nonsense "to talk about the national state dictatorships in Eastern Europe during the postwar period. Instead the region encompassed various national expressions of a single Communist dictatorship."[3]

Ulbricht's portrayal of the GDR's main economic pursuit and his demand for a peace treaty at the Fifth Party Conference were examples of this pattern of imitation. He took his cue from the CPSU's appeal to the "Soviet people . . . to catch up to and overtake the USA in the most important branches of agricultural and industrial production within a historically brief period of time." The realization of this goal would not only lay the economic foundation for a Communist society in the Soviet Union but would also represent the "victory" of Socialist order in the competitive fight against capitalism. Following this example, the SED developed the "main economic endeavor" of the GDR: "The people's economy of the German Democratic Republic must be developed in the span of so few years that it proves unambiguously the superiority of the GDR's Socialist society compared to the rule of imperialist forces in the Bonn state. As a result, the per-capita consumption of our working population with all of the important food and consumer goods will match and exceed the per-capita consumption of the entire population in West Germany. (Emphatic applause)."[4]

But the concept of exceeding West Germany was unrealistic: the economic basis of the GDR was much too narrow, and SED leadership knew it. At a conference of the Council for Mutual Economic Assistance (Comecon) in May 1958, Ulbricht had explained "that the cooperative task of making the GDR 'appealing to workers and the working class through high living standards and democratic and cultural development' had not been achieved. 'The original concept of turning the GDR into a showcase of the Socialist camp for the West could not yet be realized.'"[5] In reaction to this speech, Khrushchev approved the request by GDR leaders for economic aid, which strongly encouraged the SED to formulate its "overtaking concept" above. This, in turn, tied in directly to the demand for a peace treaty with Germany.

The Question of a Peace Treaty with Germany

Standing before the Fifth SED Party Congress, Ulbricht recalled the Soviet draft of a peace treaty with and about Germany from 1952. Now, six years later, he was following yet another Soviet impulse. Khrushchev had sent a letter to American President Eisenhower in June 1958 pushing for a peace treaty. Building continuity with the draft of 1952, Ulbricht enumerated six conditions for the conclusion of such a treaty: (1) a confederation between the two German states, (2) the two states' nonalignment with the two blocs, (3) a guarantee of human rights, but one that required ending "the domination of military and fascist powers" in West Germany, (4) the development of a "peaceful economy," (5) a drawing of Germany's borders according to the Potsdam Agreement, and (6) the deployment of national military forces in Germany. Ulbricht added that "securing peace has become the heart of the German question."[6]

The invocation of peace as the core of the German question had a solid foundation in 1958 but was still ambiguous. The two German states provided marching ground for NATO and the Warsaw Pact, and a military conflict would most likely culminate in the use of nuclear weapons, which would potentially lead to Germany's total destruction. At the same time, it was the Soviet troops in the GDR who protected the totalitarian power of the state party against its people on 17 June 1953, making these troops indispensible to the SED.

The resolution from the SED Party Congress "on the Struggle for Peace, for the Victory of Socialism, for Germany's National Rebirth as a Peace-Loving, Democratic State" took the line of peaceful coexistence and applied it to the German question.[7] The SED clarified its vision of how the two states with different social orders would coexist in Germany and how this would lead to reunification. As the Socialist core state, the GDR would take on an active role for historical reasons and reasons of international law.[8] The social conditions in the Federal Republic would have to change, but the GDR would address this through "peaceful means." The SED thus claimed its right to intervene in the Federal Republic. Indeed, there was no such thing as peaceful coexistence between the GDR and the

FRG in Germany; the GDR was "the rightful, sovereign, German state."[9] Follow-ing the logic of the SED, ending "German imperialism" was a precondition for "a policy of reunification, of Germany's national rebirth."[10]

Khrushchev Demands a Peace Agreement and a Solution to the Problem of West Berlin

Logically, for Ulbricht, the perspective presented at the Fifth Party Congress required the GDR's internal consolidation and international recognition. How-ever, the existence of West Berlin posed an urgent problem for this "consolidation" of the GDR. Ulbricht declared:

> The capital of the German Democratic Republic is Berlin. A part of the capital, Westberlin, is currently being misused as a base for the Cold War, spying, and sabotage of the GDR and the other countries in the Socialist camp. Our task is to change this unnatural situation that has been put in place (against the interests of the residents of Westberlin), to normalize relations in Berlin, and to turn the entire city into a city of peace and progress.
>
> In Berlin, it is necessary to fight this crucial battle against the American way of living and its decadence, which have settled into certain circles of Westberlin.[11]

This demand that the situation in West Berlin change became the core of the Soviet Berlin Ultimatum. It set the stage for Khrushchev's appearance at the Party Congress, during which he presented his offer for a peace treaty with Germany and demanded that West Berlin be transformed into a "Free City." He hailed the strength of the Socialist camp and positioned himself in a demonstrative gesture behind the SED's Germany policy, behind the party's proposal to build a confed-eration out of the two German states. In the end, he stated, the question of reuni-fication was an internal affair of the Germans. The Federal Republic's policy of Western integration had built a "wall" in Germany: "No one can deny that West Germany's accession into NATO, its introduction of compulsory military service, and now its decision to arm the Bundeswehr with nuclear and missile weapons, has further exacerbated international relations, especially relations between the two German states. Brick for brick, the Bonn government has erected a wall between the two parts of Germany."[12]

In examining the political maneuvers of the politicians involved in the sec-ond Berlin Crisis, it is important to remember their generational experience. This applies to Khrushchev as well. Speaking to an assembly of employees at an electro-chemical firm in East Germany, he recounted his World War II experiences from the Battle of Stalingrad in order to support his attack on the Federal Republic's security policy. He accused the FRG of

> preparing for a third world war, a world war that would be catastrophic for mankind. Hitler once chased the Germans east to create "Lebensraum." And what did he accomplish? Those who followed Hitler lost their heads. Comrades, I was a member

of the military council on the Stalingrad front. I know what kind of dogged fighting happened there. I saw the mountains of corpses of Soviet soldiers, and I saw the mountains of corpses of German soldiers. If you had seen what I saw, what Marshal [Rodion] Malinovsky saw—who is here with us today and commanded the Stalingrad front when he led the battle against [Erich von] Manstein—then you would know we must do everything possible to ensure that what happened in the past never happens again.[13]

Of course, it was a clever propaganda move to remind the Germans of this decisive battle and the lesson they should glean from it just thirteen years after the war. But the American and French presidents and the British prime minister had memories from that period, too. None of them had forgotten the war against National Socialist Germany, nor could they forget the Soviet Union's membership in the Anti-Hitler Coalition.

At the Party Congress, Khrushchev launched a massive attack on the Federal Government and its Germany policy. The FRG clearly believed, he said, that the Soviet Union "could agree to and even participate in the liquidation of the German Democratic Republic." Rhetorically, over the applause of the SED functionaries, he asked: "But can Communists really help remove a Socialist system? Can we really help turn the entire German people into cannon fodder for the American generals?"[14] In its final resolution, the SED reiterated its support for the Soviet peace program and formulated a list of basic demands for cooperation with the "working class and popular masses" of West Germany:

Collaboration in formulating the principles of a peace treaty with Germany. This would support détente and create a productive atmosphere of rapprochement between the two German states;

Rapprochement between the two German states through a path of negotiations based on equal standing and the signing of an agreement to build a confederation of the two German states in a step toward Germany's reunification;

Berlin is to be transformed into a city of peace and progress;

In connection with the establishment of a nuclear-free zone in Europe, it will be essential to eliminate the frontline politics of Westberlin by creating normal, peaceful, and democratic conditions in all of Berlin. This will lead to normalization in the relationship between Westberlin and the German Democratic Republic.[15]

Khrushchev's speech and the final resolution of the SED Party Conference were part of the propaganda preparation for and staging of the coming ultimatum. Since early 1958, Moscow had worked on a draft of a peace treaty for Germany, about which the SED was also informed.[16] In August of the same year, Secretary of the Central Committee Yuri V. Andropov submitted a report to the CPSU executive presidium on the alarming increase in the number of refugees fleeing the GDR compared to the previous year. He especially stressed their social composition: many were urgently needed specialists from the intelligentsia. "The unspoken message was that something definitely had to be done."[17] The party apparatus of the CPSU remembered all too well the rising refugee numbers in 1952–53, which signaled the first existential crisis of the SED state and went ignored in Moscow until after Stalin's death. This time, after consulting with the Kremlin, the GDR government opened the diplomatic discussion. In a note to the four powers on 4 September 1958, the SED demanded that they sign a peace treaty with Germany as soon as possible. The Soviet Union reacted positively; among the Western powers, the note had no effect.

SED Propaganda and the West Berlin Elections of 1958

The SED attempted to turn the West Berlin parliamentary elections of 1958 into an open discussion of its demand to change Berlin's status.[18] During the final phase of the elections, Ulbricht positioned himself fundamentally on the status of Berlin. In his speech, which had been approved by Moscow, he repeated his assertion that Berlin was the capital of the GDR and the entire city lay on the GDR's territory. The "occupation authority of the Western powers" in West Berlin, he stated, no longer had any legal basis but was "presently still a fact." The Western powers had broken the Potsdam Agreement, thereby "burying the legal basis of their presence in Berlin and forfeiting any moral-political claim to the continuation of their occupation in Westberlin."[19] The Soviet threat to hold separate negotiations with the GDR regarding Allied rights in Berlin only had a chance internationally if the GDR presented itself as a sovereign state and was dealt with as such. Ulbricht demanded respect for the sovereignty of the GDR over its capital, Berlin, including control of the transit routes between the Western sectors and West Germany: "The German Democratic Republic, which does not recognize any limitation on its sovereignty and exercises supreme authority in and for Berlin, bases its policies on the reality of the situation."[20] He then referred to an exchange of letters between the Ministry for Foreign Affairs of the GDR and its Soviet counterpart in 1955 in connection with a treaty between the Soviet Union and the GDR, in which the GDR confirmed

> that, for the time being, Soviet armed forces in the German Democratic Republic would exercise control over the transportation of troops and goods by the three garrisons stationed in Westberlin, namely France, England, and the USA, between West Germany and Westberlin. This regulation does not rule out the GDR's authority over these issues. Transportation between the German Democratic Republic and the Western sectors of Berlin, as well as transportation inside of Berlin, will not be affected by any of these agreements. This also applies to flying over the territory of the GDR in the air corridors between West Germany and Berlin, beyond the transport of supplies to the Westberlin garrisons of the USA, England, and France. In negotiations regarding the creation of a federation between the two German states, these types of issues will, of course, be subject to debate.[21]

The voters of West Berlin answered Ulbricht's threats unequivocally on 7 December 1958 in the Abgeordnetenhaus elections: with a participation rate of 93 percent, it represented a popular referendum against the SED, which only received 1.9 percent of the vote. Just a few days after Ulbricht announced the necessary changes in Berlin, Khrushchev took the stage at the Moscow Sports Palace on 10 November and repeated Ulbricht's demands. The second Berlin Crisis had begun.[22]

Notes

1. Nikita S. Khrushchev, *Khrushchev Remembers*, trans. and ed. Strobe Talbott (Boston, 1970), 452–53.

2. Gerhard Wettig, *Sowjetische Deutschland-Politik 1953 bis 1958: Korrekturen an Stalins Erbe, Chruschtschows Aufstieg und der Weg zum Berlin-Ultimatum* (Munich, 2011), 140.

3. Alexander Vatlin, "Die unvollendete Vergangenheit: über den Umgang mit der kommunistischen Geschichte im heutigen Russland," *Jahrbuch für Historische Kommunismusforschung* (2010): 288–89.

4. Walter Ulbricht, "Der Kampf um den Frieden, für den Sieg des Sozialismus, für die nationale Wiedergeburt Deutschlands als friedliebender, demokratischer Staat: Aus dem Referat auf dem V. Parteitag der SED vom 10. bis 16. Juli 1958," 10 July 1958, in Ulbricht, *Arbeiterbewegung*, vol. 7, 319.

5. Lemke, *Einheit*, 417.

6. Ulbricht, "Der Kampf um den Frieden, für den Sieg des Sozialismus, für die nationale Wiedergeburt Deutschlands als friedliebender, demokratischer Staat," in Ulbricht, *Arbeiterbewegung*, vol. 7, 293–94.

7. See "Beschluss des V. Parteitages der SED über den Kampf um den Frieden, für den Sieg des Sozialismus, für die nationale Wiedergeburt Deutschlands als friedliebender, demokratischer Staat," in *Protokoll der Verhandlungen des V. Parteitages der Sozialistischen Einheitspartei Deutschlands, 10. bis 16. Juli 1958 in der Werner-Seelenbinder-Halle zu Berlin* (Berlin (East), 1959), vol. 2, 1329–1416.

8. Lemke, *Einheit*, 377.

9. "Beschluss des V. Parteitages der SED," in *Protokoll der Verhandlungen des V. Parteitags der SED*, vol. 2, 1347.

10. Lemke, *Einheit*, 377.

11. "Beschluss des V. Parteitages der SED," in *Protokoll der Verhandlungen des V. Parteitags der SED*, vol. 2, 1348.

12. "Begrüßungsansprache (KPdSU)," speech by Nikita S. Khrushchev, 11 July 1958, in *Protokoll des V. Parteitags der SED*, vol. 1, 279.

13. "Die Rede des Genossen Chruschtschow am 9.7.1958 vor der Belegschaft im Kulturhaus des EKB [Elektrochemisches Kombinat Bitterfeld]," Ministry for State Security, Erich Mielke to Walter Ulbricht, Berlin, 21 July 1958, SAPMO-BArch, NY 4182/1096.

14. "Begrüßungsansprache (KPdSU)," speech by Nikita S. Khrushchev, 11 July 1958, in *Protokoll des V. Parteitags der SED*, vol. 1, 278.

15. "Beschluss des V. Parteitages der SED," in *Protokoll der Verhandlungen des V. Parteitags der SED*, vol. 2, 1336.

16. See Michael Lemke, *Die Berlinkrise 1958 bis 1963: Interessen und Handlungsspielräume der SED im Ost-West-Konflikt* (Berlin, 1995), 99.

17. Gerhard Wettig, *Chruschtschows Berlin-Krise 1958 bis 1963: Drohpolitik und Mauerbau* (Munich, 2006), 21.

18. Since 1957, the SED's district headquarters in Berlin had been preparing for the party to participate in the 1958 elections to West Berlin's Abgeordnetenhaus, even though the SED had not taken part in any Abgeordnetenhaus election since 1948. The district headquarters established an "agitation commission," laid out the role of the party newspaper and the Berlin radio stations in the elections, and determined that the choice of candidates would be "undertaken well in advance by the office of the district headquarters." Büro der SED-Bezirksleitung Groß-Berlin, Material, "Die Lage in Westberlin und unsere Aufgaben," SAPMO-BArch, NY 4182/1096.

19. Walter Ulbricht, "An die Arbeiterschaft und an alle friedliebenden Bürger Westberlins!: Aus der Rede vor Westberliner Wählern," 27 October 1958, in Ulbricht, *Arbeiterbewegung*, vol. 7, 649.

20. Ibid..

21. Ibid., 649–50. On approving this speech with Moscow, see Wettig, *Chruschtschows Berlin-Krise*, 24.

22. "'Westmächte zerstörten Rechtsgrundlage ihres Aufenthaltes in Berlin—UdSSR fest an der Seite der DDR,' Aus der Erklärung des Vorsitzenden des Ministerrates der UdSSR, Nikita S. Chruschtschow, zur Deutschlandfrage und über Berlin, 10.11.1958," in *Dokumente zur Deutschlandpolitik der Sowjetunion*, vol. 2, *Vom IV. Parteitag der SED (30.3.–6.4.1954) bis zur Überreichung des zweiten sowjetischen Entwurfs für einen Friedensvertrag mit Deutschland (10.1.1959)* (Berlin (East), 1963), 655.

Chapter 9

THE SOVIET UNION'S 1958 BERLIN ULTIMATUM

A Bolt of Lightning: Khrushchev's Speech on 10 November 1958

Khrushchev's appearance at the Moscow Sports Palace on 10 November 1958 was the bolt of lightning that sparked the second Berlin Crisis. A few days earlier, on 6 November, the presidium of the CPSU Central Committee had advised Khrushchev on his "Thoughts on Germany"; only Anastas Mikoyan contradicted the party leader's approach. Mikoyan feared "a drastic deterioration in the East–West conflict."[1] Khrushchev directed his main attack toward the West German government, which he accused of planning a new war. He warned:

> To march against the East would mean marching to death for Western Germany.
>
> It is high time to realize that the times when the imperialists could act from "positions of strength" with impunity have gone never to return, and try as they may, the imperialists will not be able to change the balance of forces in their favour. Nor should they forget the geographical position of Western Germany which—with military techniques as they are today—would not survive a single day of modern warfare. We do not want another military conflict. It would be fatal to Western Germany and would bring untold calamities to the peoples of other countries. The Soviet Union and the other socialist countries are doing everything to keep the adventurists dreaming of new wars from taking the fatal step.[2]

Addressing the three Western powers, he explained: "The German question, in the sense of the reunification of the two German states now in existence, can only be settled by the German people themselves along the lines of *rapprochement* between these states. The conclusion of a peace treaty with Germany is an entirely different matter which, indeed, should be settled primarily by the four powers which formed the anti-Hitler coalition, in co-operation with representatives of Germany. The signing of a peace treaty with Germany would help to normalise the entire situation in Germany and in Europe in general."[3] The Potsdam Agreement of 1945 stood at the center of Khrushchev's argument, and he accused the Western powers of breaking their Allied accords on Germany by creating the Federal Republic and rearming the new country. He claimed that the Western powers only ever referred to the Allied agreements when doing so boosted their stance vis-à-vis their rights in Berlin. Now it was time "to set ourselves free from obligations under the Potsdam Agreement, obligations which have outlived themselves and which the western powers are clinging to, and to pursue with regard to Berlin a policy that would spring from the interests of the Warsaw Treaty,"[4] of which the GDR was a member. Khrushchev called the Berlin regulation of 1944–45 outdated and annulled it unilaterally. "The SED highlighted one passage of the speech in particular explaining that the time had come 'for the signatories of the Potsdam Agreement to renounce the remnants of the occupation régime in Berlin.'"[5] The party hoped that this would apply not only to the Western powers but also to the Soviet Union, which still directly infringed on the sovereignty of the GDR.

The Soviet Union's threat to unilaterally eliminate the four-power status in Berlin triggered great anxiety in the West and precipitated hectic diplomatic activity. The West German government declared on 12 November that the Soviet decision would be a "breach of valid international law" and would aggravate the "current political tensions worldwide," an escalation for which the Soviet Union would be "solely responsible." The Federal Government reminded the Western powers of their pledge to maintain the four-power status of Berlin and to counteract any "threat to Berlin." The statement's conclusion reiterates once more the alarm that Khrushchev's speech elicited from the Federal Government and the German public: "The Federal Government, the people of Berlin, the whole German population, and the entire free world trust in the declarations of the Western powers and in the effective protection that their guarantees confer upon the German people."[6]

A few days later, American Secretary of State John F. Dulles assured Wilhelm Grewe, the West German ambassador, that "neither in Congress nor in the government circles of Washington were there differences in opinion regarding the necessity to defend Berlin and its connection routes—even at the risk of military entanglement. The only uncertainty lay in the methods of crisis management and the development of a tactical consensus with Britain and France."[7] The British Foreign Office reacted pragmatically. In a memorandum from 14 November, the Office listed three alternatives at the West's disposal: "'(a.) Depart from Berlin; (b.) Use force; (c.) Remain in Berlin, although this would mean negotiating with the GDR and, if necessary, recognising it.' For London it was 'clear . . . that course (a.) was out of the question, and that course (c.) should definitely be prioritised over course (b.).' The memorandum was sent as a telegram to the British embassy in Washington."[8] With this statement, the British tried to take the lead in formulating an appropriate reaction within the Western alliance—but the attempt failed. "In Washington and Paris, people were more than surprised by the British memorandum; in Bonn they were appalled."[9] In contrast to the British, French President Charles de Gaulle presented himself to Adenauer as a reliable partner in his insistence upon retaining the status quo. For Adenauer and de Gaulle, "there was nothing to negotiate because it was impossible to offer Khrushchev anything that would satisfy him."[10]

Khrushchev's Motives

In retrospect, it is clear that Khrushchev seriously misjudged the situation when he began this political offensive. He saw differences among the Western powers with respect to the German question but underestimated the readiness of the United States to hold its position in Berlin, the political weight of the Federal Republic in NATO, and the ability of the Western powers to agree on a joint strategy against the Soviet Union despite their differences. In 1957, he had asserted himself over Molotov and Malenkov during the inner-party power struggle and had now become the unchallenged leader of party and state.[11] By 1958, the situation looked much more conducive to the fulfillment of Khrushchev's goals: with Sputnik's launch and Soviet nuclear armament, the Soviet Union appeared to have finally risen to a position of nearly equal military standing with the United States.

Khrushchev considered his own decisions to be in harmony with Soviet policy on Berlin after 1945.[12] Stalin's successor wanted to transform the Soviet defeat of 1949 into victory. Henry Kissinger cites two central areas of interest in Soviet policy that were responsible for the Berlin offensive: first, the confrontation between the Soviet Union and the United States in Germany and Europe, and second, the stability of the USSR's own bloc. West Berlin's geopolitical significance, along with the lack of agreement between the USSR and the Western powers on the transit routes to West Berlin, had become an Achilles' heel for the Western powers' position in Europe. Khrushchev skillfully selected his point of attack: "The challenge inherent in East German control of the access routes to Berlin was indirect. It confronted the democracies with the choice of recognizing the East German satellite or threatening to go to war over the technical issue of who was to stamp transit documents." In Kissinger's view, the Soviet Union was also protecting the "most fragile link" in its sphere of influence:

> Faced with the larger, more prosperous West Germany on its border, and recognized diplomatically only by its fellow Soviet satellite states, East Germany lacked legitimacy. The manpower drain through Berlin threatened its very survival. If something was not done, the leaders of East Berlin reasoned, the whole state could collapse in a matter of years. That would mean a devastating blow to the Soviet sphere of influence, which Khrushchev was attempting to consolidate. By cutting off the escape route, Khrushchev hoped to give his East German satellite a new lease on life. And by forcing a Western retreat, he sought to weaken the Federal Republic's Western ties.[13]

Weakening the West—especially the American position in Europe—was precisely Khrushchev's goal, according to Gerhard Wettig's semantic analysis:

Khrushchev's use of the Russian term *vol'nyi gorod* indicated that he had a different "freedom" in mind than that of the West.* By claiming to support the freedom of the city, he attempted to deprive the Western powers of their justification to remain in Berlin. They were nothing more than occupiers, he argued, who in reality pursued aggressive goals. According to [Khrushchev's] convictions—which he only expressed openly in his own camp—the issue was not simply an isolated outpost with two million people, as he portrayed it to most of his conversation partners. Since the Soviet blockade of 1948–49, the defense of West Berlin had come to symbolize the American pledge to Western Europe. If the United States were to give up the city, NATO would lose its political foundation because the partners' trust in the protection of the leading power would be destroyed. This was precisely what Khrushchev wanted: changes in Berlin and Germany should make the Atlantic Treaty untenable, relaxing the situation in Europe by getting rid of his Western opponent.

But the intention to dramatically weaken the West was supposed to remain hidden. Therefore, the Kremlin decided not to demand the Federal Republic's immediate departure from the alliance. Generally Khrushchev avoided revealing his real goal: to question the existential foundations of the Western alliance.[14]

---

* In Russian, *vol'nyi* means "free" in the sense of not being bound to anything. If, however, the speaker means personal freedom along the lines of human rights, he or she uses the word *svobodnyi*.

According to Russian historians Vladislav Zubok and Constantine Pleshakov, a further motive behind the Soviet Ultimatum was the debate in NATO around the creation of European nuclear forces, in the context of which the Federal Republic could have come into possession of nuclear weapons.[15] This aspect is relevant to the Berlin Crisis as well. The idea of the Federal Republic having nuclear weapon capabilities at its disposal through NATO was unbearable to Soviet leadership. But the subject was not clear-cut in the Western camp, either; British Prime Minister Harold Macmillan rejected the idea as well.[16]

The maximum goal of the Soviet peace treaty was the demilitarization and neutralization of Germany and the transformation of West Berlin into a "Free City" on the territory of the GDR. If this dream had materialized, it would have undermined the security policy of the Western powers and "led to the collapse of NATO," according to Soviet Foreign Minister Gromyko.[17] Khrushchev was concerned with effecting a fundamental shift in the power relationship between the Soviet Empire and the United States in Europe. Just before the end of the Geneva conference of foreign ministers in 1959, as Khrushchev prepared to meet with the American president, he remarked: "I think it will be impossible to talk to the USA about signing a peace treaty with Germany. To them it would amount to capitulation."[18] This clearly indicated the goal behind Khrushchev's offensive in Berlin, and at the same time it described his dilemma: he could not use negotiations to force the Western powers to abandon their position in Berlin. Gerhard Wettig examines the strategy more closely:

Victory without war would come by shifting the decision to take military action and thereby the risk of war onto the other side. The defensive West rather than the Soviet aggressor would be pressured into choosing war. Khrushchev felt that if the USSR signed a peace treaty with the GDR and established the closed access routes as a fait accompli, the Western powers would not be able to prevent a change in the status quo; they could only try to reverse it after the fact. This, in turn, would mean launching an armed attack on the new status quo. In order to keep West Berlin, they would have to decide to go to war with the Soviet Union. And according to [Khrushchev's] calculations, they would avoid taking this step at all costs.[19]

Henry Kissinger considers Khrushchev's behavior to embody an "oddly inconclusive quality" of Soviet conduct. "Khrushchev pursued neither confrontation nor negotiation consistently"—with positive implications for the Western democracies, which were not in agreement on the topic either. Thus, Khrushchev "spared the Atlantic Alliance what might have turned into its greatest crisis," despite his threats of nuclear war.[20]

The Berlin Ultimatum

The Soviet Union's note to the Western powers on 27 November 1958 paraphrased Khrushchev's speech in the Moscow Sports Palace and turned it into a diplomatic document. Khrushchev informed the Western powers that an "independent solution" to the Berlin question must be found. After a lengthy historical summary, the Soviet government began a discussion of the wartime Allied agreements, which it now regarded as "null and void":

> The USA, Great Britain, and France have long since rejected the essentials of the treaties and agreements concluded during the war against Hitler Germany and after its defeat. The Soviet Government is doing no more than drawing conclusions that inevitably ensue for the Soviet Union from this actual state of affairs.
>
> Pursuant to the foregoing and proceeding from the principle of respect for the sovereignty of the German Democratic Republic, the Soviet Government will enter into negotiations with the Government of the GDR at an appropriate time with a view to transferring to the German Democratic Republic the functions temporarily performed by the Soviet authorities by virtue of the above-mentioned Allied agreements and under the agreement between the USSR and the GDR of September 20, 1955....
>
> Should the Government of the United States be unwilling to contribute ... to the implementation of the political principles of the Allied agreements on Germany, it will have no reason, either legal or moral, for insisting on the preservation of the Four-Power status of Berlin.[21]

This was the fundamental reasoning behind Khrushchev's ultimatum. With it, the Soviet Union put pressure on the Western powers to act soon; the note referred to a transitional period of six months: "The Soviet Government proposes to make no changes in the present procedure for military traffic of the USA, Great Britain, and France from West Berlin to the FRG for half a year. It regards such a period as fully sufficient to provide a sound basis for the solution of the questions connected with the change in Berlin's situation and to prevent a possibility of any complications, provided, naturally, that the governments of the Western powers do not deliberately seek such complications."[22] This sounded like an order to leave, but it was actually an offer to negotiate with the Western powers on the basis of inter-Allied rights—whose future validity, however, the Soviet government denied. As the ultimatum laid out, the Western powers' departure was the only logical step: "The Soviet Government makes this approach to the Government of the USA, guided by the desire to achieve a relaxation of international tension. . . . Of course, the most correct and natural way to solve the problem would be for the western part of Berlin, now actually detached from the GDR, to be reunited with its eastern part and for Berlin to become a unified city within the state in whose territory it is situated."[23]

The Soviet note used the term "occupation regime" to describe the Western powers in their sectors of Berlin, which fundamentally ignored the right of West Berliners to self-determination. Following the blockade of 1948–49, the overwhelming majority of West Berlin residents entrusted the Western powers as "protector states" with guarding their freedom. For Moscow, Article 6 of the Germany Treaty between the Federal Republic and its partners, which stipulated the protection of West Berlin and the city's ties to the alliance until reunification in freedom (as it was still formulated at the time) only had negative implications. From Khrushchev and Ulbricht's perspective, it was precisely these ties that had to be cut. The Germany Treaty also arranged for reciprocal consultation between the West German government and its partners: "The Three Powers will consult with the Federal Republic in regard to the exercise of their rights relating to Berlin" ("Convention on Relations Between the Three Powers and the Federal Republic of Germany, May 26, 1952," in U.S. Dept. of State, *Documents on Germany*, 427).

Naturally Khrushchev was aware of this reality and respected it to the extent that he offered to negotiate with the Federal Republic even while exerting political pressure. Soviet policy on Berlin did not presume a quick reunification of the divided city; it acknowledged and accounted for the diverging developments in the two city halves. The Soviet government offered the Western powers a compromise for future negotiations:

> The Soviet Government on its part would consider it possible to solve the West Berlin question at the present time by the conversion of West Berlin into an independent political unit—a free city, without any state, including both existing German states, interfering in its life. Specifically, it might be possible to agree that the territory of the free city be demilitarized and that no armed forces be contained therein. . . .
>
> The Four Powers which shared in the administration of Berlin after the war could, as well as both of the German states, undertake to respect the status of West Berlin as a free city. . . .

It is obvious that, considering the specific position of West Berlin, which lies within the territory of the GDR and is cut off from the outside world, the question would arise of some kind of arrangement with the German Democratic Republic concerning guarantees of unhindered communications between the free city and the outside world—both to the East and to the West—with the object of free movement of passenger and freight traffic. In its turn West Berlin would undertake not to permit on its territory any hostile subversive activity directed against the GDR or any other state.

The above-mentioned solution of the problem of West Berlin's status would be an important step toward normalizing the situation in Berlin. ("Note From the Soviet Union to the United States Regarding the Status of Berlin and the Potsdam Agreements, November 27, 1958," extracts, in U.S. Dept. of State, *Documents on Germany*, 557.)

The threat to the Western powers lay in the announcement that they would have to negotiate directly with the GDR regarding transit routes to Berlin starting at the end of May 1959. The second Berlin Crisis, which would last for four years, had begun.

Since NATO's guarantee of protection included the Western forces stationed in Berlin, the Soviet Union's unilateral decision to terminate Berlin's status and transfer control of the Western powers' transit routes to the GDR entailed the risk of war. If the Western powers refused to accept that GDR institutions would control all connections between the Federal Republic and West Berlin, then they would have to take military measures. And if they consented to this step, they would enter into a military conflict with the Soviet Union, which could lead to nuclear escalation. Evidently, in Khrushchev's assessment of this war scenario, he was confident that the West would shy away from the risk of nuclear war. And if NATO did attempt to keep the transit routes open through military force, the West would be exposed to the rest of the world as the true aggressor.

In terms of security policy, the nuclear standoff between the two superpowers marked a major difference between the second Berlin Crisis and the first in 1948–49. After Sputnik's successful launch into the earth's orbit in 1957, Khrushchev understood "that nuclear bipolarity became the basic feature of the Cold War, as both the Soviet Union and the United States gained the capacity to destroy each other and the entire world. . . . Khrushchev, for all his later bravado, developed a sense of the ultimate limits imposed by nuclear weapons on statesmanship."[24] The Soviet Union went on to test its hydrogen bomb in 1958. Analyzing the American reaction to the Soviet Ultimatum, Henry Kissinger begins by assessing the consequences for U.S. foreign policy that arose from losing its monopoly on nuclear weapons. The United States had to face its own "willingness to run risks" in terms of using military force in international crisis situations, and this "constrained its freedom of diplomatic maneuver."[25] In other words, avoiding nuclear war slowly became the top priority in the politics of both nuclear powers—even though Khrushchev still made use of his potential nuclear threat. At the time of the Berlin Ultimatum, however, he bluffed that the Americans were still superior to the Soviet Union regarding the number of strategic, long-range missiles, a logic that allowed Khrushchev to launch his offensive from a position of supposed inferiority.

Another serious difference existed between the blockade of transit routes in 1948–49 and the situation ten years later. The first Berlin Crisis took place in a destroyed city with a population that had grown accustomed to years of food rationing, hunger, and destitution. By 1958, the state of the Western sectors had completely changed. West Berlin had transformed into a prosperous metropolis, which, if it came down to it, could no longer be supplied adequately through an airlift. Since there was still no contract to regulate the transit routes to West Germany, West Berlin was extremely susceptible to pressure from the East.

Multiple Reactions from the West

The ultimatum had immediate consequences within the Western alliance and brought out the differing interests among its member states. It represented a direct affront to Adenauer's course: the Western integration of the Federal Republic and continued insistence on German reunification based on free elections in all of Germany. Kissinger agreed with Adenauer that isolating the Federal Republic from the West represented one of the main goals of the Soviet offensive:

> The Soviet agenda for negotiations placed Bonn in a no-win situation. In return for any concessions it might make, the West would at best receive what it already had: access to Berlin. At the same time, the East German satellite would be given a veto on German unification which would lead either to a stalemate or to an outcome Adenauer described in his memoirs as follows: " . . . we could not buy the reunification of Germany at the price of loosening Germany from the Western bloc and giving up the achievements of European integration. Because the result would be that a defenseless, unbound Germany in the middle of Europe would be created, that necessarily would be tempted to play off the East against the West."[26]

The Soviet sources available today confirm the chancellor's suspicion. Adenauer saw no reason to negotiate at all under Khrushchev's conditions. But as Kissinger puts it, West Germany's problem was that Adenauer's views "were not shared by his Anglo-American allies, least of all by Great Britain."[27]

At the Paris conference of foreign ministers in 1949, the four powers had already made the status quo in Germany the basis of their agreement to lift the Berlin Blockade and regulate German interzonal trade. The Western powers did not understand why Khrushchev had decided to terminate this modus vivendi, which had even allowed for the establishment of two German states. The United States and Great Britain tried feverishly to compromise with the Soviet Union, willing to grant the GDR more recognition internationally and concede to other Soviet demands. Kissinger notes the internal danger of these negotiations for West Germany: "It was ironic that Great Britain and the United States should be urging Germany onto a course that would almost certainly lead to greater German nationalism, while Adenauer, having far less confidence in his own countrymen, remained determined not to expose them to that temptation. Eisenhower and Macmillan were placing their faith in the Germans' conversion; Adenauer could not forget their original sin."[28]

In Adenauer's view, an agreement between the Western powers and the Soviet Union that went over the heads of the Germans would destroy the foreign policy foundation of his push for the Federal Republic's Western integration. After all, his government had used the Germany Treaty to tie Western integration to a promise by the Western powers that they would not recognize the GDR as a second German state.

The Federal Republic and West Berlin were dependent upon the protection of the Western powers, in particular the United States, against Soviet dominance. This relationship of dependency was even clear to the Social Democratic opposition, which, in contrast to Adenauer, prioritized German reunification over the FRG's Western integration. Willy Brandt, the Social Democratic governing mayor of Berlin, presented the SPD's plan for Germany in Washington in February 1959.[29] The plan had been drafted in time for the coming conference of foreign ministers in Geneva and advocated the neutralization of a unified Germany. Secretary of State Dulles answered Brandt by firmly confronting him with American interests, citing the reality of the international political situation. Détente between the two blocs in Europe would only be possible based on the status quo of divided Germany. Therefore, the Geneva conference would no longer discuss the topic of German unity:

> Dulles impressed upon [Brandt] that "standard demands for free elections would not lead to progress." As for Brandt's inquiry into the "possibility of a special status for Germany," [Dulles] replied "icily," as Brandt recalled later, "We and the Russians might disagree on a thousand things. But there is one point on which we have exactly the same opinion: we will not allow for a reunified, armed Germany to float around in no man's land between the East and the West." For Brandt this was clear: there was "something of an unspoken compact between Moscow and Washington to respect the spheres of influence in Europe," and this included accepting the division of Germany in the long term.[30]

Opposition parties in Central and Eastern Europe summed up this unspoken arrangement between Washington and Moscow a few years later with the saying, "Yalta endures." After Brandt's conversation with Dulles, the fate of the SPD's Germany plan was sealed: it disappeared from the political agenda altogether. Elements of it reappeared in Social Democratic Ostpolitik after 1969, when the Federal Republic faced a reassessment of the status quo in Germany and the recognition of the GDR.

The FRG could hardly change the constellation of world politics through its strength alone. The West German government and the (West) Berlin Senate had to simply accept the state of affairs, which meant accepting the impossibility of rapid reunification. The status quo of division became a new starting point for West German Ostpolitik after the construction of the Berlin Wall, even though the Federal Government never abandoned its constitutional mandate for German reunification. But only through a new strategy of Ostpolitik did the Federal

Republic have any chance at all of participating constructively in the regulation of the status quo in divided Germany; it marked the beginning of a learning process that would last for years.

In 1958, NATO served as the headquarters from which to formulate a joint response by the West to the Soviet Ultimatum. The Federal Republic appealed to the alliance to stand firm in order to maintain the status quo in Berlin. John F. Dulles set the tone: "Confidence, clear lines, no faltering!" Drawing a comparison to Hitler, the secretary of state "pointed out that it was imperative to put the aggressor in his place from the very beginning."[31] The communiqué from NATO's ministerial meeting on 16 December 1958 warned the Soviet Union that its ultimatum had already provoked a serious situation—one that the alliance would have to address with resolve: "The member states of NATO could not approve a solution of the Berlin question which jeopardized the right of the three Western Powers to remain in Berlin . . . and did not assure freedom of communication between that city and the free world. The Soviet Union would be responsible for any action which had the effect of hampering this free communication or endangering this freedom."[32] At the same time, the member states declared their readiness to consider the problem of "Germany as a whole. . . . as well as those of European security and disarmament."[33] With this response, the Western powers rejected the ultimatum but simultaneously signaled their willingness to negotiate. The alliance had to feel out the real intentions of the Soviet Union. In case conflict did arise, Dulles announced to French Foreign Minister Maurice Couve de Murville his intention "to maneuver the Soviets into a situation where they would fire the first shot."[34] That was his answer to Khrushchev. Dulles did not believe in the immediate threat of Soviet attack; the Soviet Army was still in a transitional phase, converting their nuclear delivery systems from bombers to missiles.

It was only after the Western powers had positioned themselves that the Soviet government presented its draft of a peace treaty with Germany.

Notes

1. Wettig, *Chruschtschows Berlin-Krise*, 25.
2. "Address by the Chairman Khrushchev Proposing That the Western Powers Thenceforth Deal Directly with the German Democratic Republic on Any Questions Concerning Berlin," Moscow, 10 November 1958, extract, in U.S. Dept. of State, *Documents on Germany*, 542.
3. Ibid., 543.
4. Ibid., 546.
5. Lemke, *Berlinkrise*, 100.
6. "Erklärung der Bundesregierung zur sowjetischen Berlin-Politik vom 12.11.1958," in Auswärtiges Amt, *40 Jahre Außenpolitik*, 112–13.

7. Wilhelm G. Grewe, *Rückblenden 1976–1951: Aufzeichnungen eines Augenzeugen deutscher Außenpolitik von Adenauer bis Schmidt* (Frankfurt am Main, 1979), 364.

8. Rolf Steininger, *Der Mauerbau: Die Westmächte und Adenauer in der Berlinkrise 1958–1963* (Munich, 2001), 30.

9. Ibid., 31.

10. Ibid., 48.

11. See Michael S. Voslensky, *Sterbliche Götter: Die Lehrmeister der Nomenklatura* (Vienna, 1989), 205–6.

12. This was also a reflection of Khrushchev's character. American Secretary of State Dulles gave his assessment of Khrushchev at the NATO conference of foreign ministers in 1958. Dulles called him "impulsive, with certain characteristics of a gambler"; it was important to anticipate this character trait and especially to consider that the gambler wanted to win. "Telegram From the Delegation to the North Atlantic Council Ministerial Meeting to the Department of State," Paris, 17 December 1958, in U.S. Dept. of State, *FRUS, 1958–1960*, vol. 8, *Berlin Crisis, 1958–1959*, ed. Charles S. Sampson (Washington, 1993), 210.

13. Kissinger, *Diplomacy*, 571.

14. Gerhard Wettig, "Chruščev und die Berliner Mauer: Forderung nach einem Friedensvertrag 1961–1963," in Karner et al., *Wiener Gipfel*, 646–47. Khrushchev emphasized often that his demand for the creation of a "Free City" championed the freedom of West Berlin and its residents, who would no longer need to be defended by the Western powers.

15. See Zubok and Pleshakov, *Inside the Kremlin's Cold War*, 195–96.

16. See Steininger, *Mauerbau*, 32.

17. Wettig, *Chruschtschows Berlin-Krise*, 35.

18. Notes by Nikita S. Khrushchev, 10 August 1959, *Archive of the Ludwig Boltzmann Institute for Research on War Consequences (AdBIK)*.

19. Wettig, "Chruščev," 651.

20. Kissinger, *Diplomacy*, 580.

21. "Note From the Soviet Union to the United States Regarding the Status of Berlin and the Potsdam Agreements, November 27, 1958," extracts, in U.S. Dept. of State, *Documents on Germany*, 555–56.

22. Ibid., 559.

23. Ibid., 556.

24. Zubok and Pleshakov, *Inside the Kremlin's Cold War*, 189.

25. Kissinger, *Diplomacy*, 573.

26. Ibid., 572.

27. Ibid., 572–73.

28. Ibid., 578.

29. See Theo Pirker, *Die SPD nach Hitler: Die Geschichte der Sozialdemokratischen Partei Deutschlands, 1945–1964* (Munich, 1965), 268–73.

30. Steininger, *Deutsche Geschichte*, vol. 3, 51–52.

31. Steininger, *Mauerbau*, 53–54.

32. NATO, "Declaration on Berlin," 16–18 December 1958, *NATO e-Library*, http://www.nato.int/cps/en/SID-0F390516-41373721/natolive/official_texts_17646.htm.

33. Ibid.

34. Steininger, *Mauerbau*, 54.

Chapter 10

NEGOTIATIONS OVER A PEACE TREATY AND THE "FREE CITY OF WESTBERLIN"

Moscow Drafts

After the Soviet Ultimatum and the first shocked reactions from the Western powers, the Soviet Ministry of Foreign Affairs produced drafts related to a peace treaty with Germany, a statute for the "Free City of Westberlin," and a separate peace treaty between the Socialist states and the GDR. The USSR first submitted the draft of a peace treaty with Germany to Poland and Czechoslovakia for their approval. Ulbricht then informed Khrushchev on 3 January 1959 that the SED Politburo was also "satisfied [with] the draft of the 'Peace Treaty with Germany.'"[1] Ulbricht announced that the GDR's Council of Ministers planned to conclude a treaty between the GDR and the Federal Republic to build a confederation as soon as the Western powers received the draft of the peace treaty in March.

The GDR Ministry for Foreign Affairs worked on an interpretation of the Soviet draft that maintained the line of peaceful coexistence and emphasized the offensive character of the Soviet advance. The peace treaty, the document argued, would make it easier for the Germans to find a solution to the national question because it would enable "significant success" in the struggle to "overcome the aggressive powers of imperialism and militarism in West Germany." SED leaders viewed the document as a foundation upon which to solve the national question according to their vision. However, the Ministry for Foreign Affairs was also prepared to face a negative outcome from the Soviet advance: if the Western powers rejected the proposal, "German reunification would have to be shelved again."[2]

On 5 January 1959, Soviet Deputy Prime Minister Anastas Mikoyan arrived in Washington to clarify the Soviet position to John F. Dulles, the American secretary of state, before the peace treaty was put forth. The visit embodied the polarized world order and underlined the two world powers' joint responsibility for Germany as a whole. As Mikoyan emphasized in Washington: "Since the conference of

1945, the Soviet Union had accepted an unspoken agreement among the Allies to undertake changes in Germany within the respective areas of power but to leave the legal basis of the four-power agreements untouched. Mikoyan suggested now that the Soviet Union was ready to give up these positions."[3]

In a conversation with Dulles on 5 January, Mikoyan emphasized the following points:

> First, he demanded the recognition of three state entities in Germany: the Federal Republic, the GDR, and Berlin, which was occupied by the Allies. Second, the Soviet government expected the Western powers to recognize the GDR. Third, he cited Adenauer's intent to topple the government of the GDR as a reason to delay reunification for the foreseeable future. Fourth, Mikoyan conceded Adenauer's right not to recognize the GDR, but he could not understand [Adenauer's] disrespect toward Poland and Czechoslovakia. Fifth, he demanded solving the question of [Germany's] borders through the peace treaty. Sixth, he reiterated the assertion that signing a peace treaty did not mean reunification. Full German reunification was unrealistic; a confederation was the only viable possibility. Seventh, Mikoyan emphasized that the Soviet Union did not wish to start a military confrontation. The USSR hoped to resolve negotiations on Berlin within the next six months. Thus, Mikoyan expressly distanced himself from the ultimatum or any other threat.[4]

The Soviet Ministry of Foreign Affairs informed several foreign ambassadors of Mikoyan's visit Washington so that they could confidentially convey the information back to their respective governments. Among them were the Scandinavian countries, including NATO members Denmark and Norway, but also India, Indonesia, Egypt, Yugoslavia, and Austria. At the focus of this communication were the German question and the Berlin problem, as well as a prophylactic attribution of guilt. A complete resolution of the German question was not possible, the message said, considering the existence of the two German states. But the peace treaty might be "a good start that helps bring the two German states closer together, that helps them to agree on a way to unify the country at some point in the future." The foreign ministry suggested that Mikoyan appealed to the shared interests of the United States and the Soviet Union, thus offering a concession to the other side. Moreover, Moscow declared that the peace treaty with Germany would decide whether "developments evolved toward war or sustained peace." Regarding Berlin, the message stated: "the Soviet Union hopes that Westberlin will not support itself on the bayonets of the occupying troops but will rather become a free city whose position is guaranteed by the four powers [as well as] by the two German states and the United Nations Organization." The foreign ministry insisted that the Soviet note on the peace treaty was not an "ultimatum" or a "threat." It painted the United States as an obstacle to the peace process. Although Dulles had agreed to negotiations on Germany, the note read, he remained elusive "with regard to the Berlin question or the question of a peace treaty." To conclude, the foreign ministry framed Mikoyan's efforts in Washington as proof that the United States held fast to its positions and had no desire "to undertake any step whatsoever toward finding a solution to this question that would both satisfy the interests of the German people and provide for long-term peace throughout the world."[5]

The Soviet government sent its draft of a peace treaty with Germany to the Western powers and the two German states on 10 January 1959.[6] The document contained similarities to other Soviet drafts of peace agreements before it but differed drastically in Article 25: "Until the reestablishment of the unity of Germany and the creation of a unified German State, West Berlin will be in the position of a demilitarized free city on the basis of its own special statute."[7]

The SED Politburo had approved this proposal on 2 December 1958. A four-power agreement would solve a problem that, in the view of the SED, was actually the responsibility of West Berlin's population: namely, to achieve "normalization." This was East Berlin's answer to the anticipated results of elections to West Berlin's Abgeordnetenhaus on 7 December 1958. The SED expressed its decisive stance in a letter to the Central Committee of the CPSU: the situation in West Berlin would "radically change if the Western occupation powers withdrew from Berlin."[8] Concerning the stipulations on Berlin, the SED went on: "Regarding the suggestion to grant Westberlin the status of a Free City and, under these conditions, provide it with support from all sides, especially with respect to the economy—yes, this is an unusual way to solve the problem of the GDR's capital. Still, even we can recognize the advantage of this stipulation under the present conditions."[9] The Soviet government wanted to solve the Berlin question to its satisfaction through negotiation, and the SED Politburo understood this.

For the foreign ministry of the GDR, finding a solution to the Berlin problem held top priority:

> Since Westberlin is the most dangerous source of tension in Europe right now, the resolution of the Westberlin issue cannot be delayed. The necessity of solving the Westberlin problem is independent of a peace treaty with Germany and should not require that a peace treaty be signed.
>
> The most urgent measure to curb danger arising from the existence of this pressure cooker Westberlin is to terminate the unlawful occupation regime that the Western powers continue to perpetuate: a departure of all foreign troops from Westberlin and an end to the use of Westberlin as a political tool in the Cold War against the German Democratic Republic and the Socialist camp. The implementation of these measures would have a positive effect on arriving at a peace treaty with Germany.[10]

Addressing the problem of West Berlin took urgent priority over signing a peace treaty. At the beginning of negotiations, Otto Winzer, first deputy foreign minister of the GDR, articulated his skepticism regarding the success of the Soviet offensive and conveyed it to Ulbricht. At the same time, Winzer emphasized the importance of the "Westberlin problem" for the GDR. It needed to be solved regardless of how the peace negotiations concluded. Resolving the "frontline city" issue was a question of survival for the SED state.

In early February 1959, Moscow sent drafts of four documents to East Berlin that were intended to push forward the transformation of West Berlin: the agreement with the Western powers, the statute for a "Free City of Westberlin," a protocol on the guarantees of the city's statute, and the "Declaration on the Establishment of a Free City of Westberlin." The communication also included a draft of a peace treaty with the GDR, on which the politburo of the SED then positioned itself. On 27 February 1959, Ulbricht responded to Khrushchev with "a few proposed changes" and "proposals on how to transfer the rights and functions of the Soviet Union in Berlin to the German Democratic Republic." Cautiously Ulbricht added, "Please consider these proposals simply as suggestions."[11]

The authors in the Moscow foreign ministry did not want to commit themselves to the GDR in a binding way concerning transit routes to and from Berlin. They assumed that the United States would take a contrary position, as President John F. Kennedy later did in his "three essentials" at the Vienna Summit with Khrushchev and again on 28 June 1961, declaring that "a separate peace treaty between the USSR and the GDR would have no bearing on the Allied rights in Berlin."[12] Ulbricht, too, saw this gap in the draft of a separate peace treaty and decided to couple the two demands, at least symbolically. The SED Politburo conveyed its proposed changes to the peace treaty together with its "suggestions" on how to handle the transfer of Soviet authority to the government of the GDR.

By emphasizing the "special status" of West Berlin in its draft of a German peace treaty, the Soviet Union was already sending a signal to the Western powers. The USSR was not willing to transfer its authority the GDR unconditionally without examining Western interests first. A procedural stipulation in the draft underlined the Soviets' desire to negotiate: "If, however, the Western powers consider it expedient before the calling of a peace conference preliminarily to exchange opinions with the Soviet Union about the content of a peace treaty, then the Soviet Government will be agreeable to that. In this case it will be essential to insure the appropriate participation of the German Democratic Republic and the Federal Republic of Germany as the states directly interested in the conclusion of a German peace treaty."[13] Thus, Khrushchev did manage to achieve one thing with his ultimatum: although they rejected the idea of separate negotiations on the status of Berlin, the Western powers at least agreed to enter negotiations on the German problem.

Ulbricht's Plans: Full Sovereignty and a Solution to the "Westberlin Problem"

The Transfer of Soviet Rights in Berlin to the Government of the GDR

The Soviet Union's Berlin Ultimatum and its bid for a peace treaty with the two German states presented Ulbricht with two new possibilities: he could finally close the hole in the inner-German border to refugees escaping the GDR, and he could insist upon international recognition of the GDR. Moreover, the transformation of West Berlin into a "Free City" on the territory of the GDR, along with new control over its access routes and the all-important withdrawal of Western troops from the city would fundamentally change the status quo in Germany. Ulbricht's hopes corresponded to Adenauer and Brandt's acute fears.

In terms of a withdrawal of Western troops from Berlin, Khrushchev and Ulbricht's interests were identical. So far, building a wall through Berlin had not entered their discussion at all. But in the SED's view, the ultimate test to Soviet policy on Berlin was the Soviet Union's attitude toward its status rights. In this vein, Ulbricht had already mentioned the control of transit routes to Khrushchev on 2 December 1958:

> The Central Committee of the SED welcomes the intention of the Soviet govern-ment to transfer all functions to institutions of the GDR that have been temporar-ily exercised by Soviet bodies in Berlin on the basis of inter-Allied agreements and the agreement between the USSR and the GDR of 20.9.1955, so that the GDR might be able to make decisions exclusively at its own discretion on all questions concerning its territory. I have no doubt that negotiations on this topic between the governments of our two countries will lead without difficulty to the necessary arrangements, which can then be realized within the period already discussed [by May 1959].[14]

Shortly thereafter, in January 1959, Ulbricht requested a meeting with Khrushchev in order to determine "how to prepare for USSR representatives to transfer the rights that arose from the four-power status of Berlin."[15]

To Ulbricht, the Soviet Union's transfer of control over the transit routes to and from West Berlin would be the benchmark of sovereignty for the GDR. The draft of a separate peace treaty with the GDR, to be signed if the Western pow-ers and the FRG could not agree on a peace treaty for Germany, did not address this question at all. The signatory powers were only obliged through Article 23 "to try constantly to end the foreign occupation of Westberlin and work toward its transformation from a source of tension in international relations, a source of the Cold War and countless other provocations that pose a serious threat to the peace and security of Europe, into a demilitarized Free City on the basis of a special status."[16]

The SED's goals in Germany policy corresponded to the economic concept of overtaking the Federal Republic in terms of living standards—a goal that finally seemed attainable with the Soviet Ultimatum. However, only the Soviet Union could make it possible: to realize its plan, the SED required a change in Berlin's four-power status and the withdrawal of the Western powers. Throughout the sec-ond Berlin Crisis, Ulbricht's primary objective—also vis-à-vis the Soviet Union—was to secure unlimited sovereignty. But his dilemma had not changed; he was still at the mercy of Soviet foreign policy. Ulbricht's most pressing issue was whether the Soviet Union was truly ready to give up its "occupation rights" in Berlin, or whether the threat only served as leverage in negotiations with the Western powers.

A working paper, presumably from the GDR's foreign ministry, summarizes the need for clarity on seven points and also provides information about the goals of the SED. The first point requests the creation of a new legal structure to monitor the movement of the Western garrisons in Berlin: "It must be established that the issue of these connections is exclusively an affair of the GDR." The only transit routes controlled by neither the GDR nor the Soviet armed forces were the air corridors to West Berlin. This situation had to be changed: "For air traffic, we will instate a permission procedure to be determined by contract. Regarding the so-called 'Allied air traffic control,' it shall be replaced by an air traffic control of the GDR." Until this existed, the GDR intended to "take over the Soviet position in the air traffic control." With the collapse of the Control Council and the creation of two German states, "the foundation of the existence and purpose of the military mission was terminated." Thus, the working paper suggests "dissolving the [Western] military missions in Potsdam, since there is no longer an occupation regime."[17]

According to the foreign ministry, the rules for citizens of the GDR traveling abroad also had to change. Left over from the period of the Control Council, the Allied Travel Bureau still existed in West Berlin to grant visas to travel abroad to Western countries. Because the GDR required its citizens to obtain an exit visa to leave the country, the procedure of visiting the Allied Travel Bureau applied almost exclusively to party and state functionaries, and they felt pained by the limited sovereignty of their Socialist state. Therefore, the foreign ministry proposed that "citizens of the GDR should no longer apply for 'preliminary passports' through the Allied bureau. For states that do not recognize our passports, negotiations will be initiated with the goal of achieving recognition of our travel documents." Berlin's four-power status allowed family members of military personnel in the Western garrisons unrestricted access to East Berlin. In the future they would have to present an "entry permit." The prison for war criminals in Spandau would be closed; of the three remaining prisoners (Rudolf Heß, Baldur von Schirach, and Albert Speer), two would be transferred to the Federal Republic and one to the GDR to serve the rest of their sentences. The last point in the working paper focused on eliminating the Allied Billing Office for Postal and Long-Distance Communication in West Berlin. The office was established in 1947 under the Control Council in order to deal with postal and telephone billing between the occupation zones; from 1959 onward, it operated under the direction of the Western powers. To replace the office, the SED proposed reaching an agreement among the postal administration of the GDR, the West German postal service, and the postal service of West Berlin. SED leadership tied the transfer of Soviet occupation rights in Berlin to dismantling all structures that still retained traces of Berlin's four-power status.[18]

This list of demands laid the foundation for a resolution by the SED Politburo on the transfer of Soviet rights in Berlin to the government of the GDR.[19] The resolution was conveyed to Khrushchev on 27 February 1959 along with a response to the Soviet draft of a separate peace treaty with the GDR. The SED demanded a clear outline of the legal status of West Berlin and expanded Article 23 of the peace treaty to include the following statement: "Independent of the creation of a demilitarized Free City of West Berlin, the government of the USSR transfers all functions to the government of the GDR that it has exercised until now in connection with the four-power administration and the presence of foreign troops in Westberlin."[20] The SED detailed exactly how this transfer would take place and listed precisely the rights to be transferred. After signing the separate peace treaty, the government of the GDR would submit an offer to the Western powers "to enter negotiations concerning all questions that arise from the transfer of functions to the GDR that were previously exercised by the Soviet Union." During these negotiations, the "movement of troops" by the Western powers along the transit routes would be supervised by "representatives of the Soviet Union and the GDR."[21] The SED planned to implement this measure even if the Western powers refused to enter into negotiations at all.

According to the SED's general policy to regulate civilian travel between West Berlin and the Federal Republic, transit and entry would be "subject to control procedures determined by the GDR." In order to enter East Berlin, "citizens of the Federal Republic need a visa. The government of the GDR reserves the right to require a special permit for travel by residents of Westberlin and the Federal Republic, as it sees fit." These were the control procedures with which the GDR wished to register and monitor inter-German movement, regardless of whether a peace treaty was signed. After the end of the Soviet Military Command in Berlin, all contact by the Soviet Union to the Western powers and the official institutions of West Berlin would only be permitted through the Soviet embassy in the GDR: "No contact will be maintained between the Soviet embassy or other Soviet entities and branches of the Bonn government in Westberlin."[22]

The "Free City of Westberlin": The Statute by the SED

According to Soviet plans, an agreement on the "Free City" was to be reached by the Soviet Union, Great Britain, France, the United States, and the two German states. The legal and economic structures, private ownership, and political order of the city would remain unchanged. At the center of the agreement was the "Statute of the Free City," which would have "binding power" over West Berlin and, of course, would heavily influence the character of the city. In the Soviet version of the agreement, Article 4 included a variety of prohibitions for West Berliners: "On the territory of the Free City, it is forbidden for organizations or individual persons to undertake any kind of activity, antagonistic or otherwise—including subversive propaganda—against any other state including the Free City itself."[23] Paul Verner, the Central Committee secretary responsible for the SED's "Western operations," requested that the article also include the word "diversion" (*Diversion*).[24] With just one word, Verner's demand exposed the intention behind this article and the rest of the statute: at issue was the suppression of free media that served as a forum to criticize SED rule. The SED understood the fundamental Soviet concept of ideological "diversion" to mean the West's targeted influence over public opinion in the GDR with the goal of impeding the establishment of socialism. By 1960, the word had come to designate a criminal act.[25]

The SED's draft of the statute aligned itself with the Soviet version and, in Article 21, banned all "fascist and otherwise antidemocratic organizations, as well as organizations that conduct enemy activities against other states." Article 2 required that the Constitution of West Berlin "reflect the principles of this statute." Until reunification, the citizens of West Berlin would have their own nationality. Article 9 specified that the citizens would not be free to practice "a profession on the territory of the GDR," and likewise, no citizens of the GDR would be allowed to work in West Berlin. The economic relations of West Berlin were to be guaranteed by all other countries, and the city would possess its own currency system. The GDR would provide "the Free City [with] unobstructed communication to the rest of the world." The "Free City" would be demilitarized but could still have its own police force; however, the police would not be allowed to join alliances "of a military or military-political nature."[26] NATO, which guaranteed the protection of West Berlin, represented exactly this type of military alliance.

Because of the movement to flee the GDR through West Berlin, the SED had special interest in defining the exact terms of citizenship in the "Free City." In contrast to contemporary practice, whereby residents of the GDR who crossed the sector border were immediately considered "Germans" according to the Basic Law of the Federal Republic, the SED's draft of a statute stipulated that people could only become citizens of the Free City "with the approval of the responsible offices in their respective home countries."[27] Putting an end to emigration from the GDR was a goal shared by leaders in Moscow and East Berlin, and the Soviet draft contained a clear message that the SED version lacked: "In the Free City of Westberlin, no asylum of any kind will be granted. The government of the German Democratic Republic maintains its right to veto the acquisition of citizenship in the Free City as well as the application for permanent or temporary residence in the Free City by persons who, at the time this statute enters into effect, are not citizens of the Free City of Westberlin."[28]

On 14 February 1959, Ulbricht sent Khrushchev the SED Politburo's draft of the statute and included further requests in an accompanying letter. Since West Berlin fundamentally "belonged to the territory of the German Democratic Republic," it made sense to refer to it as an "administrative area." And since it could not be ruled out that West Berlin would conduct "its foreign affairs through the Bonn government," Ulbricht proposed amending the statute to say that the "Free City" could only transfer its foreign representation "to another state" if all states involved in the contract agreed. Likewise, he wrote, the statute should designate that the Deutsche Reichsbahn and the waterways "are the property of the GDR and will remain under its administration."[29]

The plans were part of Soviet preparations for the upcoming conference of foreign ministers with the Western powers. In Geneva, it was already clear that the Western powers were unwilling to hold serious negotiations on the "Free City of Westberlin." But the drafts by Khrushchev and Ulbricht discussed above demonstrate unequivocally that at the beginning of the crisis, they were focused on changing the status quo in Berlin and Germany and not on building a wall through Berlin.

The Geneva Conference of Foreign Ministers, 1959

On the basis of the Soviet proposal for how to proceed, the three Western powers and the Soviet Union agreed to hold a conference of foreign ministers in Geneva. The conference ran from May to August 1959, with some interruptions. For the first time, the two German states also took part in a four-power conference on Germany, although they were not permitted to participate in full. This signaled a first step toward recognition of the GDR. The two German states were treated equally in Geneva, but internationally they carried very different weight. In contrast to the GDR, the Federal Republic had democratic legitimacy, enjoyed international recognition, and had economic strength. The FRG needed the United States as its leading power, "but did not operate under its supervision as the GDR did [with the USSR]."[30]

Preparing for this conference, the Western powers and the Federal Republic conferred during a meeting of the NATO Council in April 1959 but could

> only agree on what they did not want: a neutralized Germany in Europe, the withdrawal of American and Canadian troops from the European continent, and reunification without free elections. They could also agree on one other thing: if they were forced to accept a modus vivendi for Berlin in order to solve the problem of reunification, then negotiating with the Soviets made no sense from the beginning. By this time, the Kremlin had long possessed an "elaborate statute for a demilitarized Free City of West Berlin," which, for tactical reasons, the Soviets had not presented [to the West]. They wanted to keep the Western powers in the dark with regard to Soviet intentions and hoped to elicit Western proposals for a solution first.[31]

Before the NATO conference, American Secretary of State Dulles visited Chancellor Adenauer in order to discuss military preparations for a potential conflict over the transit routes. The conversation revolved around the use of nuclear weapons by NATO. As long as the crisis continued, the danger existed of war over Berlin—even if neither side wanted it. The two statesmen spoke in Bonn about NATO's defense strategy. Dulles described the Western powers' significant inferiority to the Soviet Union in terms of the conventional armament of their military forces; at the same time, he emphasized the superiority of the United States when it came to nuclear weapons. He argued for a confrontational course:

> "If we convince the Soviets of our willingness to wage a general war to defend our rights, down to the last consequence, this steadfastness will do more to maintain peace than if we end up looking weak and fickle." . . . He seemed ready to deploy nuclear weapons in the framework of a two-stage plan. If, in the first stage of escalation, it became necessary to use force, then there would be no reason to shy

away from deploying this type of weapon in the second stage. Feeling cornered, the chancellor replied that all other means should be exhausted before the decision was made to use nuclear weapons in order to break through a blockade of access routes to West Berlin. After a long discussion, Adenauer finally consented to the two-stage plan. However, it was only a very general understanding.[32]

As a member of the Four-Power Working Group initiated by the three Western powers in preparation for the conference of foreign ministers, the Federal Republic was integrated into the coordination process through the Western side and could actively influence Western negotiation strategy.[33] For example, the Soviet Union demanded the creation of a committee composed equally of representatives from East and West Germany, which would advise the confederation of the two German states. In July, Ulbricht received a message from Geneva that, according to information from Soviet Foreign Minister Gromyko, the Western powers were not entirely opposed to the formation of such a committee, "but—and this is where Bonn's influence showed—[they] disapproved of the parity principle."[34]

The presence of the Western powers in their sectors of Berlin, as well as the control of the city's access routes, constituted the central international conflicts of the second Berlin Crisis. Ulbricht's hope that the GDR would attain full sovereignty over its territory, including the capital and its transit routes, was already dissipating during the first phase of the conference. After a conversation with Valerian Zorin, a member of the Soviet delegation, Otto Winzer, head of the GDR delegation, reported to Ulbricht on the state of negotiations:

> Thus Ulbricht learned that the USSR considered it impossible to implement the status of a Free City in Westberlin. According to Zorin, the only alternatives were "either to enter into a temporary agreement on Westberlin or for the Soviet Union and the GDR to take action on their own." Zorin suggested that [the GDR] recognize the current situation for the period of one year on the condition that the number of Western troops in the Western part of the city decrease, no nuclear weapons or missiles be stationed there, and enemy propaganda and "subversive activity" coming out of [Westberlin] toward the GDR be stopped.[35]

This was the gist of the Soviet proposal for an interim agreement, which Foreign Minister Gromyko submitted to the Western powers without waiting for the GDR's input. He "denied having ever formulated an ultimatum, and, in response to the question of whether Western rights would still be recognized after the end of the one-year period, stated that his country would never approve of an indefinite continuation of the Western occupation regime."[36] In the last phase of the conference, Gromyko increased the period to one and a half years. Nevertheless, "for Ulbricht, [this was] a first step back from the announced intention to sign a separate peace treaty."[37] This gesture from the Soviet foreign ministry coincided with an invitation by President Eisenhower to Khrushchev to visit the United States. On 22 July, the head of the Kremlin accepted the invitation and announced that he would come in September for ten to fifteen days. "He did not care whether it was an official or an unofficial visit, and he only mentioned the Geneva conference in passing. Regardless of the conference's results, he felt that conversations were necessary 'at the highest level.'"[38]

A few months later, preparing to meet with President Eisenhower, Khrushchev sketched out his thoughts on a solution to the German problem: "The superpowers [are under] no obligation whatsoever to reunify Germany. It is useful to remember here that situations similar to Germany (GDR and FRG) have developed in Korea (DPRK and South Korea), and Vietnam (North and South Vietnam), for example."[39]

On 28 July 1959, the Western powers, too, submitted a proposal for an interim agreement. In it they accepted the Soviet demand for a Free City of Berlin but applied it to Greater Berlin. All of Berlin would assume the status of a Free City and would become a third independent state entity in Germany along with the Federal Republic and the GDR. However, the responsibility of the four Allied powers would remain unchanged:

> In order to create a normal situation and maintain integrity, the plan stated, it would be necessary to form a joint administration for the undivided territory of Greater Berlin under the supervision of the Four Powers. Within 60 days, general, free, secret, and direct elections would be held for a constitutional council, which would formulate a constitution and an election law within the following 60 days; these documents would be approved by popular referendum within the next 30 days. Berlin's government would be free to negotiate with the other parts of Germany over its administrative, economic, financial, and legal relations, but could not be integrated into one of the German states before reunification. The Four Powers would enjoy free and unrestricted access between Berlin and the other parts of Germany. The city's security would remain guaranteed by the armed forces of the Allied powers on the basis of their original rights and other rules that had yet to be determined. Berlin would not be allowed to gain membership in the defense organizations to which the Federal Republic and the GDR belonged, so that the armed forces of other powers could not enter Berlin.[40]

Adenauer saw danger in this draft of an agreement: in his view, it would mean giving up Berlin's four-power status, forming a direct relationship between the Western powers and the GDR, and leveling the path to a Free City of West Berlin.

However, this type of interim agreement never materialized, and the Geneva conference of foreign ministers ended in failure. The deadline set in Khrushchev's first ultimatum had expired without the Soviet Union signing a separate peace treaty with the GDR. In the words of West German Ambassador Grewe, the Geneva conference of 1959 concluded "a five-year period in which the German question had been the subject of four-power conferences and remained at the top of the agenda in diplomatic negotiations between the major powers. From that point onward, other questions, topics, and themes increasingly gained priority. For a long time, the German question would disappear from the agenda of major international conferences."[41] The Federal Republic's leeway in terms of Germany policy was very limited. Ralf Dahrendorf, a contemporary, described it concisely and precisely for the Bundestag Committee on Domestic Affairs: "[The Federal Republic] could do nothing more than fundamentally insist upon the goal of reunification, wait for a major shift in the international climate, and, on a practical level, ensure that the German question remained open and that no provisions or decisions to waive certain rights were set in place that would rule out the reestablishment of unity."[42]

Nevertheless, the Berlin Crisis did remain on the international political agenda. Willy Brandt laid out his views to the federal chancellor on 28 October 1959:

"1. Any agreement on West Berlin must explicitly remain valid until *German reunification*. 2. The plan to create a 'Free City of West Berlin' would justify to some extent the *demand for a withdrawal of Western troops*, later for the reduction of troops to a purely symbolic strength." 3. Ulbricht's suggestion to make West Berlin into an entity modeled on the Vatican only aims to eliminate West Berlin's constitutional ties to the Federal Republic and represents the "most serious attack on the existence of a free Berlin." It was clear that a free Berlin could "not survive as a third fragmental state." 4. Allied control of the access routes to and from West Berlin had to be sustained. Brandt urged [Adenauer] to "voice these points soon" in order to present a "coordinated German position."[43]

Just a few days later, writing to Federal Foreign Minister Heinrich von Brentano, Brandt sketched out his ideas for the Western summit conference that would take place in Paris in December 1959:

1. The Western powers must be encouraged to declare West Berlin an integral part of the Federal Republic and to insist upon the continuation of the present legal situation until reunification. 2. The suggestions put forth in Geneva by the Western side represented "the limits of what we can bear." . . . 3. The Western powers have to remain guarantors of free access to West Berlin. Whether the UN might be able to take over surveillance duties through a four-power commission should be looked into. It would be extraordinarily alarming "if the Western powers' responsibility for maintaining free movement to and from Berlin were curtailed in any way."[44]

These views were diametrically opposed to the position of Ulbricht and his politburo.

Notes

1. Walter Ulbricht to Nikita S. Khrushchev, 3 January 1959, SAPMO-BArch, DY 30/3505.
2. "Material für die Argumentation zum Friedensvertragsvorschlag der Sowjetunion," Berlin, 16 January 1959, SAPMO-BArch, DY 30/3505.

3. Küsters, *Integrationsfriede*, 770.

4. Ibid., 769.

5. Central Committee of the CPSU to Mikhail Suslov, 21 November 1959, RGANI, F. 5, op. 30, d. 300. The irony or arrogance of power: the image of Western "bayonets" in Berlin, used here and in other Soviet documents, was relatively harmless compared to the Soviet tanks deployed in Berlin in 1953 and Hungary in 1956, which protected both regimes against their own populations.

6. "Note from the Soviet Union to the United States, Transmitting a Draft Peace Treaty for Germany, 10 January 1959," in U.S. Dept. of State, *Documents on Germany*, 585–607.

7. Ibid., 601.

8. SAPMO-BArch, DY 30/J IV 2/2A/668.

9. Central Committee of the SED to the Central Committee of the CPSU, draft, 2 December 1958, SAPMO-BArch, DY 30/J IV 2/2A/668.

10. "Material für die Argumentation zum Friedensvertragsvorschlag der Sowjetunion," Berlin, 16 January 1959, SAPMO-BArch, DY 30/3505.

11. SAPMO-BArch, DY 30/3505.

12. Harald Biermann, *John F. Kennedy und der Kalte Krieg* (Paderborn, 1997), 123.

13. "Note from the Soviet Union to the United States, Transmitting a Draft Peace Treaty for Germany," 10 January 1959, in U.S. Dept. of State, *Documents on Germany*, 593.

14. SAPMO-BArch, DY 30/J IV 2/2A/668. In the draft of this letter from Ulbricht's office, these sentences appear on the reverse side of the paper with a handwritten note in the margin: "Page 1." This became the wording of the official version.

15. Walter Ulbricht to Nikita S. Khrushchev, Moscow, 31 January 1959, SAPMO-BArch, DY 30/3505.

16. SAPMO-BArch, DY 30/3505.

17. "Probleme im Zusammenhang mit der Übergabe der Rechte der sowjetischen Vertreter betreffend Westberlin an die Regierung der Deutschen Demokratischen Republik," SAPMO-BArch, DY 30/3505.

18. Ibid.

19. "Beschluss der Vorschläge zur Regelung der Übergabe der Rechte und Funktionen der Sowjetunion hinsichtlich Westberlins an die DDR," politbüro of the Central Committee of the SED, 17 February 1959, SAPMO-BArch, DY 30/3506.

20. Proposed changes by the politbüro of the SED on the draft of a peace treaty with the GDR, SAPMO-BArch, DY 30/3506.

21. Ibid.

22. Ibid.

23. "Abkommen über die Freie Stadt Westberlin" (draft), SAPMO-BArch, DY 30/3505.

24. Paul Verner to Walter Ulbricht, "Zum Abkommen und zum Statut von Westberlin," SAPMO-BArch, DY 30/3505.

25. See "Stichwort Diversion," in Ulrich Weißgerber, *Giftige Worte der SED-Diktatur: Sprache als Instrument von Machtausübung und Ausgrenzung in der SBZ und der DDR* (Berlin, 2010), 94–99.

26. "Statut der Freien Stadt Westberlin" (SED draft), SAPMO-BArch DY 30/3505.

27. Ibid.

28. SAPMO-BArch, DY 30/3505.

29. Walter Ulbricht to Nikita S. Khrushchev, Berlin, 15 February 1959, SAPMO-BArch, DY 30/3505.

30. Lemke, *Berlinkrise*, 137.

31. Hanns Jürgen Küsters, "Die Reaktionen der Bundesregierung und des Senats von Berlin auf die Berlin-Krise," in Karner et al., *Wiener Gipfel*, 722.

32. Küsters, "Reaktionen," 721.

33. See Steininger, *Mauerbau*, 87–94.

34. Lemke, *Berlinkrise*, 135.

35. Ibid., 130.
36. Wettig, *Chruschtschows Berlin-Krise*, 61–62.
37. Küsters, *Integrationsfriede*, 790.
38. Steininger, *Mauerbau*, 130.
39. Notes by Nikita S. Khrushchev, 10 August 1959, AdBIK.
40. Küsters, "Reaktionen," 722–23.
41. Grewe, *Rückblenden*, 410.
42. Quoted in ibid., 415.
43. Willy Brandt to Konrad Adenauer, 28 October 1959, quoted in Hanns Jürgen Küsters, "Konrad Adenauer und Willy Brandt in der Berlin-Krise 1958–1963," *Vierteljahreshefte für Zeitgeschichte* 40 (1992): 502.
44. Willy Brandt to Heinrich von Brentano, 10 December 1959, quoted in ibid., 504.

Chapter 11

THE SECOND BERLIN CRISIS AND A SHIFT IN THE COLD WAR

The International Character of the Second Berlin Crisis

The second Berlin Crisis was an international conflict and became the longest period of heightened tension in Central Europe during the Cold War. Contention over the Western powers' rights in Berlin, the status of West Berlin, and unobstructed movement to the Federal Republic became questions of war and peace between the Soviet Union and the United States. Both countries understood that a war over Berlin would end in nuclear inferno. The Soviet Union aimed to elicit certain changes in Germany and Berlin in agreement with the Western powers, especially the United States, through an internationally binding peace treaty that would prevent another world war. Thus, the summit meetings between Khrushchev and American presidents Eisenhower and Kennedy in 1959 and 1961 represented major junctures in the Soviet decision-making process.

The latter, the Vienna Summit, differed from the meetings before it in that the resolutions from the Potsdam Conference of 1945 no longer applied after 1960. According to these resolutions, the four powers exercised their rights together in order to negotiate a peace treaty with both German states. In Vienna, though, only the highest representatives of the nuclear superpowers discussed the international conflicts at hand, their respective positions, and their leeway to negotiate solutions to the conflicts. Between the 1959 conference of foreign ministers in Geneva and the 1961 summit in Vienna, the nuclear standoff and the decolonization process combined to reduce France and Great Britain to regional powers. Meanwhile, the American president pushed to shape the agenda in Vienna around the central topic in the conflict between the two nuclear powers: namely, checks on nuclear armament in order to avoid nuclear war. For Khrushchev, however, Berlin and a peace treaty with Germany took priority. The Vienna Summit assumed a combative character, encouraging both sides to harden their stances on the issue of Berlin;

this, in turn, led the two powers to rev up their armament efforts. The American president ordered a fleet of nuclear submarines armed with Polaris missiles to be built in preparation for a nuclear counterattack.

Leading up to the summit in Vienna, the crisis in the GDR dramatically altered Khrushchev's negotiating position vis-à-vis the United States. He was now under pressure to act quickly. The Soviet leader renewed his 1958 ultimatum for Kennedy: if the West refused to change its position on Berlin, the Soviet Union would sign a separate peace treaty with the GDR in December 1961. Kennedy responded to this threat by asserting the Western powers' hard-fought right to remain in Berlin. In this atmosphere of open confrontation, securing the existence of the GDR became the Soviet Union's primary area of crisis management. It was also crucial to Soviet security policy; after all, the GDR served as a "garrison state"[1] for the Soviet Union, housing hundreds of thousands of Soviet soldiers.

Summits rarely lend themselves to international treaty negotiations, and Vienna was no exception. The proceedings were little more than a big show. Even Khrushchev saw the conference realistically as a "game": "If we cannot find a solution, then we will use the ministers' discussions to distract the general public. Sometimes it is useful to give people the impression that a question is being solved, when in principle the question is not being solved but rather the decision postponed. We can accept this, but not indefinitely."[2]

Khrushchev's meeting with Eisenhower, the following summit in Paris that he terminated, and his subsequent conversations with Kennedy in Vienna all led nowhere: none of the occasions yielded a peace treaty with Germany or a new agreement on Berlin. Thus, the Soviet Union's summit diplomacy ultimately proved ineffective as a way to implement its goals. In light of the GDR's existential crisis, the Soviet Union felt forced to take unilateral measures within its sphere of influence in order to stop the mass exodus from the GDR. Indeed, Khrushchev's desired changes to the status quo made way for a reinforcement of the same through the closure of the sector border in Berlin. This outcome did not reflect the original goals of either Soviet or German Communist leaders.

Khrushchev and Ulbricht hoped that their Berlin policy would fundamentally alter the status quo to their advantage. It is important to emphasize here that by strategically inflating the GDR's importance as the Socialist core state in Germany, the Soviet Union hoped to weaken West Germany's international position, forcing it to accept the de facto division of Germany into three parts. The Soviet Union demanded that the Federal Republic relinquish the Germans' democratic right to self-determination in the long term. Furthermore, Khrushchev intended to isolate the Federal Republic in NATO by using Communist propaganda to denounce West Germany as an "aggressive militaristic state" that endangered European peace with its "revanchist policy." These ideological formulations especially targeted two principled positions of West German foreign policy: the refusal to officially recognize the Oder-Neisse line before a peace treaty was signed with a unified Germany, and the claim to be the sole legitimate representative of the German people. Demands for a peace treaty with the two German states and a transformation of West Berlin into a "Free City" were intended to cause conflict within NATO and, as Khrushchev stated himself, shred the organization to pieces.[3] As in the first Berlin Crisis, Soviet policy in the second Berlin Crisis extended well beyond Berlin: both episodes represented Soviet attempts to shift the spheres of influence in Germany and Europe and weaken the power of the United States, the Soviet Union's rival on the continent. This was the strategic goal behind Khrushchev's motion to transform West Berlin into a "Free City" and force the Western powers to withdraw their troops.

The CPSU and the SED were unequal partners during the Berlin Crisis, as the SED relied in many ways on Soviet decisions. For all questions concerning Berlin, the Soviet Union retained control over the conflict in each phase of the crisis, and the SED had to seek the "approval" of Soviet leadership before making any decisions. Coordination throughout this decision-making process relied heavily on the first secretaries of the CPSU and the SED, Khrushchev and Ulbricht. But the latter pursued his own interests, too. Throughout the Soviet offensive, the SED wished above all to solve its "Westberlin problem" and close the open gateway to the West. Ulbricht's main concern was ending Berlin's four-power status. He hoped that Khrushchev would transfer Soviet authority to the GDR and thereby grant sovereignty to the SED state within its capital city and along the transit routes to West Berlin; had he succeeded, it would have been superfluous to build a wall through the city. In addition, Ulbricht wanted to assert the GDR's position internationally as the Socialist core state in Germany.

While the whole world was fixated on summit choreography between the two dominant powers of this polarized world order, the international conditions changed dramatically for the Soviet Union—to the great disadvantage of its policy on Berlin and Germany. When Khrushchev began his Berlin offensive in 1958, the CPSU stood at the helm of an international Communist movement. But independent of the Berlin Crisis, 1961 brought a fundamental change in the East–West conflict: the schism between the Soviet and Chinese Communist parties grew so deep that it became irreversible, and the Eastern bloc as a monolithic adversary to the West fell to pieces.

The Soviet–Chinese Schism and the Position of the SED

At the 22nd Party Congress of the CPSU in October 1961, the ideological and political conflict between the Soviet and Chinese Communist parties—and therefore between the two states—came into the open. First, Khrushchev openly criticized Albanian party leaders for aligning themselves with China in 1960 and closing the Soviet submarine docking station in Albania. In his initial remarks, Zhou Enlai, vice chairman of the Communist Party of China and the Chinese premier, then publicly scolded Khrushchev for his actions. It was unheard of to question the authority of the CPSU party leader in this way. After emphasizing the necessity of maintaining unity among the Socialist states and within the international Communist movement on the basis of Marxist-Leninist thought, Zhou came to the point:

> We believe that if, unfortunately, disagreements and differences in opinion arise between brother parties and between brother countries, it is necessary to address them patiently and to be guided by the spirit of proletariat internationalism, by the principles of equality, and to arrive at a shared perspective through consultation with one another. The public, unilateral condemnation of a brother party goes against this unity and will not lead to solving the problem. Openly dragging out disagreements between brother parties and brother countries before the eyes of the enemy cannot be considered a serious Marxist-Leninist approach. This type of action only serves to embitter friends and please enemies.[4]

By highlighting the principle of "equality" among the Communist parties, the Chinese premier sent a clear message: we will no longer accept the unchecked leadership role of the CPSU and hereby declare ourselves to be on equal standing. Moscow thus found itself in an ideological conflict with Beijing that would change the character of the Cold War with the West. One aspect of this debate was the question of whether war between socialism and capitalism could be avoided. While Khrushchev advocated "peaceful coexistence" and thus avoidance of war—especially considering the development of nuclear weapons—the Chinese Communists took the opposite view, citing Lenin. They believed that if American imperialists decided to unleash a nuclear war against the will of the People, its end would "certainly not be the obliteration of mankind." The People would emerge victorious over imperialism and "then, in great leaps, establish a civilization upon the ruins of imperialism a thousand times superior to the capitalist system, and would build for themselves a bright future."[5] "Radiant future" would have more aptly described the outcome of such a war.

Khrushchev had already faced Chinese critique of his peaceful coexistence policy at the conference of governing Communist parties in Bucharest on 24 June 1960. In reaction, the SED took a clear position. Ulbricht informed his Central Committee of the controversy at the ninth plenum in July 1960. He reported that a few Chinese functionaries had recently focused on "only one aspect of the modern era," namely, that of "imperialist war and revolutions." But these characterizations, he declared, were "one-sided because they do not take into consideration the transition from capitalism to socialism and the emergence and establishment of the Socialist world system. Today it is impossible to understand any isolated incident in the world without looking first at the Socialist world system."[6]

He then launched a direct attack on Peng Chen, representative of the Communist Party of China at the Bucharest meeting: "Of course, as long as imperialism exists there is cause for war. For that reason we must remain constantly vigilant. It is not that we underestimate the danger of war but rather that we concentrate our efforts on moving forward in the struggle for peace and not, as some of our Chinese comrades would prefer, on the philosophy of whether or not it is possible to avoid war." If the imperialist power did choose to start a war, the Socialist camp would have the military strength "to put a stop to the war"; after all, the working class had "long-range missiles" at its disposal. In this respect, Ulbricht clearly toed the Soviet line. He continued: "For the revolutionary struggle and war for liberation, Communists are the protectors of independence, and wars against the yoke of colonialism are just wars indeed. The CPSU has always actively supported wars of this kind." Ulbricht also rejected the way in which his Chinese counterparts equated the concept of peaceful coexistence "with a policy of internal class peace." To the contrary, he argued, "peaceful coexistence means that states with different social orders can live together, side by side. In other words, coexistence is a specific form of class struggle between socialism and capitalism on a world scale—a form that is advantageous for socialism."[7]

Despite these fractured developments, the West still believed in the existence of a monolithic Eastern bloc. But the constellation of the Cold War changed when China questioned its own loyalty to the alliance with the Soviet Union. This pivotal moment in the history of the international Communist movement naturally had implications for international politics and the end of the Berlin Crisis:

> This was to alter the geopolitics of the Cold War entirely. For the USSR and China it meant that in the very near future they would have to wage the Cold War on their own, regarding each other as traitors. For the United States it meant two major adversaries instead of one (although Washington failed to understand this until the late 1960s). On the one hand, it was a positive change: the efforts of the USSR and China could neutralize each other. On the other hand, it introduced new uncertainty into the Cold War relationship and made the behavior of the East even less predictable than before.
>
> . . . Bipolarity was becoming obsolete by 1960, when military cooperation between China and the Soviet Union ended, and the Eastern bloc ceased being a monolith. It was not coincidental that the Sino-Soviet split and Soviet-American détente occurred at the same time. The whole Cold War system began to change as the new elites came to power in the USSR. The spontaneous changes in the revolutionary–imperial paradigm had both split the Socialist bloc and built some bridges between Moscow and the West.[8]

Khrushchev's Trip to the United States in 1959

While the Geneva conference of foreign ministers was still in progress, Eisenhower invited Khrushchev to visit the United States. Khrushchev's trip to America in 1959 was not a summit meeting in the narrow sense of the term, since no negotiations took place. The American president had assured his partners beforehand that there would be no substantial negotiations on Berlin or Germany during the visit.

However, it was clear that the leaders of the two superpowers would discuss their countries' differences without consulting their respective partners; in light of the ongoing international crisis, both men had to decide how much risk they were willing to take. Kissinger saw it this way, too: "Of all the heads of the allies,

Eisenhower bore the gravest burden of responsibility, because the decision to risk nuclear war ultimately rested on his shoulders." Kissinger's assessment applied to Khrushchev as well. Even before the conference of foreign ministers, the American president had publicly stated "that America's willingness to risk war over Berlin was very limited." Eisenhower's knowledge that a war with nuclear weapons could have apocalyptic consequences largely determined his approach to the Soviet Union. "A general nuclear war would, in a matter of days, produce casualties that dwarfed the cumulative totals of both world wars."[9]

Eisenhower saw the Berlin problem and the German question in the context of his larger vision. "He wanted to couple the discussion of Berlin with an agreement to stop nuclear testing—which, in his view, would be a decisive step toward détente, providing the psychological conditions for an amicable solution to the Berlin question and representing a Western offer that rewarded the Soviets for cooperating on the Berlin question. Contrary to Dulles's wishes, disarmament now took priority over the German question."[10] Khrushchev's visit did contribute to a positive change in climate, and the Soviet guest emphasized that he would stop making threats with regard to Berlin. Eisenhower was invited to visit the Soviet Union.

Under the improved conditions, the American president was ready to hold a new summit meeting. Adenauer, Eisenhower, de Gaulle, and Macmillan decided on a Western negotiation strategy in December 1959. "(1) No concession of Western rights in Berlin, (2) It is up to Khrushchev to enable progress in the German question. If he causes difficulties, then it is clear he does not want détente."[11] The Western powers and the Soviet Union agreed on a time and place for the next summit conference: Paris, 16 May 1960.

The Summit that Khrushchev Cut Short: Paris 1960

Unlike at the conference of foreign ministers in Geneva, the Federal Republic and the GDR were not granted observer status in Paris. Nevertheless, the Soviet Union did not ignore the West German position, which comes through in a report to Ulbricht by the East German ambassador to Moscow on a conversation between Khrushchev and the West German ambassador. According to this report, West German Ambassador Hans Kroll told Khrushchev in December 1959: "Regarding the Berlin question, the Federal Republic will not change its position: Berlin must be seen as the capital of Germany. Thus, the Berlin question can only be resolved in the interest of the German people and the West German population. A change in position by the Federal Republic with respect to the Berlin question cannot be expected."[12]

In early January 1960, Khrushchev informed Ulbricht confidentially of his preparations for the upcoming summit, and his letter provides insight into his strategy at the time. In order "to ensure that [the Socialist camp] maintained the upper hand in the struggle for peace," Soviet party leadership decided to reduce the size of the Soviet Army by 1.2 million persons over the following two years.

This step was meant to demonstrate the seriousness of Soviet appeals for disarmament. Positive propaganda was also part of the diplomatic game, a tool that could be used to launch an even stronger attack on Western nuclear armament later—especially since Khrushchev believed that the international power constellation was shifting in favor of the Socialist camp. It was important to him that Soviet forces be "armed with the most modern rockets and nuclear weapons, to whatever extent suffices to accomplish any military task at hand. The possession of powerful rockets and nuclear weapons allows us not only to retaliate, if necessary, against an imperialist attack on the Soviet Union and the other countries in the Soviet camp but also to obliterate countries from the face of the earth that house these aggressors." Disarmament propaganda was one side of the coin; armament was the other. "At the same time, the power of our armed forces to defend themselves using the newest technical achievements will continue to grow."[13]

Khrushchev's plans were also carried out, as evidenced by Soviet military and security policy during the second Berlin Crisis. They help explain the relationship between the political offensive and Soviet military planning, which was intended to help Moscow achieve its goals even against the resistance of the Western powers. Nuclear weapons and their deployment in a theoretical war over Berlin played a central role.

At the beginning of the Berlin Crisis in 1958, the Soviet Union's strategic nuclear weapons were inferior in quality to those of the United States. The Soviet air force possessed just eighty-seven strategic bombers that it could use as a potential threat against the American adversary. In light of this, the USSR initiated a feverish armament policy to catch up; military expenditures increased dramatically in 1961. "These funds were used to build 125 intercontinental rockets, 530 mid-range rockets, and 1,254 short-range rockets, as well as 1,188 wingtip missiles and their corresponding launchers. The great majority of these weapons could be loaded with nuclear warheads."[14] The Soviet armament industry aimed to close the gap on American nuclear capacities.

Not only Eisenhower but also the Soviet leadership set new priorities for the summit: they both placed disarmament at the top of the agenda, relegating the German question to the background. The politburo of the SED formally approved of Khrushchev's letter[15] but internally held fast to its own policy. Ulbricht's office put together a separate plan in preparation for the summit conference. The SED was especially interested in three things: (1) The consequences of Soviet disarmament targets for Germany and Europe, (2) "Preparing for and signing a peace treaty with both German states," and (3) "Addressing the Westberlin question."[16] The Ministry for Foreign Affairs drafted a series of proposals, among them a sketch of a "pre-peace treaty" with the two German states that would also include an interim solution for West Berlin. From the perspective of the SED, signing this type of agreement would have several advantages: the debate over a peace treaty would be "rejuvenated"; the West German government would "encounter new difficulties"; and the GDR and USSR would demonstrate their "willingness to compromise." The proposal itself would only be introduced during or after the conference.[17]

The plan recalled visions of an interim solution for Berlin that had been negotiated among the four powers during the Geneva conference of foreign ministers. At the Paris summit, the Soviet Union hoped to resume these negotiations where the parties had left off in Geneva, and the Western powers had exactly the same plan.

Leading up to the summit meeting, Wilhelm Grewe summarized for the Federal Government the dangers facing West Berlin if the powers were to sign this type of interim agreement (the Federal Government also considered it to be a real possibility). Grewe placed special emphasis on the psychological impact it would have on the city. Any deadline for the Western powers to withdraw their troops according to such an agreement "will be seen by the population of West Berlin as an execution date. Outside Berlin, too, the feeling toward this 'interim' will hardly differ. Investments in Berlin will come to a halt. A process of migration and relocation to the West will commence, and this will increasingly cripple Berlin's economic life."[18] The issue of a Communist "takeover" of the city would only be shelved temporarily. In its proposal for a "pre-peace treaty," the foreign ministry of the GDR also discussed implementing a peace treaty "in two steps." Adenauer and Ulbricht were well aware that Berlin's future represented the fate of the two political systems in Germany, and any solution depended entirely on the policy of the four powers.

Overshadowed by an espionage scandal, the summit conference went differently than the Western diplomats had expected. Before the use of satellites began, the United States depended on U-2 reconnaissance aircraft to collect intelligence on the Soviet Union's strategic armament. On 1 May 1960, the Soviet anti-aircraft defense system shot down a plane of this type over Siberia. Khrushchev used the episode to tout the USSR's success in propaganda against the Chinese. He claimed that it proved "the Americans would not be allowed to 'spit in the face' of the Soviet military-industrial complex any longer. His widely publicized anti-American show after May Day had to send a clear message both to adversaries and to friends: the USSR *really* is as strong militarily as Khrushchev had always claimed. The more hype over the latest U-2 incident, the better."[19]

Khrushchev hoped to use this incident at the Paris summit as well. As the Soviet delegates set off for the conference, they were still instructed to reach an agreement with the Western powers if possible. But at the Moscow airport, Khrushchev changed his mind: "Any negotiations with Eisenhower should begin only when he offered excuses for the spy flights."[20] This is precisely how things played out. At the first session of the summit, Khrushchev declared the Soviet Union unwilling to enter negotiations on account of the spy flight and the still pending American apology. He rescinded his invitation to Eisenhower to visit the Soviet Union and suggested "pushing the summit conference back six months—an especially perfidious insult to Eisenhower, since Eisenhower would no longer be in office six months later."[21] Behind Khrushchev's strategy was likely a recognition that the United States and France's stance on the Berlin question would not produce the result that he desired.

Since Khrushchev broke off rather than canceled the four-power negotiations, the failed conference did not lead the USSR to sign a separate peace treaty with the GDR, a move that the West dreaded. The Berlin Ultimatum entered its second year; Khrushchev wanted to wait out the results of the American presidential elections. For the SED, this meant that the situation in Berlin would remain "unchanged"[22] until the summit could finally take place. Ulbricht insisted that in light of the summit's failure, this tactic "was correct. Because the Soviet Union had not signed a peace treaty with the GDR directly after the failed summit conference in Paris, [its] position had improved. The opponent could not claim that the Soviet Union had provoked the summit's failure as an excuse to sign a peace treaty with the GDR."[23]

Khrushchev could do the West German government no greater favor "than prevent the conference from convening. In his native Cologne dialect, Adenauer expressed his feelings in dramatic terms: 'We were terribly lucky once again,' he said to [Felix] von Eckardt after receiving news of the éclat in Paris."[24]

The four powers had not reached a decision on Germany and Berlin, thereby leaving the German question open. Khrushchev postponed all decisions on Berlin until the next summit meeting with the newly elected American president; before then nothing would change on the Soviet side, as Khrushchev announced publicly. The Soviet leader took this opportunity to consider the SED's role moving forward; meanwhile, the situation "prompted the SED to think about how it could harness the latest development toward the GDR's goal of international recognition. Soviet and East German visions seemed to converge in the late summer of 1960 in the tactic of allowing the GDR de facto to gradually take over Allied rights. Maintain a policy of faits accomplis—this was the motto of the Eastern alliance."[25]

Notes

1. Michael Stürmer, "Der lange Schatten des Tyrannen: Westbindung und Geschichtsbild in Deutschland," in *Von Geschichte umgeben: Joachim Fest zum Sechzigsten*, ed. Karl Dietrich Bracher et al. (Berlin (West), 1986), 259.
2. Notes by Nikita S. Khrushchev, 10 August 1959, AdBIK.
3. "Gespräch Chruschtschows mit dem Ersten Sekretär der SED, Walter Ulbricht, am 31. März 1961," excerpt, in Wettig, *Chruschtschows Westpolitik*, 112.
4. Presseamt beim Vorsitzenden des Ministerrates der DDR, ed., *XXII. Parteitag der Kommunistischen Partei der Sowjetunion, 17.–31.10.1961, Protokoll* (Berlin (East), n.d.), 3036.
5. "Es lebe der Leninismus, Peking 1960," quoted in *Konflikte im Weltkommunismus: Eine Dokumentation zur Krise Moskau–Peking*, ed. Hermann Weber (Munich, 1964), 82.
6. Speech by Walter Ulbricht, in " Protokoll des 9. Plenums des ZK der SED," 20–23 July 1960, SAPMO-BArch, NY 4182/633, 4–5.

7. Ibid.

8. Zubok and Pleshakov, *Inside the Kremlin's Cold War*, 234–35.

9. Kissinger, *Diplomacy*, 573–74.

10. Schwabe, *Weltmacht*, 264–65.

11. Steininger, *Mauerbau*, 141.

12. Abteilung Information des MfAA, "Information zu den Beziehungen West-Deutschland–UdSSR" (handwritten to Walter Ulbricht), Berlin, 7 January 1960, SAPMO-BArch, DY 30/3497.

13. Nikita S. Khrushchev to Walter Ulbricht, 4 January 1960, SAPMO-BArch, DY 30/3507.

14. See Matthias Uhl, *Krieg um Berlin? Die sowjetische Militär- und Sicherheitspolitik in der zweiten Berlin-Krise 1958–1962* (Munich, 2008), 114–15.

15. Telegram from Walter Ulbricht to Nikita S. Khrushchev, Berlin, 31 January 1960, SAPMO-BArch, DY 30/3507.

16. "Plan für die Vorbereitungen der Gipfelkonferenz," 13 January 1960, SAPMO-BArch DY 30/3507.

17. MfAA, "Vorschlag für den Abschluss eines Friedensvertrages mit den beiden deutschen Staaten," 26 January 1960, SAPMO-BArch, DY 30/3507.

18. Grewe, *Rückblenden*, 435.

19. Zubok and Pleshakov, *Inside the Kremlin's Cold War*, 205. Italics in original.

20. Ibid.

21. Steininger, *Mauerbau*, 158.

22. Walter Ulbricht to Nikita S. Khrushchev, 22 November 1960, SAPMO-BArch, DY 30/3507.

23. File note on a conversation between Walter Ulbricht and Nikita S. Khrushchev, Moscow, 2 February 1961, SAPMO-BArch, DY 30/3506.

24. Grewe, *Rückblenden*, 437.

25. Lemke, *Berlinkrise*, 150.

Chapter 12

CRISIS IN THE GDR, CHANGES TO THE BORDER REGIME, AND INTERZONAL TRADE

A Supply Crisis and the Exodus Movement from the GDR

Simultaneous to fundamental changes in the international political constellation of 1960–61, the Berlin confrontation took on new dimensions with the crisis in East Germany. In the fall of 1960, while the GDR's economic troubles intensified, leaders in East Berlin and Moscow began to discuss "security measures" for West Berlin in order to address the open sector borders and the growing number of refugees fleeing the GDR. The SED had caused its own crisis by setting unrealistic economic goals and forcing agricultural collectivization. Fifteen thousand farmers fled, and "the yield per hectare of wheat, potatoes, and root vegetables sank by 25 percent."[1] Food rationing ended in 1958, but it was reintroduced in 1960 in the form of customer lists at grocery stores.

The most important indicator of the GDR's acute state crisis was the snowball-ing number of refugees fleeing to West Berlin, similar to the situation in 1952–53, through the one hole in the "fortified state border" between the GDR and the Federal Republic. In 1959, 143,917 refugees left the GDR and East Berlin; in 1960 the number rose to 199,188, and in 1961, 207,026 GDR citizens found their way to West Berlin. Nearly half of the refugees in all three years were under the age of twenty-five. The numbers from June to August 1961 reflect the dramatic escalation in this wave of emigration: 19,198 in June, 30,415 in July, and 47,433 in August. In just three months, 96,946 people voted with their feet against the SED state.[2] Ulbricht provided Khrushchev with an unembellished description of the GDR's economic situation in January 1961, urging the Soviet leader to find a swift solution to the "Westberlin question." The SED's most pressing issue in Berlin was the open sector border and with it the city-wide S- and U-Bahn metro systems (the networks of East and West Berlin were not separated until 13 August

1961). Ulbricht repeatedly voiced these concerns to Khrushchev in order to elicit a rapid decision on Berlin.

At the Fifth Party Congress of the SED in 1958, Ulbricht and Khrushchev had begun their Berlin offensive with a fanfare of propaganda. Just three years later, it was already necessary to seal off the sector border in order to prevent the GDR from "bleeding" further. In negotiations with the United States, Khrushchev's position changed significantly in response to the crisis in East Germany; suddenly he found himself under pressure to act quickly. Renewing his ultimatum from 1958, the Soviet party leader threatened to sign a separate peace treaty with the GDR in December 1961 if the West refused to make concessions on the Berlin question. Kennedy reacted to this threat by reiterating the rights of the Western powers to remain in Berlin. In this atmosphere of open confrontation, securing the GDR became the main objective of Soviet crisis management. The Vienna Summit ended as fruitlessly as its predecessor, and then came the decision: with the approval of the Soviet Union, the GDR closed Berlin's sector border on 13 August 1961.

Border Controls and Special Permits to Enter East Berlin

In late August 1960, the SED decided to demonstrate the GDR's sovereignty within is capital. Citizens of West Germany now required special approval to pass through border crossings to East Berlin, and the rules for West Berliners traveling to and through the GDR changed as well. Both measures were taken according to plans for the "Free City of Westberlin," building a system to monitor people's movement that would remain in place until 1989. Beginning on 8 September 1960, citizens of the Federal Republic needed a permit to visit the "capital of the GDR." The American government protested to the Soviet foreign ministry, accurately describing the action by the East German authorities as an attempt "to control the movement of persons between the eastern and western sectors of Greater Berlin." The American government saw this as a "grave violation of Berlin's four-power status." The United States would never accept "that the eastern sector of Berlin forms part of the territory of the 'German Democratic Republic' or that Berlin is 'on the territory of the German Democratic Republic.'"[3] The Soviet foreign ministry's response cited the sovereignty of the GDR, which existed since 1955 and allowed East Germany to make decisions on "questions of movement of the German population between the G.D.R. and the F.R.G." The note went on: "The Soviet Government considers that the note of the Government of the United States in connection with measures of the Government of the German Democratic Republic for the regulation of the entrance into the limits of its capital by citizens of the F.R.G. represents an effort to interfere in the internal affairs of a sovereign government." Moreover, the Soviet government insisted "that the Government of the United States undertake necessary measures for the suppression of revanchist activity in West Berlin."[4] In this way, the Soviet Union defended the SED's actions to the Western powers.

In terms of propaganda, the occasion for this step by the East German government was the Tag der Heimat (roughly, "Homeland Day") commemorated by the associations of expellees on 29 August 1960 in West Berlin. The GDR's Ministry of the Interior used this gathering to justify "refusing entry into East Berlin to citizens of the Federal Republic for the period of 31 August to 4 September 1960 if they did not possess the required permit."[5] The politburo of the SED also informed Khrushchev of its decision to only allow West Berlin residents to travel to or through the GDR if they carried a personal identification card issued by West Berlin rather than a passport from the Federal Republic: "The institutions of the GDR have been instructed to no longer recognize as valid personal documents the passports issued unlawfully by the Federal Republic to residents of Westberlin."[6]

The Berlin Crisis of 1958–61 added the term "revanchism" to the political vocabulary of the SED.[7] The West German government never gave up its hope for reunification based on free elections, nor was it ready to recognize the Oder-Neisse line before a peace treaty was signed with a unified Germany. Since the Soviet Union pushed for a peace treaty that would make the outcome of the Second World War and the division of Germany irreversible, both of the Federal Republic's positions became "revanchist." In order to achieve its political goal, the USSR used propaganda to concoct an image of the Federal Republic as the enemy of peace in Europe. The "revanchism campaign against the associations of expellees and the Federal Republic began in 1959–60."[8] The Tag der Heimat in Berlin provided an ideal excuse for the SED to implement its new mechanisms of control over the movement of people to East Berlin and, as the "anti-fascist"—and therefore the sole legitimate—German state, to demonstrate that the GDR was no longer willing, in its own words, to silently tolerate "revanchist activities" in West Berlin. Likewise, the SED's draft of a statute for the "Free City of Westberlin" also prohibited "revanchist organizations."

The introduction of required permits to enter the GDR and East Berlin did not occur without coordination with Moscow, as indicated in a letter to Ulbricht from Johannes König, deputy foreign minister of the GDR, accompanying a draft for a joint declaration by the Socialist States of Europe (except for the Soviet Union) on "Revanchism in West Germany." The declaration included propaganda that explained the new security measures for FRG citizens who wished to visit East Berlin. König told Ulbricht that the draft was based on suggestions by "our Soviet friends."[9] The declaration also tried to stigmatize the Federal Republic as an obstacle in the way of European peace: "The government of the German Federal Republic propagates the spirit of revanche, ethnic hatred, and war in a planned and systematic manner to prepare the West German population for new, aggressive adventures that aim to reverse the outcome not only of World War II but also of World War I. To this end, [the FRG] has refused to recognize the legally determined German borders. Revanchism is the official state policy of the West German government today." In addition, the signatory governments also demanded signing a peace treaty with both German states "in order to rein in the revanchism in West Germany and to secure peace in Europe."[10]

On 13 September, Ulbricht implemented the next step discussed with Khrushchev: "The SED introduced a visa requirement for West Berliners who used the territory of the GDR as a transit route."[11] When the inter-German trade authority of the FRG requested the decree's reversal, the GDR responded with a blunt rejection. Ulbricht had already informed Khrushchev that the SED expected West Germany to enact trade sanctions against the GDR.[12] The SED leader took calculated risks in order to push forward a solution to the "Westberlin question" using the tools at his disposal, namely, the control of people's movement within and to Berlin. Along with these measures, the Volkspolizei began to monitor the movement of foreign diplomats across the checkpoints within the city. The Papal Nuncio, for example, was no longer allowed to enter East Berlin. On 22 September, the American ambassador to the Federal Republic was stopped by the Volkspolizei at the Brandenburg Gate and asked to identify himself. This led to increased diplomatic activity over the following days, and the Soviet embassy asked the GDR's foreign ministry to inform it "if new measures were taken to control the entry of Western diplomats into democratic Berlin."[13]

Ulbricht reacted to Khrushchev in a letter: "There have been no special regulations for foreigners and stateless persons in our ordinances so far. In the accompanying document, we have included a draft of a communiqué and a draft of an order by the minister of the interior addressing these points. The politburo has decided to issue the communiqué and the order only when an appropriate occasion presents itself and only with the approval of our Soviet friends." Furthermore, new signs at the checkpoints would present a loud visual cue telling visitors where they were: "'You are entering the Capital of the German Democratic Republic' (until now the signs read: 'You are entering the democratic sector')."[14]

The situation in Berlin was not supposed to change before the summit meeting between Khrushchev and Kennedy. Ulbricht, however, stressed to Khrushchev that the Western powers had not respected Berlin's status in their sectors either. They had allowed the Federal Government to make West Berlin the "most prominent base . . . for its revanchist policy, for foreign agent activities targeting the Socialist countries, and for the organization of desertion from the GDR." Ulbricht urged Khrushchev to position himself on the SED's proposals to improve the surveillance of people's movement: in addition to the already existing requirement that West German visitors to the GDR register themselves, Ulbricht also wished to introduce a visa requirement for foreigners. However, "the militaries and diplomats of the Western powers" would "only have to show their identification documents." The laws of the GDR would also apply to its capital city, although representation for Berlin's population in the People's Chamber of the GDR would be "postponed for now." Evoking the events of 17 June 1953, the term "security measures" encompassed the SED's response to continued attempts by the "Adenauer government" to "light little fires in the GDR. This occurs by engaging repatriates and influencing groups of Westberlin youth, as well as through the leaders of some churches, who are active in organizing a semi-legal resistance movement. Therefore, we must improve our security measures." Against the backdrop of these supposed security threats to the GDR emanating from West Berlin, Ulbricht suggested that an upcoming meeting between CPSU and SED party delegations address tactics for the city, deciding "which security measures the GDR should implement."[15] Closing the sector border in Berlin was now on the table.

The Conflict over Interzonal Trade

After the GDR refused to negotiate over its new rules regulating the movement of persons within and to Berlin, the Federal Government announced on 30 September 1960 that it would terminate the agreement on inter-German trade—which provided advantageous conditions to the GDR—at the end of the year.[16] At the same time, the FRG declared itself ready to reverse its course if the SED stopped requiring West German citizens to seek permission to enter East Berlin at the inner-city checkpoints. In Ulbricht's opinion, the United States, Adenauer, and Willy Brandt were responsible for taking this step. Writing to Khrushchev, he was certain that the termination of trade represented a "preparatory measure to avoid holding a peace conference and signing a peace treaty."[17] He assured Khrushchev that the GDR was willing to negotiate with the Federal Republic over a new trade agreement.

Ulbricht was well aware that the economy of the GDR relied on supplies from the Federal Republic, as he stressed to Khrushchev in another letter. Gerhard Wettig summarizes this letter as follows:

> The GDR's economy faced a serious deficit in the goods it needed to achieve its production goals. Deliveries from the West, especially from West Germany, constituted far more than half of the required goods in some important categories, in one case as much as 92 percent. Of course the GDR could obtain these materials elsewhere, but there was not enough money. This argumentation was meant to convince Soviet leaders to guarantee supplies for the GDR's economy. If the USSR did not jump in and provide massive deliveries, the already difficult state of production would become a catastrophe within the following year.[18]

Only with the Soviet Union's help would the orchestrators of the SED's planned economy be able to meet their goal of building closer ties to the Soviet economy and breaking free of economic dependence on the Federal Republic. Ulbricht listed the GDR's economic wishes to Khrushchev: the state needed secure supplies of several raw materials, a stronger expansion of its steel industry for the production of special steel plates, and a steady supply of semi-finished products. For December 1960 alone, the GDR would need 20,000 tons of meat, along with at least 75,000 tons of meat and 47,000 tons of butter for 1961.[19] It was Ulbricht's goal "to reach joint agreements to entwine the economies of the GDR and the Soviet Union in order to stabilize the economy of the GDR and achieve economic independence from the disruptive maneuvers of the imperialist and militaristic circles of West Germany."[20] The SED state's political separation from West Germany should be reflected in its economy as well.

Khrushchev learned in the autumn of 1960 that stabilizing the GDR was not only a political task but also an economic one: "Both sides are insufficiently prepared to formulate a precise strategy and measures to free the GDR economically from West Germany ([Khrushchev] apparently did not know that the GDR is dependent upon West Germany). Adenauer's announcement has really forced us to face the situation."[21] Khrushchev approved plans to integrate the East German economy into the division of labor among the Socialist states, but at the same time he urged Ulbricht to initiate results-oriented negotiations to spur West Germany to resume interzonal trade. Regarding these negotiations, the Soviet leader told Ulbricht that he had already spoken to Kroll, the West German ambassador in Moscow. He suggested to Ulbricht that Adenauer might "give [the GDR] room to come up for air."[22] Khrushchev's conversation with Kroll on a solution to the conflict over inter-German trade demonstrates the Soviet Union's pursuit of a split Germany policy while always keeping an eye on both states and West Berlin.

During negotiations between the CPSU and the SED on 30 November in Moscow, Khrushchev suggested "formulating a maximal and a minimal economic program that would lead to the GDR's independence. Maximal for the case of total severance, minimal if the trade agreement can be renewed. We do not want to reach into our pockets right now."[23] According to the Russian protocol, Khrushchev brusquely rejected Ulbricht's request for a credit in the amount of 500 million marks: "And now you are asking for nearly 68 tons of gold. That is unthinkable. It cannot be the case that you are purchasing goods but we have to pay for them. We have very little gold ourselves and need to save what we have for an emergency."[24] With respect to the GDR's long-term economic security, Khrushchev suggested creating a joint working group "to guarantee a continual provision of raw materials to the GDR and avoid the constant occurrence of new negotiations and consultations."[25] Moscow's position was clear: the GDR should do everything possible to hold constructive negotiations over the resumption of interzonal trade. In return, Moscow promised to compensate for the GDR's problems in its own economic planning.

In February 1961, Anastas I. Mikoyan and Heinrich Rau, the East German minister of foreign trade, discussed inter-German trade and the economic relations between the Soviet Union and the GDR. The question of credit came up once more, and Mikoyan replied: "It doesn't hurt to be in debt to West Germany." Regarding their tactics toward the Federal Republic on the question of trade, he continued: "The GDR has to let WG [West Germany] know that it is not dependent upon WG ('if they are not willing to change, we can just let things be'). If difficulties arise, the SU [Soviet Union] will jump in. With a production of six million tons of milled material, the SU does not have a problem sending the GDR 200,000 tons. Comrade Mikoyan is in favor of expanding trade further—not for political reasons but rather for national reasons. This point should be impressed upon West Germany (subtly, 'throwing in a word or two here and there' in conversations with the capitalists)." The two men also agreed that the Soviet Union should be sent a list of goods "that the GDR receives from WG so that the SU can supply these things in the future."[26] Mikoyan encouraged the SED to present itself to the Federal Republic as more independent than it actually was, disputing the Federal Republic's claim to control inter-German trade throughout all of Germany.

The termination of interzonal trade presented the SED and the CPSU directly with the contradiction between political desire and economic feasibility. The GDR's economy relied on supplies from the Federal Republic in many areas. When the FRG ended the agreement on interzonal trade, this dependency upon deliveries of special types of steel, steel sheets, and raw materials became obvious. Two months later, Ulbricht reminded Moscow that the GDR was once part of a unified economic area: "We are a state that came into being and still exists without a foundation of raw materials, and—with open borders—must struggle to win the contest between two competing systems."[27] Ulbricht's wish to integrate the economy of the GDR into that of the Soviet Union in order to sever the GDR from the Federal Republic was only logical, especially as the positive effects of West German economic integration into the European Economic Community stood on display just across the border. The plan failed, however, because the Soviet Union lacked the necessary economic strength. In reality, the GDR's economy continued to depend on the Federal Republic. The Soviet Union urged the SED to seek a compromise with Bonn on the procedures for West German citizens entering East Berlin so that the Federal Republic would resume interzonal trade, at least temporarily, and let the GDR "come up for air."

Negotiations on Interzonal Trade

At the outset of negotiations between representatives from the two "currency areas" Deutsche Mark (DM) West and DM East, Kurt Leopold, head of the West German Interzonal Trade Bureau, declared: "Inter-German trade is inextricably tied to free movement along the access routes to West Berlin. Without it, trade would not exist at all."[28] Before resuming inter-German trade, Bonn expected a concession from the GDR on its visa requirements for West German citizens entering East Berlin. In an informal conversation, however, Leopold told a representative from the GDR's Ministry for Foreign Trade and Inter-German Trade that the Western side would not necessarily "demand the retraction of the inner-city measures put in place by the GDR."[29] Nonetheless, Ulbricht informed Khrushchev in a telegram that the West German government "wished for an end to controls at the sector border (Brandenburg Gate), which means lifting the orders of the GDR regarding visas for West German citizens in the capital of the GDR."[30] But on 20 December,

Leopold only asked for suggestions from the GDR to "change the 'visuals' of the checkpoints."[31]

That same day, Minister Rau informed Ulbricht and Grotewohl of the developments. Rau proposed a solution to the problem of "the visuals": it might be possible, he wrote, "to issue pre-printed visas valid for one day (the date of issue) at the passport controls, and the validity of the visa could be tied to the passport number. If this were in place, the Volkspolizei officer would only have to enter the passport number into the visa, which would speed up the entire process."[32] Moscow answered Ulbricht's telegram by advising him to act "with elasticity," especially concerning passport controls for West Germans. He should assure the FRG in negotiations "that the government of the GDR did not wish to impede visits by citizens of the Federal Republic to democratic Berlin, as long as they respected the sovereignty of the GDR." The letter contained a further suggestion regarding the surveillance of "people's movement at the sector border": since the control mechanisms were not yet operating "to their full extent," it would be expedient for reasons "discussed thoroughly [in Moscow] to avoid escalating the situation at the present time."[33] Rau's suggestion went into effect, and the final protocol of negotiations over the resumption of interzonal trade included an agreement to improve "procedural specifications" in the GDR's decree of 8 September on the control of movement for West German citizens visiting the GDR.[34] Interzonal trade resumed on 1 January 1961.

Mikoyan stayed abreast of the negotiations through the GDR's chief negotiator, Heinz Behrendt, and requested detailed information on the process of inter-German trade. Behrendt informed him of a disruption in deliveries of steel products. Mikoyan also asked why the projected quantities for inter-German trade in 1961 were lower than those in 1960. Behrendt blamed the cancellation of the interzonal trade agreement; missing deliveries from West Germany had to be offset by imports from other countries. "Since we have paid for those imports with deliveries of goods, the goods ready for export to West Germany are only available to a limited extent."[35]

According to Khrushchev's own account, this conflict over inter-German trade convinced the Soviet leader that there was more at stake than simply the GDR's international recognition. Because the East German economy was so weak, an absence of West German supplies could force the Soviet Union to step in with aid deliveries in order to stabilize the GDR. Indeed, this danger influenced the Soviet Union's approach to the second Berlin Crisis: in negotiations with the Federal Republic to resume inter-German trade, Khrushchev urged Ulbricht to compromise.

After the construction of the Berlin Wall, the GDR's economic weakness was one of Khrushchev's central arguments before the presidium of the CPSU Central Committee in January 1962 to explain why the Wall represented the maximum that the Soviet Union could have achieved. Before the "final battle over Westberlin could be fought, the economy of the GDR had to be integrated more completely into that of the Soviet Union."[36]

Notes

1. Rainer Karlsch, "Krise als Chance? Die DDR-Wirtschaft nach dem Volksaufstand und dem Mauerbau," in *Staatsgründung auf Raten? Auswirkungen des Volksaufstandes 1953 und des Mauerbaus 1961 auf Staat, Militär und Gesellschaft der DDR*, ed. Torsten Diedrich and Ilko-Sascha Kowalczuk (Berlin, 2005), 197.
2. "Statistiken und Dokumente," in Hertle et al., *Mauerbau und Mauerfall*, 312–14.
3. "Note From the United States to the Soviet Union Protesting the Extension of East German Travel Restrictions on Entry into East Berlin, September 12, 1960," in U.S. Dept. of State, *Documents on Germany*, 719.
4. "Note From the Soviet Union to the United States Asserting the Right of the German Democratic Republic to Regulate Travel Into East Berlin, September 26, 1960," in U.S. Dept. of State, *Documents on Germany*, 720–21.
5. Lemke, *Berlinkrise*, 150.
6. Telegram from Walter Ulbricht to Nikita S. Khrushchev, 5 September 1960, SAPMO-BArch, DY 30/3507. Since West Berlin did not formally belong to the Federal Republic, residents of West Berlin were not granted West German passports; instead, they were issued special, "provisional" (*vorläufige*) personal identification documents. However, many residents of West Berlin also had a formal place of residence in the Federal Republic and used their West German passports to travel.
7. See "Stichwort 'Revanchismus,'" in Weißgerber, *Giftige Worte*, 271–73.
8. Heike Amos, "SED und MfS gegen die Vertriebenenverbände in der Bundesrepublik Deutschland 1949 bis 1989," (manuscript, Berlin, 2010), 60.
9. Johannes König to Walter Ulbricht, Berlin, 6 September 1960, SAPMO-BArch, DY 30/3497. This letter to Ulbricht was sent along with the text of the declaration.
10. "Gemeinsame Erklärung der Regierungen der Volksrepubliken Albanien, Bulgarien, Rumänien, Polen, Ungarn, der ČSSR und der DDR zur verstärkten revanchistischen Aktivität in Westdeutschland" (draft), 6 September 1960, SAPMO-BArch, DY 30/3497.
11. Lemke, *Berlinkrise*, 151.
12. See ibid., 150.
13. Johannes König to Walter Ulbricht, Berlin, 27 September 1960, SAPMO-BArch, DY 30/3497.
14. Walter Ulbricht to Nikita S. Khrushchev, Berlin, 18 October 1960, SAPMO-BArch, DY 30/3507.
15. Ibid.
16. See also the section on "Interzonal Trade" in chapter 2 of this volume. Gradually the term "inter-German trade" (*innerdeutscher Handel*) grew more common to describe the trade activity at this time, even though its legal basis in the 1949 agreement still remained valid—allowing the GDR to participate indirectly in the European Economic Community.
17. Walter Ulbricht to Nikita S. Khrushchev, Berlin, 18 October 1960, SAPMO-BArch, DY 30/3507.
18. Wettig, *Chruschtschows Berlin-Krise*, 110.
19. Walter Ulbricht to Nikita S. Khrushchev, Moscow, 22 November 1960, SAPMO-BArch, DY 30/3507.
20. Walter Ulbricht to Nikita S. Khrushchev, Berlin, 18 January 1961, SAPMO-BArch, DY 30/3508.
21. File note on a conversation between Walter Ulbricht and Nikita S. Khrushchev, 30 November 1960, SAPMO-BArch, DY 30/3566.
22. "Gespräch Chruschtschows mit dem Ersten Sekretär der SED, Walter Ulbricht, am 30. November 1960," Russian protocol, in Wettig, *Chruschtschows Westpolitik*, 47. On the Soviet side, Gromyko and Alexei N. Kosygin, first deputy chairman of the Council of Ministers, also par-

ticipated in this meeting; the German delegation included Bruno Leuschner, head of the State Planning Commission, and Heinrich Rau, minister of foreign trade.

23. File note on a conversation between Walter Ulbricht and Nikita S. Khrushchev, 30 November 1960, SAPMO-BArch, DY 30/3566.

24. "Gespräch Chruschtschows mit dem Ersten Sekretär der SED, Walter Ulbricht, am 30. November 1960," Russian protocol, in Wettig, *Chruschtschows Westpolitik*, 47.

25. File note on a conversation between Walter Ulbricht and Nikita S. Khrushchev, 30 November 1960, SAPMO-BArch, DY 30/3566.

26. File note on a conversation between Anastas I. Mikoyan and Heinrich Rau at the signing of an agreement, Moscow, 23 February 1961, SAPMO-BArch, DY 30/3566. The passages cited here are marked in the original document.

27. Walter Ulbricht to Nikita S. Khrushchev, Berlin, 18 January 1961, SAPMO-BArch, DY 30/3508.

28. Wettig, *Chruschtschows Berlin-Krise*, 114.

29. Hauptabteilung Innerdeutscher Handel, note on an unofficial conversation at the Interzonal Trade Bureau, Berlin, 12 December 1960, SAPMO-BArch, DY 30/3566.

30. Telegram from Walter Ulbricht to Nikita S. Khrushchev, 14 December 1960, SAPMO-BArch, DY 30/3566.

31. Heinz Behrendt, note on conversations with Kurt Leopold, 20 December 1960, SAPMO-BArch, DY 30/3566.

32. Heinrich Rau to Walter Ulbricht and Otto Grotewohl, Berlin, 20 December 1960, SAPMO-BArch, DY 30/3566.

33. This document provides neither a date nor the name of its author, but contains the handwritten note "strictly confidential" from 22 December 1960. In the protocol it appears as an answer to Ulbricht's telegram, and the sender was very likely Khrushchev. SAPMO-BArch, DY 30/3566.

34. Kurt Leopold to Heinz Behrendt, attachment: "Ergebnisprotokoll der Verhandlungen über die Wiederaufnahme des innerdeutschen Handels," 29 December 1960, SAPMO-BArch, DY 30/3566.

35. Note on a conversation between Heinz Behrendt and Anastas I. Mikoyan, 28 January 1961, SAPMO-BArch, DY 30/3566.

36. "Stenogram der Sitzung des Präsidiums des ZK der KPdSU am 8. Januar 1962," in Wettig, *Chruschtschows Westpolitik*, 509. See also chapter 18 of this volume.

Chapter 13

ULBRICHT: RESOLVE THE "WESTBERLIN QUESTION" NOW!

The Status Quo in Berlin before Khrushchev's Summit with President Kennedy

From summit meeting to summit meeting, Khrushchev repeatedly extended the Berlin Ultimatum of 1958 and instructed the SED to keep waiting on a solution to the question of West Berlin. Reaching an agreement with the United States took priority over signing a peace treaty with the GDR, and it was important to see what would come out of talks with newly elected American President John F. Kennedy. The Soviet head of party and state adhered to this position in a conversation with Ulbricht on 30 November 1960:

> *Khrushchev:* Another question is whether we should pursue a peace treaty with the GDR in 1961. It is unlikely that a peace treaty will be signed with both German states. If we bring up this issue of a peace treaty, then we are also open to the possibility of signing an interim agreement—in other words, an agreement among the four powers on a preliminary status for West Berlin, tied to a deadline before which the two Germanys must negotiate their problems. If they cannot reach an agreement, we would be free to sign a peace treaty with the GDR. That would be our concession to Eisenhower, to save his reputation and refrain from giving the impression that we want to chase them out of West Berlin. Now more than ever before, this is still the right approach. You, the Germans, will not negotiate with each other; we will then sign a peace treaty with you, and the Western powers will end up with no peace treaty at all. This does not bother us. We do not get anything from them anyway. We will have to accept the escalation and sign a peace treaty. When will we sign it, in 1961?
>
> *Ulbricht:* No!
>
> *Khrushchev:* Why not?
>
> *Ulbricht:* We do not have the capacities.

Khrushchev: Politically or economically?

Ulbricht: Only economically. Politically I am in favor of it.

Khrushchev: In terms of politics, we are almost certain that the Western powers will not start a war if we sign a peace treaty with the GDR. And economically—do you really believe they are going to declare a blockade, meaning economic war? I don't think so.[1]

In order to put pressure on the Soviet Union, Ulbricht argued with Khrushchev in November 1960 over the danger posed by Bonn: "Conflict in Berlin will increase. The Bonn government has changed its position since the government's declaration of 30 June at the Bundestag; it sees the Federal Republic as the final German state and insists upon maintaining the status quo, perpetuating these lingering traces of war. Bonn envisions a solution to the German question not from a national and European perspective, but as a satellite state of the United States." The SPD was not a viable alternative either, Ulbricht continued, since its candidate for chancellor, Willy Brandt, was already preparing to build a "Grand Coalition" with the CDU after the Bundestag elections of 1961. Therefore, it was "imperative" to try to force Adenauer into peaceful coexistence.[2] The portrayal of the Federal Republic as a "satellite state" caused a dispute between Gromyko and Ulbricht, exemplifying the way in which Soviet Germany policy always took both German states into consideration:

Gromyko: In the GDR right now, propaganda is being spread that the FRG is not a legitimate state. That is not entirely in line with our position that there are two German states.

Ulbricht: We mean to say that two states exist in Germany, but the West German state never implemented the resolutions of the Potsdam Conference and therefore has no legitimacy.[3]

Gromyko: But how can a peace treaty be signed with an illegitimate state?

Ulbricht: A state is a state no matter what.

Gromyko: But do you mean to say that the FRG is not a sovereign state?

Ulbricht: According to the Paris agreement, the FRG has relinquished some of its rights.[4] In this regard, it is important to differentiate between political and legal aspects. Politically it is possible and necessary to sign a peace treaty with them. But legally, they do not recognize us and we do not recognize them.

Gromyko: One can criticize the FRG as a militaristic state. But to criticize it as a non-sovereign state—that would be harmful to our tactic.

Ulbricht: This is more of an issue concerning the awareness of our population. Our population says that the GDR is a legitimate state that has fulfilled the Potsdam Agreement. The Bonn state, however, is illegitimate.

Khrushchev: How the GDR addresses this question internally, that is a domestic affair. But we are maintaining our position. We are not obliged to share your interpretation. We have diplomatic relations with both German states and believe that both are sovereign.[5]

Despite his political refusal to recognize the Federal Republic, Ulbricht knew all too well that the Soviet Union was concerned with Germany as a whole. Even

before the meeting in Moscow, Ulbricht conveyed to Khrushchev that the SED was
planning to intervene in the upcoming Bundestag elections "in order to bring about
change in the politics of West Germany. We must sway the Bonn government to
transition to a policy of compromise [*Politik der Verständigung*]. Through this strategy,
we will bring the fight over general and complete disarmament and the neutrality
of Germany to the center of West German election campaigns. We wish to thwart
plans by the right-leaning Social Democratic leaders who, in these elections, hope to
exceed the Adenauer government in revanchism and chauvinism and shape the election campaign primarily around socio-political issues."[6] Ulbricht's declaration was
followed by action: in Stuttgart, the illegal apparatus of the KPD helped organize a
new party, the German Peace Union (Deutsche Friedensunion) in December 1960.[7]
The SED/KPD developed a new approach to the Confederation of German Trade
Unions in order to change the internal power constellation of the SPD.[8] For the
SED's own policy toward the West as well, it was "essential to assess the viability of
the struggle for a peace treaty and the resolution of the Westberlin question."[9]

Responding to Ulbricht at their 30 November meeting, Khrushchev painted a
different picture of the Federal Republic's policies, referring among other things
to a conversation with the West German ambassador to Moscow. Ambassador
Kroll had declared "that no one in West Germany intended to swallow the GDR
or change the borders."[10] With this in mind, the Soviet leader admitted that everyone had underestimated the challenge of "freeing" the GDR from its economic
dependence upon West Germany. Thus the argument was born that socialism in
the GDR could only flourish within secure borders—an argument that SED propaganda would later use to justify building the Berlin Wall. In Moscow, Ulbricht
forcefully emphasized the problem of West Berlin and signaled that there would
be further conflict to come:

> However, the situation in Berlin has grown more complicated, much to our disad-
> vantage. West Berlin has become stronger economically. This is also evident in the
> fact that about 50,000 workers from East Berlin work permanently in West Berlin.
> This means that part of our qualified workforce goes over to West Berlin because
> they can earn higher wages there. We have not yet taken action against this. The state
> of the intelligentsia is also a disgrace. For example, a teacher in the West earns 200
> to 300 Marks more than in the East. Doctors earn twice as much. Moreover, they
> receive a significant one-time sum of money just for going over to West Germany.
> All of these circumstances influence the segment of the intelligentsia that otherwise
> has little to do with politics. Why don't we raise the salaries for these social groups?
> First, our resources are inadequate. Second, even if we did raise their salaries, we
> would not be able to match their purchasing power with the goods we have on hand,
> so they would spend the money in West Berlin anyway. Still, we are going to try.
> Another issue is that many children from East Berlin go to school in West Berlin.
> We have a law against this, but so far we have not enforced it because we do not want
> to provoke a major conflict. From now on we are going to try to protect ourselves
> against these unpleasant developments, but the number of conflicts in Berlin will
> only increase.[11]

Khrushchev did not relinquish control over the conflict, even though he acknowledged that in Berlin, "many vestiges have endured after the war that jeopardize the sovereignty of the GDR." However, he took a clear position on the strategy required to change the situation, and this was not up for discussion:

> *Khrushchev:* They will not withdraw their troops from West Berlin if we have no agreement to that extent. But we are not going to send our troops over there to force them to withdraw theirs. We will work out a tactic with you to gradually push the Western powers out of West Berlin—but without war. For this we will use leverage that the GDR already possesses.
> *Ulbricht:* Fine.[12]

Khrushchev still counted on the possibility of a "transitional treaty" among the four status powers, by which the two German states would be obligated to reach a "settlement." The GDR's participation in negotiating such a four-power agreement did not even come under consideration. This aspect alone must have led the SED delegation to wonder "whether the USSR planned to hand over individual rights in Germany and Berlin to the GDR at all. Reserving certain rights meant maintaining some level of control, though not so much in relation to the GDR specifically—it was much more important to Moscow to remain present in Germany as a (theoretical) whole and, through the mechanism of shared Allied rights, to ensure its ability to 'lawfully' interfere in any potential development."[13] As Khrushchev's conversation with Kroll demonstrated, the Soviet premier personally intervened in the negotiations over interzonal trade, which had functioned so far on the basis of an inter-Allied agreement to end the Berlin Blockade.

Khrushchev made one thing clear to the SED delegation: only if it proved impossible to reach an understanding with the Western powers and between the two German states "would the Soviet Union be free to conclude a peace treaty with the GDR. If the Western powers are unresponsive, it will be necessary to increase the urgency of the situation and sign a peace treaty."[14] With this statement, Ulbricht received the clarity he needed on the question of a peace treaty. Reaching an agreement with the Western powers still took priority. What Khrushchev underestimated, however, was the severity of the crisis in the GDR.

Ulbricht Pushes for a Solution to the "Westberlin Question," 1961

The crisis that resulted from the SED's "overtaking principle," announced at the Fifth Party Congress in 1958, led significant portions of the workforce to emigrate over the open border in Berlin. A situation emerged in the GDR so dire that the SED could no longer await the outcome of Soviet summit diplomacy. In January 1961, SED leaders discussed how to proceed on the question of West Berlin.

Speaking to the politburo on 4 January, Ulbricht called for a "battle against desertion of the Republic. If we improve our work with the people, we will be able to rein in desertion." The phrase "work with the people" (*Arbeit mit den Menschen*) was used by the SED to mean that all party functionaries—indeed, all party members—were expected to stay alert to the behavior of their colleagues and friends in conversations at work, in schools, etc., to determine whether they planned to flee the GDR. Party loyals were instructed to dissuade others from leaving, or else inform the security apparatus in order to prevent them forcefully from taking this step. Emigration also factored in to international negotiations on a peace treaty. "I am in favor of calling together a group of comrades to come up with several suggestions for how to decisively stop desertion of the republic. This way, we will not end up in international negotiations faced with the argument that 'desertion is increasing.' It must be stopped to a great extent."[15] Most certainly, these statements marked the beginning of Ulbricht's plans to close the sector border in Berlin; "battle against desertion" became the political code word under which the SED carried out its preparations.

Ulbricht's decision to build a special working group leaves little doubt that this was the case. The group comprised the SED's highest ranking officials responsible for internal affairs: Erich Honecker, secretary of security in the Central Committee and also secretary of the National Defense Council; Minister of the Interior Karl Maron, who oversaw the border police and the Volkspolizei; and Erich Mielke, minister of state security. In addition to this working group, another committee seems to have existed under Ulbricht's personal leadership, mainly consisting of members of government. Hans Bentzien mentions this second body in his 1995 memoirs. Bentzien began his tenure in office in the GDR as minister of culture on 23 February 1961. He describes a meeting on his first day of work that included Chairman of the State Planning Commission "Bruno Leuschner, Minister of Transportation Erwin Kramer, and Minister of Construction Ernst Scholz. . . . 'I was at a conference of the Planning Commission to build the wall,' writes Bentzien. 'However, military questions were not discussed. The generals made their preparations separately with the Soviet staff in Wünsdorf.'"[16]

In January 1961, Ulbricht instructed Minister of Defense Heinz Hoffmann "to discuss several military questions with Colonel General Ivan I. Yakubovsky, commander of the Group of Soviet Forces in Germany [GSFG]. [Ulbricht] was interested to know which crisis situations would elicit intervention by the GSFG in the GDR and on what scale, and whether [the GSFG] considered it advisable to create a barrier system that could be implemented at any time." Hoffmann's meeting with Yakubovsky took place on 10 February and also included Marshal Andrei A. Grechko, commander-in-chief of the Warsaw Pact Forces. The militaries then consulted Hoffmann "on questions regarding the practical organization of deploying Soviet troops in the GDR."[17] When Khrushchev decided in July to close the sector border in Berlin, the Soviet ambassador to the GDR, Mikhail G. Pervukhin, and the deputy head of operations for the GSFG, Colonel Anatoli G. Mereshko, were surprised at how well prepared Ulbricht, Maron, Mielke, and Hoffmann were for the operational issues posed by closing the border.[18]

Otto Winzer sent Ulbricht a paper on 10 January describing "possible strategies for a tactical approach to the question of a peace treaty and Westberlin." The paper addressed two main issues. First, it proposed a "transitional peace treaty" to create the Free City of Westberlin "independent of a [real] peace treaty." This was based on the draft of an interim treaty put forth at the Geneva conference of foreign ministers in the summer of 1959. Winzer emphasized to Ulbricht that "the idea of a transitional treaty might in fact be effective to revive the discussion of a peace treaty in general."[19] Second, the paper examined the measures and tactics necessary for the GDR to sign a separate peace treaty with the Soviet Union and resolve the "Westberlin question" once and for all.

Ulbricht reminded Khrushchev once again of the GDR's crisis situation in a letter of 18 January 1961, leading up to the Vienna Summit. Finding a solution to the "Westberlin problem" had become an existential question for the SED state. In Ulbricht's view, the chances of making progress in Berlin were quite good, since the West German government found itself in the middle of a Bundestag election campaign, and the American president did not want an "escalation of the situation."[20] According to Ulbricht, a compromise on West Berlin should be reached before the Bundestag elections in September. This was the SED's approach to negotiations based on the constellation in Germany. But Khrushchev had other plans, which he conveyed to Ulbricht two months later in Moscow. In his letter, Ulbricht clearly described what the SED saw as the most urgent problem: "Desertion of the republic is the most important argument our opponent will make in negotiations. Therefore, it will be essential in 1961 to achieve economic stability in the GDR in order to reduce desertion."[21]

Regarding relations between the GDR and the Soviet Union, Ulbricht suggested holding a council between delegations of the GDR and the USSR, "with the goal of increasing the GDR's authority in future negotiations." Moreover, he asserted that most states in the Warsaw Pact saw a solution to the West Berlin question "as an affair that only affected the Soviet Union and the GDR." In order to change this, the SED proposed convening the Political Consultative Committee of the Warsaw Pact in March, following the meeting between government delegations of the GDR and the Soviet Union.[22]

The GDR's economic problem intensified further through the country's competition with the flourishing West. Ulbricht's goal at the Fifth Party Congress—to overtake the Federal Republic in terms of workers' living standards—had been rooted in a faulty evaluation of West German development, which took a more prosperous path than the SED had predicted: "Regarding the increase in production and consumption, West Germany demonstrated the strongest growth in 1960 since the end of the war, and nothing indicates that this will change."[23] In the Federal Republic, wages increased by 9 percent and working hours were shortened. Workers in the metal industry reached a contractual agreement for a five-day week through 1965. In the GDR, by contrast, "these types of wage increases and reductions in working hours are not part of the plan."[24] In fact, the goals set for 1961 were probably not attainable at all, and the GDR operated with a foreign trade deficit of about 1.35 billion marks in foreign currency; of that amount, 800 million were owed to the Soviet Union and 500 million to the "capitalist economic area." If the Soviet Union refused to issue foreign currency credit to the GDR, this would have dire consequences for the population's living standards, leading to a situation in which "we would be faced with serious crisis phenomena."[25]

If the discrepancy in living standards between the GDR and the FRG continued to increase, the emigration movement would grow as well. In order to solve the GDR's fundamental economic problem in the conflict of systems with the Federal Republic, in order to "catch up" to the FRG, Ulbricht insisted that more funds be invested in the GDR over the following years and that "a close economic community—intertwined with the economy of the USSR—be developed. There is no other way."[26] The economic rebound in the Federal Republic, which "is visible to every resident of the GDR, is the main reason why about two million people have left our republic over the course of ten years."[27] Ulbricht did not explicitly highlight the decisive condition enabling this movement: the open sector border in Berlin. But to him it represented the core of the West Berlin problem.

Khrushchev's answer made one thing clear to the SED: the line fixed on 30 November 1960 had not changed. There would be no further debate over the path moving forward on the West Berlin question:

> We know you are also of the opinion that in the present situation, now that the new American president has entered into office, it is important and necessary to try and address the question of a peace treaty with Germany and the normalization of the situation in West Berlin on the basis of an understanding with the United States and the other Western powers. At the moment, we are beginning to initiate a straightforward discussion of these questions with Kennedy. Our efforts so far have shown that it will require some time before Kennedy defines his position on the German question more precisely and it becomes clear whether or not the government of the United States is willing to aim for mutually acceptable resolutions.[28]

Only after this question was clarified and no understanding with the United States could be reached would it be appropriate to plan further measures with the GDR. However, Khrushchev agreed to convene the Political Consultative Committee of the Warsaw Pact to discuss a peace treaty with both German states.

Ulbricht's letter of 18 January was tantamount to a declaration of bankruptcy by the SED and represented an important turning point in the course of the Berlin Crisis. It pushed the security of the GDR to the foreground of the political process. His haste to resolve the West Berlin question in order to avert the existential danger that desertion posed to the GDR in 1961 separates the two phases of the crisis. Since it proved impossible to reach a settlement with the Western powers, especially with the United States, on a peace treaty for all of Germany or West

Berlin, ensuring the existence of the GDR by closing Berlin's sector border rose to the top of the agenda for Moscow and East Berlin and determined the subsequent course of events.

Khrushchev's Time Frame in March 1961

At the conference of the Warsaw Pact's Political Consultative Committee on 28 and 29 March 1961, Ulbricht reported on the situation in the GDR.[29] The literature has suggested that at this meeting, Ulbricht proposed closing the sector border with a "barbed wire barrier running straight through Berlin," to which the gathered leaders of the Eastern bloc states allegedly reacted "in horror."[30] But the script of Ulbricht's speech does not contain any mention of this proposal; according to this document, he primarily discussed the planned peace treaty and the resolution of the West Berlin question. However, Wettig cites a conversation between Ulbricht and Soviet Ambassador Pervukhin on 22 March 1961 in which the SED leader referred to "closing the border in Berlin"[31] as an urgent and necessary step to stop the mass exodus.

Ulbricht opened his remarks in Moscow with the prediction that Kennedy would turn his political focus to Africa and Asia and would therefore show "no initiative" on the German question. Kennedy would "avoid negotiations over a peace treaty with both German states." The West German government, "Hitler's successor," wanted "to take revenge for the defeat of the German militarists in two world wars" and was not ready to sign a peace treaty with "anti-imperialist content"; its refusal was "supported by the NATO states."[32] This description of the situation represented a harsh critique by Ulbricht of Khrushchev's illusory negotiation strategy. To counter Khrushchev, Ulbricht demanded that "the Soviet Union and all states that are ready to do so [sign] a peace treaty with the German Democratic Republic." This peace treaty with the GDR "would also put a stop to the hotbed of war propaganda against the Socialist countries in Westberlin." It would "benefit" not only the GDR, but also all other states in the Warsaw Pact and, naturally, peace in Europe.[33]

After finalizing this peace treaty, the GDR hoped to sign treaties and agreements with the Western powers and the Federal Republic "in which all questions of movement to, from, and through the GDR could be addressed."[34] Treaties of this kind could also be signed with West Berlin in order to grant the city unimpeded movement in all directions. Although Ulbricht did not mention Soviet occupation rights in Berlin, he portrayed a future in which these rights—along with control over the Western troops' transit routes to Berlin—had already been transferred from the Soviet Union to the GDR through a peace treaty. This had been Ulbricht's goal since 1959. The GDR would agree to transitional regulations for the presence of Western troops under the condition that the withdrawal "be completed within a specific timeframe." Ulbricht stressed the link between signing this type of peace treaty and "ending the abnormality of the situation in West-berlin. Here, we reiterate the sovereignty of the GDR, whose capital is democratic Berlin."[35]

With respect to West Berlin, Ulbricht explained that the SED aimed for a long-term transition into a "Free City." In negotiations with the Western powers fol-lowing the hypothetical peace treaty, the GDR would have to focus on "gradually reducing the occupation troops in Westberlin."[36] The second point on Ulbricht's agenda was effecting change in the political climate and public opinion in West Berlin: "Every revanchist, militaristic, and neo-Nazi activity against the GDR and the Socialist countries" had to be eliminated. "Spy and sabotage organizations in Westberlin must be dissolved, along with RIAS, the U.S. radio broadcaster." All of these arrangements and regulations "will bring a gradual transformation of the frontline city of West Berlin into a demilitarized Free City. We do not envision a sudden change to the entire situation but rather a transitional period that brings feasible and reasonable solutions to everyone involved."[37]

This type of strategy to strengthen the position of the GDR "as a bastion of peace in Germany" would ultimately benefit the entire Socialist camp. "We will also have to make sacrifices," Ulbricht continued, since the Federal Republic would most likely answer these actions with economic sanctions on the GDR. If this became the case, the GDR would be able to use the access routes to West Berlin for significant leverage: "Every boycott and blockade measure against our republic will also disrupt the unobstructed movement to and from Westberlin."[38] In other words: Ulbricht considered repeating the blockade of transit routes following the 1948 model. His speech, however, neglected to specify any kind of schedule for negotiations. He had only suggested to Khrushchev that they should take place before the Bundestag elections of September 1961.

In Khrushchev's presentation on further action toward the West, he cited Len-in's remarks on the art of nuanced observation of the opponent:

> Lenin taught us that it is only possible to win the battle "by carefully, precisely, and meticulously taking advantage of every single 'split' among the enemies, no matter how tiny, every conflicting interest among the bourgeoisies of different countries, among different groups and variations of the bourgeoisie within each country, and every possibility, no matter how remote, to win over an ally—even if the ally is tem-porary, clumsy, weak, or unreliable in character."
>
> In the present situation, Lenin's advice takes on special weight.[39]

Khrushchev provided a detailed description of Soviet–American relations, which he saw as critically important to the question of war and peace between the two international political camps. He informed the committee of Kennedy's suggestion to meet in either Vienna or Stockholm in May—a discussion that Khrushchev wanted to have as well. Fundamentally, Khrushchev stressed: "The policy of the Soviet government toward the United States of America is based on the assumption that we really do desire and believe in a serious improvement in relations with this country, that this kind of improvement would provide the foundation for peaceful coexistence between the two camps and would benefit the entire Socialist camp."[40]

The peace treaty and a solution to the Berlin problem were major touchstones in a potential improvement in relations. "It is important to remember that broad circles of the international public would not understand us properly if we were to start forcing a German peace treaty without even waiting to assess the results of my meeting with Kennedy, which is set for May."[41] Khrushchev was skeptical about the chances of reaching an agreement. But at least for the sake of propaganda, he insisted that preparations for a separate peace treaty with the GDR only begin after the Vienna meeting.

> If the upcoming meeting with Kennedy and other contact with the Western powers do not produce a sign of their readiness to realistically address the question of a peace treaty with both German states, then our countries will naturally begin energetic preparations to sign a peace treaty with the German Democratic Republic.
>
> The Soviet government still believes that the question of a German peace treaty must be addressed. But to reach a final decision on the topic and determine the appropriate measures, our governments will need to hold an additional exchange of views to consider the concrete circumstances. Therefore, we feel obliged at least to try to explore all possibilities in this respect, even if we cannot be sure of their success.[42]

After the end of the conference, delegations met from the SED and the CPSU. Ulbricht was now familiar with the time frame Khrushchev envisioned for signing a separate peace treaty with the GDR, and he knew that it did not correspond to his own. At this meeting, Ulbricht did not bring up the necessity of closing Berlin's sector border in order to stop the mass exodus, a point he had already conveyed to Pervukhin. Instead he described his Germany-centered negotiation plan, which focused on taking advantage of the Bundestag elections. Khrushchev responded by questioning the strength of the GDR's economy: "When will you be in an economic position to bring relations with Adenauer to a head at minimal risk to the GDR, a position in which all of your plans to transform the economy have already been prepared? The significance of these questions is not irrelevant for you. You need to prepare yourself better. The issue of setting a date should not be forced."[43] Khrushchev went on to rebuff Ulbricht's time frame and propose his own instead:

> I am of the opinion that we should [only] pose the question of signing a peace treaty after the October celebrations, i.e., in the second half of November. This date should remain confidential.
>
> If we use this date, you will be able to prepare yourself more thoroughly. But I am not only considering your side; I am also thinking of the Soviet side. On 13 October our party congress begins.[44] Before the party congress we do not want to have to worry about the peace treaty because it will distract us. It would cause quite a stir. This question [of a peace treaty] is not irrelevant for us, since we were the ones who requested it in the first place. Are we to go through with our party congress

under such circumstances? Our people would not be able to understand it; we would be forced to give militant speeches and exert pressure. . . .

At the same time, it would be better to make a decision on the topic before the Bundestag elections. But ultimately we will have to do it afterward. The party congress must be held in a building with a hall for six thousand people, because four thousand delegates will be at the party congress. We had thought of holding the party congress in February or May, but the construction people said the hall would not be ready before June. Since we understand the value of the construction workers' promises, we decided to plan the party congress for October. Second, this date for the party congress is better for our guests, the delegations from the Communist and workers' parties. They will come for the party congress and then stay for the celebrations [to mark the anniversary of the October Revolution].[45]

It was impossible to overlook the difference in priorities between the supreme power and its satellite. While the SED hoped to use the peace treaty to solve its West Berlin problem, Khrushchev aimed for nothing less than a shift in the international power constellation: "In conversations with Kennedy, the peace treaty will be a central issue. If we can wrestle a peace treaty out of him, it will rip NATO to pieces; the German question is holding NATO together."[46] Looking to the upcoming meeting, Khrushchev assured Ulbricht that he knew the Americans were playing for time and would want to consult their allies, but he was unwilling to wait any longer: "With regard to the German question, they also say: Let's not rush [the issue], let's examine it more closely. I know how they examine things. But then we will tell them that they have had enough time. We have already told Kennedy, as we explained in a memorandum to Adenauer,[47] that the former American president claimed he could not do it because he was about to step down, and the new president claims he cannot do it because he just entered into office. But then we will tell him: One year has passed and you have done nothing. Public opinion will be on our side."[48]

The two leaders' diverging visions also reflected a difference in the perceived significance of the mass "desertion" through Berlin:

Khrushchev: Of course you are struggling somewhat because the door [in Berlin] is open.
Ulbricht: We are struggling quite a lot. In fact, it is the only point in which we are really struggling right now.
Khrushchev: And you only recognize now that you are having difficulty because of this? Did you think eleven years ago that you would find yourself in this position?
Ulbricht: We didn't think about it then; we thought about other things.
Khrushchev: Of course you are encountering some difficulties, but the GDR grows from these difficulties. You have already created a Socialist economy. If we hold up your losses and your achievements next to each other, then the GDR wins and Adenauer loses. Do not beg for my pity.
Ulbricht: But right now it bothers us more than ever before. Desertion has taken on greater dimensions than it had two years ago.
Khrushchev: If we announce a peace treaty, the fever in your country will only get worse. And I do not know yet how this can be prevented.[49]

With this conversation, Khrushchev once again delayed signing a separate peace treaty and solving the West Berlin problem. Ulbricht had to keep waiting, especially as Khrushchev conveyed the unmistakable position that concerning the peace treaty, "it was not the Germans who would decide."[50] In his 1961 message to the Soviet Union, Ulbricht cited the first flight into outer space by Soviet astronaut Yuri Gagarin as proof of the "certainty of socialism's victory in the entire world." While praising the USSR's strength, Ulbricht also reminded Khrushchev of the still outstanding issue of the "peace treaty with both German states."[51]

Khrushchev did not waver from his agenda, but he never lost sight of the SED's difficulties either. On 24 April 1961, he told the West German ambassador that "control over entry to and exit from West Berlin through the territory of the GDR—as it would occur on the basis of a peace treaty—was essential; otherwise it would be necessary 'to construct a fortification wall around West Berlin or establish a special regime. [But] this is impossible because Berlin is a single, uniform economic area, and the inhabitants of Berlin work in different parts of the city, have relatives [there], etc.'"[52] Khrushchev obviously did not have a clear idea of Berlin's divided economy: East Berlin was part of the GDR's planned economy, while West Berlin was integrated into the market economy of the Federal Republic. At this time, Khrushchev and Ulbricht were still considering two different strategies to address the refugee question. Khrushchev envisaged controlling the access routes to West Berlin through a peace treaty. Ulbricht was skeptical as to whether this goal was feasible at all, and, in light of the GDR's crisis, contemplated sealing the sector border—a possibility that Khrushchev still ruled out.

Notes

1. "Gespräch Chruschtschows mit dem Ersten Sekretär der SED, Walter Ulbricht, am 30. November 1960," Russian protocol, in Wettig, *Chruschtschows Westpolitik*, 41.
2. File note on a conversation between Walter Ulbricht and Nikita S. Khrushchev, 30 November 1960, SAPMO-BArch, DY 30/3566.
3. The provisions of the Potsdam Agreement (based on an American draft) between the United States, the USSR, and Great Britain on 2 August 1945 included "4 Ds" to be carried out in occupied Germany: denazification, demilitarization, decartelization, and democratization. After the Paris conference of foreign ministers in 1946, the Kremlin interpreted this to mean that the Germans had to organize their political, social, and economic affairs as they did in the Soviet zone/GDR.
4. Through the Paris Treaties of 23 October 1954, which cemented the Federal Republic's entry into the Western alliance, West Germany assumed its sovereign rights—with the exception of its right to and responsibility for Berlin and Germany as a whole, which the Western powers still reserved.

5. "Gespräch Chruschtschows mit dem Ersten Sekretär der SED, Walter Ulbricht, am 30. November 1960," Russian protocol, in Wettig, *Chruschtschows Westpolitik*, 48–49. The SED's notes from the conversation ignore this controversy altogether.

6. Walter Ulbricht to Nikita S. Khrushchev, Berlin, 22 November 1960, SAPMO-BArch, DY 30/3507.

7. See Heike Amos and Manfred Wilke, "Die Deutschlandpolitik der SED und ihre 'bürgerlichen' Bündnispartner' in der Bundesrepublik 1949 bis 1989," *Jahrbuch für Historische Kommunismusforschung* (2010): 53–61.

8. See Manfred Wilke and Hans-Peter Müller, *SED-Politik gegen die Realitäten: Verlauf und Funktion der Diskussion über die westdeutschen Gewerkschaften in SED und KPD/DKP 1961 bis 1972* (Cologne, 1990).

9. Walter Ulbricht to Nikita S. Khrushchev, Berlin, 22 November 1960, SAPMO-BArch, DY 30/3507.

10. "Gespräch Chruschtschows mit dem Ersten Sekretär der SED, Walter Ulbricht, am 30. November 1960," Russian protocol, in Wettig, *Chruschtschows Westpolitik*, 40.

11. Ibid., 35.

12. Ibid.

13. Lemke, *Berlinkrise*, 153.

14. File note on a conversation between Walter Ulbricht and Nikita S. Khrushchev, 30 November 1960, SAPMO-BArch, DY 30/3566.

15. Bullet-point protocol of a politburo meeting, "Die gegenwärtige Lage und die Hauptaufgabe 1961," 4 January 1961, SAPMO-BArch, DY JIVZ/2/747.

16. Armin Wagner, "Stacheldrahtsicherheit: Die politische und militärische Planung und Durchführung des Mauerbaus 1961," in Hertle et al., *Mauerbau und Mauerfall*, 121–22.

17. Uhl, *Krieg um Berlin?*, 116.

18. See "Secrecy and Conspiratorial Communication" in chapter 15 of this volume.

19. Otto Winzer to Walter Ulbricht, 10 January 1961, SAPMO-BArch, DY 30/3508.

20. Walter Ulbricht to Nikita S. Khrushchev, Berlin, 18 January 1961, SAPMO-BArch, DY 30/3508.

21. Ibid.

22. Ibid.

23. Ibid.

24. Ibid.

25. Ibid.

26. Ibid.

27. Ibid.

28. Nikita S. Khrushchev to Walter Ulbricht, 30 January 1961, SAPMO-BArch, DY 30/3508.

29. Walter Ulbricht, "Rede auf der Tagung des Politischen Beratenden Ausschusses der Teilnehmerstaaten des Warschauer Vertrages," Moscow, 29 March 1961, SAPMO-BArch, DY 30/3586. The Political Consultative Committee was an advisory body that did not make decisions.

30. See Lemke, *Berlinkrise*, 157. The source of this account is the former deputy defense minister of Czechoslovakia, Jan Sejna, who participated in the meeting of the Political Consultative Committee and claimed that the gathered representatives refused to support Ulbricht's proposal.

31. Gerhard Wettig, "Chruschtschow, die Berliner Mauer und das Friedensvertragsultimatum" (manuscript, 2009).

32. Walter Ulbricht, "Rede auf der Tagung des Politischen Beratenden Ausschusses der Teilnehmerstaaten des Warschauer Vertrages," Moscow, 29 March 1961, SAPMO-BArch, DY 30/3586.

33. Ibid.

34. Ibid.

35. Ibid.

36. Ibid.

37. Ibid.

38. Ibid.

39. "Ausführungen Chruschtschows vor dem Politischen Konsultativkomitee der Mitgliedsstaaten des Warschauer Pakts am 29. März 1961," in Wettig, *Chruschtschows Westpolitik*, 71.

40. Ibid., 76.

41. Ibid., 82.

42. Ibid.

43. "Gespräch Chruschtschows mit dem Ersten Sekretär der SED, Walter Ulbricht am 31. März 1961," excerpt, in Wettig, *Chruschtschows Westpolitik*, 110.

44. The beginning of the CPSU's 22nd Party Congress was later pushed back to 17 October 1961.

45. "Gespräch Chruschtschows mit dem Ersten Sekretär der SED, Walter Ulbricht am 31. März 1961," excerpt, in Wettig, *Chruschtschows Westpolitik*, 110–11.

46. Ibid., 112.

47. The Soviet "aide-mémoire" of 17 February 1961 listed the usual demands without indicating a readiness to compromise. The memorandum aimed to make signing a peace treaty—along with participation in advisory committees and even the possibility of Bonn exercising influence—more attractive to the West German government. The message contained sharp attacks on the Federal Republic and ended in a general appeal to improve bilateral relations. See "Aide-mémoire der Regierung der UdSSR an die Regierung der Bundesrepublik Deutschland," in *Dokumente zur Deutschlandpolitik*, ed. Bundesministerium für innerdeutsche Beziehungen, series 4, vol. 6/1, *1. Januar bis 31. Mai 1961* (Frankfurt am Main, 1975), 340–50.

48. "Gespräch Chruschtschows mit dem Ersten Sekretär der SED, Walter Ulbricht am 31. März 1961," excerpt, in Wettig, *Chruschtschows Westpolitik*, 114–15.

49. Ibid., 113.

50. Ibid., 111.

51. Walter Ulbricht, "Grußbotschaft an die Sowjetunion," 13 April 1961, SAPMO-BArch, NY 4182/652.

52. "Gespräch Chruschtschows mit dem Botschafter der Bundesrepublik Hans Kroll am 24. April 1961," in Wettig, *Chruschtschows Westpolitik*, 145–46.

Chapter 14

THE VIENNA SUMMIT, 1961
The Second Soviet Ultimatum

Moscow's Expectations before the Summit

After Kennedy entered office, Llewellyn E. Thompson, American ambassador to Moscow, warned the president not to underestimate the issue of Berlin in navigating relations with the Soviet Union. He advised Kennedy to negotiate with Khrushchev, if only to prevent a separate peace treaty between Moscow and East Berlin. "Lastly, Thompson warned that, at the very least, the East Germans would have to seal off their sector boundary in order to stop the refugee flow."[1] The idea of separating the spheres of influence in Berlin thus entered the conversation as a potential line of compromise in American policy. Kennedy consented to a meeting, and Thompson conveyed the message to Khrushchev on 9 March 1961. The Soviet leader took the opportunity to emphasize the importance of reaching an understanding between the United States and the Soviet Union on the Berlin question. He referred to West Berlin as a "bone in the throat" of Soviet–American relations. "A rapid agreement on this point could lead to major progress in disarmament negotiations. But the diplomats already realized that Khrushchev would introduce the Berlin question to the agenda and aimed to achieve definitive results. Charles 'Chip' Bohlen, former US ambassador to Moscow, urged Kennedy not to sit down with Khrushchev until he had met and consulted with the principal Western European allies. Bohlen, the experienced 'Atlanticist,' advised [Kennedy] to protect [himself] by embedding the summit with Khrushchev in extensive conversations with the Allies."[2]

In early May, Khrushchev sent Kennedy a letter indicating that "in addition to the Laos problem, the German question (that is, Berlin) and disarmament should be on the agenda of their one-on-one meeting."[3] The Soviet foreign ministry informed representatives of the Socialist countries in Moscow on 19 May that Khrushchev would meet with Kennedy on 3 and 4 June 1961 in Vienna. Both parties agreed "that at this meeting, they did not intend to hold negotiations or draft a treaty on the fundamental international problems that also affected the interests of other countries."[4] Berlin, however, would naturally enter the discussion:

> Before meeting with the U.S. president, Khrushchev tried to find out what kind of response he was going to elicit. When Ambassador Llewellyn Thompson told him on 24 May that his demands would be rejected, he angrily asked whether the United States wanted war. This would amount to sheer madness. Shortly afterward, he assured the members of the presidium of the Central Committee that he would under all circumstances overcome the resistance of this "son of a bitch." If the Americans failed to withdraw from West Berlin, the air routes would be blocked. If they then wanted to resort to the use of arms, they would be stopped by their European allies who, in the deployment of nuclear weapons that would surely follow, foresaw their own annihilation. Mikoyan was the only one to raise objections. Khrushchev became very upset and reiterated his resolve to go through with any military action necessary.[5]

On 26 May 1961, based on secret intelligence, Khrushchev informed the presidium of the Central Committee of a NATO session on Germany. After analyzing the NATO meeting, Khrushchev drew a clear conclusion: the Soviet Union was "not afraid of German aggression," believing the FRG would "not start a new war." Khrushchev went on: "The most dangerous [country] is America," he said. "America could easily start a war," but "[French President Charles] de Gaulle and [British Prime Minister Harold] Macmillan will never side with the Americans in unleashing war in Europe now . . . because the main deployment of nuclear weapons will be in the territory of West Germany, France, and England." The Soviet leader offered the following assessment: "If we look at it in terms of a percentage, there is more than a 95 percent probability that there will be no war."[6]

In his conversation with Thompson, which took place one month after the disastrous American invasion of Cuba, Khrushchev emphasized that he could no longer postpone the peace treaty with Germany: "If no agreement were reached in Vienna, he would sign a separate treaty with the GDR that winter, probably right after the party congress." This time, according to Thompson, Khrushchev "did not show any signs of accommodation on Berlin; Allied access to West Berlin would require an agreement with the East Germans." Thompson responded "with uncharacteristic anger that Khrushchev should not misunderstand the US position, which was: Khrushchev could sign any peace treaty he wanted but interference with Allied access to Berlin would be met with force. It was a preview of Kennedy's own unequivocal position as far as Berlin went and should have been a warning to Khrushchev that this really was the line in the sand."[7]

Khrushchev approached Kennedy in Vienna with a policy of strength through fear—perhaps because he knew that little had changed in Kennedy's position. Khrushchev's initial hope to reach an agreement with the new president had disappeared. The "situation is exactly the same as it was under Eisenhower," the 26 May protocol notes, and Khrushchev believed that the Soviets would "definitely not be able to agree with the Germans and the Americans. . . . Because for them, West Berlin is truly a [Gordian] knot that we will simply cut through, and that will have major consequences for NATO. And they, for example von Brentano, even say that West Germany might [then] leave NATO. But it will not leave, he is [just] making a threat."[8] Khrushchev's assessment of West Berlin as a "knot" holding together the Western alliance was just as astute as his sense that there would be no peace treaty with the Federal Republic and the United States on a solution to the West Berlin problem. It was also clear to Khrushchev that no one would start a war to force the Western troops out of Berlin, and that the Americans did not want war either. Despite these insights, he still insisted on the original goal of the Berlin offensive, to undo the knot holding together the Western alliance in Berlin. If the Soviet Union was to assert the authority of its "garrison state," the GDR, and put a stop to the flow of refugees from that country, the only option left to Khrushchev was to close the sector border in Berlin; after all, even he had no intention of going to war over Berlin. Ulbricht's demand thus provided a way out of the Soviet dilemma: a retreat back to the borders of the spheres of influence, even in Berlin.

Kennedy: Balancing Détente and an Assertion of the Western Positions

In the words of Günter Bischof and Martin Kofler, Kennedy was a pragmatist and "a child of the Cold War." To him, the greatest challenge of foreign policy was maintaining peace with the Soviets in the nuclear era. He had already realized as senator that a policy of coexistence with the Soviet Union was the only possible approach, and that negotiated settlements must be the goal. Even during his election campaign, he argued that topics such as nuclear disarmament and a ban on nuclear tests should be negotiated if necessary "at summits or elsewhere."[9]

The American president primarily hoped that the Vienna Summit would address arms control and the conflicts in the third world. But Khrushchev's reaction to Kennedy's suggestion to meet, which Kennedy received through Ambassador Thompson, showed that the Berlin question still stood at the top of the Soviet agenda. Even though nuclear arms control, not to mention disarmament, was an affair of both superpowers, Kennedy had to reconcile two separate goals when dealing with Berlin: achieving détente in relations with the Soviet Union and preserving the unity of the Western alliance.

Before the summit, Kennedy invited Federal Chancellor Adenauer and British Prime Minister Macmillan to Washington. The Berlin problem, along with other questions facing the alliance, formed the heart of the discussions. "Kennedy impressed on Chancellor Adenauer the importance of Berlin and the United States' commitment to defend West Berlin and his opposition to negotiating on Berlin with the Soviets. He reviewed U.S. contingency planning with his German counterpart, and Adenauer was promised to be included in future military planning."[10] Leading up to this meeting, Henry Kissinger had advised the president in a memorandum to take the Federal Republic's concerns seriously. "Strategically, the Germans were 'a candidate for nervous breakdown': 'The fear of being left alone or sold out [in a nuclear war in Europe] is, in my judgment, a quest for emotional security.' Kissinger professed his admiration for Adenauer's historic achievement of having transformed the FRG 'into a responsible member of the Western community.'"[11]

Neither Adenauer nor Macmillan had any idea that Kennedy was about to experience his first foreign policy defeat. The CIA-supported invasion of Cuba by 1,500 Cuban exiles turned into a fiasco. Fidel Castro emerged victorious, in part because Kennedy—with an eye on the crisis in Berlin—stopped short of "helping the landed forces to victory through American support from the air. Such direct American military deployment could have quickly triggered a larger East–West crisis—exactly the type of thing the new president hoped to avoid in the nuclear era."[12] Simultaneous to the Bay of Pigs disaster, the Soviet Union succeeded in sending Yuri Gagarin into space.

In Paris, on his way to Vienna, Kennedy met with French President Charles de Gaulle, who had two pieces of advice with respect to the summit meeting. The first concerned Laos: he suggested that the United States refrain from military intervention there, just as it should in Vietnam. The second recommendation had to do with Berlin: there, the West "must not retreat before Soviet dictation." "If Khrushchev actually followed through on his threats to sign a separate peace treaty with the East Germans, then this would mean war: 'If he wants war, we must make it clear to him that he can have war,' de Gaulle emphasized. But one should not take Khrushchev's warmongering too seriously, the general went on dryly, since he had been spouting ultimatums for the past two and a half years without ever mustering the courage to unleash a war."[13] Fundamentally, the French president was against Western initiatives to negotiate on Berlin: "In general, Paris was of the opinion that the current situation in Berlin 'was doubtlessly the least bad compromise possible.' As nothing new could be offered to Moscow, it 'did not seem very desirable to propose new negotiations.' This position was solidified because the French did not believe that Khrushchev would start a war over Berlin—it was assumed that his political and military saber-rattling was merely designed to bring the Western powers to the negotiating table. France would not alter its opinion on this during the weeks and months that followed."[14]

Confrontation at the Summit: Khrushchev's "Vienna Ultimatum"

Kennedy's and Khrushchev's expectations before their meeting were informed by "fundamental misunderstandings." Kennedy "simply ignored the Berlin issue, *the top priority of the Soviet premier*," while his counterpart "showed no interest whatsoever in moving forward on the president's main issues: disarmament and ending nuclear tests. Thus, [the two] entered into negotiations blind and without an agenda, which ultimately proved fatal for the three planned rounds of talks."[15]

The question of a peace treaty with the two German states and a solution to the Berlin question formed the focus of the last round of talks. With the two leaders' opposing interests, the conversation became combative. Khrushchev began by stressing that "he would like to reach agreement with the President—and he said he wanted to emphasize the words 'with you'"—on the Berlin question. But he immediately coupled the offer with a threat: "If the US should fail to understand this desire the USSR will sign a peace treaty alone."[16] This was Lenin's maxim: in the end, the only thing that mattered was who defeated whom. The first controversy over Berlin seemed to be of a geographic nature: Kennedy stated that West Berlin was not situated in the territory of the GDR. "Khrushchev replied that the USSR considered all of Berlin to be GDR territory."[17] Kennedy responded with the official American position: "This may be [the] Soviet view but [it is] not ours. If the USSR transfers its rights, that is a matter for its own decision; however, it is an altogether different matter for the USSR to give [away?] our rights which we have on [a] contractual basis." The president argued "that the USSR could not break the agreement and give US rights to the GDR."[18] Furthermore, Kennedy stressed once again the origin of these rights in the first place: "We are in Berlin not because of someone's sufferance. We fought our way there, although our casualties may have been not as high as the USSR's. We are in Berlin not by agreement of East Germans but by contractual rights."[19]

Khrushchev wondered why Kennedy saw West Berlin as such an important issue. Before this point, the two had discussed Laos and reassured each other that neither side had any interests there. Kennedy responded by accusing the Soviet chairman of trying to drive the United States into political "isolation." He underscored Berlin's direct impact on American interests: "How can the US agree to East Germany's preventing it from exercising our rights [that we have] won by war? The United States cannot accept an ultimatum. Our leaving West Berlin would result in the US becoming isolated. The President emphasized that he is not President of the US to preside over [the] isolation of his country just as Mr. Khrushchev, as leader of the USSR, would not want to see his own country isolated." Khrushchev then "interjected that he understood this to mean that the President did not want a peace treaty." Kennedy replied "that the US was interested in maintaining its position in Berlin and its rights of access to that city."[20] He did not want to alter the position of the Soviet side, but appealed to Khrushchev not to "disturb the balance of power"[21] in light of the present situation. Khrushchev then returned to his previous threat, to sign a peace treaty at the end of the year. Kennedy clarified that a peace treaty with the GDR was not the issue. "However, a peace treaty denying us our contractual rights is a belligerent act."[22]

Therefore, a formal transfer of rights in Berlin from the Soviet Union to the GDR would not solve the problem at all; an attempt by the GDR to implement these rights vis-à-vis the Western powers would provoke a military conflict. Kennedy had found the weakness in Khrushchev's threat to sign a separate peace treaty and highlighted it as such. He went on to say that the United States did not see West Berlin as a springboard from which to launch an attack against the Soviet

Union. At the same time, the United States had contractual commitments to Germany: "If the US were driven out of West Berlin by unilateral action, and if we were deprived of our contractual rights by East Germany, then no one would believe the US now or in the future. US commitments would be regarded as a mere scrap of paper."[23]

Khrushchev returned to this point at their last meeting that afternoon, saying that "if the President insisted on US rights after the signing of a peace treaty and that if the borders of the GDR—land, air, or sea borders—were violated, they would be defended. . . . He must warn the President that if he envisages any action that might bring about unhappy consequences, force would be met with force."[24] Kennedy retorted that, "it was the Chairman, not he, who wanted to force a change."[25] Khrushchev assured him that he only wanted peace. "War will take place only if the US imposes it on the USSR. It is up to the US to decide whether there will be war or peace. This, he said, can be told [to] Macmillan, de Gaulle and Adenauer. The decision to sign a peace treaty is firm and irrevocable and the Soviet Union will sign it in December if the US refuses an interim agreement." Kennedy replied "by observing that it would be a cold winter."[26]

Kennedy fought back against the ultimatum, but in principle he was in favor of negotiating over the status quo in Germany. In the discussions with Khrushchev, he took the position that "it would be well if relations between East Germany and West Germany improved and if the development of US–USSR relations were such as to permit [a] solution of the whole German problem. During his stay in office, Mr. Khrushchev has seen many changes, and changes will go on. But now he wants a peace treaty in six months."[27] Khrushchev had handed Kennedy a prepared memorandum that summarized the Soviet positions once more. Its last point gave a deadline of six months to end negotiations on a peace treaty and find a solution to the Berlin problem.

The Outcome: A Policy of Force

The summit did not come close to meeting American expectations. "Kennedy left Vienna entirely shocked by Khrushchev. The young president's charm simply ricocheted off the shrewd tactician from the Kremlin."[28] Khrushchev, in contrast, was pleased with his strategy of brusque confrontation; he felt like the victor and saw the discussions as an agreeable preview for future negotiations. He adhered to the schedule he had laid out for Ulbricht, planning to hold off on a decisive confrontation with the Western powers until after the 22nd Party Congress. Soon, however, he realized this would not be so simple:

> Only gradually did Khrushchev recognize that the injuries he had inflicted on Kennedy through his gruff behavior actually strengthened [Kennedy's] will to resist. [Khrushchev's] goal would be harder to attain than he had previously thought. Considering the USSR's military weakness in the area of global strategy, it could hardly

be expected that this would rein in the United States. To remedy the situation, he called a meeting with the heads of the Soviet nuclear program on 10 July 1961 and ordered them to prepare to launch a 100-megaton explosive device at the end of October—timed to coincide with the Western powers' decision. This superbomb, he explained, should make an impression that would elicit compliance.[29]

The physicist Andrei D. Sakharov spoke out against this plan right away. It was the first time he intervened in world politics, and it marked the beginning of his path as a dissident. At the time, the physicist had no notion of the broader political context, and Khrushchev did not mention it, much less discuss it. Sakharov, however, passed Khrushchev a note warning the leader of the consequences that would arise from taking this step, arguing that it would be tantamount to ending discussions over disarmament and would trigger a new round in the arms race. Khrushchev's response provided a lesson in the maxims of Soviet foreign policy: "One can be a good scientist and still understand nothing about political issues. So please leave the politics to us, the specialists in this area. And test out your bomb; in that regard we will not bother you but rather help you. We have to define our policy from a position of strength. We do not say this out loud, but it is true! Any other policy would be impossible, since our opponents understand no other language."[30] To reiterate this point, Khrushchev elaborated on his experience with Kennedy. He claimed that the Soviet leadership had helped Kennedy in the election campaign. In Vienna, Khrushchev had hoped the meeting would change relations between the two superpowers: "But what did Kennedy say? 'Don't make such big demands of me, don't put me in a vulnerable situation. If I make such great concessions, I will be ruined!' I like the lad! But he comes to a meeting and cannot do anything. Why the devil do we need him, then? Should we simply chat with him and waste time? Sakharov, do not try to tell us politicians what we should do and what we should let happen. I would be a weakling rather than chairman of the Council of Ministers if I listened to people like Sakharov!"[31]

The ineffectiveness of Sakharov's internally conveyed, scientifically grounded arguments to prevent testing the nuclear bomb changed the physicist's worldview. He decided from that point forward to intervene publicly in politics. His memorandum seven years later, a programmatic alternative to the policies of the CPSU, opened the chapter on "Dangers" with the following sentence: "Three technical aspects of thermonuclear weapons have made nuclear war a threat against the continued existence of civilization. These are the enormous destructive power of a nuclear explosion, the relatively low production costs of nuclear weapons, and the essential impossibility of effective defense against a massive thermonuclear attack."[32] The person who built the Soviet hydrogen bomb understood the danger of his weapon and assumed political responsibility for his physical "invention." Out of a will to save human civilization and follow his ethical convictions, Sakharov presented his evaluation of politics and thereby stood in open opposition to the CPSU's monopoly on power.

Not only Khrushchev adhered to the logic of the Cold War, however; Kennedy did as well. On the flight back to the United States, he discussed the outcome of the Vienna Summit with the British government. One topic addressed military planning for potential crisis situations in Berlin. British Foreign Minister Alexander Douglas-Home reduced the Berlin problem to the question of refugees in order to explain Ulbricht's pressure on Khrushchev. Macmillan compared Kennedy's disaster in Vienna to someone meeting Napoleon "at the height of his power for the first time."[33]

Back in the United States, "Kennedy wanted above all to demonstrate his strength. Right away, he risked worsening the anticipated Berlin crisis with Moscow by announcing further increases to the defense budget."[34] In the formulation of this policy, a veteran of the first Berlin Crisis, Dean Acheson, secretary of state under President Truman, played an important role. Acheson's expertise focused on "exerting influence on the decision-makers in the Kremlin at the right time." His theory was that "an early willingness by the United States to escalate the situation, along with drastic armament measures," would be sufficient to attain the U.S. goal in Berlin: to maintain the status quo.[35] The president followed Acheson's advice. In July 1961, the Kennedy administration asked Congress to approve eleven armament programs amounting to $3.45 billion. The funds were allocated to expanding the various armed forces, strengthening civil defense, and armament through nuclear weapon systems.[36] Kennedy announced this armament program in his Report to the Nation on 25 July 1961, a speech that also contained the three essential components of his policy on Berlin.

The American dilemma during the Berlin Crisis elicited a strategic shift in favor of "Flexible Response." In the aftermath of the Vienna fiasco and the reality of nuclear stalemate, the Western militaries discussed the predicament they faced in the conflict over West Berlin and its access routes. It seemed unrealistic, for instance, that the United States would risk mutual destruction in order to disentangle a convoy held up by GDR troops near Magdeburg. American General Lauris Norstad, NATO's supreme commander, told the worried head of the British general staff that he found it intolerable to have no other options than to declare nuclear war or accept Soviet–East German conditions.[37] In light of this problem, more began to doubt the wisdom of a "massive retaliation" strategy. Even the Pentagon's escalation scale for the case of a Berlin conflict contained the option of halting or reversing escalation at one of several predefined phases. The inclusion of more flexible options had begun, particularly in the context of a potential threat to Berlin.[38]

After the Soviet Union's failed attempt to shift the spheres of influence in Germany to its own advantage in Berlin, movement began to regularize the current status quo through international treaties, including the Federal Republic's "Eastern Treaties" (Ostverträge), in which it officially recognized the GDR. The Berlin Wall came to symbolize the transition from confrontation to a cooperative competition of systems and "peaceful coexistence" during the Cold War. Over the entire decade of the 1960s, U.S. security policy was based on further developing the 1961 approach. Crucial to this was the willingness of Kennedy's and Johnson's Democratic administrations to stimulate the economy through government spending, including an expanded military budget, as well as the Vietnam War, which demonstrated that conventional warfare could still be planned and waged. NATO officially adopted the "Flexible Response" strategy in January 1968 with document MC 14/3, drafted by the alliance's military committee.[39]

The SED Reacts to Khrushchev's "Vienna Ultimatum"

The memorandum that Khrushchev handed to Kennedy gave a six-month deadline to "[put] an end to the vestiges of the Second World War in Europe."[40] The most important "vestige" was the right of the Western powers to occupy West Berlin. On this point, the memorandum stated:

> The peace treaty would specifically define the status of West Berlin as a free city and the Soviet Union, just as the other parties to the treaty, would of course observe it strictly; measures would also be taken to ensure that this status be respected by other countries as well. At the same time, this would mean putting an end to the occupation regime in West Berlin with all its implications. In particular, questions of using the means of communication by land, water or air within the territory of the G.D.R. would have to be settled solely by appropriate agreements with the G.D.R. That is but natural, since control over such means of communication is an unalienable right of every sovereign State.[41]

It still remained to be seen how the Soviet Union would force the United States, Great Britain, and France to voluntarily relinquish their position in Berlin without risking war. Ulbricht understood this dilemma in the Soviet negotiating position as well. But the ultimatum laid out Moscow's approach to solving the West Berlin problem, and this determined his own path forward. Ulbricht thanked Khrushchev: "You have represented in an extraordinary way not only the position of the CPSU and the Soviet Union but also that of the other states in the Socialist camp based on the joint declaration of the Communist and workers' parties. This was a major political achievement, and it presented a solution to the growing disputes by way of negotiations in a peaceful manner."[42]

The confrontation in Vienna created an international political constellation in which Ulbricht could almost sense the favorable resolution of his "Westberlin problem." But it was still unclear to him how the negotiations over a peace treaty would actually take shape. If the Soviet Union were to reach an agreement with the Western powers after all, the GDR would still be left out. The most crucial question facing the SED was whether Khrushchev was truly prepared to sign a separate peace treaty with the GDR if negotiations with the United States fell through. Khrushchev had not yet approved of closing the border in Berlin, as Ulbricht's letter after the Vienna Summit shows: Ulbricht included two attachments that dealt with "containing the movement of border crossers," meaning the sixty-five thousand workers who lived in East Berlin and the surrounding area but worked in West Berlin. The solutions formulated by the SED at this point were all based a situation in which the sector border stayed open.[43]

Ulbricht urged Khrushchev in his letter to find a solution: "Since this is an important political question affecting the peace treaty and the resolution of the Westberlin question, we would like to share our thoughts with you." Ulbricht wanted to know which economic measures would "best serve our purposes" and "when the best moment would be" to implement them. He only indirectly mentioned the pressure facing the SED: "If it is politically necessary, we will have to postpone the whole thing until after a peace treaty is signed, but that will create immense difficulties for us over the next six months." By focusing on the peripheral issue in order to get at Khrushchev's intentions toward the peace treaty, the letter reveals East Berlin's uncertainty about the current schedule. At the same time, the letter provides rare evidence of the conspiratorial character with which Ulbricht prepared to close the border. He asked Khrushchev to keep both documents confidential, since copies did "not exist at our party headquarters."[44]

Soviet Ambassador Pervukhin had conveyed a message from Khrushchev to Ulbricht stating the CPSU's wish for the SED to convene a meeting among the heads of state of the Warsaw Pact nations. The Central Committee of the SED took care of the necessary invitations, proposing that the council meet from 20 to 21 July in Moscow. On 5 July, Ulbricht forwarded Khrushchev the letter that he had already sent, "according to plans," to the first secretaries of the governing Communist parties.[45] The final dates of the conference were set as 3 to 5 August, 1961.

Notes

1. Jenny Thompson-Vujacic and Sherry Thompson-Miller, "Botschafter Thompson zwischen den politischen Strömungen auf dem Wiener Gipfel," in Karner et al., *Wiener Gipfel*, 607.
2. Günter Bischof and Martin Kofler, "'Vienna, a City that is Symbolic of the Possibility of Finding Equitable Solutions': John F. Kennedys Gipfeldiplomatie mit Freund und Feind in Europa im Mai/Juni 1961," in Karner et al., *Wiener Gipfel*, 147.
3. Ibid., 150.
4. "Information, die der stellvertretende Außenminister der UdSSR, Sobolew, gestern den Chefs der Vertretungen der sozialistischen Länder gegeben hat (keine Veröffentlichung)," SAPMO-BArch, DY 30/3497.
5. Wettig, "Chruščev," 657–58.
6. "Protocol 331," 26 May 1961, quoted in Aleksandr Fursenko and Timothy Naftali, *Khrushchev's Cold War: The Inside Story of an American Adversary* (New York, 2006), 356–57.
7. Thompson-Vujacic and Thompson-Miller, "Botschafter Thompson," 608.
8. "Stellungnahme Chruschtschows im Präsidium des Zentralkomitees der KPdSU am 26. Mai 1961," in Wettig, *Chruschtschows Westpolitik*, 155–56.
9. Bischof and Kofler, "Kennedys Gipfeldiplomatie," 144.

10. Ibid., 147.

11. Ibid., 148.

12. Ibid., 149.

13. Ibid., 155–56.

14. Georges-Henri Soutou, "Paris as Beneficiary of the Unsuccessful Vienna Summit," in *The Vienna Summit and Its Importance in International History*, ed. Günter Bischof, Stefan Karner, and Barbara Stelzl-Marx (Lanham, MD, 2013), 145–46.

15. Bischof and Kofler, "Kennedys Gipfeldiplomatie," 153.

16. "Memorandum of Conversation: Meeting Between The President and Chairman Khrushchev in Vienna," Vienna, 4 June 1961, 10:15 a.m.," in U.S. Dept. of State, *FRUS, 1961–1963*, vol. 14, *Berlin Crisis, 1961–1962*, ed. Charles S. Sampson (Washington, 1993), 88. A German translation of the Russian protocols from the Vienna Summit can be found in Wettig, *Chruschtschows Westpolitik*, 189–251.

17. "Memorandum of Conversation: Meeting Between The President and Chairman Khrushchev in Vienna" Vienna, 4 June 1961, 10:15 a.m.," in U.S. Dept. of State, *FRUS, 1961–1963*, vol. 14, 92.

18. Ibid.

19. Ibid., 88.

20. Ibid., 89.

21. Ibid.

22. Ibid., 94.

23. Ibid., 91.

24. "Memorandum of Conversation: Vienna Meeting Between The President And Chairman Khrushchev," Vienna, 4 June 1961, 3:15 p.m., in U.S. Dept of State, *FRUS 1961–1963*, vol. 14, 97.

25. Ibid., 98.

26. Ibid.

27. "Memorandum of Conversation: Meeting Between The President and Chairman Khrushchev in Vienna" Vienna, 4 June 1961, 10:15 a.m.," in U.S. Dept. of State, *FRUS, 1961–1963*, vol. 14, 95.

28. Bischof and Kofler, "Kennedys Gipfeldiplomatie," 159.

29. Wettig, "Chruschtschow."

30. Andrej D. Sacharow, *Mein Leben* (Munich, 1990), 249–50.

31. Ibid., 250.

32. Andrej D. Sacharow, *Memorandum: Gedanken über Fortschritt, friedliche Koexistenz und geistige Freiheit* (Frankfurt am Main, 1968), 7.

33. Rolf Steininger, *Berlinkrise und Mauerbau 1958 bis 1963* (Munich, 2009), 195.

34. Bischof and Kofler, "Kennedys Gipfeldiplomatie," 161.

35. Biermann, *John F. Kennedy*, 124.

36. Heribert Gerlach, *Die Berlinpolitik der Kennedy-Administration: Eine Fallstudie zum außenpolitischen Verhalten der Kennedy-Regierung in der Berlinkrise 1961* (Frankfurt am Main, 1977), 176.

37. Gregory W. Pedlow, "Allied Crisis Management for Berlin: The Live Oak Organization, 1959–1963," in *International Cold War Military Records and History: Proceedings of the International Conference on Cold War Military Records and History Held in Washington, D.C., 21–26 March 1994*, ed. William W. Epley (Washington, 1996), 94.

38. See Gregory W. Pedlow, "Flexible Response Before MC 14/3: General Norstad and the Second Berlin Crisis, 1958–62," *Storia delle relazioni internazionali* 13 (1998), special issue: *Dividing the Atom: Essays on the History of Nuclear Sharing and Nuclear Proliferation*, ed. Cyril Buffet and Leopoldo Nuti, 235–68; Gregory W. Pedlow, "The Evolution of NATO Strategy 1949–1969," in *NATO Strategy Documents, 1949–1969*, ed. Gregory W. Pedlow (Brussels, 1997), ix–xxv.

39. See Christian Tuschhoff, "Strategiepoker: Massive Vergeltung—flexible Antwort," in *Das Zeitalter der Bombe: Die Geschichte der atomaren Bedrohung von Hiroshima bis heute*, ed. Michael Salewski

(Munich, 1995), 167–88; Reiner Pommerin, "Von der 'massive retaliation' zur 'flexible response': Zum Strategiewechsel der sechziger Jahre," in *Vom Kalten Krieg zur deutschen Einheit: Analysen und Zeitzeugenberichte zur deutschen Militärgeschichte 1945 bis 1995*, ed. Bruno Thoß (Munich, 1995), 525–42. For the full text of this document, see "Final Decision on MC 14/3: A Report by the Military Committee to the Defence Planning Committee on Overall Strategic Concept for the Defense of the North Atlantic Treaty Organization Area," 16 January 1968, in Pedlow, *NATO Strategy Documents*, 345–70.

40. "Aide-Mémoire From the Soviet Union to the United States on the German Question, Handed by Chairman Khrushchev to President Kennedy at Vienna, June 4, 1961," in U.S. Dept. of State, *Documents on Germany*, 732.

41. Ibid.

42. Handwritten letter from Walter Ulbricht to Nikita S. Khrushchev, n.d. (probably June 1961), SAPMO-BArch, DY 30/3508. The letter's second attachment is dated 6 June; unknown is only the date on which the letter was sent.

43. "Vorschläge zur weitgehenden Eindämmung der Grenzgänger-Bewegung aus der Hauptstadt und den Grenzkreisen um Berlin nach Westberlin," March 1961, SAPMO-BArch, DY 30/3682; "Maßnahmen zur weitgehenden Eindämmung der Grenzgänger-Bewegung aus dem demokratischen Berlin und den Grenzkreisen um Berlin nach Westberlin," 6 June 1961, SAPMO-BArch, DY 30/3682.

44. Handwritten letter from Walter Ulbricht to Nikita S. Khrushchev, n.d. (probably June 1961), SAPMO-BArch, DY 30/3508.

45. Walter Ulbricht to Nikita S. Khrushchev, 5 July 1961, SAPMO-BArch, DY 30/3386.

Chapter 15

THE DECISION TO CLOSE THE
SECTOR BORDER IN BERLIN

Khrushchev's decision to allow Ulbricht to seal off the sector border to West Berlin in the "capital of the GDR" occurred on 20 July 1961.[1] Ulbricht and Khrushchev communicated about the decision-making process via Mikhail G. Pervukhin, Soviet ambassador to East Berlin. Directly after the Vienna Summit, however, this measure was not yet on the table and Ulbricht remained unsure of how to proceed. He began by focusing propaganda entirely on the swift conclusion of a peace treaty, the same demand that Khrushchev had presented to Kennedy in his second ultimatum.

"No One Has the Intention of Building a Wall"

The "Vienna Ultimatum" elicited fear and helplessness in West Berlin and a new wave of panicked flight out of the GDR. One alarm signal came from Hennigsdorf in early June: The engineer Helmut Newrzella at the Lokomotivbau-Elektrotechnische Werke (Locomotive and Electrotechnical Works, or LEW) sent a letter to Ulbricht with the signatures of thirty coworkers. The letter protested inadequate conditions and demanded that those responsible for the situation be removed from their positions. Since the responsible party was the SED leadership itself, Newrzella's letter represented a thinly disguised demand that the heads of the party and state step down. The original document never reached Ulbricht; it was destroyed at the plant. But the Ministry for State Security (MfS) opened investigations to find out whether this provocation could "be traced directly to the adversary." Ulbricht was informed of the letter's contents as well as the conflict resolution procedure within the factory: "Exact information on the petition's signatories cannot be obtained at this time, since the original document was destroyed following the instructions of the first secretary at LEW, Comrade Steinbach, without recording the thirty signatures elsewhere. In a conversation between LEW's party newspaper and Newrzella, [Newrzella] stated that he had aimed to collect 300 signatures by noon on 2 June 1961. N. came across in the discussion as very provocative and did not comprehend the outrageousness of his behavior."[2] Only after Newrzella escaped to West Berlin did the exact content of the letter to Ulbricht become known; RIAS (Radio in the American Sector) broadcast the document on 21 June 1961 at 5:35 a.m. The letter also provides an authentic representation of working-class living standards in the "State of Workers and Peasants" in June 1961:

Subject: Questions on the supply situation in the GDR

With great concern, we are witnessing the reinstatement of butter rations, at 1/8 kilo per family according to the customer list, along with insufficient supplies of the most important basic food staples such as potatoes, bread, fruit, and vegetables, as well as meat and sausage products. We demand the following:

1. An immediate end to these abnormal conditions!
2. A concrete explanation for the origins of this unacceptable state of affairs. In our opinion, it resulted from the rushed collectivization of agriculture.
3. The dismissal of all persons responsible for this unacceptable state of affairs.

Is this our reward for years of intensive cooperation to build the people's economy of the GDR?[3]

According to the MfS's assessment, RIAS operated as an "American espionage broadcaster," but the MfS confirmed that RIAS did in fact broadcast the letter of 1 June. Ulbricht would use this incident later in an exchange with Khrushchev as evidence of a Western campaign against the GDR.

In light of the GDR's miserable state of supplies and the outcome of the Vienna Summit, Ulbricht decided to launch a propaganda offensive with a clear message that the peace treaty and a solution to the West Berlin problem were on their way. The SED leader set the date for a spectacular international press conference in East Berlin on 15 June 1961. Topics included the draft of a peace treaty with both German states, the resolution of the "Westberlin question," and the complete disarmament of Germany. Questions from the numerous West German journalists focused on Ulbricht's vision of the border in Berlin, future control of the transit routes through the GDR, and the issue of refugees from the GDR. The record of this press conference is a remarkable contemporary document that registers the shock that Khrushchev's second ultimatum provoked in Berlin and Germany, as well as Ulbricht's extreme self-confidence, which left no room for doubt that a peace treaty would be signed. A correspondent from the *Frankfurter Rundschau* asked: "In your opinion, does the establishment of a Free City mean that the state border will be erected at the Brandenburg Gate? And are you determined to go through with this, with everything it entails?"[4] Ulbricht's response still shapes his image in German public opinion today as the cold and calculating "builder of the Wall," who fooled the public just two months before 13 August to hide his intention and disguise preparations that were already in place: "As I understand your question, there are people in West Germany who would like us to mobilize construction workers in the capital of the GDR in order to build a wall. I am not aware that this intention exists. The construction workers of our capital are mostly busy building apartments, and their manpower has been fully deployed to that end. No one has the intention of building a wall." To reinforce this statement, he declared (and this was the truth), "As I have said before: We are in favor of regulating relations between Westberlin and the government of the German Democratic Republic through a treaty. That is the most simple and most normal way to address these matters."[5]

Indeed, Khrushchev had not yet decided on 15 June whether to close the sector border, and Ulbricht saw this as "the truth." At the same time he used this truth to lie, since plans in the GDR to take this step were already in motion. The question from Karlheinz Vater, editor at *Der Spiegel*, was right on target: "Can the strictly neutral status [of a Free City] be reconciled with the fact that refugees from the GDR continue to be received in West Berlin?" Ulbricht left no doubt as to what he expected from the administration of the "Free City": "We consider it a matter of course that the so-called 'refugee camps' in Westberlin will be closed and the people involved in human trafficking will leave Westberlin. This includes not only the espionage headquarters of the West German Federal Republic, but also the espionage agencies of the United States, France, and England." In Ulbricht's portrayal, it was these agencies that organized "human trafficking" from the GDR. He explicitly emphasized that it would still be possible for people to change their places of residence, to move from the Federal Republic to the GDR and vice versa, but this would have to "occur in a legal manner." For Ulbricht, the solution was very simple and would shape the exit procedure for decades to come: "Whoever receives permission from the institutions of the German Democratic Republic—that is, the Ministry of the Interior—can leave the GDR. Whoever does not receive it, cannot leave."[6]

Responding to a question about smooth passage to and from West Berlin and the control of transit routes through the GDR following the conclusion of a peace treaty, the chairman of the State Council explained that a new situation would emerge: "No one will be able to avoid negotiating with the GDR on these issues. I would like to ask the foreign press correspondents to understand that we only demand the same rights in this regard that every other state already possesses. We are no less sensitive in this matter than the United States, Great Britain, and France with respect to their own territories." A central issue at the press conference was the question of air transportation to West Berlin. Karlheinz Vater voiced the problem of air control. Ulbricht's answer showed that this was at the very core of his concerns, and he referred to the international rules on tourist traffic: "Whether people arrive in the GDR by water, by land, or by air, they are subject to our procedures. They are our transit routes." Concluding, Ulbricht stressed: the peace treaty would come. The treaty and the creation of a demilitarized Free City of Westberlin were the "key to peace and the reunification of Germany!"[7]

It was only after this press conference, in early July 1961, that Ulbricht prepared the leading cadre of the party for a separate peace treaty between the USSR and its allied Socialist states. He was unwavering in this goal, especially since the Vienna Summit had demonstrated Khrushchev's inability to push forward his peace treaty with the United States through negotiations. The phrase "border closure" did not appear in Ulbricht's speech to the Central Committee of the SED, even though he had already informed Khrushchev that he could no longer guarantee the survival of the GDR without closing the border in Berlin. Unflinching, Ulbricht oriented the cadre of the SED toward the conclusion of a peace treaty. It would create "a new legal and political situation in Germany and also in Berlin" and lead to "a whole series of consequences. One of these consequences, for example, will be that all traffic through the GDR to Westberlin by land, by water, and by air will be subject to the control of the sovereign GDR. Transit to Westberlin will only be possible on the basis of respect for the sovereignty of the GDR, that is, only on a foundation of proper treaties, as are typical for any interstate movement."[8] In order for this to become reality, the Soviet Union would have to transfer its rights in Berlin to the GDR; the GDR would have to secure the border to West Berlin; and the Western powers would have to officially recognize the GDR under international law.

The SED integrated state security into a propaganda offensive for a "German Peace Plan," proposing the immediate establishment of a German peace commission with members from both German administrations as well as the West German Bundestag and the East German People's Chamber. The "Peace Plan," however, also had the "character of a last-ditch offer, since [Ulbricht] was attempting one last time to reinforce the Soviet Union's maximum goal of a peace treaty and a Free City through propaganda and cause the West to suddenly buckle under pressure." The politburo of the SED had decided on this course in January, and Khrushchev had signaled in March that the SED could begin the operation after his meeting with Kennedy. "The 'Peace Plan' contained a prophylactic justification for building the Wall," and the SED used a "false and primitive chain of arguments" to intensify the issue over the following weeks: "The SED wanted peace. The Federal Government rejected all offers to that extent and, to the contrary, armed the Nazi-led Bundeswehr. And it was planning an attack on the GDR. [The GDR] had to be prepared."[9] The only questions still open for Ulbricht were when and how Khrushchev would act.

Ulbricht Demands Closing the Sector Border in Berlin

With a growing number of refugees fleeing the GDR, Berlin's open sector border increasingly held sway over the fate of the SED state. In view of this situation, Ulbricht decided to take an unusual step, requesting to see the Soviet ambassador, Mikhail G. Pervukhin, in late June or early July 1961 in order to convey a personal message to Khrushchev. The content was at once capitulation and ultimatum: "If the present situation with the open border went on, collapse would be inevitable. As a Communist, he warned against [permitting this to happen] and shirked all responsibility for whatever ensued afterward. This time he could not guarantee that he would be able to maintain control of the situation. Moscow should know this."[10] In connection with Ulbricht's statement, Pervukhin assessed the consequences arising from the stalemate situation between the Soviet Union and the Western powers in Berlin. He wrote to Moscow that "closing the border would be difficult technically and damaging politically, but 'with the exacerbation of the political situation,' dividing Berlin 'could be necessary.'"[11]

By this time, Ulbricht had already begun initial preparations to close the border permanently; it remains unclear, however, when he became "conscious of the acute necessity and then the practical possibility of closing the border."[12] Pervukhin, too, had clearly been aware of the SED's preparations even before the Vienna Summit; he wrote to Foreign Minister Gromyko in May that the East Germans were on the verge of closing the border in Berlin unilaterally: "Our friends would now like to impose controls at the sector border between Democratic Berlin and West Berlin enabling them to close the 'gateway to the West,' as they call it, to reduce the bleeding of the Republic's population, and to weaken economic diversion operations against the GDR, which stem directly from Westberlin."[13] These plans contradicted the line agreed upon by Khrushchev and Ulbricht (to keep things quiet in Berlin), but the dreaded unilateral border closure never took place.

It was not the SED but in fact the people of East Germany who disrupted the two leaders' strategic schedule with their mass exodus from the GDR. In terms of refugee numbers, the spring of 1961 mirrored the situation in the crisis year of 1953. Up to twenty thousand people turned their backs on the GDR each month. Ulbricht was especially bothered by their average age: "If 75 percent of deserters are youths under the age of twenty-five," he reasoned, this showed "that schools are not adequately fulfilling their duties."[14] As in 1953, the path to the West for refugees led through Berlin. With increasing urgency, closing the border became a question of the SED state's survival.

Before Khrushchev made his final decision on 20 July to seal the sector border in Berlin, he consulted the foreign military intelligence service (officially the Main Intelligence Directorate, or GRU) and the KGB, especially concerning American policy. These sources apparently played just as important a role in Khrushchev's decision-making process as the negative responses from the three Western powers on 17 July to the Soviet memorandum of 4 June. The Western powers adamantly denied that Berlin lay on the territory of the GDR and reiterated their own rights to remain in Berlin on the basis of Allied agreements from 1945.

The GRU reported on the rapid expansion of the United States' nuclear submarine fleet, which posed a new security challenge to the Soviet Union. "By the end of 1964, Kennedy hoped to have a total of twenty-nine George Washington-class nuclear submarines at his disposal, each equipped with sixteen Polaris missiles. For the first time, these would give the United States the real capacity to launch a counterattack, and the Soviet Union possessed no adequate defense."[15] According to research by historian Matthias Uhl, this news shattered Khrushchev's "previous strategic concept for a military-political confrontation with the United States."[16] His own plan had been to keep the United States in check with 150 to 200 intercontinental missiles well into the mid 1960s. The military intelligence service also contradicted the propaganda-fueled image of Soviet superiority and emphasized the risks of a military advance against the Western powers: "The Soviet Union would encounter an armed and well-prepared opponent."[17] Moreover, the GRU reported on the strength of the U.S. Air Force in Europe and its plans in the event of an air blockade of West Berlin. In reaction to this information, Khrushchev canceled his original plans for an air blockade (for which "special troops" had already been deployed) and put a stop to any preparations by the National People's Army (NVA) of the GDR.[18]

The KGB reported to Khrushchev on the political reaction planned by the Western powers if a peace treaty were to be signed with the GDR; according to their information, the Western powers had not yet agreed on a joint plan by July 1961. But the decision makers at the Kremlin found another point disquieting, namely, that the American State Department had seen through the Soviet ruse in Berlin: "In its reasoning, the American State Department assumed 'that the policies of the USSR with regard to the Berlin question contained a significant element of bluff, and that the Soviet Union would not likely risk the outbreak of nuclear war over West Berlin.'" The State Department recommended that Western policy "remain tough and the Soviet Union be warned through all channels of the potential consequences of armed conflict over Berlin."[19] This is precisely what Kennedy did, and the NATO Council's resolution followed the tactic as well. The alliance intended "to answer the prevention of free access to West Berlin with measures 'whose outcome [could] pose a real danger to the security of the Soviet Union.' The West added weight to its threat by ordering troop reinforcements."[20]

Khrushchev received all of this information on 20 July 1961, and it led him to draw only one conclusion: NATO would regard any encroachment upon free access to West Berlin as a military emergency—a position that Kennedy reaffirmed in his speech five days later. Khrushchev's "yes" to closing the border in Berlin came at the end of a long political decision-making process.

Secrecy and Conspiratorial Communication

The coordination between Ulbricht and Khrushchev has been described by Yuli A. Kvizinski, who served at the time as an attaché to Soviet Ambassador Pervukhin in East Berlin. According to Kvizinski, Pervukhin delivered Khrushchev's answer to Ulbricht (Kvizinski does not name a date), instructing him to "close the border to Westberlin and begin practical preparations for this measure under conditions of utmost secrecy." Ulbricht acknowledged the message impassively and asked Pervukhin to thank Khrushchev for his decision. He then spoke in detail about the implementation of the operation. In order to seal off the entire length of the border to West Berlin, the SED would need a sufficient amount of barbed wire and "stakes, and everything had to be brought to Berlin in secret. The U-Bahn and S-Bahn [underground and overground] metro connections to Westberlin would have to be discontinued as well."[21] The Soviet ambassador was apparently taken aback by Ulbricht's familiarity with the details, which signaled that the SED had been thinking through the operation for quite some time. Ulbricht also knew that they "should take action on a Sunday"; 13 August would be a good date. Secrecy was of central importance to the preparations and success of "Operation Rose."[22]

Kvizinski characterizes Ulbricht as a multilayered figure. "In every respect, as an apparatchik of the Party, he still stayed true to himself in all of his habits and behaviors. Both of these aspects converged wonderfully in his person."[23] Kvizinski goes on to describe the conspiratorial communication between Ulbricht and Khrushchev during "Operation Rose," as well as the preparations by the SED: "Ulbricht determined that the head of his bodyguard, Wagler, would maintain contact with us, and [Wagler] brought the documents from his boss to the embassy and only handed them to me personally. Later, Wagler was replaced by Otto, head of state security in the division for security matters at the Central Committee of the SED. We translated the documents and passed them on to Moscow."[24] This did not take place via radio, since both sides feared that the code lacked security, but rather via courier. Pervukhin personally wrote the letters for Khrushchev and did not know whether he was even allowed to share the information with Foreign Minister Gromyko (he eventually did).

The head of the SED decided to "only inform Erich Mielke, minister of state security, Minister of the Interior Karl Maron, Minister of Defense Heinz Hoffmann, and Minister of Transportation Erwin Kramer."[25] Except for Hoffmann, all persons named were members of both working groups tasked by the SED in January 1961 with containing "desertion of the republic." All of those responsible for "Operation Rose" had been members of the Moscow cadre in Soviet exile. The transportation minister had a particularly difficult task, as he was responsible for disrupting the S-Bahn and U-Bahn networks in Berlin.[26] For these men, too, utmost secrecy was paramount: "They all received the order to only prepare this material personally, to write it with their own hands and lock it in their own safes. Ulbricht assumed responsibility for developing the overall concept, and it was just a few days later that he announced his decision to appoint Erich Honecker to chief of staff."[27] The politburo of the Central Committee, formally the party's highest leadership body, did not learn about the operation until all decisions had been made and only the implementation itself remained up in the air. This reflected a common pattern: "As a rule, Ulbricht always discussed faits accomplis and then waited to hear from Moscow before informing the politburo and the secretariat."[28]

Khrushchev was not only making a political decision, however; there was also a significant military aspect to the plan's execution. The deputy head of operations for the Group of Soviet Forces in Germany (GSFG) at the time, Colonel Anatoli Grigoryevich Mereshko,[29] was told to "draw up a plan to secure the border control barrier between East- and Westberlin." In an interview with the author and Alexander Vatlin, Mereshko recalled how instructions were passed down from Khrushchev to General of the Army Ivan I. Yakubovsky:

Mereshko: On about 22, 23, or 24 July, the top Commander of the GSFG, General of the Army Ivan I. Yakubovsky, ordered me to bring the topographical maps of the GDR denoting the exact border between the GDR and the FRG, along with the map of Berlin with the demarcation line between East and West Berlin. And we were to take these maps directly to the ambassador of the Soviet Union; he had called us in for an important conversation. The ambassador at that time was Mikhail G. Pervukhin.

When we entered Pervukhin's office, he looked astonished and said to Yakubovsky, "Ivan Ignatyevich, I requested that you come with the chief of staff of the Group, and you have come with a colonel." To which Yakubovsky replied in quite a harsh tone that he had come with the deputy chief of staff of the Group. Then Pervukhin explained: "Ivan Ignatyevich, we are here to discuss a state secret. Nikita Sergeyevich [Khrushchev] has instructed me to inform you of a plan to introduce a border regime between the two parts of Berlin, which you are to draw up." . . .

He asked: "How much time to you need to formulate this plan? You should know that only three people from the government of the GDR will take part: as we see it, Defense Minister [Heinz] Hoffmann, Interior Minister [Karl] Maron, and Minister for State Security [Erich] Mielke."

Wilke: There was also a fourth person, Erwin Kramer, Minister of Transportation, who was responsible for splitting the U-Bahn and S-Bahn systems in Berlin.

Mereshko: During my work on the plan, I only dealt with these three people.

So Pervukhin asks, "How much time do you need in order to draw up this plan?" Yakubovsky looked at me, and I said: "Comrade Ambassador, if the situation is so complicated (and we knew all about it of course), and [the plan] needs to be ready within a short period of time, we will prepare the plan within one week."[i]

Pervukhin looked at me carefully and said: "The plan is very complicated, we should not rush ourselves. Let's give ourselves a period of two weeks." . . . Yakubovsky replied, again in quite a harsh tone, "If my staff says that we only need one week, you can rest assured that the plan will be finished within one week. But we will gladly accept your deadline."

We leave the embassy and he tells me that Pervukhin will be recalled soon and a new ambassador will come. This was his way of explaining why he had spoken to the ambassador in such a sharp tone.[ii]

Yes, before we left the ambassador said: "I will now go to Comrade Ulbricht, and we will confirm that these three ministers will take part in drawing up the plan, and on our side the colonel will work on the technicalities of the plan." Yakubovsky answered: "I request that these ministers come to Wünsdorf[iii] at 15:00, and we will plan out our contact and the collaborative process together."

And sure enough, at 15:00—we had returned earlier—these three ministers were there. We discussed how we would work together, how we would stay in contact; the main problem was the language barrier. The task at hand was aided by the fact that Ulbricht had repeatedly brought up the issue to Khrushchev ever since the introduction of border controls. Khrushchev held off from taking this step for a long time. But the preparations in the governing organs of the GDR were certainly in full swing. . . .

The ministers could already give full answers to practically any question.[30]

---

i. Based on this deadline of one week, the conversation would have presumably taken place on 23 July. The plan would then have been ready by 1 August, in time for the conversation between Ulbricht and Khrushchev that day in Moscow.

ii. In fact, Pervukhin remained ambassador to East Berlin until late 1962, when he was replaced by Piotr A. Abrassimov on November 30.

iii. The headquarters of the Supreme Command of the GSFG, south of Berlin.

The rule of secrecy and conspiracy applied to Mereshko as well:

Before I began to draw up the plan, Yakubovsky ordered: "Do not to say anything to anyone about your work, neither to your superior nor to the chief of staff. I will decide myself who needs to know. You will work silently."

The plan was developed in seven to ten days; in any case, we took less than two weeks to do it. The plan was plotted onto the maps in duplicate. Then Yakubovsky signed the plan, and if I remember correctly, the three ministers' signatures are also on the plan for some reason. I do not remember Kramer. In the top right corner, "Approved. Ulbricht," on the left "Approved. Khrushchev." It was always the case that the left side was more important. One copy of the plan was sent immediately to our general staff via courier, and one copy remained with the GSFG.[31]

Kennedy's Three Essentials and Khrushchev's Response

Khrushchev's decision occurred shortly before Kennedy's 25 July 1961 radio and television Report to the Nation, in which he laid out the basic principles of his Berlin policy. The speech grew out of Kennedy's evaluation of the Vienna Summit. When he returned to Washington from Vienna, he immediately reviewed the Pentagon's emergency plan for a blockade of West Berlin toward the United States and the West. At the same time, he did not allow himself to overreact and decided against declaring a state of emergency or voicing new military threats, as others had recommended. Evidently he felt that he had asserted the United States' determination to do everything necessary to guarantee its own national security interests while maintaining peace in West Berlin. "American experts in both Moscow and Washington advised that the Soviets were more likely to be impressed by quiet substantive moves than by dramatic threats and by a build-up in our readiness, all on a low key, than by loudly flailing about." Kennedy followed this advice: "We do not intend to leave it to others to choose and monopolize the forum and the framework of discussion."[32]

The president opened his Report to the Nation with a historical reflection—one that he had already cited in Vienna while speaking with the Soviet Premier:

234 | *The Path to the Berlin Wall*

"I hear it said that West Berlin is militarily untenable. So was Bastogne. So, in fact, was Stalingrad. Any dangerous spot is tenable if brave men will make it so. We do not want to fight—but we have fought before."[33] Kennedy informed the American public of his administration's decisions regarding the U.S. armament program and future Berlin policy. The United States was matching the Soviet armament program with one of its own and taking precautions in case of a conflict situation in Berlin. Half of the aircraft in the nuclear-armed Strategic Air Command would be "on ground alert which would send them on their way within 15 minutes of warning."[34] In his address, Kennedy reiterated the three essentials of American policy on Berlin, "which would apply from that point forward and would be defended through all possible means: the right of the Western powers to remain in Berlin, their rights of access to the city, and the security of its inhabitants' freedom. West Berlin stood under the protection of NATO's shield, 'and we have given our word that an attack in that city will be regarded as an attack upon us all.' Moreover, Kennedy stated unequivocally who was responsible for the crisis, namely Moscow."[35]

Kennedy added that if the situation were to culminate in war, then it would be Moscow, not Berlin, that sparked it. The president's message had two components: in addition to scare tactics, it also contained an offer to compromise on the basis of Berlin's four-power status. Kennedy limited his guarantees, consciously speaking of "West Berlin" and not "Berlin" as a whole. This choice of words signaled to Moscow that the United States was also willing to respect the original Allied rights of the Soviet Union within its own sector, as long as the Soviet Union reciprocated with respect to the Western powers' rights. At the same time, the speech represented "a new definition of Western interests, which in large part [remained] hidden to the German side, including Adenauer, until August 13."[36] It closely followed the strategy of the Western powers and NATO during the Ostbloc crises of 1953 and 1956 to not interfere in the territory of the other side. Kennedy now applied this rule to Berlin. If the West Germans failed to notice, that was their own problem. Thus, an unspoken consensus emerged between Moscow and Washington with regard to their actions in Berlin, reflecting a conviction shared by the two men with nuclear arsenals: no war over Berlin.

Within West German politics, Khrushchev's Vienna Ultimatum sparked contradictory reactions in the Federal Government and the Berlin Senate regarding policy on Germany:

> In Early July, [Governing Mayor of West Berlin Willy] Brandt had already tried to get a sense from the Federal Government of whether a May 1960 suggestion by the West to reunify Berlin should enter into the discussion after all, "in order to escape the increasingly narrow scope of conversation." This proposal met with rejection, both at the leadership level of the Federal Foreign Office and in a conversation with [Minister for Foreign Affairs Heinrich] von Brentano on 11 August [1961]. The Federal Foreign Office insisted that the Western Allies should not be distracted from the central issue—the potential conclusion of a separate peace treaty with the GDR—that resulted from the crisis in Berlin. Brandt's public demands to open

negotiations over a German peace treaty, to take Khrushchev at his word, and to confront the needs of the other fifty-two states that had waged war against Germany likewise found little resonance.

Adenauer took a decisive stance against the suggestion, which would turn the Germans into a ping-pong ball for the interests of half the world. He also considered Kennedy's television address of 25 July 1961 to be ruinous and absolutely wrong, in which the president reiterated the validity of the three essentials that he had also conveyed to the federal chancellor in writing a few days prior. Internally Adenauer called for deliberate steps, even though he was, in fact, inclined to open negotiations with the Soviets if the right moment presented itself.

Brandt, however, supported Kennedy's line of maintaining a fundamental willingness to negotiate—under the condition that the Americans not allow themselves to be gradually driven out of Berlin.[37]

But driving the Americans out of Berlin was the central goal of the Soviet demand—and Ulbricht's hope—to transform West Berlin into a "Free City."

Only on 7 August, after Moscow had reached its final decision to close the sector border in Berlin, did Khrushchev respond to the American president in a public address. For propaganda purposes, he stuck by his intention to use the Soviet peace treaty to change the power constellation in Europe; he then projected this same logic onto the Americans in order to attack and condemn their strategy: "For them, the question of access to Westberlin and the question of a peace treaty altogether is only a smokescreen. If we were to refrain from signing a peace treaty, they would take it as a strategic breakthrough and would increase their demands. They would aim to eliminate the Socialist order in the German Democratic Republic." Moreover, Khrushchev declared, Kennedy wanted to alter the eastern border of Germany as it was set in 1945 in Potsdam and ultimately "lay out [his] greatest demand: an end to the Socialist order in all countries in the Socialist camp. This is already their goal." History, he argued, showed that when aggressors "grow impertinent" without being kept in check, they simply become more aggressive.[38] With that, he announced the reinforcement of Soviet troops at the "Western border."

The bipolar power structure of the nuclear stalemate came into clear focus, but simultaneously forced both sides to adopt a policy of calculated risk. In Kennedy's report to the nation, the president addressed both elements thoughtfully, including in his line of compromise concerning the Berlin question. The Americans insisted upon maintaining the Western presence in Berlin, but only within the Western sectors; this enabled the Soviet Union to permit its satellite state, the GDR, to secure the sector border to West Berlin in order to stop the flow of refugees. Khrushchev respected this new interpretation of the four-power status of Greater Berlin. His concession during the process of conflict resolution was to refrain from signing a separate peace treaty with the GDR—if he ever saw this as a serious alternative in the first place. His conversations with Ulbricht suggest that the separate peace treaty was, from the beginning, no more than a propaganda tool to exert pressure, and the Soviet Union never truly considered transferring Soviet rights in Berlin to the GDR. Respecting the status quo of European postwar borders became the key to resolving the second Berlin Crisis and the starting point in regulating the status quo of a divided Germany and Europe.

Notes

1. See Wettig, "Chruschtschow."
2. "Bericht 272/61 über Provokationen in Hennigsdorf/Bezirk Potsdam, 2.6.1961," Bundesbeauftragte für die Unterlagen des Staatssicherheitsdienstes der ehemaligen DDR (BStU), MfS, ZAIG no. 454. The recipient list read: "1. Comrade Ulbricht, 2. Comrade Honecker [with a check next to both names], 3. Comrade Irmler, 4. HA V, 5. Files."
3. Abteilung Information RIAS, workday 5:35 a.m., 21 June 1961, broadcast manuscript, Attachment 7, "Gutachten: Die Rolle der Westberliner, der westdeutschen Presse und des Rundfunks in Zusammenhang mit der Provokation in Hennigsdorf," 26 October 1961, BStU, MfS, AU 16144/62.
4. "Protokoll der Internationalen Pressekonferenz mit Walter Ulbricht," 15 June 1961, SAPMO-BArch, NY 4182/653.
5. Ibid.
6. Ibid.
7. Ibid.
8. Walter Ulbricht, "Rede auf der 13. Tagung des ZK der SED am 3. und 4. Juli 1961," in "Protokoll der 13. Tagung des ZK der SED, 3./4.7.1961," 7, SAPMO-BArch, NY 4182/654.
9. Lemke, *Berlinkrise*, 163.
10. Julij A. Kwizinskij, *Vor dem Sturm: Erinnerungen eines Diplomaten* (Berlin, 1993), 179; see also 180–81.
11. Zubok and Pleshakov, *Inside the Kremlin's Cold War*, 250.
12. Lemke, *Berlinkrise*, 162.
13. Mikhail G. Pervukhin to Andrei A. Gromyko, 19 May 1961, quoted in Hope M. Harrison, "Wie die Sowjetunion zum Mauerbau getrieben wurde: Ein Superalliierter, eine Supermacht und der Bau der Berliner Mauer," in Hertle et al., *Mauerbau und Mauerfall*, 86.
14. Report by Walter Ulbricht and bullet-point protocol by the advisory board of the politburo on "Die gegenwärtige Lage und die Hauptaufgabe 1961," 4 January 1961, SAPMO-BArch, DY JIVZ/2/747.
15. Uhl, *Krieg um Berlin?*, 224.
16. Ibid.
17. Ibid., 223.
18. Ibid., 225.
19. Ibid., 226.
20. Wettig, *Chruschtschows Berlin-Krise*, 169.
21. Kwizinskij, *Vor dem Sturm*, 180.
22. This was the code name for the operation to close the sector border in Berlin.
23. Kwizinskij, *Vor dem Sturm*, 178.
24. Ibid., 181.
25. Ibid., 180.
26. Erwin Kramer, Minister of Transportation, emigrated to the Soviet Union in 1932 and worked in transportation there. In 1937 he completed a training program on the tactics of pioneer

troops at a Soviet military academy, then took part in the Spanish Civil War and became an instructor for the engineering corps of an army battalion.

27. Kwizinskij, *Vor dem Sturm*, 180.

28. "Wortlaut eines Gesprächs von Wilfriede Otto mit Werner Eberlein am 5. September 1996 über die Beratung der Ersten Sekretäre des ZK der kommunistischen und Arbeiterparteien der Staaten des Warschauer Vertrages vom 3. bis 5. August 1961 in Moskau," in Wilfriede Otto, "13. August 1961: Eine Zäsur in der europäischen Nachkriegsgeschichte: Dokumente und Materialien," *Beiträge zur Geschichte der Arbeiterbewegung* 39, no. 2 (1997): 85. At this time, Eberlein was Ulbricht's chief interpreter.

29. Colonel General Anatoli Grigoryevich Mereshko, born in 1921, fought in Stalingrad as a lieutenant in the 62nd Army and was a graduate of the Frunze Military Academy. After his service in the GSFG from 1957 to 1962 and other functions, he became deputy chief of staff of the Unified Armed Forces of the Warsaw Treaty Organization in 1983. Today he lives in Moscow.

30. Manfred Wilke and Alexander Vatlin, "'Arbeiten Sie einen Plan zur Grenzordnung zwischen beiden Teilen Berlins aus!': Interview mit Generaloberst Anatolij Grigorjewitsch Mereschko," trans. Tatiana Timofeeva, *Deutschland Archiv* 44, no. 2 (2011): 91–92.

31. Ibid., 93.

32. Ted Sorensen, "The Personal Recollections of a Presidential Adviser in Vienna," in Bischof et al., *Vienna Summit*, 352.

33. John F. Kennedy, "Radio and Television Report to the American People on the Berlin Crisis," 25 July 1961, online by Gerhard Peters and John T. Woolley, *The American Presidency Project*, http://www.presidency.ucsb.edu/ws/?pid=8259.

34. Ibid.

35. Steininger, *Mauerbau*, 227.

36. Schwarz, *Adenauer: Der Staatsmann*, 654.

37. Küsters, "Reaktionen," 729.

38. "Aus der Rundfunk- und Fernsehansprache Chruschtschows," 7 August 1961, in Jürgen Rühle and Gunter Holzweißig, *13. August 1961: Die Mauer von Berlin*, 3rd. rev. ed. (Cologne, 1988), 84.

Chapter 16

THE CONSTRUCTION OF THE BERLIN WALL, 1961

Germany's Division Gains a Symbol

"They Will Feel Your Power!": Khrushchev and Ulbricht on the Wall's Construction

After the completion of plans to seal the sector border, as Anatoli Mereshko recalled in his interview, a meeting with Ulbricht took place, probably toward the end of July:

Mereshko: On about 2 August, we (Yakubovsky and I) went to Ulbricht with the finished plan. The three ministers were already gathered in his residence; they each reported briefly on their own preparations to introduce the new border regime.

Wilke: Then we have a problem regarding the dates. There is no doubt that Ulbricht discussed this issue with Khrushchev in Moscow on 1 August. And on 3 [August], the Political Consultative Committee of the Warsaw Pact commenced its conference. Could your meeting have been on 31 July?

Mereshko: I have somewhat different dates. From 5 to 6 August, the conference of general secretaries of the Communist and workers' parties took place.

Wilke: No, from 3 to 5 August. But that is nothing more than a different name for the same thing. You could not have gone to Ulbricht in Berlin on 2 August. Ulbricht was in Moscow from 1 to 5 August.

Mereshko: I only knew that the conference took place from 5 to 6 August. I could not participate, but I knew about it. That is why I was surprised that Pervukhin suggested this deadline of two weeks, but he probably knew that the conference of the first secretaries would take place, and then Khrushchev would approve our plan. So I am saying that it happened on 5 and 6 [August]; if you have other dates, then go ahead.

Wilke: All of the documents give the dates from 3 to 5 August.

Mereshko: I am not writing a historical document; I am just recounting what I know from memory. If the official sources say something else, then that must be true.

Wilke: There is nothing wrong with your memory. You said that the plan was finished before Ulbricht flew to Moscow.

Mereshko: Exactly.

Wilke: The only issue is that the day you recall as being early August was probably 31 July.

Mereshko: Sure, it's possible. I did say *about* when I mentioned 2 August.[1]

After this meeting in Berlin, Ulbricht traveled to Moscow. He had an appointment with Khrushchev on 1 August, at which the two presumably agreed upon the schedule to close the border. After that, everything proceeded quickly: the Political Consultative Committee of the Warsaw Pact legitimated the GDR's planned border closure in Berlin; the SED Politburo drafted declarations for the People's Chamber and the Council of Ministers and decided on the exact moment at which the procedure would begin (13 August 1961 at 12:00 a.m.); and Marshal Ivan S. Konev took over as commander-in-chief of the GSFG.

At the Kremlin on 1 August, Ulbricht and Khrushchev discussed the GDR's economic problems, which urgently called for Soviet aid, and the details of the border closure in Berlin. The protocol from this conversation is among the central documents on the Wall's construction. It was not until 2009, however, that it was released for publication as part of Gerhard Wettig's edited collection of Khrushchev's conversations. In it, Wettig documents crucial passages of the 1 August meeting and shows that both dictators viewed these issues—which would decide the fate of so many people—as solvable technical problems along the path to their consolidation of power:

Khrushchev: Comrade Pervukhin informed me that heightened controls will be needed along Berlin's outer ring.[2]

Ulbricht: That is the standard position of the foreign ministries, which take for granted the four-power status of the city.

Khrushchev: Comrade Pervukhin said: If the refugees from the GDR do creep over to West Berlin, then ultimately they will not be able to go further than that. But this is unthinkable, since enormous [refugee] camps will be built in West Berlin, and they will show them to tourists.

Ulbricht: Yes, ultimately the border does go right through Berlin itself.

Khrushchev: I would implement controls only within Berlin, but not along the outer ring.

Ulbricht: At the beginning, controls along the outer ring will be necessary to prevent people from congregating in Berlin. This outer ring exists in accordance with the four-power status, but we are of the opinion that the border runs through Berlin. In any case, everything has to move quickly.

Khrushchev: When the border is closed, both the Americans and the West Germans will be happy. Ambassador Thompson told me that this exodus is inconvenient for the West Germans. Therefore, when you implement these controls, everyone will be satisfied. Moreover, they will feel your power.

Ulbricht: Yes, it will achieve stability.

Khrushchev: I have a technical question: What will the controls look like on streets where one side is in the GDR and the other in West Berlin?

Ulbricht: We have a precise plan. In houses that have an exit to West Berlin, we will wall up that exit. In other places we will erect barricades of barbed wire. The wire has already been acquired. All of this can be done very quickly. Transportation is more difficult. We are reconstructing the S- and U-Bahn platforms to accommodate people changing trains to West Berlin.

Khrushchev: But who is going to change trains?

Ulbricht: The segment of the population that has received permission to cross [the border]. For example, about fourteen thousand people—many of whom are members of the intelligentsia—live in West Berlin but work for us.

Khrushchev: I have another question. If you let your people live in West Berlin, will people who live on your side be allowed to work there?

Ulbricht: No, that will not be allowed, that is different. However, there are several thousand children, particularly from the lower-middle classes, who live in East Berlin but attend schools in West Berlin.

Khrushchev: That must come to an end.

Ulbricht: Right, we will no longer allow it. Up until now, our trains to Potsdam went through West Berlin. Now they will have to take a detour through the territory of the GDR. However, there is a danger that the authorities of West Berlin and the occupation powers will take over the train stations in West Berlin that belong to us.[3] But this will make it difficult for them, since the trains that depart from there [to West Germany] still need to travel through our territory.

Khrushchev: Then they will not be able to do it, since you would then have to block the transportation route.

Ulbricht: That leads to the problem of the [Western] military trains that we have to clear through.[4] In other words, these types of conflict are going to arise.

Khrushchev: Small conflicts—that doesn't matter. But it is important to do all of this cleverly so that no one can accuse us of anything.

Ulbricht: We have now initiated the fight against human trafficking.[5] The opponent can feel that we are preparing to close the border. For example, yesterday an English journalist asked me: "Are you closing the border today?" I said that it depended on the Western powers.[6]

Khrushchev: I can see that we have a real understanding on these points.[7]

This conversation gives some indication of the provisional character of the border closure, which, according to the Eastern side, would no longer be necessary after a peace treaty was signed. After speaking to Khrushchev, Ulbricht noted "wire" as the material with which to draw the border, a decision that reflected military planning as well. Barbed wire was well suited to quickly and provisionally delineating the border in and around the city. "Wire" as a material also corresponded to Moscow's political plans, since the act of temporarily sealing off West Berlin was meant to stop the mass exodus from the GDR but should only represent a first step along the path to a peace treaty. The Soviet leader "wanted to get rid of the border barricade by the end of the year if a peace treaty could transfer control of the access routes into the Western sectors to the GDR and the mass exodus from East Germany could be stopped through other means."[8]

In order to conclude this peace treaty, the Western powers had to be on board; the Soviet Union clearly prioritized this over a unilateral peace treaty with the GDR. Therefore, the GDR's measures to secure the border could not in any way infringe upon the rights of the Western powers in Berlin, affecting neither control over the airways nor the unimpeded access of the Western military forces to East Berlin. To this end, Ulbricht noted that the existing procedure for the militaries and diplomats of the four powers at the Berlin border should remain in place, unchanged. His notes also give a clear indication of whom he really wished to target in closing the border: it would "prevent residents of the GDR from visiting West Berlin without special permission."[9] During their discussion on 1 August, the two party leaders agreed on the night from Saturday, 12 August to Sunday, 13 August as the date to close the border.[10]

One part of the meeting also addressed the reaction of the GDR's population. Khrushchev wanted to know how serious the danger was of sparking another 17 June (he only mentioned the event obliquely by referring to the Soviet army's conflict resolution). This part of the conversation gives a previously unknown glimpse into Khrushchev's and Ulbricht's perceptions of the GDR's crisis. Ulbricht was primarily concerned with securing his own power and defending it against threats from "our people" either voting with their feet or rebelling. Both the Wall itself and the GDR's new border regime suggested that SED leadership considered the refugee movement—and even a general readiness to emigrate—to be a mass revolt against the authority of the SED in the GDR.[11] The Wall was also predicated on the Communists' fear for their own power, as the conversation between the two leaders makes clear:

> *Khrushchev:* I have another question. I have read reliable secret reports from the West,[12] and they assess the situation in the GDR as such that conditions are ripe for an uprising. Following their own political line, they recommend not allowing it to become an uprising, since nothing good can come of this. They say: "We will not be able to help, and the Russians will crush everything with tanks." So they advise waiting until conditions are ripe.
>
> *Is this truly the case? I do not really know, since I can only depend on the Western reports.*
>
> *Ulbricht:* We have information that the Bonn government is gradually laying the groundwork to organize an uprising through recruitment and organized resistance so that the uprising can take place in the fall of 1961. We can see the methods of our opponent: The church encourages farmers to withdraw from the cooperatives, although the results are not very significant.[13] There are also acts of sabotage. Is all of this real? An uprising is not realistic. But some actions are possible that could cause serious international damage.
>
> *For instance, in a factory in Hennigsdorf near Potsdam, previously owned by AEG, antagonistically inclined engineers organized a petition. They demanded not signing a peace treaty because that would cement the division of Germany. They did not directly state that*

*they supported Adenauer but suggested holding a free referendum and electing an adminis-
tration to govern Germany. In this sense, the struggle is playing out in a number of state
enterprises. When we conducted a search of these people's homes, we found that one of them
is an American agent and four are former fascists.*[14] *Thus, not even the Eastern office of the
SPD*[15] *had anything to do with it; these were operations by American agents.*

*In this district, the number of sabotage acts within the agricultural collectives increased,
and there was a malicious slaughter of livestock. The Party's district leadership did not
actively run the plant, and hostile forces, primarily resettlers from West Germany, were
able to unfurl their plan. Among the agents are a lot of resettlers. If they were to succeed
in organizing a demonstration in Hennigsdorf, the farmers would support them. There are
many other districts where the opponent engages in these kinds of operations. But now we
are addressing the problem, and nothing serious will happen.*

Khrushchev: Did these people resettle in the GDR a long time ago?

Ulbricht: About two or three years ago.

Khrushchev: Why?

Ulbricht: They say that they did not like it in West Germany. Some of them are quite
primitive, and the enemy takes advantage of them.

Khrushchev: Perhaps it would be better to send them back to West Germany than to lock
them up in prison?

Ulbricht: I have thought about that as well.[16]

For Ulbricht, it was history that gave such weight to this letter from Hennigsdorf, written by engineer Helmut Newrzella and signed by thirty of his co-work-
ers. A similar letter, addressed to Prime Minister Otto Grotewohl and requesting
direct negotiations over salary cuts, had unleashed the demonstrations by construction workers in Berlin on 16 June 1953. When the prime minister refused to talk
to the construction workers, they took to the streets of Berlin with the slogan,
"We want to be free people!" (*Wir wollen freie Menschen sein!*). Clearly Ulbricht had
not forgotten the roots of this popular uprising; neither had the Ministry for State
Security (MfS), which reminded the SED leader on 3 June 1961 that this same
division of LEW had participated in the uprising on 17 June 1953.[17]

West Germany Is Superior: The GDR's Economic Crisis

Before the meeting of the Political Consultative Committee, Khrushchev asked
Ulbricht for a thorough report on the causes of the GDR's economic difficulties.
Ulbricht replied with the requested memorandum. His analysis began by listing
the structural causes of the country's economic struggle.

- The GDR was founded as a state with "practically no raw materials industry at its disposal." Until 1955, the GDR was forced to pay comprehensive
  reparations.
- The GDR was the second "industrialized country in the Socialist camp," but
  its economy was still coupled with West Germany's. The export of industrial
  equipment to other Socialist countries meant that the GDR's own mechanical

engineering industry had to "increase imports from West Germany and other capitalist countries." This structural dependence upon West Germany and the Western-dominated global market is underscored elsewhere in the memorandum because of its significance for the GDR's foreign debt: "Our economic difficulties and significant debt to capitalist countries have arisen in large part because we have had to buy material from West Germany and other capitalist countries in order to maintain our high exports of systems and machines to the Socialist countries."

- As a result of "the open border to West Germany, which is superior to us in terms of the industrial level in many branches of production and the living standards of its population, we have been unable to abide by several economic laws. Especially in recent years, we have observed very significant losses of highly qualified workers through recruitment by the West German monopoly. This fact, along with our insufficient ability to mechanize and automatize processes, has had direct influence on the development of production."

- "Berlin's division" necessitated economically unwise investments, such as the construction of a street detour and a detour for the train route in order to avoid running through West Berlin.

- "In the interest of supplying Socialist countries with heavy equipment," heavy machinery operations, shipyards, and an international port were built. The expansion in Rostock was intended to make the GDR independent "of West German ports, especially Hamburg." Ulbricht pointed to one investment that had particular importance for Soviet nuclear armament: "The Wismut joint-share company was established under the most difficult circumstances, the largest company in the GDR at that time."[18]

Ulbricht then laid out for Khrushchev three structural problems facing the GDR's economy:

1. The GDR was a state carved out of a single, unified German economic area and had had to provide reparations, particularly to the Soviet Union. Because of Germany's division, the GDR was forced to make investments in its infrastructure that were not economically advantageous.

2. West German industry was superior to that of the GDR, and the living standards of the population in the West were higher. In other words, socialism had lost the competition of systems in Germany to capitalism.

3. As the second industrialized country in the Socialist camp, the GDR sent machines and industrial systems to the Comecon (Council for Mutual Economic Assistance) states. In order to produce these investment goods, the close ties of the GDR's economy to that of the FRG were still a prerequisite. East Germany received important materials and pre-products from the Federal Republic that the economy of the Socialist camp could not deliver at the necessary quality. The price of this arrangement was the GDR's increasing debt to

the West, which it then had to repay in exports. Due to these imbalanced economic relations, the GDR lacked the resources to modernize its industry and improve the living standards of its population.[19]

Khrushchev was also interested to know why the economic program unveiled at the Fifth Party Congress of the SED in 1958 had failed. Ulbricht repeated the arguments that he had already laid out for Khrushchev in January. The unrealistic program presented at the congress had been based on an increase in the GDR's economic productivity in 1958, as well as on crisis developments in the economy of the Federal Republic such as a coal-mining crisis in the Ruhr Valley. In 1958 and 1959, the "gap [between East and] West Germany [could be] reduced, in terms of living standards as well."[20] But hopes for further crises in the Federal Republic were deceptive: rather than falling into despair, the Federal Republic witnessed an economic boom and a shortage of labor. The educated labor force of the GDR was welcomed with open arms on the West German job market.

For SED leaders, the refugee numbers were a strong indicator of the crisis in their own country: "Recruitment [by West Germany] had already decreased significantly in 1958 and, in 1959, reached its lowest point since the establishment of the GDR. In 1960, however, 200,000 people left the republic; in 1961, the number amounted to 330,000 people by the end of July." As a consequence of the country's population loss, the number of employees in many key areas of the economy decreased. East Berlin, the center of the electrotechnical industry, was hit especially hard. Economic plans could not be fulfilled, and a disparity emerged between rising consumption and slow developments in productivity. "But the open border, the economic boom in West Germany, and the labor shortage there also meant that we were unable to maintain the fixed relationship between increases in labor productivity and average wages." The "open border" created an ideological problem for the SED, forcing the party to consider the daily needs of its working classes in the workplace: "The open border and the influence of consumer ideology from Westberlin and West Germany prevented us from consistently making the necessary corrections to certain prices, and also corrections to unrealistic production requirements and the elimination of disproportionate wage structures." When the SED had attempted exactly these changes in 1953, employees of the GDR's largest firms reacted with strikes and demonstrations on 17 June. In Ulbricht's closing summary of the major reasons for the GDR's current economic difficulties, "the consequences of the open border" stood at the top of the list.[21]

The political function of this "report" from Ulbricht is obvious: it suggested to Khrushchev that closing the sector border in Berlin would end the GDR's instability and win time for the SED to solve the problems facing the East German economy. Independent of this purpose, however, the document reveals that Ulbricht did indeed understand why people were fleeing his state.

Legitimizing the Border Closure through the Warsaw Pact

After Ulbricht and Khrushchev's bilateral decision on 1 August 1961 to close the border, the party leaders of the states in the Warsaw Pact convened from 3 to 5 August in Moscow to discuss the situation in the GDR and the Berlin problem. The Political Consultative Committee was not a body that would debate the pros and cons of closing the sector border in Berlin with any controversy. The decision had already been made. When exactly this took place remained unclear for a very long time, as did the real purpose of this conference for the decision-making process. Bernd Bonwetsch and Alexei Filitow provide one example of this obscurity in their introduction to the published protocol:

> To this day, a written resolution to close the border has never been found. Nevertheless, it is quite certain that the actual decision only occurred in connection with the conference of first secretaries from the Communist and workers' parties of the states in the Warsaw Pact from 3 to 5 August 1961 in Moscow, which Ulbricht had requested on 24 June. This is supported primarily by protocols from a meeting of the SED Politburo on 7 August 1961, at which Ulbricht gave a report from the Moscow conference. The protocols do not contain direct reference to border blockades, but rather to the "commencement of the foreseen control measures," which would take place "during the night from Saturday to Sunday on the basis of a resolution by the Council of Ministers."[22]

No formal resolution to close the border emerged from the conference of party leaders because Ulbricht and Khrushchev had already conspired confidentially to take this action, just as the SED itself had already begun preparations for the appropriate "measures." Ulbricht's decision to convene the Political Consultative Committee was prompted by a "request" from Khrushchev, and as for the Council of Ministers of the GDR, its 12 August session is discussed in more depth below. But the Council's resolution and the declaration by the states of the Warsaw Pact had one thing in common: they served to legitimize the long-term division of Berlin.

Even the outcome of the Political Consultative Committee's meeting was already set from the beginning: "Files from the Russian State Archive of Contemporary History show that all of the resolutions and documents presented by the Political Consultative Committee had already been approved by the presidium of the Central Committee of the CPSU on the morning of 3 August."[23] But the conference declaration gave the GDR legitimacy in closing the sector border in Berlin—an operation that Ulbricht had desired and Khrushchev had decided. In line with other propaganda, the declaration placed blame on the West: "So far, the governments of the Western powers have not proven themselves willing to reach a reasonable solution through negotiations with all interested countries. Moreover, in response to suggestions put forth by the Socialist countries out of love for peace, the Western powers answer with heightened preparations for war, with an outburst of war hysteria, and with the threat of military force."[24]

Drawing a historical analogy to 17 June 1953, Ulbricht painted a picture in his speech at the conference of an external threat to the GDR by the Federal Republic:

> Both Adenauer and Brandt have claimed in conversations with leading politicians from the United States that with external assistance, it would be possible to organize uprisings in the German Democratic Republic with the goal of toppling the power of the workers and peasants. This was, however, before the miserable shipwreck of the American-armed and commanded invasion of the revolutionary people's power in Cuba. Still, it should not be overlooked that the West German extremists are toying with the idea of unleashing civil war in Germany to pull the Western powers into a military adventure against the Socialist camp.[25]

In the joint declaration of the Warsaw Pact, these threat scenarios concentrated themselves in the hotbed of West Berlin: "There is no other place on earth with such a high concentration of foreign espionage and intelligence headquarters, where they can go about their business so freely as in West Berlin. These numerous intelligence headquarters sneak agents into the GDR to undertake various acts of diversion; they recruit spies and incite enemy elements to organize acts of sabotage and unrest in the GDR." The declaration also highlighted the detriment to the East German economy from the targeted "recruitment" of laborers, which Ulbricht had also mentioned in his speech: "Through fraud, corruption, and blackmail, government bodies and arms firms in the Federal Republic prompt a certain susceptible faction of GDR residents to leave for West Germany." Ideologically correct in its formulation, this statement indicates that the mass exodus from the GDR—supposedly initiated by "external" forces—was the real reason to close the border in Berlin.[26]

In Moscow, Ulbricht presented his plan to close the sector border in Berlin for GDR citizens and openly acknowledged the real targets of the measure. In the same way that the SED co-opted the population of the GDR for its propaganda purposes, Ulbricht spoke now of "our people": "This situation necessitates that in due course, the state border of the German Democratic Republic (which runs straight through Berlin) will only be crossable by citizens of the German Democratic Republic with special exit permits or, concerning visits to Westberlin by citizens of the capital of the GDR, with special attestation."[27]

He elaborated thoroughly on the economic difficulties facing the GDR and warned that the West could enact a trade embargo in reaction to the border closure in Berlin. The committee took note of Ulbricht's speech, and the Polish party leader Władysław Gomułka gave an expressive response of "internationalist solidarity":

> The GDR could close the border in Berlin as soon as possible, he said, but without involving the brother countries in the affair and thereby triggering reprisals against them from the West. The party leaders from Hungary and Czechoslovakia, [János] Kádár and [Antonín] Novotny, adroitly played up the danger of war and supported broad measures in the area of the military—knowing, of course, that Khrushchev adamantly strove to avoid any escalation of this kind. Conversely, all speakers rejected on principle the option of offering stronger economic aid to the GDR,

which Khrushchev had distinctly advocated; their entirely plausible reason was that a total economic embargo by the West would also have disastrous consequences for their own countries. The Soviet Union should therefore assume most of the burden in saving the East German economy.[28]

Ulbricht's apprehension likely derived from his experiences of the fallout after the Federal Republic terminated inter-German trade in 1960, and he hoped to use this episode to emphasize the importance of comprehensive aid to the GDR from its "brother countries." But his concerns proved unfounded: neither the Federal Republic nor the United States or other Western powers initiated a trade embargo against the GDR or the other Socialist states after 13 August.[29]

The scenarios threatening the existence of the GDR provided the propaganda basis for the Warsaw Pact to recommend that the People's Chamber and the GDR government "introduce a system at the Westberlin border such that clandestine operations against the countries of the Socialist camp are completely deterred, and all around the territory of Westberlin, including its border to democratic Berlin, reliable surveillance and effective controls are put in place. Naturally these measures will not affect the existing stipulations on the control of and movement along the transit routes between Westberlin and West Germany."[30] The states of the Warsaw Pact explicitly described "heightened controls at the Westberlin border" as a transitional measure that "will cease to apply once the peace settlements with Germany have been realized and the pressing issues have been resolved accordingly."[31] In this respect, Ulbricht was skeptical. He recalled all of the futile attempts by the Soviet Union to sign a peace treaty with the Western powers, and drew the logical conclusion: "In this situation, concluding a peace treaty between the German Democratic Republic and the states of the Anti-Hitler Coalition that are willing to do so will take top priority." On the basis of such a peace treaty, a "reassessment of the Westberlin question must follow."[32]

Ulbricht, however, was not in charge of the process; Khrushchev had the last word at the conference. After giving an overview of his conversations with the Western politicians, he requested economic aid for the GDR from the Socialist states and reminded the other party leaders of East Germany's political significance for the security of the entire Socialist camp. He asked: "What does it mean for the GDR to be liquidated? It means that the Bundeswehr advances to the Polish border, to the border of Czechoslovakia. It means that the Bundeswehr comes closer to our Soviet border and to the borders of other countries. I believe that if we allow this to happen as a result of our lack of understanding, then it would be costly—much more costly, not only politically but also materially, than if we now do what is necessary to aid the GDR in growing stronger." He added: "If we attempt to lower the living standards of the East German population to match our own, then the government and the party of the GDR will collapse; in other words, Adenauer will take over." He continued: "So, comrades, we must keep these things in mind—even more so because Berlin will be an open city. Indeed, even if the GDR is closed off, we still cannot even consider allowing this to happen and must not permit it."[33] This was the only place in Khrushchev's speech where he hinted at closing the border in Berlin. He emphasized the point further by mentioning coordination between the Soviet and East German militaries on certain "measures": "We are considering placing tanks along the entire border for defense reasons."[34] Khrushchev's reference to the "open city" in this context could only have meant the "Free City" of West Berlin as the Soviet draft of a peace treaty and the Vienna Ultimatum demanded.

Regarding the conclusion of a peace treaty on Germany, Khrushchev did not want to commit himself either way, which amounted indirectly to rejecting Ulbricht's request for a separate agreement. Khrushchev suggested that the Western powers wanted a four-power conference. "One can accept [such a conference] as a preparatory measure because it will not elicit an immediate decision on the peace treaty, so it will simply freeze the present situation." As for Soviet aid to the SED, Khrushchev referred to the Soviet troops stationed in East Germany "totaling several hundred thousand men, and each battalion costs us many times more there than it would cost us to have them stationed at home." He added rhetorically: "What does the GDR mean to us—we are strong, we have weapons, etc., we can defend our borders. But in fact, this [mentality] would be national narrow-mindedness and not a Communist understanding of the tasks that stand before us Communists."[35]

The draft of the declaration by the governments in the Warsaw Pact was approved without discussion. It culminated in a recommendation to the People's Chamber and the government of the GDR to "ensure reliable surveillance and effective controls around the entire territory of Westberlin, including its border to democratic Berlin."[36]

The SED implemented Moscow's recommendations at an extraordinary session of the politburo on 7 August. The declaration by the states of the Warsaw Pact became the basis of the politburo's resolutions, which were then approved unanimously—and thus "democratically"—by the People's Chamber and the Council of Ministers. Concerning the Council of Ministers, the politburo stated: "The commencement of the foreseen control measures will take place in the night from Saturday to Sunday based on a resolution by the Council of Ministers. Comrade Ulbricht will invite the Council of Ministers to a gathering that weekend."[37] On the evening of 12 August, Ulbricht—in his function as chairman of the State Council—ended the conspiratorial preparation of the border closure vis-à-vis the Council of Ministers. The politburo's resolution would be transformed into a state operation, and the border closure would move forward following a resolution by the Council of Ministers.

The Operation to Close the Border: Planning and Troop Deployment

Ulbricht had stated unequivocally in Moscow that closing the gateway to the West in Berlin was an action directed specifically at the population of the GDR. Leaving the SED state without official permission was already criminalized as "desertion of the republic," and now the route over Berlin would finally be closed to those who attempted it anyway. This political goal determined the shape of the barrier to close the sector border. In terms of security policy, this was quite a complex task, and it was incumbent upon the Soviet forces and the National People's Army (NVA) of the GDR to secure the operation militarily. They were prepared for the possibility that the action could trigger a military conflict with NATO, even though Khrushchev wanted desperately to avoid it.

Sealing the border in Berlin fell under the responsibilities of the Ministry of the Interior, which oversaw the Volkspolizei, the border police, and the "Combat Groups of the Working Class," the SED's party army.[38] Only these forces would be deployed to Berlin in order to lend the operation the character of a "police action." That it was embedded in a larger military action is evident in the fact that the Soviet army developed the concrete plans for the operation. The SED's decision to close the border under the auspices of a police action had to do with Berlin's four-power standing; German military operations would have gone against the demilitarized status of the city.

Khrushchev had announced his military plans on 4 August to the party leaders of the states in the Warsaw Pact with a remark that the Soviet army might position tanks along the border of the GDR; it was a misleading way to downplay the extensive deployment that actually took place. At the end of June, as Ulbricht warned Khrushchev that he could not guarantee the GDR's survival if the sector border remained open, Commander-in-Chief of the GSFG Yakubovsky received "personal instructions from Khrushchev to look into the possibility of closing the border in Berlin completely." In connection with the Vienna Ultimatum to Kennedy, the presidium of the CPSU had already approved a plan from the military on 1 July concerning "measures to implement heightened controls and surveillance at the external and sector borders of Greater Berlin."[39] Between 22 and 24 July, Khrushchev had asked Yakubovsky to draw up concrete plans to execute the border closure in Berlin.[40]

Between May and August 1961, the number of Soviet troops in the GDR increased by 37,500 to a total of 380,000 soldiers. 70,000 more soldiers were stationed at the western border of Poland, and troop levels in Hungary increased by 10,000 men. "The manpower of Soviet troops in Central Europe was increased by about 25 percent to more than 545,000 men prior to the construction of the Wall. The Soviet Union concentrated nearly one-third of its entire land forces in the GDR, Poland, and Hungary in order to secure the border closure in Berlin." Naturally the Soviet Union also increased its air force presence in the GDR, and the planes were equipped with "special ammunition." "In Soviet military talk, this term was used as a cover for nuclear weapons."[41]

The Soviet approach in Berlin during "Operation Rose" always kept the interests of the Western powers in mind. Air traffic to and from West Berlin was a particularly sensitive issue. For the Western powers, but also for the GDR, the air corridors were of great significance because refugees were evacuated from West

Berlin by air. Ever since Khrushchev's ultimatum of November 1958, Ulbricht had tried to win control over West Berlin's air traffic by planning to transfer the functions of the international air traffic control center to the GDR, thus enabling the SED to end the evacuation of refugees by air. In connection with closing the border, the National People's Army planned flight-related measures to address the urgent Berlin problem, as the SED called it. The party hoped for "a possible blockade of the West Berlin airfields Tempelhof, Tegel, and Gatow, as well as their flight lanes, through interception aircraft, barrage balloons, and the targeted deployment of radio interference measures."[42] Khrushchev, however, put a stop to these plans. He understood that proceeding as Ulbricht suggested would have severely infringed upon the rights of the Western powers and therefore contained incalculable military risks.

Closing and securing the border in Berlin fell under the authority of the Volkspolizei and border police; Minister of the Interior Maron was in charge, whom Ulbricht had already summoned in January as part of the working group to come up with "measures" to "contain" desertion of the republic. The National Defense Council of the GDR ordered the presidium of the Volkspolizei in Berlin to establish a "security commando of 1,500 men." The commando would be responsible for "protecting the border in Berlin, controlling the movement of persons and vehicles, and organizing deep security along the border by stationing guards at posts and throughout the security strip."[43] The Ministry for State Security also concentrated its efforts on "containing" desertion: "A decree from Mielke on 4 May stated that 'the political operative work in all branches of defense and intelligence' should serve this goal. This also meant that the entire network of unofficial intelligence workers should focus on combatting emigration in addition to any 'special assignments.' In every district administration and county authority, a top employee would be in charge of this task."[44] With these directives, the MfS created an invisible but very tangible wall against "desertion of the republic" in the society of the GDR—a wall that claimed many more victims than its visible counterpart made out of brick and concrete.

On 24 July, the Department for Security Questions at the Central Committee of the SED provided Ulbricht with an overview of the "extent of pioneer measures on Berlin's outer western ring." Along this border, 52.2 kilometers were already "wired shut" with barricades; "92.2 km still have to be closed." A list followed of the amounts of material such as wood, fasteners, barbed wire, and wire mesh needed to close the "outer western ring" of Berlin, meaning the border between West Berlin and the surrounding region of Brandenburg, which belonged to the GDR. The measures required 47,900 concrete columns, 473 tons of barbed wire, and 31.9 tons of wire mesh. As the list of materials shows, the pioneer troops were preparing to close the border to West Berlin with barbed wire. The department of the Central Committee then informed the coordinator of these measures of a logistical problem: the GDR was short 303 tons of barbed wire, not a single meter of wire mesh was available, and the number of concrete columns was 21,000 pieces too low.[45]

On 25 July, the chiefs of staff of the GSFG and the NVA, Lieutenant General Grigori I. Ariko and Major General Siegfried Riedel, met in order to coordinate military measures on the "state border west" to the Federal Republic. With the help of the Ministry of the Interior, the GSFG developed the plans to close the sector border. Plans for the border closure thus lay in Soviet hands. The division of labor between the GSFG and the NVA during the process of closing the sector border was set: while the People's Army would secure the operation beyond eyeshot of the border, the Soviet troops would stand ready "for combat as a backup force."[46] Neither Soviet troops nor members of the NVA would be stationed in Berlin; only forces from the Ministry of the Interior and the Combat Groups of the Working Class would appear there. In addition, the GSFG drew up plans to guard the "state border west," and three divisions of the NVA were deployed to support the Soviet 8th Guards Army in Thuringia.[47] Military preparations by the Soviet army and the NVA were such that they "could be applied to both a peace treaty and sealing off the border."[48]

Khrushchev informed Ulbricht of the Soviet Union's military planning on 1 August.

> Moreover, we need to reach a joint decision regarding measures to demonstrate our heightened military strength. I listened to the report from our general staff, and we are doing everything necessary. We are entrenching our tanks along the border to the FRG, behind your soldiers' posts. We are going to do this "secretly" so that the West finds out. This is not bad at all. We might even transfer several divisions into the GDR. I told Kennedy's advisors: for each of your divisions, we will deploy two; if you initiate a mobilization, then we will initiate one too.[49]
>
> Our military comrades have suggested that we also do something for the Germans; perhaps it might be worthwhile to augment their divisions. But I said that we have to ask Comrade Ulbricht how the Germans would react. Maybe this would only trigger a negative reaction, and for the purposes of demonstrating [our power], this measure would not have central significance.[50]

Following the final political decision to close the border, several preparation units were established within the NVA.

> On 9 August, in the Schloss Wilkendorf near Strausberg [in Brandenburg], an operations group from the Ministry for National Defense convened. It was headed directly by Defense Minister Hoffmann and Chief-of-Staff Major General Riedel and included eleven other officers. For the sake of secrecy, this group circumvented the military levels of command in the military district and divisions and drew up all of the operational plans down to the regiment level for the 1st and 8th Motorized Guard Divisions, as well as all necessary measures for the heightened combat readiness of the entire NVA. Orders and documents had to be ready by 12 August at 6:00 am.[51]

Riedel had taken care of coordination with the GSFG. The operations group was responsible for securing the border closure in Berlin militarily. Parallel to this, a second group from the Ministry of the Interior was formed at the police academy of the German Volkspolizei in Biesenthal (near Berlin) under the direction of the deputy minister, Major General Willi Seifert.[52] This second group included Colonel Horst Ende, chief-of-staff in the interior ministry, and five other officers belonging to the staff of the interior ministry, the border police, the East Berlin presidium of the Volkspolizei, and the interior ministry's main department of transportation police: "Confidentially, they drew up all of the plans to close the border crossing points to West Berlin, including those in the S- and U-Bahn as well as some of the long-distance train lines. Furthermore, like the NVA group in Wilkendorf, the Biesenthal group also circumvented the command of the border police and Volkspolizei presidiums, drafting orders directly for the German border police and the Berlin brigade of the riot police."[53] The principle of secrecy also applied to the military operations to close the sector border in Berlin, just as it had characterized the political decision-making process between Moscow and East Berlin.

In order to exaggerate the threat that went along with strengthening the Soviet troops, Marshal of the Soviet Union Ivan S. Konev was recalled to active duty and appointed commander of the GSFG. It was a symbolic gesture that personalized the Soviet Union's resolve to assert its rights as victor in Germany. Valentin Falin, a Germany expert in the Soviet foreign ministry at the time and a personal advisor to the party leader, witnessed the transfer of command from Khrushchev to Konev: "I have decided to send Marshal Konev as commander of the Soviet forces in the GDR. He will be equipped with comprehensive authorities. If the Americans move their tanks to starting position, we will bring ours to full combat readiness." Falin also noted Khrushchev's expectation that this decision would have deterrent effects: "Konev's character is well known. His appearance in the GDR will certainly cool off a few hotheads."[54] Khrushchev signed off on the operation plans on 8 August. This date, along with Konev's assumption of command on 10 August in Wünsdorf and his orders to the three GDR ministers, left a lasting impression on Colonel General Anatoli G. Mereshko:

> On 7 August, Yakubovsky calls the GSFG from Moscow and orders Chief-of-Staff Ariko and me to come to Moscow with the original copy of the plan to close the border. We boarded the plane, ignoring the bad weather. As we flew to Moscow, we encountered such strong turbulence that the plane nearly fell from a height of about 5,000 meters onto the tops of the trees. I am sharing these details to show you that this is really how things were. When the pilot told us that we had just narrowly escaped death, I could only respond that it was my lucky day, my birthday. The storm front over the GDR, Poland, the western territories of the Soviet Union was so dangerous that we were advised to land in Minsk. We departed Minsk in the night and were set to arrive in Moscow on 8 August around 10 or 11 a.m. Khrushchev had scheduled the meeting with Yakubovsky about the plan at 10 a.m. We were nervous boarding the train in Minsk because we could not possibly arrive on time. When we got to Moscow, an officer from the General Staff picked us up at the train station and reported that Yakubovsky

had already met with Khrushchev and the plan had been approved. A while later we saw Yakubovsky, and he was very pleased that everything had gone well; both the conversation with Ulbricht and the meeting with Khrushchev had gone off without a single word of criticism. He thanked us for our work, and on 8 August, on that very same day, we flew back to Wünsdorf.

On 10 August, we received the news in the GSFG that two marshals were about to fly in. Neither Yakubovsky nor anyone on the staff knew the reason for the visit. We only knew that the men were Marshal of the Soviet Union Chuikov[i] and Marshal of the Soviet Union Konev.[ii] A meeting was called of the Military Council of the Group, and we joined them. Participants were the members of the Military Council: Yakubovsky, [Semen P.] Vassyagin, Ariko, and Yakubovsky's first deputy, General [Petr A.] Belik. As guests, the three ministers of the GDR were also present: Hoffmann, Mielke, and Maron. I sat with the folio of documents (the plan and the explanatory documents) on the edge [of the meeting] at the small table. Chuikov comes and sees me right away: "I ordered only the Military Council to meet, why is this Colonel [Mereshko] here?" Yakubovsky explained that the colonel had drawn up the plan and was ready to provide information on all of the materials. Chuikov looked at me: "Alright, he is my Stalingrader. Then stay."[iii]

He sits down at the place of chairman, Konev and Yakubovsky sit next to him, and Chuikov explains that the presidium of the Central Committee of our party, Comrade Khrushchev, has granted him the authority to say that Ivan Stepanovich Konev, hero of the Soviet Union, marshal of the Soviet Union, will be appointed to commander-in-chief of the GSFG, and [Chuikov] then lists all of his functions and assets. All members of the Military Council had long faces, nobody expected anything like this. Chuikov goes on to explain: "Ivan Ignatyevich [Yakubovsky], you will remain first deputy of Comrade Konev; Konev will deal with military political questions, and you will still be responsible for the combat readiness of the Group, for the military preparations and the supply [of the troops] with everything necessary, Ivan Stepanovich will release you from the [military political] duties. Whatever you did before, you will continue to do that." Then he turns to the ministers of the GDR and asks them to report on the state of readiness to carry out the plans. Each of them, with the exception of Hoffmann, stated that he was ready; Hoffmann said that he would be ready to carry out the plan within six hours of receiving the order—others had asked for one week. Chuikov says: "Two days. And no postponement. The 'X' hour at which the plan will be implemented will be conveyed to you by Ivan Stepanovich Konev." After that he instructed me to take him to another room where the high-frequency radio communication was situated. He ordered: "Connect me with Khrushchev." And then he reported: "Nikita Sergeyevich, Ivan Stepanovich has assumed the office of commander-in-chief, and the German ministers have received the order to stand ready." The appointment of Ivan Stepanovich as commander-in-chief was a surprise to everyone; obviously the secrecy of this plan had completely worked. With this, the meeting ended. Chuikov flew back.

At 12 a.m. on 13 August, Konev set the plan in motion and the operation began. From 10 to 12 August, the Combat Groups of the Working Class were called from the large cities of the GDR, from Leipzig, Dresden, Halle, etc., and gathered in Berlin. Before point "X," two divisions of the National People's Army of the GDR had been led to Berlin. And the divisions of the GSFG, especially the 3rd and 20th Armies, were stationed along the outer ring of the city.[55]

---

i. Vasily I. Chuikov commanded the 62nd Army at the Battle of Stalingrad. From 1949 to 1953, he was commander-in-chief of the GSFG and at the same time head of the Soviet Control Commission in the GDR. From 1960 to 1964, he was head of the infantry divisions of the Soviet army.

ii. As commander of the 1st Ukrainian Front in 1945, Ivan S. Konev captured Berlin with Marshal Zhukov. From 1956 to 1960, he was first deputy defense minister and also commander-in-chief of the united forces of the Warsaw Pact. From August 1961 to April 1962, he was commander-in-chief of the GSFG.

iii. Mereshko fought as lieutenant under Chuikov's command from 1942 to 1943 in Stalingrad.

That very same evening, Konev promised the Western city commanders at a reception in West Berlin: "You can rest assured. Whatever happens in the near future, your rights will remain untouched and nothing will be directed toward West Berlin."[56]

The Ministry for State Security was the last of the three security ministries to examine the final plans; concerning the development of an operations group within the MfS itself in preparation to close the border, nothing is known. "In any case, the entire leadership ranks of the ministry were only informed by Mielke on the early evening of 11 August. Even in this instance, the protocol does not mention the precise nature of the imminent measures." During "Operation Rose," the MfS sent a total of twelve reports to the central staff of the KGB on "reactions" to the border closure: "Characteristic of many reports from the MfS on the construction of the Wall is the combination of domestic information from the GDR and dispatches from the West, mainly through the HVA."[57]

Preparations were completed according to plan, and on 12 August at about 21:00, Hoffmann gave the two NVA divisions their orders. The Potsdam-based 1st Motorized Guard Division would secure the outer city border, while Schwerin's Guard Division was to station itself directly in East Berlin. "Operation Rose" had begun.

13 August 1961: The Division of Berlin

The SED Mobilizes Its Party against "Desertion of the Republic"

The planned border closure was even kept secret from the party cadre; however, the party was mobilized against desertion of the republic in late July. On 28 July, the politburo charged Bruno Leuschner, chairman of the of the State Planning Commission, and Erwin Kramer, minister of transportation, with "drawing up a train schedule according to which trains from the GDR no longer stop in Berlin or only pass through. As a general rule, youths under the age of twenty-five should not be allowed to travel to West Germany or Westberlin."[58] The polit-buro had compiled a list of planned measures to counter the increasing refugee numbers over the previous two months. The party itself founded a "Committee against Human Trafficking" (Komitee gegen den Menschenhandel), which began its work on 3 August and was disbanded by the end of the month. This consti-tuted a concealed mobilization of the party cadre, as similar committees were established in all branches of the party and state-run enterprises. Their purpose was to heighten surveillance of the social environment, as revealed in the official list of duties:

- The Volkspolizei shall remove personal identification documents from any suspi-cious persons.
- Youths of military age (18–23) are not permitted to travel to West Germany or Berlin.
- Registration of persons working in Westberlin.
- Border crossers are required to pay their rent, electricity, etc., in West German marks.
- This requirement shall be extended to households in which only one family member works in Westberlin.
- Increased control of packages at customs.[59]

These committees were intended to be active in the enterprises of the GDR, run by each firm's party organization. Party leaders used the party organizations within the state enterprises to ensure that any measures put forth by the state executive were in fact implemented at all levels.

The Decision by the Council of Ministers on 12 August

On the evening of 12 August, Ulbricht ended the conspiratorial preparation of the border closure vis-à-vis the Council of Ministers. The politburo's resolution would become a state operation, and the border closure would follow from a reso-lution by the Council of Ministers. The session started as a summer garden party at Ulbricht's country home on Döllnsee. It began with coffee and cake, followed later by dinner. As Werner Eberlein[60] recalled:

The session of the Council of Ministers would take place afterwards, during which the Council would pass a resolution on the border closure. . . . I do not think that anyone even suspected what was really going on. . . . After dinner, at about 21:00 or 21:30, everything was cleared and Ulbricht said: "Now we will hold a brief session." . . . Then Ulbricht gave a speech stating that the measures would be implemented on 13 August. He did not go into detail, but simply read out the resolution that was to be written and then passed by a general vote. Only a few people said anything about it. That night, around 22:30 or 23:00, the resolution was passed. When the party ended at about 23:30 or a little bit later and everyone drove home, the avenue leading into Berlin was already full of Soviet tanks. The decision had thus already been made.[61]

The key sentences of the resolution were: On the borders of the GDR "including the border to the Western sectors of Greater Berlin," border controls should be introduced "as they normally occur along the borders of any sovereign state. . . . Citizens of the GDR may only cross these borders with special permission. . . . As long as Westberlin has not been transformed into a demilitarized, neutral Free City, residents of the capital of the GDR will require a special permit to cross the border into Westberlin." The ministers of the interior and transportation were tasked with "issuing the necessary regulatory statutes."[62]

At a meeting in November 1961, the SED and CPSU party delegations praised the resolution by the Council of Ministers. Ulbricht claimed there that the Council had spent the entire day discussing the matter. For the Communists, the resolution represented a democratic process, since the decision of the party was transformed into a state operation following formal and proper official procedure. Khrushchev applauded himself afterward for knowing that the measures in Berlin had taken place at just the right moment:

> *Khrushchev:* Could we have closed the border earlier than 13 August? No! If we had closed it earlier, people in democratic Berlin would not have supported it.
>
> *Ulbricht:* Moreover, our opponents would have been able to take retaliatory measures, whereas they were completely exhausted by 13 August.
>
> *Khrushchev:* You implemented it very well, quickly and under conditions of total secrecy.
>
> *Ulbricht:* And in doing so, we also adhered to democracy.
>
> *Khrushchev:* I wondered myself how you managed that.
>
> *Ulbricht:* On Saturday [12 August], I invited the entire Council of Ministers to my dacha, and we spent the whole day discussing these measures. By about 23:00, everyone had given their approval and went home. They needed about an hour to reach Berlin, and in Berlin they already encountered the tanks. Nevertheless, everything had been discussed.[63]

The published resolution by the Council of Ministers catered to East Berliners' hopes that the situation begun on 13 August could change rapidly if the four powers agreed on regulations for Berlin as part of a peace treaty. This hope, however, proved deceptive.

Barbed Wire through Berlin

The operation began at midnight from 12 to 13 August; by 3:00 a.m., units of border police, riot police, and combat groups were instructed to stand in position along Berlin's sector border. "Most of the inner-city border checkpoints were to be closed during this period and sealed off through pioneer measures. Simultaneously, S- and U-Bahn traffic to and from Berlin was interrupted."[64] With more than 5,000 border police, 5,000 guard and riot police, and 4,500 members of the combat groups, it was possible to barricade the entire border in and around West Berlin by the morning of 13 August.[65] Streets were torn up, chevaux-de-frise were erected, and barbed wire was stretched along the length of the border. Interior Minister Maron gave the units deployed to the western outer ring eight days beginning on 12 August to complete the pioneer measures to expand that border. Closing the sector border in Berlin during the night spanning 12 to 13 August was a military success that took the West entirely by surprise.

The man of the hour was Erich Honecker, secretary for security in the Central Committee. He headed the Central Staff of the National Defense Council during the operation—a body that had only been established on 9 August.[66] The group also included the four ministers, Hoffmann, Kramer, Maron, and Mielke, and "one representative each from the Soviet embassy and the GSFG were present" during the meetings as well.[67] From 13 to 21 August, this committee convened fifteen times to assess the situation. Three of these discussions were led by Ulbricht, including one on 17 August at which the gathered officials concluded "that the West will not undertake anything special."[68]

Honecker's group was not the only body with its headquarters at the presidium of the Berlin Volkspolizei; the secretariat of the SED's district office in Berlin also moved its headquarters there that night. As a member of the SED faction in the People's Chamber, Hans Modrow had approved the security measures at the border on 11 August. Looking back, he writes that while he did feel obliged to vote according to a party resolution, he was also personally convinced that something needed to be done to improve the economic situation. For him, there is no question: without 13 August, the GDR could not have survived until 1990. "We might not have had the better arguments in erecting the Wall, but in terms of contemporary politics, we definitely had the better cards." On 12 August, simultaneous to the resolution by the Council of Ministers, the SED's district office fetched Modrow and brought him to the presidium of the Volkspolizei. After midnight, Paul Verner, first secretary of the Berlin SED, informed the functionaries that the border was closed and tasked them with "mobilizing the combat groups and informing the active district party members as quickly as possible of the security measures being carried out at border." In addition to organizational measures, it was the duty of the party functionaries to make sure that "no onlookers gathered at the border," and especially "that on Monday, work in Berlin's state enterprises resumed smoothly. The only phrase missing was, 'as if nothing had happened.'"[69]

The minister of transportation announced on 13 August that "the direct S-Bahn connection between the border areas of the GDR and Westberlin" would be interrupted. The separation of S-Bahn networks in East and West Berlin was carried out accordingly, along with the closure of certain stations; the same procedure applied to the U-Bahn.[70]

Protests in East Berlin and the GDR against the sealed border were nipped in the bud. "From 13 August to 4 September 1961, a total of 6,000 arrests took place; of them, about 3,100 led to incarceration."[71] The security apparatus now faced critics head on, knowing that they could no longer flee: "'There will be no discussion with provocateurs'; this was the solution."[72]

Regulations at the Border

The most important consequence of closing the border was shutting the door to the West for citizens of the GDR, who could only cross the border with explicit permission from the state. Maron set these rules and selected certain checkpoints for street traffic. Of the thirteen checkpoints, twelve were designated for West Germans and West Berliners, while "Checkpoint Charlie" on Friedrichstraße let through members of the Western powers, diplomats, and foreigners. Given the current situation, citizens of the GDR who did not work in Berlin were instructed not to travel to Berlin for the time being.[73] The number of checkpoints shrank to seven before the end of August.

On 13 August, the lord mayor of East Berlin announced an ordinance from the Magistrat stating that it would no longer be possible for residents of East Berlin to work in West Berlin.[74] Thus, the SED's exasperating problem of border crossers suddenly solved itself.

Visits by West Berliners to the other part of the city developed into a drama. At first, border police were content with strict controls at the point of border crossing. But beginning on 15 August, all vehicles from West Berlin needed special permits, and on 22 August, the GDR's Ministry of the Interior introduced a visa requirement to visit the Eastern sector. "At the same time, it was announced that people could submit the appropriate [visa] applications at two branches of the GDR travel agency in West Berlin."[75] The political backdrop of this measure and its immediate rejection by West Berlin during this phase of open confrontation is unmistakable: the GDR intended these travel agencies to assume quasi-consular functions in West Berlin. On the same day that the ordinance was issued, the West Berlin Senate made clear "that it would not tolerate any institutions on the territory of West Berlin that operated on instructions from the authorities of the GDR. Three days later, the Allied Command issued [order] BK/O(61) 11, which prohibited the establishment and operation of GDR bureaus for the purpose of issuing visas and instructed West Berlin authorities to take whatever measures necessary to carry out this order."[76] With these developments, movement between the two halves of the city essentially came to a standstill: "For normal West Berliners, it was no longer possible to visit their relatives. Only residents of the Western sectors whose visit was in the interest of the GDR and the SED (salespeople, artists, SED functionaries) could continue to enter East Berlin."[77]

An important background event that influenced the decision by the Senate and Western city commanders was an operation by the Combat Groups of the Working Class in East Berlin to close the SPD's local office on 21 August (the office had existed since 1946). In response, the Berlin SPD dissolved its party organization in East Berlin, promising its members that it would return to the Eastern part of the city as soon as the situation changed fundamentally.

The SED's position remained firm: either the West would permit offices of the (East German) Reichsbahn to issue special permits or reach an equivalent solution through direct negotiations with the Berlin Senate, or West Berlin residents would not be allowed to enter East Berlin. It was not until Christmas of 1963 that the first Permit Agreement (Passierscheinabkommen) finally allowed West Berliners to visit their friends and family on the other side of the Wall. This agreement followed a shift in the Germany policy of Willy Brandt, West Berlin's governing mayor, who advocated a new Ostpolitik for the Federal Republic beginning in July 1963.[78]

The Border Regime: The Wall and the Command to Shoot

The SED now established a border regime in Berlin comparable to the system along the inner-German border, which heavily relied on armed force. Since 1952, guards along the inner-German border and Berlin's outer ring acted upon the command to shoot people fleeing across the border if their flight could not be stopped in any other way; now this order also applied to the center of Berlin, a move that was accompanied by an intensive propaganda campaign.[79] On 16 August, speaking in West Berlin, Willy Brandt appealed to soldiers and officers of the border police and combat groups to not allow themselves to be turned into "scoundrels" (*Lumpen*), to hold on to their humanity, and especially to not shoot their fellow "countrymen."[80] In reaction to this speech and over the course of the campaign accompanying the new orders, the politburo instructed Albert Norden, Central Committee secretary for agitation and propaganda, to elicit "written statements" from all groups, platoons, and companies stationed at the border "that anyone who breaks the laws of our German Democratic Republic will be called to order, even—if necessary—through the use of armed force."[81]

The reaction to Brandt's speech resonated in a front-page article in the SED party newspaper, *Neues Deutschland*, on 23 August: "And concerning the 'countrymen' that we are not supposed to shoot: Since when are burglars, highwaymen, and murderers 'countrymen'? . . . We know the difference between friend and enemy! The enemies of our people will hit a brick wall when they reach us and—depending on how outlandish they wish to be—lose teeth, hair, or their lives."[82] When this coldhearted commentary appeared, Conrad Schumann had already leapt over the barbed wire on Bernauer Straße; Ida Siekmann had already jumped to her death into the street below trying to flee her apartment building. One day after this infamous commentary, Günter Litfin died from a shot to the head by a member of the transportation police as he tried to escape to West Berlin; a "breach of the border" was thus "successfully thwarted."[83] The SED state had already found language to justify the border regime in its propaganda.

Ulbricht believed that barbed wire was the appropriate material to quickly seal the sector border. On 20 August, as Yuli A. Kvizinski recalled later, a meeting took place among him, Pervukhin, and Marshal Konev. Ulbricht explained to his Soviet guests that "the heated phase of the operation was over; now it was important to consolidate the situation and strengthen the border. Barbed wire could not remain in the city forever—it irritated the people and provoked them to make fresh attempts to breach the border. 'We will build a concrete wall to replace the barbed wire,' Ulbricht said, 'and even plaster it. We will have to reduce our [national] construction program somewhat, but we have no other choice.'"[84]

Marshal Konev had considerable influence over the shape of the border regime. Konev ordered the establishment of a "strict military regime" in the 100-meter exclusion zone in front of the border, instructing that "weapons be used . . . [against] traitors and violators of the border."[85] He demanded that Army General Hoffmann "do more to hold members of the German border police accountable who intentionally cross into the Federal Republic. Such transgressions are to be interpreted not as desertion but as treason against the German Democratic Republic."[86] These demands demonstrate the extent to which the Soviet army controlled the configuration of the border regime, down to the last detail. This applies to the inner-German border as well, along which Konev explicitly ordered the laying of mines.[87] Thus, the Soviet military exercised lasting influence on the character of the border. Marshal Konev pointed out to General Hoffmann on 14 September that the border fortification did not have "any preventative military function" against a Western attack "but rather a repressive function, oriented inward."[88]

Cementing the border in Berlin also had consequences for people living near the inner-German border. After the hole in Berlin was sealed, an expansion of structures along the inner-German border began as well.[89] "Operation Fortification" (Aktion Festigung) kicked off a wave of resettlement on 1 September "to forcibly relocate 3,000 'unreliable elements' from along the border to the interior [of the country]." This occurred on the orders of the interior minister, who selected residents to be deported from the area within the "5 km exclusion zone and the 500 m protective strip."[90]

Four days before the meeting of the Central Staff on 20 September, convening once more at the behest of the SED Politburo, Ulbricht informed Khrushchev of his plans: "Now the further fortification of the border is taking place. Our tactic of implementing measures little by little has made it difficult for the opponent to gain an understanding of the extent of our measures and has made it easier for us to identify the weak points along the border."[91] At the 20 September session, the Central Staff took stock of the closed border so far. Honecker reported that the politburo had "criticized the inadequate pioneer measures to secure the state border in Berlin"; after all, the assignment had ordered that "all attempts to break through must be rendered impossible."[92]

Major General Seifert from the Ministry of the Interior went through the planned measures to stabilize border security. In order to prevent emigration via motorized vehicles, pioneer measures were put in place such as "digging trenches, laying concrete plates and concrete ties," tearing "through streets," and dumping piles of sand. For the inner-city border, the interior ministry planned "to construct 18 to 20 km of wall along the border. Until this is complete, trenches will be dug." The sewage system would also be sealed with barricades. "Decisive measures" would be taken on Bernauer Straße, among other places, "where the border runs along the edges of property lines." In these cases, a "complete eviction or a more rapid eviction of unreliable elements [must] occur." Responding to follow-up questions, he explained that the wall would be 2 meters high.[93]

Honecker summarized the results of this advisory session in eleven points. Two of them concerned the establishment of an exclusion zone behind the Wall, as ordered by Konev, as well as the command to shoot: "The exclusion zone of 100 m must be enforced consistently, with a strict military regime put in place." Within this exclusion zone, sole responsibility would belong to the commanders of the border brigades. "Firearms are to be used against traitors and violators of the border."[94] On 2 November, Khrushchev approved of the planned expansion.

With his Soviet "friends," however, Ulbricht encountered certain coordination problems regarding the border regime. On the occasion of official congratulations for his sixty-ninth birthday on 30 June 1962, Ulbricht responded to the congratulatory note from Moscow with a list of grievances, which he set down to protocol for Soviet diplomat A. I. Gorchakov. The list provides a rare glimpse into Ulbricht's issues with the Soviet supreme power during this early period of the Wall's construction. The source feeding these quiet complaints was information Ulbricht received on conversations between American Secretary of State Dean Rusk and Soviet Ambassador to Washington Anatoly F. Dobrynin, in which Rusk requested that the border to West Berlin be made even "more secure." It was not without irony that Ulbricht dismissed this request and, to counter, demanded that his Soviet "friends" convince the Americans to get the West German government to "stop its public appeals to destroy the wall." Gorchakov noted:

> Furthermore, I informed Comrade W. Ulbricht about the content of the unofficial conversation between Rusk and Comrade Dobrynin. Comrade Ulbricht paid particular attention to Rusk's reply concerning the use of additional protective measures at the border to Westberlin.
>
> We foresaw, said Comrade Ulbricht, that things would develop exactly in this direction. As early as 21 August of last year, we suggested following through on the measures we drew up to create a prohibitive border zone in Berlin. It is clear that without a prohibitive zone, it is impossible to maintain order and calm at the border. A prohibitive zone of this type is indispensible. Before the Moscow conference, we sent materials to the Central Committee of the CPSU that addressed precisely this question. Some of the Soviet comrades, however, had a series of objections to these measures because they believed that we would be fine without them.
>
> Now, Comrade Ulbricht continued, Rusk himself wants us to build a second wall so that violators of the border who cross over the first wall will still be on the territory of the GDR, and the GDR police who open fire will be shooting within the state border. On a practical level, we are talking about the creation of a prohibitive border zone with a width of 10 to 100 meters, depending on the location-specific conditions and the evacuation of the population that lives in these areas.
>
> In January 1962, Ulbricht went on, we sent a letter to the commander-in-chief of the Group of Soviet Forces in Germany with questions concerning the creation of a border zone along the borders to Westberlin. To this day, we still have not received an answer to this letter, since the Soviet comrades were apparently against the implementation of such measures. Still, said Ulbricht, we have partially realized

some of these foreseen measures already, for instance by evacuating residents from the city districts in direct proximity to the border. This was undertaken without any special instructions or orders, without noise. If we had not done it, there would have been many more conflicts and incidents at the border. Special crossing documents will be issued to persons living within 100 meters of the border strip; they will be prohibited from receiving any visitors at all. Going forward, we have drawn up new measures to fortify the state border, and we foresee in particular the creation of a border zone. We will send these measures to Moscow soon. The Western powers must ensure that there is a kind of prohibitive border strip on the Western side as well, in order to prevent explosions at the Wall and other attempts from the Westberlin side to destroy the border fortifications. Rusk must force Brandt to stop his public appeals for the Wall's destruction and hinder the organization of incidents and conflicts at the border.[95]

It was Pervukhin, the Soviet ambassador to East Berlin, who had most strongly opposed the creation of a special border zone in the middle of Berlin. Ulbricht repeated his request in a letter to Khrushchev on 23 July 1962, shortly after his conversation with Gorchakov. By June 1963, a border zone was established that remained in place to varying degrees until 1989.[96]

Notes

1. Wilke and Vatlin, "Arbeiten Sie einen Plan," 93.
2. The outer ring circumscribed Greater Berlin and thus included both halves of the city.
3. Ulbricht is referring to the West Berlin S-Bahn metro system, which was still operated by the East German Deutsche Reichsbahn. This continued even after Berlin's division.
4. Ulbricht was thinking about the period between closing the border in Berlin and signing the (still planned) peace treaty at the end of the year; during these months, he would still respect the occupation rights of the Western powers. With the conclusion of the peace treaty, the problem would naturally take care of itself.
5. The SED considered emigration from the GDR to be the result of targeted "solicitation" by West German companies or the Federal Government or Berlin Senate. The term "human trafficking" (*Menschenhandel*) was used in East German criminal law to punish those who helped citizens of the GDR to emigrate "abroad" (§132, criminal code of the GDR).
6. On 2 August 1961, the SED's party newspaper, *Neues Deutschland*, published an interview of Ulbricht by the deputy editor-in-chief of the British *Evening Standard*, Mark Wilson. In it, Ulbricht denied that there was "any kind of threat . . . to close the border," adding that the decision was not up to the GDR but rather to the Western powers. If they were prepared to regulate by contract the use of the "transit lines" through East German territory, there would be no reason to close the border. Closing the border would also be unnecessary if "the other side [indicated] peaceful intentions . . . by transitioning to normal relations." The *Evening Standard* contained neither a report nor even a note about the conversation.

7. "Gespräch Chruschtschows mit dem Ersten Sekretär der SED, Walter Ulbricht, am 1. August 1961," in Wettig, *Chruschtschows Westpolitik*, 311–13. This conversation was adapted into a play in Berlin in 2009: http://www.spiegel.de/kultur/gesellschaft/0,1518,626153,00.html.

8. Wettig, *Chruschtschows Berlin-Krise*, 181.

9. "Handschriftliche Notiz Ulbrichts über das Treffen mit Chruschtschow am 1.8.," in Matthias Uhl and Armin Wagner, eds., *Ulbricht, Chruschtschow und die Mauer: Eine Dokumentation* (Munich, 2003), 94; erroneously dated 3 August.

10. Uhl, *Krieg um Berlin?*, 227.

11. See Sälter, *Grenzpolizisten*, 7–8, 15–24, 437–38.

12. Khrushchev is referring to internal reports by Western governments obtained by Soviet intelligence.

13. In March 1960, a pastor from the countryside of Brandenburg was asked by SED functionaries for his opinion on agricultural collectivization, especially the recruitment methods. He answered "that they were inhuman, that the comrades had no heart and would never be able to compensate for the sorrow and heartbreak that they had caused." Ulrich Woronowicz, *Tagebuch 1958 bis 1960: Als Dorfpfarrer in Brandenburg* (Halle, 2011), 116.

14. According to internal information at the Ministry for State Security (MfS), it was not until 10 and 11 August—after the conversation between Ulbricht and Khrushchev—that six people were arrested in connection with the Hennigsdorf case. See BStU, MfS, ZAIG no. 454. The district court of Potsdam sentenced five of the arrested men on 25 January 1961 to long prison sentences: Herbert Siegmund for nine years and six months; Heinz Dehler for seven years; Heinz Schilling for six years; Günter Baasch for five years and six months; and Dietrich Wendt for five years. All were charged with "serious acts of agitation against the state." See BStU, MfS, AU 16144/62, vol. 9, "Gerichtsakte."

15. The Eastern office of the SPD tried to maintain contact with former party members in the GDR, systematically collected information on the situation in the GDR, and, in the eyes of SED leadership, was an extremely dangerous organization.

16. "Gespräch Chruschtschows mit dem Ersten Sekretär der SED, Walter Ulbricht, am 1. August 1961," in Wettig, *Chruschtschows Westpolitik*, 300–301.

17. On 3 June 1961, the MfS also informed Ulbricht of the following: "There has been no significant political influence in this division from either the party organization or the union, even though it was known that not a single SED member worked in the entire division and that this division was already the source of provocations in LEW on 17.6.1953." See BStU, MfS, ZAIG no. 454.

18. "Information über die Ursache der wirtschaftlichen Schwierigkeiten der DDR," 4 August 1961, SAPMO-BArch, DY 30/3709.

19. Ibid.

20. Ibid.

21. Ibid.

22. Bernd Bonwetsch and Alexei Filitow, "Chruschtschow und der Mauerbau: Die Gipfelkonferenz der Warschauer-Pakt-Staaten vom 3.–5. August 1961," *Vierteljahreshefte für Zeitgeschichte* 48, no. 1 (2000): 158.

23. Uhl, *Krieg um Berlin?*, 135.

24. "Erklärung der Regierungen der Warschauer Vertragsstaaten," draft, n.d., SAPMO-BArch, DY 30/3386. The document is classified as "top secret."

25. Walter Ulbricht, "Rede auf dem Treffen der Ersten Sekretäre der ZKs der kommunistischen und Arbeiterparteien der sozialistischen Staaten," Moscow, 3 August 1961, SAPMO-BArch, DY 30/3478.

26. "Erklärung der Regierungen der Warschauer Vertragsstaaten," draft, n.d., SAPMO-BArch, DY 30/3386.

27. Walter Ulbricht, "Rede auf dem Treffen der Ersten Sekretäre der ZKs der kommunistischen und Arbeiterparteien der sozialistischen Staaten," Moscow, 3 August 1961, SAPMO-BArch, DY 30/3478.

28. Bonwetsch and Filitow, "Chruschtschow," 166.

29. See Steininger, *Berlinkrise*, 258.

30. "Erklärung der Regierungen der Warschauer Vertragsstaaten," draft, n.d., SAPMO-BArch, DY 30/3386.

31. Ibid.

32. Walter Ulbricht, "Rede auf dem Treffen der Ersten Sekretäre der ZKs der kommunistischen und Arbeiterparteien der sozialistischen Staaten," Moscow, 3 August 1961, SAPMO-BArch, DY 30/3478.

33. "Die Rede des Gen. N. S. Chruschtschow," in Bonwetsch and Filitow, "Chruschtschow," 191.

34. Ibid., 189.

35. Ibid., 192.

36. "Erklärung der Regierungen der Warschauer Vertragsstaaten," in Rühle and Holzweißig, *13. August 1961*, 94.

37. "Protokoll Nr. 39/61 der außerordentlichen Sitzung des Politbüros des ZK der SED, 7.8.1961," quoted in Uhl and Wagner, *Ulbricht*, 97.

38. These were paramilitary units organized in the enterprises of the GDR. The "combat groups" were established after the popular uprising on 17 June 1953 and were led as divisions in the Ministry of the Interior.

39. Uhl, *Krieg um Berlin?*, 126–27. Uhl emphasizes that this plan is still not accessible for historical research.

40. See "Secrecy and Conspiratorial Communication" in chapter 15 of this volume.

41. Uhl, *Krieg um Berlin?*, 128–29.

42. Uhl and Wagner, *Ulbricht*, 28.

43. Uhl, *Krieg um Berlin?*, 90. See also Gerhard Sälter, "Zur Restrukturierung von Polizeieinheiten der DDR im Kontext des Mauerbaus," *Archiv für Polizeigeschichte* 13 (2002): 66–73.

44. Bernd Eisenfeld and Roger Engelmann, *13.8.1961: Mauerbau. Fluchtbewegung und Machtsicherung* (Bremen, 2001), 29–30.

45. "Übersicht der Abteilung Sicherheitsfragen des ZK der SED über die Pioniermaßnahmen am westlichen Außenring von Berlin," 24 July 1961, SAPMO-BArch, DY 30/3682.

46. Uhl, *Krieg um Berlin?*, 127.

47. See "Notiz über die Absprache zwischen dem Chef des Stabes der GSSD und dem Chef des Hauptstabes der NVA," in Uhl and Wagner, *Ulbricht*, 89–90.

48. Ibid., 123.

49. Khrushchev made a declaration to this effect on 27 July 1961 to John McCloy. Khrushchev had just received a report on the content of Kennedy's radio and television Report to the Nation of 25 July, in which the president announced a strengthening of American forces as a demonstration of his unwavering defense of West Berlin.

50. "Gespräch Chruschtschows mit dem Ersten Sekretär der SED, Walter Ulbricht, am 1. August 1961," quoted from Wettig, *Chruschtschows Westpolitik*, 297.

51. Wagner, "Stacheldrahtsicherheit," 127.

52. Willi Seifert (1915–86) became a member of the KPD in 1930. He was imprisoned from 1934 to 1945, including in the Buchenwald concentration camp from 1938 to 1945. He held a leadership position in the Volkspolizei from 1948 to 1956 and served from 1957 to 1983 as deputy minister of the interior. As such, he was also responsible for the Combat Groups of the Working Class.

53. Wagner, "Stacheldrahtsicherheit," 127.

54. Valentin Falin, *Politische Erinnerungen*, trans. Heddy Pross-Weerth (Munich, 1993), 346.

55. Wilke and Vatlin, "Arbeiten Sie einen Plan," 94–95.

56. Quoted in Wettig, *Chruschtschows Berlin-Krise*, 185.

57. Daniela Münkel, "Der Mauerbau im Blick der Stasi," *Frankfurter Rundschau*, 13 August 2010, 21. The HVA was the foreign intelligence service of the GDR.

58. Gerhard Sälter, "Der Bau der Berliner Mauer 1961 und seine Auswirkung auf die Gesellschaft der DDR" (manuscript, Berlin, 2003), 38.

59. "Anlage 5 zum Protokoll Nr. 38 des Politbüros vom 28.7.1961," quoted in Sälter, "Der Bau der Berliner Mauer," 39.

60. Werner Eberlein (1919–2002) was the son of Hugo Eberlein, a cofounder of the KPD who was murdered in the Soviet Union in 1937. Werner Eberlein grew up in the Soviet Union and became Ulbricht's interpreter in 1961. From 1986 to 1989 he was a member of the politburo of the Central Committee of the SED.

61. "Wortlaut eines Gesprächs von Wilfriede Otto mit Werner Eberlein am 5. September 1996 über die Beratung der Ersten Sekretäre des ZK der kommunistischen und Arbeiterparteien der Staaten des Warschauer Vertrages vom 3. bis 5. August 1961 in Moskau," in Otto, "13. August 1961," 88.

62. "Beschluss des Ministerrates der Deutschen Demokratischen Republik, 12.8.1961," in Rühle and Holzweißig, *13. August 1961*, 95.

63. "Gespräch Chruschtschows mit dem Ersten Sekretär des ZK der SED, Walter Ulbricht, am 2. November 1961," in Wettig, *Chruschtschows Westpolitik*, 483–84.

64. Wagner, "Stacheldrahtsicherheit," 129.

65. Torsten Diedrich, "Die militärische Grenzsicherung an der innerdeutschen Demarkationslinie und der Mauerbau 1961," in *Vom Kalten Krieg zur deutschen Einheit: Analysen und Zeitzeugenberichte zur deutschen Militärgeschichte 1945 bis 1995*, ed. Bruno Thoß (Munich, 1995), 138.

66. Sälter, "Der Bau der Berliner Mauer," 50.

67. Uhl, *Krieg um Berlin?*, 139.

68. Uhl and Wagner, *Ulbricht*, 48.

69. Hans Modrow, *Ich wollte ein neues Deutschland* (Berlin, 1998), 85–86.

70. "Bekanntmachung des Ministeriums für Verkehrswesen der DDR über Veränderungen im Nah- und Fernverkehr," 12 August 1961, in Rühle and Holzweißig, *13. August 1961*, 96–97.

71. Eisenfeld and Engelmann, *13.8.1961*, 77.

72. Lemke, *Berlinkrise*, 170.

73. "Bekanntmachung des Ministeriums des Innern der DDR über den Zugang nach Ost-Berlin," 12 August 1961, in Rühle and Holzweißig, *13. August 1961*, 96.

74. "Bekanntmachung des Magistrats von Groß-Berlin," 12 August 1961, in Rühle and Holzweißig, *13. August 1961*, 98.

75. Kunze, *Grenzerfahrungen*, 41.

76. Ibid.

77. Ibid., 42.

78. On the Berlin permit agreements, see ibid., 79–229.

79. On these orders and the propaganda used in 1961, see Sälter, *Grenzpolizisten*, 162–76.

80. "Aus der Rede des Regierenden Bürgermeisters von Berlin, Brandt, auf einer Kundgebung in Berlin," 16 August 1961, in Rühle and Holzweißig, *13. August 1961*, 106.

81. Lemke, *Berlinkrise*, 170; see also Sälter, *Grenzpolizisten*, 172–75.

82. *Neues Deutschland*, 23 August 1961, quoted in Grafe, *Die Grenze*, 102.

83. On Litfin, see Stiftung Berliner Mauer and Zentrum für Zeithistorische Forschung, ed., *Die Todesopfer an der Berliner Mauer 1961–1989: Ein biographisches Handbuch* (Berlin, 2009), 37–39.

84. Kwizinskij, *Vor dem Sturm*, 187.

85. Uhl, *Krieg um Berlin?*, 139.

86. "Übersetzung des Schreibens des Oberkommandierenden der Gruppe der sowjetischen Truppen in Deutschland, Marschall Konew, vom 14. Sept. 1961 an den Minister für Nationale Verteidigung der DDR, Armeegeneral Hoffmann," in Otto, "13. August 1961," 92.

87. Sälter, *Grenzpolizisten*, 57–58.

88. Uhl, *Krieg um Berlin?*, 139.

89. Sälter, *Grenzpolizisten*, 53–60.

90. Jürgen Ritter and Peter Joachim Lapp, *Die Grenze: Ein deutsches Bauwerk* (Berlin, 2007), 28–30.

91. Walter Ulbricht to Nikita S. Khrushchev, 16 September 1961, SAPMO-BArch, DY 30/3509.

92. "Protokoll über die Lagebesprechung des zentralen Stabes am 20.9.1961, von 08:30 Uhr bis 09:30 Uhr," in Werner Filmer and Heribert Schwan, *Opfer der Mauer: Die geheimen Protokolle des Todes* (Munich, 1991), 374.

93. Ibid., 375–77.

94. Ibid., 379.

95. From the service log of the provisional chargé d'affaires of the USSR in the GDR, A. I. Gorchakov, 4 July 1962, No. 0427/DDR, RGANI, F. 5 (r. 9017), op. 49, d. 480, 101–3.

96. See Sälter, "Der Bau der Berliner Mauer," 67; Gerhard Sälter, "Mauer, Grenzgebiet und Hinterlandsicherung in Ost-Berlin in den achtziger Jahren," in *Weltende: Die Ostseite der Berliner Mauer. Mit heimlichen Fotos von Detlef Matthes*, ed. Gerhard Sälter, Tina Schaller, and Anna Kaminsky (Berlin, 2011).

Part III

THE END OF THE
SECOND BERLIN CRISIS

Chapter 17

NEGOTIATIONS, BUT NO WAR!

13 August and the Berlin Crisis: Berlin–Bonn–Washington

In August 1961, Khrushchev let the Germans feel Soviet power. In shock over the division of Berlin, many Germans wondered whether the Wall signaled their country's permanent division and whether all hopes for reunification were now no more than an illusion. Media and politics reacted immediately to these sentiments and to the diffuse uncertainty of the German population. The unbelievable act of dividing a European metropolis with barbed wire became an international media sensation, and television cameras captured the event in real time.

Interestingly, in their declarations after 13 August, none of Germany's leading politicians indicated that they would abandon the goal of national unity. The opposing systems in Germany endured; the Soviet Union had demonstrated that it would stay true to its GDR. But the ongoing emigration movement out of East Germany evidenced the reality that the German question remained open, even if no one knew when or how it would finally be resolved:

> The border closure and the commencement of the Wall's construction in Berlin during the night before 13 August hit the Federal Government and the Berlin Senate without any advance intelligence warning. Adenauer was vaguely aware of future operations but did not know the exact timing or nature of the measures. Brandt only learned of them the following day through the Federal Intelligence Service. No direct contact took place that Sunday between the federal chancellor and the governing mayor. Von Brentano simply told Brandt by phone that evening that it would be important to "cooperate closely."[1]

On 13 August, Federal Chancellor Adenauer pinpointed the real cause behind the Wall's construction: "This measure has been taken because the regime, forced upon the Central German people by an external power, was unable to adequately address the internal problems of its own territory." However, the SED's demonstration of power had no bearing on the Federal Republic's constitutional mission to achieve German unity through peaceful means. "Now more than ever, we feel intimately connected to the Germans in the Soviet zone and in East Berlin; they are and will remain our German brothers and sisters. The Federal Government is unwavering in its commitment to the goal of German unity in freedom. Considering the significance of this act, I have asked the foreign minister to brief all foreign governments through the German embassies." This declaration was a promise, especially to the people of the GDR. Adenauer stated clearly that the German question could not be resolved through the unilateral use of force, and the West German government continued to insist upon the right of the German people to self-determination. In the same statement, however, Adenauer declared: "It is the order of the day to confront this challenge by the East with steadfastness but also with calm, and not to undertake anything that will worsen the situation without improving it."[2]

Now entirely enclosed, West Berlin became a hotbed of protest against the barbed wire barricade. West Berliners were particularly troubled by the way in which the Western powers accepted the closed border, which unleashed a second shock wave throughout the city. Fears for the future and a crisis of trust in the United States' guarantees toward the alliance became pervasive. Was it time to rent moving vans and abandon the abandoned city? The *Bild* newspaper summarized the uneasy mood in its front-page headline: "The East acts—What does the West do? The West does NOTHING!" Below the headline, the paper bluntly declared: "US President Kennedy remains silent . . . Macmillian goes hunting . . . and Adenauer scolds Brandt."[3]

Willy Brandt gave voice to the political climate in a powerful, frank speech before the German Bundestag. In it he described the way in which the Western powers were being squeezed out of their responsibilities to Berlin as a whole and the consequences this would have for their responsibilities to the rest of Germany. His words addressed the chasm that had emerged in German politics: "Even a worm curls up if you step on it. For the forces of the Western Allies, last Sunday means that they have been pushed out of the four-power agreements that apply to Berlin as a whole. The declaration by the nations of the Warsaw Pact and the subsequent announcements by the Eastern zone government also mean, in effect, that they wish to challenge the joint responsibility of the Western powers for Germany as a whole, even before the separate peace treaty of which there is so much talk." Brandt was pleased, but not without bitter irony, that the Western powers lodged "serious" protests in Moscow on 17 August and demanded a retraction of the measures. These protests reflected the position of the Berlin Senate and the people of the city, he said. Responsibility for the increasing tension of the international situation rested solely with the government of the Soviet Union, "which refuses to stop supporting the brutal and incompetent Ulbricht regime." Brandt not only offered his analysis of the current constellation, but, like Adenauer, also insisted on maintaining unity among the German people: "Our compatriots will not be sacrificed. We are one people—Berliners have shown that again in their own special way, in the face of the threats of recent days—a people with self-respect. Justice and morality allow us no other option."[4]

West Berlin remained an erratic element disrupting the German two-state system. In a sense, the scenario of 1948 simply repeated itself. Willy Brandt took the place of Ernst Reuter; like Reuter, he became the political spokesperson of West Berlin. It was in front of Berlin's City Hall in Schöneberg, not in front of the Reichstag, that two hundred and fifty thousand Berliners gathered on 16 August 1961. With his speech to the crowd, Brandt transformed the powerless outrage of West Berliners over the forced division of their city into resolute self-assertion. He reminded the people that "our neighbors in the [Eastern] sector and the [Soviet] zone" had the heaviest burden, and no one could relieve them of it right away. "And that is the most bitter part! We can only join them in shouldering [the burden] by showing them that we have risen to the occasion! They are wondering now whether we will write them off. To this we answer: No, never! They ask us whether we will betray them, and to this the only answer is: No, never!"[5] Brandt also took a stance against the passive acceptance of the closed border and demanded that the Federal Government aggressively advocate for the interests of West Berlin on the international stage. The Federal Government, he declared, should not sign a single nonmilitary agreement that did not "secure the interests of free Berlin." As an expression of solidarity with the people of the GDR, he requested that artists and athletes from West Germany and West Berlin refrain from partaking in events sponsored by the "Zonal regime," and he proposed a boycott of the Leipzig Trade Fair. He demanded that the public ostracize the SED state.[6]

Adenauer was not present for Brandt's speech in front of City Hall on 16 August. When confronted later with critical questions regarding his reaction on 13 August, "he frequently pardoned himself with the excuse that he did not want to inflame the atmosphere. He claimed to have been told that his appearance at the border would unleash an uprising, and he could not be held responsible for that."[7] Adenauer's plan to fly to Berlin with American Vice-President Lyndon B. Johnson on 19 August met with Johnson's rejection. "It was not until 22 August that the chancellor visited the German capital. His reception in Berlin was cool but not hostile."[8]

In terms of West Berlin's future, a lot depended on Kennedy's reaction. He was briefed on the situation in Berlin on 14 August, and his response was supposedly calm: "This is the end of the Berlin crisis. The other side panicked—not we. We're going to do nothing now because there is no alternative except war. It's all over, they're not going to overrun Berlin."[9] For Brandt, however, nothing was over; a new development had begun. On the day of his speech before City Hall, he drafted a letter to Kennedy laying out his view on the situation in Berlin and the obligations of the Western powers: "This development has not changed the will to resist among the West Berlin population, but has sufficed to raise doubts as to the determination of the three powers and their ability to react. In this regard, the decisive factor is that the West has always specifically invoked the existing four-power status." Brandt knew very well that these guarantees of freedom for the Berliners had always applied to the Western sectors only. But the political-psychological danger in Berlin was twofold:

1. Inactivity and a merely defensive posture can bring about a crisis of confidence in the Western powers.
2. Inactivity and a merely defensive posture can lead to exaggerated self-confidence on the part of the East German regime, whose newspapers are already boasting today about the success of its demonstration of military power.[10]

Kennedy, though, saw the border closure as "proof of how 'empty' talk of a 'Free City' had been and how despicable the GDR regime, which the Soviet Union was now trying to make 'respectable,' really was."[11] Brandt disagreed with this inter-pretation as well: "The Soviet Union has achieved half of its free city proposal by deploying the German People's Army. The second act is a question of time. After the second act, a Berlin would exist quite like a ghetto that has not only lost its function as a refuge of freedom and a symbol of hope for reunification, but has also been severed from the free part of Germany. Instead of a refugee movement to Berlin, we might experience the beginning of an exodus from Berlin."[12] With the abolition of the four-power status in Greater Berlin, Brandt requested a three-power status in West Berlin, a reaffirmation of the Western powers' guarantee to remain present in the city until German reunification, and a declaration that the Western powers considered the German question in no way resolved. Brandt also took a position on negotiations that sharply contrasted Kennedy's stance: "I expect from such steps no significant material change in the present situation and recall—not without bitterness—declarations rejecting negotiations with the USSR on the principle that one should not negotiate under pressure. We now have a state of accomplished extortion, and I already hear that it will not be possible to turn down negotiations. In such a situation, when the possibility of taking initiative to act is already so small, it is all the more important to demonstrate at least political initia-tive." An initiative of this kind would have meant a "demonstrative strengthening" of the American garrison in Berlin. In closing, Brandt wrote: "I consider the situ-ation serious enough, Honorable Mr. President, to write to you in all frankness as is possible only between friends who trust each other completely."[13]

For Willy Brandt, it was less the 13 August border closure itself than the reac-tion of the Western powers that marked a turning point in his political thinking. As he wrote later, he abandoned all illusions and gained a greater sense of reality: "Ulbricht was allowed to give the West's supremacy a hard kick in the shin—and the United States only grimaced, annoyed. My political thought over the following years was heavily influenced by my experiences that day. What people later called my Ostpolitik took shape before this backdrop."[14]

While leaders in Washington believed in the days after 13 August that "the crisis, which in Washington's view did not constitute a crisis at all, could be kept under control with tired gestures of protest, alarms were sounding for Americans . . . [stationed] in Berlin and Bonn. This was evident in the telegrams they sent to

Washington on 16 and 17 August."[15] American journalists in Berlin also provided accurate accounts to shape public opinion on the situation in Berlin; among them was Robert H. Lochner, director of Radio in the American Sector (RIAS), who had been appointed by the U.S. State Department.[16]

By 17 August Kennedy had received Brandt's letter, which "elicited irritation in Washington at the time." Kennedy himself was "extraordinarily angry. He refused to tolerate advice of this nature, and his answer reflected it—at the same time showing Brandt the limits of German politics and American engagement. No word on reunification; this was only about West Berlin."[17] The president wrote: "The link of West Berlin to the Free World is not a matter of rhetoric. Important as the ties to the East have been, painful as is their violation, the life of the city, as I understand it, runs primarily to the West—its economic life, its moral basis, and its military security."[18]

Nevertheless, the protests from West Berlin seemed to have an effect on Washington, and the United States moved forward with measures that many in Berlin had hoped for: "Everything coincided to bring about a gradual change in American policy—if only in terms of climate. Kennedy decided to strengthen the US garrison in Berlin by one more brigade group (1,500 to 1,800 men) . . . and send Vice President Lyndon B. Johnson along with the 'hero' of the 1948–49 Berlin Airlift, General Lucius D. Clay, as his personal representatives on a short visit to Berlin. At the same time, the United States wanted to accelerate progress in its military armament—without making it public. The construction of the Wall, the president criticized, should have been anticipated sooner."[19] As early as 14 August, however, Kennedy was already thinking about ways in which to use Berlin's border closure for propaganda purposes. Johnson's trip gave him the media opportunity to disseminate the basic pattern of this propaganda through a gesture of solidarity. Johnson stressed that the Americans vouched for the city's viability. The "barrier of barbed wire" had "broken . . . vital human and communal ties." Regarding those in power in the East, Johnson declared: "What a victory they claim! What a failure they prove! I tell you, the Communists congratulate themselves much too soon." The cause of Berlin's division, as Johnson saw it, was the Soviet defeat in the competition of systems in Germany after 1945. While Germans in the Federal Republic had "built a vital democratic life," in East Germany "there has been a terrible and tragic failure." "They" were trying now

> to interpose barbed wire, bayonets, and tanks against the forces of history. In the short run, the barbed wire is there, and it will not go away by a wave of the hand. But in the long run, this unwise effort will fail. Lift your eyes from these barriers and ask yourselves: Who can really believe that history will deny Germany and Berlin their national unity? Who can really believe that the German people will choose Communism after what they have seen on their own German soil? But we must understand that this is just a beginning. This is a time for confidence, and for poise, and for faith—faith in ourselves. It is also a time for faith in your allies everywhere in the world. This island does not stand alone. You are a vital part of the whole community of free men.[20]

In other words, the division of the city would endure—even the United States could not change it with a "wave of the hand"—but the "island" itself would still belong to the Western community. What remained was the certainty of Communist defeat, which the Communists trumpeted as victory, and faith in history and its laws to end the unnatural division of Germany and Berlin. The message for Germans to trust in themselves and their allies also provided an indirect answer to Brandt's warning of a crisis of trust.

The Soviet side feared precisely this type of propaganda, with its duality of freedom and force; after all, it worked. "In terms of propaganda, the Wall, which Ulbricht dubbed the 'Antifascist Protection Rampart,' gave the West a permanent trump card against the GDR and the Soviet Union. This trump was played consistently over the following years. Ultimately, history proved that the Socialist experiment on German soil could only be maintained within closed borders."[21]

Henry Kissinger analyzed the consequences of 13 August for German politicians with respect to reunification. Internationally, barbed wire and the Wall were a clear negation of German hopes for reunification. Nevertheless, these hopes would continue to exist and exert pressure on politics in the Federal Republic. Kissinger conceived of politics over longer periods of time, and he knew in particular how important public opinion was for the self-image of a society. Thus, despite the dismal scenes in Berlin, he encouraged the American administration to continue advocating for German reunification. To him, this position was not simply "political daydreaming" but rather an "absolute necessity in order to do justice to the aspirations of the German people." Kissinger was especially concerned with American Germany policy, which aimed above all to keep the Federal Republic in the Western alliance and prevent another Rapallo. Among the Western governments, fear of a new neutralist equilibrium between the Federal Republic and the Soviet Union remained virulent, but Kissinger wanted to rule this out permanently: "The best strategy to accomplish this was to continue blaming the USSR for the enduring division."[22]

In fact, the Federal Republic did not even consider formulating a Berlin policy without the approval of the Western alliance. In the Bundestag debates on the division of Berlin, Adenauer adhered to his administration's declaration of 13 August, emphasizing the necessity of retaining "very close ties" to the FRG's three Western allies. "Together with them," he stated, the Federal Government would "prepare and implement the required measures." At the same time, he expressed the conviction that negotiations were still possible "in order to find a way out of the situation in which the world now finds itself."[23]

Coordination between the policies of the Federal Republic and the Berlin Senate became more difficult with the Bundestag elections. Adenauer and Brandt were rivals, and the heated phase of the election campaign had just begun. During this time, the campaigns took priority and influenced political decisions. Adenauer wanted to follow "the laws of polarization": "Adenauer had done splendidly in the past with this recipe for success. On top of that, he was resolved to carry on according to the maxim, 'business as usual.' This led to his decision to go through with major campaign events on the evening of 14 August in Regensburg, on 16 August in Bonn, and on 18 August in Essen."[24] A campaign of maximum polarization through massive attacks on Brandt would hardly have been possible had Adenauer stood by the governing mayor on 16 August on the balcony of West Berlin's City Hall, showing solidarity with the Social Democrats. The dynamic that emerged was exactly as Ulbricht had predicted, validating his (fruitless) suggestion to Khrushchev that they should take advantage of the elections to sway the discussion of a peace treaty. Now it was the closure of Berlin's sector border that coincided with the peak of the election campaigns.

On 1 August, Khrushchev and Ulbricht had discussed the possible outcomes of the Bundestag elections and their implications for the Federal Republic's willingness to negotiate. Khrushchev assured Ulbricht that the Soviet Union backed only him in Germany; Adenauer and Brandt were "two scoundrels." Adenauer would win the elections, and after that the Federal Republic would negotiate:

> *Khrushchev:* Brandt is worse than Adenauer. Here we only support you.
>
> *Ulbricht:* No one knows what to expect of Brandt since he has nothing to lose.
>
> *Khrushchev:* I think Adenauer will behave differently after the elections. I know from secret documents that the Western powers are getting ready to present their proposals after the elections in the FRG. If they present us with hard conditions, it would be advantageous for them to lay them on the table before the elections in order to help the chancellor. But then they would only block their own path to negotiations with us. They want to present their proposals after the elections to retain the possibility of softening them. Kroll has indicated as much to me. He said that these elections are pure rhetoric. He is an intelligent man.[25]

Ulbricht held a radio address on 18 August in which he described the closed border as a savior of European peace against the impending aggression of the Federal Republic toward the GDR. In addition, he described the moment of future German reunification. He began the address with an obligatory shift of blame to the West, which he held responsible for the division:

> Now, those who did not believe it before will understand more readily that it is useless—ever since West Germany joined NATO through the Paris Treaties—to hope that German unity under NATO's command can be achieved through whatever secret means the Western powers might possess.
>
> By now it should be clear to everyone that the division of the German nation can only be overcome through a tremendous struggle by the people to banish militarism and imperialism. At the head of this people's struggle are the laborers and other working persons of the GDR and their state. They are more confident of their power today than they were yesterday. They have wreaked defeat upon militarism and know that one billion people in the Socialist camp are behind them. No one should think, however, that the strict security of our borders means that we have written off the workers and the peace-loving people in West Germany. No, no one has been written off.[26]

With this speech, Ulbricht stated definitively that the day of reunification would only come after the victory of socialism in Germany. Comparing the declarations by various German politicians directly after 13 August on the subject of reunification, it becomes clear that no one had given up faith in national unification—even as the permanent division of the country seemed to become an irreversible fact. This also applies to Ulbricht, who, as Kvizinski attested after 1989, had a far-reaching vision on the national question:

> Of course Ulbricht did not want reunification, since it was obvious to him that the GDR would be trampled by the Federal Republic. But since he knew how charged this national question was in Germany, he was constantly working on all kinds of plans for reunification. . . . He did not want to give up control of the problem itself or the position of political initiative on the German question, and he believed it was necessary to have a well thought-out plan—down to the last detail—for how to proceed in case the situation sharpened. If we and the SED had had this type of plan in 1989, who knows how things might have developed and whether it could have been possible for the GDR to join a confederation with the Federal Republic in one form or another. But in 1989, the GDR did not have any thought-out policy whatsoever in terms of the national issue—aside from the stubborn position that reunification was off the agenda.[27]

Khrushchev and the German Question after the Construction of the Wall

The border closure in Berlin resonated internationally as containment of a crisis situation. The difficulties this event signified for the Germans, especially for Berliners and citizens of the GDR, were seen as the unavoidable price of maintaining the status quo in a bipolar world order that divided Germany into two states. Even after the Wall's construction, however, Soviet demands to conclude a peace treaty and resolve the "Westberlin problem" did not subside until 31 December 1961.

In an exploratory meeting with former NATO General Secretary and Belgian Foreign Minister Paul-Henri Spaak, Khrushchev laid out his conditions for negotiations on a peace treaty. He asked for realism with regard to the German question by pointing out that two German states could continue to exist very well. Spaak and Khrushchev both entered the conversation on 19 September 1961 in Moscow looking for signs of how East–West relations would move forward. Khrushchev gave a thorough presentation of the Soviet perspective. He began with an anecdote to highlight the double standards in international public debates on Germany and to illustrate what he saw as the hypocrisy of the Western powers with respect to the German question:

> *Khrushchev:* Pavel Pavlovich, I will give you an anecdote from the first years of Soviet power. If you don't mind, I would like to call you Pavel Pavlovich as I did back when we first met and spoke to each other. You don't mind, do you?[28]

Spaak: No.

Khrushchev: As I will tell you, the anecdote is as follows. There used to be many surveys to test civil servants [of the party and state], and there were many questions of a certain kind. One features writer used this and wrote a satire about it. A man asks a Soviet civil servant: Do you believe in God? He says: At work, no, but at home, yes. This is your approach to the issues concerning Germany. At home he says no, at work, yes. De Gaulle has never acknowledged that there are two Germanys, he has never stated it publicly, but in conversation he does not shy away from the topic. He says openly that it would never be permissible to have one Germany; it is imperative that there are two Germanys.

The English, they are more diplomatic. They do not say such things in conversation; one has to read in their eyes that they will never agree to have just one Germany.

Spaak: You can read my eyes.[29]

Khrushchev: The civil servant says: at home, yes; at work, no. The Western powers do the opposite with Germany: at home, no; at work, yes.

I have spoken to Eisenhower.[30] He also did not say that he was in favor of having two Germanys, but he did not commit very adamantly to the arguments that there should be one Germany. . . .

The perspective on Germany is not realistic here, not thought through. We believe that there are two Germanys. And this is the reality. You, the West, want one single Germany, which you also declare—but without sincerity. We do not speak of one single Germany, but even we go on to say that a single Germany with Ulbricht at the head would be a good thing. It would be better than two Germanys with Ulbricht and Adenauer.

The West says that one Germany with Chancellor Adenauer at the head without Ulbricht would be good. The wish of each side is understandable. But it is also unrealistic. We are clear on this, but the West—I do not know if it realizes this or not. And if it does, then it acts as if it does not. We take reality as our starting point. If the wish endures [despite this], then it is no longer relevant.

In order to arrive at a unified Germany with Ulbricht at the head, there will need to be war. In order to have a Germany with Chancellor Adenauer at the head, there will need to be war. We are against war. We are in favor of the situation that has emerged at present.

Adenauer said privately to our Ambassador Comrade Smirnov: I know that Germany can no longer be reunified. And I am not aiming for that. But I can [only] tell this to you, not to the Germans. If I say it [to them], they throw stones at me. So that is how things really stand right now.[31]

On Khrushchev's portrayal of Adenauer's position in conversation with the Soviet ambassador, Gerhard Wettig remarks:

Discussing the German question on 7 March 1958, the federal chancellor told Ambassador Smirnov that "for questions that cannot be solved on the first attempt," one must make a "second attempt." The "problem of the Germans in the Soviet zone" was "not a question of nationalism, not a question of strengthening Germany's political influence." In his wish to endow the people of the Soviet zone with a right to self-determination, he focused "not on national considerations." Instead, he wanted to end the experiment undertaken there "to copy the Soviet system," which was so inappropriate for the German people. With this in mind, on 19 March he proposed giving the Soviet zone the status of Austria.[32]

Toward the end of his meeting with Spaak, the Soviet premier underscored the "honest" realism of his own position and repeated his offer to conclude a treaty based on the realities of postwar Europe. Khrushchev stressed emphatically that an attempt to force reunification under either Ulbricht or Adenauer would inevitably lead to a war that the Soviet Union did not wish to fight. Khrushchev's strength lay in his reference to the real situation and the obligation of the two involved superpowers to avoid war. "No war over Berlin" was his common denominator with American President Kennedy and the reason why negotiations resumed between the two world powers to find a solution to the Berlin problem. The question of German reunification had been shelved long before.

In his conversation with Spaak, Khrushchev saw only one way out of the confrontation: "the recognition of two Germanys and the conclusion of a peace treaty. This would be most fair because if we were to sign a peace treaty now with the major powers that fought a war against Germany, then we would not only resolve the German question but also clear the air and bring about the necessary conditions for peaceful coexistence. We are in favor of this solution. But there could also be an interim solution based on compromise."[33]

Conflicting Positions among the Western Powers, and Kennedy's Decision to Negotiate

After the Wall's construction, it was not easy for the Western powers, including the Federal Republic, to find agreement on how to proceed with the Berlin Crisis despite the present situation. On the question of whether to negotiate with Khrushchev, conflicts within the Western alliance had persisted up until the Wall was built. In his Vienna Ultimatum, Khrushchev had not necessarily insisted on a "two-plus-four agreement": "If the United States is not prepared to sign a joint peace treaty with the two German States, a peaceful settlement could be achieved on the basis of two treaties. In that case the State[s] that participated in the anti-Hitlerite coalition would sign a peace treaty with two German States or with one German State, at their own discretion. These treaties need not be completely identical in wording but they must contain the same kind of provisions on the most important points of a peaceful settlement." Moscow had wanted to lure Washington with the offer of a new four-power conference at which the cornerstones of a German peace settlement would be set, based on the reserved rights of the four powers from Potsdam. In the next step, this would provide a foundation to conclude peace treaties with the respective German state in each side's sphere of power. At the same time, the Soviet Union could imagine no better solution to normalize the situation in West Berlin than to "transfor[m] it into a demilitarized free city."[34] Willy Brandt had compared this vision of the future to a "ghetto."

Khrushchev's proposal would have cemented Germany's three-part division under international law. On paper this already existed, but in the daily lives of the German people, the strong ties between West Berlin and the Federal Republic outweighed the fact that Berlin was not a federal state. Khrushchev pointed out this reality to Paul-Henri Spaak after the barbed wire had been erected to cut through the city. He emphasized his "categorical objection to the fact that the four major powers are supposed to take responsibility for Germany's reunification. We say that German reunification is a German affair. But this is just a formal declaration."[35]

Just a few days before 13 August, the Western foreign ministers and NATO's Council of Ministers convened to discuss how to move forward with the Soviet Union. The round began on 5 August with a conference of foreign ministers from the three Western powers in Paris, at which the topic of negotiating over the Soviet Ultimatum led to heated disagreement among the three powers—a conflict that would have critical significance for the course of the crisis. American Secretary of State Rusk and British Foreign Minister Douglas-Home advocated taking the initiative to begin negotiations in the fall. French Foreign Minister Maurice Couve de Murville adamantly disagreed, adhering to the position of his president. Couve de Murville believed that the Soviets wanted "only to negotiate on Berlin; but any Berlin agreement would change the status of Berlin and the [Allied] access rights." He did not consider this a tactical question, since the French interpreted the Berlin Crisis as "a power struggle between East and West. Thus, he believed it was essential 'to show no weakness,' no negotiations. If they were to propose negotiations, it would only show that they feared war 'at the bottom of [their] hearts.' This was exactly what Khrushchev had been saying all along, and therefore it was wrong to reinforce this impression."[36] The British and American foreign ministers held fast to their proposed course of action as West German Foreign Minster von Brentano was called in to the meeting. Acknowledging the French veto, Rusk suggested a compromise of "signaling readiness to negotiate through diplomatic channels while also speaking with Gromyko at the UN General Assembly"[37]; Couve de Murville and von Brentano rejected this approach.

French President de Gaulle took the same position as his foreign minister. De Gaulle accepted the value of exploratory talks but categorically rejected negotiations "in which one did not know what to negotiate about. Regarding the Berlin question, he still saw nothing that needed to be negotiated; [the West] should lay down the situation for Khrushchev in plain terms, namely, that the West would refuse to accept any change to their status in Berlin, would not tolerate interference in their legitimate rights, and would react appropriately to any change by force."[38] At the end of the meeting, Rusk told Adenauer that even Great Britain and France now accepted the Federal Republic "as a full-fledged partner in discussing plans for Berlin and Germany." In contrast to de Gaulle,

Adenauer was not fundamentally opposed to negotiating with the Soviet Union, especially considering that a war over Berlin would use West Germany as its battlefield. The outcome of the conference left the Western powers at odds with each other before 13 August regarding the question of negotiations with the Soviet Union on Berlin. Rusk acknowledged to Adenauer that there was not much room for compromise with Khrushchev—"there is little meat on this bone"—and, as Steininger argues, he was right: "in principle, there really was little to negotiate with Khrushchev, aside from things at the Germans' expense. But he could not say this openly to the Germans at that point. When it became clear in the fall [that Rusk had been right], Adenauer was grateful for de Gaulle's continued opposition to negotiations."[39]

On 14 August, Frank Roberts, British ambassador to Moscow, stressed to the British Foreign Office that it was important to remember "that the Russians have been careful to stop the refugee flow by measures on their side of the Iron Curtain and have done nothing yet to interfere with West Berlin and its communications, nor with Western rights and communications."[40] This was also Washington's assessment that day and was consistent with Kennedy's three essentials. Macmillan implied to his foreign minister, Douglas-Home, what he believed to be most important: "The world should know that there will be negotiations, that the West will make an appropriate proposal, and that the Russians should accept it."[41]

After the border was closed, Kennedy became more resolved than ever to negotiate with Moscow. On 21 August, he confided in Rusk "that going forward, he wanted to take the lead more strongly on the Berlin question." At the same time, he criticized the outcome of the voting procedure within the alliance, which could agree on neither negotiation goals nor a specific time frame. He was convinced that this could not go on for much longer: his administration "should just put together a clear American position right away, very quickly, and make it clear that they would not accept a veto from any of the other Allies."[42] The Vienna Ultimatum still lay fresh on the table and dictated Kennedy's time frame: he wanted to invite the Soviet side to negotiations before 1 September, conduct preparatory discussions by 1 October, and begin official negotiations after that. On 12 September, Kennedy and Rusk reached an agreement on three points:

1. Convene a "peace conference" with the goal of concluding two parallel peace treaties.
2. Ambassador Thompson should begin negotiations with the Soviets with respect to point 1.
3. Adenauer should be informed as soon as possible.[43]

On point 1, Kennedy accepted the Soviet proposal of signing separate peace treaties with each of the German states. The president hoped for a new beginning that focused on finding a solution to the Berlin problem. Regarding the "well-known demands for an immediate reunification of Germany or Berlin on the basis of free elections," there was "nothing to negotiate."[44] Parallel to these preparations for negotiations, military plans for the case of an emergency proceeded.

In early September, the United States and the Soviet Union initiated contact. Thompson asked Gromyko on 7 September whether he would meet with Rusk, his American counterpart, during the upcoming UN General Assembly. Concerning a separate peace treaty with the GDR, the Soviet foreign minister asserted that "its conclusion was 'the only possible solution.' When Thompson disagreed, Gromyko wanted to know if there were other solutions." Khrushchev had already signaled to Kennedy by letter that he was not averse to "establishing a kind of informal contact with Kennedy in order to find a way to end the crisis without detracting from the prestige of the United States—as long as it was based on a peace treaty and a 'Free City' of Westberlin." Kennedy, he wrote, should "articulate his vision of a solution to the crisis if he accepts the principle of a peace treaty and 'Free City.'"[45] Through a press release, Kennedy responded that Rusk would attend the UN General Assembly, and if Gromyko also participated, then they could engage in conversations. "This would be an opportunity to discuss Germany and other issues." One day later, the Soviet foreign ministry announced that Rusk and Gromyko would meet for a "serious exchange of ideas." According to Kennedy's vision, the foreign ministers' discussions would culminate in a "peace conference" at which "two peace treaties—one with the FRG, one with the GDR—would be signed."[46]

Kennedy, however, had made his calculations without taking de Gaulle into consideration. During the conference of the Western foreign ministers in preparation for the Rusk–Gromyko talks, the French foreign minister categorically declared that France would not participate in any peace conference. Couve de Murville stressed that "it was unacceptable to discuss the agenda of a conference with Gromyko that was only taking place because of a Soviet threat." German Foreign Minister von Brentano agreed. Baffled, Douglas-Home countered "that the populations who stood before potential nuclear war and would be turned into nuclear dust would surely insist on holding a conference." The French foreign minister eventually accepted the exploratory talks, "but reiterated once more that a conference with French participation was out of the question for Paris."[47]

The discussions between Rusk and Gromyko were successful in the sense that the Soviet Union retracted its second ultimatum to Kennedy in October and expressed a desire to resume negotiations with the Western powers on Berlin:

> From Britain's perspective, Gromyko's conversations with Rusk, Kennedy, and Macmillan had one advantage: for the first time, the Soviets realized what a dangerous game they were playing in Berlin; Gromyko revealed this in his remark that any potential solution would have to avoid injuring the prestige of the participating powers. This was an entirely new tone. For Ambassador Thompson, a potential solution to the Berlin question emerged on the following basis:

1. Preservation of the Western position in West Berlin;
2. "Very significant concessions concerning the recognition of the GDR."[48]

Notes

1. Küsters, "Reaktionen," 730.
2. "Erklärung von Bundeskanzler Adenauer," 13 August 1961, in Rühle and Holzweißig, *13. August 1961*, 98.
3. "Titelseite der Bildzeitung," 16 August 1961, in Rühle and Holzweißig, *13. August 1961*, 101.
4. "Erklärung des Regierenden Bürgermeisters von Berlin, Willy Brandt, anlässlich der Sondersitzung des Deutschen Bundestages über den Bau der Mauer," 18 August 1961, in *40 Jahre Außenpolitik der Bundesrepublik Deutschland*, 133–34.
5. "Aus der Rede des Regierenden Bürgermeisters von Berlin, Brandt, auf einer Kundgebung in Berlin," 16 August 1961, in Rühle and Holzweißig, *13. August 1961*, 106.
6. Ibid.
7. Schwarz, *Adenauer: Der Staatsmann*, 661.
8. Köhler, *Adenauer*, vol. 2, 554.
9. Quoted in Peter Wyden, *Wall: The Inside Story of Divided Berlin* (New York, 1989), 218.
10. "Schreiben des Regierenden Bürgermeisters von Berlin, Brandt, an Präsident Kennedy," 16 August 1961, in *Dokumente zur Deutschlandpolitik*, ed. Bundesministerium für innerdeutsche Beziehungen, series IV, vol. 7/1, *12. August bis 30. September 1961* (Frankfurt am Main, 1976), 49. For the letter's contemporary English translation, see "Telegram from the Mission at Berlin to the Department of State," Berlin, 16 August 1961, in U.S. Dept. of State, *FRUS 1961–1963*, vol. 14, 345–46.
11. Steininger, *Berlinkrise*, 255.
12. "Schreiben des Regierenden Bürgermeisters von Berlin, Brandt, an Präsident Kennedy," 16 August 1961, in Bundesministerium für innerdeutsche Beziehungen, *Dokumente zur Deutschlandpolitik*, vol. 7/1, 49.
13. Ibid.
14. Willy Brandt, *Begegnungen und Einsichten: Die Jahre 1960–1975* (Hamburg, 1976), 17.
15. Steininger, *Berlinkrise*, 260.
16. See Frederick Taylor, *The Berlin Wall: A World Divided, 1961–1989* (New York, 2007), 167–85.
17. Steininger, *Berlinkrise*, 262.
18. "Letter from President Kennedy to Governing Mayor Brandt," Washington, 18 August 1961, in U.S. Dept. of State, *FRUS 1961–1963*, vol. 14, 352–53.
19. Steininger, *Berlinkrise*, 267.
20. "Rede des amerikanischen Vizepräsidenten Johnson auf einer gemeinsamen Sitzung des Berliner Senats und des Berliner Abgeordnetenhauses," 19 August 1961, in Rühle and Holzweißig, *13. August 1961*, 108–9. For original audio, see Lyndon B. Johnson, "Speech to House of Rep. in Berlin," 19 August 1961, online by George Washington University, National Security Archive, *The Berlin Wall, Fifty Years Ago*, http://www2.gwu.edu/~nsarchiv/NSAEBB/NSAEBB354.
21. Kwizinskij, *Vor dem Sturm*, 188.
22. Biermann, *John F. Kennedy*, 136–37.
23. "Aus der Regierungserklärung, abgegeben von Bundeskanzler Adenauer auf der Sondersitzung des Deutschen Bundestages," 18 August 1961, in Rühle and Holzweißig, *13. August 1961*, 107.

24. Schwarz, *Adenauer: Der Staatsmann*, 662.

25. "Gespräch Chruschtschows mit dem Ersten Sekretär der SED, Walter Ulbricht, am 1 August 1961," in Wettig, *Chruschtschows Westpolitik*, 309.

26. "Ansprache des Vorsitzenden des Staatsrates der DDR Walter Ulbricht im Fernsehen und Rundfunk," 18 August 1961, manuscript, SAPMO-BArch, NY 4182/657.

27. Kwizinskij, *Vor dem Sturm*, 177–78.

28. By addressing Spaak by his first name and his father's name as it is common in Russia, Khrushchev tried to give the conversation a level of personal intimacy.

29. It is unclear whether Spaak meant this ironically or whether he wanted to agree with Khrushchev.

30. Khrushchev is referring to conversations with Eisenhower during his visit to the United States. Their meeting at Camp David on 27 September 1959 was especially significant.

31. "Gespräch Chruschtschows mit dem belgischen Außenminister Paul-Henri Spaak, am 19. September 1961," in Wettig, *Chruschtschows Westpolitik*, 449–51.

32. Wettig, *Chruschtschows Westpolitik*, 451, footnote 863.

33. "Gespräch Chruschtschows mit dem belgischen Außenminister Paul-Henri Spaak, am 19. September 1961," in Wettig, *Chruschtschows Westpolitik*, 451.

34. "Aide-Mémoire From the Soviet Union to the United States on the German Question, Handed by Chairman Khrushchev to President Kennedy at Vienna, June 4, 1961," in U.S. Dept. of State, *Documents on Germany*, 730.

35. "Gespräch Chruschtschows mit dem belgischen Außenminister Paul-Henri Spaak, am 19. September 1961," in Wettig, *Chruschtschows Westpolitik*, 451.

36. Steininger, *Berlinkrise*, 243. For the American protocols of the Paris meetings, see U.S. Dept. of State, *FRUS 1961–1963*, vol. 14, documents 94–102.

37. Steininger, *Berlinkrise*, 245.

38. Ibid., 245–46.

39. Ibid., 248.

40. "Moscow tel 1514 to FO," 16 August 1961, secret, in *Documents on British Policy Overseas*, series 3, vol. 6, *Berlin in the Cold War: 1948–1990*, ed. Foreign & Commonwealth Office (London, 2009), DVD, document 292.

41. Quoted in Steininger, *Berlinkrise*, 267.

42. Steininger, *Berlinkrise*, 267.

43. Ibid., 270.

44. Ibid.

45. Ibid., 273.

46. Ibid., 274.

47. Ibid.

48. Ibid., 279.

Chapter 18

A WALL IN BERLIN BUT NO PEACE TREATY WITH THE GDR

Khrushchev Retracts His Ultimatum

Khrushchev accepted Kennedy's offer to talk. Even before the meetings between Secretary of State Rusk and Foreign Minister Gromyko began in late September, Khrushchev dictated a telegram to Moscow from his vacation. First, the presidium of the CPSU should decide on a "course correction" to be undertaken immediately, and second, Pervukhin should inform Ulbricht of the new negotiations with the United States:

> I would think that the presidium must immediately reach an agreement to undertake these changes so that it can be read to me today, and it would be good to deliver this document, perhaps even now, by courier to Germany, so that Ambassador Pervukhin can go to Comrade Ulbricht and personally communicate with him, requesting on our behalf, on behalf of the Central Committee, that [Ulbricht] agree to comply (in order not to injure his pride). So that Comrade Ulbricht is not presented with a fait accompli, it is important to tell him that we are making concessions on the positions that we have already agreed to with him. (They are concessions at the expense of the GDR, which is why we have to discuss it with Comrade Ulbricht).[1]

No documents have surfaced from the conversation between Ulbricht and Pervukhin. Thus, it is impossible to determine whether the question of a separate peace treaty with the GDR was already off the table at that point or only postponed. Khrushchev's remark at the end of his dictation, that an understanding with the Western powers would occur "at the expense of the GDR," repeated the phrase from his instructions to Gromyko on the details of regulating Berlin's air traffic in a future agreement with the Western powers. In Khrushchev's words:

> If you have the impression that President Kennedy really wants to reach an agreement, but for reasons of prestige, as he has said, so that our countries do not suffer

either morally or in terms of prestige, so that no one has the impression that the prestige of the United States has been damaged, we would negotiate with them keeping this in mind—we would take responsibility for discussing the issue (of course, it would be at the expense of the GDR's prestige), and until a treaty has been signed, we would assume the obligation of negotiating with the GDR so that they would accept the infringement upon their sovereignty with respect to controlling the airways, so that the four states with symbolic troops in Westberlin could exercise a joint [air traffic] control.[2]

Khrushchev's instructions to Gromyko continue:

> Tell him that we will make concessions on the Western powers' air traffic and military transport planes, and we hope that this receives due recognition on the part of the United States. However, after the conclusion of a peace treaty, the occupation rights deriving from the conditions of surrender for Hitler Germany will cease to be valid. But here, too, we wish to reach an understanding with the Western powers that no damage shall be done to the prestige of one side or the other; with the consent of the government of the GDR, we believe it is possible to reach a tentative agreement on these air traffic conditions.[3]

The threat that a settlement between the Soviets and Americans would occur at Ulbricht's expense might explain the SED leader's highhandedness in imposing mandatory document checks for members of the American garrison upon their entry into East Berlin in October 1961.

In his Moscow conversations of 19 September, Belgian Foreign Minister Spaak also addressed the time frame of the Soviet Ultimatum. He posed "a question [to Khrushchev] that might be indiscreet. How much time is left to reach a [peace] treaty?" The Soviet protocol of this conversation does not contain an answer to the question.[4] But in Spaak's report to the NATO Council, he described the situation as follows: "Khrushchev is not in any particular hurry. He is not tied to a specific date, but he does not wish for the problem's resolution to be pushed back indefinitely."[5]

In terms of content as well, the two sides seemed to be drawing closer. After the second conversation between Rusk and Gromyko, Khrushchev dictated to his foreign minister further instructions that included an assessment of the situation: "It is evident after Comrade Gromyko's last conversation with Rusk that the Americans have recognized the following points: First, the U.S. government takes the position that two Germanys exist and this should be taken into account. Second, the U.S. government is not satisfied with the situation in Germany, and the same goes for Berlin vis-à-vis both sides' interests. Third, concerning the measures of 13 August along the sector border of Berlin, Rusk stated that they serve to defend the interests of East Germany and the USSR. This is an important acknowledgment."[6] In the bilateral conversations, the Soviet Union slowly backed down from its maximum demands. By Gromyko's third meeting with Rusk on 30 September, he no longer mentioned the Soviet Ultimatum with its threat to unilaterally sign a peace treaty with the GDR at the end of the year and hand over control of the access routes to West Berlin. Rusk had admitted to Gromyko at their second meeting on 27 September "that the situation in Germany and Berlin was 'not entirely satisfactory' to either side—which Gromyko was pleased to hear."[7] The peace treaty as a final, official way to regulate the German question under international law no longer seemed to dominate Soviet policy on Germany. In his argumentation, Gromyko used the logic of the Vienna Ultimatum but also integrated Kennedy's three essentials:

> Gromyko could imagine an agreement based on the following:
>
> 1. Recognition of the borders (GDR, FRG, Poland);
> 2. "Respect" for the GDR's sovereignty ([but] no diplomatic recognition);
> 3. Non-proliferation of nuclear weapons (no transfer to the FRG);
> 4. "Free City" of Westberlin (with Soviet guarantees concerning entry, etc.)."[8]

Khrushchev concluded from the meetings of the two foreign ministers that the United States was ready for negotiations. In his instructions to Gromyko for a conversation with Kennedy at the White House on 6 October, he wrote: "There is no final deadline for the Soviet Union. If negotiations begin, then it is the obligation of everyone involved to do everything to ensure that they proceed successfully and achieve the best solution. The Soviet Union, at any rate, will act according to this principle. But it must be understood that the negotiations should not be extended artificially, and the resolution of these long overdue questions cannot be pushed back indefinitely."[9] At the White House, Gromyko reiterated the cornerstones of Soviet policy as he had formulated them for Rusk. On behalf of Khrushchev, he conveyed to Kennedy the de facto retraction of the June ultimatum. For the Soviet government, "the date by which to conclude a peace treaty was no longer essential."[10]

Publicly—and probably to Ulbricht's surprise—Khrushchev retracted his Vienna Ultimatum on 17 October during his address at the 22nd Party Congress of the CPSU. He reiterated the retraction once more on 27 October, the day on which tanks from both sides ended their standoff in Berlin. At the Party Congress, the Soviet leader declared that the date itself was only of secondary importance: "We are not superstitious and believe that both 31 and 13 can be lucky numbers. (Movement in the room, applause.) Important is not this or that date but rather finding a purposeful and honest solution to the question. We want the Western powers to recognize the necessity of clearing out the vestiges of the Second World War in order to maintain peace on earth in the interest of all countries, in the interest of all of humanity."[11]

Ulbricht used his opening remarks at the Party Congress to emphasize the importance of the GDR's contribution to the "struggle for peace" in surrounding West Berlin with the construction of its "Antifascist Protection Rampart" (*antifaschistischer Schutzwall*) on 13 August. He evoked this propaganda image of the Wall at just the right moment, and this description of its purpose would endure in the GDR as an obligatory turn of phrase until 1989. He continued by stating that all measures had been taken with the "consent" of the Warsaw Pact nations and especially the government of the USSR. Ulbricht deviated slightly from Khrushchev's line only on the issue of a peace treaty, which he said should be "achieved as soon as possible."[12]

Abandoning the peace treaty's deadline seemed to give the situation breathing room:

> Khrushchev decided to give up his June ultimatum because he believed he would achieve his goal through patient, grinding pressure rather than hasty force.
>
> As he first announced internally in early November, the Eastern side was in a very good position compared to the West after closing the border in Berlin, and they should take advantage of this without having to resort to risky action. He clearly believed that the city of West Berlin would die out. "The capitalists are already running away from there; the workers are running away too. And the time will come when those who remain in West Berlin will turn to us and ask for reunification with the GDR."[13]

Military Exercises for an Unwanted War over Berlin

As long as the Soviet Union did not retract the threat issued in its ultimatum, a military conflict over the access routes to West Berlin was still possible. If it came down to this, Germany would become a battlefield—and the Americans wanted to know what risks the West German government was willing to help shoulder in the case of war:

> In late July 1961, [West German Defense Minister Franz Josef] Strauß and the American security expert Paul Nitze discussed potential military reactions in the case of a blockade. Both agreed that if a blockade occurred, they would test Soviet readiness to go to war by waging a trial attack on the transit Autobahn to West Berlin. On 3 August, Strauß reported to the chancellor [on vacation] in Cadenabbia on the American preparedness for war if the Federal Republic was on board. The defense minister requested the deployment of three divisions that would have to be ready by the end of the year. Considering the Western powers' inferiority in conventional weapons, it would be impossible to avoid confronting the choice of risking a nuclear counterattack or else suffering a diplomatic defeat.[14]

The West German government was forced to position itself on this question—perhaps central to the country's own survival—both within the Western alliance and vis-à-vis the Soviet Union. The federal chancellor and foreign minister were "recognizably at pains to avoid worsening the situation and increasing the agitation of the German public, trying instead with all their strength to reduce [agitation] as much as possible." As evidence of this, Arnulf Baring quotes Heinrich von Brentano's letter accompanying a draft of the administration's declaration on 18 August 1961: "'I have tried to find an objective tone and to direct criticism especially at the Soviet zone; everything that needed to be said to the Soviet Union I formulated into an appeal.' . . . The previous day, on 16 August, the head of the government had already assured the Soviet ambassador in Brentano's presence that West Germany would not undertake any steps that could complicate relations between the Federal Republic and the USSR and worsen the international situation."[15] Hanns Jürgen Küsters reaffirms the importance of this conversation between the Soviet ambassador and Adenauer in terms of how the chancellor assessed the question of war and peace in the Berlin conflict:

> Since the Soviet Union avoided encroachments upon the territory of West Berlin and intended to respect its own sphere of influence in the GDR and East Berlin—Adenauer could gather as much from his conversation with Soviet Ambassador Smirnov on 16 August 1961—neither the Western powers nor the chancellor was ready to risk nuclear war over Berlin. Indeed, on 7 September, Adenauer and [NATO Supreme Allied Commander Lauris] Norstad had come to an agreement that it would be possible to limit the use of military means to conventional weapons in protecting the Western Allies' access routes to Berlin. However, Bonn recognized quickly that none of the three Western powers wanted to initiate military measures, much less fight a war over Berlin.[16]

The Central Committee of the CPSU informed the SED in "strict confidence" of upcoming tests for new types of nuclear weapons. Specifically it was referring to the mega-bombs that Khrushchev had discussed in July with the Soviet physicists. These nuclear tests stood in direct relation to the Soviet leader's negotiations on a peace treaty. Khrushchev intended for them to intimidate the "hotheads in the West" and, "on the issue of a German peace treaty, to increase preparations for war, foment war hysteria, and speak the language of menace. These tests demonstrate clearly the readiness of the USSR and the entire Socialist camp to use weapons to confront any adventure on the side of the aggressive states." The Central Committee of the CPSU assumed that this position was supported by the Central Committee of the SED and "understood correctly by the workers of the GDR."[17] During the 22nd Party Congress and the conflict over Allied access rights in Berlin, the Soviet Union detonated fifty-megaton nuclear bombs on 24 and 30 October. The tests unleashed protests worldwide. However, these demonstrations did not make much of an impression upon the American government; it was doubtful that the Soviet Union already possessed launching capabilities for their bombs. Moreover, Khrushchev was well aware of the consequences arising from nuclear war. Speaking to Belgian Foreign Minister Spaak, he described the theoretical fate of individual countries in order to boost his argument for a peace treaty with both German states as an alternative to the war that nobody wanted: "These days, a mutual threat is also a suicidal threat. I am not saying this only with respect to the West. I am not saying that it will only hurt the West while [we][18] remain unscathed. We will also suffer enormous sacrifices, but we will not be obliterated, we will survive. France and Germany will not survive; America will also survive despite heavy losses. That is the true reality."[19] The United States, in contrast, was certain that it could win a nuclear war, notwithstanding the significant losses in Europe and America. Directly before the Soviet Union's tests, U.S. Deputy Defense Minister Roswell L. Gilpatric asserted on 21 October "that the United States had such a strong advantage in the area of strategic nuclear weapons that it would still be superior even after an initial strike by the Soviet Union."[20]

The militaries of both sides tested out scenarios at this time for the case of nuclear war. In the Soviet Union, the second Berlin Crisis helped "crystallize the strategy of comprehensive nuclear war. Political leadership and especially the Soviet military adhered to a theory of 'inevitable escalation' and assumed that every contained conflict would develop into a contained nuclear war within a short period of time. Through an offensive approach and the massive deployment of nuclear weapons, the war would be decided in favor of the Socialist camp."[21] The supreme command of the Warsaw Pact played out the military scenario in the commando staff's "Burja" (storm) exercise from 28 September to 10 October 1961:

> The training scenario, which envisioned the commencement of combat operations between NATO and the Warsaw Pact in the fall of 1961, was directly tied in to the Berlin Crisis and the situation of the divided city after the Wall's construction. Thus, planning for Burja followed from the real conditions of combat forces from both military blocks stationed on the western theater of war. The field of operations for the maneuver covered the western Soviet Union, Poland, Czechoslovakia, and the GDR. The participating militaries of the Eastern alliance practiced combat operations and advances for the territory of the Federal Republic, Denmark, Belgium, and France.[22]

In the exercise scenario, war broke out after the conclusion of a separate peace treaty with the GDR and the transfer of Soviet status rights for the transit routes to West Berlin. According to the exercise, these routes were then blockaded by the GDR. We are familiar with the starting point of the combat scenario thanks to a lecture by the defense minister of the GDR, Army General Heinz Hoffmann, to evaluate the exercise:

> The Soviet Union signs the peace treaty with the GDR in early October 1961. Starting on 4 October at 24:00, the Western powers' connection to their garrisons in West Berlin is only possible with permission from the GDR. This leads to the closure of control checkpoints and the blockade of the air corridor for planes belonging to the Western powers. In reaction, the Western powers try to reestablish communications to West Berlin using military force. On 5 October at 15:00, forces from a US division advance along the Autobahn from Helmstedt to Berlin; at the same time, transport planes, followed by reinforcement from combat planes, try to break through to West Berlin. After the West realizes that penetration by force will fail because of resistance from the GSFG and the NVA, it unleashes war in Europe on 6 October at 12:00 with a nuclear missile strike.[23]

In the maneuver, the Soviet General Staff's combat goals on the western front were achieved on the fifth day at war. Soviet troops stood at the Rhine and crossed the river with a line of attack toward Paris and the coast of the English Channel. It was an attack led by tactical nuclear weapons; the Soviet Supreme Command calculated the "deployment of more than 2,200 nuclear weapons" in Burja. The preemptive nuclear strike would come from troops of the Warsaw Pact in order to break Western resistance.[24] In the exercise, this strike was a success: "75 percent of nuclear potential stationed in the Federal Republic would be destroyed immediately, along with 90 percent of radar capabilities and airfields. In the area of deployment, 40 percent of the [Western] troop personnel fall victim to the nuclear weapons. The losses in weapons, equipment, and technology could be up to 60 percent. Thus, the combat capacity of the active NATO divisions in the Federal Republic would be reduced to the point that they would no longer be capable of active warfare." NATO would also deploy nuclear weapons and draw a "nuclear weapon barrier" in the "Oder-Neisse region and the Sudeten [mountains]" in order to detain reserves from the Soviet Union. According to the exercise, a war over Berlin would produce an area of 140,000 square kilometers contaminated with nuclear radiation.[25]

Even before the 22nd Party Congress began, Moscow had already evaluated the outcome of Burja and drawn direct consequences for the Kremlin's policy on Berlin: "The deficiencies and serious weaknesses that emerged during Burja, especially concerning cooperation among the participating states of the Warsaw Pact, clearly [precipitated] a revised approach by political and military leadership with regard to concluding a unilateral peace treaty with the GDR. . . . Specifically because Khrushchev could not be sure of the military strength of his own combat forces or that of his alliance partners, as the exercise by the commando staff showed, he retreated in late fall from his original political goals. In any case, signing the peace treaty was out of the question."[26]

Burja ended on 10 October; that same day, a meeting took place at the White House in Washington "to discuss military measures in both the conventional and nuclear realms. Present were: Kennedy, Rusk, McNamara, Lemnitzer, Gilpatric, Kohler, Nitze, Hillenbrand, Taylor, and Bundy." At issue was a paper from the Pentagon titled "U.S. Policy on Military Actions in a Berlin Conflict": "It was a four-step plan with which to react to a Soviet blockade of Berlin. The original version cannot be found, but the plan has been described by Nitze. It was approved by Kennedy on 20 October with minor changes."[27] Like the Soviets, the American military saw the blockade of access routes to Berlin as the catalyst of any conflict. And like the Soviet General Staff, the Pentagon also assumed that a regional Berlin conflict would escalate quickly and turn into a war fought with nuclear weapons. The Soviet military concluded from Burja that it would be best to launch a preemptive nuclear strike in order to disarm the opponent. The American plan tried to determine the individual steps of escalation in order to give political leadership the opportunity to deescalate the situation. Steps one to three on the escalation scale were identical to the starting position in the Warsaw Pact's combat scenario:

Step I: Interference with access to Berlin (short of a definitive blockage).

Reaction: Probe advance on the ground; fighter escort in the air.

Step II: Significant blockage measures.

Reaction: NATO economic embargo, maritime harassment, UN action, rapid military reinforcement.

Step III: Continuation of blockade.

Reaction in Europe: Expansion of non-nuclear operations to gain air superiority; expansion of non-nuclear ground operations on the territory of the GDR with strong air support. This aimed to show the Soviets that a point would soon be reached after which there was no turning back. "The risks rise, as do the military pressures on the Soviets."

Reaction worldwide: Maritime blockade. This was seen as relatively ineffective, but it would serve to delay nuclear conflict. The joint Chiefs of Staff demanded that this be accompanied by other military action in Europe.

Then came the decisive

Step IV: Soviet encroachment upon the Allies' vital interests.

Reaction: Use of nuclear weapons in three stages.

Stage A: Attacks on selected targets in order to demonstrate the will to use nuclear weapons.

Stage B: Limited tactical use of nuclear weapons to achieve tactical advantages.

Stage C: General nuclear war.

Here the comment read: "The Allies only partially control the timing and scale of nuclear weapons use. Such use might be initiated by the Soviets, at any time after the opening of small-scale hostilities. Allied initiation of limited nuclear action may elicit a reply in kind; it may also prompt unrestrained pre-emptive attack."[28]

Kennedy was very interested in being able to assess the risk of escalation after war had already begun:

In the meeting on 10 October, Kennedy wanted to know whether steps IV A and B were possible without IV C. McNamara and Nitze expressed differing views. McNamara believed that the result of IV C was so terrible that one would first have to take steps IV A and B, even if it would lead very quickly to IV C.

Nitze expressed a different opinion. With IV A and B, the Soviets would likely give in to the strong temptation to launch a preemptive nuclear strike. Therefore it would be best—if [the United States] was already willing to use nuclear weapons—to carry out this preventative strategic strike first. It would be possible to win the exchange of nuclear strikes that would result; if [the United States] allowed for a Soviet strike, however, it would probably lose. . . .

McNamara, who had weaker nerves, disagreed. Neither side could be sure that it would win, regardless of who struck first. And the consequences were so horrendous that both sides had significant interest in not allowing things to reach that point in the first place.

Regarding step IV, Rusk commented in general that whichever side employed nuclear weapons first had to be clear about the enormous responsibility tied to such a decision and the consequences it would have for the rest of the world.

A decision on steps III and IV was never reached [during the meeting], and the differences of opinion especially concerning step IV were never resolved. The Pentagon, in cooperation with the State Department, was asked to prepare a new draft for Kennedy, to be sent as "clear instructions" to the Supreme Commander of NATO, General Norstad.

Kennedy sent the draft mostly unchanged—but with his approval—to Norstad on 20 October.[29]

Kennedy informed Adenauer of the American plans in November 1961, and "the interpreter was asked to shred her notes" from the meeting.[30]

The Burja exercise and the Pentagon plans lay bare the serious military backdrop behind all political decisions by both nuclear powers during the Berlin conflict. De-escalation held top priority for both sides, as the end of the tank standoff on Friedrichstraße would demonstrate seventeen days later.

Ulbricht Demands a Peace Treaty

Presenting himself to the people of the GDR, Ulbricht played the role of victor. In a television and radio address discussing the "measures" of 13 August, he was unequivocal in claiming that they were an important step toward a peace treaty. 13 August made the politicians and population of the Federal Republic "aware of the real power relations in Germany and the rest of the world." He continued: "Our measures have shown that we are proceeding seriously and without hesitation in our preparations for the peace treaty. Our measures will without a doubt facilitate the conclusion of a peace treaty and the transition of Westberlin into a demilitarized Free City."[31] This was also Ulbricht's position on 20 September when he held an unofficial conference with the "brother parties" of the Socialist states in East Berlin. In his speech, the SED leader asserted that 13 August had only been the first step, and the second must follow: the peace treaty with the GDR. In his words, "At the present time, the preparation of a German peace treaty has entered its decisive phase. The measures of 13 August were necessary as an important preparatory step toward the peace treaty."[32]

Ulbricht was encouraged in his plans by a report from the GDR's ambassador to Moscow, Rudolf Dölling, on a speech by Khrushchev at his "traditional gathering" with international guests who also vacationed in Crimea. Khrushchev had declared "that the USA and Kennedy wanted to avoid a peace treaty in order to keep their options open. They only talked about the 'reunification of Germany' as a prerequisite to a peace treaty in order to hide their real intentions. He emphasized here that neither de Gaulle nor Kennedy nor Macmillan was truly interested in reunification because they feared a unified Germany." Khrushchev praised the policy of the GDR and attributed its difficulties to the economically motivated "desertion of the republic"; the Polish party leader Gomułka disagreed and posited "that the nationalism fomented by Adenauer was one of the main causes of desertion." As Ambassador Dölling remarked, Khrushchev frequently stressed that "it can be read as a success that Western politicians are forced to speak of 'coexistence,' 'Free City of Westberlin,' 'German peace treaty,' and 'necessity of negotiations.'"[33]

In September, the SED Politburo instructed the Ministry of Foreign Affairs to prepare the content of a separate peace treaty. These plans were based on the documents drafted in Moscow and East Berlin with the first Soviet ultimatum of 1958–59, in particular the Soviet draft of a peace treaty with Germany from January 1959. Otto Winzer, state secretary at the foreign ministry, sent Ulbricht an overview of the problems that still needed to be resolved in connection with a peace treaty. Winzer requested that Ulbricht take a look at "the overview before the meeting," which would take place later that day.[34] The state secretary recommended "placing more emphasis on the GDR's position as a sovereign state, i.e., emphasizing the rights that would be granted to the GDR through the conclusion of a peace treaty."[35]

The treaty's article on West Berlin was of central importance. Winzer underscored the need to decide whether to simply declare the "vestiges of the occupation regime" eliminated with the conclusion of the treaty, "or whether [these] vestiges should be listed individually. The latter does not seem appropriate to me, since it exceeds the framework of the peace treaty. The remnants should be named individually in a protocol to the peace treaty; at issue is the content of an exchange of letters between Dr. Bolz and Zorin on the movement of troops and the air traffic control, the military mission in Potsdam, the Spandau Prison for war criminals, the Billing Office for Postal and Long-Distance Communication, [and] the entry by members of the Western garrisons in West Berlin into democratic Berlin."[36] Winzer also compiled a list of settlements that still needed to be reached with the West Berlin Senate, the Federal Republic, and the Western powers. The list began with a series of agreements concerning the West Berlin Senate, among which the transportation agreements took priority. Ulbricht apparently considered three of these unnecessary and discarded them: an agreement on questions related to the employment of West Berliners in enterprises of the GDR, an agreement on catastrophe relief, and an agreement "on questions arising from the entry and visit to Westberlin by citizens of the GDR or to the GDR by citizens of Westberlin (permission procedures, questions related to insurance and liability)."[37] The implication of discarding these points was clear: the border was there to stay. Ulbricht reiterated this intent with respect to a question that would remain open after the peace treaty's conclusion and had to do with monitoring inter-German tourist travel: "Look into the form of required documents for travel by citizens of the GDR to West Germany and by citizens of West Germany to the GDR (visa requirement?)."[38]

Concerning West Germany, transportation agreements took top priority, including one that would regulate civilian air travel to and from West Berlin via "West German airlines." Agreements were also prepared to regulate "transit traffic through the GDR by troops stationed in Westberlin" from Great Britain, France, and the United States, including the "control system" and the costs of the transfer.[39]

The consultation with Ulbricht on 16 September was published as a communiqué stating "that the chairman of the State Council welcomed several ministers to discuss questions concerning preparations for a peace treaty."[40] At the meeting, Ulbricht appointed specific people to formulate a concept for the GDR's negotiation strategy. Winzer's paper served as the basis for the session. Winzer himself was to assume the key role in preparing for diplomatic negotiations. Minister of Transportation Kramer and Heinz Keßler, deputy minister of national defense, were placed in charge of the agreement on air transportation. Mielke would be partially responsible for the agreement on "legal and administrative cooperation; justice." The agreement on travel from the East to the West and vice versa, which Ulbricht had discarded, was replaced by a demand to "prohibit asylum in Westberlin." Sepp Schwab[41] was charged with this issue.

That same day, Ulbricht sent a report on the situation to the presidium of the CPSU. Key phrases in the documents were the "stability of the situation" and a "change of thought" (*Umdenken*) in the GDR, West Berlin, and the Federal Republic. Closing the border had been a prerequisite to achieving stability in the GDR. In Ulbricht's words, "The experience of the last years has proven that it is not possible for a Socialist country such as the GDR to peacefully compete with an imperialist country such as West Germany while maintaining open borders." It would only be possible to win a contest of this kind "after the Socialist world system has exceeded the capitalist countries in per-capita production." People in the GDR who still hoped for reunification in the Western sense "would now have to thoroughly think through the questions at hand; in other words, [to realize] that the solution to the national question of the German people requires the defeat of German imperialism and the victory of socialism in the GDR." The intelligentsia understood the question relatively quickly and "respected" the measures, so "there were fewer difficulties with them than before."[42]

Ulbricht blatantly expressed his irritation at Brandt's reaction after 13 August: "Brandt the adventurist has exceeded even Mr. Adenauer in terms of chauvinism and anticommunism." Nevertheless, it was clear that both West German politicians "have reached a dead end in their foreign policy." 13 August also smashed the "showcase" of West Berlin. Many residents would leave West Berlin and move to somewhere in the Federal Republic. "There are a lot of villas up for sale in Westberlin right now. The new thing about the situation is that Westberlin has exhausted its role as a showcase of the capitalist West and only partially functions as a center of unrest. Moreover, it has become clear that even with regulations on the use of communication routes through the GDR to Westberlin, that part of the city will not be able to shake its difficulties." Ulbricht drew the premature conclusion that West Berlin could only flourish through "normal relations" with the GDR.[43]

Ulbricht continued that 13 August had led to a "sobering" in the Federal Republic. However, the operation's proximity to the Bundestag elections of 18 September had been too close to influence the election results in favor of the German Peace Union—although "[the party's] solution with a neutral Germany is gradually winning ground." Admittedly, this reflected Ulbricht's dream more than anything else, but the SED leader was clear on one thing: even if the borders to the Federal Republic and West Berlin were closed, "the competition with West Germany [would] continue." This conviction carried over to the SED's next measures, the preparations for a peace treaty: "By the time we meet in the second half of October, we would like to inform you of our position on the 'question of flight connections to Westberlin.' The question of flight connections over the sovereign territory of the GDR already plays a key role in discussions among the Western powers. We have prohibited the use of the erroneous term, 'flight corridors.'"[44] In his response to Ulbricht's letter, Khrushchev confirmed the positive effects of 13 August on the Western powers: "Through [the Wall's construction], our position was strengthened with regard to the question of a German peace treaty and the normalization of the situation in West Berlin on the basis [of that treaty]."[45] He added that among the Western powers, more and more voices spoke out in favor of negotiations on the German question.

Following the session on 16 September, Schwab delivered drafts of several agreements to Ulbricht in early October. The outlines of these documents vividly depict Ulbricht's vision of Germany after a peace treaty. Compared to the Soviet draft of 1959, the most significant changes affected Article 23, calling for a Declaration on the Establishment of the Free City of Westberlin to serve as the "basis of negotiations between the four major powers" when the opportunity arose. The new declaration contained a line lifted from the Austrian State Treaty to prevent the "accession of Westberlin into the EEC," a stipulation directed clearly against the economic and political ties between West Berlin and the Federal Republic. Rules affecting the internal order of the Free City consciously mirrored the treaty between Poland and the Free City of Danzig, for example the provision on West Berlin's ability to borrow on credit. This stated that "bonds and credits of Westberlin, as well as similar benefits from other states or international organizations [required] consent from the government of the GDR." In addition, the foreign ministry drafted a series of transportation rules for the Free City "consisting of three agreements to regulate land, water, and air traffic, as well as the [East German] train stations and waterways in Westberlin."[46]

The agreement on air traffic was a sensitive issue in the transportation regulations. Article 1 of the draft read: "The GDR has full and exclusive sovereignty over the air space within its state territory including the Free City of Westberlin."[47] Out of this claim, Schwab reasoned that within its territory, West Berlin would be permitted "to operate air fields, as long as East German regulatory authorities are established simultaneously at these air fields. This applies to all airplanes that depart from or arrive to Westberlin."[48] Ulbricht requested drafts of the remaining parts of the treaty by 10 October.

These drafts paint a very clear picture: the planned statute for a Free City placed West Berlin's "administration" in the hands of the SED, weakened or destroyed ties between the city and the Federal Republic, and had the unmistakable character of a transitional solution—valid until the city's annexation to the GDR. The plans, however, were in vain; Khrushchev had already decided in favor of negotiations with the Western powers and against signing the separate peace treaty with the GDR for which Ulbricht still held out hope.

The Confrontation of Tanks at Checkpoint Charlie in October 1961

Despite their consensus on the principal necessity of resolving the West Berlin problem, the GDR and the Soviet Union chose different paths after 13 August. By sealing the border, the SED had decidedly not reached its maximum goal, "control of Westberlin." Instead, SED leaders "considered it their duty to dismantle the Allied status of Berlin and the rights of the Western powers gradually and to the GDR's advantage."[49] In contrast, Moscow saw change in the status quo as a long-term goal that could only be reached by negotiating with the Western powers. This required calm in Berlin to avoid disturbing negotiations with the United States. Ulbricht, however, counted on heightening tension to demand control over the access routes to West Berlin and push for the full integration of East Berlin into the GDR, along with international recognition of the state's sovereignty.

During the period between 13 August and around the end of October, when Khrushchev reached his decision, the different interests affecting Berlin policy emerged in full clarity. While the Soviet Union sought a compromise with the Western powers, the SED tried to implement strict controls over foreigners entering the "capital of the GDR." As Ulbricht wrote in a letter to Khrushchev, he found it crucial to "clear the table for future negotiations; in other words: it is necessary to fundamentally establish the sovereignty of the GDR within its capital."[50] Even against the stated will of Moscow leadership, the SED tried to assert this sovereignty vis-à-vis the Western powers. The first step was a restriction stating that after 23 August, foreigners would only be allowed to use the checkpoint on Friedrichstraße; the second step was the control of identification documents from personnel of the Western garrisons in West Berlin.

The 12 August resolution by the Council of Ministers regarding checkpoints at Berlin's sector border had explicitly affirmed the rights of Western military personnel to access the Eastern sector without undergoing document checks because of Berlin's four-power status. A few days later, Winzer informed Ulbricht, Willi Stoph, and Minister of the Interior Karl Maron of a problem that had arisen from closing the border: diplomats' cars could now be used as getaway vehicles for people fleeing East Berlin. Diplomats from the Socialist states accredited in East Berlin employed drivers from the GDR, and now they were requesting "permanent clearance for trips with CD [diplomatic corps] license plates traveling to Westberlin." Winzer wanted to reject this request. "Moreover, the control apparatuses at the border to Westberlin must be instructed to ask for proof that the passengers of any CD vehicle are indeed diplomats. Otherwise the danger exists that vehicles with CD license plates will be abused for other purposes." Winzer suggested extending border controls to all CD vehicles: "It would be preferable to require the same legitimation from diplomats and members of the military missions accredited in Westberlin, as well as from members of the Western occupation powers and diplomats accredited in West Germany who enter the capital of the GDR with CD vehicles. If they can cross the border without undergoing controls, these people will be able to use their vehicles for human trafficking and other enemy measures. But it is an international norm that every diplomat must show his papers when crossing a state border."[51] This suggestion led directly to a confrontation over the access rights of members of the Western armed forces and civilian employees working in the Eastern sector of Berlin. Referring to regular protests by the Western city commandants when their diplomats or employees were subject to controls by the GDR police, Winzer wrote: "In any case, this question needs clear regulation through a directive from the minister of the interior."[52] When Maron announced the decree on 23 October, the conflict escalated to a confrontation of tanks on Friedrichstraße.

Ulbricht replied to Winzer immediately, instructing him to ask the ambassador of the USSR whether the Soviet side "had anything against checking the papers of passengers in CD vehicles at the border—in accordance with normal procedure in any state—since large numbers of people ride in CD vehicles who have nothing whatsoever to do with the diplomatic missions."[53] SED leaders faced one problem in issuing these plans, namely, that the Western states did not recognize the GDR or maintain any diplomatic relations with the SED state. They addressed their grievances directly to the Soviet military leaders. Thus, the SED could not directly negotiate this passport control for Western diplomats with the states affected; instead, the new regulation had to simply be enforced by the border police upon entry into East Berlin.

Writing to Khrushchev in September, Ulbricht stressed that the Western city commandants gave the impression, even after the Wall's construction, "that the four-power status still exists in Berlin. We are of the opinion that we will no longer publish such communiqués concerning complaints from the Western commandants to the chief of the Soviet garrison in Berlin. It would be best if such complaints were no longer received at all. If the Western powers want something, they can convey it directly to the Soviet government."[54] This was Ulbricht's request to the first secretary in Moscow: the Soviet Union should make it clear to the Western powers that it would reinforce the nonexistence of four-power status not only through propaganda but also through political action. Complaints by the city commandants primarily addressed the obstruction or refusal of unrestricted access by the Volkspolizei to personnel from the Western powers traveling to the Eastern sector.

Khrushchev understood the significance of Ulbricht's indirect demand and rejected any change "to the system of controls at the border to Westberlin." Part of this system was the unhindered access of the Western powers to East Berlin and the right of the four city commandants to address conflicts among themselves— without the interference of German authorities. In light of Soviet negotiations with the United States, Khrushchev requested that the GDR avoid any steps "that could make the situation worse, especially in Berlin. In this regard, it seems especially important to refrain from new measures that would change the system instated by the government of the GDR at the border to Westberlin."[55] Ulbricht did not back down following this call for restraint, especially since Khrushchev informed him in the same letter that the Soviet city commandant would now ignore protests by the Western city commandants if the complaints fell under the GDR's scope of authority. The directive from Moscow was therefore ambiguous, as Michael Lemke has argued.[56]

Moscow and East Berlin never entirely clarified the question of whether passport control for Western diplomats and military personnel upon entry into the Eastern sector fell under the authority of the GDR:

> In a conversation with Mikoyan on 7 October, Ulbricht maintained the position that he should decide on Western access to the "capital of the GDR" at his own discretion. The freedom of the Americans to enter East Berlin had a demoralizing effect on the population, prompting people to question the ability of the Socialist power to assert itself. The GDR would no longer accept this violation of its sovereignty by the United States but would refrain from [new] measures for the moment, while negotiations were still in progress between [the United States] and the USSR. In Moscow, [Soviet leaders] were worried. On 19 October, the foreign and defense ministers presented a joint statement to the head of the Kremlin recommending that he urge Ulbricht not to take any new steps without initiating discussions with the Soviet side first. [Khrushchev] should tell him that according to current information, the Americans were planning to provoke as many incidents as possible with the Volkspolizei. Therefore, [the Volkspolizei] must be ordered to practice restraint.[57]

Meanwhile, Interior Minister Maron prepared the provision on document controls for members of the Western military missions traveling as civilians, as well as for their vehicles, per Winzer's request. SED leadership had timed this conflict well. The 22nd Party Congress of the CPSU was convening simultaneously—a meeting that marked a turning point in the course of the Berlin Crisis through Khrushchev's public retraction of his ultimatum.

Against the Soviet request to exercise restraint, the Volkspolizei began checking the documents of Western diplomats and officers in civilian clothes on 15 October. The British elected to show the Volkspolizei their papers "on their own initiative" but did not hand over their documents. "To the Americans and the French, only the Soviets—if anyone at all—had any authority in the matter, not the Volkspolizei."[58] Motions by the Western city commandants protesting the Volkspolizei's encroachments to the Soviet command were rebuffed with the argument that the new regulations were within the GDR's sovereign rights.

The introduction of document controls was not the SED's first demonstration of power after 13 August. The regime reduced Berlin's border checkpoints to just seven locations and confined foreigners to the Friedrichstraße crossing after 23 August—against protests from the Soviet ambassador. Ulbricht explained to Khrushchev that Pervukhin had evoked the four-power status of the city and "raised objections. However, we cannot accept this argument." Ulbricht then elaborated on the SED's other plans simultaneous to sealing the border that would help manifest its claims concretely. "We are taking the tactical approach of gradually increasing our security measures to the point where no serious complications can possibly arise."[59]

Pervukhin's warning, however, was not unfounded. With Clay, Ulbricht had an adversary who could see through his tactic and was unwilling to allow it. Against the backdrop of early conversations with Moscow, the United States carefully observed the infringement of its rights, which raised concerned discussions in Washington. Maxwell Taylor, Kennedy's military advisor, considered Ulbricht's measures "more serious than seem to be generally regarded." He underscored the decisive point in a memorandum for the president: the construction of the Wall was aimed "specifically and publicly at the occupying powers. . . . Its target is the Western Allies who are to be humiliated publicly before all of Germany. It is a measure aimed at further depressing the morale of West Berlin, at destroying the confidence of West Berlin in the Western Powers, and at offsetting the effects of the Johnson–Clay visit."[60] A few days later, Taylor drew the conclusion that "Khrushchev intends using military force, or the threat thereof, to gain his ends in Berlin." Therefore, "the moment has come to shift into higher gear."[61] This entailed strengthening military efforts in tandem with heightened political efforts, meaning negotiations. The SED's measure, which evidently was never an independent factor in American reasoning, made it obvious to the Kennedy administration that the crisis was not yet over.

On 22 October, one day before the GDR's Ministry of the Interior issued its new decree, everything came to a head. Volkspolizei officers stopped the deputy head of the American military mission and denied him entry into the Eastern sector after he refused to show identification. In reaction, the Americans asserted their access rights by way of military escort. The Ministry of the Interior used this incident to justify the (pre-prepared) ordinance decrying "provocative abuses of state order at the border checkpoint Friedrichstraße by members of the United States occupation power."[62] SED leadership wanted to enforce its alleged rights to control all movement across the border, and this attempt triggered the confrontation of tanks on Friedrichstraße. For Clay, the conflict did not revolve around showing identification documents but rather defending the four-power status of Berlin that Ulbricht was trying to negate: "Clay accepted neither the measures nor the allegations. He wanted the USSR to recognize its responsibility for the GDR's actions," and this also meant coaxing Khrushchev "to ensure complete respect for Western rights." Kennedy was also convinced that "calling for absolute resolve in defending [the Western powers'] own rights was extremely important for future negotiations with the USSR." Soviet leadership, according to Clay's calculations, would not forfeit control of the situation in Berlin. He was certain that they were fearful of a military conflict: "Following this logic, he tried to convince the Kremlin that the United States wanted to start an armed conflict. He instructed ten tanks to advance to Checkpoint Charlie, some of them armed with demolition equipment, apparently following orders to obliterate the obstacles blocking the way to the Soviet sector by using force."[63]

Khrushchev did indeed fear conflict but nevertheless ordered Marshal Konev to align his tanks to face the United States. The demolition equipment on the American tanks elicited its intended reaction. Khrushchev instructed Konev: "If the American machines begin to dismantle the border barricades, I give the order to shoot with live ammunition."[64] He accompanied this command with a political declaration that Gromyko handed to American Ambassador Thompson on 27 October. Gromyko protested the American advance and largely adhered to the GDR's interpretation of the law: "The regulation of movement at the border between the GDR and Westberlin is not among the functions of the American military authorities as occupiers of Westberlin. Moreover, when a visit to East Berlin is required, American personnel can cross the border unobstructed as long as they respect the necessary formalities. But it is obvious that the authorities of the GDR should have the right to check whether persons who claim to be members of the military do in fact belong to the official posts of the United States in Westberlin." In this vein, he pointed out that Soviet citizens "are subject to controls by the Westberlin police" upon entry to West Berlin. "There has never been friction or objection in that regard." Gromyko rejected the American demand that these types of controls only be carried out by Soviet officers; border checks fell under the authority of the Volkspolizei. After all, "members of the Soviet military are not traffic police, and they are not in Berlin to fulfill that purpose." If the "provocations" continued, the Soviet Union would consider it "an act of provocative, armed invasion" of the GDR and would provide adequate support "to suppress such operations." Gromyko's declaration closed with an expression of hope that the American administration would put an end to this type of "provocation" in the future.[65]

With the deployment of tanks, the situation escalated into a direct military confrontation between Soviet and American forces. It also corresponded to the aforementioned nuclear test by the Soviet Union, which Khrushchev had timed to coordinate with the 22nd Party Congress and which now lent a menacing backdrop to the conflict over the Western powers' access rights. "Lucius D. Clay wanted this showdown. Since his arrival in Berlin, he had been increasingly disappointed by what he saw as the West's weak posture. In his view, there was only one answer to Soviet Berlin policy: toughness."[66] This had already been his recipe for success during the first Berlin Crisis in 1948–49. Under utmost secrecy, he had already rehearsed the act of tearing down the Wall using tanks with bulldozers in West Berlin. The barricades on Friedrichstraße could be the starting point. He had not even requested approval for the exercise from the U.S. supreme commander in Europe, but the Soviet secret service had managed to photograph it. Moscow was informed of the operation on 20 or 21 October. On 25 October, Clay sent a secret telegram to Secretary of State Rusk: "If we are prepared to raid in force for quick penetration rather deeply tearing down the maze walls as we return I believe it would bring Soviet confrontation. Anything less at this time offers little promise."[67] Once Rusk understood what Clay meant by his telegram, he saw no reason at all to follow the general's suggestion: "Entry into East Berlin is not a vital interest which would warrant determined recourse to force to protect and sustain." For this reason, he argued, the United States had "acquiesced in the building of the wall" in the first place.[68]

In a certain way, Ulbricht interpreted Clay's motive correctly to Khrushchev: "In the mean time, the Bonn government and certain circles of the Pentagon have carried out a counter-attack in order to at least partially reverse the outcome of 13 August. In doing so, it is clearly the intent of the Western powers to rule out a satisfying solution to the Westberlin problem by creating certain faits accomplis."[69]

America's next steps were the subject of discussions at the White House on 27 October. One of the meeting's conclusions directly affected the U.S. position in the present crisis: "There would be no more test drives to East Berlin, and above all there would be no trips by American personnel in civilian clothes. With this decision, the problem seemed at least somewhat defused. Instructions to this extent were conveyed immediately to Clay. Clay was not pleased. If they made these kinds of concessions, the approach was completely wrong; after all, they wanted to intimidate the Soviets and not themselves."[70] Based on an analysis of British files, Steininger posits that Clay was generally dissatisfied with Western policy, including Kennedy's policy on Berlin. Christopher Steel, the British ambassador to Bonn, asked Clay what "the right thing would have been 'for the West to do' and received the answer: 'tear down the Wall.'" Clay was dismissed just a few months later and left Berlin depressed about [the city's] future. "Men of his making—or caliber—had no place in new American policy,"[71] Steininger writes, and attributes the resolution of the conflict to Kennedy's initiative. The president used his brother Robert's contact with Georgi Bolshakov at the Soviet embassy in Washington. Bolshakov gave Khrushchev Robert Kennedy's message, "in which he asked [Khrushchev] to withdraw the tanks with an assurance that the American tanks would be withdrawn directly afterward."[72]

Aleksandr Fursenko and Timothy Naftali confirm that Bolshakov's message arrived at the headquarters of the Main Intelligence Directorate (GRU) around 7:00 a.m. Moscow time on 28 October. Whether this message actually influenced Khrushchev's decision remains unclear. But he made his decision as if he had received the message. "'I knew Kennedy was looking for a way to back down,' he explained a few days later. 'I decided therefore that if I removed my tanks first, then he would follow suit; [and] he did.'"[73] Khrushchev gave the order for de-escalation, and on 28 October the first Soviet tanks disappeared. After that, the Americans did the same. Gerhard Wettig believes the initiative lay with Marshal Konev. Since Konev feared that a confrontation could "lead to an exchange of fire and then war, he supposedly asked Khrushchev to issue directives to de-escalate the conflict. The head of the Kremlin was also nervous and did not hesitate to give the requested order."[74] In the end, it is only of secondary importance which side took initiative to de-escalate the situation; what counts is that both leaders in Washington and Moscow wanted the same thing.

After the tank episode, the Soviet Union intensified its conflict control in Berlin. To this end, Ulbricht received "advice that it was not 'productive' to devote press coverage to the conflict over Western officials' access. [The press] should distance itself from 'exaggerated' polemics and confine its discussion to the right of the GDR as a matter of principle to exercise controls on the border to West Berlin."[75] One month before the showdown in Berlin, during his conversation with Paul-Henri Spaak, Khrushchev had already expressed his conviction that there would be no war over Berlin.[76]

While the tank confrontation was still ensuing, Ulbricht sent the SED Politburo instructions from Moscow that contained the same Soviet "advice." He emphatically approved the interior minister's decree and declared that the "exaggerated" attacks on the Western powers in the media were not "productive": "The previous instructions stating that civilian personnel of the three Western powers are obliged to show identification papers should be carried out diligently. In the press, we will take our principled position that in the capital of the GDR, controlling the Westberlin border is among the sovereign rights of the GDR's state institutions. Since we are engaged in preparations to solve other problems, it is not productive to publicly attack the three Western powers in an exaggerated way that could, for reasons of prestige, unnecessarily complicate our other measures."[77]

Two days later, Ulbricht issued instructions to expand the border barricades. He requested that "pioneer-type tank obstacles be erected at the major points along this border." He also criticized the Ministry of Defense for not implementing this order earlier, since it had already been issued by the politburo. The ministers of national defense and state security were instructed to remedy this lapse. Ulbricht was especially concerned with "the most politically significant parts of the border," meaning the Brandenburg Gate, Potsdamer Platz, and the checkpoints; these places urgently required reinforcement. "Since we can only assume that temporarily closing Friedrichstraße would prompt the occupation troops in West Berlin to try to break through the six other border crossings, preparations must be accelerated there as well." After Clay's advance, the SED leader was worried that the Western Allies might be tempted "to steamroll through our barbed wire barriers at these locations and carry out a political demonstration." Ulbricht also considered the issue of construction workers, and he was in a hurry: "It is necessary to choose not only experienced pioneer troops but also members of the police force or activists in concrete construction who can be deployed quickly at any given time."[78]

Ulbricht's attempt to deprive the Western powers of their sovereign rights in Berlin using salami tactics[79] had failed. In Moscow, he and Khrushchev decided on a procedure to be implemented at the checkpoints for members of the Western militaries. In Khrushchev's words: "Passage shall be granted as we have agreed. The militaries can cross freely, and civilians must show identification. Later, after discussions [with the United States] have taken place, things can be different."[80]

Clay's actions at Checkpoint Charlie had made one thing clear: "Four-power responsibility continued to exist in Berlin, and above all, the GDR had no authority over the three Western Allies in East Berlin."[81] Once again, SED leaders were forced—through the active participation of the Soviet Union—to face the limits of their state's sovereignty. At the same time, it became clear that neither the United States nor the USSR had any interest in deepening the conflict; one sign of this was Kennedy's request that American military personnel only enter the Eastern sector of Berlin in uniform.

Khrushchev Approves Strengthening the Border

Ulbricht and the SED delegation only learned that Khrushchev had retracted his June ultimatum to Kennedy through Khrushchev's address at the 22nd Party Congress on 17 October. Khrushchev no longer "firmly" insisted upon 31 December 1961 as the deadline by which to sign a peace treaty with the Western powers. Now he only demanded that they show "willingness to settle the German problem." This change of course in Soviet policy, as Ulbricht wrote to Khrushchev, made it necessary "to coordinate further tactics" moving forward.[82]

The economic problems facing the GDR remained a central issue, but Ulbricht was most concerned with asserting the GDR's rights to implement controls at the border to West Berlin. Although he had been briefed on the commencement of discussions between the Soviet and American foreign ministers, he was apparently unfamiliar with the detailed content of those conversations. He was aware that Soviet leadership placed absolute priority on concluding a treaty with the Americans. Perhaps he also sensed that the separate peace treaty that he had hoped for and that his foreign ministry had prepared only served as a Soviet tool to exert pressure on the United States in their negotiations. This was reason enough in October 1961 for Ulbricht to take the enforcement of the GDR's "sovereignty" in its capital city into his own hands. Through Clay's "counterstrike" and Khrushchev's decision to retract his ultimatum, a new situation emerged for the SED. In order to discuss it more thoroughly, Ulbricht asked Khrushchev to convene a meeting between the SED delegation and the presidium of the CPSU. In his letter, Ulbricht reminded the Soviet premier of their agreements so far: "In my last meeting with Comrade Khrushchev, as well as at the conference of the first secretaries of the Communist and workers' parties, it was agreed that a settlement should be reached between the Soviet Union and the Western powers on the issue of Westberlin before the conclusion of a peace treaty. The outcome of this settlement and the guarantee declaration of the Soviet Union and the government of the GDR on Westberlin should then be incorporated into the peace treaty with the GDR."[83]

Ulbricht also reminded Khrushchev of the West German government's influence on the Western powers "to hinder negotiations and thwart the conclusion of a peace treaty and the peaceful resolution of the Westberlin question. We must counter this pressure from the Bonn government on the Western powers through appropriate measures; in other words, we have to exert even greater pressure upon the Western powers." The partial blockade of West Berlin as Ulbricht proposed would have certainly escalated the conflict. Ulbricht continued: "Considering the latest provocations by the United States' military authorities on the territory of the capital of the German Democratic Republic, it will be a necessary next step to establish a system at the border to Westberlin in the capital of the GDR in order to eliminate any violation of the GDR's sovereignty." In order to put this system into place, he wrote, the following steps would have to be taken: "Enforcement of identification requirements for all military and civilian members of the three Western powers when controlled by the border police or Volkspolizei of the GDR at the border with Westberlin." Should the personnel of the Western powers refuse to comply with these controls, "then the border with Westberlin—except for the connection route[84] between Westberlin and West Germany—is to be blocked pending the outcome of government negotiations. This step can be justified with the argument that these measures are intended to prevent conflict in Berlin until the conclusion of a peace treaty."[85]

The measures that Ulbricht lists here would be directed exclusively toward the Western powers without encroaching upon the access rights of West Germans or foreigners traveling to East Berlin. Moreover, this move still respected Kennedy's essentials regarding the "security of the access routes between Westberlin and West Germany or the so-called freedom of Westberlin." Influenced by the course of the first Berlin Crisis in 1948–49, Ulbricht assumed that the Western powers would react to a partial blockade with an embargo, just as they had done in 1948. The purpose of the proposed measures was simply to "clear the playing field" (*das Vorfeld bereinigen*) for negotiations. Such steps would also "intensify" conflict within the Federal Republic over "the West German government's policy on Germany." In Berlin itself, a conflict would bring changes for the Soviet Union; the USSR would no longer be able to station troops at the Soviet memorial in the British sector or participate in "guarding the three convicted war criminals in Spandau." From the SED's perspective, the Soviet representative in the central air traffic control could "remain for the time being, although his presence there—in terms of the GDR's interests—serves no purpose."[86] In short, Ulbricht wanted to eliminate any remnants of Berlin's four-power status, including those of the Soviet Union.

In a conversation with Khrushchev in early November, Ulbricht suggested a further initiative on Germany policy that concentrated on the Federal Republic's recognition of the GDR and demanded the establishment of "correct relations." Khrushchev had nothing against this type of propaganda offensive, but he was skeptical of its significance for realpolitik. "In my view," he stated, "there is no hope that West Germany will agree to your suggestions, but obviously it would be an entirely appropriate step on your side. Therefore I support this initiative; we have no difference of opinion there."[87]

To Ulbricht, the retraction of the Soviet Ultimatum created a new situation. Khrushchev asked Ulbricht in their meeting why the deadline's postponement changed anything for the GDR. In doing so, Khrushchev declined to mention the foreign policy factors that had led the Soviet Union to take this step, focusing instead on the GDR's economic weakness, especially its continued reliance on the Federal Republic:

> *Khrushchev:* I cannot understand why the date of signing a peace treaty is so important to your economy. It seems to be an artificial argument, since [the treaty] would not change the situation for you, either within the country or with respect to foreign relations.
>
> *Ulbricht:* The hesitation to sign a peace treaty will foster uncertainty and instability. As a result, the Bonn government will refuse to sign a trade agreement with us on certain goods, for example some types of steel.[88] Before, they signed treaties with us but did not deliver specific categories of goods. Now we do not know what kind of treaty they will sign and what goods we will then receive. In other words, there is a total lack of clarity regarding certain deficit goods. If, however, the peace treaty is signed, a clear situation will emerge and we will know where we stand.
>
> *Khrushchev:* Let us assume for a moment that the peace treaty is concluded and it results in a local restriction of the economy.[89] Ultimately we know what they [the West] are preparing for: an economic blockade. Would that make things easier for you?
>
> *Ulbricht:* But I can't tell that to the people.
>
> *Khrushchev:* And I am still trying to understand what we are talking about. I do not believe that the longer the conclusion of a peace treaty is delayed, the worse the GDR's economy will get. This brings me back to one of our old topics: As long as the GDR cannot free itself from economic dependence on West Germany, Adenauer will continue to bully you in certain ways. This is a given since we represent mutually[90] antagonistic classes[91] and are constantly waging battle against each other. You can only overcome [this situation] by freeing yourself from economic dependence.[92]

The GDR's economic dependence on the Federal Republic took up much of the conversation:

> *Honecker:* It is unclear when we will free ourselves from West Germany's interference.
>
> *Khrushchev:* As long as capitalism survives, it will interfere. We will interfere [with them] whenever we are able to, and they will do the same—although both of us deny it. This is also understandable because we represent antagonistic systems.
>
> *The main thing is to free the GDR's economy from dependence on West Germany. Then Adenauer will no [longer] have such great significance.*[93]

Ulbricht blamed the problem once more on the division of Germany:

> *Ulbricht:* If the Ruhr Valley were ours, we could sit down with you and only talk about politics.
>
> *Khrushchev:* Now you are finally being honest about what you need.[94]

Ulbricht's suggestions to "clear the playing field" in Berlin did not receive direct attention at the conference of the two delegations. But the two first secretaries had probably discussed the topic earlier in their private meeting, as the following dialogue indicates:

> *Khrushchev:* Regarding the German question, it seems that we cleared up everything in our conversation yesterday.
> *Ulbricht:* [It is] clear, we will wait it out.
> *Khrushchev:* Not [that you will] wait it out, but rather that we will enter into discussions.
> *Ulbricht:* (Pointing to Gromyko) Those are his negotiations [with the United States].
> *Khrushchev:* We will be in contact with them, but action on our side is necessary too.[95]

The direction of this previous conversation can only be inferred. But two of Ulbricht's comments are revealing: "We will wait it out" and "Those are his negotiations." Read together, these two comments imply that he knew there would be no separate peace treaty with the GDR before negotiations with the United States came to a close.

Khrushchev and Ulbricht returned to the topic of a peace treaty once more during the meeting of delegations. This time they addressed the question of whether to use a tactic of gradual pressure on the West in order to push the peace treaty through:

> *Ulbricht:* It is important that this kind of tactic receives your approval. The situation is complicated. We should implement the tactic gradually and carefully think through any measures to exert pressure. By now it is clear to everyone that the peace treaty is not just going to fall out of the sky on a sunny day.
> *Khrushchev:* There is total understanding between us. It will only be possible to wrestle the peace treaty out [of them]. We have to go on the offensive. Now we are in a position to block access [to West Berlin] any day; it will not lead to war. But then we have to accept that air traffic will be monitored without us, and that will be to our disadvantage.[96]

Khrushchev gave the SED free rein to secure the border in Berlin however it saw fit:

> *Ulbricht:* I have a quick question.
> *You have told us that it would be beneficial to strengthen the border in Berlin to the point that no tanks can break through. At the moment there are barbed wire barricades, and in some places large trucks have been able to break through. Now we have prepared anti-tank obstacles. We could set them up in two nights. The question is whether we should do it now.*
> *Khrushchev:* At the places where passage is blocked? Why shouldn't you do it? Even in places where you have left room for a border crossing, you should still erect concrete barriers and a barricade bar. It should always be closed: Show your permit and you can go through.[97]

Exploratory Discussions on a Berlin Settlement

After the end of the Berlin Crisis, Kennedy visited West Berlin in 1963 and received a triumphant welcome. Particularly memorable was the climax of his speech from the balcony of City Hall in Schöneberg. Impressed by the contrast between the

Wall and the celebrating people of Berlin, the American president elevated Berlin "to a symbol of freedom par excellence. In his speech that included the endearing phrase 'Ich bin ein Berliner' and the equation of the city with freedom, Kennedy embodied the spirit that Ernst Reuter had once evoked."[98] For West Berliners and the media, Kennedy's German sentence was a sensation. It allowed people to forget that in 1961, Kennedy had been prepared to surrender Western rights to the transit routes to West Berlin.

Kennedy had already given thought on 21 August 1961 to the use of freedom rhetoric in negotiations with the Soviet Union on Berlin. That day, he asked a working group to come up with proposals for an overall concept to guide American negotiations. He wanted to break the continuity in the way the United States evoked its status rights in Berlin. The working group was "*not* to insist upon the rights that originated in the occupation as long as other strong arguments existed; for the general public, occupation rights as a basis [for the United States to be there] were less attractive than freedom and the protection of West Berliners."[99] After the exploratory talks among Gromyko, Rusk, and Kennedy, American Ambassador Thompson believed in September that it would be possible to negotiate a "solution to the Berlin question on the following basis: (1) Retention of the Western position in West Berlin; (2) 'very significant concessions with respect to recognizing the GDR.'"[100]

After the NATO Council meeting in December 1961, the Americans resumed their talks with the Soviet Union. However, the Western powers still disagreed on a central issue:

> Kennedy wanted negotiations, Macmillan wanted negotiations. In his conversations in Washington, Adenauer was forced to cave to American pressure in terms of negotiations and now seemed to favor negotiating as well. But one person had been against it from the beginning and remained so: General Charles de Gaulle. Without a common Western position, it would be difficult to negotiate with the Soviet Union; even Kennedy felt this way. In contrast, NATO General Secretary Spaak wanted to enter negotiations without France, if necessary, and isolate Paris. Adenauer rejected this idea emphatically in Washington, and Kennedy agreed.[101]

The Western discord arose from the differing interests of the states and governments involved. Great Britain was France's antipode throughout the discussion process. Facing its dramatic colonial decline, Britain evoked its traditional policy of European balance and wanted to reach a settlement with "Russia" at the expense of Germany. Macmillan's government rejected the idea of German reunification. Thus, recognizing the GDR posed no problem at all; it was only out of consideration for the Federal Republic, Britain's partner in NATO, that the administration refrained from doing so. Like Kennedy, the British wanted to reach an agreement in Berlin on the basis of the Soviet Ultimatum.

At the behest of the British ambassador to Washington, David Ormsby-Gore, the Foreign Office discussed its positions on negotiating with Moscow in November 1961. Writing to his foreign minister, Lord Douglas-Home, Ambassador Ormsby-Gore took the view that if push came to shove in Berlin, "the British would not risk nuclear war under any circumstances, and, he added, 'that goes for the other European NATO partners and for Canada as well'—a presumption that probably rang true. And then he introduced his central idea, namely to transform West Berlin into an 'independent city,' reasoning that 'with a population of 2¼ million intelligent people, it has just as much a right to an independent existence as Cyprus, Mauretania, or Kuwait.'" The government of this "independent city" could then ask the Western powers to station up to ten thousand troops in the city and request that the UN open offices there. Through an agreement with the GDR, this independent part of Germany could oversee transit to and from the Federal Republic "and thereby free the Federal Republic from its uncomfortable arrangement." Ignoring objections from the British diplomatic corps, Lord Douglas-Home accepted the ambassador's suggestion, which built on the Soviet proposal to establish a "Free City."[102]

In November, Charles de Gaulle embarked on a state visit to London, and the negotiations on Berlin were at the heart of his conversations with Macmillan. De Gaulle reiterated his absolute rejection of any negotiations. He was convinced "that Khrushchev wanted to neutralize Germany and shatter NATO, and that the West needed to take a clear position: there was a red line that could not be crossed. If the West were to accept a compromise on the Berlin question, it would only allow the Soviets to continue exerting pressure on other fronts." De Gaulle had a clear vision of the Soviet Union's goals in Berlin: "In principle the Russians wanted to cash in on Berlin, and because this would have catastrophic consequences for the Germans and the rest of Europe, it had to be prevented. The Russians began the crisis; therefore negotiations would be impossible so long as the Russians refused to stop threatening the West." Macmillan failed in his attempt to convince de Gaulle that negotiations were imperative. Independent of his general doubt as to whether there could ever be agreement with the Soviet Union, the French president also schooled Macmillan on France's geopolitical interest in "keep[ing] the Federal Republic firmly situated within the Western camp." De Gaulle's vision of Germany, just like Macmillan's, drew heavily on the First World War and the consequences of German defeat, which eventually led to the Second World War. Against this historical backdrop, de Gaulle maintained the opinion that if the new West German government accepted the Western powers' "desired concessions" to the Soviet Union, "this would be seen by the German people as betrayal. Whatever the United States and Great Britain chose to do, France would have no part in it—even if [France] did not propose starting a war with the Russians, either. In any case, the Germans would have the impression that at least one friend still remained in the West." The French president repeated that he took no issue with exploratory talks, but France would not participate in them. Recognizing the GDR was out of the question.[103]

With regard to ties between West Berlin and the Federal Republic, General de Gaulle positioned himself clearly against the British vision of an "independent city." Even though the three Western occupation powers often reiterated that Berlin did not belong to the Federal Republic by law, "in the past years it had indeed been treated [as if it did]. Adenauer, for example, was welcomed there as federal chancellor," and the governing mayor, Brandt, was the SPD's candidate for federal chancellor in 1961. On the issue of providing the Federal Republic with nuclear weapons, de Gaulle suggested to Macmillan a possible cooperation between France and the Federal Republic to develop their own nuclear weapons. "For the time being, France did not intend to share relevant information with the Germans on building nuclear weapons, but: 'This does not always have to be the case. For France, the Russian threat is too great and the Rhine too close to the Elbe for us to give up such long-term security.'" Nuclear weapons for the Federal Republic—this was precisely the issue, as Steininger argues, that the British and Americans considered "cause for particular concern." After returning to Paris, the French president briefed top officials from his foreign ministry on the outcome of his talks in London. The British "were only too ready to make concessions at the expense of the Germans and not at all prepared to take a hard line against the Russians."[104]

During these months, Adenauer's alliance with the general was especially crucial: "Over the course of American exploratory talks on Berlin, nearly every ounce of [Adenauer's] trust in the United States and Great Britain had disappeared. In his view, Kennedy increasingly showed himself to be a weak president surrounded by inexperienced advisors from the ranks of academia." Since Adenauer's thoughts were occupied at this time with "the horrific vision of nuclear war" in Europe, he was all the more concerned that the American president could "decide in favor of nuclear war" in 1962.[105]

President Kennedy had formulated the American interests in Berlin with his three essentials that July. According to his speech, the presence of the Western powers in Berlin was nonnegotiable, and this included free access to West Berlin. The worst-case-scenario military planning had shown, however, that a conflict could spark very easily over the Western powers' rights to use the transit routes between the Federal Republic and West Berlin. The military scenarios had also demonstrated that a war over Berlin would likely lead to nuclear inferno. Ultimately, Khrushchev and Kennedy were the only two parties responsible for the decision to use nuclear weapons. Kennedy's three essentials implicitly acknowledged that the Soviet Union could erect whatever border control it saw fit within its own sector. Politically, Kennedy saw the Berlin issue as a conflict of interests with the Soviet Union that contained the danger of war. Thus, in the current Berlin conflict, avoiding nuclear war took top priority—especially as he knew that he would bear responsibility if war indeed broke out. The United States' contractual obligation to help the Federal Republic reestablish German unity took diminished importance as a result. The issue simply had no place on the political agenda. Since the territorial spheres of influence in Germany seemed to have obvious outlines after the Wall's construction, reaching a settlement to ensure unimpeded access to West Berlin remained the most pressing issue in American Berlin policy to curb the danger of military conflict.

Before conversations in Moscow began, Kennedy and Macmillan met in Bermuda on 21 and 22 December 1961 in order to draw up instructions for American

Ambassador Thompson. At one point, the discussion turned to an idea to internationalize the Autobahn running through the GDR. "Couldn't [the Western powers] present an offer to the Soviets, Kennedy wondered, to internationalize just as many kilometers of Autobahn in the FRG as in the GDR?" British Foreign Minister Douglas-Home "waved [the suggestion] aside: the Soviet Union would never agree to an internationalization of the GDR's Autobahns."[106] Requesting consent from the Federal Republic did not even appear to enter the discussion.

Despite the British foreign minister's skeptical prognosis, exploratory talks between Thompson and Gromyko began in Moscow on 2 January 1962, focusing on the Western powers' free access to West Berlin. To begin, the American ambassador reiterated the Western position on a peace settlement with Germany: "The Western powers support signing a peace treaty with a unified Germany and believe that they [the Western powers] cannot unilaterally be deprived of their rights in Berlin, especially concerning free access to West Berlin. The Western powers have committed themselves to defending the freedom of West Berliners and have declared this openly."[107]

The Western powers were willing to consider the Berlin question, but only with regard to Berlin as a whole; the United States found it "illogical and contrary to the basic agreements on Berlin that it was being asked to deal with only a part of the city." Thompson interpreted the construction of the Wall to mean that the GDR aimed for the "isolation of West Berlin" and the "permanent division of Berlin." He went on to remark that "the leaders of the GDR have presented various declarations whose purpose is to prevent the free transit of our transportation vehicles on the Autobahn between West Berlin and West Germany." This was Thompson's way of transitioning to the main goal of future negotiations: ensuring the Western powers' free access to West Berlin: "The key point for the Western powers is the question of access, and we would like to devote our first talk to precisely this question. This is the point that contains a real threat and where unilateral action could have far-reaching results. In this context, we would be interested to hear any suggestions you might have in relation to access."[108]

Gromyko responded right away to the Western powers' "main interest," taking a contrary position: "The Soviet government sees the conclusion of a German peace treaty as the central question, since it would finalize the end of the Second World War." Thompson replied pragmatically: "Concerning the question of access, we do not believe it is realistic to aim for complete understanding. . . . But since one must begin negotiations somewhere, the United States has decided it would be better and easier to begin by discussing the question of access." Thompson asked Gromyko to specify more closely what the Soviet Union meant when it insisted upon respecting the sovereignty of the GDR: "For example, does this mean that the GDR would have the right to determine who could travel from West Berlin to West Germany and back?" He went on to outline two concrete ideas from the United States and the other Western powers to secure access to West Berlin: "The first version would be to establish a corridor between West Berlin and West Germany under the control of the Western powers. The second version is based on the creation of an international authority responsible for securing the access routes to Berlin." The first proposal was pure provocation; from the American perspective, the real subject of negotiations would be the second proposal. The authority would guarantee "the uninterrupted flow of normal vehicular movement along the Autobahn" rather than exercise control over the authorities of the GDR:

> It would pay for the use of required buildings, equipment, and various other instruments. It would maintain the Autobahn in good condition and ensure that no other body could collect tolls of any kind for the use of this Autobahn. Furthermore, this authority would have a representative at the central air traffic control in order to ensure uninterrupted air traffic. The establishment of such an authority would require addressing several questions, for example the question of whether or not the GDR would be allowed to use this Autobahn. It would be absolutely necessary for East Germany to draw up strict rules for entry into West Berlin and exit from West Berlin. It would also be necessary to agree on whether the connection to West Berlin could use the Autobahn that already exists for this purpose, or whether another one should be made available.[109]

The ambassador also discussed filling the Board of Governors of this future authority, for which the American administration had already drawn up a statute. In addition to equal numbers of representatives from Western and Eastern states, it would also include representatives from East and West Berlin and "from the authorities of East and West Germany. In addition, the American administration is of the opinion that representatives from three neutral states could also take part in this international authority." The statement that followed highlighted Kennedy's interests once again: "If such an authority were created, it would contribute to the avoidance of dangerous conflict and greatly reduce the possibility of friction arising from the issue of access to West Berlin. The government of the United States hopes that the Soviet Union will not categorically reject this proposal but rather give it serious consideration."[110]

Citing Khrushchev, Gromyko rejected the corridor idea as "absolutely unacceptable." Regarding the second proposal, the Soviet foreign minister stated that he could not speak "definitively," but in his view, the proposed international authority seemed to be "something like a state within a state." To evidence this, he referred to the question of whether or not the GDR "would be allowed to use the Autobahn leading to West Berlin." Thompson further specified the scope of authority, stating that the international body would "exercise its functions territorially on the Autobahn Helmstadt–West Berlin and in the central air traffic control." In principle Gromyko did not rule out the possibility of reaching a settlement on access to West Berlin, but he stressed immediately that this could only occur in the context of a settlement on the larger question of West Berlin. Thompson replied "that if the Soviet Union refused to discuss the issue of Berlin as a whole, then the Western powers could hardly discuss the Soviet suggestion to create a Free City only in West Berlin." Gromyko responded: "We cannot imagine reaching an understanding without changing the situation in West Berlin. One has to wonder what else would be the point of negotiations."[111]

The answer to this question was revealed to Gromyko just a few days later at the presidium of the CPSU, when Khrushchev announced a change of course in his Berlin policy. He wanted to continue negotiations, he declared, but no longer wished to reach an agreement with the United States.[112] He instructed the foreign ministry to continue reiterating the basic positions of Soviet Berlin policy in talks with the Western powers, and especially to refrain from saying anything that might appear to recognize the Western powers' rights. Gromyko took this line in the following four conversations with the American ambassador.

Thompson submitted a memorandum to the Soviet foreign minister on 1 February 1962 on the creation of an international authority overseeing the Autobahn between Helmstadt and West Berlin. The memo also contained a proposal for Berlin's reunification, based on a document put forth by the Western powers on 26 May 1959 at the Geneva conference of foreign ministers.[113] In the context of the 1962 negotiations, the proposal of 1959 provided the United States with a counterposition to fend off negotiations over the "Free City of Westberlin." Gromyko's internal reaction was clear: "The documents presented by Thompson are based on the United States' current position, and this position is unacceptable."[114] In their last conversation on 9 February, Gromyko's formulations were more diplomatic but still very firm: "The question of access to West Berlin is too narrow a basis for negotiations."[115] The round of talks ended fruitlessly.

On 22 February, Adenauer positioned himself in a memorandum to London and Washington. Like de Gaulle, he assumed that the Soviets would simply "pocket" any American concessions "without being prepared to engage in a negotiated solution for Berlin by which they would have to give up the leverage that city affords. Instead, the Soviet advantage rested in the fact that with any unilateral Soviet action in the future of the Berlin Crisis, [the Western] positions would already be weakened."[116] In following this logic, the chancellor grasped the exact line of Soviet Berlin policy. Kennedy had a different view; he hoped to reach an agreement with Moscow without having to consider France and West Germany's concerns. He decided "with resolve to 'take a personal day-to-day responsibility' for the Berlin question. Kennedy was convinced that Adenauer held the key to finding a solution to the problem." Based on a recommendation from Macmillan, a new Berlin concept was ready in Washington by early March. In Bermuda the previous December, Macmillan had suggested that "Khrushchev 'must be given a good smell of the dinner he can have if he leaves Berlin alone.' The problem, however, was how to accomplish this 'without getting the Germans in an uproar.'"[117] The new concept focused on cementing the status quo for the time being, "while at the same time calling for a permanent conference in Berlin composed of foreign ministers and their representatives from the Western Allies and the Soviet Union. This would be the place to discuss other questions, namely, the international access authority for Berlin; American–Soviet agreements on the non-proliferation of nuclear weapons; the exchange of non-aggression commitments between the East and West; the establishment of pan-German committees to settle technical questions; the recognition of borders in Europe, and so on."[118]

On the sidelines of the Geneva disarmament conference in March 1962, American Secretary of State Rusk had spoken to Gromyko, his Soviet counterpart, about this concept, and they agreed to continue discussions with the new Soviet ambassador to Washington, Anatoly F. Dobrynin, on 16 April 1962. Rusk also informed the new West German foreign minister, Gerhard Schröder, of this plan. While Schröder raised no objections, Adenauer "was full of mistrust, not only toward the British at the time, but now toward the Americans as well." He expressed this mistrust in a conversation with Kroll, his ambassador to Moscow: "Do not trust the Americans; they will find a way to reach an understanding with the Russians at our expense."[119]

Khrushchev's decision to stop pursuing an agreement on Berlin (in order to continue using the city for leverage) remained unnoticed in Washington. Nevertheless, there now existed an indirect, personal channel between Kennedy and Khrushchev (via Rusk, Thompson, and Gromyko) that also allowed them to exchange opposing positions. In confidence, Khrushchev shared certain details of this communication with Ulbricht:

> *Khrushchev:* I would like to say a few words about the peace treaty, about what seems to be happening in that area. The negotiations between Gromyko and Thompson were a step backward compared to the conversations that Gromyko had last fall with Kennedy and Rusk. Now they are asking for much more.[120] We have responded firmly and said that this is no basis for negotiations.
>
> *Now I would like to share with you in strict confidence that Kennedy has laid out his position in a very clear way:* The United States will not sign a peace treaty. But the United States would be ready to recognize the existing borders of Poland and Czechoslovakia. However, they cannot recognize the border between the two German states. I do not believe that we can ask this of them either, since it is really an issue between the two German states. The Germans do not recognize each other, so one cannot ask Adenauer's partners to behave otherwise.
>
> *Second, he has stated his will to find some kind of possible solution. He says that perhaps it must be done in a different way than he proposed in his interview*[121] *concerning the international commission. But some kind of commission must be created in case, as he says, Ulbricht takes action against the agreement. Some kind of body with representatives from the United States and the USSR is needed in this situation. He did not elaborate on these thoughts further but shared them with me in confidence. At issue is a commission to protect the air and land routes.*
>
> *Ulbricht:* Sometimes it happens that the Western press claims we have made various proposals, and then we have to somehow address them.
>
> *Khrushchev:* Propaganda is one thing; confidential talks are another. And there is a difference between what I suggest and whether Kennedy agrees to it.[122]

Khrushchev's Change of Course: Negotiations, but No Agreement

Just a few days after a meeting between Thompson and Gromyko in January 1962, Khrushchev took stock of the negotiations and exploratory talks so far before the presidium of the Central Committee of the CPSU. He saw no possibility of concluding a peace treaty with the United States under Soviet conditions. The passage from his speech quoted below marked a change of course in Khrushchev's political line on Berlin. Now he declared that the Wall through Berlin was the maximum that the East could push through against the Western powers. In light of the ongoing arms race and the necessity of stabilizing the GDR's economy and ending its dependence on West Germany—developments that would eventually lead to a "final battle for Westberlin," he emphasized—he wanted to continue using West Berlin to exert pressure on the United States. He was in favor of further negotiations, but an agreement to resolve the Berlin problem was no longer in the interest of the Soviet Union.

Khrushchev's change of course signaled a retreat from the Berlin policy that he had pursued since his ultimatum in 1958. In particular, it meant that all plans to sign a separate peace treaty with the GDR or even hand over control of West Berlin's transit routes were now entirely off the table. The Soviet leader's speech is among the key documents of the second Berlin Crisis and deserves ample attention. It also provides glimpses into Khrushchev's political thought: in a struggle for equal standing with the United States, it was essential to couple the goals of an ideologically based politics with a sober assessment of the real situation. Excessive threats veiled careful decisions. In the military exercise scenarios as well as negotiations between diplomats, the transit routes and access to West Berlin were the critical points with potential to spark a war. Even though Khrushchev was no longer interested in reaching an agreement because of the long-term negative effects on Soviet policy, he continued to stress the necessity of avoiding war:

> For us, it is not absolutely essential to sign a peace treaty if they refuse to sign it. In other words, we should not push things to the point of saying: either honor or war. Comrades, we mustn't be like the officer who passed a little gas at an evening soirée and then felt compelled to shoot himself. We are not like that. We are servants of the state and carry the responsibility of the state. What threat do we face, then? We are in a splendid position: our economy is developing, we have decided on a program—and now we are supposed to make all of this contingent on West Berlin? Moreover, we are making progress every year. Whose situation is getting worse? Not ours; theirs. So why do we need it?
>
> We must increase pressure; we cannot fall asleep. And while we grow, we have to let our opponent feel this growth—but without adding the straw that breaks the camel's back.[123]

After this affirmation of the USSR's power, Khrushchev asked:

What is the state of the German question, and what options do we have—what are the minimum and maximum options?

I do not believe that we will achieve the maximum because the West is not yet ready for it, neither morally nor materially. From a moral standpoint, there are still very strong reactionary powers fighting to prevent the creation of conditions that will end the tension. Materially the adversary is strong, not weaker than us; they can play the same hand that we can, meaning that they can act from a position of strength. Therefore, to address the question of war as a potential outcome of this game, no one can claim that war is out of the question. Why? Because the opponent is strong and has the same capacities at its disposal as we do. From their point of view, it is fine by the bourgeoisie (upon whom they depend) and has been [cemented] in the form of agreements and similar documents that [the Wall is] a unilateral violation; therefore it is not we, the Soviet side, but supposedly they who are in the right.

Who will actually make the decision: agreement or no agreement, or in the broadest terms, war or peace? Kennedy will decide.[124]

In other words, it would be impossible to reach a peace treaty suitable to the Soviets against the will of the West, especially since the West could "play the same hand" as the Soviet Union militarily, and no one could rule out war as the conflict's final outcome. After providing this assessment of the situation, Khrushchev evaluated the results of Soviet Berlin policy so far, giving special praise to the operations of 13 August 1961:

> *Khrushchev:* But speaking realistically, we have indeed achieved a victory on this [front], a moral victory. If we take the United States' earlier position expressed in statements by Dulles, for example, the goal of total elimination,[125] etc., that is all off the table now. Now they talk about coexistence; now they use Kennedy to sweet-talk us: "What [else] do you need, you have a prospering economy, the future is on your side, why do you need Berlin?" They didn't say things like that before. They say our strength is equal to theirs. This means that with equal strength, a clever opponent will never unleash a war because the attacking side must be absolutely confident in its superiority.
>
> In other words, I do not see any particular advantages that they would give us by signing a treaty.
>
> *Voices:* True!
>
> *Khrushchev:* We gained [our advantage] on 13 August.
>
> *Koslov:* Realized through the process of fighting for Berlin.
>
> *Khrushchev:* Well, when East Germany was an open state next to capitalism, that bone caused us quite a sore throat. When we closed the Wall, however, we pulled out the bone and passed it on to our enemy, and now that bone is no longer working against us but in our favor.[126]

After concluding that the Wall represented a Soviet victory in the Cold War, Khrushchev no longer needed to push so hard for his other goals in Berlin, especially since he had no desire to compromise with the Western powers. Khrushchev considered it more advantageous to continue reiterating the Soviet demands. This would allow him to maintain the upper hand and exert pressure on the Western powers with regard to Berlin.

Khrushchev had already discussed this tactic of exerting permanent pressure on the West with Ulbricht on 2 November 1961. Citing the ongoing arms race with the United States, Khrushchev underscored the necessity of increasing the defense budget in his speech to the presidium of the CPSU: "Right now, a transformative process is taking place on an entirely new basis; we will increase arms production and replace some of the older rockets."[127]

The Soviet leader had learned that the GDR was economically dependent upon deliveries from the Federal Republic. Ulbricht indicated repeatedly to Khrushchev that it was largely Soviet orders that forced the GDR to use inter-German trade in order to fulfill them. Politically Khrushchev and Ulbricht wanted to end this dependence on the Federal Republic, but economically the Soviet Union cemented the constellation with its orders to the capital goods industry of the GDR. Khrushchev now hoped to alter this absurd situation to clear the way for new confrontations with the West:

> I have told Ulbricht for years that it takes no effort on our part, on the part of the Soviet Union, to give the GDR a full load [of orders] because we grow each year by 10 to 10.5 percent. So whatever we produce for this growth could just as easily be ordered from the GDR. But this has shown itself to be impossible. Why? Because the GDR has its particular range of orders, and they rely not on raw materials that we produce but rather on raw materials that the West, especially West Germany, produces. This is why they hesitate on the issue. And Ulbricht says to us, "But you are forcing us to do it." And I think that in a certain way, he is right. Our state economic planners preparing the orders compel and force the GDR to accept orders that can only be filled by using West German raw materials: stainless steel, pipes, etc. Obviously this is stupid. It is unacceptable. It satisfies precisely the interests of forces within the GDR who still pursue a path to reunification based on Adenauer's vision. In my opinion, our last conversation[128] did not demonstrate that Ulbricht has understood this.
>
> But it needs time. Consequently I believe that we should already start preparing ourselves for the final battle for West Berlin. It will take time. And we will have to force this transition in the economy of the GDR so that it can reorient itself away from West Germany and toward the Soviet Union, above all, and toward the other Socialist countries. That is the most important thing.[129]

The economy's strategic significance in the competition of systems—its role in the success of class struggle between socialism and capitalism, according to the Communist understanding—was as clear to Ulbricht as it was to the Soviet leader. Ulbricht wrote to Khrushchev: "The politburo of the Central Committee of the SED believes that if tensions decrease between the USSR and the United States and West Germany, then the economic battle between West Germany and the GDR will be the primary arena upon which the larger struggle will play out. It is safe to assume that with reduced tension, the Bonn government will exert pressure on the GDR by taking advantage of its economic connections to the GDR and providing credit loans."[130] With the last sentence, Ulbricht foresaw what would become the most important lever in the Federal Republic's Germany policy after the Basic Treaty of 1973, when the FRG began trading West German subsidies for human relief measures (*menschliche Erleichterungen*). Ulbricht predicted this danger in early 1962, indirectly responding to the "main task" that Khrushchev had presented one month earlier. In light of the competing systems in Germany, Ulbricht asked the Soviet Union to help find a "solution to several economic problems in the GDR" but added that this would also create "new problems" for Comecon.[131]

Khrushchev found himself in a complex situation in January 1962, leading him to reject flatly the American negotiation offer to establish an international control authority for the transit routes to West Berlin. The question of equal military capacities played a central role in the game of Berlin poker between Moscow and Washington, and Soviet rocket armament had no end in sight. Moreover, no solution had been reached to address the GDR's economic weakness and dependence upon the Federal Republic. All of these problems required time, and this influenced Khrushchev's decisions on the Berlin question. The wall that ran through the city and closed the gateway to the West for the people of the GDR was the maximum that the Soviet Union could achieve for the time being. It was simply not feasible to hope for an agreement that would respect the GDR's sovereignty and also satisfy Soviet demands.

Speaking to the presidium, Khrushchev bluntly rejected Kennedy's offer by claiming that it clashed with Soviet interests:

> An international thoroughfare or a control authority for this international route— that is nonsense. We would agree to it if we had no other way out. One cannot accept it as the outcome of an understanding but rather [only] as the consequence of a desperate situation reflecting an ultimate demand, since it would mean giving up the rights of the GDR forever. What would cause us to do that? Right now we can take any bridge [along the transit route] and make it unusable, we can fix it up and repair it for a month, for example, and when everything is finished, we can render it unusable for another month. So no international thoroughfares, we will not allow them; it is the territory of the GDR. [With the creation of an access authority,] an international power would come in, carry out the repairs, and collect money for it. It is insanity or total brazenness to suggest a thing like that, and also insanity to accept it.
>
> So this is what I told Thompson more or less in plain terms because [the plan] gives you [the Americans] quite a lot, but for us it does nothing to improve the situation—in fact, it makes the situation worse. Do you want to force us to hang the noose around our own necks? What do you think: Are we in such a desperate situation that you are offering us a noose?[132]

The Soviet leader sharply criticized his foreign minister's conduct during negotiations and threatened him indirectly.[133] His choice of words reveals the fury that Khrushchev was feeling at the time. His most sensitive point concerned a suggestion by Gromyko that the USSR might recognize the Western powers' rights to remain in Berlin:

> Our interpretation of free access to West Berlin is exactly the opposite of the interpretation and outlook of the West. We understand freedom of access to mean precisely what they consider a violation of their rights to free access.
>
> Thompson often asks you [Gromyko]: "How do you see things? Do you mean that the GDR can decide after all?" Yes, the GDR. You interpreted this sentence a bit too liberally in your notes, Comrade Gromyko, but you correct yourself now in conversation because you allow for the possibility that an understanding might be reached on this issue. There can be no understanding on this issue, however, because we are concerned not with immediacy in the GDR but rather with the future. And with the things you say, you are digging a hole at your own expense that will block the way for the GDR's development.
>
> This is an unacceptable way to act. Why? You argue that this is truly the fundamental question, and without a decision on this question we will not reach an agreement. So you are worried that there will be no agreement. But we do not need an agreement; for us it is better to use West Berlin to aggravate [relations] with the West than to make concessions that have an immediate negative effect on the political climate for residents of the GDR. They would be concessions of principle at the expense of the GDR's sovereignty. We cannot afford to do this at all.[134]

Khrushchev insisted with unmistakable clarity that the conflict was not yet over. Once again, he returned to the question of war and peace, evoking Germany under Hitler as the ultimate deterrent:

> Logic, if we want to talk about logic—but war does not follow any logic when it begins. Take Germany: If logic had existed there, the situation would not have come to war. Following his own logic, Hitler would have shot himself. This can happen again. Man loses his balance and overestimates his own strength or his opponent's rationality. And in the present situation, we like to overestimate our opponent's rationality because according to logic, they will not start a war (since they are not losing anything right now). But there are people who do things that, according to logic, they should not do. We cannot rule it out. Therefore we must pursue a reasonable policy.
>
> Moreover, I believe that our material and intellectual wealth is growing every year, and our armed forces are growing, too. Is that a reason to force [the situation] into now or never? Is that the question right now? No, it is the other way around. We do not have to consider this question because the way we see it, if not now, then tomorrow. And if it happens tomorrow instead of now, why is that worse? Does it ruin our foundation? No, not at all. On the contrary. Our strength grows, our impact on the world grows, our influence grows. Why should we agree to take a step that only causes agitation? And imagine that they do react with war. Ultimately the logic of war means either capitulating or accepting the challenge.
>
> So let us pursue this policy logically. If we wanted to take an extreme stance on the issue, then we would have to step away from the offensive. But that is not the correct thing to do. It is important to attack, but to attack cleverly. In this game we

cannot act like the person who plays all the cards in his hand and then reaches for the pistol and shoots himself. We cannot be that player. We do not have the right, and there would be no reason for it.[135]

On the basis of Khrushchev's speech, the presidium of the CPSU approved the new "tactical positions of the government of the USSR in future negotiations with the governments of the United States, England, and France on West Berlin and the German question." The foreign ministry was instructed to gain approval from the other Socialist states on the drafted statute for the "Free City of West-berlin" and its related agreements. Khrushchev made sure to convey instructions for the new negotiation tactics to all of his diplomats:

> Ultimately the issue does not lie in these papers, since you will be conducting a conversation. But your voice should tremble out of confidence and not fear; [it should] boom! And do not be afraid to get worked up; otherwise we will not achieve anything. The last word must be ours. If we initiate our own withdrawal through diplomacy and conversations, your talks will be useless. You have to remain on the offensive in talks with the same confidence that we have had until now.
>
> Can't you see where we began and what we have achieved? The most clever observers attribute the whole thing to me personally: "He got it after all," they say, "he has his Wall." And now they wonder: What would have happened if we had sent our armed forces? Fifty–fifty. 50 percent chance there would have been no war, 50 percent there would have been war after all; the Russians would have defended themselves. And even they say that this is not the way to operate. We did the right thing.[136]

While Khrushchev's speech celebrated his victory in the Berlin Crisis, mere mention of the word "withdrawal" put a damper on his boasting.

Notes

1. To Vasili V. Kuznetsov, dictated by Nikita S. Khrushchev, Pizunda, 2 September 1961, RGANI, F. 52, op. 1, d. 581, sheet 16.
2. Remarks by Nikita S. Khrushchev on a draft of instructions for Andrei A. Gromyko before his meeting with President Kennedy, 29 September 1961, RGANI, F. 52, op. 1, d. 582.
3. Ibid.
4. "Gespräch Chruschtschows mit dem belgischen Außenminister, Paul-Henri Spaak, am 19. September 1961," in Wettig, *Chruschtschows Westpolitik*, 460.
5. "Bericht des Außenministers Spaak über ein Gespräch mit Ministerpräsident Chruščev," 21 September 1961, in Bundesministerium für innerdeutsche Beziehungen, *Dokumente zur Deutsch-landpolitik*, series IV, vol. 7/1, 482.

6. "Anweisung an Gen. Gromyko für sein Treffen mit Präsident Kennedy," dictated by Nikita S. Khrushchev, 29 September 1961, RGANI, F. 52, op. 1, d. 364, sheets 16–18.

7. Steininger, *Berlinkrise*, 275.

8. Ibid.

9. Nikita S. Khrushchev, notes for a draft of instructions to Andrei A. Gromyko before his meeting with President Kennedy, 29 September 1961, RGANI, F. 52, op. 1, d. 582.

10. Steininger, *Berlinkrise*, 276.

11. "Schlusswort des Ersten Sekretärs des ZK der KPdSU, Nikita S. Chruschtschow, auf dem XXII. Parteitag," 27 October 1961, in Presseamt des Ministerrats der DDR, *XXII. Parteitag der Kommunistischen Partei der Sowjetunion*, 3022.

12. "Rede des Genossen Walter Ulbricht auf dem XXII. Parteitag, 20.10.1961," in Presseamt des Ministerrats der DDR, *XXII. Parteitag der Kommunistischen Partei der Sowjetunion*, 3045.

13. Wettig, "Chruščev," 670.

14. Küsters, "Reaktionen," 730.

15. Arnulf Baring, *Sehr geehrter Herr Bundeskanzler! Heinrich von Brentano im Briefwechsel mit Konrad Adenauer 1949–1964* (Hamburg, 1974), 330–31.

16. Küsters, "Reaktionen," 730–31.

17. Central Committee of the CPSU to the Central Committee of the SED, strictly confidential, 28 August 1961, SAPMO-BArch, DY 30/3386.

18. The word "we" is missing in the Russian text.

19. "Gespräch Chruschtschows mit dem belgischen Außenminister, Paul-Henri Spaak, am 19. September 1961," in Wettig, *Chruschtschows Westpolitik*, 453.

20. Wettig, *Chruschtschows Berlin-Krise*, 207.

21. Uhl, *Krieg um Berlin?*, 155–56.

22. Ibid., 165.

23. "Vortrag von Armeegeneral Hoffmann zur Auswertung der Kommandostabsübung Burja," n.d., quoted in Uhl, *Krieg um Berlin?*, 168.

24. Hoffman gives the impression that NATO would make the first nuclear strike. However, planning by the Soviet General Staff suggests the opposite. Uhl discusses this contradiction in further detail. Uhl, *Krieg um Berlin?*, 168–69.

25. Ibid., 169–70.

26. Ibid., 180.

27. Steininger, *Berlinkrise*, 282. For the text of the plan approved by Kennedy, see "U.S. Policy on Military Actions in a Berlin Conflict," 20 October 1961, online by CIA, Freedom of Information Act, the Berlin Wall Collection, http://www.foia.cia.gov/collection/berlin-wall-collection.

28. Steininger, *Berlinkrise*, 282; see also Sean M. Maloney, "Notfallplanung für Berlin: Vorläufer der Flexible Response 1958–1963," *Militärgeschichte* 7, no. 1 (1997): 3–15.

29. Steininger, *Berlinkrise*, 283.

30. Ibid., 284.

31. "Ansprache des Vorsitzenden des Staatsrates der DDR Walter Ulbricht im Fernsehen und Rundfunk," 18 September 1961, manuscript, SAPMO-BArch, NY 4182/657.

32. Walter Ulbricht, 20 September 1961, SAPMO-BArch, NY 4182/660, 103. Peter Florin sent out the final version of the speech with the remark: "I have removed everything from the text indicating that this was a conference of the brother parties, since we did not keep an official protocol." Peter Florin to Walter Ulbricht, 6 October 1961, SAPMO-BArch, NY 4182/660.

33. Rudolf Dölling, "Information," strictly confidential, 28 August 1961, through politburo, 15 October 1961, SAPMO-BArch, DY 30/3497.

34. Otto Winzer to Walter Ulbricht, 16 September 1961, marked "Urgent!," SAPMO-BArch, DY 30/3509.

35. "Probleme und Aufgaben im Zusammenhang mit der Vorbereitung und dem Abschluß eines Friedensvertrages mit der DDR," SAPMO-BArch, DY 30/3509.

36. Ibid.

37. "Protokoll über Besprechung beim Genossen Walter Ulbricht am 16.9.1961," 20 September 1961, SAPMO-BArch, DY 30/3509.

38. Ibid.

39. Ibid.

40. Ibid.

41. Sepp Schwab (1897–1977) joined the KPD in 1919 and emigrated to the Soviet Union in 1930, where he worked for the Communist International. In 1944, he became a member of the Working Commission of the KPD for Postwar Planning in Moscow, and from 1956 to 1964, served as deputy foreign minister of the GDR.

42. Walter Ulbricht to Nikita S. Khrushchev, 16 September 1961, SAPMO-BArch, DY 30/3509.

43. Ibid.

44. Ibid.

45. Nikita S. Khrushchev to Walter Ulbricht, 28 September 1961, SAPMO-BArch, DY 30/3509.

46. Sepp Schwab to Walter Ulbricht, 5 October 1961, SAPMO-BArch, DY 30/3509. The document is marked "Top Secret!" At the end of the letter appears a handwritten note: "All documents exist in four copies. All drafts have been shredded."

47. "1. Entwurf des Abkommens zwischen der DDR und der Freien Stadt Westberlin über den Luftverkehr von und nach der Freien Stadt Westberlin." Handwritten note, "2. Variante." Attachment to a letter from Sepp Schwab to Walter Ulbricht, 5 October 1961, marked "Top Secret!" SAPMO-BArch, DY 30/3509.

48. Sepp Schwab to Walter Ulbricht, 5 October 1961, SAPMO-BArch, DY 30/3509.

49. Lemke, *Berlinkrise*, 174.

50. Walter Ulbricht to Nikita S. Khrushchev, Moscow, 30 October 1961, SAPMO-BArch, NY 4182/1206.

51. Otto Winzer to Walter Ulbricht, Willi Stoph, and Karl Maron, 21 August 1961, SAPMO-BArch, DY 30/3509.

52. Ibid.

53. Walter Ulbricht to Otto Winzer, 21 August 1961, SAPMO-BArch, DY 30/3509.

54. Walter Ulbricht to Nikita S. Khrushchev, 16 September 1961, SAPMO-BArch, DY 30/3509.

55. Nikita S. Khrushchev to Walter Ulbricht, 28 September 1961, SAPMO-BArch, DY 30/3509.

56. See Lemke, *Berlinkrise*, 174.

57. Wettig, *Chruschtschows Berlin-Krise*, 197.

58. Steininger, *Berlinkrise*, 291.

59. Walter Ulbricht to Nikita S. Khrushchev, Moscow, 30 October 1961, SAPMO-BArch, NY 4182/1206.

60. "Memorandum by the President's Military Representative (Taylor)," Washington, 24 August 1961, in U.S. Dept. of State, *FRUS 1961–1963*, vol. 14, 364–65.

61. "Memorandum From the President's Military Representative (Taylor) to President Kennedy," Washington, 4 September 1961, in U.S. Dept. of State, *FRUS 1961–1963*, vol. 14, 392.

62. Wettig, *Chruschtschows Berlin-Krise*, 198.

63. Ibid., 197–99.

64. Falin, *Politische Erinnerungen*, 346.

65. "Erklärung des sowjetischen Außenministers A. Gromyko an USA-Botschafter Thompson," 27 October 1961, SAPMO-BArch, DY 30/3509.

66. Steininger, *Berlinkrise*, 294.

67. "Telegram from Lucius D. Clay to Secretary of State Dean Rusk," Berlin, 25 October 1961, reproduced in Steininger, *Berlinkrise*, 296.

68. "Telegram from the Department of State to the Mission at Berlin," Washington, 26 October 1961, in U.S. Dept. of State, *FRUS 1961–1963*, vol. 14, 540.

69. Walter Ulbricht to Nikita S. Khrushchev, Moscow, 30 October 1961, SAPMO-BArch, NY 4182/1206.

70. Steininger, *Berlinkrise*, 299.

71. Ibid.

72. Ibid., 297–98.

73. Fursenko and Naftali, *Khrushchev's Cold War*, 404.

74. Wettig, *Chruschtschows Berlin-Krise*, 200.

75. Ibid.

76. See "Gespräch Chruschtschows mit dem belgischen Außenminister, Paul-Henri Spaak, am 19 September 1961," in Wettig, *Chruschtschows Westpolitik*, 465.

77. Walter Ulbricht to the SED Politburo (attn.: Hermann Matern), Moscow, 27 October 1961, SAPMO-BArch, DY 30/3291.

78. Walter Ulbricht to the SED Politburo (attn.: Hermann Matern), Moscow, 29 October 1961, SAPMO-BArch, DY 30/3291.

79. The expression "salami tactics" was coined by Mátyás Rákosi, head of the Hungarian Communist Party after 1945, to describe the way in which his party disposed of the opposition factions (like slices of salami) in order to maintain a monopoly on power.

80. "Gespräch Chruschtschows mit dem Ersten Sekretär des ZK der SED, Walter Ulbricht, am 2. November 1961," in Wettig, *Chruschtschows Westpolitik*, 485.

81. Steininger, *Mauerbau*, 313.

82. Walter Ulbricht to Nikita S. Khrushchev, Moscow, 30 October 1961, SAPMO-BArch, NY 4182/1206.

83. Ibid.

84. In the draft corrected by Ulbricht, "connection route" (*Verbindungsweg*) has been changed to "connecting traffic" (*Verbindungsverkehr*). The word "block" (*sperren*) has been changed to "close" (*schließen*).

85. Walter Ulbricht to Nikita S. Khrushchev, Moscow, 30 October 1961, SAPMO-BArch, NY 4182/1206.

86. Ibid. In his draft, Ulbricht crossed out the following sentence: "It must now be determined whether or not the departure of the Soviet officer from the central air traffic control will help advance a settlement between the USSR and the United States at this time."

87. "Gespräch Chruschtschows mit dem Ersten Sekretär des ZK der SED, Walter Ulbricht, am 2. November 1961," in Wettig, *Chruschtschows Westpolitik*, 471. The Soviet delegation at this meeting included A. Gromyko, A. Kosygin, M. Pervukhin, and A. Mikoyan; the SED delegation included E. Honecker, F. Ebert, and P. Verner.

88. Special types of steel and certain mechanical tools were among the "deficit" goods that could not be produced in either East Germany or the other Comecon countries. The GDR therefore relied on inter-German trade to acquire them from the Federal Republic, both for the country's own use and for the production of manufactured products for other Comecon countries, especially the USSR.

89. Khrushchev is referring to a situation in which an embargo by the West would restrict economic activities to the other Comecon countries.

90. The word "mutually" (*gegenseitig*) was written into the protocol by hand.

91. According to Marxist-Leninist thought, capitalism and socialism—along with the classes and forces whose interests they embodied—stood in antagonistic opposition to one another. In other words, they were eternal enemies.

92. "Gespräch Chruschtschows mit dem Ersten Sekretär des ZK der SED, Walter Ulbricht, am 2. November 1961," in Wettig, *Chruschtschows Westpolitik*, 472–73.

93. Ibid., 474.

94. Ibid., 488.

95. Ibid., 481.

96. Ibid., 486.

97. Ibid., 484.

98. Roth, *Insel*, 221.

99. Steininger, *Berlinkrise*, 268. Italics in the original.

100. Ibid., 279.

101. Ibid., 303.

102. Ibid., 300–301.

103. Ibid., 303–4.

104. Ibid., 305.

105. Schwarz, *Adenauer: Der Staatsmann*, 739.

106. Steininger, *Berlinkrise*, 307.

107. Notes from a talk between Comrade Gromyko and Ambassador Thompson, 2 January 1962, SAPMO-BArch, DY 30/3510. For Rusk's instructions to Thompson before the meeting, see "Telegram From the Department of State to the Embassy in the Soviet Union," Washington, 28 December 1961, in U.S. Dept. of State, *FRUS 1961–1963*, vol. 14, 709–13. For Thompson's report to Rusk after the meeting, see "Telegram From the Embassy in the Soviet Union to the Department of State," Moscow, 2 January 1962, in U.S. Dept. of State, *FRUS 1961–1963*, vol. 14, 720–24.

108. Notes from a talk between Comrade Gromyko and Ambassador Thompson, 2 January 1962, SAPMO-BArch, DY 30/3510.

109. Ibid.

110. Ibid.

111. Ibid.

112. A thorough discussion of this shift can be found in the next section of this chapter, "Khrushchev's Change of Course: Negotiations, but No Agreement."

113. "Kurze Darlegung der Vorschläge über die Schaffung einer internationalen Administration für Berlin in Fragen des Zuganges, überreicht vom Botschafter der USA L. Thompson an Genossen A. A. Gromyko," 1 February 1962; "Vorschlag über die Wiedervereinigung Berlins, überreicht vom Botschafter der USA L. Thompson an Genossen A. A. Gromyko," 1 February 1962, German translations from the Russian translations of the English originals, SAPMO-BArch, DY 30/3510.

114. "Kurze Information über die Zusammenkunft des Ministers für Auswärtige Angelegenheiten der UdSSR A. A. Gromyko mit dem Botschafter der USA in Moskau," undated (probably 1 February 1962), German translation of the Russian original, SAPMO-BArch, DY 30/3510.

115. "Erklärung des Ministers für Auswärtige Angelegenheiten der UdSSR A. A. Gromyko an den Botschafter der USA in Moskau L. Thompson," 9 February 1962, SAPMO-BArch, DY 30/3510. This document also contains the handwritten instruction: "Points marked in red should not be reported to Ulbricht."

116. Steininger, *Berlinkrise*, 320.

117. Ibid., 321.

118. Ibid., 321–24.

119. Ibid., 324.

120. In the fall of 1961, the Kremlin operated under the impression that an agreement to Soviet satisfaction on the key issues of the Western powers' presence in and access to Berlin was within reach. In early 1962, the United States made it clear that its stance on both of these points had not changed.

121. John F. Kennedy, interview with Aleksei Adzhubei (Khrushchev's son-in-law), Hyannis Port, MA, 25 November 1961. An excerpt from this interview can be found in U.S. Dept. of State, *Documents on Germany*, 801–4.

122. "Gespräch Chruschtschows mit dem ersten Sekretär des ZK der SED, Walter Ulbricht, 26 February 1962," excerpt, in Wettig, *Chruschtschows Westpolitik*, 531.

123. "Stenogramm der Sitzung des Präsidiums des ZK der KPdSU, am 8. Januar 1962," in Wettig, *Chruschtschows Westpolitik*, 516.

124. Ibid., 504.

125. After Eisenhower entered office in 1953, his administration announced a "rollback" policy toward communism.
126. "Stenogramm der Sitzung des Präsidiums des ZK der KPdSU, am 8. Januar 1962," in Wettig, *Chruschtschows Westpolitik*, 507.
127. Ibid., 508.
128. Khrushchev is referring to his conversation with Ulbricht on 2 November 1961.
129. "Stenogramm der Sitzung des Präsidiums des ZK der KPdSU, am 8. Januar 1962," in Wettig, *Chruschtschows Westpolitik*, 509.
130. Walter Ulbricht to Nikita S. Khrushchev, Berlin, 8 Februar 1962, SAPMO-BArch, DY 30/3510. Ulbricht was informed of the content of the conversations between Gromyko and Thompson soon after they took place.
131. Ibid.
132. "Stenogramm der Sitzung des Präsidiums des ZK der KPdSU, am 8. Januar 1962," in Wettig, *Chruschtschows Westpolitik*, 513.
133. Negotiations rely on trust between the negotiation partners, and confidential information can sometimes change hands. In the talks between Thompson and Gromyko, this confidential piece of information was the identity of the new Soviet ambassador to Washington. Drawing reference to this, Khrushchev threatened Gromyko and his entire ministry: "In fact, Comrade Gromyko, we will have to take a look at the Foreign Ministry. These days, the fear of the Stalin era has diminished and disappeared. How did Thompson find out, for example, that we will send Ambassador Dobrynin [to Washington]? Thompson received this information confidentially at a time when it had not been released to anyone. And that is the kind of thing that very few people should know. Me and you. Who else knew aside from you?" Ibid., 511.
134. Ibid., 514.
135. Ibid., 516–17.
136. Ibid., 517.

Chapter 19

REPERCUSSIONS FOR GERMANY
AND A SHIFT IN TROUBLE AREAS

Both German states had to reorient themselves to the new constellation that Khrushchev had orchestrated. The situation only affected the two German governments at first, but before long, the permanence of German division encompassed both societies separated by the Wall. Ulbricht was unable to defy Khrushchev's decision not to conclude a separate peace treaty with the GDR or transfer control rights along West Berlin's transit routes to the East German state. The SED had to acknowledge and cope with the new Soviet course; reunification propaganda gave way to the demand for international recognition. Adenauer, meanwhile, could not prevent Kennedy from continuing negotiations with the Soviet Union on Berlin. At the same time, the Wall formed the basis of a reorientation in West German Ostpolitik and policy on Germany. The beginning of this path was marked by open conflict between Kennedy and the Adenauer administration over the proposed international control authority for transit routes to West Berlin, as well as by Ulbricht's adaptation to Moscow's new Berlin policy. One thing was clear to everyone: the wall through Berlin buried German hopes of rapid reunification—an outcome that Ulbricht celebrated.

Ulbricht and the New Situation

On 8 February 1962, Ulbricht requested an urgent meeting with Khrushchev, preferably before the end of the month.[1] The subsequent conference of CPSU and SED delegations on 26 February 1962 in Moscow marked the hour of truth. Before the assembled delegations, Ulbricht wondered "how . . . to proceed on the issue of a peace treaty and West Berlin. We have been making propaganda for years. But where shall we go from here?"[2] Aware of the American negotiation positions and Gromyko's replies in the exploratory talks, Ulbricht continued by assessing the discussions:

> So far, Gromyko and Thompson have tried to get a feel for each other, and over the course of this process, the Americans have increased their demands. They never used to pose such enormous demands as the transfer of control along the entire Autobahn and in all of Berlin. This means that Kennedy is following Adenauer's advice—the only difference is that [Kennedy] is more flexible.
>
> We assume that if these negotiations make inroads on the question of West Berlin, then it might be possible to move closer to their position in the context of a summit conference. But we cannot imagine that this would achieve settlements significant enough that the Western troops would withdraw from Berlin and the situation there would normalize. We do not believe that results of this kind will be possible this year, or that it would be beneficial for the USSR and the GDR to give guarantees on access to West Berlin. Such guarantees would only make sense if the situation in West Berlin did in fact normalize.[3]

The SED Politburo had drawn conclusions from the course of negotiations regarding the circumstances under which a peace treaty could still be signed. Compared to Ulbricht's original goal of transforming West Berlin into a "Free City" under the SED's control and requiring all Western troops to withdraw, the new East German proposal contained severe concessions. The new peace treaty, which Ulbricht considered "bad," only strove for international recognition of the GDR and left the situation open regarding Berlin and the control of its transit routes. Also absent was any mention of the Soviet Union transferring rights in Berlin to the GDR. To the contrary: the contested issues related to West Berlin would provide the Soviet Union with adequate means of exerting pressure on the Americans without relinquishing anything to the GDR.

However, Ulbricht apparently had no knowledge of the 8 January resolution by the presidium of the CPSU approving the new Soviet line in negotiations on Berlin. Explaining the recommendations of the SED Politburo for how to move forward in negotiations, Ulbricht still referred to Khrushchev's former position of wanting to push through a peace treaty:

> We also request that negotiations between Gromyko and Thompson—or over other diplomatic channels among the four powers or at the summit meeting, if it takes place—be carried out in a way that it is possible to seriously address the question of a peace treaty by the end of the summer, that is, to hold a conference of foreign ministers from the states of the Warsaw Pact in order to prepare for a peace treaty. You will ask, "But what do we get out of this?" To respond in general terms, I can say that you would get a "bad" peace treaty, so to speak, that is the crux of the matter. The issue of the GDR's borders would be solved, along with the issue of the capital of the GDR and the elimination of remnants from the Second World War on the GDR's territory. But the issue of air traffic and all questions related to transportation routes would remain as they are today. This would mean that the GDR's positions would improve, that its authority would gradually increase and its relations

to other countries would develop. If we were to conclude this type of peace treaty, the Americans would have nothing against it. The only change would be that all foreign citizens would have to show their identification papers at the borders to the GDR.[4] This means that the Soviet government could continue using Westberlin to exert pressure. The peace treaty would not touch current regulations of the airways, so this could be used to exert pressure, too.

Thus, it is possible to conclude the peace treaty and attach a protocol stating the issues for which the Soviet government has reached an agreement with the Western powers on Westberlin, as well as the issues for which no agreement has yet been reached. From our perspective, these negotiations could continue for years to come. But it would all mean that foreign citizens, even members of the military, could not enter Democratic Berlin[5] without a visa from us. This will naturally heighten tension to a certain extent. But as long as we, the Socialist countries, do not want war, and as long as no one knows when negotiations will end, we should clarify at least some of the questions now, even if we leave others to resolve later. We believe that this would be the purpose of a peace treaty.

From an internal standpoint, [a peace treaty] is necessary in order to strengthen our position. We cannot hold elections to the People's Chamber without a peace treaty because we need an election platform.

This is the position of our politburo. We therefore suggest modifying the proposal by the Warsaw Pact as follows, in order to reach an agreement on Westberlin before concluding a peace treaty: negotiations with the Western powers should continue, but as long as there seems to be no chance of normalizing the situation in Westberlin through these negotiations, they should be postponed in favor of discussing issues that threaten us with war or economic blockade.

Of course we understand that from our vantage point in Berlin, we cannot always judge the situation comprehensively. However, it must be taken into account that after years of our propaganda for the peace treaty, the people of the GDR no longer have much faith in us.[6]

The issue of credibility and the SED's interpretive monopoly in the GDR led Ulbricht to make one more request:

Recently the Bonn government publicized the demands presented by Thompson and started a campaign in their support. We decided not to initiate a counter-campaign to avoid giving the impression of wanting to disrupt ongoing negotiations between Gromyko and Thompson by stating our positions publicly. However, the first round of these negotiations concluded without achieving results of any kind. So during the second round, we should at least be able to address Thompson's positions in the first round. We cannot allow Adenauer to be the only one employing this kind of propaganda.

We would like you to respond, in case you have any objections to this plan.[7]

Even on an issue of this kind, the SED was unable to make an independent decision. Khrushchev's response reflected the resolution by the presidium of the CPSU, but he refrained from mentioning the resolution itself to Ulbricht and his delegation—apparently it remained a party secret. Khrushchev opened his reply to

Ulbricht like an obliging father soothing his child, an attitude that highlighted the relationship of dependency in a quite humiliating way: "Comrade Ulbricht, I think your tone is too loud. There has always been propaganda from the West, but this whole thing isn't worth a hill of beans. You are getting yourself worked up for no reason. Stay calm, go easy on your nerves. Our opponent is still strong."[8]

He went on to concede that the GDR was not in the same position as the Soviet Union, and the existence of West Berlin still had a powerful negative effect on the awareness of the GDR's population. This provided a context for him to share the new course of Soviet Berlin policy with the SED:

> Of course we see that there are other circumstances [in the GDR]. A good portion of the East German population listens to West German radio, and this portion will continue to listen to it. It is all anti-Communist propaganda, and whoever wants to listen will go ahead and listen. I can see that Adenauer has hit you in a vulnerable place and is rubbing it in. We thought that West Berlin was now a lever in our hands to agitate the West. But actually it appears that things are the other way around.
>
> I believe that on 13 August, we achieved the maximum of what we could get out of West Berlin. Now it is our job to continue working diligently.[9]

Khrushchev also informed Ulbricht of his decision not to sign a separate peace treaty with the GDR. The peace treaty, he asserted, was no longer on the table: "I cannot understand you when you say that the main problem is signing a peace treaty right now. I am of a different opinion. The main problem is securing our economy."[10] To conclude, Khrushchev offered a positive evaluation of the progress so far:

> You and I have to pursue our own policies. Today we are stronger than yesterday, and tomorrow we will be even stronger. Right now there are fundamental obstacles blocking the way to a peace treaty. I said that there would *probably* be no war, *probably*. But who can vouch for those idiots? What is compelling us to sign a peace treaty? Do we lose anything without one? No.
>
> In 1958 and before 13 August, our prospects did not look promising. At that time I gave a lot of thought to how we could improve the situation. But now Ulbricht has built the Wall and laughs at the British and Americans, and they are forced to deal with it. The Americans wanted to tear down the Wall with bulldozers, but we advanced our tanks. They advanced theirs, too, but were then forced to withdraw. Now Kennedy is being pushed to do something after all. But he says, "I cannot do anything about it." Isn't this enough for you? You are insatiable!
>
> For us, the peace treaty is a means of exerting pressure on West Berlin. If we choose to, we can resolve this issue as well. But we will not sign anything without you because it is your problem.[11]

Khrushchev exhibited a certain clever cynicism in portraying his own decision not to sign an agreement with the Americans as proof of his loyalty to Ulbricht. Ulbricht informed Khrushchev that the economic situation in West Berlin had stabilized thanks to large subsidies from the West German government—in contrast to the decaying West Berlin portrayed in East German propaganda. Khrushchev summed up his position: "Our line is correct. We believe it is important to exert constant pressure and work toward a peace treaty, but we cannot view it as a matter of life or death. Instead [we must strive] tirelessly for a peace treaty. Even if we assume that capitalism will exist for fifty more years, can we still make progress now? Yes, we can, with 13 August we can."[12]

Looking back, Herbert Häber[13] comments on the outcome of Ulbricht's Berlin policy by highlighting two fundamental strategic mistakes on the part of the SED leader:

> Ulbricht's policy was based on two major strategic errors, and these became his trap:
>
> The first was Ulbricht's belief and knowledge that the Soviet Union would determine his fate—just as the entire development of the GDR cannot be extracted from Soviet policy on Germany. When the leadership of the CPSU tasked Pieck and Ulbricht with shaping the Soviet occupation zone into a democratic Germany, [the two] were already caught up in the first illusion: that the Soviet Union would overcome the devastation of war very quickly and rise up to be the leading European power politically, intellectually, and economically. They believed in the victory of communism and therefore also the Soviet Union. They thought it would be possible within the Socialist camp to develop an equal partnership between the GDR and the Soviet Union. This proved to be wrong, along with [their] evaluation of the political and economic potential of the Western zones, the future Federal Republic.
>
> The SED propagated the Soviet division of the world into two camps: one of progress and peace, the other of imperialism and war. The party's early documents claim that the West was plagued by collapse and decay, whereas the East experienced permanent growth and progress. Both were illusions.
>
> Communists in the Federal Republic were isolated quickly; the KPD was banned in 1956. Ulbricht's expectations that the West would fall into crisis turned out to be wrong. Instead, the West began a long, persistent economic recovery. Absorbed in his own belief that he could build a unity of action with the SPD, the majority party of the workers' movement, to address both the national question and the shape of internal German relations, Ulbricht made a second strategic error. His vision of the SPD as it had existed during the Weimar Republic no longer applied to the postwar SPD of West Germany.
>
> Of course, one is always wiser in hindsight. But it should have been possible even then to see some things more clearly, with greater objectivity, if Ulbricht had not always followed Moscow's line—but at that time, the GDR had no alternative.[14]

As a result of the Berlin Crisis, the SED had to accept limited territorial sovereignty in the GDR and East Berlin until the end of the state's existence. Article 6 of the 1964 "Treaty of Friendship, Mutual Assistance and Cooperation" between the Soviet Union and the GDR contained an agreement by both states to view "West Berlin as an independent political unit." But the Soviet Union did not transfer any rights to the GDR as a sovereign state to control the transit routes between the Federal Republic and West Berlin. It was only with the Quadripartite Agreement of 1971–72, in the context of the Federal Republic's Eastern treaties, that the four powers reached an understanding on the transit routes to West Berlin.

Adenauer's Conflict with Kennedy
over the Transit Routes to West Berlin

Adenauer won the Bundestag elections for the last time in 1961 and built a coalition government with the Free Democratic Party (FDP). Policy on Berlin and Germany played an important role in the coalition agreement. The FDP condoned "Adenauer's hard line toward the readiness of the Americans and British to make concessions," as stated clearly in the agreement:

> In accordance with the Basic Law and the Federal Republic's treaties, especially the Germany Treaty, the new Federal Government considers German unity to be the central goal of its policies. [The government] considers Article 7 of the Germany Treaty to be the most important basis of German hope for reunification; in it the United States, Great Britain, and France declared the restoration of German unity to be the goal of their joint policy. The Basic Law and Article 7 do not allow the following:
>
> - a reduction in the object of German unity by dissolving or loosening ties between Berlin and the Federal Republic;
> - a reduction in the object of German unity by recognizing in any way a German state on the territory of the Soviet occupation zone;
> - a reduction in the object of German unity by directly or indirectly sanctioning the unlawful measures of 13 August 1961 or augmenting these measures by recognizing the right of the Soviet Union or GDR authorities to control civilian air traffic to and from Berlin;
> - a settlement of the border issue before the conclusion of a peace treaty for all of Germany.[15]

The FDP coupled this declaration of the government's basic position on German unity with a demand that the new West German government "try to win the upper hand on Germany policy, both for itself and for the West."[16]

In late November, Adenauer visited the American president. He formulated a letter to the governing mayor of Berlin upon his return, laying out his assessment of the situation. Adenauer assured Brandt that the Federal Government would defend its ties to West Berlin politically, but that he supported Kennedy in entering exploratory talks with the Soviet Union to reach an isolated solution on the access routes:

> At their second meeting from 20 to 22 November 1961 in Washington, Adenauer got the impression that Kennedy would stand up to Khrushchev more firmly in the future. The chancellor rejected any discussion of disengagement and recognition of the GDR. Kennedy reaffirmed ties between the Federal Republic and West Berlin and asserted the need for free access to Berlin. The original four-power rights were to remain in place. Adenauer agreed to bilateral contact with East Berlin at the lowest level and was prepared to issue a renunciation of violence with regard to the Oder-Neisse question. Moreover, he conceded that in a worst-case scenario, the Bundeswehr would take part in a war to maintain the freedom of West Berlin. At

the same time, he stated his opposition to the use of nuclear weapons. Secretly he hoped for resistance from de Gaulle as well.

On 14 December 1961, Adenauer once again gave Brandt a written guarantee that the Federal Government considered "the preservation of freedom and viability in Berlin" to be an "absolute necessity," not only for Germany but also for the West as whole. The defense of the three essentials, for which the United States was prepared to take "every risk," would not suffice "to foil the Communists' salami tactics." It was beyond dispute that the West must demand the dismantling of the Wall in negotiations, a point that Adenauer had just reiterated to Kennedy directly. The East made no indication of cooperating in the foreseeable future, but it was crucial from the "national and human standpoint to insist upon these inalienable demands continually and repeatedly." Adenauer denied press reports that the Federal Government had changed its course in favor of an isolationist Berlin solution. The issue of Berlin, he argued, could only be resolved in the context of reunification. In light of "Soviet intransigence," this was unlikely. Therefore, the Federal Government should support the Western powers in trying to reach an "arrangement" on the access routes to Berlin in order to improve the situation, as long as those efforts did not interfere with prospects for reunification. If Moscow once again articulated its desire for a peace treaty, the West would reintroduce its peace plan and the Federal Republic would demand a popular referendum. The main reason not to insist upon convening a peace conference immediately was still the necessity to build a unified German government first. If [the FRG] were to agree to hold a kind of pre-peace conference to set the basic principles of a peace treaty, it would weaken [West Germany's] own position, namely, that a peace treaty could only be signed with Germany as a whole. It would endanger the credibility of [West Germany's] reunification policy and offer Moscow an "alibi to conclude a separate peace" settlement. It would also provoke the danger of relinquishing important components of the peace treaty, such as the border procedure, under pressure from the Soviets. Brandt could be pleased with the Berlin guarantee at the end of Adenauer's letter: "We will also remain dedicated to protecting the ties between West Berlin and the Federal Republic. Like you, I am of the opinion that we must show national solidarity in these difficult times. Therefore, the Federal Government will always keep Berlin abreast of new developments." With these closing words, Adenauer and Brandt's common interests were restored.[17]

Exploratory talks between the Kennedy administration and the Soviet Union took as their starting point the Soviet Ultimatum and not the Germany Treaty, whose goals the Soviet Union had already rejected in 1955. In April 1962, conflict erupted between Bonn and Washington. Before the new round of American–Soviet talks could begin in Washington, German Ambassador Grewe was "handed several papers with instructions to position ourselves on them within the next 48 hours. The content of the documents: new proposals for Rusk to submit to Dobrynin. I accepted them with reservations considering the unusual and unreasonably short deadline and conveyed them to Bonn immediately."[18]

In addition to the plan for an international authority to control the transit routes and air traffic, the American papers contained further points that Rusk intended to negotiate with the Soviet ambassador Dobrynin: "American–Soviet agreements on the non-proliferation of nuclear weapons; exchange of non-aggression agreements between the East and West (which would certainly pose delicate problems if the West forced its access to Berlin in the case of a blockade!); the establishment of Germany-wide committees to regulate 'technical' issues; and the proposal for a permanent conference of deputy foreign ministers from the Western Allies and the Soviet Union, to convene regularly in Berlin."[19] When this paper arrived at the Federal Chancellery on 11 April, it set off a "flurry of agitation." During a meeting with Foreign Minister Schröder and Schröder's state secretary, Karl Carstens, Adenauer noted that the paper only partially represented a revision of the 22 March proposal "that the Federal Foreign Office had known about for a long time. Moreover, Gerhard Schröder had met with his American counterpart Rusk in Lausanne on 13 March but never reported to the chancellery on the outcome of that talk. Adenauer's suspicion grew stronger that the soft American line found an accomplice in his own foreign minister."[20]

After this discussion, Heinrich von Brentano, head of the CDU/CSU, requested a meeting in his office with Vice Chancellor Erich Mende (FDP) and the head of the SPD, Erich Ollenhauer, on 12 April—against the will of Foreign Minister Schröder. The chancellor ordered Schröder and Carstens to report back to him "on the final version of the American plans for Berlin." Von Brentano and Heinrich Krone[21] expressed their sharp opposition to the documents. "If it came to a resolution with the Soviets on this basis, there would not be enough moving trucks in Berlin; Berlin would be a dead city."[22] The chairmen of the SPD and FDP, in contrast, were more timid in their judgment.

The Federal Republic's Ostpolitik and Germany policy were in transition. This is evident beyond Schröder's conversation with Rusk; in early April, the top ranks of the FDP had internally discussed a paper by Wolfgang Schollwer "that proposed recognizing the two-state nature of Germany and striving for a nuclear-free, militarily weakened zone in Central Europe. Eastern concessions: removal of the Ulbricht group, destalinization in the GDR, a Soviet guarantee of Berlin's freedom, and the reestablishment of unimpeded travel in Germany."[23] Schollwer's paper, along with the SPD's Germany Plan of 1959, politically manifested a Germany policy that sought intermediary solutions and a softening of the division. These positions saw recognition of the GDR as the inevitable basis of any future policy.

In the debate over the United States' negotiation concept, Mende supported Adenauer's position. Of course the American proposals were strictly confidential, and the West German government could not seriously ask Kennedy to refrain from undertaking exploratory talks with the Soviet Union. But the only hope of influencing these talks was to present the proposals for public discussion. "Adenauer knew that there was no better way to inform the press than to hold a dramatic meeting of the chairmen of the political factions right in the middle of the Bundeshaus.[24] No wonder [West German radio broadcaster] Deutschlandfunk was already reporting [on the proposals] by the evening of 13 April."[25] Schwarz suggests that it was Heinrich von Brentano who "informed the press." Dietrich Schwarzkopf, the reporter responsible for the Deutschlandfunk report, contradicts the historian somewhat. He recalls that von Brentano alerted him and Günter

Müggenburg to the American proposals without revealing their precise content. Once they were aware that the American papers existed, it was not difficult for the reporters to confirm their assumptions through a conversation with Willy Brandt. With a bit of further research, they were able to publish the content of the documents later that day:

> We informed *New York Times* correspondent Sidney Gruson, with whom we had a regular exchange of information—also to give the story more "weight." Gruson asked the Dutch ambassador (whom he knew well) whether he was aware of the American proposals. He said yes and confirmed the accuracy of our assumptions.
>
> I was the first to spread the information over Deutschlandfunk on 13 April. This elicited Kennedy's wrath, since he assumed that Ambassador Grewe had leaked the content of the papers. Grewe suspected Adenauer. Grewe, whom Kennedy disliked anyway, could not remain in his position. After publication, the American proposals were essentially "burned," especially the points concerning an access authority and a permanent Berlin conference of advisors. We did the Adenauer government a big favor but brought great harm to Ambassador Grewe, whom I respect very much. Neither outcome was our intention; we just wanted the story. A few days later, the deputy press officer, Krüger, patted me on the shoulder and warned me not to get Deutschlandfunk too involved in conflicts between the Allies. I did not promise him anything.[26]

The publication of the confidential documents led to official protests by the American government and the removal of Ambassador Grewe from Washington. Rusk could no longer convey the proposals to the new Soviet ambassador.[27]

De Gaulle reacted to the British and American negotiating positions with severity similar to that of the federal chancellor. He was Adenauer's partner in this conflict. In a note to his foreign minister on 14 April, de Gaulle "lambasted 'the insanity with which they propel themselves into negotiations' and instructed him to condemn the preparatory talks and their content. His invitation to Adenauer soon after to make a state visit to France was thus not only a strategic move in European politics but also a demonstration of solidarity on the issue of Germany and Berlin."[28] Adenauer used his spring vacation to seek clarity on the future course of West German foreign policy. To complicate matters further, Adenauer's differences with the Kennedy administration were also entangled in his conflict with Great Britain over the shape of Western Europe's political union, which London rejected entirely. "'Remain in a bloc of only France and Germany': this was the new line that crystallized more clearly every day. Adenauer now resolved to risk open conflict with Washington. He disapproved of the approach by his Federal Foreign Office, which relentlessly articulated its trust in the American negotiation strategy."[29] Adenauer chose Berlin as the stage from which to launch his critique of the Kennedy administration. Two internationally publicized press conferences on 7 and 8 May provided an ideal forum for Adenauer to openly and publicly criticize the Federal Republic's most important allies, an "unprecedented step"[30] up until this point.

Kennedy aimed to use his policies to end the Cold War and secure the status quo in Europe by exchanging interests with the Soviet Union. "Kennedy also planned to devote more attention to the problems of the Third World. It was not Europe, not Germany, but rather other political hotspots that assumed a central position in America's foreign policy."[31] The *New York Times* quoted a bitter remark from the federal chancellor on Kennedy's decision to give higher priority in American policy to development aid: "I am also against colonies and I am all for development aid. But I also demand that 16,000,000 Germans [in East Germany] be allowed to live their own lives. We shall tell that to our friends and our enemies."[32] Adenauer rejected the plan to create an international authority because he disapproved of any body in which West and East Germany held the same status. Regarding German participation in the planned thirteen-person Board of Governors of that authority, he preferred for "the Pankow people to stay off the board, and we could stay off it too. Then the ratio of votes would be exactly the same. But it seems to me that this whole plan cannot be implemented. Do you know that in the end, three countries—namely Sweden, Austria, and Switzerland—will have the decisive voice since the votes of the people from the East and West will probably cancel each other out? Well then, I should like to ask: If these countries were asked whether they wanted to take on this role, would they really answer in the affirmative? I don't think so!" Asked whether he considered it better for West Berlin if the negotiations had no outcome and the status quo remained in place, Adenauer responded unambiguously: "I believe it is much better for things to stay as they are than for this line to implemented."[33] This was a clear statement by the federal chancellor against continuing exploratory talks with the Soviet Union.

In retrospect, Henry Kissinger is astounded that Khrushchev did not take initiative in Berlin while Western unity on the issue crumbled. When Adenauer publicly articulated his objection to both the composition of the Board of Governors and the function of the access authority, "Khrushchev should have known that he held the key to unleashing a major crisis within the Atlantic Alliance. Amazingly, just as Soviet success seemed imminent, Khrushchev veered off course. Trying to achieve in one stroke the breakthrough which had eluded him for the past three years, Khrushchev placed Soviet intermediate-range missiles into Cuba. Khrushchev had obviously calculated that, if he succeeded in that adventure, his bargaining position in an eventual Berlin negotiation would be overwhelming." The decision to pull back from the Berlin offensive had already occurred in Moscow on 8 January 1962. And furthermore, there was no urgency on the issue of Berlin: the "garrison state" in the GDR had secured itself on 13 August 1961, whereas the situation in Cuba was precarious. The outcome of the Cuban Missile Crisis, however, had the opposite effect on Khrushchev's position from what he had intended, "stripp[ing] his Berlin diplomacy of whatever credibility still remained to it."[34]

Adenauer's predictions ultimately came true: the status quo between West and East endured in Berlin, ushering in a lull in politics on Germany and Berlin. However, this did not mean stagnation for West German foreign policy. First, both the Federal Government and the Kennedy administration were careful "not to push the conflict to the edge." Concerning West Berlin, Hans-Peter Schwarz adds that in the early months of 1962, "the critical phase had already been cleared in the longwinded tension surrounding Berlin. With a combination of obstinacy and vague hints at a readiness to negotiate, the chancellor did in fact succeed in steering the city unscathed through four years of heavy Soviet pressure."[35] On top of that came the will of West Berliners to determine their own future, a characteristic that their governing mayor Willy Brandt knew how to convey effectively to the greater public.

Germany Policy, or the Importance of Holding On

Just to be clear: for an entire generation of Germans, the construction of the Berlin Wall marked the end of any hope to overcome the division the country through an agreement among the four powers. The structure cemented the border in Berlin and between the two German states. The Wall delimited the edges of two systems, as that generation believed, drawing a line between freedom and dictatorship. At the same time, it was a European border separating the Soviet Empire from the democratic West. Immediately after its construction, it became an international symbol of the Cold War. Protesting the barbed wire division of Berlin on 16 August 1961, Willy Brandt laid out in emotional terms before an audience of two hundred and fifty thousand Berlin residents his refusal to abandon his compatriots in East Germany and East Berlin. The division, Brandt insisted, would not be the country's ultimate fate.

The Germans' spirit of national solidarity after 1945—throughout all four zones—was rooted above all in family ties spanning both sides the border, and also in a common language and culture. SED leaders erected the Wall not only to stop people from fleeing the GDR but also to allow the "national illusion" in the GDR to wither away. The problem of the common language, they believed, could be overcome through censorship and linguistic controls. This process of forcibly isolating people of the GDR from Germans in the Federal Republic threatened both populations' long-term perspectives to reconstruct a unified German nation-state.

Internationally, West German policy was forced to adapt to the new realities; even Adenauer acknowledged this. His thoughts focused on achieving a modus vivendi with the Soviet Union on the German question, reflecting his view that West Germany would have to "accept the Soviet zone as a state entity as soon as the people there were able to live more freely and humanely."[36] As the end of Adenauer's tenure as federal chancellor approached, there was little he could do to manifest these views in political action. Brandt had given a definitive and fundamental "no" to the division of the city, answering silent German voices in the GDR and East Berlin who wondered whether the West would "write them off" or even "betray" them. It was a question of whether West Germans would abandon their national perspective now that the Wall embodied the permanence of

Germany's division. Facing the reality of division, the Federal Government and the Berlin Senate had to develop a policy of not letting go—one that countered the logic of the Wall and the isolationist goals of the SED state.

Throughout Berlin, the Wall tore apart personal relationships. Since both the Western city commandants and the Berlin Senate forbade the GDR from opening offices in West Berlin to issue travel permits for East Berlin, West Berliners were unable to visit their relatives and friends in the Eastern part of the city after August 1961. It took two and a half years until the Berlin Senate and the GDR reached the first Border Pass Agreement (*Passierscheinregelung*) in December 1963. This settlement marked the visible beginning of a new policy in the Berlin Senate and the Federal Government to try to relieve human difficulties arising from the division. The price of the new approach was obvious, and the Berlin Senate was willing to pay: de facto recognition of the GDR as the second German state.

Ernst Richert, a contemporary scholar, brilliantly explained why this policy was a necessary step along the path to winning back national unity. After fleeing Leipzig for West Berlin in 1949, Richert became a pioneer of GDR scholarship in West Germany. He was convinced that "time works in favor of cementing the status quo" and thereby the existence of the SED. "Nothing in the world will be able to force Russia out of Central Germany before the year 2000." He went on to quote Chancellor Adenauer, who had taken the position before the Bundestag that "concerning reunification, it was crucial to brace oneself for long periods of time, similar to with Alsace-Lorraine's separation from France."[37] Out of Adenauer's statement, Richert inferred the following:

> If we let things go on as they are today, then in forty years, when our youngest generation is the oldest generation, I see a near certain probability that there will be nothing left to reunify. If the GDR were a Soviet "imperial state" (*Reichsland*), a visibly foreign protectorate on the edge of the Soviet Union, perhaps things would be different. But such a distinctly isolated state with such strong social mobility, with considerable prospects for young people to improve their standing, with such a striking lack of tradition and at the same time such a strict effort to model an entirely new type of behavior, will force its society to transform—it wants to be faster and stronger than its people can even realize. A *new self-evidence* emerges in which direct self-reflection has been vastly eliminated.[38]

This process of educating people toward a new, collective self-image occurred in parallel, but to a different end, in the Federal Republic. Richert feared that when the time eventually came for reunification, the two German societies would only retain loose ties to each other through the private contacts of "a dying older generation" and, despite sharing a common language, would fundamentally misunderstand each other. In other words: if mutual isolation efforts continued undisturbed with their piercing propaganda slogans and the closed borders of the GDR, West German politics would lose any chance it had of potential reunification in the future. "Little time remains for the West to salvage (or must we say: reinvent?) any traces of pan-German togetherness that can still be saved or reinvented."[39]

Richert demanded that "West Germany take initiative" rather than simply building on the policies of the Western powers. His goal was to "improve contact between the two societies on the basis of the status quo" and, "in the words of Golo Mann, to strive indirectly to 'establish Polish conditions' in the GDR."[40] Richert's reference to the Federal Republic's growing economic power and Moscow's integral role in influencing the largely Stalinist SED dictatorship, as well as his mention of Poland, reflect his hope that the GDR would shift toward reform Communist policies. This path—perhaps a realistic alternative to the lost national unity—could only be initiated by the Soviet Union. But all options aiming to change the status quo in the dictatorship (short of reunification itself) first required the Federal Republic's official recognition of reality, including the SED state. Only after this would it be possible to negotiate.

Richert's analysis and prognosis for the fate of German unity convey a certain shock over the Wall's potential consequences for the future of Germany. Beginning in the mid 1960s, the Federal Republic's new Ostpolitik heeded Richert's warnings and attempted to secure all common ground remaining between the two societies in divided Germany. No West German administration ever gave up the demand for national unity and the right of East Germans to self-determination. Over the twenty-eight years that the Wall stood in place, Berlin continued to function as a bustling exchange of contact and information, as well as a bridge connecting the people of the two German states.

From the Berlin Crisis to the Cuban Missile Crisis

Over the course of the Berlin Crisis, the use of nuclear weapons remained an ever-present propaganda threat, and military preparations on both sides served as the catalyst to reach political compromise based on the territorial status quo in Berlin. Khrushchev's next advance, however, truly brought the world to the brink of nuclear war: his decision to station intermediate-range weapons with nuclear capabilities on Cuba. In the broader scope of international politics, the two crises must be seen in connection to each other. A disparity still existed between the nuclear armament of the United States and that of the Soviet Union: "In the summer of 1962, the United States possessed more than seventeen times as many nuclear warheads as the Soviet Union (five thousand vs. three hundred); compared to 229 American intercontinental rockets, the Soviet side had only twenty 'usable' devices at its disposal. . . . Against this backdrop, it occurred to Khrushchev in 1962 to place intermediate-range missiles equipped with nuclear weapons on Cuba."[41] In Cuba, Khrushchev was also concerned with protecting a new satellite state; President Kennedy had already tried to topple its new Communist regime in April 1961 through the failed, secret Bay of Pigs Invasion. This motivation spurred Soviet action:

In June 1962, the secret operation "Anadyr" began. Intermediate-range missiles on Cuba would compensate for the Soviet deficit in intercontinental, strategic capabilities and enable [the Soviet Union] to pose a massive threat to American financial, government, and population centers. If the Soviet Union could conceal the transfer of this nuclear system to the Caribbean island until it was fully stationed and thus already a fait accompli, the balance of military strength between the two superpowers would shift fundamentally. This would eventually force the Western powers, as Khrushchev calculated, to reach settlements in favor of his demands. Moreover, the GDR's lacking economic strength would no longer be of any significance, since the conflict would be decided before an embargo could ever enter the discussion.[42]

Khrushchev's plan depended, however, on his erroneous assumption "that the American president and with him the Western public would simply accept the missiles pointed at American cities after they had secretly been put in place."[43]

American reconnaissance aircraft discovered the Soviet missiles on 15 October, and the American president decided to immediately confront the Soviet challenge in his own backyard. The American Marines placed Cuba under "quarantine" to prevent the transfer of more weapons to the island. The United States coupled this measure with an ultimatum to the Soviet Union demanding that it dismantle the missiles. Simultaneously, the United States presented the issue of the Soviet rockets on Cuba to the UN General Assembly. Shortly before American forces attacked Cuba, Khrushchev caved and consented to withdraw his missiles. This dramatic step followed a series of secret conversations between Khrushchev and Kennedy that culminated in an agreement: after the withdrawal of Soviet nuclear missiles from Cuba, the United States would dismantle its Jupiter rockets stationed in Turkey. Kennedy also guaranteed the "inviolability" of Cuban borders. Despite "protests from his mistrustful military, Kennedy had achieved a peaceful end to the Cuban Missile Crisis."[44]

Kennedy's resolute attitude during the Cuba crisis also prevented the Soviet Union from improving its standing in Berlin. Kissinger leaves no doubt that the Berlin and Cuba crises were pivotal moments in the Cold War, even if most governments at the time did not recognize their significance:

> Had the democracies not become so consumed by their internal disputes, they might have interpreted the Berlin crisis for what it was—a demonstration of latent Soviet weakness. . . . Thus the division of Europe into two blocks was reaffirmed again, as it had been in the Hungarian Revolution of 1956. Both sides would complain about that state of affairs, but neither ever attempted to alter it by force. The cumulative result of the failure of Khrushchev's Berlin and Cuban initiatives was that the Soviet Union did not again risk posing a direct challenge to the United States, except during a brief flare-up at the end of the 1973 Middle East War. Though the Soviets assembled a vast force of long-range missiles, the Kremlin never deemed these sufficient to mount a direct threat to established American rights.[45]

On the basis of secured borders in Europe, East–West relations entered a phase of détente accompanied by West Germany's new Ostpolitik and the establishment of the Conference on Security and Co-operation in Europe (CSCE). The Federal

Republic gradually moved to recognize the GDR in the context of this international constellation—indeed, "as a West German decision supported by all the major German parties, not as an initiative imposed by the United States. In time, the allies exploited the Soviets' eagerness for the recognition of East Germany by insisting on the precondition that the Soviet Union put in place ironclad access procedures to Berlin as well as confirm its four-power status. The Soviets formally accepted these conditions in the Quadripartite Agreement of 1971. There was no further challenge to Berlin or the access routes until the wall was pulled down in 1989, leading to German reunification. Containment had worked after all."[46]

Notes

1. Walter Ulbricht to Nikita S. Khrushchev, Berlin, 8 February 1962, SAPMO-BArch, DY 30/3510.
2. "Gespräch Chruschtschows mit dem Ersten Sekretär der SED, Walter Ulbricht, am 26. Februar 1962," in Wettig, *Chruschtschows Westpolitik*, 523. The Soviet delegation at this meeting included L. I. Brezhnev, F. R. Koslov, A. N. Kosygin, V. S. Semyonov, and M. G. Pervukhin; the East German delegation included B. Leuschner, O. Winzer, and R. Dölling.
3. Ibid.
4. In particular, the militaries and diplomats of the Western powers would only be able to use the access routes and visit East Berlin with permission from the GDR. Even if this occurred through unilateral approval, it would still represent enormous progress in Ulbricht's view because it would fundamentally acknowledge the GDR's right to control these routes. This, in turn, would enable further steps in the future.
5. The GDR's official name for East Berlin.
6. "Gespräch Chruschtschows mit dem Ersten Sekretär der SED, Walter Ulbricht, am 26. Februar 1962," in Wettig, *Chruschtschows Westpolitik*, 524–25.
7. Ibid., 524.
8. Ibid., 526.
9. Ibid., 527.
10. Ibid., 528.
11. Ibid., 528–29.
12. Ibid., 533.
13. Herbert Häber was born in 1930 and served as a member of the Central Committee of the SED from 1976 to 1986. From May 1984 to November 1985, he was also a member of the politburo. From 1973 to 1985, he was head of the Western Division/Division for International Policy in the Central Committee of the SED, which was conceptually responsible for policy toward the Federal Republic.
14. Herbert Häber, letter to the author, 5 January 2011.
15. "Koalitionsgrundsätze der FDP für eine außenpolitische Zusammenarbeit mit der CDU/CSU," quoted in Schwarz, *Adenauer: Der Staatsmann*, 682.
16. Ibid.
17. Küsters, "Reaktionen," 732–33.
18. Grewe, *Rückblenden*, 549.

19. Schwarz, *Adenauer: Der Staatsmann*, 743.

20. Ibid., 743–44.

21. Heinrich Krone (1895–1989) served as Berlin's member of the Bundestag (CDU) from 1949 to 1969. From 1961 to 1966, he was federal minister for special affairs.

22. Krone, quoted in Schwarz, *Adenauer: Der Staatsmann*, 744.

23. Schwarz, *Adenauer: Der Staatsmann*, 744.

24. The Bundeshaus housed the offices of the Federal Republic's authorized representative in Berlin from 1950 to 1990.

25. Schwarz, *Adenauer: Der Staatsmann*, 744.

26. Dietrich Schwarzkopf, letter to the author, 28 July 2010.

27. See Grewe, *Rückblenden*, 545–63.

28. Schwarz, *Adenauer: Der Staatsmann*, 745.

29. Ibid., 747.

30. Kissinger, *Diplomacy*, 590.

31. Christian Hacke, *Zur Weltmacht verdammt: Die amerikanische Außenpolitik von J. F. Kennedy bis G. W. Bush* (Munich, 2002), 91.

32. Kissinger, *Diplomacy*, 590.

33. "Aus der Pressekonferenz des Bundeskanzlers Adenauer in Berlin," 7 May 1962, in *Dokumente zur Deutschlandpolitik*, ed. Bundesministerium für innerdeutsche Beziehungen, series IV, vol. 8/1, *1. Januar bis 30. Juni 1961* (Frankfurt am Main, 1977), 487–88.

34. Kissinger, *Diplomacy*, 591.

35. Schwarz, *Adenauer: Der Staatsmann*, 749.

36. Ibid., 748.

37. Ernst Richert, *Das zweite Deutschland: Ein Staat der nicht sein darf* (Frankfurt am Main, 1964), 333.

38. Ibid., 333–34.

39. Ibid., 334.

40. Ibid., 335.

41. Wilfried Loth, "Internationale Rahmenbedingungen der Deutschlandpolitik 1961–1989," in Deutscher Bundestag, *Materialien der Enquete-Kommission: Aufarbeitung*, vol. V/2, 1746.

42. Wettig, "Chruščev," 674.

43. Loth, "Rahmenbedingungen," 1748–49.

44. Schwabe, *Weltmacht*, 288.

45. Kissinger, *Diplomacy*, 593.

46. Ibid.

CONCLUSION
Who Was Responsible for the Berlin Wall?

Until 1961, Berlin was the gateway to the West for people in the GDR. The demarcation line between East and West Germany had already been closed and fortified in 1952 following Stalin's orders. But before 13 August 1961, hundreds of thousands of people used the open door in Berlin to escape from the SED state. Without sealing and militarily securing the sector border there, the GDR likely could not have survived through the end of 1961. This, at least, was Walter Ulbricht's opinion. Going through the Soviet ambassador to East Berlin, Ulbricht sent a clear message to Soviet Premier Nikita S. Khrushchev: if the sector border in Berlin remained open, Ulbricht could no longer guarantee the survival of the GDR. Whether or not Ulbricht's concerns were justified in 1961, one thing is clear: the GDR did not exist for much longer after the inner-German border fell in 1989.

This event provokes the question of whether the GDR's borders, the border closure, and the border regime had existential significance for the East German state. Ulbricht gave an unambiguous answer in 1962: "The economic strength of the GDR and the Socialist camp did not suffice to influence the economy in Westberlin. On the contrary: Many citizens of the GDR purchased goods in Westberlin that were unavailable in the GDR or that we had to export to West Germany. On top of that, it had been apparent for quite a while that it would not be possible to catch up to West Germany and Westberlin in terms of living standards by the end of 1961."[1]

Many in the GDR reacted to the conditions described above by fleeing the country—a mass movement that the SED's economic policy of 1960–61 only encouraged. In Ulbricht's view, the GDR could only ensure its own survival within closed borders. He was convinced by 1961 that the fight against "desertion of the republic," which the SED Politburo had elevated to one of its main party goals in January, could only lead to victory if the gateway to the West was closed. However, neither West Berlin nor East Berlin was actually part of the GDR; the divided city still existed under its post–World War II four-power status. Without approval from the Soviet Union, the SED could not go through with its plan to seal the sector border.

Soviet politics after 1958 centered on resolving the "Westberlin question" to its own satisfaction through a German peace treaty with the Western powers. The Soviets hoped to transform West Berlin into a demilitarized "Free City" in order to force the withdrawal of the Western powers from their sectors. At the beginning of the second Berlin Crisis, neither the Soviet Union nor the SED planned to build a wall through the city; instead they wanted to change Berlin's status to the disadvantage of the Western powers. As in the first Berlin Crisis of 1948–49, Moscow aimed to weaken the overall position of the United States in Europe. In the context of international politics, Khrushchev's decision to allow the GDR to close Berlin's sector border on 13 August represented a retreat from the Soviet Union's political offensive, which had brought Europe to the brink of nuclear war.

But in the end, who was responsible for building the Wall in Berlin? There was no doubt that Ulbricht needed it. Only with a closed sector border in Berlin could the state party secure its monopoly on power vis-à-vis its own people. Ulbricht, however, was not ultimately in charge. The political and military authority rested in the hands of the Soviet leader of party and state, Khrushchev. Only after President John F. Kennedy refused to sign the Soviet draft of a peace treaty at the Vienna Summit in June 1961, and only after the mass exodus from the GDR assumed dramatic proportions, did a constellation emerge in which Khrushchev decided to take this step. Ulbricht had already pushed for a solution to the West Berlin question at the beginning of that year, and the SED's politburo had passed several measures to combat "desertion of the republic." But Ulbricht had to wait until after the Vienna Summit for Khrushchev to grant permission to erect a barbed wire barricade closing the sector border.

In November 1960 in Moscow, Ulbricht had laid out to Khrushchev the catastrophic situation in the GDR and the role of West Berlin as a destabilizing factor. The issue of open sector borders and the necessity of closing them did not directly enter the conversation, but Ulbricht was fully aware that the SED could not act independently to address the matter; the party was tied to whichever path Soviet leadership chose. Khrushchev still hoped at that time to negotiate a solution to the Berlin problem with the Western powers. He waited for the new American president to enter office and refused to make any decision on Berlin before their meeting in Vienna. In a letter of January 1961, Ulbricht urged Khrushchev to reach a rapid solution to the Berlin problem, stressing the growing numbers of refugees. The SED Politburo went ahead and established a working group to combat desertion of the republic; it included Karl Maron, interior minister and head of the Volkspolizei and border police, and Erich Mielke, the minister of state security. In July of that year, both ministers, along with Defense Minister Hoffmann, worked closely with Colonel Mereshko from the Group of Soviet Forces in Germany (GSFG) as Mereshko drew up concrete plans to close the sector borders.

The state of crisis in the GDR grew increasingly noticeable to decision makers in Moscow over the course of the Berlin conflict and could only be ended by closing Berlin's sector border and securing the Soviet "garrison state." The growing urgency of the situation ran against Khrushchev's plans to negotiate with the United States in hopes of reaching an agreement. Thus, Khrushchev's response to Ulbricht's cry for help maintained the Soviet position of 30 November 1960: before the summit with Kennedy, there would be no decision. Kennedy, however, refused to sign the Soviet Union's Berlin settlement in Vienna. Only after it became clear that negotiations would not elicit the withdrawal of the Western powers or the transformation of Berlin into a "Free City," and that neither the Soviet Union nor the United States wanted to start a nuclear war over Berlin, did Moscow see the Wall as a viable course of conflict resolution. Washington then accepted it as well.

After declaring the "fight against desertion of the republic" a major goal, the SED began preparations to close the border in January 1961, even though internal party documents never stated this intention directly. The operation remained a state secret, and preparations took place under conspiratorial conditions—the working group mentioned above was a clear indication of this. Ulbricht instructed his defense minister to consult the top commander of the GSFG while still maintaining utmost secrecy. After Khrushchev finally consented to closing the border on 20 July, both the Soviet ambassador and the deputy head of operations for the GSFG were surprised by how well Ulbricht, Maron, Mielke, and Hoffman were already prepared for the "measure."

Members of the Volkspolizei and border police, along with workers in Combat Group uniform, erected a barbed wire barricade on 13 August and the Wall soon after that in order to save the SED state from potential collapse. The "Antifascist Protection Rampart" (*antifaschistischer Schutzwall*), as the structure was celebrated in SED propaganda, aimed to prevent "desertion of the republic" from the GDR and thereby the "bleeding" of the country's "human capital." In order to achieve this goal, the SED deployed border troops to guard the wall, commanding them to use armed force against "unlawful breaches of the border"—an order that many troops carried out. Above all, this border targeted the GDR's own population. Walter Ulbricht was clear about this in internal discussions: "This situation necessitates that in due course, the state border of the German Democratic Republic (which runs straight through Berlin) will only be crossable by citizens of the German Democratic Republic with special exit permits or, concerning visits to Westberlin by citizens of the capital of the GDR, with special attestation."[2]

When the SED divided Berlin with barbed wire in 1961, trying to stop the flow of refugees from the GDR, it secured its own survival for the next twenty-eight years. Walter Ulbricht, builder of the Wall, presented himself as victor after 13 August 1961. However, time would show that in many ways, the structure symbolized three strategic defeats for the SED:

1. The Socialist state—and especially its centralized, planned economy—had already lost the competition of systems between the Federal Republic and the

GDR by the time the Wall was built. The GDR could only survive within hermetically sealed borders.

2. The Soviet Union did not transfer either its status rights in Berlin or its control of transit routes to West Berlin to the GDR, even though Khrushchev repeatedly announced his intention to do so. Thus, Ulbricht's goal of using the Berlin Crisis to usher in full sovereignty for the GDR vis-à-vis the Soviet Union proved to be an illusion. The SED state remained a vassal of the Soviet Union.

3. The "Westberlin question" could not be resolved. More than any other factor, this persistent and erratic disruption to the normalcy of a two-state Germany reminded people that Germany's division in a polarized Europe was, in fact, *not* normal, even if fewer and fewer people perceived it that way. Polish and Czechoslovakian civil rights activists advocated German unity after Charter 77 and Solidarność because they saw it as the only way to overcome Europe's division and achieve sovereignty for their own nations.

In the spring of 1962, with the Wall partially complete, Ulbricht sent Khrushchev a progress report in which he laid out the historic significance of the border for the future of socialism. In it he emphasized that socialism had been unable to compete with the Western democracies while the border was still open: "The disadvantage of securing the border was that it became obvious to the public that the GDR and the Socialist camp are not presently in a position to compete with the capitalist NATO states while maintaining open borders."[3]

The media's use of the term "Wall" was misleading. The structure was a multilayered fortification complex in which the so-called *Hinterlandmauer* (rear wall) that bordered East Berlin served as the real obstacle, oriented inward. This was the border that prevented citizens of the GDR from fleeing to West Berlin. People who dared to try anyway faced the weapons of the border police. In contrast to the Western side, which was photographed often and shaped people's image of the Wall internationally, the *Hinterlandmauer* was hardly visible from West Berlin and appeared in very few photos.[4] It was forbidden to photograph the Wall in East Berlin.[5] The propaganda image of an "Antifascist Protection Rampart" suppressed a truth whose acknowledgment in the GDR was considered a crime: the Berlin Wall only protected the SED dictatorship—a reality that became visible to the rest of the world when the Wall fell on 9 November 1989.

Another fact came to light that day as well: Berlin had remained an erratic disruption on the territory of the GDR that, because of its four-power status, prevented the two German states from sealing themselves off entirely (as had happened in Korea). During the Berlin Crises of 1948–49 and 1958–62, the Soviet Union attempted twice to eliminate the city's disturbance and push the Western powers out of Berlin, trying to alter the spheres of influence in Germany to its own advantage. As important as Germany was for the Soviet Union, the USSR's real opponent throughout the Berlin Crises was the United States, whose position in Europe it hoped to unsettle. Khrushchev vividly expressed this goal to Ulbricht in March 1961: if he could wrestle the peace treaty out of Kennedy, then it would "rip [NATO] to pieces."[6]

To conclude, it is important to look more closely at various positions in the historical debate over Ulbricht's influence on Khrushchev's decisions. Yuli A. Kvizinski, a former attaché to the Soviet ambassador in Berlin, describes in his memoirs how Ulbricht pressured Khrushchev to make a decision.[7] This account has convinced several contemporary historians that "Ulbricht played an integral role not only in the decision to build the Wall but also in the Soviet Union's overall Berlin policy from 1958 to 1961. With respect to the Wall, [many historians see] Ulbricht as the driver and Khrushchev as the passenger."[8] Another Russian contemporary, Oleg Troyanovsky, Khrushchev's former advisor on foreign policy, did not have the impression that Ulbricht and his politburo "were simply pushed around by Moscow like chess pieces" during the Berlin Crisis. Instead he believed "that they were 'active players' themselves, who 'constantly tried to convince Moscow to assume an offensive tactic toward West Germany and Westberlin' and intermittently 'bombarded [Moscow] with messages and telephone calls.'"[9] This interpretation is supported by SED files showing that Ulbricht actively represented the interests of his party and state to Soviet leadership. Hope Harrison has concluded from this that above all it was Ulbricht who forced Khrushchev to act.[10]

Gerhard Wettig takes the opposite position: "The fact that the GDR faced imminent collapse in 1961 certainly encouraged [Khrushchev] to take the SED leader's cries for help seriously. But for the same reason, [Khrushchev] was unwilling to follow Ulbricht's suggestions as long as he had a better alternative. He decided to close the border in Berlin after great hesitation, based on his own assessment of the situation, and he did so on the condition that it only stay closed so long as it remained impossible to stop the mass exodus from the GDR by controlling the access routes to West Berlin."[11]

Michael Lemke presents a similar argument but focuses on the GDR's economic crisis beginning in 1960. This factor forced the SED "to build even closer ties to the USSR, especially economically." For Lemke, the second Berlin Crisis shows that in viewing the relationship between the GDR and the Soviet Union, it would be inaccurate to say that the GDR displayed "one-sided dependence." In addition to maintaining its "garrison state" in the GDR, the Soviet Union also needed "the medium of the SED" to conduct its Germany policy. Through the SED the USSR was able to implement its policies in the GDR—Stalin built this constellation with the KPD in 1945—and it could harness the SED's Western Operations to "transport and propagate [those policies] into the Federal Republic." This level of cooperation implied a certain operative independence of the SED. Fundamentally, however, Lemke does not dispute the asymmetrical relationship between the USSR and the GDR: "The Berlin Crisis demonstrated that the USSR, which clearly held East Berlin under its authority, was not only the SED's primary ally but also its guarantor, without which the SED could not have acted on its power-political interests, security interests, or even the special interests of the East German state. Thus, without the Soviet Union it would have been impossible to make headway in stabilizing the SED, achieving international recognition for the GDR, or implementing political goals in Berlin."[12]

Also contradicting Harrison's argument is the fact that Ulbricht often had to cope with Khrushchev's tendency to prioritize his own international ambitions for a German peace treaty with the United States over the interests of the SED state. Wettig presents the plausible thesis that Khrushchev only decided to close the sector border after he was convinced following the Vienna Summit that the mass exodus from the GDR endangered that state's very survival. Lemke points to the asymmetrical relationship of dependency between the Soviet Union and the GDR, which called for a measure to secure the GDR and thereby the territorial integrity of the Soviet Empire. Khrushchev himself had no doubt concerning his own responsibility for taking this step. In a conversation with West German Ambassador Kroll on 9 November 1961, he reflected on closing the border: "People also accuse us of closing the border in Berlin. I don't deny it. Of course the GDR could not have closed the border without us. Why should we hide ourselves behind Comrade Ulbricht's back? He is not large enough for us to do that. Of course we closed the border, it occurred on our initiative. Technically the GDR implemented the whole thing because it is really a German issue."[13] Khrushchev's self-assessment resonates with the Russian historians Vladislav M. Zubok and Constantine Pleshakov: "The decision to build the Wall to separate the GDR from West Berlin was the benchmark of Khrushchev's statesmanship; although something like it was expected, the decision was made spontaneously, coming as a surprise to friends and foes alike."[14]

The decision-making process that culminated in Berlin's permanent division also speaks to Khrushchev's ultimate responsibility in each phase. In early July, Ulbricht informed the Soviet leader that in light of increasing refugee numbers, he could no longer guarantee the survival of the GDR while maintaining open borders. Khrushchev reached the political decision on 20 July, instructing the supreme commander of the GSFG to draw up plans to close the sector border. After Khrushchev had "confirmed" the border plans on 8 August in Moscow, Marshal Ivan S. Konev issued the critical order to Maron, Mielke, and Hoffmann, the three East German ministers responsible for carrying it out, on 10 August at GSFG headquarters in Wünsdorf. In conversations in Moscow at the beginning of August, Ulbricht and Khrushchev had agreed upon 13 August at 0:00 as the starting point of the operation; the politburo of the SED granted its formal approval on 7 August.

Khrushchev allowed Ulbricht to divide Berlin with barbed wire and then build a wall through the city. Ulbricht, however, had to abandon all hope for a separate peace treaty that would grant him control over the transit routes to West Berlin and allow the GDR to assert its sovereignty internationally—and also toward Moscow. The Soviet Union held fast to Berlin's four-power status.

Khrushchev also decided to end his Berlin Crisis when he declared to the presidium of the Central Committee of the CPSU on 8 January 1962 that closing the sector border in Berlin was the maximum the Soviet Union could achieve at that time. He wanted to continue exploratory talks with the Americans, but no longer wished to conclude a treaty. The Eastern bloc would not be able to wage the "final battle for Westberlin" before Soviet missile armament was complete and the GDR had achieved economic stability. Until that point, the Soviet Union wanted to use West Berlin for leverage against the Western powers. When Ulbricht tried in February 1962 to discuss the next steps toward a peace treaty, Khrushchev replied with his key statement from the 8 January presidium session: "I believe that on 13 August, we achieved the maximum of what we could get out of West Berlin. Now it is our job to continue working diligently."[15]

Notes

1. Addendum to a letter to the presidium of the Central Committee of the CPSU: "Zur Entwicklung der Lage vom Juli 1961 bis Januar 1962 und zu den nächsten Aufgaben," Walter Ulbricht to Nikita S. Khrushchev, 8 February 1962, SAPMO-BArch, DY 30/3510.
2. Walter Ulbricht, "Rede auf dem Treffen der Ersten Sekretäre der ZKs der kommunistischen und Arbeiterparteien der sozialistischen Staaten," Moscow, 3 August 1961, SAPMO-BArch, DY 30/3478.
3. Addendum to a letter to the presidium of the Central Committee of the CPSU: "Zur Entwicklung der Lage vom Juli 1961 bis Januar 1962 und zu den nächsten Aufgaben," Walter Ulbricht to Nikita S. Khrushchev, 8 February 1962, SAPMO-BArch, DY 30/3510.
4. See Sälter et al., *Weltende*.
5. See Elena Demke, "Mauerfotos in der DDR: Inszenierungen, Tabus, Kontexte," in *Die DDR im Bild: Zum Gebrauch der Fotografie im anderen deutschen Staat*, ed. Karin Hartewig and Alf Lüdtke (Göttingen, 2004), 89–106.
6. "Gespräch Chruschtschows mit dem Ersten Sekretär der SED, Walter Ulbricht, am 31. März 1961," excerpt, in Wettig, *Chruschtschows Westpolitik*, 112.
7. See Kwizinskij, *Vor dem Sturm*.
8. Bonwetsch and Filitow, "Chruschtschow," 156.
9. Ibid.
10. Harrison, "Wie die Sowjetunion," 77–98.
11. Wettig, *Chruschtschows Berlin-Krise*, 286.
12. Lemke, *Berlinkrise*, 278.
13. "Gespräch Chruschtschows mit dem Botschafter der Bundesrepublik Hans Kroll, am 9. November 1961," in Wettig, *Chruschtschows Westpolitik*, 493–94.
14. Zubok and Pleshakov, *Inside the Kremlin's Cold War*, 251.
15. "Gespräch Chruschtschows mit dem Ersten Sekretär der SED, Walter Ulbricht, am 26. Februar 1962," in Wettig, *Chruschtschows Westpolitik*, 527.

BIBLIOGRAPHY

Archival Sources

Foundation Archives of Parties and Mass Organisations of the GDR in the Federal Archives (SAPMO-BArch)
SAPMO-BArch DY JIVZ 2/747; DY 30/J IV 2/2A/668; DY 30/3291; DY 30/3386; DY 30/3478; DY 30/3497; DY 30/3505; DY 30/3506; DY 30/3507; DY 30/3508; DY 30/3509; DY 30/3510; DY 30/3538; DY 30/3566; DY 30/3586; DY 30/3682; DY 30/3709; NY 4182/633; NY 4182/652; NY 4182/653; NY 4182/654; NY 4182/657; NY 4182/660; NY 4182/1096; NY 4182/1206; NY 4890/471
Russian State Archives (RGANI)
RGANI F. 5, op. 30, d. 300; F. 5 (r. 9017), op. 49, d. 480; F. 52, op. 1, d. 364; F. 52, op. 1, d. 581; F. 52, op. 1, d. 582
Archive of the Ludwig Boltzmann Institute for Research on War Consequences (AdBIK)
Archive of the Federal Commissioner for the Records of the State Security Service of the Former GDR (BStU)
BStU, MfS, AU 16144/62; ZAIG no. 454

Letters and Interviews

Häber, Herbert. Letter to the author. 5 January 2011.
Schwarzkopf, Dietrich. Letter to the author. 28 July 2010.
Wilke, Manfred, and Alexander Vatlin. "'Arbeiten Sie einen Plan zur Grenzordnung zwischen beiden Teilen Berlins aus!': Interview mit Generaloberst Anatolij Grigorjewitsch Mereschko," translated by Tatiana Timofeeva. *Deutschland Archiv* 44, no. 2 (2011): 89–96.

Collections of Primary Source Documents

Allied Control Authority Germany. *Enactments and Approved Papers of the Control Council and Coordinating Committee.* Vol. 1: *1945.* Berlin, 1946.
Allied Control Authority Germany. *Enactments and Approved Papers of the Control Council and Coordinating Committee.* Vol. 5: *1 October 1946–31 December 1946.* Berlin, n.d.
Auswärtiges Amt, ed. *40 Jahre Außenpolitik der Bundesrepublik Deutschland: Eine Dokumentation.* Stuttgart, 1989.
Badstübner, Rolf, and Wilfried Loth, eds. *Wilhelm Pieck: Aufzeichnungen zur Deutschlandpolitik 1945–1953.* Berlin, 1994.
Baring, Arnulf. *Sehr geehrter Herr Bundeskanzler! Heinrich von Brentano im Briefwechsel mit Konrad Adenauer 1949–1964.* Hamburg, 1974.

Bonwetsch, Bernd, and Alexei Filitow. "Chruschtschow und der Mauerbau: Die Gipfelkonferenz der Warschauer-Pakt-Staaten vom 3.–5. August 1961." *Vierteljahreshefte für Zeitgeschichte* 48, no. 1 (2000): 155–98.

Booms, Hans, ed. *Die Kabinettsprotokolle der Bundesregierung.* Vol. 6: *1953.* Boppard am Rhein, 1989.

Brandt, Willy. *Begegnungen und Einsichten: Die Jahre 1960–1975.* Hamburg, 1976.

Bundesministerium für innerdeutsche Beziehungen, ed. *Dokumente zur Deutschlandpolitik.* Series IV. Vol. 6/I: *1. Januar bis 31. Mai 1961.* Frankfurt am Main, 1975.

Bundesministerium für innerdeutsche Beziehungen, ed. *Dokumente zur Deutschlandpolitik.* Series IV. Vol. 7/I: *12. August bis 30. September 1961.* Frankfurt am Main, 1976.

Bundesministerium für innerdeutsche Beziehungen, ed. *Dokumente zur Deutschlandpolitik.* Series IV. Vol. 8/I: *1. Januar bis 30. Juni 1962.* Frankfurt am Main, 1977.

Chruschtschow, Nikita S. *Bericht des Zentralkomitees der KPdSU, XX. Parteitag der KPdSU.* N.c., n.d.

Deutscher Bundestag, ed. *Materialien der Enquete-Kommission: Aufarbeitung von Geschichte und Folgen der SED-Diktatur in Deutschland.* 9 vols. Baden-Baden, 1995.

Deutscher Bundestag, ed. *Materialien der Enquete-Kommission: Überwindung der Folgen der SED-Diktatur im Prozess der deutschen Einheit.* 8 vols. Baden-Baden, 1999.

Die KPD lebt und kämpft: Dokumente der KPD 1956–1962. Berlin (East), 1963.

Dimitroff, Georgi. *Tagebücher 1933–1943,* edited by Bernhard H. Bayerlein. 2 vols. Berlin, 2000.

Zentralkomitee der Sozialistischen Einheitspartei Deutschlands. *Dokumente der Sozialistischen Einheitspartei Deutschlands: Beschlüsse und Erklärungen des Zentralkomitees sowie seines Politbüros und seines Sekretariats.* Vol. 4. Berlin (East), 1954.

Dokumente zur Deutschlandpolitik der Sowjetunion. Vol. 2: *Vom IV. Parteitag der SED (30.3.–6.4.1954) bis zur Überreichung des zweiten sowjetischen Entwurfs für einen Friedensvertrag mit Deutschland (10.1.1959).* Berlin (East), 1963.

Eppelmann, Rainer, Horst Möller, Günter Nooke, and Dorothee Wilms, eds. *Lexikon des DDR-Sozialismus: Das Staats- und Gesellschaftssystem der Deutschen Demokratischen Republik.* Paderborn, 1996.

Erler, Peter, Horst Laude, and Manfred Wilke. *"Nach Hitler kommen wir": Dokumente zur Programmatik der Moskauer KPD-Führung 1944/45 für Nachkriegsdeutschland.* Berlin, 1994.

Filmer, Werner, and Heribert Schwan, *Opfer der Mauer: Die geheimen Protokolle des Todes.* Munich, 1991.

Fischer, Alexander, ed. *Teheran, Jalta, Potsdam: Die sowjetischen Protokolle von den Kriegskonferenzen der "Großen Drei."* Cologne, 1968.

Foreign & Commonwealth Office, ed. *Documents on British Policy Overseas.* Series 3. Vol. 6: *Berlin in the Cold War: 1948–1990.* DVD. London, 2009.

Fricke, Karl Wilhelm. *MfS intern: Macht, Strukturen, Auflösung der DDR-Staatssicherheit.* Cologne, 1991.

Herrnstadt, Rudolf. *Das Herrnstadt-Dokument: Das Politbüro der SED und die Geschichte des 17. Juni 1953,* edited by Nadja Stulz-Herrnstadt. Reinbek, 1990.

Hesselberger, Dieter. *Das Grundgesetz: Kommentar für die politische Bildung.* Neuwied, 1975.

Institut für Zeitgeschichte, ed. *Akten zur Auswärtigen Politik der Bundesrepublik Deutschland: 1953.* 2 vols. Munich, 2001.

Khrushchev, Nikita S. *Khrushchev Remembers,* edited and translated by Strobe Talbott. Boston, 1970.

Küsters, Hanns Jürgen, and Daniel Hofmann, eds. *Deutsche Einheit: Sonderedition aus den Akten des Bundeskanzleramtes 1989/90.* Munich, 1998.

Laufer, Jochen P., and Georgij P. Kynin, eds. *Die UdSSR und die deutsche Frage 1941–1948: Dokumente aus dem Archiv für Außenpolitik der Russischen Föderation.* 3 vols. Berlin, 2004.

Ministerium für Justiz und Akademie für Staats- und Rechtswissenschaften der DDR, ed. *Strafrecht der Deutschen Demokratischen Republik: Kommentar zum Strafgesetzbuch.* Berlin (East), 1984.

Münch, Ingo von, ed. *Dokumente des geteilten Deutschland: Quellentexte zur Rechtslage des Deutschen Reiches, der Bundesrepublik Deutschland und der Deutschen Demokratischen Republik.* Stuttgart, 1968.

Pedlow, Gregory W., ed. *NATO Strategy Documents, 1949–1969.* Brussels, 1997.

Petrov, Nikita. *Die sowjetischen Geheimdienstmitarbeiter in Deutschland: Der leitende Personalbestand der Staatssicherheitsorgane der UdSSR in der Sowjetischen Besatzungzone Deutschlands und der DDR von 1945–1954,* translated by Vera Ammer. Berlin, 2010.

Presseamt beim Vorsitzenden des Ministerrates der DDR, ed. *XXII. Parteitag der Kommunistischen Partei der Sowjetunion, 17. bis 31. Oktober 1961.* Berlin (East), n.d.

Protokoll der Verhandlungen der II. Parteikonferenz der Sozialistischen Einheitspartei Deutschlands, 9. bis 12. Juni 1952 in der Werner-Seelenbinder-Halle zu Berlin. Berlin (East), 1952.

Protokoll der Verhandlungen des V. Parteitages der Sozialistischen Einheitspartei Deutschlands, 10. bis 16. Juli 1958 in der Werner-Seelenbinder-Halle zu Berlin. 2 vols. Berlin (East), 1959.

Rauschning, Dietrich, ed. *Rechtsstellung Deutschlands: Völkerrechtliche Verträge und andere rechtsgestaltende Akte.* Munich, 1985.

Ruggenthaler, Peter, ed. *Stalins großer Bluff: Die Geschichte der Stalin-Note in Dokumenten der sowjetischen Führung.* Munich, 2007.

Rühle, Jürgen, and Gunter Holzweißig. *13. August 1961: Die Mauer von Berlin.* 3rd rev. ed. Cologne, 1988.

Schumacher, Kurt. *Nach dem Zusammenbruch: Gedanken über Demokratie und Sozialismus.* Hamburg, 1948.

Stalin, Josef W. *Reden, Interviews, Telegramme, Befehle, Briefe und Botschaften, Mai 1945–Oktober 1952,* edited by Parteihochschule "Karl Marx" beim ZK der SED. N.c., n.d.

Uhl, Matthias, and Armin Wagner, eds. *Ulbricht, Chruschtschow und die Mauer: Eine Dokumentation.* Munich, 2003.

Ulbricht, Walter. *Die Entwicklung des deutschen volksdemokratischen Staates 1945–1958.* Berlin (East), 1958.

Ulbricht, Walter. *Zur Geschichte der deutschen Arbeiterbewegung: Aus Reden und Aufsätzen.* Vol. 2: *1933–1946,* supplementary volume. Berlin (East), 1966.

Ulbricht, Walter. *Zur Geschichte der deutschen Arbeiterbewegung: Aus Reden und Aufsätzen.* Vol. 3: *1946–1950,* supplementary volume. Berlin (East), 1971.

Ulbricht, Walter. *Zur Geschichte der deutschen Arbeiterbewegung: Aus Reden und Aufsätzen.* Vol. 7: *1957–1959.* Berlin (East), 1964.

U.S. Department of State. *Documents on Germany, 1944–1985.* Washington, 1985.

U.S. Department of State. *Foreign Relations of the United States, 1948.* Vol. 2: *Germany and Austria.* Washington, 1973.

U.S. Department of State. *Foreign Relations of the United States, 1958–1960.* Vol. 8: *Berlin Crisis, 1958–1959,* edited by Charles S. Sampson. Washington, 1993.

U.S. Department of State. *Foreign Relations of the United States, 1961–1963.* Vol. 14: *Berlin Crisis, 1961–1962,* edited by Charles S. Sampson. Washington, 1993.

U.S. Department of State. *Foreign Relations of the United States, Diplomatic Papers: The Conferences at Malta and Yalta, 1945.* Washington, 1955.

U.S. Department of State. *Foreign Relations of the United States, Diplomatic Papers: The Conference of Berlin (The Potsdam Conference), 1945.* 2 vols. Washington, 1960.

Weber, Hermann, ed. *Konflikte im Weltkommunismus: Eine Dokumentation zur Krise Moskau–Peking.* Munich, 1964.

Wettig, Gerhard, ed. *Chruschtschows Westpolitik 1955–1964: Gespräche, Aufzeichnungen und Stellungnahmen.* Vol. 3: *Die Kulmination der Berlin-Krise (Herbst 1960 bis Herbst 1962).* Munich, 2011.

Wilke, Manfred. *Die Streikbrecherzentrale: Der Freie Deutsche Gewerkschaftsbund (FDGB) und der 17. Juni 1953.* Münster, 2004.

Zarusky, Jürgen, ed. *Die Stalin-Note vom 10. März 1952: Neue Quellen und Analysen.* Munich, 2002.

Other Primary Sources

"Declaration of Principles issued by the President of the United States and the Prime Minister of the United Kingdom (Atlantic Charter)," 14 August 1941. *NATO e-Library.* http://www.nato.int/cps/en/natolive/official_texts_16912.htm.

"Der Schwur von Buchenwald," 19 April 1945. Stiftung Gedenkstätte Buchenwald. http://www.buchenwald.de/files/downloads/Schwur-D.pdf.

Eisenhower, Dwight D. "Farewell Radio and Television Address to the American People," 17 January 1961. Online by Gerhard Peters and John T. Woolley. *The American Presidency Project.* http://www. presidency.ucsb.edu/ws/index.php?pid=12086&st=&st1=.

Johnson, Lyndon B. "Speech to House of Rep. in Berlin," 19 August 1961. Online by George Washington University, National Security Archive. *The Berlin Wall, Fifty Years Ago.* http://www2.gwu. edu/~nsarchiv/NSAEBB/NSAEBB354.

Kennedy, John F. "Radio and Television Report to the American People on the Berlin Crisis," 25 July 1961. Online by Gerhard Peters and John T. Woolley. *The American Presidency Project.* http://www. presidency.ucsb.edu/ws/?pid=8259.

NATO. "Declaration on Berlin," 16–18 December 1958. *NATO e-Library.* http://www.nato.int/ cps/en/SID-0F390516-41373721/natolive/official_texts_17646.htm.

NATO. "Resolution of Association by Other Parties to the North Atlantic Treaty, Annex B," 22 October 1954. *NATO e-Library.* http://www.nato.int/cps/en/SID-AC209642-068C9020/ natolive/official_texts_17412.htm.

NATO. "The North Atlantic Treaty," 4 April 1949, Washington. *NATO e-Library.* http://www.nato. int/cps/en/natolive/official_texts_17120.htm.

"US Policy on Military Actions in a Berlin Conflict," 20 October 1961. Online by CIA, Freedom of Information Act. *The Berlin Wall Collection.* http://www.foia.cia.gov/collection/ berlin-wall-collection.

Anthologies, Monographs, and Articles

Abelshauser, Werner. *Deutsche Wirtschaftsgeschichte seit 1945.* Munich, 2004.

Alisch, Steffen. *"Die Insel sollte sich das Meer nicht zum Feind machen!" Die Berlin-Politik der SED zwischen dem Bau und dem Fall der Mauer.* Munich, 2004.

Amos, Heike. *Die Vertriebenenpolitik der SED 1949 bis 1990.* Munich, 2009.

Amos, Heike. "SED und MfS gegen die Vertriebenenverbände in der Bundesrepublik Deutschland 1949 bis 1989." Manuscript. Berlin, 2010.

Amos, Heike, and Manfred Wilke. "Die Deutschlandpolitik der SED und ihre 'bürgerlichen Bündnispartner' in der Bundesrepublik 1949 bis 1989." *Jahrbuch für Historische Kommunismusforschung* (2010): 49–65.

Aron, Raymond. *Memoirs: Fifty Years of Political Reflection,* translated by George Holoch. New York, 1990.

Barclay, David E. *Schaut auf diese Stadt: Der unbekannte Ernst Reuter.* Berlin, 2000.

Behring, Rainer, and Mike Schmeitzner. *Diktaturdurchsetzung in Sachsen: Studien zur Genese der kommunistischen Herrschaft 1945–1952.* Cologne, 2003.

Bennewitz, Inge, and Rainer Potratz. *Zwangsaussiedlungen an der innerdeutschen Grenze: Analysen und Dokumente.* Berlin, 1997.

Benser, Günter. *Als der Aufbau des Sozialismus verkündet wurde: Eine Rückschau auf die II. Parteikonferenz der SED mit Dokumentenanhang.* Berlin, 2002.

Benz, Wolfgang. "Besatzungsstatut." In *Deutschland unter alliierter Besatzung 1945–1949/55,* edited by Wolfgang Benz, 333. Berlin, 1999.

Benz, Wolfgang, ed. *Deutschland unter alliierter Besatzung 1945–1949/55.* Berlin, 1999.

"Bericht der Enquete-Kommission." In *Materialien der Enquete-Kommission: Aufarbeitung von Geschichte und Folgen der SED-Diktatur in Deutschland,* edited by Deutscher Bundestag. Vol. I, 178–778. Baden-Baden, 1995.

"Berlin." In *Geschichte der Bundesrepublik Deutschland,* edited by Karl Dietrich Bracher et al. Vol. I: *Jahre der Besatzung: 1945–1949,* edited by Theodor Eschenburg, 447–58. Stuttgart, 1983.

Besson, Waldemar. *Die Außenpolitik der Bundesrepublik: Erfahrungen und Maßstäbe.* Munich, 1970.

Biermann, Harald. *John F. Kennedy und der Kalte Krieg.* Paderborn, 1997.

Bischof, Günter, and Martin Kofler. "'Vienna, a City that is Symbolic of the Possibility of Finding Equitable Solutions': John F. Kennedys Gipfeldiplomatie mit Freund und Feind in Europa im

Mai/Juni 1961." In *Der Wiener Gipfel 1961: Kennedy—Chruschtschow*, edited by Stefan Karner et al., 137–64. Innsbruck, 2011.

Bischof, Günter, Stefan Karner, and Barbara Stelzl-Marx, eds. *The Vienna Summit and Its Importance in International History*. Lanham, MD, 2013.

Blumenwitz, Dieter. "Die Bedeutung des BVG-Urteils zum Grundlagenvertrag vom 31. Juli 1973 für die deutsche Einigung 1990." Lecture. In *Materialien der Enquete-Kommission: Aufarbeitung von Geschichte und Folgen der SED-Diktatur in Deutschland*, edited by Deutscher Bundestag. Vol. 5/1, 457–67. Baden-Baden, 1995.

Brandt, Heinz. *Ein Traum, der nicht entführbar ist*. Munich, 1967.

Brzezinski, Zbigniew K. *Der Sowjetblock: Einheit und Konflikt*, translated by Karl Römer. Cologne, 1962.

Buchheim, Christoph. "Kriegsschäden, Demontagen und Reparationen: Deutschland nach dem zweiten Weltkrieg." In *Materialien der Enquete-Kommission: Aufarbeitung von Geschichte und Folgen der SED-Diktatur in Deutschland*, edited by Deutscher Bundestag. Vol. 2/2, 1030–69. Baden-Baden, 1995.

Buchheim, Christoph, ed. *Wirtschaftliche Folgelasten des Krieges in der SBZ/DDR*. Baden-Baden, 1995.

Bulletin des Presse- und Informationsamtes der Bundesregierung 122 (2 July 1953), Bonn.

Bundesministerium für gesamtdeutsche Fragen, ed. *Die Sperrmaßnahmen der Sowjetzonenregierung an der Zonengrenze und um Westberlin*. Bonn, 1953.

Bundesministerium für innerdeutsche Beziehungen, ed. *DDR-Handbuch*. 2 vols. 3rd ed. Bonn, 1985.

Crusius, Reinhard, and Manfred Wilke. "Polen und Ungarn 1956: Eine Dokumentation." In *Entstalinisierung: Der XX. Parteitag der KPdSU und seine Folgen*, edited by Reinhard Crusius and Manfred Wilke, 82–164. Frankfurt am Main, 1977.

Demke, Elena. "Mauerfotos in der DDR: Inszenierungen, Tabus, Kontexte." In *Die DDR im Bild: Zum Gebrauch der Fotografie im anderen deutschen Staat*, edited by Karin Hartewig and Alf Lüdtke, 89–106. Göttingen, 2004.

Deutscher, Isaac. *Stalin: A Political Biography*. London, 1949.

Deutsches Nationalkomitee für Denkmalschutz, ed. *Die Berliner Mauer: Vom Sperrwall zum Denkmal*. Bonn, 2009.

Diedrich, Torsten. "Die militärische Grenzsicherung an der innerdeutschen Demarkationslinie und der Mauerbau 1961." In *Vom Kalten Krieg zur deutschen Einheit: Analysen und Zeitzeugenberichte zur deutschen Militärgeschichte 1945 bis 1995*, edited by Bruno Thoß, 127–44. Munich, 1995.

Egorova, Natalja. "Die Entwicklung sowjetischer Vorschläge zur Abrüstungsfrage und die Einstellung von Atomwaffentests im Vorfeld des Wiener Gipfels und deren Erörterung zwischen Nikita S. Chruščev und John F. Kennedy." In *Der Wiener Gipfel 1961: Kennedy—Chruschtschow*, edited by Stefan Karner et al., 335–53. Innsbruck, 2011.

Eisenfeld, Bernd, and Roger Engelmann. *13.8.1961: Mauerbau. Fluchtbewegung und Machtsicherung*. Bremen, 2001.

Enders, Ulrich, and Konrad Reiser. "Einleitung: Die Bundesregierung im Wahljahr 1953." In *Die Kabinettsprotokolle der Bundesregierung*. Vol. 6: *1953*, edited by Hans Booms, 5–64. Boppard am Rhein, 1989.

Engelmann, Roger, and Karl Wilhelm Fricke. *"Konzentrierte Schläge": Staatssicherheitsaktionen und politische Prozesse in der DDR 1953–1956*. Berlin, 1998.

Eschenburg, Theodor, ed. *Jahre der Besatzung 1945–1949*. Vol. 1 of *Geschichte der Bundesrepublik Deutschland*, edited by Karl Dietrich Bracher et al. Stuttgart/Wiesbaden, 1983.

Falin, Valentin. *Politische Erinnerungen*. Translated by Heddy Pross-Weerth. Munich, 1993.

Fisch, Jörg. *Reparationen nach dem Zweiten Weltkrieg*. Munich, 1992.

Foitzik, Jan. *Sowjetische Militäradministration in Deutschland (SMAD) 1945–1949: Struktur und Funktion*. Berlin, 1999.

Fricke, Karl Wilhelm. *Opposition und Widerstand in der DDR: Ein politischer Report*. Cologne, 1984.

Friedrich, Jörg. *Yalu: An den Ufern des dritten Weltkrieges*. Berlin, 2007.

Fursenko, Aleksandr, and Timothy Naftali. *Khrushchev's Cold War: The Inside Story of an American Adversary*. New York, 2006.

Gaddis, John Lewis. *Strategies of Containment: A Critical Appraisal of American National Security Policy during the Cold War.* 1982. Rev. ed. New York, 2005.

Gehler, Michael. *Europa: Ideen, Institutionen, Vereinigung.* Munich, 2005.

Gerlach, Heribert. *Die Berlinpolitik der Kennedy-Administration: Eine Fallstudie zum außenpolitischen Verhalten der Kennedy-Regierung in der Berlinkrise 1961.* Frankfurt am Main, 1977.

Gibianskij, Leonid. "Osteuropa: Sicherheitszone der UdSSR, sowjetisiertes Protektorat des Kreml oder Sozialismus 'ohne Diktatur des Proletariats'? Zu den Diskussionen über Stalins Osteuropa-Politik am Ende des Zweiten Weltkrieges und am Anfang des Kalten Krieges." *Forum für Osteuropäische Ideen- und Zeitgeschichte* 8, no. 2 (2004): 113–38.

Görtemaker, Manfred. "Potsdamer Konferenz (17.7.–2.8.1945)." In *Deutschland unter alliierter Besatzung 1945–1949/55,* edited by Wolfgang Benz, 214–17. Berlin, 1999.

Grafe, Roman. *Die Grenze durch Deutschland: Eine Chronik von 1945 bis 1990.* Berlin, 2002.

Graml, Hermann. *Die Alliierten und die Teilung Deutschlands: Konflikte und Entscheidungen 1941–1948.* Frankfurt am Main, 1985.

Graml, Hermann. "Die deutsche Frage." In *Geschichte der Bundesrepublik Deutschland,* edited by Karl Dietrich Bracher et al. Vol. 1: *Jahre der Besatzung 1945–1949,* edited by Theodor Eschenburg, 281–374. Stuttgart, 1983.

Graml, Hermann. "Eine wichtige Quelle—aber missverstanden: Anmerkungen zu Wilfried Loth, 'Die Entstehung der ›Stalin-Note‹.' Dokumente aus Moskauer Archiven." In *Die Stalin-Note vom 10. März 1952,* edited by Jürgen Zarusky, 117–38. Munich, 2002.

Grewe, Wilhelm G. *Die Deutsche Frage in der Ost-West-Spannung: Zeitgeschichtliche Kontroversen der achtziger Jahre.* Herford, 1986.

Grewe, Wilhelm G. *Rückblenden 1976–1951: Aufzeichnungen eines Augenzeugen deutscher Außenpolitik von Adenauer bis Schmidt.* Frankfurt am Main, 1979.

Gromyko, Andrej. *Erinnerungen,* translated by Hermann Kusterer. Düsseldorf, 1989.

Hacke, Christian. *Zur Weltmacht verdammt: Die amerikanische Außenpolitik von J. F. Kennedy bis G. W. Bush.* Munich, 2002.

Hacker, Jens. *Der Ostblock: Entstehung, Entwicklung und Struktur 1939–1980.* Baden-Baden, 1983.

Hacker, Jens. *Die Rechtslage Berlins: Die Wandlungen in der sowjetischen Rechtsauffassung.* Bonn, 1965.

Haendcke-Hoppe-Arndt, Maria. "Interzonenhandel/innerdeutscher Handel." In *Materialien der Enquete-Kommission: Aufarbeitung von Geschichte und Folgen der SED-Diktatur in Deutschland,* edited by Deutscher Bundestag. Vol. 5/2, 1543–71. Baden-Baden, 1995.

Halder, Winfrid. *"Modell für Deutschland": Wirtschaftspolitik in Sachsen 1945–1948.* Paderborn, 2001.

Harrison, Hope M. "Wie die Sowjetunion zum Mauerbau getrieben wurde: Ein Superalliierter, eine Supermacht und der Bau der Berliner Mauer." In *Mauerbau und Mauerfall: Ursachen—Verlauf—Auswirkungen,* edited by Hans-Hermann Hertle et al., 77–96. Berlin, 2002.

Hegedüs, András B., and Manfred Wilke, eds. *Satelliten nach Stalins Tod: Der "Neue Kurs"; 17. Juni 1953 in der DDR, Ungarische Revolution 1956.* Berlin, 2000.

Heinemann, Winfried, and Manfred Wilke. "Kein Krieg um Berlin: Sicherheitspolitische Aspekte des Mauerbaus." In *Die Berliner Mauer: Vom Sperrwall zum Denkmal,* edited by Deutsches Nationalkomitee für Denkmalschutz, 35–51. Bonn, 2009.

Heinrich, Gerd. *Geschichte Preußens: Staat und Dynastie.* Frankfurt am Main, 1981.

Hertle, Hans-Hermann. *Chronik des Mauerfalls: Die dramatischen Ereignisse um den 9. November 1989.* Augsburg, 2006.

Hertle, Hans-Hermann, Konrad H. Jarausch, and Christoph Kleßmann, eds. *Mauerbau und Mauerfall: Ursachen—Verlauf—Auswirkungen.* Berlin, 2002.

Hesselberger, Dieter. *Das Grundgesetz: Kommentar für die politische Bildung.* Neuwied, 1975.

Hillgruber, Andreas. *Deutsche Geschichte 1945–1986: Die "deutsche Frage" in der Weltpolitik.* Stuttgart, 1987.

Hurwitz, Harold. *Demokratie und Antikommunismus in Berlin nach 1945.* Vol. 4: *Die Anfänge des Widerstandes.* Cologne, 1990.

Jäckel, Oliver. "Außenministerkonferenz Paris (25.4.–15.5. und 15.6.–12.7.1946)." In *Deutschland unter alliierter Besatzung 1945–1949/55,* edited by Wolfgang Benz, 219. Berlin, 1999.

Jaspers, Karl. *The Question of German Guilt*, translated by E. B. Ashton. New York, 2000.

Karlsch, Rainer. "Krise als Chance? Die DDR-Wirtschaft nach dem Volksaufstand und dem Mauerbau." In *Staatsgründung auf Raten? Auswirkungen des Volksaufstandes 1953 und des Mauerbaus 1961 auf Staat, Militär und Gesellschaft der DDR*, edited by Torsten Diedrich and Ilko-Sascha Kowalczuk, 189–200. Berlin, 2005.

Karlsch, Rainer. *Uran für Moskau: Die Wismut—Eine populäre Geschichte*. Bonn, 2007.

Karner, Stefan, Barbara Stelzl-Marx, Natalja Tomilina, Alexander Tschubarjan, Günter Bischof, Viktor Iščenko, Michail Prozumenščikov, Peter Ruggenthaler, Gerhard Wettig, and Manfred Wilke, eds. *Der Wiener Gipfel 1961: Kennedy—Chruschtschow*. Innsbruck, 2011.

Keiderling, Gerhard. *Berlin 1945–1986: Geschichte der Hauptstadt der DDR*. Berlin (East), 1987.

Kennan, George F. *Memoirs: 1925–1950*. Boston, 1967.

Kielmansegg, Peter Graf. *Nach der Katastrophe: Eine Geschichte des geteilten Deutschland*. Berlin, 2000.

Kissinger, Henry. *Diplomacy*. New York, 1994.

Kleßmann, Christoph. *Die doppelte Staatsgründung: Deutsche Geschichte 1945–1955*. Bonn, 1991.

Koch, Manfred. "Volkskongreßbewegung und Volksrat." In *SBZ-Handbuch: Staatliche Verwaltungen, Parteien, gesellschaftliche Organisationen und ihre Führungskräfte in der Sowjetischen Besatzungszone Deutschlands, 1945–1949*, edited by Martin Broszat and Hermann Weber, 349–57. Munich, 1990.

Köhler, Henning. *Adenauer: Eine politische Biografie*. 2 vols. Berlin, 1997.

Koop, Volker. *Kein Kampf um Berlin? Deutsche Politik zur Zeit der Berlin-Blockade 1948/1949*. Bonn, 1998.

Kowalczuk, Ilko-Sascha. *17. Juni 1953: Volksaufstand in der DDR, Ursachen—Abläufe—Folgen*. Bremen, 2003.

Kronenberg, Volker. "Die deutsche Perspektive nach der Katastrophe: Nation, Verfassung, Vaterland." Conference paper, German-Russian Conference of Historians, Moscow, 28–30 October 2005.

Kubina, Michael. "Der Aufbau des zentralen Parteiapparates der KPD 1945–1946." In *Die Anatomie der Parteizentrale: Die KPD/SED auf dem Weg zur Macht*, edited by Manfred Wilke, 49–118. Berlin, 1998.

Kubina, Michael, and Manfred Wilke. "Aufnahme von Flüchtlingen aus der SBZ/DDR in der Bundesrepublik." Manuscript. Berlin, 2005.

Kunze, Gerhard. *Grenzerfahrungen: Kontakte und Verhandlungen zwischen dem Land Berlin und der DDR 1945–1989*. Berlin, 1999.

Kupper, Siegfried. "Innerdeutscher Handel." In *DDR-Handbuch*, edited by Bundesministerium für innerdeutsche Beziehungen. Vol. 1, 643–53. 3rd ed. Bonn, 1985.

Küsters, Hanns Jürgen. *Der Integrationsfriede: Viermächte-Verhandlungen über die Friedensregelung mit Deutschland 1945–1990*. Munich, 2000.

Küsters, Hanns Jürgen. "Die Reaktionen der Bundesregierung und des Senats von Berlin auf die Berlin-Krise." In *Der Wiener Gipfel 1961: Kennedy—Chruschtschow*, edited by Stefan Karner et al., 719–34. Innsbruck, 2011.

Küsters, Hanns Jürgen. "Konrad Adenauer und Willy Brandt in der Berlin-Krise 1958–1963." *Vierteljahreshefte für Zeitgeschichte* 40 (1992): 483–542.

Kwizinskij, Julij A. *Vor dem Sturm: Erinnerungen eines Diplomaten*. Berlin, 1993.

Laufer, Jochen. "Die Reparationsplanungen im sowjetischen Außenministerium während des Zweiten Weltkrieges." In *Wirtschaftliche Folgelasten des Krieges in der SBZ/DDR*, edited by Christoph Buchheim, 21–43. Baden-Baden, 1995.

Lemke, Michael. *Die Berlinkrise 1958 bis 1963: Interessen und Handlungsspielräume der SED im Ost-West-Konflikt*. Berlin, 1995.

Lemke, Michael. *Einheit oder Sozialismus? Die Deutschlandpolitik der SED 1949–1961*. Cologne, 2001.

Lemke, Michael, ed. *Schaufenster der Systemkonkurrenz: Die Region Berlin-Brandenburg im Kalten Krieg*. Cologne, 2006.

Leonhard, Wolfgang. *Die Revolution entlässt ihre Kinder*. Cologne, 1955.

Liebmann, Irina. *Wäre es schön? Es wäre schön! Mein Vater Rudolf Herrnstadt*. Berlin, 2008.

Loth, Wilfried. "Internationale Rahmenbedingungen der Deutschlandpolitik 1961–1989." In *Materialien der Enquete-Kommission: Aufarbeitung von Geschichte und Folgen der SED-Diktatur in Deutschland*, edited by Deutscher Bundestag. Vol. 5/2, 1744–65. Baden-Baden, 1995.

Loth, Wilfried. *Stalins ungeliebtes Kind: Warum Moskau die DDR nicht wollte.* Berlin, 1994.

Mahncke, Dieter. *Berlin im geteilten Deutschland.* Munich, 1973.

Mai, Gunther. "Alliierter Kontrollrat." In *Deutschland unter alliierter Besatzung 1945–1949/55,* edited by Wolfgang Benz, 229–34. Berlin, 1999.

Mai, Gunther. *Der Alliierte Kontrollrat in Deutschland 1945–1948: Alliierte Einheit—deutsche Teilung?.* Munich, 1995.

Maloney, Sean M. "Notfallplanung für Berlin: Vorläufer der Flexible Response 1958–1963." *Militärgeschichte* 7, no. 1 (1997): 3–15.

Malycha, Andreas. *Die SED: Geschichte ihrer Stalinisierung 1946–1953.* Paderborn, 2000.

Malycha, Andreas. *Partei von Stalins Gnaden? Die Entwicklung der SED zur Partei neuen Typs in den Jahren 1946 bis 1950.* Berlin, 1996.

Malycha, Andreas, and Peter Jochen Winters. *Die SED: Geschichte einer deutschen Partei.* Munich, 2009.

Mampel, Siegfried. *Die sozialistische Verfassung der Deutschen Demokratischen Republik: Kommentar.* Frankfurt am Main, 1982.

Maruhn, Jürgen. *17. Juni 1953: Der Aufstand für die Demokratie.* Munich, 2003.

Maximytschew, Igor F. "Eine wenig bekannte Seite des 17. Juni 1953." In *Juni 1953 in Deutschland: Der Aufstand im Fadenkreuz von Kaltem Krieg, Katastrophe und Katharsis,* edited by Heiner Timmermann. Münster, 2003.

Meissner, Boris. "Die Bundesrepublik Deutschland und die Sowjetunion: Entwicklung, Stand und Perspektive ihrer Beziehungen." In *Die Sowjetunion und Deutschland von Jalta bis zur Wiedervereinigung,* edited by Boris Meissner, 132–45. Cologne, 1995.

Militärgeschichtliches Forschungsamt, ed. *Verteidigung im Bündnis: Planung, Aufbau und Bewährung der Bundeswehr 1950–1972.* Munich, 1975.

Modrow, Hans. *Ich wollte ein neues Deutschland.* Berlin, 1998.

Möller, Horst. "Die Deutschlandpolitik von 1949 bis in die sechziger Jahre." Lecture. In *Materialien der Enquete-Kommission: Aufarbeitung von Geschichte und Folgen der SED-Diktatur in Deutschland,* edited by Deutscher Bundestag. Vol. 5/1, 240–54. Baden-Baden, 1995.

Morozow, Michael. *Die Falken des Kreml: Die sowjetische Militärmacht von 1917 bis heute.* Munich, 1982.

Morsey, Rudolf. "Die Deutschlandpolitik der Bundesregierungen Adenauer und die politisch-parlamentarische Diskussion 1949–1963." In *Materialien der Enquete-Kommission: Aufarbeitung von Geschichte und Folgen der SED-Diktatur in Deutschland,* edited by Deutscher Bundestag. Vol. 5/2, 1822–67. Baden-Baden, 1995.

Müller, Hans-Peter. "'Parteiministerien' als Modell politisch zuverlässiger Verwaltungsapparate: Eine Analyse der Protokolle der SED-Innenministerkonferenzen 1946–1948." In *Die Anatomie der Parteizentrale: Die KPD/SED auf dem Weg zur Macht,* edited by Manfred Wilke, 337–412. Berlin, 1998.

Müller, Werner. "Die Zweite Parteikonferenz der SED 1952: Das Regime zeigt sein stalinistisches Gesicht." In *17. Juni 1953: Der Aufstand für die Demokratie,* edited by Jürgen Maruhn, 21–45. Munich, 2003.

Münkel, Daniela. "Der Mauerbau im Blick der Stasi." *Frankfurter Rundschau,* 13 August 2010, 21.

Naimark, Norman M. *Die Russen in Deutschland: Die sowjetische Besatzungszone 1945 bis 1949.* Berlin, 1997.

Neubert, Harald, ed. *Stalin wollte ein anderes Europa: Moskaus Außenpolitik 1940 bis 1968 und die Folgen. Eine Dokumentation von Wladimir K. Wolkow.* Berlin, 2003.

Oberreuter, Heinrich. *Wendezeiten: Zeitgeschichte als Prägekraft politischer Kultur.* Munich, 2010.

Opitz, Peter J. *Die Vereinten Nationen: Geschichte, Struktur, Perspektiven.* Munich, 2002.

Otto, Wilfriede. "13. August 1961: Eine Zäsur in der europäischen Nachkriegsgeschichte: Dokumente und Materialien." *Beiträge zur Geschichte der Arbeiterbewegung* 39, no. 2 (1997): 55–92.

Pedlow, Gregory W. "Allied Crisis Management for Berlin: The Live Oak Organization, 1959–1963." In *International Cold War Military Records and History: Proceedings of the International Conference on Cold War Military Records and History Held in Washington, D.C., 21–26 March 1994,* edited by William W. Epley, 87–116. Washington, 1996.

Pedlow, Gregory W. "Flexible Response Before MC 14/3: General Norstad and the Second Berlin Crisis, 1958–62." *Storia delle relazione internazionali* 13 (1998), special issue: *Dividing the Atom: Essays* on the History of Nuclear Sharing and Nuclear Proliferation, edited by Cyril Buffet and Leopoldo Nuti: 235–68.

Pfeiffer, Gerd, and Hans-Georg Strickert, eds. *KPD-Prozess: Dokumentarwerk zu dem Verfahren über den Antrag der Bundesregierung auf Feststellung der Verfassungswidrigkeit der Kommunistischen Partei Deutschlands vor dem Ersten Senat des Bundesverfassungsgerichts.* 3 vols. Karlsruhe, 1956.

Pirker, Theo. *Die SPD nach Hitler: Die Geschichte der Sozialdemokratischen Partei Deutschlands, 1945–1964.* Munich, 1965.

Pommerin, Reiner. "Von der 'massive retaliation' zur 'flexible response': Zum Strategiewechsel der sechziger Jahre." In *Vom Kalten Krieg zur deutschen Einheit: Analysen und Zeitzeugenberichte zur deutschen Militärgeschichte 1945 bis 1995,* edited by Bruno Thoß, 525–42. Munich, 1995.

Ribbe, Wolfgang. *Berlin 1945–2000: Grundzüge der Stadtgeschichte.* Berlin, 2002.

Richert, Ernst. *Das zweite Deutschland: Ein Staat, der nicht sein darf.* Frankfurt am Main, 1964.

Ritter, Jürgen, and Peter Joachim Lapp. *Die Grenze: Ein deutsches Bauwerk.* Berlin, 2007.

Roesler, Jörg. "Handelsgeschäfte im Kalten Krieg: Die wirtschaftlichen Motivationen für den deutsch-deutschen Handel zwischen 1949 und 1961." In *Wirtschaftliche Folgelasten des Krieges in der SBZ/DDR,* edited by Christoph Buchheim, 193–220. Baden-Baden, 1995.

Roggenbuch, Frank. *Das Berliner Grenzgängerproblem: Verflechtung und Systemkonkurrenz vor dem Mauerbau.* Berlin, 2008.

Rosenthal, Walther. *Das neue politische Strafrecht der "DDR."* Frankfurt am Main, 1968.

Roth, Winfried. *Die Insel: Eine Geschichte West-Berlins 1948 bis 1990.* Munich, 2009.

Sacharov, Vladimir V., Dmitrij N. Filippovych, and Michael Kubina. "Tschekisten in Deutschland: Organisation, Aufgaben und Aspekte der Tätigkeit der sowjetischen Sicherheitsapparate in der Sowjetischen Besatzungszone Deutschlands (1945–1949)." In *Die Anatomie der Parteizentrale: Die KPD/SED auf dem Weg zur Macht,* edited by Manfred Wilke, 293–336. Berlin, 1998.

Sacharow, Andrej D. *Mein Leben.* Munich, 1990.

Sacharow, Andrej D. *Memorandum: Gedanken über Fortschritt, friedliche Koexistenz und geistige Freiheit.* Frankfurt am Main, 1968.

Salewski, Michael, ed. *Das Zeitalter der Bombe: Die Geschichte der atomaren Bedrohung von Hiroshima bis heute.* Munich, 1995.

Sälter, Gerhard. "Der Bau der Berliner Mauer 1961 und seine Auswirkung auf die Gesellschaft der DDR." Manuscript. Berlin, 2003.

Sälter, Gerhard. "Fluchtverhinderung als gesamtgesellschaftliche Aufgabe." In *Die Mauer: Errichtung, Überwindung, Erinnerung,* edited by Klaus-Dietmar Henke, 152–62. Munich, 2011.

Sälter, Gerhard. *Grenzpolizisten: Konformität, Verweigerung und Repression in der Grenzpolizei und den Grenztruppen der DDR (1952–1965).* Berlin, 2009.

Sälter, Gerhard. "Mauer, Grenzgebiet und Hinterlandsicherung in Ost-Berlin in den achtziger Jahren." In *Weltende: Die Ostseite der Berliner Mauer. Mit heimlichen Fotos von Detlef Matthes,* edited by Gerhard Sälter, Tina Schaller, and Anna Kaminsky, 79–86. Berlin, 2011.

Sälter, Gerhard. "Zur Restrukturierung von Polizeieinheiten der DDR im Kontext des Mauerbaus." *Archiv für Polizeigeschichte* 13 (2002): 66–73.

Sälter, Gerhard, Tina Schaller, and Anna Kaminsky, eds. *Weltende: Die Ostseite der Berliner Mauer. Mit heimlichen Fotos von Detlef Matthes.* Berlin, 2011.

Sattler, Friederike. "Bündnispolitik als Problem des zentralen Parteiapparates der KPD 1945/46." In *Die Anatomie der Parteizentrale: Die KPD/SED auf dem Weg zur Macht,* edited by Manfred Wilke, 119–212. Berlin, 1998.

Sattler, Friederike. *Wirtschaftsordnung im Übergang: Politik, Organisation und Funktion der KPD/SED im Land Brandenburg bei der Etablierung der zentralen Planwirtschaft in der SBZ/DDR 1945–52.* 2 vols. Münster, 2002.

Scherstjanoi, Elke. *Das SKK Statut: Zur Geschichte der Sowjetischen Kontrollkommission in Deutschland 1949 bis 1953.* Munich, 1998.

Scherstjanoi, Elke. "'Wollen wir den Sozialismus?': Dokumente aus der Sitzung des Politbüros der ZK der SED am 6. Juni 1953." *Beiträge zur Geschichte der Arbeiterbewegung* 33, no. 5 (1991): 658–80.

Schlegelmilch, Arthur. *Hauptstadt im Zonendeutschland: Die Entstehung der Berliner Nachkriegsdemokratie 1945–1949*. Berlin, 1993.

"Schlussbericht der Enquete-Kommission." In *Materialien der Enquete-Kommission: Überwindung der Folgen der SED-Diktatur im Prozess der deutschen Einheit*, edited by Deutscher Bundestag. Vol. I, 142–803. Baden-Baden, 1999.

Schmeitzner, Mike, and Stefan Donth. *Die Partei der Diktaturdurchsetzung: KPD/SED in Sachsen 1945–1952*. Cologne, 2002.

Schmid, Carlo. *Erinnerungen*. Frankfurt am Main, 1980.

Schöne, Jens. *Frühling auf dem Lande? Die Kollektivierung der DDR-Landwirtschaft*. Berlin, 2010.

Schröder, Hans-Jürgen. "European Recovery Program (ERP)." In *Deutschland unter alliierter Besatzung 1945–1949/55*, edited by Wolfgang Benz, 260–64. Berlin, 1999.

Schumann, Karl F. "Flucht und Ausreise aus der DDR insbesondere im Jahrzehnt ihres Unterganges." In *Materialien der Enquete-Kommission: Aufarbeitung von Geschichte und Folgen der SED-Diktatur in Deutschland*, edited by Deutscher Bundestag. Vol. 5/3, 2359–405. Baden-Baden, 1995.

Schwabe, Klaus. *Weltmacht und Weltordnung: Amerikanische Außenpolitik von 1898 bis zur Gegenwart—Eine Jahrhundertgeschichte*. Paderborn, 2006.

Schwarz, Hans-Peter. *Adenauer: Der Staatsmann 1952–1967*. Stuttgart, 1991.

Schwarz, Hans-Peter. *Vom Reich zur Bundesrepublik: Deutschland im Widerstreit der außenpolitischen Konzeptionen in den Jahren der Besatzungsherrschaft 1945–1949*. 2nd ed. Stuttgart, 1980.

Schwarz, Hans-Peter, ed. *Die Ära Adenauer: Gründerjahre der Republik, 1949–1957*. Vol. 2 of *Geschichte der Bundesrepublik*, edited by Karl Dietrich Bracher et al. 5 vols. Stuttgart/Wiesbaden, 1983.

Semjonow, Wladimir S. *Von Stalin bis Gorbatschow: Ein halbes Jahrhundert in diplomatischer Mission 1939–1991*. Berlin, 1995.

Sharp, Tony. *The Wartime Alliance and the Zonal Division of Germany*. Oxford, 1975.

Sorensen, Ted. "The Personal Recollections of a Presidential Adviser in Vienna." In *The Vienna Summit and Its Importance in International History*, edited by Günter Bischof, et al., 349–55. Lanham, MD, 2013.

Soutou, Georges-Henri. "Paris as Beneficiary of the Unsuccessful Vienna Summit." In *The Vienna Summit and Its Importance in International History*, edited by Günter Bischof, et al., 145–66. Lanham, MD, 2013.

Steiner, André. *Von Plan zu Plan: Eine Wirtschaftsgeschichte der DDR*. Bonn, 2007.

Steininger, Rolf. *Berlinkrise und Mauerbau 1958 bis 1963*. Munich, 2009.

Steininger, Rolf. *Der Mauerbau: Die Westmächte und Adenauer in der Berlinkrise 1958–1963*. Munich, 2001.

Steininger, Rolf. *Deutsche Geschichte: Darstellung und Dokumente in vier Bänden*. 4 vols. Frankfurt, 2002.

Stiftung Berliner Mauer and Zentrum für Zeithistorische Forschung, eds. *Die Todesopfer an der Berliner Mauer 1961–1989: Ein biographisches Handbuch*. Berlin, 2009.

Strauß, Franz Josef. *Die Erinnerungen*. Berlin (West), 1989.

Stürmer, Michael. "Der lange Schatten des Tyrannen: Westbindung und Geschichtsbild in Deutschland." In *Von Geschichte umgeben: Joachim Fest zum Sechzigsten*, edited by Karl Dietrich Bracher et al., 255–73. Berlin (West), 1986.

Taylor, Frederick. *The Berlin Wall: A World Divided, 1961–1989*. New York, 2007.

Thilenius, Richard. *Die Teilung Deutschlands: Eine zeitgeschichtliche Analyse*. Hamburg, 1957.

Thoß, Bruno. *NATO-Strategie und nationale Verteidigungsplanungen: Planung und Aufbau der Bundeswehr unter den Bedingungen einer massiven atomaren Vergeltungsstrategie 1952–1960*. Munich, 2006.

Thoß, Bruno, ed. *Vom Kalten Krieg zur deutschen Einheit: Analysen und Zeitzeugenberichte zur deutschen Militärgeschichte 1945 bis 1995*. Munich, 1995.

Thompson-Vujacic, Jenny, and Sherry Thompson-Miller. "Botschafter Thompson zwischen den politischen Strömungen auf dem Wiener Gipfel." In *Der Wiener Gipfel 1961: Kennedy—Chruschtschow*, edited by Stefan Karner et al., 595–617. Innsbruck, 2011.

Timmermann, Heiner, ed. *Juni 1953 in Deutschland: Der Aufstand im Fadenkreuz von Kaltem Krieg, Katastrophe und Katharsis*. Münster, 2003.

Tjulpanow, Sergej I. *Deutschland nach dem Kriege (1945–1949): Erinnerungen eines Offiziers der Sowjetarmee*, edited by Stefan Doernberg, translated by Günter Gossing and Lothar Jäger. Berlin (East), 1986.

Tuschhoff, Christian. "Strategiepoker: Massive Vergeltung—flexible Antwort." In *Das Zeitalter der Bombe: Die Geschichte der atomaren Bedrohung von Hiroshima bis heute*, edited by Michael Salewski, 167–88. Munich, 1995.

Uhl, Matthias. *Krieg um Berlin? Die sowjetische Militär- und Sicherheitspolitik in der zweiten Berlin-Krise 1958– 1962.* Munich, 2008.

Vatlin, Alexander. "Die unvollendete Vergangenheit: Über den Umgang mit der kommunistischen Geschichte im heutigen Russland." *Jahrbuch für Historische Kommunismusforschung* (2010): 279–95.

Voslensky, Michael S. *Sterbliche Götter: Die Lehrmeister der Nomenklatura.* Vienna, 1989.

Wagner, Armin. "Stacheldrahtsicherheit: Die politische und militärische Planung und Durchführung des Mauerbaus 1961." In *Mauerbau und Mauerfall: Ursachen—Verlauf—Auswirkungen*, edited by Hans-Hermann Hertle et al., 119–37. Berlin, 2002.

Weber, Hermann. *Geschichte der DDR.* 1985. Rev. ed. Munich, 1999.

Weber, Hermann, and Fred Oldenburg. *25 Jahre SED: Chronik einer Partei.* Cologne, 1971.

Weber, Jürgen. *Das Entscheidungsjahr 1948.* Vol. 2 of *30 Jahre Bundesrepublik Deutschland*, edited by Bayrische Landeszentrale für politische Bildungsarbeit. Munich, 1982.

Weißgerber, Ulrich. *Giftige Worte der SED-Diktatur: Sprache als Instrument von Machtausübung und Ausgrenzung in der SBZ und der DDR.* Berlin, 2010.

Wettig, Gerhard. *Bereitschaft zu Einheit in Freiheit? Die sowjetische Deutschland-Politik 1945–1955.* Munich, 1999.

Wettig, Gerhard. "Chruščev und die Berliner Mauer: Forderung nach einem Friedensvertrag 1961– 1963." In *Der Wiener Gipfel 1961: Kennedy—Chruschtschow*, edited by Stefan Karner et al., 641–80. Innsbruck, 2011.

Wettig, Gerhard. "Chruschtschow, die Berliner Mauer und das Friedensvertragsultimatum." Manuscript. 2009.

Wettig, Gerhard. *Chruschtschows Berlin-Krise 1958 bis 1963: Drohpolitik und Mauerbau.* Munich, 2006.

Wettig, Gerhard. "Die Verhandlungen der Westmächte mit der UdSSR über die Aufhebung der Berliner Blockade 1948: Untersuchungen unter Verwendung sowjetischer Gesprächsprotokolle." *Jahrbuch des Landesarchivs Berlin* (2008): 243–73.

Wettig, Gerhard. *Sowjetische Deutschland-Politik 1953 bis 1958: Korrekturen an Stalins Erbe, Chruschtschows Aufstieg und der Weg zum Berlin-Ultimatum.* Munich, 2011.

Wettig, Gerhard. "Wiederbewaffnung." In *Lexikon des DDR-Sozialismus: Das Staats- und Gesellschaftssystem der Deutschen Demokratischen Republik*, edited by Rainer Eppelmann, Horst Möller, Günter Nooke, and Dorothee Wilms, 698–700. Paderborn, 1996.

Wetzlaugk, Udo. *Berliner Blockade und Luftbrücke 1948/49.* Berlin, 1998.

Wetzlaugk, Udo. *Berlin und die deutsche Frage.* Cologne, 1985.

Wetzlaugk, Udo, and Christian Koziol. *Im Überblick: Berlin.* Berlin (West), 1986.

Wilke, Manfred. "Sternstunde der deutsch-amerikanischen Allianz: 9. November 1989." In *Germany and America: Essays in Honor of Gerald R. Kleinfeld*, edited by Wolfgang-Uwe Friedrich, 196–228. New York, 2001.

Wilke, Manfred, ed. *Die Anatomie der Parteizentrale: Die KPD/SED auf dem Weg zur Macht.* Berlin, 1998.

Wilke, Manfred, and Tobias Voigt. "'Neuer Kurs' und 17. Juni: Die 2. Staatsgründung der DDR 1953." In *Satelliten nach Stalins Tod: Der "Neue Kurs"; 17. Juni 1953 in der DDR, Ungarische Revolution 1956*, edited by András B. Hegedüs and Manfred Wilke, 24–136. Berlin, 2000.

Wilke, Manfred, and Hans-Peter Müller. *SED-Politik gegen die Realitäten: Verlauf und Funktion der Diskussion über die westdeutschen Gewerkschaften in SED und KPD/DKP 1961 bis 1972.* Cologne, 1990.

Woronowicz, Ulrich. *Tagebuch 1958 bis 1960: Als Dorfpfarrer in Brandenburg.* Halle, 2011.

Wyden, Peter. *Wall: The Inside Story of Divided Berlin.* New York, 1989.

Zank, Wolfgang. "Wirtschaftliche Zentralverwaltungen und Deutsche Wirtschaftskommission (DWK)." In *SBZ-Handbuch: Staatliche Verwaltungen, Parteien, gesellschaftliche Organisationen und ihre Füh-*

rungskräfte in der Sowjetischen Besatzungszone Deutschlands, 1945–1949, edited by Martin Broszat and Hermann Weber, 253–90. Munich, 1990.

Zivier, Ernst R. *Der Rechtsstatus des Landes Berlin: Eine Untersuchung nach dem Viermächte-Abkommen vom 3. September 1971.* Berlin (West), 1977.

Zubok, Vladislav, and Constantine Pleshakov. *Inside the Kremlin's Cold War: From Stalin to Khrushchev.* Cambridge, MA, 1996.

INDEX OF PERSONS